1 SAMUEL

Books in the PREACHING THE WORD Series:

Unless otherwise indicated, all volumes are by R. Kent Hughes

1 SAMUEL

Looking for a Leader

John Woodhouse

R. Kent Hughes, General Editor

CROSSWAY BOOKS
WHEATON, ILLINOIS

1 Samuel

Copyright © 2008 by John Woodhouse

Published by Crossway Books
    a publishing ministry of Good News Publishers
    1300 Crescent Street
    Wheaton, Illinois 60187

Cover banner by Marge Gieser

Art direction: Amy Bristow

First printing, 2008

Printed in the United States of America

Note: Key words and phrases in Scripture quotations have been distinguished by italics (roman type in all-italics block quotations).

Library of Congress Cataloging-in-Publication Data

Woodhouse, John, 1949–
 1 Samuel : looking for a leader / John Woodhouse; R. Kent Hughes, general editor.
   p. cm. — (Preaching the word)
 Includes indexes.
 ISBN-13: 978-1-58134-873-6 (hc)
 ISBN-10: 1-58134-873-8
 1. Bible. O.T. Samuel, 1st—Commentaries. I. Hughes, R. Kent. II. Title. III. Series.
BS1325.53.W66 2007
222'.4307—dc22   2007012468

T S		17	15	14	13	12	11	10	09	08
15	14	13	12	11	10	9	8	7	6	5	4	3	2	1

For Moya

*"The L*ORD *will judge the ends of the earth;*
he will give strength to his king
and exalt the power of his anointed."
1 SAMUEL 2:10b

Contents

PART THREE
David: The Leader "According to God's Own Heart"
1 SAMUEL 16–31

A Word to Those Who Preach the Word

There are times when I am preaching that I have especially sensed the pleasure of God. I usually become aware of it through the unnatural silence. The ever-present coughing ceases, and the pews stop creaking, bringing an almost physical quiet to the sanctuary — through which my words sail like arrows. I experience a heightened eloquence, so that the cadence and volume of my voice intensify the truth I am preaching.

There is nothing quite like it — the Holy Spirit filling one's sails, the sense of his pleasure, and the awareness that something is happening among one's hearers. This experience is, of course, not unique, for thousands of preachers have similar experiences, even greater ones.

What has happened when this takes place? How do we account for this sense of his smile? The answer for me has come from the ancient rhetorical categories of *logos*, *ethos*, and *pathos*.

The first reason for his smile is the *logos* — in terms of preaching, God's Word. This means that as we stand before God's people to proclaim his Word, we have done our homework. We have exegeted the passage, mined the significance of its words in their context, and applied sound hermeneutical principles in interpreting the text so that we understand what its words meant to its hearers. And it means that we have labored long until we can express in a sentence what the theme of the text is — so that our outline springs from the text. Then our preparation will be such that as we preach, we will not be preaching our own thoughts about God's Word, but God's actual Word, his *logos*. This is fundamental to pleasing him in preaching.

The second element in knowing God's smile in preaching is *ethos* — what you are as a person. There is a danger endemic to preaching, which is having your hands and heart cauterized by holy things. Phillips Brooks illustrated it by the analogy of a train conductor who comes to believe that he has been to the places he announces because of his long and loud heralding of them. And that is why Brooks insisted that preaching must be "the bringing of truth through personality." Though we can never perfectly embody the truth we preach, we must be subject to it, long for it, and make it as much a part of our ethos as possible. As the Puritan William Ames said, "Next to the Scriptures, nothing makes a sermon more to pierce, than when it comes out of the inward affection of the heart without any affectation." When a preacher's *ethos* backs up his *logos*, there will be the pleasure of God.

Last, there is *pathos* — personal passion and conviction. David Hume, the Scottish philosopher and skeptic, was once challenged as he was seen going to hear George Whitefield preach: "I thought you do not believe in the gospel." Hume replied, "I don't, but he does." Just so! When a preacher believes what he preaches, there will be passion. And this belief and requisite passion will know the smile of God.

The pleasure of God is a matter of *logos* (the Word), *ethos* (what you are), and *pathos* (your passion). As you preach the Word may you experience his smile — the Holy Spirit in your sails!

R. Kent Hughes

Preface

I am very grateful to Kent Hughes for his invitation and generous encouragement to contribute to the Preaching the Word series of expository commentaries. It has led to a rich experience for me in studying, teaching, and preaching the Books of Samuel in many different settings. I am also indebted to many brothers and sisters who have helped me teach and preach the Books of Samuel, particularly the congregations at Christ Church St Ives and the students and faculty of Moore College in Sydney, Australia.

The commentary has been written out of three particular convictions about the wonderful task of expounding the Word of God.

The first of these is that *the richness of the Bible's message is heard when attention is given to the particular details of the text under consideration.* Certainly the major theme of a passage must be recognized — the "big idea" — but the insight of just this passage is only appreciated by taking seriously the unique way in which this text is expressed.

Therefore each of the expositions in this volume attempts to bring to light the specific shape and precise wording of the specific passage, often giving attention to fine aspects of the text. The written form of the expository commentary has often allowed me to include more of such detail than may be possible in many sermons. Some of the important discussion has been relegated to the endnotes. How much and which details to include in a particular sermon is a judgment that each preacher has to make. Nonetheless I am convinced that sermons are enriched by appropriate examination of the details of the text of Scripture. I have found this to be true in important ways in narrative texts such as the Books of Samuel.

The second conviction that underlies the expositions in this commentary is that *the key to understanding the significance of any text of the Bible lies in seeing the text in question in its context.* Furthermore the context of any Old Testament text such as those expounded in this volume includes not only the whole book in question (here 1 Samuel) or the whole epic history told from Genesis 1 to 2 Kings 25, of which 1 Samuel is part, but also the whole Bible, which is shaped by the Old Testament promises of God that find their fulfillment in the New Testament in Jesus Christ.

Stated briefly the Bible's message is this: God's good purpose in creation (Genesis 1–2) was not abandoned at the Fall (Genesis 3), but God promised to bring blessing to the whole world through Abraham's offspring (Genesis 12:1-3; cf. 22:18). The Old Testament history of Israel is the record of God's faithfulness to this promise despite repeated and disastrous human failure. The New Testament message is that in Jesus Christ God's promises are fulfilled:

> *Now the promises were made to Abraham and to his offspring. It does not say, "And to offsprings," referring to many, but referring to one, "And to your offspring," who is Christ. (Galatians 3:16)*

> *And we bring you the good news that what God promised to the fathers, this he has fulfilled to us their children by raising Jesus. . . . (Acts 13:32, 33)*

> *Paul, a servant of Christ Jesus, called to be an apostle, set apart for the gospel of God, which he promised beforehand through his prophets in the holy Scriptures. . . . (Romans 1:1, 2)*

> *For all the promises of God find their Yes in him [Jesus Christ]. (2 Corinthians 1:20)*

First Samuel is a very important part of the Old Testament history of Israel. Therefore each of the following expositions tries to show not only the place of the text in the story that 1 Samuel tells (though that certainly is important and illuminating), but also how the text relates to the complete Bible message. In particular I have tried to see each passage in the light of the fulfillment of the whole Old Testament message in the person and work of Jesus Christ.

The third conviction is even more basic than the first two. It is this: *The proper purpose of Biblical exposition is not simply to find relevant lessons for life from the texts before us but to proclaim Christ.* This ministry is wonderfully summed up in the words of the Apostle Paul:

> *Him we proclaim, warning everyone and teaching everyone with all wisdom, that we may present everyone mature in Christ. (Colossians 1:28)*

Each of these expositions therefore aims to show, by attention to detail and attention to context, how these Scriptures point us to our Lord Jesus Christ and the truth and grace that are to be found in him.

May God, whose words these Scriptures are, speak them again by the power of his Spirit and shine in our hearts "to give the light of the knowledge of the glory of God in the face of Jesus Christ" (2 Corinthians 4:6).

PART ONE

Samuel:
The Leader God Provided

1 SAMUEL 1–7

1

The Leadership Crisis

1 SAMUEL 1:1, 2

Leadership is as important in today's world as it has been in every society in every age. Some would go further and speak of a contemporary crisis of leadership. There is now widespread cynicism expressed, especially in the media, toward those in leadership. Confidence in our elected leaders is at a low ebb.

Of course, leadership is a much bigger subject than politics. Leadership also matters in the world of business, sports, entertainment, fashion. Indeed leadership is something that touches our lives at every level and in every sphere. All of us *choose* leaders and *reject* leaders. That is to say, we allow some people to influence us, and we reject the influence of others. This happens in many different ways — as we choose a career, as we learn, as we make important decisions, as we make life choices, as we develop our values. We do not do these things in isolation from external influences. On the contrary, our lives are shaped by the influence of different people whose example or ideas or vision or teaching or values we *follow*. These are our real leaders, although it is possible that we do not always think of them, and they do not necessarily think of themselves, as leaders. By definition leaders are those who are followed!

It is interesting to reflect for a moment on the leaders who have shaped your life. Who are the leaders who are now shaping your life? Some will be obvious. Some we might hardly realize.

I recently browsed the shelves of a local bookshop and noticed the number and variety of books on leadership. There is considerable interest in the subject. There is a popular Christian journal called *Leadership*. Mind you, most of the material I have seen is about how to *be* a leader rather than how to *choose* which leaders you will follow — which is surely the more important question.

However, all of us do both. On the one hand, whether we are high-flying achievers who think of ourselves as leaders or more humble human beings who see ourselves as small players in the game of life, all of us exercise influence (I am calling it *leadership*) somewhere. It may be over your children or within your family, a circle of friends, a neighborhood. To some degree and in some respect and in some areas of our lives, we are all leaders.

What kind of leader are you? What kind of leaders should we be? How do you work that out?

On the other hand, the more important thing is that we all *follow* leaders. No matter how high up the status tree you may think you have climbed (or think you will climb), there is always someone higher. Furthermore we all *choose* to follow leaders, the leaders we decide to trust, the leaders we allow to influence us.

What kind of leaders do we follow? What kind of leaders *should* we follow? How do we work that out?

If we could answer such questions with confidence and had the wisdom to put our answers into practice, it would make a real difference in how well we lived.

I have begun this exposition of the Old Testament book of 1 Samuel with these thoughts because the book of 1 Samuel is about *leadership*. Mind you, what we will learn from this part of the Bible is very different from anything you will find in your local bookshop in the "Leadership" section. Much in these pages will take us by surprise.

ISRAEL'S LEADERSHIP CRISIS

In 1 Samuel we find the story (which continues into 2 Samuel) of three great leaders of the nation of Israel, through a period when Israel experienced a massive leadership crisis that led to an historic change in the character of the nation's leadership.

The three leaders were:[1] *Samuel* (whose story begins in 1 Samuel 1), *Saul* (the first king of Israel, who will first appear in 1 Samuel 9 and whose death occurs at the end of 1 Samuel), and *David* (Israel's second and greatest king who will enter the story in 1 Samuel 16 but will not become king until the early chapters of 2 Samuel).

Let us briefly set the scene. The book of 1 Samuel takes us back more than 3,000 years. The date was about 1050 B.C. It was a time when the question of *leadership* was very much in the air in the small and relatively young nation of Israel.

There had been about 200 years of extraordinary social upheaval, verging at times on anarchy. These were the 200 years after the Israelites had come into the land of Canaan under the leadership of Joshua. The era is often referred to as the period of the judges. Much of it is recounted in the book of Judges, which concludes with this summary: "In those days there was no king in Israel. Everyone did what was right in his own eyes" (Judges 21:25).[2] In other words, there was no established and permanent political authority in the land. Anarchy reigned. There was a crisis of leadership in Israel. Or so it seemed.

What kind of leadership did this troubled society need?

We must, of course, remember that Israel was then different from any other nation in the history of the world. Israel was God's chosen people. They had become a nation because of God's promise to their ancestor, Abraham. The promise was that God himself would make them into a great nation and that through them he would bring blessing to the whole world (Genesis 12:1-3).

So the leadership question had a particular spin to it in those days at the end of the book of Judges and the beginning of 1 Samuel. What kind of leader did Israel, God's own people, need? Through the period of the judges God had again and again raised up a leader (a "judge") according to the need of the moment. But could that unpredictable arrangement be permanent? Could Israel survive lurching from crisis to crisis, as they had for the last two centuries? As we will see, threats from other peoples, especially the Philistines, were growing. We will also see that internal instability, even corruption in the nation's leadership, was threatening Israel's life. What was the solution for this special people whom God had made his own? What kind of leadership could provide stability and security to Israel? That is the question in the air as 1 Samuel begins.

Already we should realize that the Bible will introduce an important element to the leadership question: What does *God* have to do with leadership? As we follow the unfolding leadership crisis in Israel, we cannot avoid introducing this new element into the questions of our leadership crisis: what difference does *God* make to the kind of leader I should be and (more importantly) the kind of leaders I should follow?

The book of 1 Samuel is going to tell us the extraordinary story of the leadership crisis in Israel at the end of the second millennium B.C. In ways that will surprise us, it will point us to *God's* astonishing answer to Israel's predicament. We will see that God's answer for Israel turns out to be his answer for the whole world and for each of us individually.

However, we must not jump ahead too quickly. In order to appreciate the important things that God has caused to be "written down for our instruction" (1 Corinthians 10:11)[3] in 1 Samuel, we must listen carefully and patiently to precisely what is written and consider its significance in the context of the whole Bible.

We will begin with the opening paragraph, where we are introduced to a particular family that will play a very important role in the story 1 Samuel has to tell.

"A CERTAIN MAN" (v. 1)

The first few words of 1 Samuel are like the beginnings of a number of Old Testament books. There are names of people and places that seem to the modern reader to be quite obscure. These unfamiliar details do not exactly grab our attention. However, although the writer of an Old Testament book may not have treated his opening sentence in the way of modern authors, there is good reason for us to assume that the first few lines of a book are worth our careful attention.

In the case of 1 Samuel this expectation is rewarded in a surprising and paradoxical way. Remembering that the immediate background to 1 Samuel is the end of the book of Judges, we know that there were grave matters of national importance in the air: no king in Israel, everyone doing what was right in his own eyes. The book opens with details about "a certain man" from the hill country of Ephraim:

> There was a certain man of Ramathaim-zophim of the hill country of Ephraim whose name was Elkanah the son of Jeroham, son of Elihu, son of Tohu, son of Zuph, an Ephrathite. (v. 1)

Why are we introduced to this man, Elkanah? The details given to us about him are, to say the least, perplexing.

His Town, His Family, His Connections

Ramathaim-zophim[4] (or Ramah for short, see v. 19) is not a town of great importance in the Old Testament story so far. It was at this time a relatively obscure town in the hills of Ephraim.[5] There is no obvious reason that we should be interested in "a certain man of Ramah."

Neither are the family connections of Elkanah striking in any way. Jeroham (his father), Elihu (his grandfather), Tohu (his great-grandfather), and his great-great-grandfather Zuph are all relatively "insignificant and obscure people."[6] The information in verse 1 tells us only that this man was, as we might say, a "nobody" in Israel.[7] Why, in these critical days, are we being introduced to this insignificant character?

Elkanah himself (or perhaps his great-great-grandfather) is described as an "Ephrathite." This could mean that he had family connections with Bethlehem (also known as Ephrathah).[8]

We know, of course, that Bethlehem Ephrathah would eventually become very famous indeed. In the course of this book we will meet another Ephrathite who will make Bethlehem famous for all time. David was "the son of an Ephrathite" (1 Samuel 17:12), and Bethlehem is the town where his story began (1 Samuel 16:1-13). But he is still half a book away! About three centuries later, a prophet would say:

> But you, O Bethlehem Ephrathah,
>   who are too little to be among the clans of Judah,
> from you shall come forth for me
>   one who is to be ruler in Israel,
> whose origin is from of old,
>   from ancient days. (Micah 5:2)

That very prophecy was fulfilled in the birth of Jesus (see the citation of Micah 5:2 in Matthew 2:6).

Once again we are jumping ahead too quickly! There is much for us to learn by following the path that begins here with the obscure Elkanah the Ephrathite. At the time of 1 Samuel 1:1 a connection with Bethlehem was no claim to fame.

His Important Unimportance

The very obscurity of the names and places in the opening sentence of the book is what should strike us. Their importance lies in their unimportance![9] In this case the obscurity is not a consequence of our being modern readers with little familiarity with the world of the Old Testament. These names were little known at the time referred to in 1 Samuel 1. From the point of view of social standing, fame, or power within the nation, Elkanah and his family were "nobodies."

This is the first hint of a theme that will develop in the course of 1 Samuel. The solution to Israel's leadership crisis will not be found in the expected places. We do not begin this story with the prominent and the powerful in Israel, but with an unheard of "certain man" from the hill country of Ephraim, possibly with remote family connections to the equally obscure town of Bethlehem. This book is about a God who makes something out of nothing, life out of death, rich out of poor, somebody out of nobody. This theme will be played out in a grand poetic prayer in chapter 2 (see especially vv. 6-8). The obscurity of Elkanah is the starting point of the book.

ELKANAH'S DOMESTIC SITUATION (v. 2)

From Elkanah himself, introduced in all his obscurity in verse 1, our attention is turned to his unfortunate domestic situation:

*He had two wives. The name of the one was Hannah, and the name of the
other, Peninnah. And Peninnah had children, but Hannah had no children. (v. 2)*

This suggests that Hannah was Elkanah's first wife.[10] The couple suffered the all-too-common sadness of being unable to have children, and so,
apparently, Elkanah took a second wife. Such an arrangement was not forbidden in Old Testament times but commonly led to the kind of difficulties
we will hear about in this chapter (see Deuteronomy 21:15-17). The new
wife, Peninnah by name, bore Elkanah a number of children, but Hannah
continued to have none.

Although the problem of childlessness can be a major crisis for a couple experiencing this difficulty, and perhaps particularly for a wife, we are
again struck by the ordinariness of the situation that is brought before us in
this book's second sentence. With a national crisis in the air, our attention
is drawn to the sad circumstances of one woman in Israel, the childless
Hannah.

There are two reasons, however, that the introduction of Hannah and
her troubles should catch our attention.

Where Is the Blessing?

The first is that Hannah's predicament raises a question about God's promised blessing on Israel. "There shall not be male or female barren among
you," God had said (Deuteronomy 7:14). If we were wondering about
Israel's difficulties in these days when everyone was doing what was right in
his own eyes, Hannah's troubles were *a representation of Israel's troubles.*
This nation had been promised blessing. Where was the blessing in their
threatened existence? Where was the blessing for Hannah as a member of
God's people, Israel? Her name, ironically, means "grace." What grace did
she know?

The Beginning of Something?

The second reason that Hannah's predicament should arouse our interest is
that the Bible has told us of a number of other women in her situation. In
each case the woman concerned experienced a particular act of God's grace,
by which she did bear a child, and the child played an important role in God's
purposes. Sarah "was barren; she had no child" (Genesis 11:30). But God
promised Abraham that she would bear a child, and she bore Isaac (Genesis
17:16; 21:1-7). Isaac became the bearer of the great promise of God to bring
blessing to the nations of the earth (Genesis 22:16-18). Rebekah "was barren," but Isaac prayed for her, and she conceived and bore Esau and (more

importantly, as it would turn out) Jacob, the father of the Israelite nation (Genesis 25:21-26). Jacob's wife, Rachel, too, "was barren," but "God listened to her and opened her womb," and she bore Joseph, through whom God saved many lives (Genesis 29:31; 30:22, 23; 50:20). More recently (from the point of view of 1 Samuel 1) a woman who "was barren and had no children" was visited by an angel, was promised a son, and gave birth to Samson (Judges 13:2, 3, 24). Samson delivered Israel from the Philistines and ruled Israel for twenty years (Judges 15). Each of these women had shared a sadness like Hannah's, but in each case a child was subsequently born who was God's answer to the crisis of the time.

We are therefore justified in thinking that the very unimpressiveness of the beginning of 1 Samuel may be the beginning of something that God was about to do. Certainly we are right to think that only God could bring something important out of the unimportance and "barrenness" of 1 Samuel 1:1, 2.

Perhaps as we conclude this introduction we might be excused if we look ahead just a little. Indeed, there is no need to apologize for looking ahead. The Bible has a very important story to tell about what God has done to meet the leadership crisis, not just of Israel's day, but of the human race in all of history. First Samuel is a crucial part of that story, but it will only be fully appreciated when it is seen in the light of the story's astonishing end.

Many years after Hannah, there was yet another barren woman. Her name was Elizabeth, and by God's grace she bore a child, whose name was John (see Luke 1:7, 57-60). At about the same time, the sequence of barren women who gave birth came to its climax. There was a woman who was not barren but had not given birth to a child for the more simple reason that she was a virgin. Her name was Mary. While still a virgin, she conceived and gave birth to a child, who was given the name Jesus (see Luke 1:26-38; 2:1-7). It happened in Ephrathah, that is, Bethlehem (see Luke 2:4; cf. Matthew 2:1, 5, 6)!

The lesson for us from 1 Samuel 1:1, 2 is that God's answer to the crisis in Israel, like God's answer to the crisis of the world, comes from the most unexpected quarter. If we insist on looking to the powerful, the influential, and the impressive of this world, we will miss it. It began for Israel with a childless woman with family connections to Bethlehem. That is where we must look if we want to see God's answer — just as we must look to the child of another woman, born in Bethlehem, if we are to see God's answer for the world. The story of 1 Samuel eventually leads to the one whom God has exalted "at his right hand as Leader and Savior" (Acts 5:31).

2

Does God Care?

1 SAMUEL 1:3-28

Does God care? The state of the world raises the question sharply, as does the experience of life. It is one thing to discuss abstractly the existence of "God"; it is quite another to ask whether there is a God who *cares* about the catastrophes reported in this morning's newspaper or the ups and downs of my life. The answer to the latter question matters enormously. If there is no one other than other human beings who cares about the human race and the individuals who comprise it, that is one thing. If that is the truth, then our hopes rest on the best and wisest people we can find. But if there is a God who does care about these things, we would be very foolish to carry on as though that were not true.

It would be equally foolish to imagine that God's concerns must be the same as mine. Religious people too easily make God out to be in their own image. God is then no more than a figment of their imagination, and religion is make-believe. But if God is really there, and if he really does care, we would be wise to listen and learn from him precisely what he cares about and how he has expressed or will express his care.

In our introduction to the book of 1 Samuel we began to see the leadership crisis that was facing the people of Israel about the middle of the eleventh century B.C. For some 200 years they had experienced instability as a community and insecurity as a nation. Leadership structures of a permanent and stable kind had not yet emerged in Israel, and life was far from what God had promised before they had entered this land he had given them. *Blessing* was the summary word for what they were meant to enjoy (see, for example, Deuteronomy 7:13-16), but blessing was as far from the national experience as it was from Hannah, the first wife of an obscure man from the hills, who was unable to bear a child.

"Does God care?" was a question raised by the circumstances of Israel in 1050 B.C. as sharply as it was raised by the disappointment of Hannah. If God cared, what precisely did he care about, and how was his care expressed? Did he care about Israel's suffering? Did he care about Hannah's distress?

In the opening lines of 1 Samuel 1 we met Elkanah, the man from the hills, Hannah, his first wife, unable to bear a child, and Peninnah, his second wife, who seems to have given birth to children readily. The first episode in the book of 1 Samuel is Hannah's story, which unfolds in four scenes.

SCENE 1: YEAR AFTER YEAR . . . (vv. 3-7)

In Scene 1 the particular story we are about to hear has not yet begun. We are given a glimpse of an annual event in the life of Hannah's family. We observe this yearly family custom and learn something about Elkanah, Peninnah, and Hannah.

Elkanah and His Faithfulness (vv. 3-5)

> Now this man used to go up year by year from his city to worship and to sacrifice to the LORD of hosts at Shiloh, where the two sons of Eli, Hophni and Phinehas, were priests of the LORD. (v. 3)

Shiloh was located about fifteen miles north of Elkanah's town, Ramah. It was the place where, some two centuries earlier, after the Israelites had entered the land of Canaan in the days of Joshua, the tabernacle had been set up (Joshua 18:1). It therefore became an important location in Israel's national life. A great assembly of the Israelites was held there on the occasion of the allocation of the land to the twelve tribes (Joshua 18:1-10; 19:51; 21:2).[1] On one occasion the Israelites gathered at Shiloh in preparation for war (Joshua 22:12). The tabernacle (and perhaps by now a structure somewhat more substantial that may have been constructed there with the tabernacle) was at Shiloh.[2] There was an annual "feast of the LORD" at Shiloh (Judges 21:19). Perhaps this was the occasion attended by Elkanah and his family.

At this time the priest in charge of matters at Shiloh was Eli, with his sons Hophni and Phinehas. We will hear a lot more about them in due course. For the moment we are simply given their names.

Every year Elkanah went up to Shiloh to worship "the LORD of hosts"[3] and to offer sacrifices. Our first impressions of Elkanah are of a man who took the Lord seriously and was attentive to his responsibilities before God. Elkanah was a man of faith in God. He gave thanks to God and honored him in the way appropriate to his time.

This faithfulness to God appears to have been matched by proper conduct toward his two wives. Verse 4 tells us straightforwardly that Elkanah would give portions of the sacrifice to Peninnah and her children: "On the day when Elkanah sacrificed, he would give portions to Peninnah his wife and to all her sons and daughters" (v. 4).

Despite the fact that we are about to learn that Hannah was his favorite wife, he did not neglect Peninnah. He looked after her and her children's needs. But verse 5, as translated by the ESV, suggests that he did discriminate. In the ESV verse 5 reads: "But to Hannah he gave a double portion, because he loved her, though the LORD had closed her womb" (v. 5).

This indicates that he gave Hannah "a double portion" because on the one hand "he loved her" and because, on the other hand, "the LORD had closed her womb." Motivated by his love for her, he tried to compensate for the fact that she could not have children.

However, it is not at all clear that this is what verse 5 actually says.

There are three difficulties in this verse. First, what did Elkanah do? Second, what does that have to do with his loving her? Third, where does "the LORD closed her womb" fit in? Take these three questions in turn.

What did Elkanah do? While the Hebrew text is difficult, it does seem to indicate that, contrary to the ESV,[4] Elkanah gave Hannah *one* portion, not a double portion.[5] Elkanah, it seems, was fair in his dealings with his wives. The truth was that Hannah had no children and so needed only one portion.

What does that have to do with his loving her? Elkanah acted in this fair way, which showed no improper favoritism to Hannah, *despite the fact* that Hannah was the one he really loved. The RSV captures this sense: "[A]nd, although he loved Hannah, he would give Hannah only one portion, because the LORD had closed her womb" (v. 5, RSV).

"The LORD had closed her womb," then, is the explanation of why the loved wife received less than the other. It was a simple, though of course sad, matter of fact that Hannah had no other mouths to feed.[6]

"The LORD had closed her womb," then, expresses to us Elkanah's own perspective on the situation. He did not understand why his loved wife was suffering this sorrow. But he did know that their circumstances were given to them by the God he worshiped. And, of course, he saw rightly. His behavior toward his childless wife was affected by his understanding. He did not express resentment toward her. He did not blame her. He loved her.

Elkanah saw these circumstances in the way in which we should see all of our circumstances, and especially those that are not welcome. All things that come our way (or do not come our way) are God's doing. He is sovereign over all that happens in his world. He is therefore sovereign over everything that happens (and that does not happen) in our lives. We will see shortly that this does not necessarily mean passive acceptance of the permanence of whatever happens to us. But it does mean humble recognition of God's hand behind the circumstances in which we find ourselves. This understanding will affect our behavior, especially in difficult and unwelcome circumstances.

Elkanah knew that, and his conduct in this first scene is an expression of that knowledge.

Peninnah and Her Taunts (vv. 6, 7a-b)

From Elkanah's exemplary conduct, we turn to Peninnah, described in verse 6 as Hannah's "rival": "And her rival used to provoke her grievously to irritate her, because the LORD had closed her womb" (v. 6).

It is possible for the human mind to twist and distort a theological truth, so that it produces not righteous conduct, as we saw in Elkanah, but the opposite. Verse 6 repeats, word for word, the entirely correct understanding of Elkanah reported in verse 5: "the LORD had closed her womb." Now, however, this understanding is part of Peninnah's perspective on the situation, which she makes into a reason to taunt and provoke her "rival."

We can imagine the harsh and hurtful words. "What have *you* got to thank the Lord for, Hannah? It's a bit of a joke, Hannah, *you* coming here to give thanks to the Lord year after year when the one thing you want he won't give you!" "The Lord has closed your womb, Hannah. Isn't it obvious that he does not care about you?"

Exactly the same correct theological understanding of a situation can lead to proper conduct like Elkanah's or can be misused as an excuse for improper conduct like Peninnah's.[7] "So it went on year by year. As often as she went up to the house of the LORD, she used to provoke her" (v. 7a-b).

Hannah and Her Suffering (v. 7c)

At last our attention comes to Hannah herself. There is little to say: "Therefore Hannah wept and would not eat" (v. 7c).

So distraught was she that she would not even eat the one portion Elkanah had given her. So it happened year after year, on these visits to Shiloh. That is our first scene.

SCENE 2: ONE DAY AT SHILOH . . . (vv. 8-18)

Scene 2 takes us to one particular occasion, one of these annual visits to Shiloh.[8] On this occasion Elkanah found his sobbing wife:

> And Elkanah, her husband, said to her, "Hannah, why do you weep? And why do you not eat? And why is your heart sad? Am I not more to you than ten sons?" (v. 8)

He treated her gently, tenderly. While he was powerless to change her circumstances, there is no suggestion that his words were other than understanding and kind.[9] He really did, as we heard in verse 5, love her.

Hannah's Prayer (vv. 9-11)

Hannah, who has so far in the story been the passive recipient of the actions of others (of the Lord's closing of her womb, of Peninnah's taunts, and of Elkanah's words of comfort), now acted. Her action (to all appearances an insignificant action) will turn out to change not only her life but the life of the nation and, indeed, if we dare to see it, the history of the world.

Follow what Hannah did: "After they had eaten and drunk in Shiloh, Hannah rose" (v. 9a).

Elkanah's words of comfort in verse 8 seem to have had some effect, so that Hannah, on this occasion, participated in the eating and drinking referred to in verse 9.[10] "They" in verse 9 seems to include Hannah.[11]

Hannah "rose" from her place at the table. This is the first action of Hannah in the story so far.

Before we hear what she stood up to do, we are pointed to the other character who will play a role in this scene: "Now Eli the priest was sitting on the seat beside the doorpost of the temple of the LORD" (v. 9b).

There, seated by the door of the Shiloh temple,[12] was Eli the priest. We will hear much more about Eli in the following chapters. He was effectively the human leader of the people of Israel at this time. At this point he is portrayed as a passive figure ("sitting"). Hannah is the active one.

Our attention returns to Hannah: "She was deeply distressed and prayed to the LORD and wept bitterly" (v. 10).

"Deeply distressed" (literally, "bitter of soul") implies Hannah's "disappointment, dissatisfaction, discontent"[13] with her circumstances. She was a deeply unhappy woman. But out of her misery and through her tears, Hannah "prayed to the LORD."

It should be clear now that Hannah knew what the narrator has told us twice — namely, that it was the Lord who had closed Hannah's womb.[14] This knowledge, however, led Hannah to act in a way different from both her husband and her rival. She "prayed to the LORD."

There is a special logic behind Hannah's action. We might call it the logic of faith. To know that your suffering has come, ultimately, from God's hand could lead to fatalism: "If God is sovereign, then who am I to do anything but passively accept my lot?" But that is not the logic of real faith in God. Alternatively the knowledge that God is Lord, even over my tragic experiences, could lead to resentment: "If God has done this to me, then I want nothing to do with him!" Again, this is not the logic of faith. Faith in God means knowing and trusting God's sovereignty *and his goodness* toward us. The logic of faith says, "we know that for those who love God all things work together for good, for those who are called according to his purpose," and therefore nothing in all of God's creation "will be able to separate us from the love of God that is in Christ Jesus our Lord" (Romans 8:28, 39). Faith in God, therefore, leads us in our troubles to pray to the God who is sovereign over all things. That is what Hannah did.

Where did Hannah's faith come from? Was it make-believe, like so much religion? There is a valuable hint in the language of Hannah's prayer:

> *And she vowed a vow and said, "O Lord of hosts, if you will indeed look on the affliction of your servant and remember me and not forget your servant, but will give to your servant a son, then I will give him to the Lord all the days of his life, and no razor shall touch his head." (v. 11)*

When Hannah asked God to "look on [her] affliction," she was echoing the language of God's dealings with Israel. The exodus from Egypt in the days of Moses — that historic act by which God redeemed his people and brought them to himself to be his people — is typically described like this: "I have surely *seen* the *affliction* of my people," "when they heard that the Lord . . . had *seen* their *affliction*, they bowed their heads and worshiped," "the Lord . . . *saw* our *affliction*," "you *saw* the *affliction* of our fathers in Egypt" (Exodus 3:7; 4:31; Deuteronomy 26:7; Nehemiah 9:9). The words in italics represent the same Hebrew words translated "look" and "affliction" in 1 Samuel 1:11. Hannah begged God to do for her what he had done for Israel in the days of Moses. She was asking God to do what God had shown to be his characteristic behavior toward his people.[15]

In other words, Hannah's faith, expressed in her prayer, was not make-believe. It was confidence based on knowledge of what God is like and what God had done.

At the same time the language of Hannah's prayer strengthens the impression we have already noted that Hannah's experience can be seen as a reflection of the sorry condition of Israel. "Affliction" would not be a bad word for the people's experience in the last pages of the book of Judges and the beginning of 1 Samuel. We will see that God's response to Hannah's need will turn out to be also his response to Israel's need.

Hannah's prayer took the form of a vow ("she vowed a vow"). It would be a misunderstanding to think that Hannah was here bargaining with God — making a promise that she hoped would induce God's favor ("if you do this for me, I'll do that for you"). Her prayer had the following elements:

• She addressed God in terms that acknowledged his majesty: "O Lord of hosts."[16] She knew who God is. All true prayer is like that. Prayer has been made possible by God's making himself known. We dare to speak to God because he has spoken to us.

• She approached God in terms that acknowledged her place before him — "your servant."[17] She knew who she was before God. All true prayer is like that, too. We can only speak to God humbly.

• She made her request known to God (cf. Philippians 4:6). She asked God for what she deeply desired. And what was that? God's attention: "if you will indeed *look* on the affliction of your servant and *remember* me and *not forget* your servant . . . " Here again is faith's logic. Some other logic might want to escape from God if God is ultimately responsible for my sad circumstances. But faith understands that there is nowhere else to go. God is sovereign *and* good. Hannah's only hope was that God, in his goodness, would attend to her sorrow, just as he had attended to the sorrow of the people of Israel in Egypt. There is a mystery here. Some modern writers set the kind of language used here by Hannah over against other Bible statements. If Hannah asked God to look upon her, does that imply that she had been out of his sight — as though God is not in fact omniscient? But elsewhere we read, "no creature is hidden from his sight" (Hebrews 4:13). If God is to "remember" and "not forget" her, does that imply that he had actually forgotten her, as though God has lapses of memory? But in the next chapter we will hear Hannah describe the Lord as "a God of knowledge" (1 Samuel 2:3). These statements are not in opposition. The language of Hannah's prayer is the language of human experience. God's omniscience and perfect knowledge were the *presupposition* of her prayer, but she prayed that God might *so* look on her misery and *so* attend to her that he would now do for her what he had previously not done — give her a son.

• She made her vow to God. Should God grant Hannah her request, then she promised that the child would be given to the one who had given him to her. The sense in which Hannah will "give him to the LORD" is indicated in the words "no razor shall touch his head." This appears to be a way of saying that he would be a Nazirite — a person particularly dedicated to God's service. A Nazirite vow was normally a temporary matter. In this case, however, Hannah's child would be a Nazirite "all the days of his life."[18]

Such was Hannah's prayer. The narrator has given us the privilege of hearing Hannah's prayer as only Hannah and the Lord would have heard it on that day. If we had been an ordinary witness to this tearful woman's distress that day, we could not have guessed the significance of her action.

Eli's Assurance (vv. 12-17)

Certainly Eli didn't. The old priest saw her but completely misunderstood:

> *As she continued praying before the LORD, Eli observed her mouth.*
> *Hannah was speaking in her heart; only her lips moved, and her voice*
> *was not heard. Therefore Eli took her to be a drunken woman. And Eli*

said to her, "How long will you go on being drunk? Put away your wine
from you." (vv. 12-14)

In the light of what we will learn in chapter 2, it is likely that Eli's misunderstanding was based on too many experiences of improper conduct at
the Shiloh temple (see vv. 12-17). Eli's misunderstanding certainly raises
questions about his competence. If Israel had a leader who could not tell the
difference between a godly woman's heartfelt prayer and drunken rambling,
no wonder Israel had a leadership crisis! This matter will become clearer in
our study of chapter 2.

Hannah's response put Eli straight:

But Hannah answered, "No, my lord, I am a woman troubled in spirit. I have
drunk neither wine nor strong drink, but I have been pouring out my soul before
the LORD. Do not regard your servant as a worthless woman, for all along I
have been speaking out of my great anxiety and vexation." (vv. 15, 16)

Later we will hear that Eli's sons, Hophni and Phinehas, were "worthless men."[19] Hannah here insisted that she was *not* "a worthless woman."[20]
The "worthlessness" of Eli's sons was linked, as we shall see, to the fact
that "they did not know the LORD" (1 Samuel 2:12).[21] Hannah, however, was
not like that. On the contrary, she had been pouring out her troubled soul
to the Lord. In her great sadness, her prayer shows that she, unlike them,
knew the Lord.

At last Eli spoke as he should have spoken at first: "Then Eli answered,
'Go in peace, and the God of Israel grant your petition that you have made
to him'" (v. 17).

Unknown to Eli he introduced a play on words that will be developed
by the end of this chapter. "Your petition that you have made" is, very literally, "your asking that you have asked." This vocabulary of asking occurs
seven times in this chapter with interesting implications that we will see in
a moment.[22] More importantly (and equally unknown to the old priest) he
endorsed a prayer that would lead to his own demise.[23] When the God of
Israel granted what Hannah asked of him, Israel would have a new leader.

Hannah's Lifted Face (v. 18)

Hannah's prayer changed things. In the first place it changed her: "And she
said, 'Let your servant find favor in your eyes.' Then the woman went her
way and ate, and her face was no longer sad" (v. 18).

She came away from bringing her request to the Lord a different person
from the one Elkanah had tried to comfort back in verse 8. Now she was no
longer weeping, no longer refusing her food, no longer sad. We may well

say that she had cast all her anxiety on the Lord, knowing that he cared for her. Certainly she had humbled herself under God's mighty hand, and he had exalted her (cf. 1 Peter 5:6, 7).

There is Scene 2, and the turning point of this story.

SCENE 3: BACK HOME AT RAMAH . . . (vv. 19, 20)

Scene 3 is brief.

Worshiping the Lord (v. 19a)

In verse 19 we see the family of Elkanah worshiping the Lord the next morning: "They rose early in the morning and worshiped before the LORD; then they went back to their house at Ramah" (v. 19a).

I expect that Hannah's worship that morning had a different tone! This year her journey back home was no doubt in a different spirit from the earlier journey from Ramah to Shiloh.

Remembered by the Lord (v. 19b)

What happened then? Hannah had prayed in verse 11, "If you will indeed look on the affliction of your servant and *remember* me . . ." We now read: "And Elkanah knew Hannah his wife, and the LORD remembered her" (v. 19b).

Just as the Lord had "remembered" Noah in the days of the flood, Abraham when he destroyed Sodom, Rachel when she conceived Joseph, and his covenant with Abraham in the days of Moses (Genesis 8:1; 19:29; 30:22; Exodus 2:24; 6:5; cf. Numbers 10:9), so he "remembered" Hannah. Whenever God "remembered" his people, it led to his action on their behalf. We will not be mistaken if we expect that his remembering Hannah will involve his remembering his people Israel.

Samuel (v. 20)

> And in due time Hannah conceived and bore a son, and she called his name Samuel, for she said, "I have asked for him from the LORD." (v. 20)

In Hebrew "Samuel" sounds a little like "Asked for." About this lad we are going to hear very much more.

SCENE 4: AT SHILOH AGAIN . . . (vv. 21-28)

There is one final scene in this story of Hannah. Scene 4 will take us back to Shiloh again.

Vow Remembered (vv. 21-23)

The time came around for Elkanah to make the annual journey to Shiloh. "The man Elkanah and all his house went up to offer to the LORD the yearly sacrifice and to pay his vow" (v. 21).

Hannah's vow had not been forgotten, but now we see that Elkanah also had a vow. We are told nothing specific about this vow, except that he went up with his family to fulfill it.[24] However, Hannah did not go:

> *But Hannah did not go up, for she said to her husband, "As soon as the child is weaned, I will bring him, so that he may appear in the presence of the LORD and dwell there forever." (v. 22)*

Hannah would not go up to Shiloh until she was in a position to fulfill *her* vow. Elkanah was fully supportive: "Elkanah her husband said to her, 'Do what seems best to you; wait until you have weaned him; only, may the LORD establish his word'" (v. 23).

What did Elkanah mean by "may the LORD establish his word"? We might have expected him to say, "May the Lord help *you* to keep *your* word."[25] After all, it is Hannah's vow to the Lord that is under consideration here. What could Elkanah possibly mean by "*his* [the LORD's] word"?

There is no explicit "word" of the Lord in this particular narrative. However, God's "word" is in many ways the theme of the whole story of which 1 Samuel 1 is part. God's "word" is the expression of his purpose, particularly in his promises to Israel. That was "the good word that the LORD spoke to the house of Israel" (literal translation from Joshua 21:45; cf. 23:14, 15). When we hear Elkanah say, "May the LORD establish his word," we realize, if we have not realized it before, that the Lord's answer to Hannah's prayer is part of his greater purposes for his people. The Lord has answered Hannah's prayer. May he go on to bring his purposes to fulfillment! Elkanah was a man of remarkable insight. Perhaps he spoke more profoundly than he knew.

There was then a period, perhaps two or three years, during which Hannah cared for her son:[26] "So the woman remained and nursed her son until she weaned him" (v. 23b).

A Vow Kept (vv. 24-28b)

When the time eventually came, Hannah took the young boy with her to Shiloh:

And when she had weaned him, she took him up with her, along with a three-year-old bull, an ephah of flour, and a skin of wine, and she brought him to the house of the LORD at Shiloh. And the child was young. (v. 24)

And so with a thank offering of generous proportions[27] Hannah set off to keep her word. The young lad[28] was brought to Shiloh.

Then they slaughtered the bull, and they brought the child to Eli. And she said, "Oh, my lord! As you live, my lord, I am the woman who was standing here in your presence, praying to the LORD. For this child I prayed, and the LORD has granted me my petition that I made to him. Therefore I have lent him to the LORD. As long as he lives, he is lent to the LORD." (vv. 25-28b)

As we saw in verse 20, Hannah had named the boy Samuel because in Hebrew "Samuel" sounds a little like "Asked for." Now she used "ask" words four times over. We cannot see this in our English translations, but it is striking in Hebrew: "The LORD has granted me my *petition* that I *made* of him. Therefore I have *lent* him to the LORD. As long as he lives, he is *lent* to the LORD." The words in italics are all forms of the word *ask* in Hebrew. Most curious of all is the fact that while Samuel sounds a little like "Asked for," a little later in 1 Samuel we will come across a name that really does mean "Asked for." That name is identical in Hebrew to the last occurrence of this verb in verse 28. The name is Saul. From the very beginning, long before these things actually took place, Samuel's name was linked to that of Saul.

Worship (v. 28c)

For the time being our story concludes with the boy Samuel worshiping the Lord at Shiloh. "And he worshiped the LORD there" (v. 28c).

What, then, are we to make of 1 Samuel 1? If this ancient story is the Word of God, what should we learn from God here? There are a number of possibilities.

We might, for example, notice the character of the excellent Elkanah. He seems to be presented in very positive terms. He is not one of the Bible's better-known figures, but here we see this faithful, godly man and husband honoring God and loving his distressed wife in domestically difficult circumstances. We could do worse than reflect on Elkanah's example. He clearly provides a *good* example (see particularly vv. 3-5, 8, 21, 23).

However, the chapter is much more about Hannah than it is about Elkanah. We may well profit, then, from considering what Hannah did with her distress. Prayer was not for Hannah a formality. It was real. She cast her cares on the Lord, knowing that he cared for her. And indeed he did. Again we see in Hannah a clearly good example.

Nevertheless I believe that we would be quite right to feel a little unsatisfied with both of those lines of thought. Not that there is anything *wrong* with the observations made so far. This chapter does present good examples in the conduct of both Elkanah and Hannah, but that does not seem to be the central message of this chapter.

We must be very careful when we just take the human characters in a Biblical narrative as *examples*. Of course, there are times when that is exactly what they are, and even chiefly what they are. It would be wrong to deny *any* exemplary understanding of persons in the Bible. But here there is clearly a problem. Are we to conclude on the basis of 1 Samuel 1 that if you are sad because you are a woman who cannot have children (or perhaps sad because of any other disappointment in life) you should pray earnestly to the Lord and the disappointment will turn to joy because you will get what you long for? Is that the message of 1 Samuel 1? If not, why not?

The answer is obvious enough. There must have been many other childless women in Israel. It is reasonable to assume that many of those prayed sincerely for a child. It is equally reasonable to assume that many of those were still not given a child. In other words, we are told this story of Hannah not because it is *typical* of every troubled person in Israel who prayed, but precisely because her story is *unusual*. Of all the troubled women in Israel, the Lord chose to grant the prayer of this one. The unusualness of Hannah's story, then, *limits* the sense in which it can be exemplary.

Why was the prayer of Hannah granted? Was it because she was *so* sincere in her praying? No. Was it because she was the *most* miserable of all childless women? Of course not. Was it because she made such an *extraordinary* vow? Certainly not.

You see, although it is right to see Hannah as an example for us *up to a point*, taken too far the exemplary approach might mislead us into thinking one of those ideas is Biblical.

First Samuel 1 is not primarily about Hannah, any more than it is primarily about Elkanah. It is mainly about God. First Samuel begins by showing us that God cared for Hannah. We will see, as this story unfolds, that his care for Hannah was his care for Israel. What he did for Hannah would turn out to be for Israel. Samuel (and indeed the strangely hinted-at Saul) would turn out to be, in their own ways, part of God's answer to Israel's leadership troubles.

First Samuel 1 points us to a most unexpected starting point for the answer that God is going to provide for the leadership crisis. Who would have looked twice at miserable, sobbing Hannah for the answer to Israel's crisis? We expect to find answers from the powerful. Hannah was not powerful. Her family were "nobodies." The point of her story, however, is that God cares.

Does God care? Yes, he cared about the leadership of his people Israel and gave Hannah a son. Yes, he cares about the leadership of the world and of us. Hannah's son will be surpassed by Mary's son. God's care for us all finds its fullest expression in Jesus Christ. If you belong to him you can learn to "cast all your anxieties on him, because he cares for you" (1 Peter 5:7).

3

The God of Knowledge

1 SAMUEL 2:1-10

Do you believe in God? That may seem a strange question to pose to a reader of a commentary on 1 Samuel. Who would read a book like this except someone who takes God seriously and has an honest interest in his Word? And yet I ask the question with complete seriousness because those of us who do indeed "believe in God" very easily forget the astonishing difference such belief must make to our understanding of everything.

Too often to believe in God is treated as though it were simply one part of a person's outlook on life, even perhaps a quite minor part. Some people are conservative, some progressive; some are outgoing, some more introverted; some are religious, some not so. However, such a domestication of belief in God is profoundly misguided. To believe in the God of the Bible is to see the whole world and all of life in radically different terms from the person who does not hold this belief. The person for whom believing in God is a small thing, just a part of their complex of attitudes, with no more drastic consequences than possible church attendance (or reading a commentary on 1 Samuel!), does not believe in the God of whom the Bible speaks. Not really.

The person who believes (who actually does believe, not who just *says* he believes) in God (the God who is there, not just some *idea* of God) will not only understand things differently — such a person will live differently. Values will be different, as will ambitions, joys, sorrows, loves, hates, motivations, confidence, fears. Why and how this is so is the theme of 1 Samuel 2:1-10.

One area in which our belief in God must make a profound difference is our attitude to leadership. Does your belief in God make a difference regarding the kind of leaders you follow and the kind of leader you are?

Does God substantially change the confidence you place in leaders and what you expect from leaders? These are difficult questions, but very important if believing in God is real.

In 1 Samuel 2:1-10 we hear the wonderful prayer of Hannah. One of the things we are going to see in the narrative of 1 Samuel is that the writer is not always committed to recording events in strict chronological sequence. This prayer may have been prayed, as it at first appears, at Shiloh, at the time when Samuel was dedicated to the Lord's service under Eli's tutelage. It is also possible that it was prayed earlier than it appears in the story, perhaps at the time of Samuel's birth. It is not out of the question that it could have been uttered at some later time, perhaps after Hannah had given birth to more children.[1]

The precise moment it was uttered matters little. What is clear is that the birth of Samuel, in answer to her earlier prayer in chapter 1, was the occasion and reason for this prayer. It is remarkable that this event should have inspired a prayer that looks so far beyond the circumstances that gave rise to it. By its end Hannah's prayer becomes a prophecy, with implications for the whole world and all of history!

The prayer has three parts: an introduction (which I have headed "The Incomparable God," vv. 1, 2), the body of the prayer ("The Transforming God," vv. 3-8), and a conclusion ("The Victorious God," vv. 9, 10).

THE INCOMPARABLE GOD (vv. 1, 2)

The opening lines of Hannah's prayer immediately reveal that this woman could not be accused of superficiality in her faith in God. She speaks first of her joy and delight in God, and second of his utter incomparability.

Joy and Delight (v. 1)

> And Hannah prayed and said,
> "My heart exults in the LORD;
>   my strength is exalted in the LORD.
> My mouth derides my enemies,
>   because I rejoice in your salvation." (v. 1)

The last time Hannah "prayed," things had been rather different.[2] Then she had been "deeply distressed" and "wept bitterly," not only because of her childlessness, but because of the taunts of her rival, Peninnah (1 Samuel 1:10).

Hannah now spoke of the difference God had made to her "heart," her "strength," and her "mouth." The language is extreme for the very good reason that the impact that God had on her life was overwhelming. However, there was more to it than that.

Listen to what she said in these opening lines, and then consider why she spoke so extravagantly.

A little earlier Elkanah had asked Hannah, "Why is your heart sad?" — more literally, "bad." She had described herself as "a woman troubled in spirit." She had poured out her "soul" before the Lord (1 Samuel 1:8, 15). Hannah's "bad heart," troubled spirit, and distressed soul had now been transformed. "My heart exults in the LORD," she said.

In Biblical thought the heart is more than the seat of emotions. The heart is the center of the person. Thoughts and plans, will and decision, as well as deep emotions, come from the heart. In Hannah's case the Lord was now the focus of her heart's confident joy.

"My strength" is a modern English attempt to clarify a vivid Biblical animal metaphor, literally, "my horn." "The idea seems to be that the animal's horn is its glory and power, held high, perhaps in triumph after goring an enemy into submission."[3] While we might appreciate the translators' attempt to make this image's meaning clear for us, I am sure you will agree that something is lost![4] This woman who had previously prayed out of her "great anxiety and vexation" speaks very differently now. "My horn is raised high by the LORD," she said.

"My mouth derides my enemies" is another domestication of an even more severe Biblical image. The animal imagery of the previous line seems to continue, and Hannah literally says, "My mouth is wide against my enemies" — that is, like the triumphant animal ready to devour its prey![5]

On the one hand it is right to recognize that Hannah's graphic language is poetic, and we need to take this into account as we hear its violence. It *is* a metaphor. On the other hand we should appreciate that the metaphor is so forceful because Hannah understood her experience to have been very dramatic indeed. Why, we will see in a moment.

The reason for the exulting of Hannah's heart, the lifting of her "horn," and the wideness of her mouth is given in the last line of verse 1: "because I rejoice in your salvation."

Salvation is a very important word in the Bible because the Lord is a God who saves. It is unfortunate when the word becomes empty religious jargon. In Hannah's case, however, we might be excused for wondering whether "your salvation" is a rather exaggerated term for the birth of her child.

As we listen to the strong language with which Hannah's prayer began, we may well wonder whether it is not all just a little overstated. We understand that she had been a childless wife. Now she had a son. She had been the object of cruel mockery. Now her rival could laugh at her no more. She had been bitterly distressed. Now she was filled with joy. And we understand that all this was God's doing. He had answered her prayer. Nonetheless, we wonder whether Peninnah's taunts warrant the language "my enemies" and whether Hannah's happy change of circumstances should really be called God's "salvation." Her language makes her sound rather more like a victorious army than a new mother!

The incongruity between Hannah's extreme language and what was, after all, a common enough (though wonderful) experience, the birth of a child, is an important key to this remarkable prayer.

In her earlier prayer, in chapter 1, we noted that she drew on the vocabulary of Israel's history. The same is true of this prayer. Hannah sounds like a victorious army because she was echoing the language of Israel on occasions of great deliverance by God. In particular she seems to express the same sentiments as Moses and the people of Israel after they were rescued from the Egyptians:

> *I will sing to the LORD, for he has triumphed gloriously;*
> *the horse and his rider he has thrown into the sea.*
> *The LORD is my strength and my song,*
> *and he has become my salvation;*
> *this is my God, and I will praise him,*
> *my father's God, and I will exalt him. (Exodus 15:1, 2)*

When Hannah had prayed for a child, she had used language that reminded us of God's deliverance of Israel from Egypt. Hannah had cried out to the God who had "seen" the "affliction" of his people in Egypt, asking him to now "look on" her "affliction." The words of her prayer helped us to see that her suffering was, in a sense, a representation of Israel's suffering. We began to see that Hannah's story stands at the beginning of 1 Samuel because there is a connection, yet to be played out, between Hannah's story and Israel's story.

In the same way her language as she praised the God who *did* look on her affliction helps us see that God's goodness to her was in a sense a representation of God's goodness to Israel. The birth of Samuel stands at the beginning of 1 Samuel because there is a connection, yet to be played out, between Samuel and the story of God's salvation of his people Israel.

Hannah may, of course, have spoken more profoundly than she fully understood. That is a common feature of Biblical history that we will see many times in 1 Samuel. However, as we now listen to her words we will find a growing realization that the birth of Samuel, the occasion for this prayer, was part of something far, far bigger. Hannah's prayer was surely divinely inspired. By the end of the prayer she will be speaking as a prophet.

No One Like Him (v. 2)

Hannah's exuberant faith in God was the same as the faith of Moses and Israel at the time of the exodus. At the core of that faith was an appreciation of his utter uniqueness:

> *There is none holy like the LORD;*
> > *there is none besides you;*
> > *there is no rock like our God. (v. 2)*

After the exodus Moses and the people had sung:

> *Who is like you, O LORD, among the gods?*
> > *Who is like you, majestic in holiness,*
> > *awesome in glorious deeds, doing wonders? (Exodus 15:11)*

Quite simply, those, like Hannah, who know the God of the exodus know that there is no one, no thing, no power — there is *nothing* to compare to the Lord.

Hannah makes this point in three lines, the second of which sums up the general truth, "there is none besides you."[6] The first and the third lines make the slightly more particular points that the Lord is unique in holiness and in being a "rock." "Holy" speaks of God's perfection, with moral overtones,[7] while "rock" speaks of the protection and security to be found in him.[8]

This God cannot be set alongside other options that might be the focus of our hopes, our confidence, and our dreams. Nowhere will you find goodness as perfect as the holiness of the Lord; nowhere will you find safety as sure as our God provides. Hannah knew, as the Israelites who came out of Egypt knew, the stupidity of allowing *anything* to rival the Lord, this holy God, our rock. He is the incomparable God! There is no one besides him, no one like him!

Do you think you believe in God like Hannah believed in God?

THE TRANSFORMING GOD (vv. 3-8)

This introduction is followed by the body of her prayer, in which we will see the radically different view she had of everything in the world because of the faith in God expressed in verses 1, 2.

Knowledge That Answers Arrogance (v. 3)

First mentioned is human arrogance:

Talk no more so very proudly,
*   let not arrogance come from your mouth;*
for the LORD is a God of knowledge,
*   and by him actions are weighed. (v. 3)*

"A God of knowledge" is a God who knows. This is a wonderful description of God. God is not an abstract or religious *idea*. He is related to us, and to his whole creation, by knowledge. He *knows* all. There are no secrets from him; there are no mysteries to him; there is no unknown to him. There is no possibility of deceiving him (cf. Luke 16:15). Human pride and arrogance is a form of pretending. Because the Lord is a God who knows, it must *stop!*[9]

The proud and the arrogant are those who deny in their attitudes and actions, but particularly in their speaking, the uniqueness of the Lord. Self-centeredness, self-confidence, self-sufficiency is what they express. Because the Lord is a God of knowledge, such proud talk must cease.

All human actions should be seen in the light of the fact that they are weighed by the God of knowledge (cf. Romans 2:16). Look at Peninnah's hateful cruelty. Weighed by the God of knowledge, its true character is seen. Look at the things you have done today. Can you see them weighed by the God of knowledge? Particularly consider the human abilities, achievements, triumphs, and successes that lead to pride and self-confidence. When they are weighed by the God of knowledge, the arrogant mouth is silenced.

Power That Turns the World Upside Down (vv. 4-8c)

In verses 4 to 8 Hannah catalogs a series of things that generate human pride and shows how different they look when the incomparable God of knowledge is taken into account.

"The bows of the mighty are broken" (v. 4a) Perhaps she was thinking about the Egyptians again. What fearful warriors they were! Within a few pages in 1 Samuel the Philistines will appear. The people of Israel will have reason to tremble. Interestingly the "bows" of the Philistines will appear in the last chapter of 1 Samuel and will be indirectly responsible for Saul's death and a terrible defeat of the Israelites (see 31:3). We must not underestimate "the bows of the mighty." They are very powerful indeed and can do much damage.

However, Hannah saw "the bows of the mighty" in the light of the "God of knowledge," by whom actions are weighed. "The bows of the mighty are *broken*," she said. Shattered. Smashed. Like the Egyptian chariots sinking beneath the waves of the sea (Exodus 15:4). The Lord *demolishes* human power. Do you see human power in that light?[10]

The other side of this reality is: ". . . but the feeble bind on strength" (v. 4b).

In due course this book will tell us of a young lad with a few pebbles in his shepherd's pouch — "feeble" is what he looked like — who will bring down a Philistine giant (see 17:40-51). If you had seen the two facing each other, if you had heard the arrogance that came from the Philistine's mouth, you would not have held out much hope for the boy. Unless, that is, you saw things as Hannah did and knew that there really is no rock like our God. With him strength does not depend on human power. "The feeble bind on strength."

Human power and human weakness look completely different if you believe in God as Hannah believed in God.

Turn from human power to human plenty: "Those who were full have hired themselves out for bread" (v. 5a).

Much later in the story of 1 Samuel we will meet a very rich man who feasted like a king but refused to give food and drink to some strangers who asked him (see 25:1-12). We will see that his full stomach did not save him! People who have plenty can seem as though they could never be in need. Unless, that is, you see them with eyes like Hannah's, knowing that actions are weighed by the God of knowledge.

On the other hand: ". . . but those who were hungry have ceased to hunger" (v. 5b).

In the story of the very rich man, those strangers who were hungry were provided for by God's providential care (1 Samuel 25:18-35). The satisfaction of human need does not depend finally on human resources. Human security cannot be measured by human prosperity. "There is no rock like our God" (v. 2).

Once again I wonder whether you are finding that you believe in God as Hannah did?

The catalog of reversals in Hannah's faithful perception of the world now turns to her recent experience: "The barren has borne seven . . ." (v. 5c).

I am not at all sure that Hannah had borne seven children yet, but there was no reason why she could not — not if you take into account the Lord.[11]

On the other hand: ". . . but she who has many children is forlorn" (v. 5d).

Just as Hannah's misery at her barrenness was not unchangeable, so Peninnah's happiness at her many children was not secure. Life is not like that. God can reverse every human circumstance completely.

Hannah pressed the logic of this faith to the limit:

The LORD kills and brings to life;
  he brings down to Sheol and raises up. (v. 6)

Hannah's grasp of reality was extraordinary. We occasionally hear it said that the Old Testament had no concept of resurrection from the dead. Hannah did! The Lord changes life to death, and death to life. When we think of life and refuse to think of death, or when we think of death and ignore the God who raises the dead, our understanding is a distortion of the reality.

A little less dramatically, but just as radically Hannah asserted:

> The LORD makes poor and makes rich;
>> he brings low and he exalts. (v. 7)

Poverty and riches are in his power, just as are fame and ignominy. God determines these things. They are not under our control at all. Nor are they under the control of others, or of social and economic forces. The government does not determine them, nor does the stock market.

Furthermore:

> He raises up the poor from the dust;
>> he lifts the needy from the ash heap
> to make them sit with princes
>> and inherit a seat of honor. (v. 8a-c)

Hannah had a peculiar view of the world, don't you think? She was not describing the world as we ordinarily experience it, nor the world as it seems to our normal observations. She was describing how things appear, the possibilities that present themselves, when you know that "there is none holy like the LORD" (v. 2).

The book of 1 Samuel is going to tell of a remarkable sequence of events in which these possibilities were realized. It is an important part of the whole Bible that tells the full story of the God who really does make this difference to everything.

Before we look at the end of verse 8, which clinches this part of Hannah's prayer, let me ask you once again, do you see life as Hannah did? It is a searching question if we consider it honestly. What is your attitude to the various forms of human power? Do you see wealth as a means of security? Do you fear being weak or poor? Do you mind being unimportant? What do you think about life and death? Do you think that you have the power to hold on to life and avoid death? Most people seem to live as though they do.

There is a natural, understandable, defensible human answer to each of these questions. And there is an answer that comes from actually believing in the God of knowledge. As we listen to Hannah's prayer we must ask, where is the Lord, the God of knowledge, in our real thinking about life?

The Creator (v. 8d-e)

At the end of verse 8 two lines state simply why believing in God must so radically transform your attitude to everything:

> *For the pillars of the earth are the LORD's,*
> *and on them he has set the world. (v. 8d-e)*

In other words, the Lord is the Creator who established the world and sustains all existence. This world does not run along on principles that have some kind of independence from God. It all belongs to God and is utterly dependent on him in every way.

THE VICTORIOUS GOD (vv. 9, 10)

We might describe the body of Hannah's prayer, verses 3-8, as a Biblical worldview. This is what the world looks like when your heart exults in the Lord and you rejoice in his salvation. But the Biblical worldview is not static, and Hannah worked out the marvelous logic of her prayer in three final points.

The Winning Side (v. 9)

The first concluding point is this:

> *He will guard the feet of his faithful ones,*
> *but the wicked shall be cut off in darkness,*
> *for not by might shall a man prevail. (v. 9)*

The winners in the end will not be the strong, the powerful, the wealthy, the famous, the popular, the successful. He who has most toys in the end will *not* win! The Lord will bring through those who belong to him, "his faithful ones."

Those who are not "his faithful ones" are lumped together and called in verse 9 "the wicked." It does not matter what they do or what they become; without the Lord who set the world on its pillars they cannot prevail. For human might will not be the last word.

First Samuel is an account of how that happened in an important part of the whole Bible's story.

The Losing Side (v. 10a-b)

The second concluding point is a warning:

> *The adversaries of the LORD shall be broken to pieces;*
> *against them he will thunder in heaven. (v. 10a, b)*

It is not wise to set yourself against the Lord. The story 1 Samuel tells demonstrates this, and it will help us to see that it is still so.[12]

The King (v. 10c-e)

All this has been leading up to the climax of Hannah's prayer, which now clearly becomes a prophecy:

> *The LORD will judge the ends of the earth;*
> *he will give strength to his king*
> *and exalt the power of his anointed. (v. 10c-e)*

The first line, though remarkable, is not unexpected after what we have heard from Hannah. This God, who is the Creator of all things and who knows all things and by whom deeds are weighed, will certainly judge the ends of the earth.[13] Hannah's prayer now sees beyond even the people of Israel to the whole world.

It is astonishing that Hannah should speak now of God's "*king.*" At the time, of course, there was no king in Israel. It is true that occasionally in the past there had been indications that Israel would one day have a king (see Genesis 17:6, 16; 35:11; Exodus 19:6; Numbers 24:7; Deuteronomy 17:14-20). There was an occasion when kingship had been attempted in Israel, but it was an unmitigated disaster (see Judges 9). However, Hannah's reference to God's *king* is completely unexpected. There is little point in speculating what thought processes led to this weighty word coming at the climax of Hannah's prayer.[14] The prayer itself points to the true source of her insight — the God of knowledge!

Not only did she speak of God's "king," she called that king his "anointed." The Hebrew word is *messiah*; translated into Greek it becomes *christos.* Hannah could not have known who the Lord's messiah-king was to be. It is possible (but only possible) that she had her own son, Samuel, in mind. We can speculate that she may have interpreted his extraordinary birth as a sign of future greatness in God's purposes.

However, her recorded words do not identify the king. They simply tell us that the Lord will give him strength and raise his "horn" (ESV, "power"). The last line of the prayer uses the precise vocabulary we noted in verse 1.

The Lord who raised Hannah's "horn" will do the same for his anointed king!

The story of the book of 1 Samuel could be described as the extended answer to the question, who is the Lord's anointed king?[15] Hannah's prayer raises that question, with the implication that the answer to Israel's leadership crisis will be found in him.

Before we leave Hannah's prayer, we must take note of one more remarkable fact. Many years later another woman prayed a prayer that sounded astonishingly like Hannah's prayer. This is her prayer:

> *My soul magnifies the Lord,*
> > *and my spirit rejoices in God my Savior,*
> *for he has looked on the humble estate of his servant.*
> > *For behold, from now on all generations will call me blessed;*
> *for he who is mighty has done great things for me,*
> > *and holy is his name.*
> *And his mercy is for those who fear him*
> > *from generation to generation.*
> *He has shown strength with his arm;*
> > *he has scattered the proud in the thoughts of their hearts;*
> *he has brought down the mighty from their thrones*
> > *and exalted those of humble estate;*
> *he has filled the hungry with good things,*
> > *and the rich he has sent away empty.*
> *He has helped his servant Israel,*
> > *in remembrance of his mercy,*
> *as he spoke to our fathers,*
> > *to Abraham and to his offspring forever. (Luke 1:46-55)*

Mary knew what Hannah knew — and more. Mary had been told that the child she would bear was to be a very great king, the greatest, whose kingdom would never end (Luke 1:32, 33). And Mary knew that this king would turn the world upside down.

Hannah's song in the whole Bible story is an anticipation of Mary's song. The question for us, for whom God's King, Jesus, has come, is whether we believe in God with the clarity and truth we have seen in Hannah's marvelous prayer.

4

Corruption and Ineptitude

1 SAMUEL 2:11-26

There is a certain cynicism these days about leadership. We do not believe the words of political leaders. We are suspicious of the motives of business leaders. We doubt the competence of church leaders. We have come to expect that leaders will let us down. Most of us seem sure that we are better, wiser, and more able than those who lead us. Just listen to how we talk about those in leadership!

In our cynicism we seem to take some delight in being proven right in our low expectations. The media help us in this. What better front-page story than the exposure of corruption and ineptitude in high places yet once again?

The democratic form of government that many of us enjoy allows our cynicism about leadership to be expressed. When we lose whatever confidence we might once have had in the government, we elect the opposition. Things change, but only to the extent that we exchange one set of problems for another. The big problems remain, and before long we are thinking that it is time to give the opposition a go again! One of the chief attractions of democracy to those who are cynical about leadership is that we can change leaders regularly without having to shoot them! We love democracy because we love getting rid of leaders, and democracy gives us a painless way of doing it.

Is this unfair? I readily admit that I am not providing the full case for democracy, but I am suggesting that our remarkable commitment to democracy as a form of government is linked to our cynicism about leadership. Democracy is not a means of appointing the wisest possible leaders or the most able or the most honest. Democracy has the great advantage of being a mechanism for getting rid of leaders without a civil war. It is a way of ensuring that leaders do not become too powerful. We don't want leaders to become too powerful because we do not trust leaders. Leaders are not good enough or wise enough or competent enough to be trusted with too much power.

This cynicism about leaders has an obvious validity. Personally I am very much in favor of democracy, for the kind of reasons I have indicated. As Winston Churchill famously said, "Democracy is the worst form of government except all the others that have been tried." We have developed very low expectations for leaders — and not just political leaders.

And yet we expect a great deal from leaders! The paradox is that we are so cynical toward them because we think that they *could* do so much better. Yes, this is contradictory, but consistency has never been a strong human trait. We tend to get excited at a *change* of leadership, whether in government or at work or even in a church — or anywhere else. For all our cynicism we pin great hopes on leaders, especially on a new leader. We do follow some leaders, until they let us down. Our disappointment with certain leaders leads to a strong loyalty to another leader. We become polarized over leaders. We tend to see one as unable to do anything right, and another as unable to err. "I follow Paul." "I follow Apollos." "I follow Cephas" (1 Corinthians 1:12).

High expectations of leaders and high hopes for what a leader might achieve are not necessarily wrong. But there is this confusion: at the same time as expecting little from leaders, we expect much.

In this confusion one thing is common, and very clear once you see it. *God* does not feature in the attitudes of most people toward leadership. As you think, with cynicism or expectation, about leaders who affect your life, what place does God have in your thinking? What difference does having God in your thinking make to either your cynicism or your expectations?

In 1 Samuel 2:11-26 we will see that in Israel there was reason for cynicism about leadership. Was it like our cynicism? We will see something of the difference that God made to the situation. What can we learn about the difference God makes to our situation?

In chapter 1 we heard about Samuel's birth to Elkanah and Hannah, and how he was brought to Shiloh, where he was apprenticed to the priest Eli. Samuel's unusual birth and the prominence given to the story by the writer of 1 Samuel make us suspect that this lad is worth watching. Chapter 1 closed by telling us, "He worshiped the LORD there," in Shiloh.

Hannah's prayer recorded in 2:1-10 was extraordinary. It powerfully set before us a view of the world that, frankly, few of us find familiar. It is the view of the world that takes God with full seriousness. Hannah's prayer takes us to the heart of the message of 1 Samuel. We will have heard this book well if we can learn to see the world as Hannah saw it. We should keep looking back to Hannah's prayer as we move through the pages of 1 Samuel.

We take up the story in verse 11 of chapter 2, which picks up the narrative from the end of chapter 1. What happened once Samuel had been handed over to Eli at Shiloh?

> *Then Elkanah went home to Ramah. And the boy ministered to the LORD in the presence of Eli the priest. (v. 11)*

We presume that Elkanah took with him to Ramah the rest of his family, including Hannah, as on former occasions (cf. 1 Samuel 1:19).[1] On this occasion, however, one member stayed at Shiloh. Our attention is drawn to this one and to what he was doing. We are in no doubt who "the boy" was.[2] He is the one we last saw at the end of chapter 1, who "worshiped the LORD" at Shiloh. In language now appropriate to his priestly apprenticeship we learn that he was "ministering[3] to the LORD in the presence of Eli the priest."

Samuel was acting as a priest, doing what a priest was meant to do, or was at least beginning to do so, under the supervision of Eli.[4] The activities of "the boy," however, were in stark contrast to other practices at that time at Shiloh.

CORRUPTION IN ELI'S HOUSE (vv. 12-17)

When Shiloh was first mentioned in chapter 1 we were told that "the two sons of Eli, Hophni and Phinehas, were priests of the LORD" there (v. 3). We were told nothing more about these priests then. It is now time to become better acquainted with these sons of Eli.

They Did Not Know the Lord (v. 12)

Before we do so, it is instructive to recall how Eli earlier accused Hannah of being a drunken woman, and that she insisted that she was not "a worthless woman" (1 Samuel 1:16). The expression she used was harsh and vivid: "a daughter of *belial*." The Hebrew word *belial* in various contexts is associated with death, wickedness, and rebellion.[5] It later became a name for the prince of evil. In the New Testament Paul speaks of the opposite extremes: "What accord has Christ with Belial?" (2 Corinthians 6:15). While we should not read back all of these associations into 1 Samuel, we are right to hear Hannah using unusually strong language when she begged not to be seen as "a daughter of *belial*."

The last time this language was used in the Biblical narrative was Judges 19:22 and 20:13, where the gang that raped and murdered the Levite's concubine are called "sons of *belial*" (ESV, "worthless fellows"). That provides a vivid background to what we are about to hear about Eli's sons!

We now learn that Hannah's strong language had a terrible appropriateness there at the Shiloh temple: "Now the sons of Eli were worthless men. They did not know the LORD" (v. 12).

The sons of Eli were "sons of *belial*." Their character was drawn more from *belial* (destruction, wickedness, rebellion) than from Eli. This dreadful state of affairs is traced to its source: "They did not know the LORD." They were, in other words, like Pharaoh when faced with Moses. That ruler proudly boasted, "I do not know the LORD" (Exodus 5:2).[6] In his case this was not an admission of ignorance but an assertion of defiance. Pharaoh refused to acknowledge the Lord. He would therefore not heed his demands. In their own way Eli's sons were doing the same. That made them "sons of *belial*."

The description of Hophni and Phinehas as "sons of *belial*" sets them in utter contrast to Hannah who was *not* a "daughter of *belial*" (1:16). The crucial comment "They did not know the LORD" reminds us of Hannah's words, "The LORD is a God of knowledge, and by him actions are weighed" (2:3). Eli's sons may have failed to know the Lord, but the Lord would not fail to know them or their deeds.

Unfortunately, our cynicism about leadership probably means that the description of Hophni and Phinehas does not immediately shock us. We have become used to corruption in high places. It does not surprise or greatly disturb us to hear of people with great responsibilities proving unworthy. Furthermore, many of us do not find ourselves filled with respect for *religious* leaders. We know of church and denominational leaders today of whom 1 Samuel 2:12 could be said! Therefore it is probably not devastating news to our ears to hear that a couple of young priests at Shiloh were rogues.

However, verse 12 is *meant* to shock us. This was *Israel*, the nation chosen by God out of all the earth to be "a kingdom of priests and a holy nation" (Exodus 19:6). This was *Shiloh*, the place, for the time being, where the holy tabernacle was set up as God's dwelling place among his people. These young men were *priests*, with the solemn duty to teach the people God's Law and offer sacrifices for the atonement of the people's sins. Therefore the scandal that the young priests at Shiloh were "sons of *belial*" who repudiated knowledge of the Lord was appalling.

Contempt for the Offering of the Lord (vv. 13-17)

What was it like for the people to have priests like that? Verses 13-17 give us a glimpse of the behavior of young Hophni and Phinehas.

The custom of the priests with the people was that when any man offered
sacrifice, the priest's servant would come, while the meat was boiling,
with a three-pronged fork in his hand, and he would thrust it into the pan
or kettle or cauldron or pot. All that the fork brought up the priest would
take for himself. This is what they did at Shiloh to all the Israelites who
came there. (vv. 13, 14)

To be sure, priests were entitled to certain benefits from their work at
the tabernacle (see Leviticus 7:28-38; Deuteronomy 18:1-8; and note, later
in this chapter, 1 Samuel 2:28), but these priests exploited the people they
were meant to be serving. Their "custom" was a far cry from anything laid
down in the Law.

These young priests were greedy and lazy. They did even not do their
dirty work themselves but had a servant do it for them.[7] In a "frenzy of
gluttony"[8] the servant poked a pronged fork into any and every cooking pot
at hand. *All* that that the fork found, the priests would "take for [literally,
"into"] himself."[9]

This was the "custom" of the priests. There is probably a touch of bitter
irony here. The word translated "custom" has a basic meaning of "justice."[10]
It is based on the same root as the term *judge*. The leaders God provided
for Israel in these days were called "judges." "Justice" is what they were
meant to bring to Israel, by delivering them from their enemies and resolv-
ing disputes.[11] The young priests at Shiloh brought their own version of
"justice" to Israel: taking from the people as much as they could with the
threat of force.[12]

Furthermore, if that was the priests' wayward "custom," there were
times when they even surpassed that degeneracy:

Moreover, before the fat was burned, the priest's servant would come and
say to the man who was sacrificing, "Give meat for the priest to roast, for
he will not accept boiled meat from you but only raw." And if the man
said to him, "Let them burn the fat first, and then take as much as you
wish," he would say, "No, you must give it now, and if not, I will take it
by force." (vv. 15, 16)

In other words, there were times when the priests, through their servant,
stepped in earlier in the process and demanded, with the threat of force,
that meat be handed over then and there.[13] In line with their gluttony, the
only reason indicated for their conduct was their predilection for roasted
meat![14]

The sacrificers rightly protested, but to no avail. Force won the day.
These priests did not share Hannah's outlook that "not by might shall a man
prevail" (1 Samuel 2:9).

The writer sums up this situation in these solemn words:

Thus the sin of the young men was very great in the sight of the LORD, for the men treated the offering of the LORD with contempt. (v. 17)

"The young men" now refers to Hophni and Phinehas, presumably along with their servant.[15] How very different was their conduct from that of Hannah, who recognized and saw the implications of the fact that "there is none holy like the LORD" (1 Samuel 2:2).

BUT SAMUEL . . . (vv. 18-21)

But there was another young man at Shiloh. Quietly, perhaps hardly noticed, he provided a stark contrast to the hubris of the others: "Samuel was ministering before the LORD, a boy clothed with a linen ephod" (v. 18).

A "linen ephod" was a simple garment worn by priests.[16] As the sons of Eli were abusing their position as priests, Samuel did what a priest was meant to do, and looked the part.[17] There is a suggestion of progress since verse 11. There Samuel "was ministering to the LORD in the presence of Eli the priest." He was operating clearly under Eli. In verse 18, however, Eli is not mentioned. Samuel "was ministering in the presence of the LORD"[18] and was wearing the garments of a priest himself.

In total contrast to the abusive behavior of Hophni and Phinehas, we are now given a glimpse of the tender care that Samuel enjoyed from his family and that Elkanah and Hannah enjoyed from the Lord: "And his mother used to make for him a little robe and take it to him each year when she went up with her husband to offer the yearly sacrifice" (v. 19).

This reminds us of the beginning of our story. It all began with those visits to Shiloh that were so miserable for Hannah year after year (1 Samuel 1:3-7). The annual pilgrimage was still taking place, but now it was a time for Hannah's tender motherly love to find expression in the new robe she brought each year for her growing boy. We can easily picture the care with which that robe was made each year — each year a little bigger!

Samuel would wear a robe for the rest of his life (and beyond!), and his robe will feature at two important points later in the story (1 Samuel 15:27 and 28:14).[19]

It seems clear that Elkanah and Hannah were spared any contact with Eli's sons. Their experience at Shiloh year after year was a wonderful contrast to what was going on for others at the hands of those two rogues.

Then Eli would bless Elkanah and his wife, and say, "May the LORD give you children by this woman for the petition she asked of the LORD." So then they would return to their home. (v. 20)

The "petition she asked of the LORD"[20] was, of course, Samuel, who had been given back to the Lord and who was quietly serving the Lord there at Shiloh. The blessing Eli prayed for Elkanah and Hannah was granted: "Indeed the LORD visited Hannah, and she conceived and bore three sons and two daughters" (v. 21a).

"The barren has borne seven," she said in her prayer (1 Samuel 2:5). That was almost literally true! As the sons of Eli were disregarding the Lord and treating his offering with contempt, the Lord was at work turning the world upside down. And they had no idea!

This is the last we hear of Hannah and Elkanah. We must assume that they lived out their days at Ramah, busy with their large family and with their annual trips to Shiloh. Our interest is going to be on the son they left there at the temple.

"And the young man Samuel grew in the presence of the LORD" (v. 21b) — literally, "with the LORD." This is a delightful expression. It speaks not just of Samuel's activities in the Lord's service, as in verses 11, 18, but now of Samuel himself. He grew "with the LORD." It is true that Samuel's relationship with the Lord had a long way to go.[21] It is equally clear that at this stage his growth was taking place with the Lord's approval. This will be made even clearer shortly.

INEPTITUDE IN ELI'S LEADERSHIP (vv. 22-25)

It is time for our attention to turn to Eli, the senior figure at Shiloh. Our impressions of Eli so far have been a little mixed. His rebuke of Hannah in chapter 1, mistaking the poor praying woman for a drunkard, was our unfortunate first impression. He quickly recovered and has dealt kindly and well with Hannah and her family since then. For all we can tell, Samuel was prospering under his tutelage. The pressing question, of course, is, what was he doing about his wretched sons?

Old Eli Knew (v. 22)

Perhaps the most important thing for us to understand about Eli is what we are told, for the first time, at the beginning of verse 22 — he was "very old." To understand Eli, and to be fair to him, his great age must be kept in mind.

But that is not all:

Now Eli was very old, and he kept hearing all that his sons were doing to all Israel, and how they lay with the women who were serving at the entrance to the tent of meeting. (v. 22)

Because of his great age he was not directly in touch with what was happening at Shiloh. However, word would reach him. There was clearly outrage at his sons' behavior, and it was reported to the old man. He knew what they were doing.

The reports he would hear were worse than we have been told. Eli heard about the greedy bullying described in verses 13-16 ("all that his sons were doing to all Israel"). He also heard that they were turning the tent of meeting into a brothel![22] The picture is vague in some details, but clear in essentials.[23] The greed of Hophni and Phinehas had gone beyond roast meat!

Sadly, in the conduct of these young men we recognize two forms that corruption in leadership commonly takes. The greed of verses 13-17, where leaders use their position for personal gain, has damaged many in leadership. The particularly powerful and perverse form of greed mentioned in verse 22, sexual immorality, where leaders use their position to exploit others for their own sexual pleasure, is all too familiar. If we have become too cynical to be shocked, we do well to pause. Leadership like that of Hophni and Phinehas was — and is — evil.

The point made in verse 22 is that old Eli *knew*.

Old Eli Spoke (vv. 23-25a)

But what did he *do*?

> And he said to them, "Why do you do such things? For I hear of your evil dealings from all the people. No, my sons; it is no good report that I hear the people of the LORD spreading abroad. If someone sins against a man, God will mediate for him, but if someone sins against the LORD, who can intercede for him?" (vv. 23-25a)

He spoke to his sons about their perversity.

First, he called them to give an account of themselves: "Why do you do such things?" There can be no justification for the youths' wicked failure in their responsibilities. Eli's "Why?" was as close as he got to calling them to repent.

Second, he told them plainly that their conduct was "evil" and "no[t] good." Their wickedness was known by "all the people."

Third, he explained the seriousness of their deeds. The people they had abused were "the people of the LORD," and their actions were a direct offense against God. They had put themselves in terrible danger. It was not just that they had mistreated other people. In such a situation God has provided means for sins being dealt with.[24] Much of God's Law was concerned with such offenses. The God-given means of cleansing had at its heart the sacrificial system. However, the offense of the Shiloh priests (as we saw in verse

17) was that they showed contempt for the very means provided by God for dealing with their sins. This seems to be the meaning of "if someone sins against the LORD."

The New Testament equivalent to this argument is found in the Letter to the Hebrews. The person "who has spurned the Son of God, and has profaned the blood of the covenant by which he was sanctified" must understand that then "there no longer remains a sacrifice for sins" (10:29, 26; cf. 6:6). If your sin, like the sin of Hophni and Phinehas, consists of contempt for the very means God has provided for your salvation, what hope remains?

While Eli's words were true and right, there is something pathetic about them. There was not a direct rebuke and demand for repentance, but a pleading "Why?" He did not address them directly as the sons of worthlessness (v. 12) that they were, but appealed to them as "my sons" (v. 24). We sense a certain helplessness in Eli's imploring speech.

Old Eli Was Ignored (v. 25b-c)

We are therefore not entirely surprised to hear: "But they would not listen to the voice of their father . . ." (v. 25b).

These sons of Eli were really sons of *belial*. They were beyond heeding the voice of Eli.

The writer then adds these chilling words: ". . . for it was the will of the LORD to put them to death" (v. 25c).

They had gone too far. They were beyond repentance (cf. Hebrews 6:4-6). The Lord had given them up to their contempt for him and his ways (cf. Romans 1:24, 26, 28).

This is not a truth about God that we like to hear. But it is a grave mistake to think that verse 25 allows the *blame* for the young men's hardness of heart to be placed on God.[25] Their hardness was both their own choice *and* God's judgment on them for that choice. It was like the hardening of Pharaoh's heart in the days of Moses. Pharaoh hardened his own heart (Exodus 8:15, 32; 9:34; cf. 7:13, 14, 22; 8:19; 9:7, 35), and God hardened Pharaoh's heart (Exodus 4:21; 7:3; 9:12; 10:1, 20, 27; 11:10; 14:4, 8). The one truth does not exclude the other.

Eli does not seem to have been a wicked man, but in his old age he was not able to provide the leadership that Israel needed. His words to his sons expressed his sorrow and distress at their behavior, but he did not have the strength to curb their conduct. Shiloh suffered from the corruption of Eli's sons and the ineptitude of their old father.

Such was Israel's leadership in those days.

Our cynicism, again, dulls us to the horror of this situation. What was happening at Shiloh is too close to what we have come to expect from leaders.

However, by seeing how appalling it was for Israel to suffer from corrupt and inept leadership, we should be helped to see that it is an atrocious thing for anyone in God's world to endure such leadership. How dreadful it was that the leadership of God's chosen people had descended into grubby, greedy, immoral Hophni and Phinehas and their old, weak father! Is it really any less of a tragedy that human beings in many places in God's world today suffer leadership that displays just the same qualities?

BUT SAMUEL . . . (v. 26)

For the fourth time in our passage (see verses 11, 18, 21) we are now reminded that there was another young man at Shiloh: "Now the young man Samuel continued to grow both in stature and in favor with the LORD and also with man" (v. 26).

Just as Hophni and Phinehas were earning a reputation that was "no[t] good" (v. 24), Samuel's reputation was (literally) "good" with both the Lord and with men.[26] Again (as in verses 18 and 21) Eli's role with Samuel had faded. The lad was standing on his own two feet, so to speak, and was "becoming great" (as "continued to grow" could be translated) and good.

At this stage we are left wondering what this growing lad would become, and what difference he would make to the leadership crisis in Israel.

First Samuel 2:11-26 has an important twofold message for us.

On the one hand, we see corrupt and inept leadership for what it is. The situation at Shiloh has taken us to the heart of the problem: they did not know the Lord. Corruption in high places is not to be measured and understood only by the standards of the media or human laws. Corruption will be found wherever God is not honored.

Our cynicism about leadership needs to be rethought. The problem with our leaders is a problem we share with them. Corruption in high places does its own kind of damage, but so does corruption in "low places." Human sinfulness — defiance of God — is the heart of the problem with our leaders, and it is the heart of the problem with ourselves.

On the other hand, the indications are clear in 1 Samuel 2:11-26 that God was at work at this time in Israel's history to do something about Israel's leadership. Keep your eye on young Samuel! If we had been watching life at Shiloh through these years, we might hardly have noticed the quiet lad, there in the background. But our passage presents another view. It is not Samuel who was in the background; everything else that was happening at Shiloh was the background for the new thing God was doing. To see it, keep your eye on *Samuel*.

We will do that as we keep listening to the story that the book of 1 Samuel tells, but we also need to realize that this story eventually led to another story. The day came when another young lad was growing up. Luke tells us, in words that clearly echo 1 Samuel 2:26:[27] "And Jesus increased in wisdom and in stature and in favor with God and man" (Luke 2:52).

The message of the whole Bible teaches that God has acted not only in corrupt Israel long ago, but in this corrupt world, to provide the leadership needed.

If we had been watching the history of the world — if we are watching what is going on in the world today — we might hardly notice Jesus Christ, there somewhere in history's background. His death, we might think, is a footnote to the history of the world, his resurrection from the dead an interesting story. However, the Bible presents another view. Everything else in the history of the world is the background to the new thing that God is doing. To see it, keep your eye on *Jesus*. Samuel will turn out to be a shadow of him!

5

God and Corruption

1 SAMUEL 2:27-36

In the opening scenes of the book of 1 Samuel we have been presented with two starkly contrasting views of the world.

Hannah's understanding was articulated magnificently in her prayer in 1 Samuel 2:1-10. She knew that "There is none holy like the LORD . . . there is no rock like our God" (1 Samuel 2:2). Hannah saw the whole world in the light of that reality, including the circumstances of her own life. She knew that the Lord makes everything different. Power becomes weakness, and weakness becomes power, and riches become poverty, and poverty becomes wealth when you take into account the God of knowledge by whom actions are weighed. She conducted her life accordingly. Her response to her suffering was therefore prayer. Her response to blessing was praise. It seems clear that her firstborn son, Samuel, was following in her ways as he grew up at the Shiloh temple.

The other view of things was that of Eli's two sons, Hophni and Phinehas, the young priests at Shiloh. In contrast to Hannah, "They did not know the LORD" (1 Samuel 2:12). They, it seems, saw life in the darkness of that ignorance. They conducted their lives accordingly. Greed ruled them. Power served their gluttony. Their response to desire was to *take*, by force if need be. Their response to the God they did not know was contempt. And old Eli was unable to curb them.

The story of the corrupt leadership under which Israel suffered in the days of old Eli raises the question of which view of the world is true.

The Bible's message could be summed up as the news that the first view is true and a call to live in its light. Hannah's perspective is vindicated in the news about Jesus Christ who turned riches and poverty, power and weakness, triumph and tragedy upside down. The power of God, the wisdom of God, the riches of God's grace, the victory of God are all seen in an act of apparent weakness, foolishness, poverty, and defeat: Jesus' death on the cross (see, for example, 1 Corinthians 1:18-25; 2 Corinthians 8:9; Philippians 2:5-11; Colossians 1:19, 20; cf. 2 Corinthians 12:9, 10).

The state of the world could be summed up as people believing that the second view is true, and living in that darkness. The Hophni and Phinehas approach to life is well expressed in the words of Paul about all human beings:

> . . . *they are without excuse. For although they knew God, they did not honor him as God or give thanks to him, but they became futile in their thinking, and their foolish hearts were darkened. Claiming to be wise they became fools. . . . And since they did not see fit to acknowledge God, God gave them up to a debased mind to do what ought not to be done. They were filled with all manner of unrighteousness, evil, covetousness, malice. (Romans 1:20-22, 28, 29)*

A perfect description of Eli's two sons!

Do you see the world as Hannah did, or more as Hophni and Phinehas did? The true answer to that question will be seen in how you live, your response to suffering, to desire, to power, to weakness, to blessing.

The Hophni and Phinehas approach to life is more familiar to us than we like to admit. It is important, therefore, to listen carefully to the words of a certain man who came to visit Eli one day. The incident is recounted in 1 Samuel 2:27-36.

There is a degree of mystery about this visit. First Samuel 2:12-26 describes what was going on at Shiloh over a number of years, as Samuel was growing up. Biblical narratives do not always arrange events in strict chronological order. We therefore do not know when the visit mentioned in verse 27 took place. Nor do we know who the visitor was. All that we are told about him is contained in the first words of 1 Samuel 2:27: "And there came a man of God to Eli. . . ."

"A man of God" means a prophet.[1] Like many other prophets in the Bible, particular details about this man are largely hidden by the prominence given to the words of his message.

Indeed it was clear from the moment he opened his mouth that his words were of utmost importance. He began like this: "Thus the LORD has said . . ." (v. 27b).

This simple introduction, characteristic of the speech of prophets, is profound in its significance.[2] The man came as the bearer of the words that God had spoken. In this context we must understand that they were the words of the God of whom Hannah spoke so effusively: the God of knowledge by whom actions are weighed, the one who kills and brings to life, who will judge the ends of the earth (1 Samuel 2:3, 6, 10). This God had spoken, and the visit from the man of God to Eli was for the sole purpose of telling him what the Lord had said.

Therefore the rest of our passage is entirely taken up with the words God had spoken. Apart from the obvious importance of this message for Eli, these words of God are recorded here to illumine every reader of this book.

There is a clear logic to the message. The Lord had spoken, first, of what *he* had done in the past for the house of Eli; second, of what the house of Eli had done; and third, of what the Lord will therefore do — with a surprise at the end.

WHAT THE LORD DID FOR THE HOUSE OF ELI (vv. 27c, 28)

The Lord's past actions toward the house of Eli are summed up in three sentences: "I [did] reveal . . ." (v. 27c), "I [did] choose . . ." (v. 28a), "I gave . . ." (v. 28b).

"I [Did] Reveal . . . " (v. 27c)

> "Did I indeed reveal myself to the house of your father when they were in Egypt subject to the house of Pharaoh?"

The question is designed to stir Eli's conscience.[3] Eli could not deny that he occupied his position as priest at Shiloh because God revealed himself to his father's house many years previously in Egypt. The reference is to Aaron and his sons in the days of Moses.[4] The available evidence indicates that Eli was a descendant of Ithamar, Aaron's fourth son.[5]

One of the small puzzles of Biblical history (simply because we lack complete information) is how Eli came to be Israel's leading priest. Although he is never called "chief" or "high" priest, it seems clear that he was in charge at Shiloh. Aaron was the first "chief priest" (Ezra 7:5), and the priesthood was given by God to his sons "forever" (Exodus 29:9). The role of chief priest passed to Aaron's third son, Eleazar (Numbers 3:32; 20:24-29; Deuteronomy 10:6; cf. Numbers 4:16), the first two sons of Aaron having died in rather unfortunate circumstances (Leviticus 10:1, 2). From Eleazar the chief priesthood passed to his son Phinehas (who was a far cry from his later namesake at Shiloh!) and his descendants, who were given by God "the covenant of a perpetual priesthood" (Numbers 25:13; cf. Judges 20:27, 28; 1 Chronicles 9:20). While the role of chief priest appears to have been passed on from father to eldest living son for several generations, there is no clear indication that this was a divine requirement.[6] We do not know how the responsibility for the tabernacle/temple at Shiloh came to be in the hands of Eli, who was not a descendant of Eleazar but of Aaron's fourth son, Ithamar. It is possible that a chief priest in Eleazar's line may have died without leaving a son old enough to take on the role. In addition to his credentials as a descendant of Aaron, Eli may have been related to the Eleazar family by marriage. He may, therefore, have been the best available person to take over the responsibility.[7]

The point made in verse 27, however, is that the Lord had revealed himself to Aaron's family in the days before the exodus. Indeed, God spoke directly to Aaron in Egypt and told him to go out to the wilderness and meet with his brother Moses (Exodus 4:14). The Lord subsequently spoke to both Moses and Aaron about bringing the people of Israel out of Egypt and about the Passover (Exodus 6:13, 26; 7:8; 9:8; 12:1, 28, 43, 50). Just as God had made Moses "like God to Pharaoh," so he made Aaron Moses' prophet (Exodus 7:1, 2).

God's self-revelation was, as it always is, more than the disclosing of information. When God makes himself known, he makes his will known. The revelation to Aaron took place when the people of Israel were slaves in Egypt and in effect belonged to Pharaoh.[8] God's self-revelation to Eli's ancestor Aaron and his brother Moses began the great act of redemption by which the Lord liberated the Israelites to become a holy nation to the Lord (Exodus 19:6) and freed the house of Aaron to become priests of the Lord.

That is the first mentioned great act of God toward the house of Eli's "father."

"I [Did] Choose . . ." (v. 28a)

A second rhetorical question was addressed to the conscience of the old priest: "Did I choose him out of all the tribes of Israel to be my priest, to go up to my altar, to burn incense, to wear an ephod before me?" (v. 28a).

The redemptive self-revelation of God to Aaron in Egypt had benefited all Israelites. However, Aaron had the additional privilege of being chosen out of all the tribes of Israel (just as Israel had been chosen out of all the nations on earth, Exodus 19:5, 6; Deuteronomy 7:6; 10:15; Psalm 147:20; Amos 3:2). The occasion referred to is probably recorded in Exodus 28, where God said to Moses:

> Then bring near to you Aaron your brother, and his sons with him, from among the people of Israel, to serve me as priests — Aaron and Aaron's sons, Nadab and Abihu, Eleazar and Ithamar. (Exodus 28:1)

God's gracious work of choosing is an important theme of the Bible. Israel had been "chosen" by God (Deuteronomy 4:37; 7:6, 7; 10:15). In 1 Samuel we will be hearing about God's "choosing" a king for his people (see especially 1 Samuel 16:8-13). God's choice is reason for humility and praise. Eli must acknowledge the gracious sovereign choice by God not only of Israel but particularly of the house of Aaron, to which he and his family belonged.

The one chosen to be the Lord's priest had three duties. The first of these was to ascend the Lord's altar (see Exodus 28:43; Leviticus 1:5-8; 6:14; 9:7-14). The altar was the place of sacrifice. This was God's provision for the cleansing of the people of Israel and the atoning of their sins. The one chosen by God "to go up to my altar" (1 Samuel 2:28) had a supremely important task to perform.

The second duty seen in 1 Samuel 2:28 was "to burn incense" on the special gold altar of incense (see Exodus 30:7, 8; Numbers 4:16; 16:40).[9] This was a task specifically given to Aaron to be performed twice a day. It was an integral part of the regular functioning of the tabernacle and therefore represented the weighty responsibility that had been given to the house of Aaron for the tabernacle itself, God's very dwelling among his people (Leviticus 26:11).

The third duty given to Aaron was "to wear an ephod before me." This is not the linen ephod worn by ordinary priests, even young ones like Samuel (1 Samuel 2:18). This ephod was exclusive to the high priest. Within this rich and elaborate garment were two onyx stones, called "stones of remembrance for the sons of Israel," on which were engraved the names of the twelve tribes of Israel. Aaron was to "bear their names before the LORD" (Exodus 28:6-12; 39:2-7).[10] In other words, Aaron was to represent all Israel before the Lord.

Eli's "father" had been chosen by the Lord out of all the tribes of Israel for this extraordinary responsibility.[11]

"I Gave . . ." (v. 28b)

The third great and gracious act of God toward Eli's "father" was this: "I gave to the house of your father all my offerings by fire from the people of Israel" (v. 28b).

The responsibility for which Aaron was chosen was enormous, but he (and his descendants) were generously provided for. This provision came from the very offerings they were appointed to administer (see Leviticus 2:3, 10; 6:16; 7:7-10, 31-36; 10:12-15; Numbers 5:9, 10; 18:8-19; cf. Deuteronomy 18:1).

Eli and his sons were the inheritors of this immensely important role, on which the survival of Israel as God's people depended, and of the abundant provision for their needs that went with the task. This is the preamble to the terrible indictment that the Lord now brought against Eli.

WHAT THE HOUSE OF ELI DID (v. 29)

> *"Why then do you scorn my sacrifices and my offerings that I commanded, and honor your sons above me by fattening yourselves on the choicest parts of every offering of my people Israel?" (v. 29)*

Yet another rhetorical question introduces the accusation. Previously we saw the ugly greed with which Hophni and Phinehas behaved at Shiloh. We heard the narrator's comment that they "treated the offering of the LORD with contempt" (1 Samuel 2:17) by their conduct. However, now we can see the appalling nature of their crime in a still clearer light, the searching brightness of the Lord's past dealings with them.

They had "scorn[ed]" (literally "kicked"[12]) the sacrifices (*"my* sacrifices"!) and offerings (*"my* offerings"!) that the Lord had commanded for dealing with Israel's sins and for which they, the priests,[13] had been chosen, and from which they were generously provided for.[14] Why had they done that? the Lord asked.

Eli himself, by doing no more than rather feebly rebuking his sons, had honored them more than he had honored the Lord. They should have been expelled from the priesthood long ago! Why had he done that? the Lord asked.

Not content with the very great importance of their duties and the ample provision God had made for their needs, the priests had "fattened themselves" with the very parts of the people's offerings intended to be given to God. Gluttony had triumphed over honoring the gracious God who had dealt with this people, and in particular the priests, so mercifully. Why?

Here we have a clear example of the God of knowledge weighing actions (1 Samuel 2:3)!

THEREFORE WHAT THE LORD WILL DO (vv. 30-34)

The word "Therefore" in verse 30 now has an ominous ring. The behavior of Eli and his sons must now meet the Lord who will judge the ends of the earth (1 Samuel 2:10).

The Promise Forfeited (v. 30)

> *"Therefore the LORD, the God of Israel, declares: 'I promised that your house and the house of your father should go in and out before me forever,' but now the LORD declares: 'Far be it from me, for those who honor me I will honor, and those who despise me shall be lightly esteemed.'"* (v. 30)

Eli and his sons had been the objects of the extraordinary grace of the Lord, the God of Israel. It was summed up in a promise. The terms of this promise are important to understand. Eli's house (that is, of course, his family and descendants), being part of the house of his "father" (that is, of Aaron), should "go in and out before" the Lord forever. This refers to the activities of priests in the tabernacle or temple.

The promise was God's promise to the house of Aaron. It was given in connection with the consecration of Aaron and his four sons as priests. God had said, "And the priesthood shall be theirs by a statute forever" (Exodus 29:9).[15] This promise was reiterated with fresh emphasis to Aaron's grandson, Phinehas, after he had demonstrated remarkable zeal in his service of God and Israel. God said, "Behold, I give to him my covenant of peace, and it shall be to him and to his descendants after him the covenant of a perpetual priesthood, because he was jealous for his God and made atonement for the people of Israel" (Numbers 25:12, 13).

The promise was that the descendants of Aaron would serve as priests, one of them, of course, being the high priest.[16] Eli represented one family among the descendants of Aaron. He therefore enjoyed the blessing of this promise.

"But now" (1 Samuel 2:30) the Lord declared that the house of Eli had forfeited the promise. It was not that God's promise to the house of Aaron was nullified or revoked.[17] The priesthood would continue to be in the hands of descendants of Aaron. However, the present generation of serving priests would be all but destroyed, and the family of Eli would be removed from the priesthood, either by death or other means.[18]

The reason for this devastating pronouncement, said God, is that "those who honor me I will honor, and those who despise me shall be lightly esteemed" (1 Samuel 2:30).[19] The truth of God's sovereignty in revealing himself, choosing, and giving does not nullify but intensifies the demand for holiness in the recipients of his grace (cf. Leviticus 19:2; Amos 3:2; Romans 6:1, 2). God will not honor (or glorify) those who do not glorify him.[20] Hophni and Phinehas, and even old Eli, had failed to honor God as God (cf. Romans 1:21).[21] They could not, therefore, expect to continue as beneficiaries of God's promise. "God is not mocked" (Galatians 6:7).

The Punishment Incurred (vv. 31-33)

The contempt shown toward God by the house of Eli did not only mean that they forfeited any claim to the promise — they also incurred punishment:

> *"'Behold, the days are coming when I will cut off your strength and the strength of your father's house, so that there will not be an old man in your house.'" (v. 31)*

The Hebrew is more violent in expression: "I will cut off your arm and the arm of your father's house." This forceful metaphor spoke of a blow — or a number of blows — that would devastate Eli's house. The first of these will be three deaths to be reported in chapter 4. Later, in chapter 22, there will be a horrendous massacre. The consequence ("so that there will not be an old man in your house") is far from subtle when we remember verse 22: "Eli was very old"!

The coming devastation is elaborated with some vague but disturbing details:

> *"'Then in distress you will look with envious eye on all the prosperity that shall be bestowed on Israel, and there shall not be an old man in your house forever.'" (v. 32)*

Eli is included in the suffering that will come on his descendants.[22] "The prosperity that shall be bestowed on Israel" seems to allude to the coming days of Solomon's glorious kingdom. In those days there will be a surviving descendant of Eli, by the name of Abiathar. However, he will look on "in distress,"[23] for one of Solomon's early acts as king will be to expel Abiathar from the priesthood and banish him. When the historian records these events, he will add the comment, "thus fulfilling the word of the LORD that he had spoken concerning the house of Eli in Shiloh" (1 Kings 2:27).

> *"'The only one of you whom I shall not cut off from my altar shall be spared to weep his eyes out to grieve his heart, and all the descendants of your house shall die by the sword of men.'" (v. 33)*

As the story of 1 Samuel unfolds, we will learn of a terrible massacre of the priests, from which there will be one survivor. That survivor will be Eli's great-great-grandson Abiathar (see 1 Samuel 22:6-23).[24] His escape will leave him bearing the sorrow of the tragedy and the distress of his eventual banishment.[25]

A Terrible Sign (v. 34)

Much of what had been announced lay in the future, and Eli himself would not see it. However, he would see a terrible sign that would confirm the message of this man of God. The Lord was dealing with Eli's house in judgment. "'And this that shall come upon your two sons, Hophni and Phinehas, shall be the sign to you: both of them shall die on the same day'" (v. 34).

That is exactly what happened, as we shall see in 1 Samuel 4.

There is one more vital point in the message that the man of God brought to Eli that day. Before we hear it, let us take care to understand the truth of the first three points. The grace of God toward the house of Eli (vv. 27, 28), like the grace of God toward us, calls the recipients of such kindness to "renounce ungodliness and worldly passions, and to live self-controlled, upright, and godly lives in the present age" (Titus 2:12). The contempt for God displayed in the behavior of Eli's sons and in his failure to curb them is all the more serious in the light of God's grace (v. 29). It is like the contempt for God displayed today in our behavior "if we go on sinning deliberately after receiving the knowledge of the truth." We are then acting as "one who has spurned the Son of God, and has profaned the blood of the covenant by which he was sanctified, and has outraged the Spirit of grace" (Hebrews 10:26, 29). The certain consequence for such disdain toward God, whether in the house of Eli or among us, is "a fearful expectation of judgment" (Hebrews 10:27).

BUT SAMUEL . . . ? (vv. 35, 36)

The last point in the message delivered to Eli is remarkable. Wickedness would certainly bring God's judgment to the house of Eli, but judgment would not be God's last word. God's grace had been spurned, and therefore forfeited by Eli's house. However, God's grace cannot be frustrated in its good purpose by human wickedness.

Therefore the final point in the message from God to Eli began: "'And I will raise up for myself a faithful priest, who shall do according to what is in my heart and in my mind'" (v. 35a).

It is important to understand that a promise such as this does not necessarily have only one fulfillment.

From all that we have read so far in 1 Samuel we may reasonably suspect that Samuel will prove to be the "faithful priest" whom God was raising up for himself. Although Samuel will turn out to function more as a prophet than a priest, there is no doubt that with the demise of Eli and Shiloh, Samuel will take over priestly functions and will be faithful in them. He will indeed do "what is in [God's] heart and . . . mind."[26]

In the longer term it is reasonable to see the commitment of God expressed in this promise realized in the appointment of Zadok in the place of Abiathar. The house of Zadok then became the priestly line (see 1 Kings 2:35; 4:1).

Looking even further ahead, we should recognize that the faithful priest whom God finally raised up is Jesus. He became "a merciful and faithful high priest in the service of God, to make propitiation for the sins of the people" (Hebrews 2:17).

Of the "faithful priest" to be raised up for himself, God said: "'And I will build him a sure house, and he shall go in and out before my anointed forever'" (v. 35b).

This aspect of the promise does not fit Samuel. His "house" — that is, his sons — will fail, just as Eli's had (see 1 Samuel 8:1-3).[27] Zadok's "house," however, continued until the exile.

"My anointed" is a surprise again. Hannah had spoken of "his anointed," clearly identified as "his king," to whom God will "give strength" (1 Samuel

2:10). Samuel himself would serve as a faithful priest, as well as a prophet, before Israel's first two kings. Zadok and his descendants would serve "all the days"[28] of the kings in David's line.

In Jesus the work of faithful priest and anointed king would be combined in one person (see Hebrews 6:20; 7:1).

The message concludes with the assurance that the certainty of God's positive purpose does not diminish the severity of the judgment on the house of Eli already pronounced:

> "'And everyone who is left in your house shall come to implore him for a piece of silver or a loaf of bread and shall say, "Please put me in one of the priests' places, that I may eat a morsel of bread."'" (v. 36)

The punishment will fit the crime.[29] The gluttonous bullies will become hungry beggars. It is just as Hannah had said: "Those who were full have hired themselves out for bread" (1 Samuel 2:5).

The message delivered to Eli that day has been quite complex in its details. We must make sure that we do not lose sight of the forest for the trees. All of the details contribute to two major truths that are emerging as important themes of 1 Samuel.

The first is that the very great problem of leadership in Israel was the failure of human leaders to honor God as God. This failure was the root cause of corruption of various kinds. It made leadership self-serving and therefore exploitative. Its seriousness is exposed when it is set alongside the grace of God that was being spurned.

The problem is that the corruption that showed itself in the conduct of Hophni and Phinehas is common to human nature. We have noticed more than once that the Apostle Paul's analysis of the human condition in Romans 1 fits very well the character and conduct of the sons of Eli. If that is the case, we must ask what hope there is of human leadership ever doing any better than those two rogues.

The second truth answers that question. God intends to provide for himself faithful and secure leadership, "a faithful priest" and "my anointed" (v. 35). The story of how God has done that takes the rest of the Bible to tell. With Eli, Hophni, and Phinehas in mind, the New Testament words about Jesus should fill us with wonder:

> For it was indeed fitting that we should have such a high priest, holy, innocent, unstained, separated from sinners, and exalted above the heavens. (Hebrews 7:26)

6

When God Speaks

1 Samuel 3

Sometimes God is silent.

Now the young man Samuel was ministering to the Lord under Eli. And the word of the Lord was rare in those days; there was no frequent vision. (v. 1)

We take many things for granted in life. We often do not appreciate the goodness of these things until we lose them — good health, caring parents, freedom, friendships . . . The list could be extended. So long as such things are part of normal life for us, we give little thought to their importance.

It is also true that those who have never known some of these good things in their experience may not really know how good they are.

One good that is taken for granted by some, and unknown to others, is the word of God. The Old Testament prophet Amos issued a terrible threat to the people of Israel in the eighth century B.C.:

"Behold, the days are coming," declares the Lord God,
"when I will send a famine on the land—
not a famine of bread, nor a thirst for water,
but of hearing the words of the Lord.
They shall wander from sea to sea,
and from north to east;
they shall run to and fro, to seek the word of the Lord,
but they shall not find it." (Amos 8:11, 12)

God will be silent, Amos warned his hearers. It will be like a terrible famine, in which starving people search desperately for food and drink but can find nothing. But it will be worse than that: there will be no word of the Lord to be heard anywhere. That will mean, as Amos said a few lines earlier, the *end* for Israel (v. 2).

It is difficult for us to sense the horror of Amos's warning because we do not readily appreciate, on the one hand, the brilliant goodness of the word of God and, on the other, our profound dependence on God's word. This may be because we have come to take the word of the Lord for granted or because we have never known its goodness.

As we return to the days of young Samuel at Shiloh, we learn that those days were somewhat like the days that Amos, a couple of centuries later, would proclaim were about to come again to Israel. These were days when "the word of the LORD was rare."[1]

In context it is important to see that this statement is a comment on the word of the Lord that was reported at length at the end of chapter 2. That message shows clearly that in those days the Lord could, and at least on that one occasion did, speak his word. But this was a rare thing.

The reason for this famine of the word of the Lord has been presented in the previous chapter. The priests at Shiloh, in particular Eli's scurrilous sons, "did not know the LORD" and behaved with an outrageous contempt for both God and the people (1 Samuel 2:12-17). The priests, who had been appointed by God as mediators to receive his revelation, to offer the sacrifices for the sins of the people, and to represent the people before the Lord had become self-serving "worthless men" (1 Samuel 2:12). There is clearly a connection between the rarity of the word of the Lord and the failings of the priesthood. God would not speak often to such a priesthood, and when he did speak, it would be the kind of terrible word that we heard at the end of chapter 2.[2]

In this dark situation our attention is once again drawn to "the young man Samuel." Since a great deal was made of his name when it was given to him in chapter 1 (see 1 Samuel 1:20, 27, 28), each mention of his name should remind us of the unusual circumstances of his birth and his coming to be at Shiloh.[3]

This is the fifth time we have heard a brief statement about Samuel and his activities at Shiloh. These statements have been five bright spots in the otherwise dark and gloomy account of the goings on at Shiloh:

And the boy ministered to the LORD in the presence of Eli the priest. (1 Samuel 2:11)

Samuel was ministering before the LORD, a boy clothed with a linen ephod. (1 Samuel 2:18)

And the young man Samuel grew in the presence of the LORD. (1 Samuel 2:21)

Now the young man Samuel continued to grow both in stature and in favor with the LORD and also with man. (1 Samuel 2:26)

Now the young man Samuel was ministering to the LORD under Eli. (1 Samuel 3:1a)

In the very setting of the degeneracy of Hophni and Phinehas and the failing competence of Eli, Samuel progressed from being the lad who served the Lord under the direct supervision of Eli "the priest" in 1 Samuel 2:11, to taking on the priestly garment himself in 1 Samuel 2:18, to personal growth "with the LORD" (literal translation) in 1 Samuel 2:21, to a youth in good standing with God and the people in 1 Samuel 2:26, to the one we will now see at Shiloh serving the Lord, still "under Eli," but with Eli no longer called "the priest" in 1 Samuel 3:1.[4]

We now turn our attention more fully to this young man and hear about what happened one night in those dark times at Shiloh.

THE WORD OF THE LORD WAS HEARD (vv. 2-10)

Things were about to change. The situation described in verse 1 will be very different by the time we reach the end of chapter 3.

A Situation Where God Was Not Known (vv. 2-7)

The night began like any other night in those days in Shiloh.[5] Take a look at old Eli that night. Then see young Samuel. Then hear of the unusual thing that happened.

OLD ELI (v. 2)

At that time Eli, whose eyesight had begun to grow dim so that he could not see, was lying down in his own place. (v. 2)

We have already been told that Eli was "very old" (1 Samuel 2:22). His failing eyesight was, no doubt, part of the unwelcome physical deterioration that accompanies old age. However, the writer has chosen to highlight this particular aspect of Eli's decline immediately after mentioning the fact that in those days "there was no frequent *vision*." Eli's physical condition was a reflection of the spiritual reality. He could not see the light of day, nor could he "see" the word of the Lord. His darkness was deep.

The old man was "lying down." In a moment we will see that Samuel was "lying down" too. However, Eli's "lying down" will continue through this night, whereas the young Samuel will be very active. Old Eli, lying down, is part of a picture that is being built up of a man too old to do much at all. All we have seen him do in the whole story so far is sit, speak, hear, and now lie down (1 Samuel 1:9, 14; 2:22; cf. 4:13, 18)!

More pointedly Eli was lying down "in his own place." There is nothing wrong with that, of course. After all, as we will see, it was nighttime. But "in his own place" will make quite a contrast to the place we are about to see young Samuel.[6]

As we look at old Eli we ought to sense the growing crisis. Israel had always needed a mediator to receive God's word, to offer sacrifice for their sins, and to represent them before God (cf. Exodus 20:18-26; Deuteronomy 5:23-31). Here we see Israel's mediator as feeble and frail. What will happen when Eli is gone? Who will take over his role? Hophni and Phinehas are next in line!

YOUNG SAMUEL (V. 3)

Happily our attention is not directed to those two crooks, but to the boy who has been the real interest of our story so far: "The lamp of God had not yet gone out, and Samuel was lying down in the temple of the LORD, where the ark of God was" (v. 3).

Once again the writer seems to be selecting physical details with striking significance. "The lamp of God had not yet gone out." On the one hand, this was the lamp that burned "from evening to morning" in the tabernacle (Exodus 27:20, 21; Leviticus 24:1-4). If it "had not yet gone out," it was still nighttime. On the other hand, in the darkness represented by God's silence and Eli's blindness, the news that God's lamp "had not yet gone out" suggests that God had not yet abandoned his people. There was still hope.

While old Eli was lying down "in his own place," we are shown the young Samuel lying down "in the temple of the LORD." The temple of the Lord (that is, of course, the tabernacle) represented God's dwelling among his people. This was where one would expect the word of the Lord to be given, the sacrifices to be offered, and the priest to represent Israel before the Lord. The decline of Eli and the corruption of his sons threatened these necessary expressions of Israel's relationship with God. But the lamp of God had not yet gone out: young Samuel was there, in the temple of the Lord.

To underline the symbolism of the scene: "where the ark of God was." This is the first mention of the ark in 1 Samuel. It will play a major role in the story of the next three chapters.[7] At this point, however, the presence of the ark in the tabernacle reminds us of God's covenant commitment to Israel, and his covenant demand. The ark was a gold-plated wooden box that contained the two stone tablets of the Law with the engraved words, "I am the LORD your God, who brought you out of the land of Egypt, out of the house of slavery. You shall have no other gods before me" (Exodus 20:2, 3; also see Exodus 25:10-16).[8]

We see the young Samuel with the lamp of God still burning, the temple of the Lord still standing, and the ark of God in its place. The scene is set for the account of the strange thing that happened that night.

GOD'S UNRECOGNIZED WORD (vv. 4-7)

What was rare in those days, happened that night: "Then the LORD called Samuel . . ." (v. 4a).

It is clear that on this occasion the word of the Lord came, to Samuel at least, in an audible voice. Whether or not it would have been audible to anyone else present, we do not know. Eli's sleeping place may have been some distance away, and anyway his hearing was probably not much better than his eyesight.

If God called Samuel in an audible voice, Samuel's reaction is not at all surprising: ". . . and he said, 'Here I am!' and ran to Eli and said, 'Here I am, for you called me'" (vv. 4b, 5a).

Who else would have been calling the boy? But do notice his energetic responsiveness. It was immediate and fast. He ran to Eli.

Eli, of course, did not move: "But he said, 'I did not call; lie down again.' So he went and lay down" (v. 5b).

Obedient, but no doubt a little perplexed, Samuel did as he was told.

And the LORD called again, "Samuel!" and Samuel arose and went to Eli and said, "Here I am, for you called me." But he said, "I did not call, my son; lie down again." (v. 6)

Eli's affectionate way of speaking to Samuel as "my son" is poignant. His actual sons had defied him and brought God's condemnation.[9]

Neither Samuel nor Eli yet understood what was happening. The narrator has told us, twice now, that it was the Lord who was calling Samuel. He now gives us an explanation for Samuel's responses to the strange voice:

Now Samuel did not yet know the LORD. . . . (v. 7a)

This is a strange thing to say. After all, have we not been told that Samuel was ministering to the Lord, that he was growing with the Lord, that he enjoyed the favor of the Lord? What does it mean, "Samuel did not yet know the LORD"? The strangest thing about these words is that they are almost exactly the same as the critical words about Hophni and Phinehas in 1 Samuel 2:12: "They did not know the LORD." In their case that was part of the description of them as "worthless men." The description of Samuel repeats the words of 2:12, with one significant difference: "Samuel did not *yet* know the LORD."

The ignorance he shared with Hophni and Phinehas had this difference. They did not know the Lord because they had rejected knowledge of God by their contempt for God's Law. Samuel did not *yet* know the Lord because ". . . the word of the LORD had not *yet* been revealed to him" (v. 7b).

That is, this experience of being addressed by the Lord was entirely new to him.

On the one hand, in the case of Hophni and Phinehas, we see that it is not possible to know God at the same time as defying him. You cannot know God and live in disobedience to God.

On the other hand, in the case of Samuel we see that it is only possible to know God when God acts to make himself known.

We have this remarkable situation at Shiloh: God was speaking, but the word of the Lord was not recognized for what it was. For different reasons God was not known at Shiloh.

A Situation in Which God Was Heard (vv. 8-10)

That situation was about to change.

ELI'S REALIZATION (v. 8)

> *And the LORD called Samuel again the third time. And he arose and went to Eli and said, "Here I am, for you called me." Then Eli perceived that the LORD was calling the young man. (v. 8)*

Old Eli realized that something was happening that had not happened at Shiloh for a very long time. His sight had grown dim, but he was not yet completely blind.

ELI'S INSTRUCTION (v. 9)

So old Eli told young Samuel what to do:

> *Therefore Eli said to Samuel, "Go, lie down, and if he calls you, you shall say, 'Speak, LORD, for your servant hears.'" So Samuel went and lay down in his place. (v. 9)*

We wait, as no doubt both Samuel and Eli waited. Would it happen a fourth time? What would be the consequences if Samuel followed Eli's simple but awesome instructions?

SAMUEL'S HEARING (V. 10)

We are not kept waiting long: "And the LORD came and stood, calling as at other times, 'Samuel! Samuel!' And Samuel said, 'Speak, for your servant hears'" (v. 10).

This time there seems to be more than the voice. The Lord "came and stood." Without any more detail we should refrain from speculating further about the manner of God's presence. Suffice it to say that God was objectively and really present. This was no mere dream on Samuel's part.[10]

In this carefully told story, we should perhaps notice that Samuel did not quite manage to say exactly what Eli had told him to. The name of God ("LORD") did not come to his lips. His diffidence, in the circumstances, is more than understandable.[11]

It has taken half the chapter for the word of the Lord to be heard. But at last there was a servant at Shiloh who was hearing.

THE WORD OF THE LORD THAT WAS HEARD (vv. 11-18)

When God speaks, it is not some kind of mystical experience, in which it is the experience of hearing that matters. When God speaks, what matters is what God says.

The Word of Judgment (vv. 11-14)

On this occasion what God said was terrible.

EARS WILL TINGLE (V. 11)

> Then the LORD said to Samuel, "Behold, I am about to do a thing in Israel at which the two ears of everyone who hears it will tingle." (v. 11)

This vivid turn of phrase occurs a couple of times later in the Old Testament.[12] Do you know the experience of being so terrified that you cannot speak, and your lips quiver?[13] Here a similar sensation is described, in the ears of someone hearing terrible news. God was about to do something "in Israel" (therefore an event of national significance[14]) that would have that effect on the ears of everyone who heard it!

GOD WILL BE TRUE (VV. 12, 13)

> "On that day I will fulfill against Eli all that I have spoken concerning his house, from beginning to end. And I declare to him that I am about to pun-

ish his house forever, for the iniquity that he knew, because his sons were blaspheming God, and he did not restrain them." (vv. 12, 13)

The simple but terrible news was that God would do what he had said he would do. On one of the rare occasions that the word of the Lord had been spoken in those days, it was by the man of God who came to Eli and delivered the message we heard in 1 Samuel 2:27-36. The word of the Lord to Samuel was now simply that it was about to happen.

The word "punish" in verse 13 is often translated "judge." Over the previous couple of hundred years God had raised up "judges" who had delivered Israel from enemies and called Israel to obedient living (see Judges 2:16-19).[15] In this sense they had brought justice to Israel. However, with Israel's leadership in deep crisis, God himself was about to "judge" the house of Eli "forever" (v. 14).

The judgment of God against human wickedness is always a terrible thing to contemplate. It is hardly possible for us, embroiled as we are in the sinfulness of humanity, to see clearly the rightness of God's ways. It is very important for us to take care here and humbly listen to the word of God, not passing judgment on it, but allowing it to illumine our minds.

By the standards that we might apply to ourselves, Eli was not an excessively wicked man. His various failures, such as his mistaking Hannah's prayer for drunken mumbling, his inability to curb his sons, and his slowness in recognizing that God was speaking to Samuel, are all readily attributed to his advancing years. We can think of plenty of excuses for Eli, for he was (we might feel) no worse than any of us. And there are things about Eli that we admire.

The accusation in verse 13 may therefore sound harsh to us: "he did not restrain"[16] his sons. Well, we might say, it was not for want of trying!

The trouble with all this is that Eli is not being judged by *us*. It is the Lord who said that his sons were blaspheming and that he did not do what he should have done. It is not for us then to sit in judgment over the Lord. He is the God of knowledge, by whom deeds are weighed (1 Samuel 2:3). There is a certain arrogant absurdity in responding to this passage as though we know more about Eli's innocence (from the few pages that we have!) — and have a keener sense of justice — than the Lord does![17]

No Sacrifice Left (v. 14)

The worst of the rotten things that the sons of Eli did was to treat with contempt the very provision God had made for the forgiveness of sins (see 1 Samuel 2:17, 29). This had frightful consequences: "Therefore I swear to the house of Eli that the iniquity of Eli's house shall not be atoned for by sacrifice or offering forever" (v. 14).

Do you understand the horror of those words? If the gracious provision God has made for the forgiveness of sins is spurned, scorned, disdained, despised, there is nothing left but the fearful prospect of judgment.

This now makes sense of the disturbing words of 1 Samuel 2:25: "But they [Eli's sons] would not listen to the voice of their father, for it was the will of the LORD to put them to death." The sons of Eli had passed a point of no return. They had sinned with such high-handedness that they were beyond the pale.

The New Testament recognizes the same reality. If you trample the Son of God underfoot, if you treat with contempt the death of Jesus for your sins, what hope do you think there is for you? There is no sacrifice left to atone for your sins if you have discarded the death of Jesus (cf. Hebrews 10:26-31).

The Response of Fear and Submission (vv. 15-18)

That is the word of the Lord that young Samuel heard that night.

SAMUEL'S FEAR (V. 15)

It is no wonder that we now read: "Samuel lay until morning; then he opened the doors of the house of the LORD. And Samuel was afraid to tell the vision to Eli" (v. 15).

I doubt that he slept for whatever remained of that night. When he rose and opened the doors of the temple, we can imagine the morning light streaming in. But he was afraid. The word of the Lord that had come to him that night was a fearful message. He had no desire to share it with Eli, of all people.

SAMUEL'S SUBMISSION TO ELI (VV. 16-18a)

However, as Samuel might have expected, Eli was not likely to leave the matter there:

> But Eli called Samuel and said, "Samuel, my son." And he said, "Here I am." And Eli said, "What was it that he told you? Do not hide it from me. May God do so to you and more also if you hide anything from me of all that he told you." So Samuel told him everything and hid nothing from him. (vv. 16-18a)

Eli seemed to recognize the difficulty. His words to Samuel were both kind ("Samuel, my son") and very firm. In the strongest possible terms[18] he insisted that Samuel tell him all that the Lord had said.

Eli could have been in little doubt of the terrible nature of the message.

We do not know what time interval may have elapsed since the man of God had come to him in 1 Samuel 2:27, but it was not the kind of visit that could be forgotten. This word from God now, not given to Eli himself, but to the young man in his care, could only be fearful news.

Samuel's own fears gave way to submission to the old man Eli. Samuel told him all. The difficulty of that conversation we can only imagine, for the narrator gives us no more than the matter-of-fact report in verse 18a.

ELI'S SUBMISSION TO THE LORD (v. 18b)

Eli's response was rather more than matter-of-fact: "It is the LORD. Let him do what seems good to him" (v.18b).

"It is the LORD." In two words (in the Hebrew) Eli implies what Hannah had stated: "There is none holy like the LORD" (2:2). This may have been Eli's finest moment, as he acknowledged and accepted the rightness of God's judgment. His words were not unlike the one who, many years later, after God's judgment had finally fallen on Jerusalem, said, "The LORD is in the right, for I have rebelled against his word" (Lamentations 1:18).[19]

A PROPHET IN ISRAEL: GOD NO LONGER SILENT
(vv. 19-21)

Things could not be the same again in Shiloh, nor in fact in Israel. Samuel now knew the Lord, for the word of the Lord had now been revealed to him. The consequences are summed up in the last three verses of the chapter.

Samuel and His Words (v. 19)

> And Samuel grew, and the LORD was with him and let none of his words
> fall to the ground. (v. 19)

Whose words — Samuel's or the Lord's? Both, because, as we are about to hear, Samuel was now a prophet. He would speak God's words. And none of those words would fail.

This is the sixth and last of the brief summaries of Samuel's development at Shiloh. It would appear that the story of Samuel has reached its climax.

Israel and Samuel (v. 20)

That impression is strengthened as we hear of Israel's response to Samuel: "And all Israel from Dan to Beersheba knew that Samuel was established as a prophet of the LORD" (v. 20).

Samuel was "established" (the word suggests trustworthiness, reliability) as the Lord's prophet because his words did not fail.

God No Longer Silent (v. 21)

And so the situation described in verse 1 of this chapter came to an end: "And the LORD appeared again at Shiloh, for the LORD revealed himself to Samuel at Shiloh by the word of the LORD" (v. 21).

The God who had cared about childless Hannah cared about Israel in her time of leadership crisis. The word of the Lord would now come to Israel by the prophet he had called. God was no longer silent.

Let us make two observations as we conclude our consideration of 1 Samuel 3. The first is about the developments we are seeing in the Israel of Samuel's day. The second is about what is happening in our day.

Remember the severe crisis in Israel, which I have been describing as a crisis of leadership. In response to that crisis, what did God do? Did he raise up a man with what we would call leadership gifts? Did he set up a new organizational structure for the nation?

No. He sent *his word*, and he provided for his word to come to all Israel. Samuel held no recognized office. God made him a prophet, whose role was to speak God's words. God's response to Israel's leadership crisis was the provision of *his word*.

As you listen to the closing lines of chapter 3, don't you get the clear impression that it was *good* that God's word was heard again in Israel? It was *good* that Samuel was established as a prophet among them. There were terrible things yet to come, as we will see. But God was no longer silent, and that meant that it was possible for them to be Israel, God's people, again — to hear the word of the Lord, to believe him, to obey him. Read a Psalm like Psalm 19 or Psalm 119, and you will hear how good it was for God's people to have the word of the Lord.

What does all this have to do with what is happening today?

I cannot think of a better place to see it than in the well-known words of Hebrews 1: "Long ago, at many times and in many ways, God spoke to our fathers by the prophets, but in these last days he has spoken to us by his Son. . . ." (vv. 1, 2).

As then, so now God leads his people by his word. God's word to us is the word he has spoken by his Son, Jesus Christ. It is the word you hear when you hear the truth of Jesus Christ. God is not silent. We can be his people — we can hear his word, believe him, obey him.

And that is good — so very, very good!

7

The Problem of the Power of God
I

1 SAMUEL 4:1-11

It is not uncommon for human beings to long for God's power. Even if we do not understand a great deal about religion, we know that God (by definition) must be powerful. If there is some way in which God's power can be made to work for me, that is very attractive.

That, for many people, is the allure of religion. The businessman, weighed down by anxieties, problems, and decisions, may — in a desperate moment — pray. What does he pray for? Why, that God's power might somehow work to keep him afloat, to give him success, perhaps even to inhibit his competitors. If religion can do that, then the businessman can see its value. Gravely ill persons very often will pray. They may never have prayed before, but illness brings prayers out of many a prayer-less person! What do they pray for? Of course that God's power might work to make them well again. If religion can do that, then the sick person can see its value. The student approaching exams is almost as likely as a sick person to think of prayer. What does the student pray for? For the power of God to work to make the questions easy and the answers good — and the teacher generous!

We could characterize religion as human attempts to harness God's power. Of course, it can be more subtle than the rather crass examples I have given. In its more refined forms these days it is called spirituality. But it is fair to say that religious or spiritual activities generally seek to harness God's power — or spiritual power — for us and our lives, even if it is just to find peace and tranquillity.

That is probably a big part of why religion is an almost universal phenomenon in the human race and why spirituality is a current craze in many places. The fact is that life in this world is always under threat of some kind. That is literally true: our lives are never completely safe. Life is always precarious and fragile. It is also true that everything we value in life is insecure. So it is no surprise that humans everywhere seek access to whatever power might be able to protect their lives and well-being. Hence the religions and spiritualities of the world.

But religion has always had one huge problem: How can we know *what to do* to access the power of God? If there is power beyond us, how can it be brought to help us?

The bewildering range of religions and spiritualities that humans have devised are very largely attempts to guess the answer to that question. The tragedy of the religions of the world is that they are no more than that — human guesses as to how to access the power of God. The guesses are random, uncertain, confused, and contradictory. The array of activities (from crystals to fasting, from meditation to sacraments) supposed to be means of encountering spiritual power is bizarre.

But there is another tragedy, and that is to have no interest in the power of God — or as the Apostle Paul described it, "holding the form of religion but denying the power of it" (2 Timothy 3:5, RSV). Formal religion, or merely intellectualized religion that reduces God's power to a concept, an idea, is as tragic as the pursuit of the power of God in ignorant ways. What could be more bizarre than a religion that *in reality* knows nothing of the power of God?

Do you know the power of God?

In the early pages of the book of 1 Samuel we have seen and heard of the power of God. The birth of Samuel to the childless Hannah was an answer to her prayer to God, the "LORD of hosts" (1 Samuel 1:11), a title that reminds us of God's power. Hannah prayed again, in response to the birth of her son, and spoke with great eloquence of God's power before whom "the bows of the mighty are broken, but the feeble bind on strength" (1 Samuel 2:4).

In 1 Samuel 4–6 we come to an episode in which what Hannah spoke of was displayed in a most remarkable way. These chapters are about the power of God, but what we will see will surprise us and challenge, on the one hand, every religious guess about God's power and, on the other hand, every religious person who denies God's power in practice.

The scene is set with two important pieces of information.

THE WORD OF SAMUEL (v. 1a)

And the word of Samuel came to all Israel. (v. 1a)

This picks up the story from the end of chapter 3. The last three verses of chapter 3 summarized the future in broad brushstrokes after the word of the Lord came to Samuel as a boy in the Shiloh temple. The Lord was with Samuel as he grew up and became great. As he spoke God's words, none of them failed. All Israel came to recognize Samuel as a faithful prophet of the Lord. And the Lord's word continued to come to him.

Chapters 4–6 will relate more detail about the events in which Samuel's words proved true and Israel came to understand that he was the Lord's prophet.

"The word of Samuel came to all Israel," as an introduction to chapters 4–6, is not a general summary statement, like the last few lines of chapter 3, but a reference to the beginning of his role as a prophet. The word of Samuel that came to all Israel was the word of the Lord that came to Samuel that night in the temple of Shiloh: "Behold, I am about to do a thing in Israel at which the two ears of everyone who hears it will tingle" (1 Samuel 3:11). That is the word of the Lord that came to Samuel. And the word of Samuel came to all Israel.[1]

THE PHILISTINES (v. 1b)

The second piece of information that sets the scene for what is about to happen is this: "Now Israel went out to battle against the Philistines. They encamped at Ebenezer, and the Philistines encamped at Aphek" (v. 1b).

It is not clear who instigated the hostilities.[2] For the purposes of the story we are about to hear it does not matter. The point is that a battle was brewing.[3]

The Philistines are not newcomers to the Bible story,[4] although this is their first appearance in 1 Samuel. They will be major players until the end of this book, where they will again assemble at Aphek (1 Samuel 29:1), with consequences for Israel that will be terribly reminiscent of the episode before us.[5]

The Philistines were, like the Israelites, relative newcomers to the region. They had settled mainly in the coastal plain to the west of the hill country where the main Israelite occupation had taken place at roughly the same time. They had five main cities — Ekron, Ashdod, Gath, Ashkelon, and Gaza — each with a "lord" or "king."[6] Although the situation on the ground was no doubt more complex than we can now know, there appears to have been a long struggle for control of the region, in which the Philistines and the Israelites were leading protagonists. The former were based in the low land to the west, the latter in the hill country between that coastal plain and the Jordan Valley.

Aphek, where the Philistines set up camp, was to the north of their main territory suggesting that they may have been intent on expanding in that direction.[7] Ebenezer, where the Israelites set up camp ready to confront them, probably lay just a short distance to the east of Aphek, in the foothills, about twenty miles west of Shiloh.[8]

THE FIRST DEFEAT (vv. 2, 3)

What then happened was a disaster, from the Israelite point of view, and raised for them a serious question.

The Defeat (v. 2)

The disaster is reported with brevity:

> *The Philistines drew up in line against Israel, and when the battle spread, Israel was defeated by the Philistines, who killed about four thousand men on the field of battle. (v. 2)*

It sounds like a serious defeat. The number is not absolutely clear. The Hebrew word for "thousand" may also have been used for a military unit,[9] the size of which is unknown and may not have been fixed. However, even if the losses were well short of 4,000, they were serious. The defeat was a major blow to Israel.

The Question (v. 3)

Defeat in war is a crisis for any nation at any time. There are always serious consequences. If a particular defeat translates into a final victory for the enemy, then the prospects for the defeated nation are dim.

In the story of Israel, however, there was always more to it than that. This disaster fits into the pattern that had been going on for some 200 years, through the period covered by the book of Judges. Again and again the existence of the young nation of Israel was threatened.

Yet this people had entered this land with the extraordinary promises of God — promises of rest, of peace, of blessing. God had rescued this nation from more powerful enemies than the Philistines. Why, the most powerful nation of the day in the region, Egypt no less, had been forced by mighty acts of God's power to release this people from slavery so they could come and live here. Furthermore, by great acts of power God had unmistakably given the Israelites this land. All this he had done in faithfulness to the promises he had made (see Joshua 21:43-45). And yet, once again they were under threat — and were soundly defeated by the Philistines. Why?

That is the question the elders of Israel found themselves asking: "And when the troops came to the camp, the elders of Israel said, 'Why has the LORD defeated us today before the Philistines?'" (v. 3a).

The elders understood — up to a point — what had happened. They did not think that God was somehow absent from this battle. They saw their defeat as an act of God rather than as an achievement of the Philistines. In this they were right. Indeed the narrator's report in verse 2 hints as much. Literally it says, "Israel was defeated before the Philistines." The passive verb "was defeated" and the phrase "before [not "by"] the Philistines" indicate that the rout of the Israelites was the work of "a higher authority"[10] than the Philistines. This is what the elders understood: "the LORD defeated us today before the Philistines."

What they did not understand was why.

Consider this response by the elders. Three facts should be kept in mind.

Firstly, Israel had experienced defeat at the hands of enemies before, and the question "Why?" had been asked before. Indeed the previous two centuries had many instances of Israelite suffering under enemy aggression. In each case the answer to the question "Why?" lay in the conduct of Israel.[11]

Is it not surprising, then, that the elders did not say, "What have we done?"

Secondly, the corrupt behavior of Eli's sons, the priests at Shiloh, was well-known among all the people (see 1 Samuel 2:23). It is not unreasonable to suggest that the elders of Israel might have seen some connection between the wickedness of their priests and their defeat at the Lord's hands.

Thirdly, this is all the more so if, as we have suggested, the word of Samuel to all Israel was precisely the message of God's imminent punishment of the house of Eli. While it may not have been clear that this military defeat was somehow related to the punishment of Eli's house, the word of the Lord had been that he was about to do something that would make every ear that heard of it tingle.

The elders' question may be understandable enough, but we should be at least a little surprised at what they did not say. They did not "cry out to the LORD" as the people of Israel had done again and again in the period of the judges (see Judges 3:9, 15; 4:3; 6:6, 7; 10:10, 12).[12]

How far either an acknowledgment of sin or a cry for mercy was from their minds became clear with the proposal with which they answered their own "Why?" question: "Let us bring the ark of the covenant of the LORD here from Shiloh, that it may come among us and save us from the power of our enemies" (v. 3b).

Probably the end of that sentence should read, "that *he* may come among us and save us from the power of our enemies."[13]

We saw the ark in the temple at Shiloh in chapter 3 (v. 3). The elders' proposal reminds us of that night, as well as all we have seen going on at Shiloh.

The elders were probably not so crass as to think of the ark in simple magical terms, as if its presence would itself bring God's power to their side.[14] The title "the ark of the *covenant* of the Lord" suggests that it was as a symbol of the covenant — that is, the commitment of the Lord to Israel — that the ark was to be brought. They would remind the Lord, so to speak, of his obligations to them: "Let us bring the ark of the covenant, so that the Lord will do what he has promised and save us from our enemies. He is supposed to smite Philistines, not Israelites!"[15]

THE ARK OF THE COVENANT OF THE LORD OF HOSTS ENTHRONED ON THE CHERUBIM (vv. 4-9)

The next stage of the story is about what happened when the ark was fetched from Shiloh.

The Ark from Shiloh (v. 4)

> *So the people sent to Shiloh and brought from there the ark of the covenant of the LORD of hosts, who is enthroned on the cherubim. (v. 4a)*

The narrator is making a powerful point with his astonishingly elaborate description of the ark. The elders may have decided to remind the Lord of his obligations toward them. But the narrator informs us that what came down from Shiloh was "the ark of the covenant of the LORD of hosts, who is enthroned on the cherubim"! It is as though he is reminding us that he is the God of whom Hannah spoke. There is none like him, none besides him (1 Samuel 2:2)! Take care, elders of Israel. He is a God of knowledge, by whom deeds are weighed (1 Samuel 2:3). He is the mighty king.[16]

The point being made becomes blindingly obvious when the narrator tells us who was carrying the ark: "And the two sons of Eli, Hophni and Phinehas, were there with the ark of the covenant of God" (v. 4b).

The elders and the people of Israel may not yet have understood, but the answer to their "Why?" question was not God's failure to keep the promise of the covenant represented by the ark, but the failure of the two wretches who were carrying the ark down from Shiloh.

Look back for a moment at these two brothers as they have appeared in the story so far. We first met them in 1 Samuel 1:3. We took little notice of them at that point. We were simply told that they were there at Shiloh and that they were "priests of the LORD." It was in 1 Samuel 2:12-17 that we learned about their character and conduct. They were "worthless men." "They did not know the LORD." Their sin was "very great in the sight of the

LORD, for [among other things!] the men treated the offering of the LORD with contempt." In 1 Samuel 2:22-25 we heard of Eli's vain attempts to rebuke his sons. They did not listen, we are told in verse 25, "for it was the will of the LORD to put them to death." So far had they gone in their wickedness! Then in 1 Samuel 2:27-34 a man of God came to Eli with a word from the Lord, bringing the awful news that punishment was coming on Eli's house, and that it would begin with the death of his two sons on the same day. Then in chapter 3, when God called Samuel, his word was the same terrible message. He was about to do what he had said he would do with Eli's house. This message was delivered to all Israel in 1 Samuel 4:1.

Now in 1 Samuel 4:4 we might well tremble a little when we learn that the ark was being brought down from Shiloh by these two! Can Israel really appeal to the promises of God represented by the ark when that ark is being carried by reprobates who have despised God?

The Israelite Shout (v. 5)

However, these points have been made to us by the narrator. The elders and people of Israel had a rather different view of things: "As soon as the ark of the covenant of the LORD came into the camp, all Israel gave a mighty shout, so that the earth resounded" (v. 5).

The people, of course, had not read verse 4! They saw the ark as it is described here — "the ark of the covenant of the LORD." The promise of God was brought into their camp. Small wonder that pandemonium broke out! The earth shook with the sound of it!

The Philistine Fear (vv. 6-9)

A short distance away, another army heard the noise. What do you think happened down in Aphek? "And when the Philistines heard the noise of the shouting, they said, 'What does this great shouting in the camp of the Hebrews mean?'" (v. 6a).

"The Hebrews" is what foreigners often called the people of Israel, at times in an apparently derogatory tone (see 1 Samuel 4:9; 13:19; 14:11; 29:3; cf. Genesis 39:14, 17; 41:12; Exodus 1:19, 22; 2:6). "The Hebrews" had just been soundly defeated by the Philistines. What did they have to shout about?

> And when they learned that the ark of the LORD had come to the camp, the Philistines were afraid, for they said, "A god has come into the camp." And they said, "Woe to us! For nothing like this has happened before." (vv. 6b, 7)

The reaction of the Philistines is a surprise. They had just shown their military superiority over the Israelites. What made them think they had anything to fear? Remarkably it was because they had heard the gospel of the exodus. Listen to them:

> *"Woe to us! Who can deliver us from the power of these mighty gods? These are the gods who struck the Egyptians with every sort of plague in the wilderness." (v. 8)*

The news of what God had done many years earlier in Egypt had spread.[17] The Philistines, rightly, trembled at the idea of finding themselves up against this God — or these gods (they were not quite clear on that point).

If the Philistines really believed that the God/gods of the exodus had come among the Hebrews, what would be the sensible thing for them to do? What would you do if you faced the prospect of encountering God Almighty on the side of your enemies? Perhaps you would like to assess the intelligence of the Philistines, based on their plan in verse 9: "Take courage, and be men, O Philistines, lest you become slaves to the Hebrews as they have been to you; be men and fight" (v. 9).

Brave or stupid? They would have done well to have heard Hannah's prayer: "not by might shall a man prevail" (1 Samuel 2:9)!

THE SECOND DEFEAT (vv. 10, 11)

So what happened then? Given the terror of the Philistines and the elated confidence of the Israelites, the expectations of all the characters in the story lean one way (even if we readers know a little better).

The Defeat (v. 10)

This is what happened:

> *So the Philistines fought, and Israel was defeated, and they fled, every man to his home. And there was a very great slaughter, for there fell of Israel thirty thousand foot soldiers. (v. 10)*

It was a terrible slaughter! But it was all the wrong way around. Thirty thousand *Israelites* were dead. Even if "thousand" means less than a thousand, there were many more casualties this time than last! What God had done to the Egyptians, he had now done to the Israelites![18]

What could this defeat mean? There are two final pieces of information that we need to hear.

The Ark (v. 11a)

And the ark of God was captured . . . (v. 11a)

The consequences of this extraordinary fact will be played out to the end of chapter 6. For the moment consider the fact itself: the ark of the covenant of the Lord of hosts who is enthroned on the cherubim was taken by the pagan Philistines! It is worth noticing that now it is simply called "the ark of God." The fancy titles hardly seem appropriate anymore. It was beginning to look as though the Philistines were more brave than stupid after all. It is enough to make your ears tingle, don't you think?

The Sons of Eli (v. 11b)

The last note in verse 11 is: ". . . and the two sons of Eli, Hophni and Phinehas, died."

And that, we must now realize, is what this whole sorry episode was about. There is a lot more of this story to come, but to understand this beginning, we need to see that it was about these two men. The Lord did as he had said he would do.

This is a terribly disturbing story. There is much that should be said. Let us conclude with three specific reflections.

Firstly, we have seen something important in this story about God's power. The power of the God of whom the Bible speaks cannot be manipulated by human activities. In retrospect, there was a certain madness about the elders of Israel thinking that bringing the ark would bring God's power onto their side. If religion is the attempt by human beings to harness God's power to their own advantage, this story is testimony to the fact that it cannot be done. If the ark of the covenant of the Lord could not guarantee Israel's safety, then no other religious act will do it. My church attendance, my Bible reading, my prayers, my giving, my meditation — or whatever religious activities I practice — cannot manipulate God's power to bring me success, prosperity, or happiness. God's power is not like that. It is not at our disposal. God's power is *God's* power. This episode should impress on us that much.

There is a second thing to see here. The actions of the elders of Israel cannot be equated with all human attempts at religion. The ark of the covenant was not just any religious object. It was the God-given bearer of the promise of God!

We have the promise of God. It is no longer written on stone tablets in a gold-plated box. The bearer of God's promise to us is Jesus Christ. The story of the connection between the ark we have seen brought from Shiloh and the person of Jesus Christ is told through the pages of the Bible as a whole, and we will have reason to return to that story in the following chapters. At this point consider how the elders of Israel thought they could secure God's power by bringing the ark and how it is possible to think similarly that we might secure the power of God by taking hold of Jesus.

The terrible delusion we have seen is the thought that you can depend on the promises of God while paying no regard to his demands. Christian reader, hear this. You cannot put your trust in God's kindness toward you in Jesus Christ — as the Israelites shouted with joy in the promises represented by the ark of the covenant — and at the same time ignore God's demand for holiness in your life. The Israelites' joyful trust in the ark, and what the ark represented, meant nothing — it was false — so long as they paid no regard to the demands of the covenant, so flagrantly disdained by Hophni and Phinehas. The truth we are seeing here is that you cannot have Jesus Christ as Savior without having him as Lord.

Thirdly, it is appropriate to conclude with the following words from the New Testament about what it means to know the power of God. The Apostle Paul told the Ephesians he prayed:

> . . . that you may know . . . what is the immeasurable greatness of his power toward us who believe, according to the working of his great might that he worked in Christ when he raised him from the dead and seated him at his right hand in the heavenly places, far above all rule and authority and power and dominion, and above every name that is named, not only in this age but also in the one to come. . . . And you were dead in the trespasses and sins in which you once walked. . . . But God, being rich in mercy, because of the great love with which he loved us . . . made us alive together with Christ — by grace you have been saved — and raised us up with him and seated us with him in the heavenly places in Christ Jesus, so that in the coming ages he might show the immeasurable riches of his grace in kindness toward us in Christ Jesus. For by grace you have been saved through faith. And this is not your own doing; it is the gift of God, not a result of works, so that no one may boast. For we are his workmanship, created in Christ Jesus for good works, which God prepared beforehand, that we should walk in them. (Ephesians 1:18–2:10)

That is what it is to know the immeasurable greatness of God's power toward us who believe.

8

Where Is the Glory?

1 SAMUEL 4:12-22

Here is a question worth asking yourself: Where is the glory? It is a strange question — and the reason for asking it here will be clear when we reach the end of 1 Samuel 4. But it is a valuable and searching question. There are many forms of glory in life. Many of them are fleeting. Much glory fades with time. The glory of the celebrity is like that, as is the glory of wealth. Where is the glory for you? Where is the glory that matters to you? Where is the glory you seek and long for? Where is the glory?

As you consider that question, let us return to the story of Israel's experience in the days when Samuel had become a prophet and the Philistines had become a menace.

In the first half of 1 Samuel 4 we heard about how the Israelites suffered, twice over, a devastating defeat at the hands of the Philistines. Many had died. The ark of the covenant had been taken. The priests Hophni and Phinehas had been killed.

The real problem, however, was not the Philistines. Israel had encountered the problem of the power of God. God was more than powerful enough to deliver them from the Philistines. Even the Philistines knew that! But the Israelites could not *control* the power of God. They found themselves on the wrong side of that power as God came *against* them in judgment. The Philistines were just his unwitting instruments. There was absolutely nothing that the Israelites could do to save themselves.

In 1 Samuel 4:12-22 we hear how the news of this disaster reached the city of Shiloh, how Eli heard it and also Phinehas's wife. The impact of the news on Eli and the response of his daughter-in-law are the main concerns of this passage. Just as Hannah's prayer in chapter 2 gave us the most profound insight into the events of chapter 1, so now the words of another woman, after the birth of another son, will show us the extraordinary significance of what had happened.

We are shown two scenes. In the first the news of the Philistine victory reaches the city, and Eli learns of what had happened. In the second we are taken into a more intimate, private scene as the terrible news reaches the wife of Phinehas.

SHILOH AND ELI (vv. 12-18)

The News Reached the City (vv. 12, 13)

The sequence of events begins in verse 12 with a messenger who escaped from the scene of the battle and ran the twenty miles up into the hills to Shiloh. The story is now told from the perspective of the city as the escapee approached.

THE APPROACHING MESSENGER (V. 12)

> *A man of Benjamin ran from the battle line and came to Shiloh the same day, with his clothes torn and with dirt on his head. (v. 12)*

That he was a man of Benjamin is one of those details that seems of small consequence. Biblical writers, however, rarely include details for no reason at all. It will not be long before Israel's hopes will be pinned on another Benjaminite.[1] Then we will have reason to remember this man of Benjamin who, on the very day that Israel suffered that crushing defeat, ran the grueling road all the way up to Shiloh with his dreadful news.

As he approached the city, his appearance spoke volumes. His clothes were torn, and he had dirt on his head. This was more than the disheveled appearance of a man who had fled in haste from the battle and then run all the way to Shiloh. In addition to the mess he must have been, there were the clear and visible signs of mourning and grief.[2] One look at him, and it was plain that he brought bad news. I picture him with tears streaming down his face. Look at him, and you dread what he is about to say.

THE WAITING OLD MAN (V. 13a)

Before we hear him, however, our attention is drawn to the figure of an old man beside the road: "When he arrived, Eli was sitting on his seat by the road watching, for his heart trembled for the ark of God" (v. 13a).

Eli was sitting, as he had been when we first saw him in 1 Samuel 1:9. Then he was "Eli the priest," "sitting on the seat beside the doorpost of the temple of the LORD." Now he is just "Eli," and he was no longer by the temple. These were not good days for Eli. We already know that Eli was very old, and his eyesight was fading (1 Samuel 2:22; 3:2). It is no surprise to see him sitting, waiting. He was not capable of doing much more.

Unfortunately, the text in verse 13 is a little difficult in detail, and it is not clear whether, as most translations have it, Eli was seated "by the road watching" or "beside the gate, watching the road." One proposal even suggests that Eli was seated on top of the gate (which, if it was the city gate, would have been a substantial structure), watching the road.[3]

Eli's frailty is underlined by a detail unusual in Biblical narratives, an insight into the old man's emotional state. Literally it says, "His heart was trembling *on account of* the ark of God."

What was it about the ark that made Eli's heart tremble? After all, the Philistines had been terrified at the news of the ark coming into the Israelite camp (1 Samuel 4:7). What did Eli know that the Philistines did not know? The Israelites had shouted with joyful confidence at the ark's arrival (1 Samuel 4:5). Why did Eli's heart tremble? What did Eli know that the Israelites did not know? We know now that both the Philistines and the Israelites were mistaken, but that news had not yet reached Eli. Why, then, was he shaking so?

What Eli knew was that God had promised that his two sons were going to die on the same day, and he had learned that this was about to happen (1 Samuel 2:34; 3:11, 12, 18). It was not, I think, that he was anxious *for* the ark. Eli was terrified *on account of* the ark. He feared for his sons, who were carrying the ark of the God who had promised this punishment.[4]

The Israelites *should* have known this too, for the word of Samuel — which we have concluded was probably this same word of the Lord about the house of Eli — had come to all Israel (1 Samuel 4:1). They seem to have forgotten, but Eli could not forget. No wonder he was shaking!

The City's Response (v. 13b)

For the moment we leave him there on his seat, watching, waiting, trembling. For the man of Benjamin seems to have run straight past old Eli and into the city, where he told his news: "And when the man came into the city and told the news, all the city cried out" (v. 13b).

Just as the man hardly needed to speak — his appearance told it all — so we do not need to hear what he said. We know too well.

What we are told is that "all the city cried out," reminding us of the mighty shout from "all Israel" a little earlier when the ark had come down from Shiloh to the camp at Ebenezer (1 Samuel 4:5). This time, however, the cry had a different tone.

The News Reached Eli (vv. 14-17)

As the cry from the city rang out, our attention is turned back to the old man sitting, trembling with fear, beside the road (or wherever he precisely was).

ELI'S QUESTION (v. 14)

He heard the cry, and in a way strangely reminiscent of the Philistines when they heard the earlier cry (1 Samuel 4:6), he asked a question: "What is this uproar?" (v. 14a).

Unlike the Philistines, however, who answered their own question, Eli dared not draw the conclusion that he must have suspected. He did not have to wait long: "Then the man hurried and came and told Eli" (v. 14b).

ELI'S AGE (v. 15)

Before we hear what the man said to Eli, once again the narrator pauses to remind us of his age and infirmity: "Now Eli was ninety-eight years old and his eyes were set so that he could not see" (v. 15).

Some time had passed since 1 Samuel 3:2, where we learned of his failing sight.[5] Now he was completely blind. There is a touch of sad irony here. The man sitting, trembling with fear, "watching" the road in verse 13, was totally blind! That is why, of course, he had not drawn the obvious conclusions from the appearance of the bedraggled man of Benjamin who must have run right past him a short time earlier. Weak, blind, trembling old Eli — Israel's leader — needed to ask what the uproar meant.

ELI'S NEWS (vv. 16, 17)

The news was delivered in agonizing stages: "And the man said to Eli, 'I am he who has come from the battle; I fled from the battle today'" (v. 16a).

No doubt exhausted and emotionally drained, the man stammered out his words, repeating himself unnecessarily. Even as he identified himself, however, if his tone of voice did not betray him, his words already implied his bad news: "I *fled* from the battle today." "And [Eli] said, 'How did it go, my son?'" (v. 16b).

As though he needed to ask! The news came, whether deliberately or not, in dramatic sequence: "He who brought the news answered and said, 'Israel has fled before the Philistines. . . .'" (v. 17a).

Just the opposite of what had been expected by both the Israelites and the Philistines! This first piece of news was disastrous enough. But he added, "and there has also been a great defeat among the people" (v. 17b) — probably better translated "a great slaughter," as in 2 Samuel 17:9 (cf. 18:7).[6] This was not a minor setback in the ongoing conflict with the Philistines. This was a disaster of huge proportions. Many, many were dead.

In the original you can sense the man's emotion as he stuttered or blurted this news. He said, "Israel has fled before the Philistines, *and also* there was a great slaughter among the people, *and also* . . ." There was more. "Your two sons also, Hophni and Phinehas, are dead . . ." (v. 17c).

It was as Eli had feared. His heart had been right to tremble on account of the ark of God. The word of God had come to pass. Samuel's words had not fallen to the ground.

It is very important to take great care with an incident in the Bible like this. Like Hannah and her childlessness in chapter 1 and the gift of a son in answer to her prayer, the uniqueness of the particular circumstance must be appreciated. Hannah's experience had a place in God's purposes that was not the same as every childless woman in Israel then or in our world today who may have been blessed with a child in answer to prayer. Just so, the deaths of Hophni and Phinehas in the terrible battle of Aphek were not the same as the tragic deaths of many other sons that day or the many family tragedies that occur today.

Eli's tragedy was different. He had the specific word of the Lord concerning his sons and concerning his house. It was a terrible word. And the deaths of Hophni and Phinehas were the sign to Eli (1 Samuel 2:34). The word of the Lord had come to pass and would come to pass.

The man of Benjamin had one last thing to say: " . . . and the ark of God has been captured" (v. 17d).

As this messenger told it, this was the climactic piece of news. The defeat and the slaughter, including Eli's sons, were terrible. But the ark of God taken by the Philistines! What could that mean for the whole nation?

Eli's Death (v. 18)

As soon as he mentioned the ark of God, Eli fell over backward from his seat by the side of the gate, and his neck was broken and he died, for the man was old and heavy. (v. 18a)

Curiously, the writer does not tell us that it was the news that the ark had been *taken* that killed Eli. In a strange expression, he tells us that it was the mention of the ark itself.[7] This confirmed his great fear. The God of the covenant, whose ark it was, had dealt with Eli's sons. And Eli knew that this was the beginning of the judgment. It was the mention of the ark that killed him.

Notice how the old man died. If he was sitting on top of the gate, the scene was all the more dramatic! Be that as it may, the fall killed him because of his great age and his great weight.

Eli is given by the writer a brief obituary: "He had judged Israel forty years" (v. 18b).

It is possible that this is a piece of sad irony.[8] The sentence echoes the repeated summaries of the lives of Israel's "judges" through the book of Judges (10:2, 3; 12:7, 9, 11, 14; 15:20; 16:31). However, Eli is nowhere else said to have "judged" Israel, and he is nowhere called a "judge." Israel's past experience of "judges" could be summed up in these words: "Whenever the LORD raised up judges for them, the LORD was with the judge, and he saved them from the hand of their enemies all the days of the judge" (Judges 2:18).[9] In reality Eli had not "judged" Israel — not like that. We noted in 1 Samuel 3:13 that God announced he himself was about to "judge" Eli's house. After forty years of Eli's leadership, the Israelites had suffered a crushing defeat, and for the first time ever the ark of God had been taken from them. That is the kind of "judge" Israel could do without!

ELI'S DAUGHTER-IN-LAW (vv. 19-22)

From the publicly visible and audible events in the city and at the gate, the next scene takes us to a more private moment, where we will see yet another tragedy and hear a deeper insight into what had happened.

We are taken into a home in Shiloh, where the wife of Phinehas was at the point of giving birth.

The News Reached Her (v. 19a)

The news came to her in a dramatic, though unchronological sequence:

> Now his daughter-in-law, the wife of Phinehas, was pregnant, about to give birth. And when she heard the news that the ark of God was captured, and that her father-in-law and her husband were dead . . . (v. 19a)

As she heard it, the headline news was the capture of the ark, then Eli's death, then the death of her husband. The news came closer and closer to home.

A Life . . . and a Death (vv. 19b, 20)

The shock brought on her labor: ". . . she bowed and gave birth, for her pains came upon her" (v. 19b).

In this terrible story we have heard of so many deaths, and a new life.

But the new life was accompanied by yet another death, for the mother died.

The women attending her tried to comfort her as she was dying: "And about the time of her death the women attending her said to her, 'Do not be afraid, for you have borne a son'" (v. 20a).

The news did not touch her: "But she did not answer or pay attention" (v. 20b).

The earlier news was too much.

Ichabod: Where Is the Glory? (vv. 21, 22)

But she named the boy before she died. The name was her response to the news that had come:

> And she named the child Ichabod, saying, "The glory has departed from Israel!" because the ark of God had been captured and because of her father-in-law and her husband. And she said, "The glory has departed from Israel, for the ark of God has been captured." (vv. 21, 22)

"Ichabod" — "Where is the glory?"[10] The glory was exiled from Israel.

How very different from Hannah's prayer at the birth of her child! In her own way, however, this mother also understood something deeply profound. "Where is the glory?"

The story is far from over, but we might well pause at this point and reflect on these words of Phinehas's wife. Where is the glory?

There is a dreadful play on words in this story. The description of old Eli in verse 18 tells us that he "was . . . heavy." The Hebrew word is *kabed*, the verb form of *kabod*, "glory." Eli had been the glory, the *kabod*, of Israel — her priest, teacher, mediator, representative. But the glory of Eli had become no more than his old bulk — and it had killed him. Where is the glory? Dead by the road out of Shiloh.

The ark, kept in the tabernacle, had long been associated with the glory of God. In the days of Moses, "the cloud covered the tent of meeting, and the glory of the LORD filled the tabernacle. And Moses was not able to enter the tent of meeting because the cloud settled on it, and the glory of the LORD filled the tabernacle" (Exodus 40:34, 35). Where is the glory? Captured and taken by the Philistines!

The story in 1 Samuel 4 is actually a miniature of the history of Israel as it unfolds through the whole Old Testament. Eventually this nation was driven from the land by the Assyrians and then the Babylonians, and everything that represented their special relationship with God was destroyed. It was the very lowest point in Israel's long history. The experience at Aphek was a foretaste of it. In the land of Babylon Ezekiel became a prophet to the survivors. He saw a vision of the glory of the Lord departing from the temple in Jerusalem and going to Babylon (Ezekiel 10). The glory was exiled!

The Bible story calls us to think rather differently about glory. Where is the glory now? The Bible has an answer to that question, if we will hear it. John put it like this: "The Word became flesh and dwelt [tabernacled] among us, and we have seen his glory" (John 1:14). The glory has now come — in Jesus Christ.

What does that mean?

Just before his death Jesus prayed:

Father, I desire that they also, whom you have given me, may be with me where I am, to see my glory that you have given me because you loved me before the foundation of the world. (John 17:24)

Those who will be with Jesus, where he is, will see *his* glory.

Israel's experience raised a vitally important question — where is the glory? It is not just a question for Israel. Where is the glory for you?

9

The Problem of the Power of God

II

1 SAMUEL 5

Defying the power of God is a common human game. I wonder whether you have played it? This is how it goes. You know about God and his power. You have heard about some of the things that he has done. Perhaps you have even heard about some of the things that he has promised to do. Yet you respond *defiantly*. Why let the power of God disturb your life? Why doubt for a moment that your human strength and ingenuity is all you need to match God's power?

Put like that, it sounds rather stupid. And yet we are surrounded by people playing that game every day. Perhaps we join in from time to time. We live in such a brave world! The power of God causes few to tremble.

Those of us who know God know that this game is the greatest stupidity in the world. The trouble is, we have to admit that it *looks* as though you can get away with it. So often it looks like the Philistines, who faced the power of God with their brave words ("Take courage, and be men, O Philistines," 1 Samuel 4:9), got away with it! They won! They defeated the Israelites and captured the ark of the covenant as a trophy! Those around us who defy God and rely on their human strength to get on without him seem to do all right. Like the Philistines, they seem to win more than their share of life's battles.

Defying God is not something that *looks* particularly stupid. And so it is rare to meet a person who is *afraid* of defying God. Do you find yourself trembling for those you see defying God and his power? I suspect not.

Some aspects of the story we have been following in 1 Samuel 4 are strange to us. The peculiar features of the events narrated there are important (and we will be focusing on one of them shortly), but we would be foolish to overlook the obvious fact that there is something about this story with which we are very familiar. It is a story about people playing a game we all know too well: the Israelites were presuming on, and the Philistines were defying, the power of God. The Israelites' presumption turned to desperation as they suffered a crushing defeat at the hands of their enemies. What is to be said about the Philistines' defiance?

The feature of the story that inevitably strikes any reader today as strange is the role played by the gold-plated box known as the ark of the covenant. The elders of Israel thought that bringing the ark down from Shiloh to their camp in Ebenezer would result in God's saving them from the Philistines. It didn't. The Philistines thought that the ark's presence in the Israelite camp posed a terrible threat to them. It didn't. When the Philistines crushed the Israelites, killing many, they killed the two priests who carried the ark and took the ark itself.

Now we know (from the preceding narrative, particularly chapters 2–3) that these terrible events had a cause. The two priests were at the heart of it. They were wicked men. They had utterly failed in their God-given duty to be priests for the people of Israel. In particular they showed contempt for the sacrifices and offerings that God had prescribed as the means of dealing with the people's sins. The terrible defeat the Israelites suffered at the hands of the Philistines was God's judgment, on the one hand, on the priests who had so failed in their duty, but on the other hand, that judgment had dreadful consequences for the people of Israel for whom the sacrificial system had been corrupted.

The consequences for Israel were put into words by the dying mother of Ichabod: "The glory has departed [or, has gone into exile] from Israel!" (1 Samuel 4:21, 22). That was an eloquent expression of the tragedy. If God had rejected his priests, who had been appointed to provide the mediation that Israel needed with their holy God, and if God had allowed the ark of the covenant, the very sign and symbol of his commitment to Israel, to be taken by the Philistines, then Israel had lost everything that really mattered. So it certainly seemed.

As we read on into chapter 5, we leave the Israelites behind for a while. We will return to them at the end of chapter 6. In the meantime we are taken down to the victorious Philistines, who had taken the ark as a trophy of their triumph.[1]

THE DOUBLE DEFEAT OF DAGON (vv. 1-5)

Biblical narrative often does interesting things with the time sequence of events. Since 1 Samuel 5:1 ("the Philistines captured the ark of God") takes up the story from precisely 1 Samuel 4:11 ("the ark of God was captured"), the effect is to set the events that are about to be narrated *alongside* the happenings at Shiloh that we saw in 1 Samuel 4:12-22. We are about to hear what was happening among the Philistines as the news of the ark's capture brought death and despair in Shiloh.[2]

The "Defeated" Ark (vv. 1, 2)

When the Philistines captured the ark of God, they brought it from
Ebenezer to Ashdod. (v. 1)

Ebenezer was in the western foothills of the Israelite territory. Ashdod was some thirty miles to the southwest, close to the coast and in the heart of the Philistine territory. There were four other Philistine cities, two also near the coast but further south, and two to the east. Ashdod was the most centrally located of the five cities.

The Philistines did with the ark what they would have done with any religious trophy won from an enemy in war: "Then the Philistines took the ark of God and brought it into the house of Dagon and set it up beside Dagon" (v. 2).

Dagon was probably the highest of the Philistine gods (cf. Judges 16:23; 1 Chronicles 10:10).[3] He is thought to have been a god associated with vegetation and fertility. Setting up the ark of the God of the Hebrews "beside Dagon" — that is, beside the image of Dagon in the Dagon temple — was a great coup. There could be no more powerful expression of who had won. The ark of the god of the Hebrews captive in the house of Dagon showed not just which nation had triumphed, but whose god had won!

In the first few lines of the chapter you can detect the immense sense of satisfaction among the Philistines. They are the conquering subject of every verb: they "captured," they "brought," they "took," they "set up." The ark of the Hebrew god, the passive object of each verb, was completely in their power and control, just as the people of Israel had been crushed beneath their might.

The Philistines knew that even the mighty Egyptians had been unable to successfully defy the god of the Hebrews (1 Samuel 4:8)!

The Philistine treatment of the ark suggests that they thought of it as an idol, like their image of Dagon. They may have thought that they were adding the Hebrew god to Dagon's pantheon. More probably they were displaying his subservience to their deity.

Dagon's Demise (vv. 3, 4)

However, overnight something happened in Dagon's temple. We are not told what. We are simply shown what the people of Ashdod saw early the next morning: "And when the people of Ashdod rose early the next day, behold, Dagon had fallen face downward on the ground before the ark of the LORD" (v. 3a).

Since the Philistines captured the ark it has been called, simply, "the ark of God" (1 Samuel 4:11, 13, 17, 18, 19, 21, 22). It is as though, in the hands of the Philistines, the ark lost its special significance for the Israelites as "the ark of the covenant of the LORD [Yahweh]."[4] How could it be seen as representing God's commitment to Israel when it now signified Israel's defeat because it was in the enemy's hands?

But for the first time since its capture, the narrator calls it "the ark of the LORD [Yahweh]," the name by which God had made himself known to his people Israel.[5]

This title seems appropriate for the ark this morning — to the narrator, even if not yet to the people of Ashdod — for the sight of Dagon, fallen off his perch, with his face in the dirt "*before* the ark of the LORD," is delicious!

Very quickly the Ashdodites put things right again: "So they took Dagon and put him back in his place" (v. 3b).

The narrator is enjoying this and expects his hearers to enjoy it too! I wonder whether many years later Isaiah recalled this scene when he launched his biting mockery of the idols of Babylon: "They lift it to their shoulders, they carry it, they set it in its place, and it stands there; it cannot move from its place" (Isaiah 46:7). Dagon moved from his place, but he could not get back again! *They* had to lift the poor fellow back to his feet. *They* had to put him back in his place. What a god, great Dagon!

The next night there was more action in Dagon's temple. Again we see nothing of the action — we are just allowed to join the people of Ashdod when they came to the temple, once again early in the morning:

> But when they rose early on the next morning, behold, Dagon had fallen face downward on the ground before the ark of the LORD, and the head of Dagon and both his hands were lying cut off on the threshold. Only the trunk of Dagon was left to him. (v. 4)

Oh, dear!

Notice how the writer reminds us again that it was "the ark of the LORD [Yahweh]." And before the ark now was only what was left of Dagon. His head and hands had been "cut off" — "chopped off" is one translation![6] The severed bits of Dagon were lying on the threshold. The last sentence in verse 4 is delightfully curious in the Hebrew. Literally it says, "Only Dagon remained on him." No head, no hands, only Dagon — a delightful way of saying what Dagon was. He never could think or speak or act. So chop off his head and hands, and you still have Dagon left![7] Can you see the mighty

Dagon of the Philistines now? Headless, handless — only Dagon remaining on him!

"In Ashdod to This Day" (v. 5)

I sense that the narrator can hardly keep a straight face at this point, for he adds: "This is why the priests of Dagon and all who enter the house of Dagon do not tread on the threshold of Dagon in Ashdod to this day" (v. 5).

To this day, he says (no doubt writing years after these events), everyone who goes into Dagon's temple remembers this night and is not game to touch the doorstep where Dagon's head and arms were ripped off!

It is worth pausing and remembering that at about this time up in the hills at Shiloh a dying mother named her baby "Where is the glory?" She said, "The glory has departed from Israel!" (1 Samuel 4:21). Down by the coast in Ashdod, someone was getting some glory! If we can't see that yet, just read on.

THE HEAVY HAND OF GOD (vv. 6-10)

The events in the temple of Dagon were just the beginning of the Philistines' troubles. The second phase of their difficulties is introduced with the words "The hand of the LORD was heavy . . ." (v. 6a).

There are two powerful points in that phrase. As Dagon lay in the dirt, handless, the one whose name belonged to the ark was not handless![8] Dagon could do nothing. He never could, of course, but now his powerlessness was on display. The Lord, Yahweh, was the powerful one — in the temple of Dagon and, as we will see shortly, anywhere else.

The hand of the Lord was "heavy." The word play cannot be translated into English, but we noted earlier that in Hebrew one word, *kabod*, means "glory" and "heavy." The mother said in Shiloh, "Where is the *kabod*?" Now we learn that in Ashdod the hand of the Lord was *kabod*!

In Ashdod (vv. 6-8)

What did that mean for the Philistines of Ashdod? "The hand of the LORD was heavy against the people of Ashdod, and he terrified and afflicted them with tumors, both Ashdod and its territory" (v. 6).

Terror filled the people of Ashdod and the surrounding region as a plague of tumors spread.[9] It has been suggested that this may have been an outbreak of bubonic plague.[10] Whatever it was, it was sufficient to greatly frighten them.[11]

The men of Ashdod made the connection between the tumors, the smashing of Dagon, and the presence of the ark of the God of Israel in their midst.

> *And when the men of Ashdod saw how things were, they said, "The ark of the God of Israel must not remain with us, for his hand is hard against us and against Dagon our god." (v. 7)*

They were not entirely stupid, the men of Ashdod! They were precisely right in the connections drawn and the conclusion deduced.

Curiously they were in a very similar situation to the Israelites at the beginning of this saga. God's people had drawn the correct conclusion that their defeat before the Philistines was the Lord's doing (1 Samuel 4:3). Just as the Israelite elders had put their heads together to consider what to do, so now the lords of the Philistines — that is, the five kings of the five Philistine cities — were assembled for a crisis meeting. "So they sent and gathered together all the lords of the Philistines and said, 'What shall we do with the ark of the God of Israel?'" (v. 8a).

The elders of Israel had thought that the ark of the covenant of the Lord was the answer to their problems. The lords of the Philistines were sure that it was the presence of the ark in Ashdod that was the cause of their difficulties.

We might speculate as to what the wisest course of action might have been at this point. If you had been present at that crisis meeting, would you have had a proposal to put forward? We do not know whether there was a lengthy discussion or a debate. We do know that a plan of action emerged from the meeting: "They answered, 'Let the ark of the God of Israel be brought around to Gath'" (v. 8b).

The logic behind this proposal is less than transparent. I would love to know what the lord of Gath had to say about it! Still, he was outnumbered four to one. Why Gath? We can only guess. It was the Philistine city furthest to the east from Ashdod and closest to the Israelite hills. But perhaps the king of Gath was the weakest member of the meeting.[12]

Their decision does reveal one thing clearly. At this stage they had no intention of relinquishing control of the ark. "So they brought the ark of the God of Israel there" (v. 8c).

In Gath (v. 9)

We are not entirely surprised to hear what happened next:

> *But after they had brought it around, the hand of the LORD was against the city, causing a very great panic, and he afflicted the men of the city, both young and old, so that tumors broke out on them. (v. 9)*

This could be translated, "the hand of the LORD was *in* the city." The consequence was a very great panic. The word translated "panic" is extraordinary because the reaction was extraordinary. The word typically describes the terror that God brought on the enemies of Israel in war, leading to destruction, and is sometimes translated "confusion" or "tumult" (see Deuteronomy 7:23; 28:20; 1 Samuel 14:20; Isaiah 22:5; Ezekiel 7:7). The people understood themselves to be under attack from the Lord.

It is worth remembering that these are the Philistines who called on one another to "be men and fight" in 1 Samuel 4:9. But under attack from God they trembled.

In Ekron (v. 10)

There does not appear to have been another crisis meeting. Without consultation the people of Gath decided to send the thing to Ekron, the next Philistine city, the closest to Gath.

> *So they sent the ark of God to Ekron. But as soon as the ark of God came to Ekron, the people of Ekron cried out, "They have brought around to us the ark of the God of Israel to kill us and our people." (v. 10)*

They protested vehemently, before anything even happened. Whatever happened to "Be men and fight"? There was now nothing but terrified panic.

THE GLORY (vv. 11, 12)

Our chapter concludes with the complete capitulation of the Philistines.

Surrender (v. 11a)

Another desperate meeting of the lords was called. The people did not seem now to ask the lords for advice, as last time. They gave them instructions:[13]

> *They sent therefore and gathered together all the lords of the Philistines and said, "Send away the ark of the God of Israel, and let it return to its own place, that it may not kill us and our people." (v. 11a)*

Just as they had put Dagon back "in his place" (v. 3), they thought it was time to return the ark of the God of Israel "to its [or his] own place." This, however, was an act of complete surrender.

Terror (v. 11b)

The reason for the decision was simple: "For there was a deathly panic throughout the whole city" (v. 11b). Literally, "a panic of death."

The Heavy Hand (vv. 11c, 12)

The hand of God was very heavy there. (v. 11c)

If you have been wondering where was the glory, here is the answer.

The chapter concludes: "The men who did not die were struck with tumors, and the cry of the city went up to heaven" (v. 12).

It was like the cry of the Israelites in Egypt.[14] Is this not a remarkable turn of events? The Philistines who had defied God, fearing that they would become slaves of the Hebrews, found themselves crying out to heaven, just like the Hebrews when they were slaves of the Egyptians.[15]

All this happened a long time ago. It is, however, part of a pattern. This is how it is with defiance of God. For a time people get away with it, and it looks as though defying God is feasible. But it is not feasible.

We cannot but hear this story alongside another story, which is about the greatest of all God's defeats over his enemies. It was when Jesus died on the cross.

That was the moment in the history of the world when defiance of God had "got away with it." God's Christ, God's Son, was nailed to a cross, executed in weakness. When you look at the cross, who is the defeated one? As Jesus was crucified, it was like the ark being taken captive. Who was the victorious one then?

But early on another morning something had happened in the tomb where they had laid him, which leaves the surprise in the temple in Ashdod far behind. And the Bible tells us that the apparently defeated one was in fact the powerful victor:

He disarmed the rulers and authorities and put them to open shame, by triumphing over them in it [literal translation, referring to the cross]. (Colossians 2:15)

To defy God is as stupid as it sounds, and far more stupid than it often looks. Don't do it.

10

Knowing the Power of God

1 SAMUEL 6

Someone somewhere once devised a little ditty, evidently designed to motivate Christian people to take their service for the Lord seriously. It went like this: "He has no other hands than our hands; he has no other feet than our feet." The point was that God works in this world *through us*. As we who have come to know and love God through Jesus Christ do good, as we speak truth, care for others, work for justice, oppose evil, God is at work. Furthermore, is it not clear that the gospel of Jesus Christ will only reach the peoples of the world — not to mention the people of my neighborhood — if we who know and believe this gospel take it to them? How will my friends and family ever hear the news of the forgiveness of sins and eternal life if I do not tell them? How will the people of our world learn of the Savior every human being needs if Christian people (like us!) do not tell them? These thoughts were summed up in the catchy words, "He has no other hands than our hands; he has no other feet than our feet."

However, 1 Samuel 6 will teach us that this way of thinking, and the jingle that sums it up, is missing something very important.

The circumstances of the story we are about to hear are summed up in the first sentence of the chapter: "The ark of the LORD was in the country of the Philistines seven months" (v. 1).

Those words put in a nutshell the very great calamity that had occurred for the people of Israel. In the history of Israel this was a monumental crisis. We have seen in the preceding two chapters (especially 1 Samuel 4:8, and we will see it again in chapter 6) references and allusions to the great defining experience of Israel — namely, the exodus from Egypt. While it would be an exaggeration to regard the experience of these days as of equal importance to the exodus, we do need to appreciate that it was another time that would change Israel forever.

The brief summing up of the crisis is that *the ark* was in the land of *the Philistines*. The significance of this can hardly be overstated. The ark represented the covenant, that arrangement by which God was to be Israel's God, and Israel was to be God's people (see Exodus 19:4-6; 29:45, 46; Leviticus 11:45; 26:12). Israel knew God, for God had made himself known to them by his name Yahweh.[1] Now "the ark of Yahweh was in the country of the Philistines." The Philistines were, at this time, Israel's archenemy. A vital aspect of the covenant was that Yahweh would deliver Israel from her enemies (for example, Leviticus 26:7; Deuteronomy 23:14; 28:7). The first words engraved on the stone tablets carried in the ark were "I am Yahweh your God, who *brought you out of the land of Egypt*, out of the house of slavery" (Exodus 20:2). Although there had been difficulties in Israel's subsequent experience, never before had Israel lost possession of the ark. They had suffered setbacks from enemies, but no enemy had ever taken the ark of the covenant of Yahweh. "The ark *of Yahweh* was in the country of *the Philistines*." What did this mean for Israel?[2]

Before we learn what it meant for Israel, we have been hearing what it meant for the Philistines. In short, abject terror, as we saw in chapter 5. This lasted, we are told in 6:1, for seven months. First Samuel 6 is the account of how those seven months came to an end and where that left Israel.

PHILISTINE PERPLEXITY (vv. 2-9)

The Philistines had a problem. They had deduced that the plagues that came upon them were connected with the Israelite ark. Eventually they wanted to be rid of the wretched thing. They instructed their rulers to "return [it] to its own place" (1 Samuel 5:11), but no one seemed to know how to go about that without bringing more troubles. Clearly acknowledging that their problem was beyond the capacity of their "lords," advice was sought from their "priests and . . . diviners" (6:2).

Their Question (v. 2)

> And the Philistines called for the priests and the diviners and said, "What shall we do with the ark of the LORD? Tell us with what we shall send it to its place." (v. 2)

The location is still Ekron.[3] "The Philistines" took the initiative again, the "lords" (5:11) having failed to solve the problem.[4] But they simply did not know what to do. The lords had sent the ark from place to place in their own land, from Ashdod to Gath to Ekron. That had been a disaster. They were now very keen to "send it to its place," by which they presumably meant the land of Israel (although I doubt they had any clear idea what they meant). "With what shall we send it . . . ?" suggests they were aware that simply dumping the ark up in the hills might not be the wisest course of action. So they asked the people they hoped might know about this sort of thing, the priests and diviners.[5]

Their Answer (v. 3)

Here is the answer they were given:

> They said, "If you send away the ark of the God of Israel, do not send it empty, but by all means return him a guilt offering. Then you will be healed, and it will be known to you why his hand does not turn away from you." (v. 3)

It is fairly clear that the priests and diviners had no sure answer. They simply advised what should be done *if* it was decided to send the ark away.

However, in Biblical narratives we often hear words spoken that are more significant than the speakers themselves could have known. This is the case here. The whole account of the sending of the ark out of the land of the Philistines and back to the land of Israel contains numerous reminders of the story of the exodus from Egypt. In these words of the Philistine advisers there are four surprising echoes of the exodus!

First, the verb "send away" itself is the word used many times for Pharaoh's dismissal of Israel from Egypt. It is the word Moses used when he famously said "Let my people go" (Exodus 5:1).[6] The ark's departure from the country of the Philistines would in some sense be like the departure of Israel from Egypt.

Second, the Israelites were not to leave Egypt "empty." They were to take gold and silver jewelry from the Egyptians with them (Exodus 3:21, 22; 11:2, 3).[7] Just so, the advisers say (unaware, no doubt, of the analogy they were helping to develop), the ark must not be sent away "empty." They would shortly advise that gold objects from the Philistines should go with it.

Third, the most surprising piece of advice is that the Philistines should return to the God of Israel a "guilt offering," or as this Hebrew term might be better translated, "reparation offering."[8] While we ought not to imagine that the Philistine clergy knew the Law of Moses, it is striking to hear from them an important term in the Law given to Israel after the exodus (see Leviticus

5:14–6:7).[9] In the book of Leviticus the "guilt/reparation offering" contributes to the complex of symbols representing the seriousness of human sin in the face of the holiness of God. This particular offering "presents a commercial picture of sin. Sin is a debt which man incurs against God. The debt is paid through the offered animal."[10] While we need not try to guess what precisely was in the mind of the Philistine advisers, we can be confident that the narrator and informed readers of this story will see in the term "guilt/reparation offering" an implicit (possibly unconscious!) acknowledgment by the Philistines that they had incurred a debt against the God of Israel that must be repaid.[11]

The fourth allusion to the exodus in the advice of the Philistine experts is the expectation that when it is all over they will know something about God. A great theme in the Bible's account of the exodus is that by the mighty display of the power of God, the Israelites, the Egyptians, and indeed all the earth would "know" something about the God who did this.[12] In this case the Philistine professionals anticipated that if their afflictions were healed,[13] then they would know that it had been the hand of the Lord against them because of the guilt they had incurred.

Their Uncertainty (vv. 4-9)

Do not be deceived by the surprising insights the Philistines appeared to display. They were uncertain and confused, ready to give anything a try. The fact that they happened to speak more truly than they knew is further evidence of the hand of the Lord in this whole situation. Their confused uncertainty soon became evident.

Tumors and Mice (vv. 4, 5)

The bit about a guilt/reparation offering caught the attention of the Philistine questioners: "And they said, 'What is the guilt offering that we shall return to him?'" (v. 4a).

How do you repay a debt you cannot assess to a God you do not know?

> They answered, "Five golden tumors and five golden mice, according to the number of the lords of the Philistines, for the same plague was on all of you and on your lords. So you must make images of your tumors and images of your mice that ravage the land, and give glory to the God of Israel. Perhaps he will lighten his hand from off you and your gods and your land." (vv. 4b, 5)

This is very strange! As in the previous chapter, it is difficult to imagine the narrator keeping a straight face as he tells the story! The advice of the Philistine clergy was to make five little golden models of their tumors. Perhaps one of the lords of the Philistines could pose for the craftsman![14]

The five golden mice are a surprise but indicate that the afflictions on the Philistines were more extensive than reported in the previous chapter. There was also a plague of mice that "ravage[d] the land." The making of five models of the mice out of gold is almost as comical as the five golden tumors.[15]

The fact that they were to be of gold, however, reminds us again of the Israelites who "plundered the Egyptians" (Exodus 12:35, 36) when they were sent away carrying Egyptian gold.

The call to give glory to the God of Israel is yet another echo of the exodus, as well as of more recent events. God had said, "I will get glory over Pharaoh and all his host" (Exodus 14:4). In this event the God of Israel will "get glory" from the Philistines. We also remember that in Israel the question had been asked, "Where is the glory?" and it had been said, "The glory has departed from Israel" (1 Samuel 4:21, 22). That may be so, but the "glory" or "weight" of the God of Israel was being recognized by the Philistines. They longed for that which was mourned in Israel — namely, that the "weight" would depart from them.

The hand of the God of Israel was heavy on "you and your gods and your land." This supports the suggestion that only some of the troubles experienced by the Philistines were reported in chapter 5. Certainly if we take the words of the clergy literally here, something had happened to other gods, in addition to Dagon.[16]

It is important to notice the word "perhaps." These advisers were able to promise nothing. They did not *know* what to do. All they could offer was "perhaps."[17]

EXODUS ANALOGY (V. 6)

> "Why should you harden your hearts as the Egyptians and Pharaoh hardened their hearts? After he had dealt severely with them, did they not send the people away, and they departed?" (v. 6)

The allusions we have seen to the exodus story were no doubt largely unconscious, but the Philistines knew of the exodus (slightly confused though their understanding may have been; see 1 Samuel 4:8) and saw their situation as analogous to that of the Egyptians.

The play on the ideas of "glory" and "weight" expressed in one Hebrew word (*kabod*) continues. Literally verse 6 says, "Why should you *make heavy* your heart as the Egyptians and Pharaoh *made heavy* their heart?"[18]

The heavy or hard heart describes defiance toward God, like that of Pharaoh, and now of the Philistines. Such defiance brings God's *heavy* hand of judgment, as the Egyptians learned (see Exodus 3:19, 20; 6:1; 7:4, 5; 9:3, 15; 13:3, 9, 14; 15:6, 12), and as the Philistines had now experienced (1 Samuel 5:6, 7, 9, 11; 6:3, 5, 9). The only answer for the Egyptians was to "send away" the Israelites (1 Samuel 6:6). So, by implication, the Philistines must "send away" the ark (v. 3).

CAUTIOUS INSTRUCTIONS (vv. 7-9)

For all that, the Philistines were not sure. They did not *know* that it was the God of Israel behind their troubles. So the priests and diviners devised very cautious instructions, attempting to keep their options open.

> *"Now then, take and prepare a new cart and two milk cows on which there has never come a yoke, and yoke the cows to the cart, but take their calves home, away from them. And take the ark of the LORD and place it on the cart and put in a box at its side the figures of gold, which you are returning to him as a guilt offering. Then send it off and let it go its way and watch. If it goes up on the way to its own land, to Beth-shemesh, then it is he who has done us this great harm, but if not, then we shall know that it is not his hand that struck us; it happened to us by coincidence." (vv. 7-9)*

All precautions were to be taken. A new cart would avoid any offense from previous uses to which a cart may have been put. The two milk cows, however, were part of an ingenious test. It might remind us of Elijah's later test on Mount Carmel (1 Kings 18).[19] A situation was devised in which the probability was so strongly stacked in one direction that only the power of God could bring about a different outcome. The cows had not been yoked before — they would be unlikely to cooperate. Furthermore they were feeding calves, which were to be penned up; the cows would not naturally go away from them.[20] The cows were then to be let go, harnessed to the cart carrying the ark and the gold objects. If in these unlikely circumstances the cows pulled the cart to its destination, then the Philistines could be sure that their guesses were right — their troubles had indeed been inflicted by the God of Israel. But if the cows did something more natural, then they could safely conclude that it had all been a horrible coincidence.

Beth-shemesh was located about seven miles east of Ekron in the foothills of the central mountain range, in the territory of Judah.[21] It was probably chosen as the nearest Israelite settlement to which the ark could be sent. It also happened to be a Levitical city, the point of which will become clear shortly (Joshua 21:16).[22]

THE NEW EXODUS (vv. 10-18)

The advice of the priests and diviners was followed to the letter (and a bit beyond, as we will see), and the outcome was astonishing.

The Highway for Our God (vv. 10-12)

> The men did so, and took two milk cows and yoked them to the cart and shut up their calves at home. And they put the ark of the LORD on the cart and the box with the golden mice and the images of their tumors. And the cows went straight in the direction of Beth-shemesh along one highway, lowing as they went. They turned neither to the right nor to the left, and the lords of the Philistines went after them as far as the border of Beth-shemesh. (vv. 10-12)

The direct, straight route taken by the cows is emphasized. It was as though they were on a highway! Mind you, the cows "lowing as they went" suggests they were being driven against their natural inclinations by a power beyond them, as, of course, they were.

Many years later Isaiah looked forward to the day when God would save his people from the exile and bring them back home in a new exodus. His language would be reminiscent of this scene:

> . . . prepare the way of the LORD;
>   make straight in the desert a highway for our God.
> Every valley shall be lifted up,
>   and every mountain and hill be made low;
> the uneven ground shall become level,
>   and the rough places a plain.
> And the glory of the LORD shall be revealed,
>   and all flesh shall see it together. . . . (Isaiah 40:3-5)

That day the road from Ekron to Beth-shemesh became "a highway for our God."[23] It was like the exodus again, except that rather than the people of Israel coming up out of Egypt, the ark of the Lord was coming up from the land of the Philistines.

The lords of the Philistines watched and no doubt wondered.

The Arrival (vv. 13-15)

Suddenly our perspective shifts, and we join the workers in the fields of Beth-shemesh. For them seven months had passed since the dreadful defeat of the Israelites at Aphek. Clearly life went on for these people, but we know nothing of their experiences over the seven months since the Philistines had taken the ark.

It was a day they would never forget. They probably heard the strange, constant lowing of two cows before they saw anything. When they lifted their eyes, they saw the bizarre noisy procession making its way up the hill toward them from the Philistine land:

> Now the people of Beth-shemesh were reaping their wheat harvest in the valley. And when they lifted up their eyes and saw the ark, they rejoiced to see it. (v. 13)

This was the reversal of Ichabod. The captured ark was returning. Did that mean the glory too? The joyful reaction of the people of Beth-shemesh suggests they may have thought so.

The cart apparently (and actually!) guided by an unseen hand came nearer: "The cart came into the field of Joshua of Beth-shemesh and stopped there. A great stone was there" (v. 14a).

We know nothing else about this Joshua, but his name is enough to catch our attention. The ark's reentry to the land is associated with a man named Joshua, namesake of the famous Joshua who led the Israelites into the land after the exodus (Deuteronomy 3:28; 31:3, 7, 23; Joshua *passim*).

The cart carrying the ark that had moved so directly up to Beth-shemesh stopped there in Joshua's field, beside a great stone.[24]

The implication was apparently obvious to those people of Beth-shemesh: "And they split up the wood of the cart and offered the cows as a burnt offering to the LORD" (v. 14b).

In Israel's Law the burnt offering was "the commonest of all the Old Testament sacrifices."[25] We cannot tell the thoughts and motivations of those who offered this sacrifice, but like the "guilt offering" of the Philistines, this offering was at least an implicit acknowledgment of Israel's guilt before the Lord of the ark.

The response of the people in joy (v. 13) and burnt offering (v. 14) were the first things the narrator tells us. He then goes back for a moment to tell us about the taking down of the ark (presumably before the cart was chopped up and burnt!):[26]

> And the Levites took down the ark of the LORD and the box that was beside it, in which were the golden figures, and set them upon the great stone. (v. 15a)

The Levites were the appropriate people to handle the ark (Numbers 3:31; Deuteronomy 10:8; 31:9, 25; Joshua 3:3; 8:33).[27] Their presence is no surprise as Beth-shemesh was (as we have noted) a Levitical city.

It seems that so far at least all was well. The people responded gladly, but with humble reverence at the unexpected arrival of the ark of the Lord among them. This response is elaborated: "And the men of Beth-shemesh offered burnt offerings and sacrificed sacrifices on that day to the LORD" (v. 15b).

Further burnt offerings and also sacrifices were made "on that day."[28] There was a clear recognition that the occasion was of very great importance.

The Witnesses (vv. 16-18)

The whole remarkable sequence of events had a number of witnesses. In verse 12 we heard that the lords of the Philistines followed the cart as far as the border of Beth-shemesh. Astonished, no doubt, they watched the cart make its remarkable way straight to Joshua's field. Then in verse 16 we see the lords of the Philistines still watching with wonder: "And when the five lords of the Philistines saw it, they returned that day to Ekron" (v. 16).

In verse 13, from a different vantage point (and with a different mood), the people of Beth-shemesh saw it all.

To these eyewitnesses the narrator adds further "witnesses" to the remarkable events of this day in Beth-shemesh:

> These are the golden tumors that the Philistines returned as a guilt offering to the LORD: one for Ashdod, one for Gaza, one for Ashkelon, one for Gath, one for Ekron, and the golden mice, according to the number of all the cities of the Philistines belonging to the five lords, both fortified cities and unwalled villages. (vv. 17, 18a)

It sounds as though these golden objects were still around as the narrator wrote this account. His readers knew of them. The known golden articles testify that the Philistines followed the advice of the priests and diviners with regard to the golden tumors. There were five of them, one for each of the Philistine cities. With the mice, however, they went way beyond the suggested offering. Perhaps because the mice plague was more widespread, they decided to add a golden mouse for every city, town, and village.[29] Better to be sure than sorry! However, the point is that the evidence for this great day was still there as this account was being written.[30]

Furthermore:[31] "The great stone beside which they set down the ark of the LORD is a witness to this day in the field of Joshua of Beth-shemesh" (v. 18b).

It is still there, the writer was telling his readers, for anyone to go and see where these great things happened.

THE PROBLEM WITH THE POWER OF GOD (vv. 19-21)

It would be nice if the story ended at verse 18. You might recall that we began looking at the story of the ark in chapter 4 by considering the problem of the power of God. We have seen that the Israelites could not presume on the power of God, and the Philistines could not defy the power of God. At the end of this extraordinary story we learn the sobering news that the power of God was no less terrifying at the end than it was at the beginning of this sequence of events.

The Disaster at Beth-shemesh (v. 19)

> And he struck some of the men of Beth-shemesh, because they looked upon the ark of the LORD. He struck seventy men of them, and the people mourned because the LORD had struck the people with a great blow. (v. 19)

All the humor that has been part of this story and the mockery of the foolish Philistines stops at this point. There is nothing funny now. The return of the ark did not signal that God was less terrifying than he had ever been. If he was not to be mocked and ridiculed in the pagan land, set up beside the god Dagon, he was not to be taken lightly in Israel either.

It seems that some of the men of Beth-shemesh looked at the ark in some improper way. This cannot mean simply that they saw it. Everyone saw it. But some gazed as they should not have gazed.[32] The description is no clearer than that. But the consequence was terrible. Seventy died.[33]

Furthermore the last words of verse 19 make clear that the problem Israel had seven months earlier had not been solved. A "great blow" is the same expression in Hebrew as "great slaughter" in 1 Samuel 4:10. The numbers, of course, are different, but the power of God was still a terrible threat to the Israelite people.[34] Precisely why will not be made clear until chapter 7.

The Question at Beth-shemesh (v. 20)

At the beginning of the chapter the Philistines had their perplexed question ("What shall we do with the ark of the LORD?"). At the end of the chapter the people of Beth-shemesh had a similar question about God himself: "Then the men of Beth-shemesh said, 'Who is able to stand before the LORD, this holy God? And to whom shall he go up away from us?'" (v. 20).

They found themselves no more comfortable with the God of the ark than did the Philistines. Hannah had said in her prayer, "There is none holy like the LORD" (1 Samuel 2:2). The people of Beth-shemesh learned from experience, as the Israelites had earlier, that this can be a very disconcerting truth.

No Answer at Beth-shemesh (v. 21)

This chapter concludes:

> *So they sent messengers to the inhabitants of Kiriath-jearim, saying, "The Philistines have returned the ark of the LORD. Come down and take it up to you." (v. 21)*

Kiriath-jearim was a town not far from Beth-shemesh, further to the northeast, and therefore both away from the Philistines and toward Shiloh, from whence the ark had been taken. These geographical facts may account for the appeal being directed there.[35] The impression is given that the messengers from Beth-shemesh did not tell the whole story of what had happened and why they were so keen for the ark to be taken away from them.[36]

What then happened to the ark and what then happened in Israel is the story that will be taken up in chapter 7.

What are we to make of this story of the ark of the covenant of the Lord? There is so much that is strange (we might be tempted even to say weird!) about the events that have been recounted in these three chapters of 1 Samuel. In due course we will reflect on the important message of these chapters in the unfolding story of the book of 1 Samuel. At this point, however, I would like to think about the place of this story in the Bible as a whole.

We have already heard numerous echoes of the exodus story. Just as the people of Israel went down into Egypt and became slaves, so the ark was taken captive into the land of the Philistines. Just as the Israelites were liberated from their captors by the mighty hand of God, so the ark was brought out of Philistia by God's hand. Like the story of the exodus, this has been a story of bondage and liberation, humiliation and vindication, suffering and glory.

It is important to see that both of these stories are part of a bigger pattern still. This is the way of the God of Israel. Hannah saw it: "The LORD kills and brings to life; he brings down to Sheol and raises up . . . he brings low and he exalts" (1 Samuel 2:6, 7). Israel was to experience this again toward the end of the Old Testament period when the Babylonian exile would be followed by the return from exile. Suffering was followed by glory.

This pattern came to its climactic expression in the person of Jesus:

> *. . . who, though he was in the form of God, did not count equality with God a thing to be grasped, but made himself nothing, taking the form of a servant, being born in the likeness of men. And being found in human form, he humbled himself by becoming obedient to the point of death, even death on a cross. Therefore God has highly exalted him and bestowed on*

him the name that is above every name, so that at the name of Jesus every
knee should bow, in heaven and on earth and under the earth, and every
tongue confess that Jesus Christ is Lord, to the glory of God the Father.
(Philippians 2:6-11)

Humiliation followed by glory.

This is the pattern of life for all those who come to belong to Jesus. "[T]he sufferings of this present time are not worth comparing with the glory that is to be revealed to us" (Romans 8:18).

The strange story of the ark of the covenant of the Lord in 1 Samuel 4–6 is part of the whole Bible message that the God of Israel, the God and Father of our Lord Jesus Christ, is the one whose power always and inevitably accomplishes his purpose. He does bring low, and he does exalt.

As we stand beside the lords of the Philistines, watching the ark making its way straight up to Beth-shemesh, we should see that this God has the power to raise the dead, to turn humiliation to triumph and suffering to joy, to wipe away every tear. As we stand beside the people of Beth-shemesh and see the ark coming up the hill, dragged by those protesting cattle, what do you think of "he has no other hands than our hands; he has no other feet than our feet"?

We should now hear that ditty for the nonsense that it is. One writer has described the sentiment in that jingle as "cowardly modernity that leads us to exhaustion and despair."[37] He is right.

Some of us would do well to reflect on our plans, strategies, programs, goals, and targets to see whether our energetic activity has something of "cowardly modernity" about it, something that *does* assume "he has no other hands . . ." Is it possible that some of our exhaustion and despair, our frustrations and disappointments, our endless activism and busyness, our difficulty in finding contentment, our inability to relax might have something to do with our assumptions about the power of God and his pathetic dependence on our little hands and feet?

The truth is, we serve a God who is immeasurably powerful. The one who brought the ark up from the Philistines is the one who raised Jesus from the dead, and he will accomplish his purposes. His victory does not depend on me or on you any more than it depended on the people of Beth-shemesh.

Trust him — but do not, whatever you do, defy him.

11

Effective Leadership

1 SAMUEL 7

The Bible calls us to a fresh understanding of everything in life — an understanding in which God is no longer ignored or marginalized, and the person of Jesus Christ is no longer unimportant. It should not, therefore, surprise us to find that the book of 1 Samuel presents its theme (which I have suggested is leadership) in an unexpected, even perplexing way. Indeed as we have followed the story of the loss and return of the ark of the covenant in chapters 4–6, we may have begun to wonder whether the subject of leadership had been forgotten.

We are about to see that is not the case.

One striking feature of chapters 4–6 has been the absence of Samuel (apart from 4:1). The man who was established as a prophet in Israel according to the last sentences of chapter 3 plays no active role in the dramatic events of the following three chapters. Indeed in chapters 5, 6 no Israelite at all plays any active role. At the end of the story, to be sure, there are the astounded witnesses to the return of the ark to Israelite soil, but they played no part whatsoever in bringing it back.

In the context of Israel's leadership crisis the story of chapters 4–6 testifies to the fact that God is perfectly capable of dealing with Israel's wicked leaders without any help from the Israelites (chapter 4), and he is fully competent to deal with Israel's enemies, again without any involvement of the Israelites (chapters 5, 6). In other words, the very things that we might have described as constituting what we have been calling a leadership crisis in Israel — namely, the internal threat of corrupt people in power and the external threat of mighty enemies — are things that God had now demonstrated he can deal with for Israel without the help of any human leader at all!

This means that Israel's problem was not fundamentally their corrupt and inept leaders (God dealt with them decisively), nor was it the Philistine threat (they could not prevail against God's heavy hand). If Israel had a problem (and they certainly did), it was with God himself!

It is perfectly clear that the relationship between Israel and God was in serious difficulties. Up until now it has not been clear why. It seems to be the case that the Israelites themselves did not understand why all was not well. After the first battle of Aphek, when the Israelites were thoroughly defeated, and four "thousand"[1] died, the elders of Israel asked, "Why?" (1 Samuel 4:3). After the second battle of Aphek there was a terrible slaughter, and you can feel the sense of utter dismay in the latter part of chapter 4. God had not merely judged Hophni, Phinehas, and Eli, but another thirty "thousand" Israelites died, and the ark of the covenant was taken. The obvious question raised by these events is, why?

The issue came to its clearest expression at the end of chapter 6, when for a reason that is again not fully explained, God struck down a number of the men of Beth-shemesh. The people mourned, apparently realizing that their situation had not improved since the defeats at Aphek some seven months earlier (1 Samuel 6:19). Their question was very much to the point: "Who is able to stand before the LORD, this holy God? And to whom shall he go up away from us?" (v. 20). The first question is rhetorical. They had come to the conclusion that no one could stand before him. Therefore, the second question was pressing. The disturbing fact is that it was the same as the question of the Philistines. They had asked, "What shall we do with the ark of the LORD?" (1 Samuel 6:2), meaning, "How do we get rid of the Lord's heavy hand on us?" The Israelites now asked in essence, "What shall we do with the Lord?" meaning, "Where will we send the ark?"

At the very end of chapter 6 we saw that the people of Beth-shemesh sent a request to the inhabitants of Kiriath-jearim to come and take the ark.

Why was Israel (like the Philistines) experiencing the heavy hand of God?[2] That is the question that the events of the last three chapters have powerfully raised.

THE SITUATION NOW (vv. 1, 2)

First Samuel 7 begins by reporting the response of the people of Kiriath-jearim to the request from Beth-shemesh:[3]

> And the men of Kiriath-jearim came and took up the ark of the LORD and brought it to the house of Abinadab on the hill. And they consecrated his son Eleazar to have charge of the ark of the LORD. (v. 1)

Abinadab is a name that we will hear again in the story of 1 Samuel. One of David's older brothers bore it (1 Samuel 16:8; 17:13; also 1 Chronicles

2:13), as did one of Saul's sons (1 Samuel 31:2; also 1 Chronicles 8:33; 9:39; 10:2). This Abinadab, however, is only known to us in connection with the ark and its care at Kiriath-jearim (see also 2 Samuel 6:3; 1 Chronicles 13:7). No reason is given for the choice of the house of Abinadab as the place to which the ark was brought. Some have argued that Abinadab must have been a well-known priest.[4] Others have argued that, since he is not identified as such, he was not.[5] Since the proper handling of the ark by Levites was mentioned earlier (1 Samuel 6:15), and care was taken to "consecrate" Eleazar for the task of keeping the ark, there is an implication that Abinadab and consequently his son Eleazar were proper persons for this task — that is, Levites (Numbers 3:31; Deuteronomy 10:8; 31:9, 25; Joshua 3:3; 8:33).

At the same time Kiriath-jearim had no particular prominence in Israel's past history and did not now become important because of the ark's presence there. In other words, it seems that Kiriath-jearim did not become the new Shiloh. It was not the site of the tabernacle (as far as we know), and no known assembly or other significant event took place there.[6] A little later in the story there will be a passing reference to the ark, indicating that it accompanied Saul and his army on at least one occasion (1 Samuel 14:18).[7] Otherwise the ark seems to have been left in Abinadab's house until David decided to bring it up to Jerusalem in 2 Samuel 6 (see 2 Samuel 6:3; also 1 Chronicles 13:5, 6; 2 Chronicles 1:4).

This situation continued for a long time: "From the day that the ark was lodged at Kiriath-jearim, a long time passed, some twenty years . . ." (v. 2a).

This is one of those points in the Biblical narrative where the passage of a considerable period of time is noted but passed over.[8] There is a difficulty, however. Some have suggested that the twenty years during which the ark lodged at Kiriath-jearim refers to the time until David sent for it in 2 Samuel 6.[9] This would mean that the events from 1 Samuel 7:1 to 2 Samuel 6 took place over twenty years. While this is possible, it is a less natural reading of the present context and also creates certain other problems.[10] The twenty years is best understood as the long period of time before the next reported event, which is presented as (in some sense) a consequence of the long time in which Israel had little or nothing to do with the ark.[11] The next significant event, from the narrator's point of view, was this: ". . . and all the house of Israel lamented after the LORD" (v. 2b).

It is not that Israel lamented after the Lord *for* twenty years, but that *after* twenty years they did so.

What happened during those twenty years? No doubt we are expected to be wondering just that. The implication, to be confirmed shortly when we hear from Samuel, is that during these twenty years the Israelites had little or nothing to do with the Lord. The ark "lodged" at Kiriath-jearim, and the people lived without regard for it or what it stood for — namely, the covenant between Israel and the Lord.

We are not told yet whether those days were peaceful and prosperous for Israel or otherwise. Perhaps there was a time when things went reasonably well. But it will soon become apparent that at least toward the end of the period the Philistine threat was very real again.

In other words, this period of twenty years was very much like the periods of apostasy that had recurred during the era of the book of Judges. As on those previous occasions "they abandoned the LORD, the God of their fathers, who had brought them out of the land of Egypt," and the Lord responded by giving them over to their enemies, in this case to the Philistines (cf. Judges 2:12-14).

What did Israel do at the end of those twenty years? On the previous occasions Israel had typically "cried out to the LORD" (see Judges 3:9, 15; 4:3; 6:6, 7; 10:10; cf. 1 Samuel 12:10). The wording this time is different, but the sense is similar.[12] After twenty years, Israel experienced yet another change of heart and turned yet again to the Lord, with (it seems) tears.

The record is remarkably brief, but after twenty years there was the sound of wailing in Israel. The words of Jeremiah from many years later could have applied here: "A voice is heard in Ramah, lamentation and bitter weeping" (Jeremiah 31:15a).

THE GOSPEL ACCORDING TO SAMUEL (vv. 3, 4)

Suddenly, without warning, in verse 3 Samuel appears again in the narrative.

More than twenty years previously Samuel had last appeared when "The word of Samuel came to all Israel" (1 Samuel 4:1). The events that were the fulfillment of Samuel's word had then taken place, leading to these twenty years. Although the details are not given, it is as though Samuel had been waiting twenty years for this moment. Israel's tears were the sign that the time had come for them to hear the word of Samuel again. What they heard was the gospel according to Samuel.

Return (v. 3a)

> And Samuel said to all the house of Israel, "If you are returning to the LORD with all your heart . . ." (v. 3a)

Here is Samuel's confirmation of what the last twenty years had involved. Samuel did not assume that the weeping and wailing amounted to a true returning to the Lord. His words did, however, assume that they had been away from the Lord in their hearts. Through these twenty years Israel had not recovered from the Eli era. They had attempted to put the ark out of sight, and so out of mind. The same applied to the Lord himself. Unable to bear his hard hand against them, they had sought to be rid of him (see 1 Samuel 6:20). After twenty years, however, it was just possible that there had been a change of heart.

In another context the Bible would call the possible change in the Israelites repentance. Repentance, however, is not just weeping. It is "returning to the LORD with all your heart." This is the first point in Samuel's gospel.

Put Away (v. 3b)

Samuel spelled out the necessary consequence of genuine repentance: ". . . then put away the foreign gods and the Ashtaroth from among you . . ." (v. 3b).

"Ashtaroth" is the plural form of Ashtoreth, the Canaanite goddess also called Astarte, who was (in Canaanite religion) the wife of Baal, the storm and fertility god. The plural probably indicates many images of Astarte.[13] It is probable that the worship of these deities involved various practices.

The implication of Samuel's call to "put away" these pagan gods is clear. Over the past twenty years the Israelites had taken on the Canaanite lifestyle. They had learned Canaanite ways. If those ways were as perverse as we might suppose, perhaps the narrator had good reason to pass over those two decades in a single verse!

When did this apostate behavior begin?[14] It is difficult to avoid the impression that it all goes back to the perversions of the Eli era. Eli's sons themselves engaged in immoral sexual practices at the tabernacle; they treated the Lord's ways with contempt; indeed they did not know the Lord (1 Samuel 2:22, 17, 12). If the people under such a priesthood abandoned faithfulness to the Lord, much of the story that has been perplexing now makes sense. Corrupt priests led the people into apostasy, so that God's judgment fell not only on Eli and his sons, but on Israel as a whole (chapter 4). That is why the return of the ark was not the joyous occasion some thought it might have been (chapter 6). As so often before, the people of Israel had provoked the Lord to anger by abandoning him and going after other gods (see Judges 2:12, 14, 20; 3:8; 10:7).

The second point in Samuel's gospel is that you must put away the pagan gods. The pagan ways must be repudiated.

Heart (v. 3c)

The third point is this: " . . . and direct your heart to the LORD and serve him only. . . ." (v. 3c).

This speaks of exclusive, single-minded, wholehearted commitment. The Lord, and the Lord alone, must hold their hearts.

Promise (v. 3d)

The final point of Samuel's gospel on this occasion supports the three preceding imperatives. It is the promise, " . . . and he will deliver you out of the hand of the Philistines" (v. 3d).

Now we learn something else about the twenty-year period, or at least the most recent part of it. The Philistine threat had not been suppressed. The Philistines continued to menace Israel. If the previous history of this people is taken seriously, we may suppose that their sufferings at the hands of the Philistines had a great deal to do with the fact that now, at last, they were "lamenting after the LORD" (v. 2).[15]

That previous history is the key to understanding what was going on. The Lord gave Israel over to their enemies as judgment for their apostasy (see Judges 2:11-15). The Philistines, therefore, had been the instrument of God's judgment on Israel.

The gospel Samuel proclaimed that day was a simple but wonderful promise: return to the Lord with your whole heart (which will mean putting away your pagan gods and setting your heart on the Lord alone), and he will save you from your enemies and from judgment.

Israel's Response (v. 4)

According to verse 4 Israel obeyed Samuel's gospel: "So the people of Israel put away the Baals and the Ashtaroth, and they served the LORD only" (v. 4).

This was a remarkably important moment for the people of Israel. We will miss the importance if we overlook the more than twenty years of apostasy that preceded it. At last that era was brought to an end.

I have been calling Samuel's message "Samuel's gospel" because the response of Israel that day will have its echo in the experience of Christian people. Paul later described that experience in terms that correspond strikingly to Israel's experience: "you turned to God from idols to serve the living and true God, and to wait for his Son from heaven, whom he raised from the dead, Jesus who delivers us from the wrath to come" (1 Thessalonians 1:9, 10).

ISRAEL: GOD'S PEOPLE AGAIN (vv. 5-12)

This moment in Israel's history was so important that the summary description in verses 3, 4 is now elaborated in the details of verses 5-12.[16]

Israel at Mizpah (vv. 5, 6)

Samuel summoned a great assembly of all Israel at Mizpah. Mizpah was a city in the territory of the tribe of Benjamin (Joshua 18:11, 26).[17] It will not be long before this narrative takes a particular interest in the tribe, land, and one particular family of Benjamin (see 1 Samuel 9:1, 4, 16, 21; 10:2, 20, 21; 13:2, 15, 16; 14:16; 22:7).[18] However, at this point Mizpah was already a place where Israel had gathered on a significant and solemn occasion. In the last three chapters of the book of Judges there is the dreadful account of the crime of Gibeah and the war that broke out between Benjamin and the rest of the Israelite tribes. Mizpah was the place where all the tribes (except Benjamin) assembled "to the LORD" to determine what to do (Judges 20:1, 3).[19]

THE INTERCESSOR (v. 5)

Samuel called this assembly in circumstances as dire as those of the earlier assembly. Israel's future as God's people was at stake. "Then Samuel said, 'Gather all Israel at Mizpah, and I will pray to the LORD for you'" (v. 5).

Israel needed an intercessor. The relationship with the Lord had been broken because they had departed from him and gone after other gods. They had provoked him to anger and had come to understand that they could not stand before him. After twenty years of this situation, God provided, in the person of Samuel, an intercessor for his people.

The difference it made for Israel to have an intercessor able to do what they plainly could not do — namely, effectively pray for themselves — cannot be overstated. In verse 8 the people will beg Samuel to keep praying for them. A little later Samuel would underline his responsibility to pray for the people of Israel with the words, "far be it from me that I should sin against the LORD by ceasing to pray for you" (1 Samuel 12:23).[20]

THE REPENTANT SINNERS (v. 6a)

> *So they gathered at Mizpah and drew water and poured it out before the LORD and fasted on that day and said there, "We have sinned against the LORD." (v. 6a)*

The pouring of water and the fasting were both expressions of the people's repentance, which was also expressed there in words.[21] The actions may be best seen not so much as symbolic rituals, but as real acts of self-denial as the people turned from their self-centered ways back to the Lord.[22]

The words are clear. The cause of Israel's troubles over these past twenty years and more was at last recognized and acknowledged: "We have sinned against the LORD."

THE JUDGE (v. 6b)

Samuel's role in all this is summed up in these interesting terms: "And Samuel judged the people of Israel at Mizpah" (v. 6b).

While Samuel's "judging" the people may well include what follows, it is right to see this sentence as a summary of what he had done up to this point. He had called Israel back to the Lord and prayed for them. This is not what the word "judged" usually means in English, but the Hebrew word is used in the Old Testament for precisely this. Samuel set things right in Israel by his words to the people from God and by his words to God for the people.[23]

This statement draws our attention to the contrast between Eli's failed leadership and, at this point, Samuel's effective leadership. Eli "judged" Israel for forty years, and at the end of it, all the glory had departed from Israel (1 Samuel 4:18, 22). At Mizpah Samuel had "judged" Israel, and the glory had returned. They were God's people again.[24]

Israel and the Philistines (vv. 7-9)

It took no time at all for this new situation to be put to the test. Very quickly the people of Israel found themselves in precisely the position they had been in some twenty years earlier at Ebenezer. They faced the hostility of their old enemy again. The outcome this time, however, would be very different.

PHILISTINE THREAT (v. 7a)

Now when the Philistines heard that the people of Israel had gathered at Mizpah, the lords of the Philistines went up against Israel. (v. 7a)

Our last glimpse of the five lords of the Philistines in the narrative was as they made their way back to Ekron after witnessing the return of the ark (1 Samuel 6:16). But that was twenty years ago! We have already heard indications that in those twenty years, or at least in recent times, the Philistines had again been menacing Israel.[25] Now, however, with "all Israel" gathered at Mizpah (v. 5), the Philistines had the opportunity for a decisive strike. The situation was very like that twenty years earlier when "the Philistines drew up in line against Israel" (1 Samuel 4:2).

ISRAELITE FEAR (v. 7b)

No doubt the people of Israel remembered all too well that earlier occasion: "And when the people of Israel heard of it, they were afraid of the Philistines" (v. 7b).

Paradoxically, on the earlier occasion it had been the Philistines who were afraid (1 Samuel 4:7). In the accounts of both of the battles at Aphek/Ebenezer there is no indication that the Israelites were afraid of their adversary, although events proved that they had every reason to be. On this occasion we notice at least this difference in the people of Israel. They were afraid.

I do not think that it is reading too much into the account to suggest that there was a new humility in Israel now. The earlier confidence can now be seen to have been presumption. They now knew better — and they were afraid.

SAMUEL'S PRAYER (vv. 8, 9b)

Notice now the response of the people to their fear: "And the people of Israel said to Samuel, 'Do not cease to cry out to the LORD our God for us, that he may save us from the hand of the Philistines'" (v. 8).

The similarity to and difference from the earlier response to the Philistine threat is striking. Twenty years earlier they had said, "Let us bring the ark of the covenant of the LORD here from Shiloh, that he may come among us and save us from the hand of our enemies" (1 Samuel 4:3).[26] The hoped-for outcome was the same — that God would save them from the Philistines. The obvious difference between the two occasions lay in the means by which the people hoped this result would be brought about. Twenty years earlier they proposed bringing the ark from Shiloh. The outcome was the opposite of what was hoped for. Now they begged Samuel to cry out to the Lord "our God" for them.

We now understand that in chapter 4 the people, under the influence of their apostate priesthood, had departed from following the Lord and had pursued other gods. In chapter 4 the Israelites did not call the Lord "our God"! Calling for the ark in that situation was a preposterous arrogance. They were expecting the Lord to honor his covenant with them, even though they had broken it. No wonder the whole thing led to disaster.

Now, however, at Mizpah the people have returned to the Lord. They have obeyed Samuel's gospel and now asked him to cry out to the Lord "our God" for them. God's people — when they are God's people — can expect him to hear their cries. "So Samuel took a nursing lamb and offered it as a whole burnt offering to the LORD" (v. 9a).

Once again the contrast to the situation in chapter 4 is stark. It was the contempt shown by Hophni and Phinehas toward the Lord's offering (1 Samuel 2:17) that began the sequence of events that led to the disaster of chapters 4–6.[27] Samuel's intercession for the people began with the sacrifice that acknowledged and provided cleansing for the people's sins.[28] "And Samuel cried out to the LORD for Israel . . ." (v. 9b).

The intercessor interceded.

THE LORD'S ANSWER (v. 9c)

The difference from the earlier occasion, twenty years previously, is expressed in two words in Hebrew (though it takes five in English): ". . . and the LORD answered him" (v. 9c).

This is an extraordinary moment. In the story that 1 Samuel tells, this is the first time that the Lord has acted positively toward Israel or an Israelite since chapter 1, verse 19 when he heard and answered Hannah's prayer and Samuel was born![29] Now, after all these years, he heard and answered Samuel's prayer, and Israel was delivered.

The Philistines, Israel, and the Lord (vv. 10, 11)

The details of that deliverance (that is, the Lord's answer to Samuel's cry) are now elaborated, and we see the relationship between the Lord and his people restored to its proper state.

THE THREAT (v. 10a)

The threat took shape at the very time of the burnt offering: "As Samuel was offering up the burnt offering, the Philistines drew near to attack Israel" (v. 10a).

The contrast to the earlier occasion continues to be drawn. Samuel's proper offering of the burnt offering is utterly different from the corrupt sacrificial practices of the earlier time.[30] The Philistines drawing near to attack Israel in these circumstances is therefore very different from their earlier assaults.

BUT THE LORD . . . (v. 10b)

The Lord's answer came unmistakably:

> But the LORD thundered with a mighty sound that day against the
> Philistines and threw them into confusion, and they were routed before
> Israel. (v. 10b)

It was just as Hannah had said: "The adversaries of the LORD shall be broken in pieces; against them he will thunder in heaven" (1 Samuel 2:10).[31]

The situation that had prevailed in chapter 4 was exactly reversed. Then Israel had been "defeated before the Philistines." Now the Philistines were "defeated before Israel."[32] In both cases the expression used ("defeated before") alludes to the fact that the defeat was God's doing. In chapter 4 God was acting in judgment against his apostate people. In chapter 7 he was acting in deliverance of his repentant people.

VICTORY (v. 11)

The contrasting outcome is filled out with a description of the Israelite victory: "And the men of Israel went out from Mizpah and pursued the Philistines and struck them, as far as below Beth-car" (v. 11).

How very different from the time when every man of Israel had fled, and "there was a very great slaughter" among them (1 Samuel 4:10)![33]

The Gospel Rock (v. 12)

In case anyone has missed the connections and contrasts we have been observing between these events and the horrors of twenty years previously, Samuel made the link clear and permanent.

> *Then Samuel took a stone and set it up between Mizpah and Shen and called its name Ebenezer; for he said, "Till now the LORD has helped us."* (v. 12)

While it is possible, it seems unlikely that this Ebenezer is the same as the Ebenezer of 1 Samuel 4:1. That location seems too far north.[34] Giving this memorial stone the name of the earlier locality, however, and drawing attention to the meaning of the name underlines the reversal that had taken place. The earlier Ebenezer had a terribly ironic name. At "stone of help" Israel had *not* been helped! Now, however, the new Ebenezer stood as a testimony to the Lord's help, which was once again enjoyed by Israel.

Samuel's words of explanation have a curious ambiguity, as though he had said, "*So far* the Lord has helped us." This may be understood spatially ("*As far as this place* the Lord has helped us") or temporally ("*Until now* the Lord has helped us"). The former sense is straightforward: the Lord had helped Israel all the way from Mizpah to this stone. The second sense is suggestive. The Lord had helped Israel so far — but what of the future? Will Israel and the Lord continue into the future as we have seen them in chapter 7, or will the situation of chapter 4 somehow return?

VICTORY AND PEACE (vv. 13-17)

These questions will have to wait for the following chapters. At this point our writer provides us with an extravagant description of the outcome of these dramatic events, which (for reasons I will explain) I will call Israel's justification and Israel's sanctification.[35]

Israel's Justification (vv. 13, 14)

> So the Philistines were subdued and did not again enter the territory of Israel. And the hand of the LORD was against the Philistines all the days of Samuel. The cities that the Philistines had taken from Israel were restored to Israel, from Ekron to Gath, and Israel delivered their territory from the hand of the Philistines. There was peace also between Israel and the Amorites. (vv. 13, 14)

The great enemy of Israel was subdued and kept from Israelite territory "all the days of Samuel." In the light of ensuing events this seems to refer only to the days of Samuel's exclusive leadership of the nation. Even then it might be seen as a simplification of the situation.[36] The point being made is clear, however. After Mizpah the enemy was defeated. What the Philistines had taken from Israel was recovered.[37] The Philistines were no longer a cause of fear in Israel. The indigenous Canaanite peoples ("the Amorites") also ceased to be a threat, perhaps because of Israel's supremacy over their common enemy. Israel enjoyed, in other words, a period of peace, the likes of which had not been known for a very long time.

This is what God did for Israel. They could hold their heads high again — not because of their virtue or strength (don't forget the last twenty years) — but because of what the Lord their God had done *for* them.

That is why I have called this Israel's *justification*. I do not want the term to be pressed too far, but there is a similarity here to our justification in Jesus Christ. Our enemy has been defeated. This is what God has done *for* us. We can hold our heads high — not because of our own virtue or strength (you don't need twenty years of life to learn that) — but because of what the Lord our God has done for us in the victory of Jesus on the cross.

Israel's Sanctification (vv. 15-17)

> Samuel judged Israel all the days of his life. And he went on a circuit year by year to Bethel, Gilgal, and Mizpah. And he judged Israel in all these places. Then he would return to Ramah, for his home was there, and there also he judged Israel. And he built there an altar to the LORD. (vv. 15-17)

Samuel's "judging" was presumably like the judging we have seen in this chapter: calling Israel to wholehearted devotion to the Lord alone and to put away pagan ways, interceding for them, offering sacrifices for their sins, as well as a more general administration of justice.[38]

In other words, with the enemy defeated, Samuel's job was to lead Israel in righteousness. That is why I have called this Israel's *sanctification*, because again Israel's experience is a shadow of our own. With our enemy defeated, it is time for righteousness of life.

First Samuel 7 has brought us to a climactic moment in the story that this book has to tell. It is a high point in the history of Israel, when Israel became again what Israel was meant to be.

The chapter has displayed the kind of leader that Israel actually needed. Their need was not for a great military hero or genius. God had demonstrated unambiguously that he could deal with their enemies without such a champion. Their need was not for a brilliant political giant who could organize the nation efficiently. Israel's need could not be met by management abilities. Israel's great need was a leader who would bring them back to God. They needed a leader who would lead them in righteousness. They needed a Samuel. And God gave them Samuel!

As we read on into chapter 8 we will see that the lessons of this moment were not remembered well in Israel. But we should pause and see that we learn them. If we have learned well from Israel's experience, I hope that we can see how these chapters point us clearly to the leader we need. He is the one sent by God to bring us back to God, to intercede for us, to lead us in righteousness. The Lord Jesus Christ is the leader of whom Samuel was a faint shadow.

What a great day it was for Israel when God gave them Samuel!

What a brilliant day it is for those of us who have Jesus as our Lord!

PART TWO

Saul:
The Leader the People
Asked for

1 SAMUEL 8–15

12

The Leader Israel Wanted

1 SAMUEL 8

Most human beings spend a great deal of their lives trying to find or win or buy or build *security* for themselves and for those they love. Have you found it yet? Are there enough locks and alarms on your home? Do you hold adequate insurance for property and person? Have you accumulated sufficient savings? Are you in possession of satisfactory health and strength? Have you made enough contacts, acquired enough power, generated enough influence, exerted enough control, earned enough affection? It is an insecure world, and life itself is insecure. How far are you from finding adequate security?

Such thoughts raise the question of whom you believe. What are the dangers we should be worried about? What actions on our part will provide security? Don't smoke if you want to avoid lung cancer. Recycle if you want to avoid ecological disaster. Many of us can remember a time when some people were spending tens or even hundreds of thousands of dollars building their own personal nuclear fallout shelters — and going to great lengths to keep it secret, because, of course, if the whole neighborhood tried to force themselves into your shelter when the time came, all your efforts would have been wasted! Were the rest of us who built no shelters smart or just lucky?

Some exploit our sense of insecurity in various ways. Whom do you believe? Do you believe the home security salesman who says you must have a particular sophisticated burglar alarm system? Do you believe the insurance company that tells you how important it is to have coverage for accidental loss of life or limb? Do you believe the health food people? Do you believe those who say you must get a good education or you must find a well-paying job?

Not only do we find it hard to know if we have adequate security — we are not even sure what security is!

And yet, one thing we expect from leaders is that they will provide us with security. We recognize that a fundamental responsibility of governments is the security of the nations they lead. At the top of the agenda for leaders at any level is the safety of those they lead. Leadership that does not provide security risks the loss of any other good that may have been achieved.

In 1 Samuel 7 we saw that Samuel was the kind of leader Israel needed to provide them with security. That was because, on the one hand, the one who could certainly deliver them from any threat was God, and on the other hand, their greatest danger was the anger to which they had provoked the Lord by their apostasy. The heart of Samuel's leadership was calling the people back to the Lord (v. 3) and praying to the Lord for the people (v. 9b). That was the kind of leader Israel needed, and Samuel was the leader God provided. The chapter closed with a summary description of the rest of Samuel's life and the leadership he provided Israel (vv. 15-17). He "judged" Israel in the sense that he led them in justice and righteousness.

SECURITY THREATENED (vv. 1-3)

Chapter 8 takes us forward, apparently many years, to the time "when Samuel became old." We are to understand that the peaceful situation described at the end of chapter 7 continued through these many years. They stand, therefore, in sharp contrast to the earlier two decades, when Israel had lived away from the Lord (see 1 Samuel 7:2, 3).

As Samuel reached old age, however, the security Israel had enjoyed came under serious threat. Three factors contributed to the crisis.

Samuel's Age (v. 1a)

The first of these is indicated by the opening words of the chapter: "When Samuel became old . . ." (v. 1a).

The story of 1 Samuel began with another old man leading Israel. We learned as early as 1 Samuel 2:22 that "Eli was very old." References and allusions to Eli's great age were repeated through the ensuing narrative until his death, where we were finally reminded that "the man was old and heavy"(1 Samuel 4:18; cf. 2:32; 3:2; 4:15).

Growing old has advantages and disadvantages. On the negative side are decreasing energy, aches and pains, and the growing certainty that death is close. Israel's years of security and peace under Samuel were no doubt something to be thankful for, but the man was now old. Insofar as this stability depended on him, it was all put in jeopardy by this simple predictable fact: Samuel grew old — as Eli had, and as all leaders must.

Samuel's Experiment (vv. 1b, 2)

Samuel attempted a possible solution to the difficulties of his old age and the approaching crisis of his own demise. It was a bold experiment: ". . . he made his sons judges over Israel. The name of his firstborn son was Joel, and the name of his second, Abijah; they were judges in Beersheba" (vv. 1b, 2).

The old leader sharing his responsibilities with his two sons adds to the impression that this is a situation we have seen before. Old Eli's two sons shared the responsibilities of the priesthood with their father at Shiloh, as we learned in the third verse of this book.

However, there was a difference. The priestly office in Israel had always been hereditary in some sense. There is no surprise in Eli's sons functioning as priests. The priesthood was passed on through the descendants of Aaron (see 1 Samuel 2:30). However, the role of judge in Israel was not hereditary. Indeed on one famous occasion the judge Gideon had been asked by the people of Israel to establish a dynasty. "Rule over us," they had said, "you and your son and your grandson also." Gideon had emphatically refused, on powerful theological grounds. "I will not rule over you," he said, "and my son will not rule over you; the LORD will rule over you"(Judges 8:22, 23).[1]

Why, then, did Samuel make his sons judges? It is difficult to know, although it seems that it was less a dynastic arrangement that he had specifically in mind than a practical sharing of the burdens of the work in the present.[2] It is worth noting that Joel and Abijah were judges in the far south, in Beersheba, some fifty miles from Samuel's home in Ramah. It is reasonable to see in Samuel's appointment of them an attempt to see the justice of the judge extended throughout the land.[3]

This introduces a further difference between Samuel and his two sons and the earlier situation with Eli and his boys. Hophni and Phinehas were working in Shiloh under the direct supervision of Eli. Eli could not escape some considerable measure of responsibility for the conduct of his sons (see 1 Samuel 2:29). However, Joel and Abijah were a long way from Samuel's direct observation and influence.[4]

The Failure (v. 3)

Unfortunately, for all concerned there was a further shocking similarity between the situation of Samuel and sons and that of Eli and sons: "Yet his sons did not walk in his ways but turned aside after gain. They took bribes and perverted justice" (v. 3).

Samuel's sons were no better than Eli's sons! Indeed their perverting of "justice" reminds us of those priests whose "custom" (same Hebrew word!) was described in 1 Samuel 2:13. Although the conduct of the young judges took different specific forms than the behavior of the young priests, each selfishly exploited his position of responsibility. Entrusted with the service of the people, both the sons of Eli and now the sons of Samuel abused their trust by putting themselves before those they were supposed to serve. They were users, not servers; they were takers, not givers.

The distance between Samuel and his sons was not only in terms of miles. Unlike Eli, Samuel was so far from being implicated in the guilt of his sons that he remained the standard of conduct against which they were measured.[5] They "did not walk in *his ways.*"

The specifics of the young judges' misconduct are briefly but starkly described. They "turned aside"; that is, they deviated from the straight and narrow. Instead of pursuing "justice," which is the task of a "judge," they went after "gain." This word seems to have a violent connotation.[6] The sense is "a piece that is cut off, (illegal) profit or gain."[7] A basic requirement of a judge in the days of Moses was to hate "dishonest gain" (Exodus 18:21, same Hebrew word [ESV has "a bribe"]; cf. Proverbs 28:16 [ESV, "unjust gain"]).

These words could just as well describe the conduct of Hophni and Phinehas, who *turned aside* from the proper offering of sacrifices (which was their task) to pursue personal *gain.* The way in which Joel and Abijah did this included the "taking" of "bribes." This verb is used four times in the description of the conduct of Eli's sons in 1 Samuel 2:14-16. It will be important again a little later in this chapter. In summary, Samuel's sons did not administer "justice," as Samuel was doing (1 Samuel 7:15-17); they "perverted" justice.[8]

The clear parallel that the narrator has presented between the situation toward the end of Eli's life and the situation now in Samuel's old age makes one thing clear. Israel's well-being cannot be guaranteed by the *sons* of their leaders. The best of leaders can have the worst of sons. The old age of a great leader like Samuel was, therefore, a serious crisis. The peace, security, and prosperity of the years under Samuel were in jeopardy if his sons were to play any role in Israel's future.

A PROPOSAL FOR SECURITY (vv. 4-18)

In these circumstances a proposal emerged for establishing the security of the nation that was to change Israel forever. The proposal came from the people, via their elders. The rest of the chapter in effect reports the conversation between the people and God about this proposal, with Samuel as the mediator who spoke to God for the people and to the people from God.

The dynamics of the conversation are therefore essentially simple. Each exchange involved: People → Samuel → God → Samuel → People. The conversation involved two such exchanges:[9]

(a)	The people	to	Samuel	(vv. 4, 5	&	19, 20)
(b)	Samuel	to	the Lord	(vv. 6	&	21)
(c)	The Lord	to	Samuel	(vv. 7-9	&	22a)
(d)	Samuel	to	the people	(vv. 10-18	&	22b)

The complicating factor is that Samuel does more than simply report the words of the people and the Lord respectively. He has his own contribution to the conversation. We will listen to each stage of this conversation in turn.

The People to Samuel: A King to Judge Us (vv. 4, 5)

It all begins with the proposal that came from the elders of Israel:

> Then all the elders of Israel gathered together and came to Samuel at Ramah and said to him, "Behold, you are old and your sons do not walk in your ways. Now appoint for us a king to judge us like all the nations." (vv. 4, 5)

It was the elders of Israel who, on a much earlier occasion, had come up with a proposal to solve a national security crisis — a military defeat by the Philistines. That proposal was to bring down the ark of the covenant of the Lord from Shiloh (1 Samuel 4:3). The idea was a historic failure. Now, faced with another crisis, which (as we will see a little later, v. 20 and 12:12) also involved a military threat, they met together, apparently agreed on their proposal, and brought it to Samuel at Ramah.

However, as stated, their proposal was astonishing and perplexing. What was the problem as they saw it? And how was their proposal meant to solve the problem?

The problem, as they described it, was Samuel's old age and his sons' misconduct. We are well aware, from the first three verses of the chapter, that these two observations were true. It is less clear (because it is unstated) what conclusions the elders drew from these observations. Did they see the analogy to the earlier situation under Eli and fear the consequences? Last time they had an old leader with corrupt sons, disaster came on them.[10] While I believe the narrator intends *his readers* to see this analogy, I see no evidence that *the elders* made the connection. They simply pointed to the deficiencies in the present leadership. The old man was no doubt unable to lead as effectively as he once did (at least in their view), and in any case it was clear to all that his life was nearing its end. At the same time, those to whom he had delegated some of the work were corrupt. The system was not delivering the leadership the nation needed.

However, the proposal advanced to deal with the problem is astonishing: "Now appoint for us a king to judge us like all the nations" (v. 5b).

The elders failed to see the point that is so obvious to us as we read this narrative. One lesson that the recent history of Israel should have taught unambiguously is that the best of leaders can have the worst of sons. The elders themselves have drawn this fact to our attention again by their opening words. And yet their proposal in the present circumstances was to institute a new form of leadership in Israel that was based on the hereditary principle of a father being succeeded by his son! This inner contradiction in the elders' proposal had obviously escaped their attention. Their failure to see that the proposal was undermined by their own analysis of the crisis it was meant to address is stunning in its stupidity!

The proposal is also astonishing in its unfaithfulness. We learned in chapter 7 that under the failed leadership of Eli and his sons, the people had abandoned the Lord and had gone after the Baals and the Ashtaroth — the gods of the nations around them (see 1 Samuel 7:3, 4). The proposal of the elders in chapter 8 reveals that the similarity between the situations under old Samuel and under old Eli had this additional element. Under Samuel, too, the people were prepared to abandon the Lord and adopt the ways of the pagan nations.

That their proposal amounted to an abandonment of the Lord is indicated by two things. First, they asked for "a king *to judge us*." Samuel had "judged" the people (1 Samuel 7:15-17), as had numerous judges before him. The proposal was that this arrangement (which was clearly the arrangement by which the Lord had "judged" Israel for many years) should be *replaced* by a "king."[11] Whatever else they had in mind when they spoke of a "king,"[12] it is clear that it was something different from Samuel and his predecessors.

The second indication is clearer still. In proposing that they should have a king to judge them, they were asking for an arrangement "like all the nations." This was a remarkable rejection of Israel's calling to be the Lord's "treasured possession among all peoples," "a kingdom of priests and a holy nation," "separated . . . from the peoples," a "great nation," "in praise and in fame and in honor high above all nations," "a people for himself" (Exodus 19:5, 6; Leviticus 20:26; Deuteronomy 4:6; 26:19; 1 Samuel 12:22). It was, in other words, the political equivalent to pursuing foreign gods and Ashtaroth (1 Samuel 7:3)!

It is important to understand that the problem with the elders' proposition was not kingship *as such*. True, the hereditary principle entailed in kingship made it a very strange thing to propose in the circumstances. However, as we will see, the great weight of the criticism of the elders' request arose from the last phrase, "like all the nations."

The proposal was anticipated centuries earlier in the laws given by Moses in Deuteronomy 17. There Moses spoke of the day when Israel would say, "I will set a king over me, like all the nations that are around me" (v. 14). Moses, perhaps surprisingly, said that Israel may indeed have a king, but on certain very specific conditions, which amounted to the fact that the arrangement would *not* be "like all the nations."[13] The elders' request, therefore, while specifically anticipated in the Law, was a direct challenge to the Law.

The elders were asking, in effect, to opt out of the covenant with the Lord and to adopt a pagan model of being a nation.[14]

What motivated the elders' appeal? What was it about kingship, in particular kingship "like all the nations," that was so appealing?

Kingship is not an easy concept to define. It can take many different forms. The common features of these seem to be: (a) the rule of one man over a larger group where his authority derives simply from his being the king rather than from some other source (such as position in family, some other form of seniority, or appointment)[15] and (b) the hereditary principle that the kingship is passed down from father to son.[16]

A king therefore offered a strong, stable, and predictable center of political authority for a nation that otherwise had to depend on an unseen God to unite them. Furthermore, kingship held out the promise of efficient central organization to a nation that, lacking such structures, tended to lurch from one crisis to the next. After many years of such instability, it is not difficult to see how reasonable the proposal must have seemed to the elders.

I cannot help thinking of some proposals that come forward today to make the church more efficient, strong, and effective. The proven experience of the world of business management offers methods that have made other organizations strong and growing. If only the churches would implement some of the strategies of the business schools or recruit leaders like some of the successful companies, the churches could make an impact! They could expand their market share! I wonder whether you can hear a faint echo of the elders of Israel: "Give us a king . . . like all the nations."

We have spent a lot of time considering the proposal that came from the elders of Israel that day because it was so important. This request would change the history of Israel and, in a sense, the history of the world. We must now follow the way in which God responded to this request through Samuel, the mediator.

Samuel to the Lord: Evil in Samuel's Eyes (v. 6)

Samuel did not simply report the request to the Lord and wait for an answer. He did not like the proposal, and for this reason he "prayed to the LORD":

"But the thing displeased Samuel when they said, 'Give us a king to judge us.' And Samuel prayed to the LORD" (v. 6).

The Hebrew is stronger: "the thing was evil in the eyes of Samuel." Curiously, when the narrator indicates "the thing" that Samuel saw as evil, he cites only part of the elders' speech: "Give us a king to judge us." This, it would seem, is what Samuel saw as "evil."[17] Samuel deeply disapproved of the demand that the role of judging Israel should be transferred from himself to a king. It is unlikely that this was simply personal resentment. Samuel understood that he had been raised up by the Lord to judge Israel, as had so many before him (see Judges 2:16). The innovation proposed by the elders was a rejection of God's ways and an attempt to find security elsewhere. Therefore it was "evil in the eyes of Samuel."

For this reason Samuel "prayed to the LORD." We are not told what he prayed. However, the last time Samuel "prayed to the LORD" concerning the people of Israel it was an intercession for the people who had abandoned the Lord and had gone after other gods (1 Samuel 7:5). Some time after these events in chapter 8, when the people recognized that their request for a king had been "evil," they begged Samuel to "pray . . . to the LORD" for them (1 Samuel 12:19). It is reasonable to assume that as Samuel saw their request as "evil" in 1 Samuel 8:6, he prayed for the Lord's mercy toward them (cf. 1 Samuel 12:23).

The Lord to Samuel: Obey Their Voice (vv. 7-9)

The Lord's response to Samuel's prayer was full of surprises and a puzzle:

> And the LORD said to Samuel, "Obey the voice of the people in all that they say to you, for they have not rejected you, but they have rejected me from being king over them. According to all the deeds that they have done, from the day I brought them up out of Egypt even to this day, forsaking me and serving other gods, so they are also doing to you. Now then, obey their voice; only you shall solemnly warn them and show them the ways of the king who shall reign over them." (vv. 7-9)

The first surprise is the puzzle. Samuel was told by the Lord to "Obey [or listen to] the voice of the people."[18] This was hardly what Samuel expected. He considered the request to be "evil." We will see shortly that he was right. Why then did the Lord tell him to heed the voice of the people?

Perhaps there is a hint in the words, "in all that they say to you."[19] Samuel's response had been to the request for "a king to judge us" (vv. 5, 6). Had he overlooked the implications of the phrase "like all the nations"? "Listen to . . . all that they are saying to you, Samuel, and you will understand that this request is more serious than you have yet understood." Still we wonder, why did the Lord say that Samuel was to "obey" the people in this matter?

The second surprise is the radical interpretation that the Lord put on the proposed leadership change in Israel. It was not so much that the people had rejected Samuel (which they had, according to the end of verse 8),[20] but they had rejected God from being king over them. All acceptable forms of leadership in Israel had always acknowledged the absolute priority of the Lord's rule over his people (cf. Judges 8:23). It is interesting to note that prior to this point in the Biblical narrative God had only occasionally been called "king" (Exodus 15:18; Numbers 23:21; Deuteronomy 33:5).[21] This may have something to do with the negative connotations of the term that we are about to hear from Samuel (1 Samuel 8:11-17). The much more frequent use of the vocabulary of kingship applied to God after Israel had a king (more than twenty times in the Psalms alone!) may reflect the need then to emphasize the kingship of God over against human kingship. Be that as it may, the request here for a king "like all the nations" was a clear repudiation of their calling as the Lord's people. Tragically this was not a new thing in Israel. Since the days of Moses it had been a repeated pattern (see Exodus 32; Numbers 14; 25; Judges 2:11, 12). The people's rejection of Samuel, implicit in their request, was of a piece with these repeated acts of apostasy.

It is clear, therefore, that the thing was not only "evil in the eyes of Samuel"; it was evil in the eyes of the Lord![22] This makes the repetition of the opening instruction, "Obey [or listen to] their voice" (v. 9), all the more perplexing.

A third surprise (in which we begin to see the terrible solution to the puzzle) is the Lord's instruction to Samuel to "solemnly warn them." This strikes an ominous note. The people were about to be given the king they had asked for. Before that happened, Samuel was to warn them of the ways of this king. It is becoming clear that the Lord's willingness to grant the people their request was an act of judgment on their foolish and faithless request. In due course we will see that the judgment was accompanied by mercy. For now, however, we are beginning to see that should the people persist in their desire to be free from the Lord's rule and to have a king "like all the nations," their request would be granted, up to a point, and they would suffer the consequences of their rebellion. I say "up to a point" because in fact the Lord would not allow the people's rebellious request fully. In this very matter of requesting a king, the Lord refused to forsake his people, even though they were seeking to reject him (see 1 Samuel 12:22).

For now we should observe the profound link between human sin and its punishment. The desire to be free from God's good rule is punished by the experience of being given up to godless ways (cf. Romans 1:24, 26, 28). This principle was about to be worked out in Israel's experience.

There is a note of irony in verse 9. "The ways of the king" is, more literally, "the *justice* of the king."[23] They had asked for a king to "judge" them. Samuel was about to warn them of the kind of "justice" they could expect from this king. In the story of 1 Samuel we have seen the "justice" of the wicked sons of Eli (1 Samuel 2:13, where ESV has "custom"). Similarly the wicked sons of Samuel "perverted justice" (1 Samuel 8:3). As we will see, Samuel warned the people that they could expect from their king the very same kind of "justice" that Hophni, Phinehas, Joel, and Abijah had delivered.

Samuel to the People: The "Justice" of the King (vv. 10-18)

Samuel, the mediator who had spoken to the Lord concerning the people, now turned back to the people who had made the historic request. "So Samuel told all the words of the LORD to the people who were asking for a king from him" (v. 10).

Samuel, the faithful prophet, did what a prophet should do. He spoke the Lord's words, all of them, to the people.[24] In other words, the people were fully informed of what the Lord said in verses 7-9. The people who were asking for a king were left in no doubt about the Lord's view of this proposal.

Samuel then proceeded to "solemnly warn them and show them the ways of the king who shall reign over them" (v. 9):

> He said, "These will be the ways of the king who will reign over you: he will take your sons and appoint them to his chariots and to be his horsemen and to run before his chariots. And he will appoint for himself commanders of thousands and commanders of fifties, and some to plow his ground and to reap his harvest, and to make his implements of war and the equipment of his chariots. He will take your daughters to be perfumers and cooks and bakers. He will take the best of your fields and vineyards and olive orchards and give them to his servants. He will take the tenth of your grain and of your vineyards and give it to his officers and to his servants. He will take your male servants and female servants and the best of your young men and your donkeys, and put them to his work. He will take the tenth of your flocks, and you shall be his slaves. (vv. 11-17)

The "ways" (or the "justice") of the king who would reign over them are characterized by the repeated verb "take." He will "take" their sons (v. 11), their daughters (v. 13), the best of their fields, vineyards, and olive orchards (v. 14), a tenth of their produce (v. 15), their servants, young men, and donkeys (v. 16). The verb "take" also characterized the "ways" of Eli's sons (see 1 Samuel 2:14, 16), as well as those of Samuel's sons (8:3). The implication seems to be that with the king they had asked for, the problems of self-serving power that they had experienced at the hands of these young men would only be intensified.

How foolish they were to think that a king "like all the nations" could be good for them. Samuel's catalog of the "justice" they could expect from their king came to a dramatic climax with the words, "and you shall be his slaves" (v. 17)! If they insisted on rejecting the divine King who redeemed them from slavery in Egypt, they would find themselves in slavery again.

This time their cries would not be heard (contrast Exodus 2:23, 24): "And in that day you will cry out because of your king, whom you have chosen for yourselves, but the LORD will not answer you in that day" (v. 18).

Under Samuel, the Lord had answered their cry for help (1 Samuel 7:9b). Things would be different under the leadership change they had proposed. Note carefully the terms in which Samuel described the requested king: "*your* king, whom *you* have chosen for *yourselves*."

The warning could not have been more serious. This request, if granted, would lead to disaster for Israel.

THE PROPOSAL CONFIRMED (vv. 19-22)

The warning, however, fell on deaf ears. The second exchange between the people and the Lord, via Samuel the mediator, confirmed the people's intransigence as well as the Lord's intention to grant this terrible request.

The People to Samuel: A King to Judge Us (vv. 19, 20)

> But the people refused to obey the voice of Samuel. And they said, "No! But there shall be a king over us, that we also may be like all the nations, and that our king may judge us and go out before us and fight our battles." (vv. 19, 20)

Samuel was the last of the "judges" whom the Lord raised up to save Israel from their enemies (see Judges 2:16). The book of Judges records how the people typically "did not listen to their judges" (Judges 2:17). The era of the judges ended with the people's refusal to listen to (or obey) the voice of Samuel.

The refusal was expressed in words. The people's position had hardened. The request of verse 5 had become a demand: "There *shall be* a king over us." The proposal that they might have a *king* "like all the nations" had become a firm intention that *they themselves* would become "like all the nations." Their king would not only "judge" them, but specifically he would "go out before us and fight our battles." He would do, in other words, what the Lord had previously done for Israel (see Deuteronomy 20:4; Judges

4:14). In such an arrangement Israel's battles would no longer be the Lord's battles (see 1 Samuel 2:10; 17:47; 2 Chronicles 20:15; Psalm 24:8; Proverbs 21:31) but "*our* battles."

Samuel to the Lord (v. 21)

We may suppose that the thing was still "evil in the eyes of Samuel" (v. 6). This time, however, he simply performed his role as intermediary: "And when Samuel had heard all the words of the people, he repeated them in the ears of the LORD" (v. 21).

Samuel had now taken in the full and terrible importance of the people's demand ("all the words of the people") and was perhaps overwhelmed. This time he did not "pray," as in verse 6 but simply "repeated" (literally, "spoke") the people's words to the Lord.

The Lord to Samuel: Obey Their Voice (v. 22a)

Just as the people had not changed their demand, so the Lord had not changed his intention to grant this ominous petition:

> "And the LORD said to Samuel, 'Obey their voice and make them a king'"
> (v. 22a).

There is another touch of irony here. The consequence of the people's refusal to obey Samuel's voice is that Samuel will obey their voice. The people's refusal to hear the voice of the prophet meant that the voice of the people would prevail. What would that mean for this people who had been formed by the voice of God (see Deuteronomy 4:9-14)? What future could there be for this new institution of monarchy, given *because* the people refused to hear the voice of their prophet and judge?

Samuel to the People: Go Home (v. 22b)

Surprisingly the chapter closes, not with Samuel making a king as the Lord told him to do, but with his dismissal of the people: "Samuel then said to the men of Israel, 'Go every man to his city'" (v. 22b).

While it is too much to say that Samuel here disobeyed the Lord's command,[25] it is at least clear that he did not *immediately* carry out God's instruction. No reason is given, but the delay leaves big questions in the air. Who will the king be? How will he be chosen?[26] What will happen to the people of Israel[27] ruled in this radically new way?

For the moment we must leave these questions unanswered and allow the book of 1 Samuel to inform us in its own time and in its own way. Before

we proceed, however, we must ask what we are to learn from the extraordinary moment in the history of Israel that we have witnessed in 1 Samuel 8.

Its lesson for us comes into clear focus when we look at it from another
vantage point — from another day, many years later.

On the day I have in mind a man stood before the great pagan political power of *that* day — the Roman governor Pontius Pilate. Pilate put a
question to this man: "Are *you* the king of the Jews?" His reply was: "My
kingdom is *not* of this world. If my kingdom were *of this world*, my servants
would have been fighting, that I might not be delivered over to the Jews. But
my kingdom is not *from the world*" (John 18:36).

Do you see what he was saying? "I am *not* a king *like all the other
nations.*"

The gospel of the New Testament is that there *is* a king worth having, but he is a king whose kingship is altogether different from the king
demanded by the elders of Israel in 1 Samuel 8. His is not "of this world."
To want a leader like the leaders of this world is foolish and faithless. To
think that leaders like the leaders of this world can give us security, peace,
and justice is very foolish.

Indeed the message of the gospel is that there is a king whose justice is
altogether different from the "justice" Samuel warned the people they would
get from *their* king. For Jesus is a king who does not *take*, he *gives*.

> The justice of God has been manifested . . . the justice of God through the
> faithfulness of King Jesus to all who believe. For there is no distinction:
> for all have sinned and fall short of the glory of God, and are justified [this
> is God's justice!] by his grace as a gift, through the redemption that is in
> King Jesus. . . . This was to show God's justice. . . . It was to show his
> justice at the present time, so that he might be just and the justifier of the
> one who has faith in Jesus.[28]

Here is "a king to judge us," who brings a very different security, a very
different peace, a very different justice. How different he is from the king
demanded in 1 Samuel 8! How different from the leadership in which we
are all inclined to put our trust and hopes.

13

Lost Donkeys and the Word of God

1 SAMUEL 9

We have been seeing that the book of 1 Samuel deals with the complex and important subject of *leadership*. Of course, the theme is presented in a peculiar way. First Samuel recounts a turbulent period in the history of Israel, during which the leadership of that nation went through a radical change, from the occasional and unpredictable *judges* (of whom Samuel was the last, and arguably the greatest) to a *monarchy*, which will eventually be the rule of the great King David. However, the *issue* that was being worked out through these turbulent days in Israel, and the issue with which this account centrally deals, is *the leadership of God's people, Israel.*

As we have followed the account of these days — the plight of the people under the corrupt leadership of Eli and his sons (1 Samuel 2), the obvious need of an adequate leader in the face of a terrifying enemy (1 Samuel 4–6), and then the emerging leadership of the righteous, godly, and very powerful Samuel (1 Samuel 1, 3, 7) — we are forced to ask questions about leadership that may never have crossed our minds before. These questions go beyond leadership skills or techniques or styles. What kind of leader does *God* want *his* people to have? What should *God's* people look for from a leader?

In 1 Samuel 8 we saw the elders of the people, and then the people, demand that the old judge Samuel give them "a king . . . like all the nations" (1 Samuel 8:5, 19, 20). The demand was apparently motivated by Samuel's old age, the disastrous conduct of his sons, and the ongoing threat from their enemies (see 1 Samuel 8:5a, 20b). While we might feel some sympathy for the people's concerns, we saw that Samuel was not at all pleased with their proposal. It was "*evil* in the eyes of Samuel" (1 Samuel 8:6, literal translation). Samuel was right. The request for a king "*like all the nations*" was in fact a direct rejection of the Lord as their king (1 Samuel 8:7), who had called them to be *unlike* all the nations (Exodus 19:5, 6). Nonetheless, surprisingly, the Lord told Samuel to "make them a king" (1 Samuel 8:22a). Samuel responded by sending everyone home (1 Samuel 8:22b).

What do you think happened next? The people were rebelliously demanding a king like the other nations, God was apparently willing to give them their king, but Samuel had not yet acted on this matter.

This complicated situation was not resolved quickly. Furthermore, the process by which a king was eventually given to Israel is important to understand. It is an involved story, which will take from 1 Samuel 9:1 through 1 Samuel 12:25 to tell.[1]

MEET SAUL (vv. 1, 2)

Chapter 9 begins abruptly: "There was a man . . ." This gives the impression that a new story begins here. Just as the story of Samuel had begun with the words, "There was a certain man" (1 Samuel 1:1), so this fresh story line begins, "There was a man . . ."[2]

There is no indication (at this stage) of when the events about to be told occurred in relation to the momentous meeting between Samuel and the elders of Israel at Ramah recounted in chapter 8. Certainly we begin reading chapter 9 aware of the questions that were raised at Ramah: Will Israel be given a king? Who will it be? What will this mean for Israel?

However, we must be patient. The questions will only be answered through the complex story that begins, "There was a man . . ."

His Pedigree (v. 1)

> There was a man of Benjamin whose name was Kish, the son of Abiel, son of Zeror, son of Becorath, son of Aphiah, a Benjaminite, a man of wealth. (v. 1)

In terms of ancestry Kish was, like Elkanah in 1 Samuel 1:1, a nobody. Abiel, Zeror, Becorath, and Aphiah are hardly mentioned elsewhere in the Bible (see only 1 Samuel 14:51). Kish was apparently wealthy,[3] but he had no significant family background.[4]

Kish belonged to the tribe and the land of Benjamin.[5] This was no claim to fame. Benjamin was the smallest of Israel's tribes (see v. 21 of this chapter). We should remember that another man of Benjamin has already played a brief but important role in the story of 1 Samuel. "A man of Benjamin" brought the news of Israel's terrible defeat and the capture of the ark by the Philistines (1 Samuel 4:12).[6] The introduction of a new "man of Benjamin" reminds us of that earlier day. Soon we will see that the threat of the Philistines was still alive (1 Samuel 9:16). What will happen with this man of Benjamin?

His Person (v. 2)

The interest of the narrative is not really in Kish (any more than it was in Elkanah in 1 Samuel 1:1), but in his son:

> *And he had a son whose name was Saul, a handsome young man. There was not a man among the people of Israel more handsome than he. From his shoulders upward he was taller than any of the people. (v. 2)*

With these words we are introduced to the man whose story will occupy the many remaining pages of 1 Samuel. First impressions are not always reliable, but the narrator has taken some care in shaping our initial perception of this man.

First, his name is striking. The Hebrew word for "Saul" is a form of the verb "to ask." Saul's name was surprisingly anticipated in the account of the birth of Samuel ("I have *asked for* him from the LORD," said Hannah in 1 Samuel 1:20). We noticed that this verb was used repeatedly in 1 Samuel 1. Indeed the exact form of the verb that corresponds to the name "Saul" occurred at the end of that chapter (1 Samuel 1:28)![7] This seems to hint at a connection between Samuel and the son of Kish whom we now meet. But what will the nature of that connection be?

Furthermore, the name "Saul" (which we might translate "Asked For") subtly reminds us of the request of the people in the previous chapter "who were *asking for* a king" (1 Samuel 8:10). How strange that we should now be introduced to a man named "Asked For"!

Second, he was "a handsome young man." Again the Hebrew has some subtleties that are lost in translation. "Young man" translates a word that can also mean "chosen one."[8] We are reminded of Samuel's words in the previous chapter: "your king, whom you have *chosen* for yourselves" (1 Samuel 8:18). Is this the one they had "chosen"?

Furthermore, "handsome" interprets the Hebrew adjective "good." The same vocabulary was used by Samuel in his warning about the requested king: "He will take . . . the *best* of your *young men*" (1 Samuel 8:16). How strange that the sequel to chapter 8 introduces us to one of Israel's "best . . . young men"!

Third, he was not just *one* of Israel's best — he was *the* best! "There was not a man among the people of Israel *better* than he" (v. 2b, literal translation). The interpretation of the sense in which Saul was so "good" found in various translations ("handsome") is almost certainly correct. He was good in appearance. This is made explicit by reference to his height. He was head and shoulders above any other Israelite. He was a very impressive young man!

Such are the first impressions we are given of Saul. We have not yet been told explicitly what role he will play in the drama that is unfolding, but our expectations have been raised.

SAUL AND THE DONKEYS (vv. 3-10)

The Problem: Lost Donkeys (v. 3)

The story of the impressive son of Kish begins on a remarkably ordinary note: "Now the donkeys of Kish, Saul's father, were lost" (v. 3a).

The future of Israel was in the balance. A political revolution was simmering. But we are taken out into the country, to a rural family who had lost some donkeys.[9] This is as far from the crisis of chapter 8 as you could imagine!

Kish sent his son, with a servant,[10] to find the lost animals: "So Kish said to Saul his son, 'Take one of the young men with you, and arise, go and look for the donkeys'" (v. 3b).

Notice the focus on the father-son relationship: "Kish, Saul's father," "Saul, his son." Our previous story has been dominated by father-son relationships gone bad: Eli and his boys (1 Samuel 2:12ff.), then Samuel and his sons (1 Samuel 8:1-3). But now we see a son who gladly did his father's bidding.[11]

The story of Saul's obedience to his father will take us all the way up to 1 Samuel 10:16. It will turn out to be the story of much more than a search for some lost donkeys.

The Search (vv. 4-10)

That, however, is how it begins:

> *And he passed through the hill country of Ephraim and passed through the land of Shalishah, but they did not find them. And they passed through the land of Shaalim, but they were not there. Then they passed through the land of Benjamin, but did not find them. (v. 4)*

Saul and his servant evidently searched far and wide, but in vain.[12] The donkeys were nowhere to be found. This is hardly surprising. Lost donkeys would not be easy to find in the hills of Ephraim! Saul saw the futility of their search:

When they came to the land of Zuph, Saul said to his servant who was with him, "Come, let us go back, lest my father cease to care about the donkeys and become anxious about us." (v. 5)

These are the first words spoken by Saul in the Bible. Again, first impressions can be misleading, but they are unavoidable. Saul's concern for his father (more than for the donkeys) makes a welcome contrast to the failure of Eli's and Samuel's sons to care about their fathers. On the other hand, Saul's words reveal his (fully understandable at this stage) limited commitment to this journey. He is ready to "go back." We might be excused for wondering where this strange story is leading. What on earth can be the point of telling us about this country lad who honors his dad but can't find the donkeys?

The mention of "the land of Zuph" is worth noting. For those with ears to hear, here is a subtle hint of where this story is heading. Zuph was none other than the great-great-great-grandfather of Samuel (1 Samuel 1:1)! The land of Zuph was named after him and was apparently the region around Samuel's hometown of Ramathaim-zophim.[13] Saul had come to the territory of Samuel! We might expect that the anticipated connection between the great prophet and this young man will soon become apparent. It is clear that Saul had no idea of any of this.

At this point Saul's servant took a remarkable (and puzzling) initiative:

But he said to him, "Behold, there is a man of God in this city, and he is a man who is held in honor; all that he says comes true. So now let us go there. Perhaps he can tell us the way we should go." (v. 6)

Suddenly this rather ordinary story about lost donkeys becomes strange. How did Saul's companion know about this "man of God" in a city in the land of Zuph? We may have our suspicions as to who the man of God will turn out to be, but we cannot yet be sure. Of course, if this man of God turns out to be (as we suspect) Samuel, the question is, how could Saul *not* know of the great prophet (cf. 1 Samuel 3:20)? How was it that his servant had only vague knowledge of Israel's great leader? He did not know his name, only that he was "held in honor"[14] and that "all that he says comes true" (cf. 1 Samuel 3:19).

Perhaps, however, this is to miss the point.[15] Saul was seeking lost donkeys. He had no idea where this journey would lead. His lack of awareness of Samuel was part of his general ignorance of what was going on.

The oddest thing about the servant's words, however, is what he hoped to learn from the man of God. The ESV suggests that he might have been hoping for advice about where to find the donkeys. However, a more literal translation is, "Perhaps he can tell us *our way on which we have walked.*" It is as though this young man sensed that their journey had a significance that had little to do with lost donkeys but which they may learn from the man of God in the nearby city.

Saul was hesitant:

> Then Saul said to his servant, "But if we go, what can we bring the man? For the bread in our sacks is gone, and there is no present to bring to the man of God. What do we have?" (v. 7)

At one level the son of Kish continues to commend himself to us. Unlike the greedy, corrupt sons earlier in the narrative, he was not going to ask for something for nothing (contrast 1 Samuel 2:15 and 8:3). But perhaps we also notice again Saul's lack of commitment. He seems very willing to turn back.

In this regard the servant was quite different from Saul. He had another surprise:

> The servant answered Saul again, "Here, I have with me a quarter of a shekel of silver, and I will give it to the man of God to tell us our way." (v. 8)

Literally he said, "There is found in my hand a quarter of a shekel . . ." Where did that come from? It is very strange! Furthermore the servant sounds particularly determined. Our story is no longer quite so ordinary.

The narrator interrupts the conversation between Saul and his servant to tell us something, in case we have missed his earlier hints:

> (Formerly in Israel, when a man went to inquire of God, he said, "Come, let us go to the seer," for today's "prophet" was formerly called a seer.) (v. 9)

Do you get the hint? The man they were talking about going to see is what we would call these days a "prophet," says the narrator. Now I wonder who that might be (see 1 Samuel 3:20).

Notice that our narrator is telling us what people were doing when they said, "Come, let us go . . . ," as the servant had said, "let us go . . ." (v. 6; cf. v. 10). They were going "to inquire of God." The journey that had begun as a search for lost donkeys had become a search for a word from God!

The hesitant Saul was at last persuaded: "And Saul said to his servant, 'Well said; come, let us go.' So they went to the city where the man of God was" (v. 10).

Alongside the favorable impression we might be forming about this young man's character, we should note (for future reference) that he was not the leader in this situation but followed the word of another — here his servant.[16]

SAUL AND SAMUEL (vv. 11-27)

Directions from the Young Women (vv. 11-13)

The city they approached was probably Ramah.[17] Events now moved rather quickly. As the pair approached the city, a strangely familiar scene took shape: "As they went up the hill to the city, they met young women coming out to draw water and said to them, 'Is the seer here?'" (v. 11).

Anyone familiar with Biblical history will recall that there have been a number of occasions when an encounter with young women at a well turned out to be very significant. The stories of Isaac, Jacob, and Moses each include a scene like this that was a defining moment in each life (Genesis 24:10-61; 29:1-20; Exodus 2:15-21; cf. John 4:1-42). We cannot help wondering what this encounter will mean for Saul.[18]

The young women's reply to the travelers' question about the seer reveals that the timing of the arrival of Saul and his companion was remarkable:

> They answered, "He is; behold, he is just ahead of you. Hurry. He has come just now to the city, because the people have a sacrifice today on the high place." (v. 12)

What a remarkable "coincidence"! The world of Saul and his family's problem of lost donkeys was for the first time coming into contact with the world we left in chapter 8. That chapter ended with Samuel sending every man from Ramah "to his city" (v. 22). We do not know how much time passed between that dismissal and this day when the "seer" (who by now we have guessed was indeed Samuel) was approaching this city at the very moment that Saul and his servant arrived. If we are correct in assuming that the city was Ramah, it is possible that Samuel was returning to Ramah after one of his circuits (cf. 1 Samuel 7:16, 17).[19] Perhaps, then, Samuel had set out from Ramah after the events of chapter 8 at the very time Saul had set out in search of the donkeys.

"The people have a sacrifice today" may be better translated, "There is a sacrifice today *for the people*."[20] The last time we heard of "the people" was in chapter 8 where they had demanded a king after refusing to listen to Samuel (v. 19).[21] Now Samuel was coming to the city when the country boys happened to be passing because there was to be a sacrifice *for the people* that very day. Do you think there might be some connection between what happened in chapter 8 and this situation unfolding in this city? Did the sacrifice "for the people" have anything to do with "the people" who earlier rejected the Lord from being King over them (1 Samuel 8:7) and refused "to obey the voice of Samuel" (1 Samuel 8:19)? Had Samuel been presiding at sacrifices "for the people" in various places before returning now to Ramah? If so, this occasion will turn out to be different from all the others.

The country lads, of course, knew nothing of all this. We have no reason to think that they had any knowledge of the events of chapter 8.

The young women continued:

> *"As soon as you enter the city you will find him, before he goes up to the high place to eat. For the people will not eat till he comes, since he must bless the sacrifice; afterward those who are invited will eat. Now go up, for you will meet him immediately." (v. 13)*

The "high place" was presumably the location of the altar that Samuel had built in or near Ramah (1 Samuel 7:17b).

The focus of the young women's words was on the seer, the one whom Saul and his companion were about to meet.[22] The people were waiting for him. They were dependent on him. The sacrifice could not go ahead without him. At least in this matter of the sacrifice he was clearly the people's leader. Not only was he a seer, or prophet, to whom one would go "to inquire of God" (v. 9), but he also acted as a priest for the people, blessing the sacrifice.[23] All of this reminds us of Samuel, the man who had been brought up under the tutelage of Eli the priest at Shiloh (1 Samuel 2:11, 18, 21b, 26) and whom the Lord had established as a prophet in Israel (1 Samuel 3:20).

The urgency of the girls' words is a direct consequence of the remarkable fact that Saul and his servant had arrived at just the right moment. If they went up "now" they would meet him "immediately," "as soon as you enter the city."

The importance of the occasion, while not explained, is hinted at by the mention of "those who are invited." It is possible, in the light of what we are about to learn in verse 15, that the seer had called people together deliberately for the momentous event that was about to occur. The significance of the occasion seems to have been, as yet, unknown to the women, and perhaps even to the invitees. Certainly Saul had no idea of the "coincidence" that the timing of his arrival would turn out to be.

Samuel (v. 14)

Our expectation that the seer was Samuel is at last confirmed as we hear what happened when Saul and his servant reached the city: "So they went up to the city. As they were entering the city, they saw Samuel coming out toward them on his way up to the high place" (v. 14).

Despite the remarkably precise predictions of the young women, Saul did not yet know that the man they saw was the seer (see v. 18). Nor, of course, did he yet know his identity. The narrator — perhaps assuming that his readers would by now have guessed — confirms for us that it was indeed *Samuel* into whose presence Saul "happened" to come.

Samuel was last mentioned by name at the end of the previous chapter, as he dismissed "the men of Israel," sending them all home (1 Samuel 8:22b). The matter of the king the people were "asking for" (1 Samuel 8:10) was left hanging, as we have followed a young man whose name meant "Asked For" pursuing lost donkeys. At last "Asked For" has been brought to Samuel.

It was a memorable moment. The lives of these two men would be closely intertwined until their deaths (indeed beyond the death of one of them, 1 Samuel 28). Here Saul and Samuel encountered one another for the first time. More precisely, at this point they saw one another (see v. 17). The encounter will come in verse 18.

The Day Before . . . (vv. 15, 16)

The significance of this encounter can only be understood in the light of something that had happened the previous day. In a manner common in Biblical narrative, the narrator only now reveals what it was:

> *Now the day before Saul came, the LORD had revealed to Samuel: "Tomorrow about this time I will send to you a man from the land of Benjamin, and you shall anoint him to be prince over my people Israel. He shall save my people from the hand of the Philistines. For I have seen my people, because their cry has come to me." (vv. 15, 16)*

This brief flashback to the day before Saul and his servant had arrived at Ramah changes everything! We now see that the curiously ordinary sequence of events, beginning with the lost donkeys and the failed search for them, had been much more than it seemed. The Lord was "sending" Saul to Samuel! The remarkable coincidence of the timing of their arrival at Ramah now makes sense. It was God's doing. All that has happened so far in this chapter (the straying of the donkeys, the failure of the lads to find them, the servant's idea of consulting a seer, the quarter shekel he so strangely found in his hand, and the timing of their arrival at Ramah) can now be seen from a more significant point of view: the Lord was sending a man from the land of Benjamin to Samuel!

This was something that had been made known to Samuel by revelation.

That is the only way in which God's purposes can be discerned in the events of this world. No one can deduce God's purpose merely by observing events (either historical or contemporary). Only when God reveals his purpose (as he did on this day for Samuel and as he has done on a larger scale in the whole Bible) can any human know the purpose of God in human events. The important theological principle here is that we only understand the work of God because God has spoken.[24]

God's word to Samuel is the sequel to his earlier word: "Obey their voice and make them a king" (1 Samuel 8:22a). Now the Lord was sending a man from the land of Benjamin to Samuel.[25] Notice carefully what the Lord said to Samuel about this man.

First, note what Samuel was to do: "anoint him." We may reasonably deduce that this is how Samuel was to "make them a king" (1 Samuel 8:22). This should remind us of the last words of Hannah's prayer: "He will give strength to his king and exalt the power of his anointed" (1 Samuel 2:10), but also indicates Samuel's ongoing authority. Samuel was the one who would do the anointing.

However, notice, second, what the anointed man was to be. Whereas the people had demanded "a king over us, that we also may be like all the nations" (1 Samuel 8:19, 20), God was about to provide "a *prince* over my people Israel." It is striking that the expected word, "king," was *not* used. Although in due course Saul would be called king (1 Samuel 10:24; 11:15; 12:1), God's purpose for him was not the same as the people's purpose in their request. ("Leader" is a better word here than "prince," which in English has royal associations.[26]) Israel would continue to be *the Lord's* people, and therefore not "like the nations." The Lord calls them "*my* people" three times in verse 16! Their new leader, for the time being, will not be given the troublesome title "king." Indeed, were it not for the earlier word of the Lord to Samuel (1 Samuel 8:22), we would not think that the word in 1 Samuel 9:16 was about a king.

Third, notice what the anointed man was to do: "He shall save my people from the hand of the Philistines." On the one hand, the people had asked for a king so that he would "go out before us and fight our battles" (1 Samuel 8:20b). The man from the land of Benjamin was to do that. The Lord seems to have seen the people's request for a king to have arisen from their fear of the Philistines. On the other hand, saving his people from the hand of their enemies is what the Lord had been doing for Israel since he brought them out of Egypt. In particular he had provided "judges" who had saved them from their enemies again and again (see Judges 2:16, 18; 3:9, 31; 6:14; 10:11-14). Most recently the Lord had saved Israel from the hand of the Philistines in answer to Samuel's prayer (1 Samuel 7:8-11). There was nothing new about what the man from Benjamin was to do.

Fourth, consider why the Lord was doing this: "For I have seen my people, because their cry has come to me." The Lord was not sending the man from Benjamin because the people had asked for a king, but because he had seen their need. Curiously, Samuel had warned them that if they were to be given the king they asked for, they would "cry out because of your king," but "the LORD will not answer you in that day" (1 Samuel 8:18). That situation had not yet come. The Lord had heard their cry and was sending Saul.

Of course, the Lord had often heard the cry of his people and had come to save them (for example, Exodus 2:23; 3:7, 9; Judges 3:9, 15; 4:3). Again, in this respect the sending of the man from Benjamin was in keeping with the Lord's goodness toward his people in the past.

Samuel and Saul (vv. 17, 18)

The narrator returns to the next day, when Saul arrived in Ramah. Saul was, of course, completely ignorant of what had been revealed the previous day to Samuel: "When Samuel saw Saul, the LORD told him, 'Here is the man of whom I spoke to you! He it is who shall restrain my people'" (v. 17).

Saul saw Samuel in verse 14. Now, for the first time, Samuel saw Saul, and the Lord identified him as the promised man from the land of Benjamin.

Now, however, the Lord indicated that Saul was the one who would "restrain" Israel. Although some have argued that the Hebrew word here simply means "rule,"[27] it does not have that meaning anywhere else in the Old Testament. Saul was sent to Samuel as the one who would *hold back* the people of Israel from their determination to become "like all the nations" (1 Samuel 8:20a).[28] How this was to happen is yet to be disclosed.

Saul's complete unawareness of all that we have learned in verses 15-17 is clear: "Then Saul approached Samuel in the gate and said, 'Tell me where is the house of the seer?'" (v. 18).

The lad did not even know that the man before him was the seer he sought, let alone that he was Samuel or anything that Samuel had been told by God. He still had donkeys on his mind!

Samuel's Surprise for Saul (vv. 19-27)

Try to imagine Saul's surprise at the first words (the first of many words!) he heard from Samuel:

> Samuel answered Saul, "I am the seer. Go up before me to the high place, for today you shall eat with me, and in the morning I will let you go and will tell you all that is on your mind. As for your donkeys that were lost three days ago, do not set your mind on them, for they have been found.

And for whom is all that is desirable in Israel? Is it not for you and for all
your father's house?" (vv. 19, 20)

I wish we could see the expression on Saul's face! He no doubt heard
the bit about the donkeys. That is what had been on his "mind" (literally,
"heart"). At least, that is what he *thought* had been on his mind! Samuel
suggested that there was much more. What on earth did he mean by "all that
is desirable in Israel"?

We readers, of course, know all too well what had only recently been
"desirable in Israel," or rather what had been demanded in Israel (see
1 Samuel 8:19).[29] If we recall Samuel's attitude in chapter 8 to the people's
demand, we might hear a note of sarcasm in his expression "all that is
desirable in Israel." We can be sure, however, that Saul heard no such
thing.

> *Saul answered, "Am I not a Benjaminite, from the least of the tribes of*
> *Israel? And is not my clan the humblest of all the clans of the tribe of*
> *Benjamin? Why then have you spoken to me in this way?" (v. 21)*

Saul simply had no idea what was going on. He was a humble country
boy. As we saw at the beginning of this chapter, he had no claims to greatness.[30] Samuel's enigmatic words made no sense to him.

The reluctant Saul was then escorted by the decisive Samuel:

> *Then Samuel took Saul and his young man and brought them into the hall*
> *and gave them a place at the head of those who had been invited, who were*
> *about thirty persons. (v. 22)*

Again, it would be good to be able to see the faces of Saul and his companion, suddenly guests of honor at an important banquet for a select group
of invited persons.

Hannah knew, many years earlier, that the Lord "raises up . . . the needy"
and makes them "inherit a seat of honor" (1 Samuel 2:8).

Since we are not told directly the purpose of the meal, we cannot be
sure whether the invited guests would have made any connection between
Samuel's treatment of Saul and the great national issue of the day, the matter
of the kingship. It is certainly possible that they did.

> *And Samuel said to the cook, "Bring the portion I gave you, of which I*
> *said to you, 'Put it aside.'" So the cook took up the leg and what was on*
> *it and set them before Saul. And Samuel said, "See, what was kept is set*
> *before you. Eat, because it was kept for you until the hour appointed, that*
> *you might eat with the guests." (vv. 23, 24a)*

Rather elaborate preparations had been made for the utterly bewildered guest of honor. This was "the hour appointed." Choice food, normally the priests' portion (Exodus 29:27, 28), had been set aside for this point of time and for this special guest.[31] "So Saul ate with Samuel that day" (v. 24b).

And he had only been looking for his dad's donkeys!

We are told no more about the feast, but follow Saul's moves after it was over: "And when they came down from the high place into the city, a bed was spread for Saul on the roof, and he lay down to sleep." (v. 25).

The Hebrew is followed more closely by the NIV in the second half of this verse: "Samuel talked with Saul on the roof of his house."[32] We are told nothing of what was said. Certainly Samuel did not yet explain to Saul all that had happened that day.

> Then at the break of dawn Samuel called to Saul on the roof, "Up, that I may send you on your way." So Saul arose, and both he and Samuel went out into the street. (v. 26)

The suspense must have been intense for Saul. Was the mysterious seer ever going to tell him what was going on?

> As they were going down to the outskirts of the city, Samuel said to Saul, "Tell the servant to pass on before us, and when he has passed on, stop here yourself for a while, that I may make known to you the word of God." (v. 27)

The what? "The word of God, Saul."

I cannot help wondering whether someone put the chapter break at this strange point in order to draw attention to this climactic moment.

The very ordinary life of Saul, who three days earlier had set out to search for nothing more significant than donkeys, was about to encounter "*the word of God.*" And as we will soon see, he would never be the same again. This strange story has been leading to this point — the word of God that is going to change everything for Saul and change everything for Israel.

As we pause, only partway through this story, it is worth reflecting on the word of God.

The Bible teaches us that God speaks. God's word expresses and enacts his purpose. God rules all things by his word (see Hebrews 1:3). By his word creation was brought into being (see Genesis 1; Psalm 33:6; Hebrews 11:3). Jesus Christ is God's word become flesh (John 1:14). The news about Jesus is now God's word to the world (Colossians 1:25).

We see the significance of the events recounted in 1 Samuel 9 only when we see that the word of God was at the heart of it all. Saul was oblivious to this, but God had said to Samuel, "Obey their voice and make them a king" (1 Samuel 8:22a). Then he had said, "Tomorrow . . . I will send you a man from the land of Benjamin" (1 Samuel 9:16). Everything that happened in this chapter was according to the word of God. In due course Saul will become Israel's king by the word of God, and he will be required to listen to and obey the word of God (see 1 Samuel 12:14; 15:1).

Samuel was about to make known to Saul, for the first time, the word of God, just as the word of the Lord had come to Samuel for the first time many years earlier at Shiloh (see 1 Samuel 3:7). Saul should certainly turn his mind and heart away from donkeys! The word he was about to hear would change everything.

The contrast between the beginning and the end of this chapter is astonishing — from lost donkeys to the word of God, from the utterly mundane to the infinitely significant! The chapter shows, however, that the God whose word was about to be made known to Saul was sovereign over every mundane detail that had occurred. God was directing all things to the point where the word of God would make Saul Israel's new leader.

The plan God had for Saul and Israel was a very small-scale reflection of the plan God has for Jesus and the whole of creation. He will rule over "all things" (see Ephesians 1:10). God's rule over the mundane details to bring Saul to be Israel's leader points us to God's rule over all things that happen to us to achieve God's purpose for us under Jesus Christ's rule (see Romans 8:28-30).

14

The Secret of the Kingdom

1 SAMUEL 10:1-16

The most striking thing about the early part of the story we have been following since the beginning of 1 Samuel 9 is the utter ordinariness of it. The tall, good-looking son of Kish, the wealthy farmer from the land of Benjamin, would hardly have thought that his frustrating expedition searching for his father's lost donkeys was of historic importance. This country lad from an otherwise unknown family of the minor tribe of Benjamin was simply on an errand for his father. The circumstances and events of at least the early part of 1 Samuel 9 were evidently mundane, undramatic, we might even say trivial in nature.

However as *we* hear the account we are aware (as Saul was apparently unaware) of the great crisis in Israel that was narrated in chapter 8. Israel's leader Samuel was old, his sons were a nightmare, and the people of Israel were asking for the greatest change in the nation's constitution since the days of Moses — a king so they could be "like all the nations" (1 Samuel 8:1-5). We know that both Samuel and the Lord disapproved of the proposal (1 Samuel 8:6-9). However, the Lord told Samuel to make them a king (1 Samuel 8:22). Samuel did not do that, at least not immediately. Instead he sent everyone home (1 Samuel 8:22). When we are then introduced to an impressive young man named "Asked For" (1 Samuel 9:2), we suspect there was more going on than lost donkeys.

Our expectations are confirmed when the donkey chaser found himself in the presence of none other than Samuel (1 Samuel 9:14), the prophet who had been told by God to make a king for Israel. Saul was still apparently completely unaware of the national crisis that was occupying Samuel's mind.

By the end of chapter 9 the theme of Saul's pursuit of the donkeys gives way to Samuel's promise that he would make known to Saul "the word of God" (1 Samuel 9:27). We have come to see that the God who had said to Samuel, "Obey their voice and make them a king" (1 Samuel 8:22) had been in control of all the apparently trivial circumstances that had led to this moment. Not one of the seemingly mundane events had occurred by chance. All had been worked together by God to bring Saul, the son of Kish, to this point where he would hear "*the word of God.*"

What was the word of God that Samuel made known to Saul, and what effect did that word have?

THE WORD OF GOD MADE KNOWN TO SAUL (vv. 1-8)

The story continues seamlessly into chapter 10, where we read that Saul and Samuel were alone together for the first time. Saul's servant had been sent on ahead (1 Samuel 9:27).

The Anointing and Its Meaning (v. 1)

The way in which Samuel made known the word of God to Saul is described in verses 1-8. Unfortunately, as the footnote in the ESV indicates, there is a relatively major textual problem in verse 1. The main text of the ESV follows the Septuagint:

> *Then Samuel took a flask of oil and poured it on his head and kissed him and said, "Has not the LORD anointed you to be prince* over his people Israel? And you shall reign over the people of the LORD and you will save them from the hand of their surrounding enemies. And this shall be the sign to you that the LORD has anointed you to be prince *over his heritage."*

The Hebrew is much shorter, with only the words in italics above. The verse in the Hebrew would be translated:

> *Then Samuel took a flask of oil and poured it on his head and kissed him and said, "Has not the LORD anointed you to be prince over his heritage?"*
> *(v. 1)*

The arguments as to which of these represents the better text go both ways. While most commentators seem to favor the Septuagint,[1] I do not find the arguments compelling.[2] However, as so often in difficult text critical questions, not a lot hangs on the outcome. We will base our comments on the Hebrew — that is, the shorter — text.[3]

The Lord had said to Samuel two days earlier, "You shall anoint him to be prince over my people Israel" (1 Samuel 9:16). Samuel's actions and words now corresponded precisely to the Lord's command.[4] The actions alone were dramatic enough — the great prophet pouring the oil on the head of the young man from Benjamin and kissing him. Although we who know the events of chapter 8 may guess the significance of this, Saul could only wonder what it meant. The words Samuel then spoke explained the actions.[5]

The words were even more dramatic than the actions! According to Samuel's words (which, remember, were "the word of God" that Samuel had promised to make known to Saul, 1 Samuel 9:27), it was the Lord who had poured the oil on Saul's head ("Has not *the LORD* anointed you?")! Of course, at one level Samuel did the pouring, but since this was done in exact obedience to the Lord's command in 1 Samuel 9:16, Samuel was but the Lord's agent in this action. Saul needed to understand that he had been anointed not just by Samuel, but by the Lord!

Further, Samuel's words indicated the significance of the anointing: "to be prince." As we noted at 1 Samuel 9:16, "leader" is a better translation here because the Hebrew word does not necessarily have royal connotations. While it was extraordinary enough for this country lad to hear that God was making him the nation's *leader*, Saul was not yet told about the great issue of the day — the people's demand for a *king*.

Samuel's words differed slightly from the Lord's earlier command to him. Whereas the Lord had called the nation "my people Israel" (1 Samuel 9:16), Samuel now called them the Lord's "heritage." The idea expressed by this word seems to be the permanency of the Lord's possession. A "heritage" is an indisputable possession that cannot be transferred to another.[6] According to the Old Testament, the Lord chose the people of Israel to be his "heritage" or "inheritance" (1 Kings 8:53; Psalm 33:12; cf. Exodus 19:5, 6; Deuteronomy 7:6; 9:26, 29; 14:2; 32:8, 9).[7] Of course, all the earth belongs to the Lord (Exodus 19:5), and the Lord will "inherit all the nations" (Psalm 82:8). However, in the meantime, and as the means to that end, he chose to make Israel his "heritage" by rescuing them from their bondage in Egypt. By choosing this word as he spoke to Saul, Samuel emphasized as strongly as he possibly could the fact that the Lord was not surrendering his claim on this people. Although they had rejected him (1 Samuel 8:7), they remained *his* "heritage." Whatever else the new form of leadership Israel was receiving might mean, it would *not* mean that the Lord's possession of this people had been surrendered. In other words, he would not allow them to become "like all the nations" (1 Samuel 8:20)! (See further 1 Samuel 12:22.)

At this point we should note that only Saul and Samuel saw and heard these things. We can imagine how utterly bemused the young man from Benjamin must have been. But for now this "word of God" was a secret shared only by the youth and the prophet.

Three Signs (vv. 2-6)

Samuel had not finished speaking the word of God to Saul. As he continued he predicted three events that would shortly take place and that he will call "signs" in verse 7. The power of these events as signs lies not only in the fact that Samuel predicted them in advance, but in each case there is an astonishing echo of something that had happened earlier, before Saul had met Samuel.[8] Samuel's words (which, again, were "the word of God" that he was making known to Saul) demonstrated that all the details of Saul's journey as well as the path that lay ahead for him were under the careful, sovereign attention of God.

AT RACHEL'S TOMB (V. 2)

Here is the first sign:

> *"When you depart from me today, you will meet two men by Rachel's tomb in the territory of Benjamin at Zelzah, and they will say to you, 'The donkeys that you went to seek are found, and now your father has ceased to care about the donkeys and is anxious about you, saying, "What shall I do about my son?"'" (v. 2)*

Samuel was again exhibiting supernatural insight (as he had about the donkeys in 1 Samuel 9:20). Before Saul and Samuel had met, Saul had said to his servant, "Come, let us go back, lest my father cease to care about the donkeys and become anxious about us" (1 Samuel 9:5). Samuel now anticipated that he would meet two men who would repeat Saul's words almost exactly!

The place where Saul would encounter these two men was precisely indicated.[9] Although we no longer know where Zelzah was,[10] the fact that it was the location of Rachel's tomb is suggestive. Rachel's tomb was apparently in the vicinity of Ramah (see Jeremiah 31:15), where Saul's meeting with Samuel had probably taken place.[11]

The physical geography is less important than the historical associations suggested by "Rachel's tomb." Immediately following Saul's anointing we are reminded of Israel's origins. The future of the Lord's "heritage" is connected with its beginnings. Rachel was Jacob's second wife and the mother of Joseph and Benjamin. She had died giving birth to Benjamin (Genesis 35:16-20). She was therefore not only Israel's matriarch, but her tomb was a particular reminder of the origins of Saul's own tribe, Benjamin. By reminding us of the beginnings of Israel, and in particular of Benjamin, Rachel's tomb points us back to the book of Genesis where the promises of God that defined Israel's existence were repeatedly heard (see, for example, just before the birth of Benjamin and the death of Rachel, Genesis 35:9-12).

There at Rachel's tomb Saul would meet two men who would announce the end of the original search for the donkeys. The significance of their words cannot lie in the information they conveyed, for Samuel had already told Saul as much (1 Samuel 9:20). They were a *sign* (see 1 Samuel 10:7). On the one hand there was the inexplicable power of Samuel to predict the meeting and the unaccountable knowledge of the two men about Saul's and his father's concerns. On the other hand the words of the two men suggested that Saul's future would take a new and different path, of which even his father knew nothing.

AT THE OAK OF TABOR (vv. 3, 4)

The second sign would follow:

> *"Then you shall go on from there farther and come to the oak of Tabor. Three men going up to God at Bethel will meet you there, one carrying three young goats, another carrying three loaves of bread, and another carrying a skin of wine. And they will greet you and give you two loaves of bread, which you shall accept from their hand."*
> *(vv. 3, 4)*

Earlier Saul had spoken of the fact that he and his servant had no bread left (1 Samuel 9:7). The three men on their way to Bethel would give him three loaves of bread. His need would be met in this remarkable way.

Furthermore the meat, bread, and wine ("the three symbolic staffs of life"[12]) borne by the three men were apparently intended for some sacrificial ritual at Bethel. The presentation of some of the bread to Saul suggests a recognition that Saul now had a special (perhaps we should say, holy) status in God's purposes.

"The oak of Tabor" is not mentioned anywhere else in the Bible, but we might be reminded again of Genesis 35, where an oak is mentioned "below Bethel" (v. 8). At the oak of Tabor, Saul would meet three men "going up to . . . Bethel"![13]

Once again the significance of the place lies in its associations in the book of Genesis. Bethel ("house of God") received its name from Jacob's extraordinary encounter with God there (see Genesis 28:10-22 and 35:1-15; cf. 12:8; 13:3, 4). Bethel was the place where God repeated his astonishing promise to Jacob, the promise that defined Israel (Genesis 28:13-15; 35:9-12).

AT GIBEATH-ELOHIM (VV. 5, 6)

The third sign would be stranger still: "After that you shall come to Gibeath-elohim, where there is a garrison of the Philistines" (v. 5a).

From Rachel's tomb, via the oak on the way to Bethel, Saul would come to Gibeath-elohim, or "the hill of God." This is a reference to Gibeah ("the hill"), the home of Saul (see vv. 10, 26)[14] and therefore the end of his return journey.

The first surprise (at least for us readers) is that there was "a garrison [or governor[15]] of the Philistines" there. That there was a garrison (or garrisons[16]) of Philistines so far into Israelite territory is alarming and suggests that the Philistines had become a serious threat again.[17] That the Philistine presence was located at a place known as "the hill *of God*" added insult to injury.

By 1 Samuel 13:3 there was a Philistine garrison at Geba, located by most about three miles northeast of Gibeah.[18] The Philistine presence at Gibeath-elohim may by then have moved the short distance to Geba. Alternatively it is possible that Gibeah and Geba refer to the same place.[19] Be that as it may, we are sharply reminded of the fact (as yet not explicitly spoken to Saul) that the Lord had chosen him to save Israel from the Philistines (1 Samuel 9:16). This garrison of Philistines therefore represented the very problem Saul had been anointed to solve. The mention of the Philistines here was the first indication given to Saul of the specific task for which he had been anointed.

How could an unknown lad from Benjamin be expected to do anything about the Philistine threat to Israel? Read on:

> "And there, as soon as you come to the city, you will meet a group of prophets coming down from the high place with harp, tambourine, flute, and lyre before them, prophesying. Then the Spirit of the LORD will rush upon you, and you will prophesy with them and be turned into another man." (vv. 5b, 6)

We do not know a lot about the bands of prophets that appear from time to time in Israel's story in this period. There were pagan groups of prophets as well as Israelite (see, most famously, 1 Kings 18:19). We may reasonably guess that the designation *prophets* did not carry all the weight of that term in some other contexts. These were not, we might say, Prophets with a capital *P*. Nonetheless in this case they were, it seems, people moved by the Spirit, or breath, of God.[20]

This may not have been the first time that Saul had encountered such a group. However, Samuel told him in effect, "on this occasion the breath of God will rush upon *you* — and *you* will prophesy with the others."[21] "And you . . . will be turned into another man."

The breath (or Spirit) of God rushing upon a man had happened before. Indeed the presence of the threatening Philistines here reminds us of Samson, on whom the powerful Spirit of God "rushed" (Judges 14:6, 19; 15:14), empowering him to be a mighty savior of Israel from the Philistines. Is that what was meant by Saul's being "turned into another man"?

If Saul understood it like this (and I think that is the *most* he could have understood at this stage), his astonishment at the outcome of the donkey search must have been growing with every word he heard from Samuel! The word of God that Samuel made known to him was mind-blowing!

However, we have more questions in our minds. We cannot forget that God had said to Samuel, "Make them a *king*" (1 Samuel 8:22). The word *king*, which has not appeared since 1 Samuel 8:22, had still not been heard by Saul.

What Saul Was Then to Do (vv. 7, 8)

Our questions will have to wait, for Samuel had still not finished speaking the word of God to Saul. The predicted signs were the prelude to two instructions. The first was this: "Now when these signs meet you, do what your hand finds to do, for God is with you" (v. 7).

Empowered by the Spirit of God, Saul was to act, assured of God's presence with him. But what was he to do? "Do what your hand finds to do" does not mean that Saul would be free to do whatever he liked.[22] Rather, the words indicate that there would be a task for Saul to do.[23] What was the task?

The idiom, "Do what your hand finds to do" is also found in Judges 9:33, where the context makes clear that it refers to military action against an enemy.[24] Together with the promise that God would be "with" him (again a promise that is associated with battle against Israel's enemies; see, for example, Judges 6:12), Samuel's words were a summons to Saul, once the Spirit of the Lord had rushed upon him, to act against the enemies of Israel. The Philistine garrison there at Gibeath-elohim presented an obvious opportunity to do that![25]

The second instruction, then, was what Saul was to do when the Philistines had been defeated. He was to wait for further directions from Samuel to determine his future actions:

> *"Then go down before me to Gilgal. And behold, I am coming to you to offer burnt offerings and to sacrifice peace offerings. Seven days you shall wait, until I come to you and show you what you shall do." (v. 8)*

Samuel's words to Saul (still "the word of God" of 1 Samuel 9:27) culminated in these two instructions. The first (v. 7) was, by implication, to attack the Philistine presence at Gibeath-elohim. The defeat of this local Philistine presence within Israelite territory would not in itself bring the Philistine threat to an end. Therefore Samuel's second instruction to Saul (v. 8) was to go to Gilgal after he had done "what his hand finds to do" and wait there for further direction.[26]

Samuel would come to Saul at Gilgal "to offer burnt offerings and to sacrifice peace offerings." In 1 Samuel a burnt offering had been offered once before, when the Philistines had been subdued by God and forced to return the ark of the covenant (1 Samuel 6:14; but see also 15:22). Peace offerings seem appropriate after the overthrow of an enemy (cf. 1 Samuel 11:15). The anticipated meeting at Gilgal therefore seems to have been intended as a thankful celebration of the victory that Saul would by then have won over the Philistine garrison at Gibeah. It would also serve as a starting point for the next stage of Saul's God-ordained mission to save Israel from the Philistines (1 Samuel 9:16). There at Gilgal Samuel would show him what he was to do next.

Gilgal was about fifteen miles northeast of Gibeah, down (hence "go down"[27]) from the hills, in the Jordon Valley (near Jericho).[28] As we have noted the historical associations of the places mentioned so far in Samuel's speech (Rachel's tomb, v. 2, the oak and Bethel, v. 3), we should now notice that Gilgal was the first resting place for the Israelites in the promised land (Joshua 4:19). Gilgal was the place where the wilderness wanderings ended for Israel, and life in the land began (see Joshua 5:11, 12). Circumcision (the mark of God's promise to Abraham) and the Passover (the memorial of the redemption from Egypt) were celebrated at Gilgal as the nation began its new life in the land God was giving them (Joshua 5:1-10). Gilgal's name provided a wordplay with the Hebrew verb "to roll": there the Lord said to Joshua, "Today I have rolled away the reproach of Egypt from you" (Joshua 5:9). Gilgal was a very appropriate place for Saul to learn what his responsibilities as Israel's new leader would be.

It is now clear that Saul's leadership of Israel was to be subordinate to Samuel. Later he would be told that his fundamental responsibility as the one anointed king over the Lord's people was to "listen to the words of the LORD" (1 Samuel 15:1). This was to be a characteristic requirement of the monarchy in Israel (cf. Deuteronomy 17:18-20) and was the feature that distinguished Israelite kings from the kings of "all the nations" (cf. 1 Samuel 8:5). The king in Israel was subordinate to the prophet; he was to heed the words of the Lord.

WHAT SAUL DID (vv. 9-12)

"The word of God" that Samuel had promised to make known to Saul (1 Samuel 9:27) concludes at verse 8 of chapter 10. What do we expect will happen now that the word of God has been heard? We might reasonably expect to read of Saul experiencing the predicted three signs (vv. 2-6) and obeying the two instructions (vv. 7, 8). However the course of events did not unfold according to these expectations.

"Another Heart" (v. 9a)

Things began well, but surprisingly: "When he turned his back to leave Samuel, God gave him another heart" (v. 9a).

We had been led to think that Saul would become "another man" only after encountering the prophets at Gibeah (vv. 5, 6). However, God's work of changing Saul began immediately.[29] Whatever it meant for Saul to be given "another heart," it meant a profound change. The country lad was not in himself equipped for the task ahead of him. God changed him, and the change began without delay. God was not slow in keeping his word!

The Three Signs (v. 9b)

Furthermore the predicted signs occurred, just as Samuel had said, that very day: "And all these signs came to pass that day" (v.9b).

There is no need for these things now to be recounted in detail. We are to understand that what Samuel predicted in verses 2-6 happened precisely as he had said. The word of God came to pass.

The Third Sign (v. 10)

The writer is particularly interested to focus our attention on the coming to pass of the third sign, presumably because of the consequences that flowed from it: "When they came to Gibeah, behold, a group of prophets met him, and the Spirit of God rushed upon him, and he prophesied among them" (v. 10).

Clearly Gibeah ("the hill") is the Gibeath-elohim ("the hill of God") of verse 5. Although some details are omitted, verse 10 is a summary of the main points of Samuel's prediction in verses 5, 6. Prominent among the omissions in verse 10 is any mention of the garrison of the Philistines that was there (v. 5). This is astonishing if we have correctly understood that Saul was now expected to act against these Philistines.

Indeed this is the point at which the word of God had instructed him to act. The three signs had occurred. The consequence of the third sign was supposed to be action from Saul.[30] He was now to "do what your hand finds to do, for God is with you" (v. 7). We have concluded that this meant to do something about the Philistine presence there in Gibeah. Therefore this is the moment at which we have been led to expect Saul, like the judges

before him, to launch some kind of attack on the enemy and to defeat them
by God's power.

The failure to mention the Philistines in verse 10 seems therefore
to reflect Saul's own failure to turn his attention to this crucial matter. Notice that from the beginning of this chapter we have not heard a
word from Saul. We have no indication of what he thought of the things
Samuel told him, nor of his reaction to the things that happened to him.
Now we see no action at the very point where action had been called
for. Saul did *nothing*.

The Response of the People (vv. 11, 12)

Instead of the expected action from Saul following his empowerment by
the Spirit of God, we hear simply of the response of the people to what had
happened to Saul:

> And when all who knew him previously saw how he prophesied with the
> prophets, the people said to one another, "What has come over the son of
> Kish? Is Saul also among the prophets?" (v. 11)

Gibeah was Saul's hometown (1 Samuel 10:26), and so the third sign
had taken place in the presence of people who had known him previously. It
was clear to them that Saul had been changed. Obviously he had not previously associated with the prophets.

There is a certain irony to the people's reaction.[31] They did not know
what to make of the change in Saul. They, of course, had not heard the word
of God that Samuel had made known to Saul. *We* know that Saul had been
anointed and empowered to be Israel's new leader and their deliverer from
the Philistines. Because Saul had not yet acted as instructed, the only change
the people could see was his presence and behavior "among the prophets."[32] Saul's life from this point on would be shaped by his relationship to
a prophet more profoundly than he or they yet knew.

"And a man of the place answered, 'And who is their father?'" (v. 12a).
This further question is also more significant than the man who asked it
could have known. Much later we will learn that Samuel himself was the
head[33] of a company of prophets (1 Samuel 19:20). Was it the same group of
prophets as here? Certainly the critical relationship for Saul's future would
be that with Samuel. The man may well have been asking just the right
question![34]

However, none of these questions received an answer. The people were
perplexed about Saul but did not yet receive any explanation of why he had
been "turned into another man" (v. 6).[35]

Therefore it became a proverb, "Is Saul also among the prophets?"
(v. 12b)

The failure to understand Saul and the perplexity the people felt about him were expressed in the repetition of the question to such an extent that it became a proverb. As such it may have become an expression of "astonishment at the appearance of any man in a sphere of life which had hitherto been altogether strange to him."[36] The proverb, first heard here as Saul was in the process of becoming Israel's new leader, will be recorded again as Saul loses the capacity to lead Israel anymore (see 1 Samuel 19:24).

The reaction of the people who had known Saul is a remarkable anticlimax. While we expected to see the commencement of Israel's deliverance from the Philistines, anticipated in 1 Samuel 9:16 and 10:7, we have only heard bewildered questions.

WHAT SAUL SAID (vv. 13-16)

Still Saul made no move against the Philistine garrison: "When he had finished prophesying, he came to the high place" (v. 13).

That is all! He climbed the hill from which the group of prophets had descended (see v. 5). This does not look like what Samuel had in mind when he said, "Do what your hand finds to do, for God is with you" (v. 7)! The Philistines are still ignored — by the narrator as well as by Saul.

The Uncle's Question (v. 14a)

To our surprise, and perhaps also to Saul's, a relative of Saul was there at the high place: "Saul's uncle said to him and to his servant, 'Where did you go?'" (v. 14a).

Saul's uncle[37] may or may not have known of the search for the donkeys on which Saul and his servant had set out some time previously. His question, like those of the people in verses 11, 12, seems to have arisen from the evident fact that something had happened to Saul. "Where did you go?" was not simply asking for an itinerary but for an explanation of the change that everyone who had known Saul now seemed to recognize. "Where *have* you been?"

What Saul Said (vv. 14b-16a)

Saul's response is a spectacular case of dissimulation without actual dishonesty: "And he said, 'To seek the donkeys. And when we saw they were not to be found, we went to Samuel'" (v. 14b).

As a report of Saul's experience since he left home in 1 Samuel 9:4, that is astonishing for what was *not* said. The donkeys had not been a concern since Saul learned in 1 Samuel 9:20 that they had been found. Why did Saul speak of nothing other than the donkeys?

Saul's uncle was no fool. The mention of Samuel immediately gave him the clue: "And Saul's uncle said, 'Please tell me what Samuel said to you'" (v. 15).

It sounds as though the uncle knew more than Saul about the national crisis of 1 Samuel 8 and Samuel's involvement. Certainly he seems to have been more familiar with the great prophet than Saul had been. The uncle apparently realized, correctly, that the key to what had happened to his nephew must lie in what Samuel had said to him.

Unwittingly the older man gave Saul the cue to explain it to him. The Hebrew word translated "tell" is the verb form of the word translated "prince" in verse 1 of this chapter. This may seem a mere coincidence, until we hear Saul's reply to his uncle: "And Saul said to his uncle, 'He *told* us *plainly* that the donkeys had been found'" (v. 16a).

Again "told plainly" represents a *double* use of the same Hebrew word!

Perhaps we should be careful not to read too much into this. But we can imagine that readers of this story in Hebrew could well feel that Saul came within a whisker of telling his uncle the most important thing that had happened to him. He *almost* used the word! But he didn't tell him. Why not?

The reason for Saul's silence is not spelled out. Could it be related to the failure of the young man to do what he had been instructed to do? He had not obeyed "the word of God" that Samuel had made known to him. Could it be that having failed to act as the leader he had been anointed to be, he was not about to disclose this embarrassing, not to say shameful, fact to his uncle?

What Saul Did Not Say (v. 16b)

This episode in the story of Saul concludes by underlining what Saul did *not* say, letting us in on a bigger secret than Saul had yet been told: "But about the matter of the kingdom, of which Samuel had spoken, he did not tell him anything" (v. 16b).

"Tell" is that same verb again!

More importantly, "the matter of the kingdom" should probably be translated "the word of the kingdom" (literally, "But the word of the kingdom that Samuel had spoken he did not tell him"). For the first time since chapter 8, the *king* vocabulary is heard again. The people had asked for a "king," and the Lord had told Samuel to "make them a king" (1 Samuel 8:19, 22). The word of God, which Samuel had spoken to Saul, is now called "the word of *the kingdom*." The crucial term "kingdom" is heard by us, but not yet by any of the participants in the story. The narrator lets us in at last on the secret that *the word of God* that Samuel made known to Saul in verses 1-8 (cf. 1 Samuel 9:27) was in fact "the word of *the kingdom.*"

What does the narrator mean by "the kingdom"? It could, of course, be the kingdom of Saul that was about to be inaugurated. The narrator would then be giving us his first explicit confirmation of our suspicions that the appointment of Saul as Israel's new leader was indeed the establishment of Saul's *kingdom.*

However "the word of the kingdom" is a surprising expression. It seems appropriate to recognize another possible meaning. Three points suggest this alternative understanding. First, Saul has not yet been called "king" by the narrator, Samuel, the Lord, or anyone else. This seems to be deliberate. It is certainly striking. It is not therefore obvious that Samuel's words about Saul as Israel's new leader should be described as "the word of [Saul's] *kingdom.*" Second, the people's request for a king was interpreted by God as a rejection of *him* from being King over Israel (1 Samuel 8:7). The proper King of Israel was the Lord. "The kingdom" that mattered most was the Lord's kingdom, his rule as King over Israel. Third, all that God had said so far about Saul emphasized that God was not giving up his claim on this people. They were "my people Israel" (1 Samuel 9:16), "his heritage" (1 Samuel 10:1).

It seems therefore appropriate to see a subtle ambiguity in the expression "the word of the kingdom." It is not a matter of choosing between the two meanings. Samuel's speech in verses 1-8 was (we will see in due course) about the kingdom of Saul. More fundamentally, however, as we will see in the following chapters, the word of God to Saul was about the Lord's kingdom that he would not allow to be destroyed.[38] The word of God (1 Samuel 9:27) to Saul was in fact the word of *his* kingdom (1 Samuel 10:16).

The journey of Saul from his home and back again was a small episode in the history of Israel. The whole thing took just a few days. It is a tiny fragment of world history. However, *we* have been given the secret of the kingdom. The word of God that Samuel spoke to Saul will turn out to be the most powerful factor not just in his life, not just in Israel's life, but in the history of the whole world. It was "the word of the kingdom"!

A day eventually came when another man, not very far from the scene of the events of 1 Samuel 9–10, would come saying, "The kingdom of God is *at hand*" (Mark 1:15). The kingdom of God, which was the real concern of the word of God spoken by Samuel to Saul, eventually came into this world in the person and work of Jesus Christ. Before long the whole secret would be out. A message that became known as "the word of the kingdom" (Matthew 13:19) or "the gospel of the kingdom" (Matthew 4:23; 9:35; 24:14; cf. Luke 4:43; 8:1; 16:16) would soon be proclaimed through the Roman Empire and then to the ends of the earth!

There is still much for us to see about what God was doing with Saul, but we are beginning to see that it had to do with the kingdom that God would not give up, as we will see clearly when we reach 1 Samuel 12. Make no mistake: through the twists and turns of history, indeed through the apparently meaningless meanderings of human lives (like the donkey chase), what will matter in the end is the word of God, the word of the *kingdom*. We can only understand what matters in history and in our own lives by hearing the word of the kingdom, which for us is now the gospel of our Lord Jesus Christ. We are very privileged people to be "given," as Jesus said to his disciples, "the secret of the kingdom" (Mark 4:11; Matthew 13:11; Luke 8:10).

15

The King and the Kingdom

1 SAMUEL 10:17-27

W hat hope is there that the kingdom of God will advance in this world? What hope do you have that our prayer will be answered: "Your kingdom come . . . on earth . . ." (Matthew 6:10)?

As I write these words I find myself living and working in an evangelical theological college that has more students in training for gospel ministry than ever before. Should that give me hope? The missionary society with which I have closest links has a record number of candidates for overseas missionary work. Should that give me hope? In the city in which I live, these are exciting days for the gospel of Jesus. Plans and strategies for gospel growth are being formed and tried. Some of them are working! Church planting is the latest focus. We have Christian leaders with vision and quite remarkable ability. Should all that give me hope?

Many of the students at our college have come because they have been inspired by what is going on. They are hopeful that the kingdom of God *is* advancing in our day, and in various ways they hope to be part of the action. They see the value of giving their lives to this movement.

One of my longings for each of these students is this: Without dampening their excitement or cooling their enthusiasm or quelling their delight in the work of God that appears to be happening, I pray that their hopes will be given deeper roots. I long that they will so know God and his ways that their joy will survive — no, thrive — even when or if the numbers in church go into decline, and the strategy turns out to be a failure, and the church plant withers, and the movement that may have inspired them seems, to all appearances, to be over.

I share these thoughts here because I believe that the engaging story of Saul coming to the throne of Israel at the end of the second millennium B.C. can help this very thing to happen! The story of Saul is an account of the remarkable commitment of God to establish *his* kingdom.

The people of Israel had a strategy of their own for securing their nation. They had asked the prophet Samuel to give them a king (1 Samuel 8:5) so they could be "like all the nations" (1 Samuel 8:20). The account then followed a young man named Saul ("Asked For") who (unknown to him) was sent by God to Samuel to be anointed as "leader" (not yet "king") of God's people and to save them from the Philistines (1 Samuel 9:16). Samuel made known the word of God to Saul (1 Samuel 9:27), which included the instruction to act against the Philistines at Gibeah once the Spirit of the Lord had "rushed" upon him (1 Samuel 10:5-7). However, Saul did nothing, and when interrogated by his uncle, he said nothing about the momentous word that had been spoken to him (1 Samuel 10:16).

SAMUEL'S SPEECH (vv. 17-19)

The anointing of Saul and his commission to act against the Philistines, and so save Israel, remained a secret known only to Saul and Samuel. Some (unspecified) time passed. The next stage of the story was initiated by Samuel: "Now Samuel called the people together to the LORD at Mizpah" (v. 17).

We are not told how much time elapsed between Saul's conversation with his uncle in 1 Samuel 10:14-16 and Samuel's call to the people to assemble at Mizpah. I imagine it was not long.

Mizpah was the place Samuel had assembled the people in chapter 7 (v. 5), and had been one of the centers visited annually by Samuel as he "judged" Israel (1 Samuel 7:16). Apostasy had led to the first assembly at Mizpah (1 Samuel 7:3, 4). The purpose of that assembly had been Samuel's prayer for all Israel and their confession of their sin against the Lord (see 1 Samuel 7:5, 6). It had been a great day that culminated in a mighty victory over the Philistines (1 Samuel 7:11). Samuel's summons to assemble once again "to the LORD" at Mizpah suggests that the problem of apostasy had arisen again. It was time for renewed repentance if Israel were to experience again deliverance from the fearful Philistines.[1]

This expectation is confirmed in Samuel's speech to the people gathered at Mizpah. The speech had three simple but devastating points.

What the Lord Had Done (v. 18)

First, there was a reminder of all that the Lord had done for Israel:

And he said to the people of Israel, "Thus says the LORD, the God of Israel,
'I brought up Israel out of Egypt, and I delivered you from the hand of
the Egyptians and from the hand of all the kingdoms that were oppressing
you.'" (v. 18)

Samuel was still the Lord's prophet to Israel (1 Samuel 3:20). "Thus says the LORD" is, of course, what prophets say (cf. 1 Samuel 2:27). In the following speech Samuel was bringing the word of the Lord to Israel.[2]

The rehearsal of God's great acts for Israel focused on the exodus ("I brought up Israel out of Egypt"), the event that founded this nation (see Exodus 19:4-6; 20:2). The God who had so redeemed Israel in the beginning had also proven faithful in delivering this people from all oppressors ("all the kingdoms that were oppressing you"). This is what God is like.[3] He delivers his people from the powers that would do them harm.

The implication is obvious. The God of Israel could be trusted to save his people from the hand of the Philistines. Indeed we (the readers of this account) know that he had already begun to accomplish this purpose (1 Samuel 9:16), even though we have noticed that Saul had not yet acted as expected.

What Israel Had Done (v. 19a)

The second point of Samuel's speech was his indictment of the people for what they had done in asking for a king so they could be "like all the nations."

"But today you have rejected your God, who saves you from all your
calamities and your distresses, and you have said to him, 'Set a king over
us.'" (v. 19a)

"But *you*" is an emphatic contrast to "*I*" in verse 18 (this is even clearer in Hebrew). There was a terrible disparity between what the Lord had done (v. 18) and what Israel had done (v. 19a).[4] The Lord had proven himself to be the one who saved Israel from their "calamities and . . . distresses." The people of Israel had responded by demanding "a king over us" as a *replacement* for the Lord (see 1 Samuel 8:7, 19).[5]

There was a certain madness in Israel's heart. What they had done made no sense at all. To reject God was to reject their Savior!

It is not simply the idea of a king, as such, that is condemned here. It is, rather, Israel's rejection of God. In other words, the request for a king was not simply a political request, an alternative arrangement for the affairs of state. The people had betrayed themselves with the words "that we also may be like all the nations" (1 Samuel 8:20). Their desire for a king was in fact a desire to no longer be the Lord's people.

Anyone who was taking the prophet's words seriously that day would have trembled in anticipation of what he would say next. When a prophet reminded the people of God's goodness, then of their guilt, it was usual for him then to pronounce the coming punishment.[6]

Therefore . . . (v. 19b)

Samuel's third point begins with the frightening words "Now therefore":[7] "Now therefore present yourselves before the LORD by your tribes and by your thousands" (v. 19b).

Samuel gave them no hint of what was about to happen. At this point, however, it sounded as though it would be something terrible, a fitting punishment for the apostasy behind the demand for a king.[8]

The people of Israel being brought before the Lord by their tribes and by their thousands[9] sounds very like an occasion that had taken place some time earlier. Shortly after Israel had entered the promised land, they had found themselves threatened with punishment because of Achan's act of disobedience (see Joshua 7, especially vv. 14, 16). Anyone who remembered that day may well have trembled as Samuel called the people to "present yourselves before the LORD by your tribes."[10]

THE LORD'S CHOICE (vv. 20-24)

The account continues with more echoes of Joshua 7 (compare Joshua 7:16): "Then Samuel brought all the tribes of Israel near, and the tribe of Benjamin was taken by lot" (v. 20).

If the other tribes were thinking of that day when Achan had brought trouble on Israel, I am sure they breathed a sigh of relief when Benjamin was taken! As on that earlier day, the process continued (compare Joshua 7:17): "He brought the tribe of Benjamin near by its clans, and the clan of the Matrites was taken by lot" (v. 21a).

As with the Achan incident, we are to understand this to be some kind of lot process,[11] which is under the sovereign control of the Lord. He will bring it to his intended outcome.[12] If we find ourselves thinking of the Achan story, we can only catch our breath when we hear the next words: ". . . and Saul the son of Kish was taken by lot" (v. 21b).

"Asked For" was his name. We first met him in 1 Samuel 9:2. We have followed his search for donkeys (1 Samuel 9:3-5). We witnessed his anointing by Samuel (at the Lord's command) to be Israel's leader and to save them from the hand of the Philistines (1 Samuel 9:16; 10:1). Why would Saul be selected in this Achan-like process, which we (and the people) have been led to believe is a punishment? We might remember that Saul had not yet acted to save the Israelites from the Philistines, although the word of God to him had led us to expect him to do so (1 Samuel 10:7). Was Saul in fact about to be punished for this?

Saul may well have wondered the same thing: "But when they sought him, he could not be found" (v. 21c).

We should not press the Achan parallel too far.[13] However, even apart from that, the tone Samuel had set in verses 18, 19 was terrifying. The selection process that narrowed down to Saul was presented as the consequence of what *Israel* had done in asking for a king, seen in the light of what *God* had done in his great acts of salvation for them. I am not at all surprised that Saul, as the lot drew closer, made himself scarce! "So they inquired again of the LORD, 'Is there a man still to come?'" (v. 22a).

Literally they "asked" again, a pun on Saul's name.[14] The process that led to the lot falling to someone who was not present, and then the people asking of the Lord whether someone was missing is not explained. It does not matter.[15] What matters is that the Lord brought the process to his intended end: ". . . and the LORD said, 'Behold, he has hidden himself among the baggage'" (v. 22b).

The word "baggage" is vague. It can refer to almost any physical object (utensils, weapons, musical instruments, furniture).[16] It does not matter where he was hiding. He was hiding. Is it too much to suggest that Saul's hiding was, like what he did not say to his uncle (1 Samuel 10:16), evidence of a troubled conscience?[17] If so, the Achan-like process must have terrified him.[18] "Then they ran and took him from there" (v. 23a).

When Achan had been identified by lot, the people *ran* to his tent to find the hidden things (Joshua 7:22). So now they *ran* to find Saul.

At this point the echoes of the Achan story seem to fade. We may wonder what will happen with the young man about whom we know so much. First we see him among the people: "And when he stood among the people, he was taller than any of the people from his shoulders upward" (v. 23b).

We have already been told that Saul was the tallest man in Israel in 1 Samuel 9:2, when we were first introduced to him. But now, for the first time, all the people of Israel saw this towering young man.

The kind of king the people were guilty of asking for (one who would make them "like all the nations" and who would go out before them and fight their battles, 1 Samuel 8:20) would need to be a man who made an impression on others. The man who stood now in their midst was evidently just such a man. Most impressive was his sheer physical size. If we are still thinking of Achan, we might observe that while Saul was not guilty in the same way that Achan was,[19] the process had led to the tangible expression of the people's guilt, and here was their rebellious request embodied.[20]

Samuel's words to the people were then astonishing: "And Samuel said to all the people, 'Do you see him whom the LORD has chosen? There is none like him among all the people'" (v. 24a).

We noted at 1 Samuel 9:2, when Saul was introduced as "a handsome young man," that "young man" translates a word that can also mean "chosen one." We were reminded then that the matter of the king had begun as a choice of *the people*: "*your* king, whom *you* have chosen for *yourselves*" (1 Samuel 8:18). In that choice the people had rejected God as their king (1 Samuel 10:19; cf. 8:7). This vocabulary of choosing was now used to introduce Saul to the people.

It would not have been surprising if Samuel had said, "Do you see him whom *you* have chosen?" The surprise is that Samuel informed the people, for the first time, that "*the LORD*" had "chosen" the man before them.[21] "Chosen" is an extraordinary word in Biblical vocabulary when God is the subject. God *chose* Abraham (Nehemiah 9:7), he *chose* Israel (Isaiah 14:1; 41:8; 44:1; 49:7), he *chose* Aaron (Psalm 105:26), and he will *choose* David (1 Kings 8:16) and Jerusalem (1 Kings 11:32).

Of course, Samuel's words do not take us (the readers of the record) entirely by surprise. The story from the beginning of chapter 9 has clearly shown us that Saul had been selected by God to be Israel's new leader and savior from the Philistines (1 Samuel 9:16; 10:1). The puzzle for us is how God's choice of a "leader" could be brought together with the people's choice of a "king." We have this perplexing situation: the people had *chosen* to reject the Lord and have a king for themselves. However, the man before them, who was the obvious choice for such a king (there was no one "like him among all the people"), was "him whom *the LORD* has chosen."

However perplexing that may have seemed, the Lord's choice became the people's choice: "And all the people shouted, 'Long live the king!'" (v. 24b).

At last the people got it — or thought they did. What could be more obvious? Who better than this huge fellow to be a king for us, so that we may be like all the nations? Who better to "go out before us and fight our battles" (1 Samuel 8:20)?

In all the excitement it would be easy to overlook the fact that calling him "king" was the people's idea. Neither the Lord nor Samuel had yet called Saul "king." But "all the people" acclaimed the tall, good-looking young man as their *king*.

At this stage we might wonder what hope there could be for this king. It appears that God had given the people what they had wickedly asked for, and we might well fear for the consequences. Does this mean that Israel would now be "like all the nations"? Would Israel now cease to be the Lord's people? We know (as the people could not yet know) that it was not as simple as that. The Lord's purpose for Saul was that Israel would continue to be "my people" (1 Samuel 9:16), "his heritage" (1 Samuel 10:1), despite their attempt to reject the Lord.

THE KINGDOM (vv. 25-27)

The sequence of events has been perplexing. The people's demand for a king was a rejection of God as their king (1 Samuel 8:7), and yet God told Samuel to "make them a king" (1 Samuel 8:22). God brought Saul to Samuel to be secretly anointed as *leader* (ESV, "prince") over his people Israel (1 Samuel 9:16; 10:1). The narrator told us, tantalizingly, that had to do with "the kingdom" (1 Samuel 10:16), with no more explanation yet. Now, here at Mizpah, Samuel told the people how wicked was their demand for a king. Without explanation, and through a process that sounded and looked like a divinely guided prelude to punishment, Saul was identified, designated as the Lord's choice, and acclaimed by the people as their king.

What Samuel did at this point is very important: "Then Samuel told the people the rights and duties of the kingship, and he wrote them in a book and laid it up before the LORD" (v. 25a).

"The rights and duties of the kingship" is an interpretation of a Hebrew phrase that is very difficult.[22] In Hebrew it is strikingly similar to the expression translated "the ways of the king" in 1 Samuel 8:9, 11. In chapter 8 we noted that a more literal translation is "the justice of the king." A more literal translation of the expression here in 1 Samuel 10:25 would be "the justice of the kingdom." A crucial line of thought comes to a climax here. At the end of chapter 7, Samuel had "judged" Israel (v. 15). The "justice" he brought was deliverance from their enemies (1 Samuel 7:13), peace with their neighbors (1 Samuel 7:14), and social order throughout the nation (1 Samuel 7:16). When the elders of Israel first asked for a king, it was "to judge us" in the same sense (1 Samuel 8:6, 20). God told Samuel to tell the people the "justice" of the king who would reign over them (ESV, "the ways of the king," 1 Samuel 8:9). With some degree of cutting irony, Samuel told them of the "justice" of the king who would reign over them in 1 Samuel 8:11-18: "he will take, take, take." "In that day you will cry out because of your king, whom you have chosen for yourselves" (1 Samuel 8:18). Such would be the "justice of the king"!

Now at Mizpah, with the bemused Saul acclaimed as their king, Samuel told the people the "justice of the kingdom" or, we might say, "the ways of the kingdom." "Kingdom" is the same word that was used with tantalizing ambiguity in 1 Samuel 10:16. What does our narrator mean by "the justice/ways of the kingdom"?

Samuel wrote "the justice/ways of the kingdom" in a book and laid it up before the Lord. It seems very unlikely that "the justice of the kingdom" was the same as the ironic "justice of the king" that the people had chosen for themselves, rehearsed by Samuel in 1 Samuel 8:11-18.[23] In my opinion Samuel wrote the following or something very like it:[24]

*When you come to the land that the L*ORD *your God is giving you, and you*
possess it and dwell in it and then say, "I will set a king over me, like all
the nations that are around me," you may indeed set a king over you whom
*the L*ORD *your God will choose* [the word we saw in 1 Samuel 10:24]. *One*
from among your brothers you shall set as king over you. You may not put
a foreigner over you, who is not your brother. Only he must not acquire
many horses for himself or cause the people to return to Egypt in order
*to acquire many horses, since the L*ORD *has said to you, "You shall never*
return that way again." And he shall not acquire many wives for himself,
lest his heart turn away, nor shall he acquire for himself excessive silver
and gold.

And when he sits on the throne of his kingdom, he shall write for himself
in a book a copy of this law, approved by the Levitical priests; and it shall
be with him, and he shall read in it all the days of his life, that he may
*learn to fear the L*ORD *his God, by keeping all the words of this law and*
these statutes, and doing them, that his heart may not be lifted up above his
brothers, and that he may not turn aside from the commandment, either to
the right hand or to the left, so that he may continue long in his kingdom,
he and his children, in Israel. (cf. Deuteronomy 17:14-20)

"The justice of the kingdom," you see, had been given by Moses in the
very early days of this nation. It was, in brief, that a king in Israel was *not* to
be like all the nations. He was *not* to take, take, take, and was to reign *only*
under the Lord his God, keeping and doing all the words of *his* law.

See what had happened at Mizpah. God had outmaneuvered the people!
They were bent on abandoning the kingship of God by getting a king *for*
themselves so they could be like all the nations. But now they had a king,
and they had the written terms by which *God's* kingdom must nonetheless
be preserved. They had a king, but they were *not* to be like all the nations.

As though to underline this strange arrangement we read: "Then Samuel
sent all the people away, each one to his home" (v. 25b).

Hadn't a king just been appointed? Indeed he had. But *Samuel* sent
everyone home. In case we haven't yet got the point: "Saul also went to his
home at Gibeah . . ." (v. 26a).

Some king! Saul's first act as the king of Israel was an act of obedience to the prophet Samuel! From this moment it is clear who was really in
charge in Israel. Even Saul submitted to the prophet.[25] That is the "justice"
of this kingdom: the king must submit to the prophet. In other words, king
or no king, God will rule his people (and now their king) by his word. This
theme will be developed throughout the story of Saul's reign (see especially
1 Samuel 12:14, 15; 13:13; 15:1, 22, 23).

Saul's hometown was notorious in Israel's recent history. A terrible rape and murder in Gibeah (Judges 19:22-30) had led to a bloody conflict between the tribe of Benjamin and the rest of the tribes of Israel (Judges 20). Curiously the account that preserves Gibeah's infamy is framed by a reference to the fact that "in those days there was no king in Israel" (Judges 19:1; 21:25). That Israel's first king should come from the very town that was the source of such trouble reminds us that God reverses things (see 1 Samuel 2:6-8).

Saul's return to Gibeah raises the question of the Philistines who were, presumably, still garrisoned there (1 Samuel 10:5) or nearby (1 Samuel 13:3). Surely the new king would be expected now to take some action against the Philistines.

This expectation is increased when we learn that God was at work actively supporting this new arrangement: ". . . and with him went men of valor whose hearts God had touched" (v. 26b).

The expression "men of valor" could mean "the army" (cf. 1 Samuel 17:20, where the same word is translated "the host"; cf. Exodus 14:28; also 1 Samuel 14:52).[26] If this is the case, God had provided both the constitution for the new monarchy (v. 25) and now the military support that may be needed to establish it, by touching the hearts of the fighting men, just as he had changed the heart of Saul himself (1 Samuel 10:9).[27] They appear to have gladly accepted the new arrangement: the king (Saul) *and* the kingdom (of God).[28]

Furthermore, the prospect of the new king at last dealing with the Philistine presence at Gibeah is sharpened by the divinely inspired fighters who accompanied Saul back to Gibeah.

But there was a problem: "But some worthless fellows said, 'How can this man save us?' And they despised him and brought him no present" (v. 27a).

If these men were among "all the people" who only a little earlier had shouted "Long live the king!" (1 Samuel 10:24), what was it that now caused them to despise him? It seems reasonable to assume it was "the justice of this kingdom," which they now understood.[29] It was now clear that Saul was not to be a king who would make them "like all the nations," but a king who was still subject to the Lord's prophet, still subordinate to the word of God. These "worthless fellows" apparently accepted Saul (v. 24) until they saw that his appointment did not accomplish the intention of rejecting God's kingship (v. 19).

These "worthless fellows" remind us of the sons of Eli,[30] who did not know the Lord and treated the Lord's offering with contempt (see 1 Samuel 2:12, 17). These men persisted in the spirit denounced by Samuel in verse 19: "You have rejected your God who *saves* you. . . ." They asked, "How can this man *save* us?" These men's doubts about Saul could not have been based on his physical stature.[31] In those terms, if Saul could not save them, then no one in Israel could ("There is none like him among all the people," v. 24). Like the sons of Eli, these sons of *belial*[32] were showing contempt for the Lord (cf. 1 Samuel 2:17), who had chosen Saul (1 Samuel 10:24) for the very purpose of *saving* his people (1 Samuel 9:16).[33] The answer to their question will come dramatically in the next chapter.

The last words of this chapter tell us what Saul then did: "But he held his peace" (v. 27b).

He said nothing.[34] He did nothing. He just went home quietly. While this might add to an impression of a mild-mannered young man,[35] we must be struck by the continuing passivity of the new king. Did the objectors have a point, after all? How could this inactive man save anyone? The Philistine garrison, after all, was still at Gibeah (1 Samuel 10:5)!

The story of King Saul has only just begun. However, the crucial thing is now clear. Whether Israel had a king or did not have a king, what mattered was *the kingdom*. And *the kingdom* — the *kingdom of God* — must prevail.

Do you see what this says to our strategies, schemes, plans, training, abilities, and leadership models? The kingdom of *God* must prevail. Some will be unimpressed and despise the ways of this kingdom. They will want strategies "like all the nations," plans like the corporate world, methods like the world of power politics and marketing. The ways of the kingdom of God are foolish and weak to them (cf. 1 Corinthians 1:25). Indeed it will only be those whose hearts are touched by God who will welcome an arrangement where all human power and cleverness is called to submit to the word of God. This is why we must "renounce disgraceful, underhanded ways." We "refuse to practice cunning or to tamper" with the word of God, but by "open statement of the truth" we proclaim "Jesus Christ as Lord" (cf. 2 Corinthians 4:2-5). Our hope that the kingdom of God will come rests not on any form of human power or cleverness, but on the one whose kingdom it is.

16

The Kingdom at War

1 SAMUEL 11:1-11

Have you noticed how often the New Testament employs military and warfare language and images for the proclamation of the gospel of Jesus Christ? It is true that this way of speaking is often used negatively, underlining its *metaphorical* character: "we are *not* waging war according to the flesh" (2 Corinthians 10:3), wrote Paul. "We do *not* wrestle against flesh and blood" (Ephesians 6:12). "The weapons of our warfare are *not* of the flesh" (2 Corinthians 10:4). However, although we are not engaged in a literal and physical war, "the weapons of our warfare . . . have divine power to destroy strongholds" (2 Corinthians 10:4). Paul wrote of "the weapons of righteousness" (2 Corinthians 6:7). "The word of God" is "the sword of the Spirit" (Ephesians 6:17). We are called to "put on the whole armor of God" (Ephesians 6:11). Furthermore Paul described his gospel preaching around the Mediterranean world as a "triumphal procession" (2 Corinthians 2:14), although, importantly, that is hardly what it would have looked like to most observers.

The metaphorical character of these expressions is important. The cause of Jesus Christ *cannot* be advanced by literal, physical violence on our part, any more than by "cunning" and "disgraceful, underhanded ways" (see 2 Corinthians 4:2). In an age of terrorism this distinctive of the Christian gospel needs to be clearly understood. We refuse to fight this war with worldly weapons.

As we engage in efforts to win our neighbors, friends, relatives, and everyone else for Christ, we must remember this lesson. Never allow your longing for victory to tempt you into thinking that it may be won by worldly means, whether by human power, human cleverness, or human impressiveness. No. It must be won (to quote the apostle again) "by purity, knowledge, patience, kindness, the Holy Spirit, genuine love; by truthful speech, and the power of God; with the weapons of righteousness for the right hand and for the left" (2 Corinthians 6:6, 7).

However it is also important to be reminded that the proclamation of the gospel *is* war. As we take the word of Christ to an unbelieving world, we go to *do battle*. It is right to feel apprehensive. "Who is sufficient for these things?" (2 Corinthians 2:16). It is also right to sense the excitement of gospel work. War is like that.

I suspect that in our day we have a problem with this kind of talk. We are not entirely comfortable with the language of aggression applied to Christian work. "Going to do battle" is *not* how we like to think of our evangelistic efforts. This Biblical language does not fit comfortably with our approaches to making Christ known. In many ways the business world has replaced the battlefield as a source of categories for thinking about this work. Gospel work is then not war but *commerce*: we go to sell a product, not to fight a battle. We are marketers, not soldiers. We have merchandise, not weapons. We face potential customers, not an enemy. We are out to expand our market share and increase our customer base, not to capture, defeat, and destroy a foe. We form a business plan, not a battle plan. The conflict we face arises from the competition in the marketplace of ideas where our product is not the only one offered, rather than the hostile wiles of an enemy. The language of war, weapons, and battle is too extreme for the way we think about evangelism. We are more like advertisers than fighters.

If this description is approximately correct, then we need to think again. We need to allow God's Word to show us what we are engaged in. If we are uncomfortable with the battle language, it may well be because we are not seeing the task before us as clearly as we must. How are we to understand the military language of the New Testament?

Behind the warfare language of the New Testament, we need to see the actual warfare of the Old Testament. Just as we should look back to the Old Testament to understand the New Testament's language of sacrifice, election, redemption, and so much more, we ought to see the language of war associated with the Christian gospel against its necessary and clarifying background in the Old Testament.

In 1 Samuel 11 we find one graphic example of Old Testament warfare. We will see how the battle recounted in this chapter helps us to understand that our gospel endeavors are combat.

You may recall where we are in the story of Saul. The people of Israel had asked old Samuel for a king so they could be "like all the nations" (1 Samuel 8:19, 20). This was a very low point in Israel's history. In this demand the people were rejecting God's way of being King over them (1 Samuel 8:7; 10:19).

However, as the story has unfolded since chapter 8, we have seen God's hand on the course of events, leading to the anointing of Saul as Israel's new leader who would save the Lord's people Israel from the Philistines (1 Samuel 9:16; 10:1). So far, however, Saul seems to have made no active response to his commission. He did not act against the Philistines at Gibeah (1 Samuel 10:5), nor did he tell his uncle about "the word of the kingdom" that Samuel had spoken to him (1 Samuel 10:16). Nonetheless when Samuel ominously (see 1 Samuel 10:18, 19) presented Saul to the people as the Lord's choice, they acclaimed him as their king with a great shout (1 Samuel 10:24). Samuel then told the people the terms of this kingship, "the justice of the kingdom" (1 Samuel 10:25, literal translation), which we had reason to understand meant that Saul's kingship was still to be subordinate to God's kingship, as had been anticipated long before by Moses (Deuteronomy 17:14-20). He was *not* to be the kind of king they had asked for, one who would make them "like all the nations" (1 Samuel 8:5, 20).

At the end of chapter 10, Saul had not yet done anything as king. The question raised by some disgruntled fellows had not been answered: "How can this man save us?" (1 Samuel 10:27). Saul appears to have made no difference whatsoever to Israel at the end of 1 Samuel 10. Everyone, including Saul, had simply gone home (1 Samuel 10:25b, 26a), as Samuel told them to! Importantly, the Philistine problem had still not been addressed. The menacing presence in the Israelite heartland, in Gibeah (1 Samuel 10:5), does not appear to have received attention from anyone — certainly not from Saul. As time passed, the question asked by the "worthless fellows" in 1 Samuel 10:27 must have seemed more and more legitimate.

THE CRISIS IN JABESH-GILEAD (vv. 1-3)

Saul returned to his home at Gibeah (1 Samuel 10:26). For a time nothing came of the kingship matter. Saul's passive inactivity continued. As we will see in due course, the Philistine presence in Israelite territory (1 Samuel 10:5) remained (see 1 Samuel 13:3). Saul did nothing about the problem.

We cannot know how much time passed between chapters 10 and 11. Indeed it is likely that the events of chapter 11 began *before* the end of chapter 10.[1]

The Threat from Nahash (v. 1a)

The point is that across the Jordan River, some forty miles northeast of Saul's home in Gibeah, there was a crisis: "Then Nahash the Ammonite went up and besieged Jabesh-gilead . . ." (v. 1a).

Previously in 1 Samuel it had been the Philistines, from the west, who had threatened Israel (1 Samuel 4:1; 7:7). That threat was to remain for the rest of Saul's life (see 1 Samuel 14:52). Now, however, the Ammonites from the east menaced the people of Jabesh-gilead, who were therefore in grave danger.[2]

Jabesh-gilead, on the east side of the Jordan River, in the territory of the tribe Manasseh, had featured in the closing pages of the book of Judges.

In the events of 1 Samuel 11 we will see a remarkable number of reminders of the horrendous events recorded in Judges 19–21. Significantly the earlier period involved an assembly "to the LORD" at Mizpah, just as 1 Samuel 11 is the sequel to a similar assembly there (compare Judges 20:1, 1 Samuel 7:5, and 1 Samuel 10:17). In the dreadful internal conflict that is recounted in Judges 19–21 Jabesh-gilead did not join in the retributive attack on the tribe of Benjamin (see Judges 21:8) for the appalling crime committed in Gibeah (see Judges 19:22-30). For this the people of Jabesh-gilead had suffered terribly at the hands of their fellow Israelites (see Judges 21:1-15). That episode had brought Jabesh-gilead into a peculiar relationship with the tribe of Benjamin, because 400 virgins from Jabesh were given as wives to the devastated tribe of Benjamin (Judges 21:14). This makes it likely that Saul may have had a family connection with Jabesh-gilead.

The location of Jabesh-gilead was exposed to an old enemy of Israel. Nahash, the Ammonite king, is a new character in our story.[3] However, the Ammonites have a colorful history in relation to the Israelites.[4] Their ancestor, Ben-ammi, was (like his half-brother Moab) a son of Abraham's nephew, Lot, by incest with one of his daughters (Genesis 19:38). The Ammonites (with the Moabites) were eventually included by the prophets among Israel's traditional enemies (see, for example, Isaiah 11:14; Jeremiah 9:25 26; 25:21; 27:3; 49:1-6; Ezekiel 25:1-7; Daniel 11:41; Amos 1:13-15; Zephaniah 2:8, 9).[5] The antagonism can be traced back to Israel's encounters with the Ammonites on the journey to the promised land (see Deuteronomy 23:3-6). More recently (from the point of view of 1 Samuel 11) the Ammonites had repeatedly been involved in aggression against the Israelites (see Judges 3:13; 10:7-9, 17, 18). Jephthah had roundly defeated them and delivered Israel from their threat for a time (Judges 11:1-33).

The Proposal from the Men of Jabesh (v. 1b)

Listen to the response of the people of Jabesh-gilead to the threat from Nahash the Ammonite: ". . . and all the men of Jabesh said to Nahash, 'Make a treaty with us, and we will serve you'" (v. 1b).

This was an astonishing thing for the people of Jabesh ("all" of them!) to say. No doubt they hoped this would avoid violence, but they were doing more than offering to make friends with this old enemy. By offering to make a treaty (or covenant) with Nahash, they were in effect asking Nahash to become their king![6]

Two things in the context add to our surprise at the words of the people of Jabesh. On the one hand, we remember how recently (in the narrative) the people of Israel had been asking for a king "like all the nations" (1 Samuel 8:19, 20)![7] The request for a covenant with Nahash is a shocking expression of that idea: their king would be one of the nations' kings!

On the other hand, it is perplexing that the people of Jabesh made no reference *whatsoever* to the one who so recently (in the narrative at least) had been acclaimed by "all the people" as Israel's new king (1 Samuel 10:24). The people had wanted a king so that he would "go out before us and fight our battles" (1 Samuel 8:20). The failure of the folk of Jabesh to call on Saul raises a major question about his kingship. Indeed it is the question raised by the "worthless fellows" at the end of chapter 10: "How can this man save us?" (v. 27)! They seem to have assumed that he could not![8]

The request from the people of Jabesh-gilead appears as a massive vote of no confidence in the new regime established at Mizpah and a reversion to the desires expressed in chapter 8.[9]

The Condition from Nahash (v. 2)

I doubt the people of Jabesh-gilead were expecting Nahash's reply:

> But Nahash the Ammonite said to them, "On this condition I will make a treaty with you, that I gouge out all your right eyes, and thus bring disgrace on all Israel." (v. 2)

Now we see something of the character of Nahash, this king from the nations. This enemy is a real enemy. He despised the people of Jabesh — indeed all the people of Israel. He mocked their request for a treaty and turned it into an occasion to abuse and humiliate them.

Gouging out the eyes appears to have been a means of degradation imposed on an enemy (see Judges 16:21; 2 Kings 25:7). No doubt Nahash was motivated, at least in part, by a desire for revenge for the defeat inflicted by Jephthah (Judges 11:32, 33). The tables would be turned. If the people of Jabesh could be so ill treated without any kind of defense from their fellow Israelites, that would bring disgrace on the whole nation that had previously subdued the Ammonites.

As we hear Nahash's reference to "all Israel" we are reminded that it was "all" the people who had recently acclaimed Saul as their king (see the four occurrences of "all" in 1 Samuel 10:20, 24). Nahash probably knew nothing of this, but the "disgrace" that would be brought on "all Israel" would have this added dimension: their newly appointed king could not save the people of Jabesh-gilead from this enemy. If Nahash got his way, the "worthless fellows" of 1 Samuel 10:27 would be vindicated!

This was a very low point in Israel's history. "Disgrace" is something with which Israel and her leaders were threatened if an enemy were to defeat her despite the claim to be the Lord's people (see 1 Samuel 17:26 [ESV, "reproach"]; Isaiah 25:8 [ESV, "reproach"]; Ezekiel 36:15 [ESV, "reproach"]; cf. 1 Samuel 25:39 [ESV, "insult"]). The exodus from Egypt and the conquest of Canaan had meant the rolling away of "disgrace" from Israel (Joshua 5:9; ESV, "reproach"). Eventually, when the nation was finally destroyed, "disgrace" returned (Lamentations 5:1). On this day Nahash threatened to bring the shame of an utterly humiliating defeat for the people who were called the Lord's people.

The unpleasant violence of 1 Samuel 11 begins with the character and intentions of the enemy. He was bent on brutal cruelty and degradation.

The Response from Jabesh (v. 3)

Listen to the response of the elders of Jabesh:

> The elders of Jabesh said to him, "Give us seven days respite that we may send messengers through all the territory of Israel. Then, if there is no one to save us, we will give ourselves up to you." (v. 3)

They sound pathetic. Remember what Samuel said in 1 Samuel 10:19: "you have rejected *your God*, who saves you." As though to demonstrate the accuracy of Samuel's words, in this crisis the elders did not cry out to God (as the people did, for example, in Exodus 14:10; Judges 3:9, 15; 4:3; 6:7; 10:10, 12; cf. 1 Samuel 7:9; 12:8, 10; Nehemiah 9:27). They did not even send for "the ark of the covenant of the LORD" as they once did (1 Samuel 4:4). They certainly did not send for Saul who had been chosen by God to save them (1 Samuel 9:16). Like the men at the end of chapter 10, they did not expect *him* to save them. Saul did not even come to their minds.[10] They proposed to "send messengers through all the territory of Israel" in the vague hope that there might be *someone* to save them.

Why they thought Nahash might agree to such a proposal is difficult to guess, but that they would make such a request underlines their wretched plight. Apparently Nahash thought so little of Israel's strength that he played with them, like a cat with a mouse.[11] He let them have their seven days.[12] After seven days, however, everyone knew that there would be violence. This enemy was real.

THE SAVIOR IN GIBEAH (vv. 4-7)

The News Reached Gibeah (v. 4)

The account does not waste time following the messengers as they went all over Israel. We are taken straight to the moment when they "happened" to arrive at Gibeah, Saul's town.[13] But even then, the messengers did not seek out Saul:[14] "When the messengers came to Gibeah of Saul, they reported the matter in the ears of the people, and all the people wept aloud" (v. 4).

The unlikelihood of a savior for Jabesh-gilead emerging from Gibeah, of all places, is clear when we recall how Gibeah had been at the center and was the cause of the terrible and gory internal conflict recounted in Judges 19–21. The people of Gibeah, by a dreadful crime, had come close to destroying one of the tribes of Israel (see Judges 21:3) and were also the cause of a deadly attack on Jabesh-gilead (see Judges 21:10, 11).

The mention of "Gibeah *of Saul*" reminds us, however, that this was the home to which Saul had returned after the king-making assembly at Mizpah (1 Samuel 10:26).[15] Careful hearers of this story will remember that God had said of Saul, "He shall save my people" (1 Samuel 9:16). At this point the people either did not know that or they did not believe it. The thought does not appear to have crossed the minds of even Saul's own townsfolk. They did not send for Saul. Indeed they seem to have gone beyond those who asked at the end of chapter 10, "How can this man save us?" to the point of giving "this man" no thought at all. They just wept.[16]

The News Reached Saul (v. 5)

As they were weeping, someone who had missed the arrival of the messengers "happened" to appear: "Now, behold, Saul was coming from the field behind the oxen" (v. 5a).

We first met him pursuing donkeys (1 Samuel 9:3). Saul's appearance now behind the oxen is incongruous. Not much seems to have changed for this man despite his acclamation as Israel's king (1 Samuel 10:24)![17] Our impression of Saul as a man who had not yet done anything king-like continues.

And as though to underline the fact that no one was looking to Saul for help here, Saul had to *ask* what was going on: "And Saul said, 'What is wrong with the people, that they are weeping?' So they told him the news of the men of Jabesh" (v. 5b).

Do you see the situation? Terrible violence threatened. Saul was the one who had been anointed by God as king to save his people (1 Samuel 9:16; 10:1). He had been acclaimed by all the people as king (1 Samuel 10:24). The terms of his kingship had been spelled out (1 Samuel 10:25). But now, even here in his own hometown, no one looked to him for help. We are even left wondering where those men were now "whose hearts God had touched" (1 Samuel 10:26).

The Spirit of God (v. 6)

That situation was about to change, but not by Saul's initiative, nor by the people's. "And the Spirit of God rushed upon Saul when he heard these words, and his anger was greatly kindled" (v. 6).

This was God-inspired rage. The anger inspired in Saul by the Spirit of

God was obviously directed at the threat posed to the people of Jabesh-gilead by Nahash and the Ammonites. The association between God's Spirit (or Breath) and his wrath against evil is an important Biblical theme (see Isaiah 40:7; 61:1-3; Matthew 3:11, 12). It was prominent in the book of Judges, where the Spirit drove the judges to violent action against the oppressors of God's people (see particularly Judges 14:19).

In itself Saul's experience seems almost identical to that of the earlier judges (see Othniel in Judges 3:10, Gideon in Judges 6:34, Jephthah in Judges 11:29, and especially Samson in Judges 14:6, 19 and 15:14 where the same verb "rushed" is used to describe the Spirit's coming).[18]

However, the Spirit of God had "rushed" on Saul earlier (1 Samuel 10:10). On that occasion the event should have been the precursor to action from Saul (1 Samuel 10:7), presumably against the Philistines (1 Samuel 10:5). In fact Saul did nothing then, and so this second "rushing" of the Spirit on Saul might be seen as "a booster shot to stir him into action."[19]

Action from Saul (v. 7)

On this occasion Saul was at last stirred to action:

> *He took a yoke of oxen and cut them in pieces and sent them throughout all the territory of Israel by the hand of messengers, saying, "Whoever does not come out after Saul and Samuel, so shall it be done to his oxen!"* (v. 7a)

It was just as well the donkeys weren't around!

Saul sent the messengers (the same messengers as in verse 4[20]) on the same course ("throughout all the territory of Israel," see verse 3), but with a rather different message. They had gone out on a search for a deliverer. Now the God-appointed deliverer powerfully challenged those who had apparently failed to see him as their savior to come out and follow him or else![21]

We have noticed that various elements in the present context are reminders of Judges 19–21 (the assembly at Mizpah, see Judges 20:1; the tribe of Benjamin, Judges 20:14; the town of Gibeah, Judges 19:14; and the trans-Jordan town of Jabesh-gilead, Judges 21:8; as well as the matter of kingship, Judges 19:1 and 21:25). The first of the horrors recounted in the earlier episode was the gang rape and murder in Gibeah of the Levite's concubine, who was then cut into twelve pieces and sent "throughout all the territory of Israel" (Judges 19:29). Saul's action (again from Gibeah!) with the oxen was an awful reminder[22] of those days when "there was no king in Israel" and "Everyone did what was right in his own eyes" (Judges 21:25; cf. 19:1). Saul's action marked the new beginning. Now there *was* a king in Israel! What difference would that make?[23]

Notice carefully how the call was to "come out after Saul *and Samuel.*" Like it or not, Saul was *not* going to be a king "like the nations." It was not a matter of rejecting Samuel and choosing Saul (cf. 1 Samuel 8:7, 8). That kind of kingship (the kind of king they had demanded in 1 Samuel 8:19, 20) was not on offer to God's people Israel.

So what happened? "Then the dread of the LORD fell upon the people, and they came out as one man" (v. 7b).

There was nothing heroic in this. It was not noble or virtuous. Just as Saul's rage was inspired by God's Spirit, so the people's response to Saul was brought about by the hand of God upon them.[24] The men who had stuck with Saul in 1 Samuel 10:26 were men "whose hearts God had touched." Now God touched many more hearts, and out they came — trembling.

THE VICTORY FROM BEZEK (vv. 8-11)

The Muster at Bezek (v. 8)

> When he mustered them at Bezek, the people of Israel were three hundred thousand, and the men of Judah thirty thousand. (v. 8)

Bezek was well north of Gibeah, approximately as far north as Jabesh-gilead, but still in the hills on the western side of the Jordan River. Although we have previously noted that "thousand" may refer to a body of people considerably less than a thousand (see 1 Samuel 4:2, 10; 8:12; 10:19; 13:2, 5; 15:4), the gathering at Bezek was still very considerable.

There may be a veiled irony in the reference to Israel and Judah.[25] Saul's kingship began with a remarkable union of the people "as one man," united by the dread of the Lord (v. 7). It was, however, a fragile unity, for a later king would cause this people to be divided into the kingdoms mentioned (in anticipation) here, Israel and Judah (1 Kings 12:16-20).

The "Gospel" for Jabesh-gilead (v. 9)

> And they said to the messengers who had come, "Thus shall you say to the men of Jabesh-gilead: 'Tomorrow, by the time the sun is hot, you shall have deliverance.'" (v. 9a)

The messengers were sent on a third mission, with yet another message. They were to return to Jabesh-gilead with the good news that deliverance was at hand! What a gospel they had to proclaim: news of a savior![26]

We should notice, however, the remarkable fact that this gospel (if we may call it that) was now believed by the large body of people who had gathered at Bezek. "They" told the messengers to take the good news back to Jabesh-gilead. Therefore we must conclude that not only had "the dread of the LORD" fallen on them, but also a new confidence in his power and goodwill toward them.

The promise of salvation before midday the next day suggests that Saul and the people would cover the twenty miles or so from Bezek east across the Jordan Valley to Jabesh-gilead by night to avoid detection and ensure a surprise attack. "When the messengers came and told the men of Jabesh, they were glad" (v. 9b).

Of course they were glad! The news the messengers brought was better than they could have hoped for! However, they could have been in no doubt that "salvation" (ESV, "deliverance") for them would mean violence. Tomorrow, before noon, there would be bloodshed.

The Victory (vv. 10, 11)

With some cunning the Jabesh people gave the Ammonites the impression that their search had failed: "Therefore the men of Jabesh said, 'Tomorrow we will give ourselves up to you, and you may do to us whatever seems good to you'" (v. 10).

"We will give ourselves up to you" is, more literally, "we will come out to you" (the same verb as in verse 7). This is also the verb that was used in the people's promise to Nahash in verse 3. It can mean "come out to fight" (see Genesis 14:8; 1 Samuel 8:20; 18:30; 2 Samuel 18:2-4, 6; Amos 5:3[27]). The ambiguity would have escaped Nahash, who was, no doubt, confirmed in his complacency by the apparent promise of the men of Jabesh.

Events unfolded, however, rather differently from Nahash's expectations:

> And the next day Saul put the people in three companies. And they came into the midst of the camp in the morning watch and struck down the Ammonites until the heat of the day. And those who survived were scattered, so that no two of them were left together. (v. 11)

The "morning watch" would have been from about 2 to 6 A.M. The night crossing of the Jordan is implied. The three companies probably came at the Ammonite camp from three different directions (cf. Judges 7:16-18, 20, 21; 9:43; 1 Samuel 13:17, 18).[28] The details of the bloody battle, beginning just before dawn and lasting until about noon, do not need to be labored. It is clear that many Ammonites fell in battle that day. In striking contrast to the people of Israel who had come out "as one man" (v. 7), the surviving Ammonites were scattered "so that no two of them were left together."

And so the violent enemy was violently defeated, just as the Philistines had been smitten under Samuel's leadership earlier (1 Samuel 7:11). But, of course, we must remember that back on the western side of the Jordan Valley, the Philistine problem remained.[29]

Before we see the consequences that flowed from this remarkable victory (1 Samuel 11:12-15), let us come back to our earlier questions about Christian evangelism as warfare. What light is shed on our efforts to proclaim the gospel of Jesus by Saul's conquest of Nahash?

Let me draw to your attention just two things.

First, Christian evangelism has this in common with Saul's conflict: the enemy is real. Precisely because the enemy in this case is not a physical enemy, evangelism cannot and must not be physically violent. However, we do not take the gospel into a happy marketplace, selling an idea to eager customers. There is an enemy. An evil enemy. An enemy hostile to God, God's purposes, and God's people. The enemy has an army: unbelief, godlessness, pride, ignorance, sin. And the proclamation of the gospel is a war against the enemy and his forces. Do not forget that the war is not a worldly war. Our weapons must be the weapons of righteousness — and no other. But do not think that what we go to do can be painless.

Second, and even more important, we must see that the New Testament uses battle language for gospel proclamation only *after* it shows us God's appointed King has already won the victory. What God did through Saul that day is a pale shadow of what God did to the great enemy when King Jesus died on the cross. We go to battle only after the decisive battle. The blood has been shed. The enemy has in fact fallen. Do not be afraid. Just as Saul said "Today the LORD has worked salvation in Israel" (1 Samuel 11:13), we hear the New Testament word:

> . . . behold, now is the day of salvation. We put no obstacle in anyone's way, so that no fault may be found with our ministry, but as servants of God we commend ourselves in every way: by great endurance, in afflictions, hardships, calamities, beatings, imprisonments, riots, labors, sleepless nights, hunger; by purity, knowledge, patience, kindness, the Holy Spirit, genuine love; by truthful speech, and the power of God; with the weapons of righteousness for the right hand and for the left; through honor and dishonor, through slander and praise. We are treated as impostors, and yet are true; as unknown, and yet well known; as dying, and behold, we live; as punished, and yet not killed; as sorrowful, yet always rejoicing; as poor, yet making many rich; as having nothing, and yet possessing everything. (2 Corinthians 6:2b-10)

The proclamation of the gospel is rarely impressive in worldly terms. But the God who wrought salvation in Israel that day long ago is doing it still.

17

Kingdom Renewal

I

1 SAMUEL 11:12-15

The claim of the Christian gospel is extraordinary. "Christ Jesus came into the world to save sinners" (1 Timothy 1:15). Are you convinced that Jesus Christ *can* save sinners? Of course, you would need some understanding of what he came to save sinners *from* before you could answer that question sensibly. The truth is that he came to save sinners from a terrible enemy. The powers of evil that enslave human beings in their rebellion against God will bring their captives to death and hell. Jesus Christ came into the world to save sinners. Are you persuaded that this man can save you?

If your answer is yes, then I strongly suspect that you are a Christian. This man, Christ Jesus, is your King, whom you gladly love and serve. If, however, you find that your honest answer to my question is uncertain, or even negative, then it is likely that this is the reason you are *not* a Christian. In order to become a Christian perhaps this is the question you need answered: How can this man save me?

Many years ago some people in Israel found themselves asking precisely that question about Saul, the newly designated leader, chosen by God to "save" them from their enemies, the Philistines (1 Samuel 9:16). "How can this man save us?" they asked (1 Samuel 10:27). Frankly, in their case the question was not serious. It was a mocking question. They were quite sure that this man could *not* save them. They despised him. Our narrator judged them to be "worthless fellows."

Their question, however, expressed a lack of conviction about Saul's capacities that proved to be widespread in Israel. In the same way we find that many, many people today think little of Jesus Christ, presumably because they do not believe that he can save them.

We have seen that in Saul's case his capacity to save the people of Israel was demonstrated in a rather dramatic fashion as he rescued the terrified people of Jabesh-gilead from the dreadful threats of Nahash and the Ammonites. The story was told in the first eleven verses of 1 Samuel 11. It is right for us to observe that Jesus Christ has also demonstrated, in no less a dramatic manner, his capacity to save. He overcame evil by never once yielding to it. When wicked men eventually put him to death, he conquered death and rose from the grave, never to die again. "Consequently he is able to save to the uttermost those who draw near to God through him" (Hebrews 7:25).

The question asked by the "worthless fellows" in 1 Samuel 10:27 was answered as powerfully as could be imagined. The question about Jesus Christ's ability to save has been answered even more powerfully.

The consequences that flowed from the demonstration of Saul's power to save were huge for the people of Israel. As we follow the brief description of the immediate aftermath of his victory over the Ammonites, we will also see something of the consequences of Jesus Christ's demonstrated power to save.

THEY RECOGNIZED THE WICKEDNESS OF REJECTING GOD'S KING (v. 12)

Now that it was obvious to everyone that those who doubted Saul's ability to save at the end of chapter 10 were wrong, the people recognized the wickedness of rejecting God's king. "This man" had decisively and powerfully "saved" them. "The people" therefore distanced themselves from those "worthless fellows" who had despised him: "Then the people said to Samuel, 'Who is it that said, "Shall Saul reign over us?" Bring the men, that we may put them to death.'" (v. 12)

Too much should not be made of the fact that the question here is different in wording from the question in 1 Samuel 10:27. The doubt expressed about Saul's ability to save in 1 Samuel 10:27 is reasonably interpreted as an unwillingness to have him as king.[1] After all, who would want to have a man who could not save them as their king?

We have observed, however, through the narrative of chapter 11 that almost everyone seemed to have doubted Saul's ability to save. If we take the account of the assembly at Mizpah seriously (1 Samuel 10:17-27), with its references to "all the people" (three times in verse 24!), the only explanation for the fact that no one in 1 Samuel 11:1-4 thought to send for Saul is that no one thought that he would be able to save the people of Jabesh-gilead. Admittedly it was only the people of Jabesh and of Gibeah who appear in 1 Samuel 11:1-4 with the opportunity to call on Saul. However, throughout the land the people only came out to follow Saul after a severe threat and an act of God (1 Samuel 11:7). The doubt expressed by the "worthless men" in 1 Samuel 10:27 seems to hang over all Israel in 1 Samuel 11, at least until verse 7.

Now, however, "the people" were keen to lay blame for this attitude on others, not on themselves. "Who was it that said . . . ?" The human habit of shifting blame and pointing the finger is as old as Genesis 3 (see vv. 12, 13). What they *did* understand, however, was the seriousness of rejecting the one they now saw was God's king. What arrogance it was for people to refuse the one chosen by God to reign over them, with the excuse that they doubted he was up to the job!

Jesus revealed the wickedness of this attitude in his parable of the ten minas (Luke 19:11-27). In an only slightly veiled reference to himself, the man who had gone away to be appointed king was hated by the citizens. "We do not want this man to reign over us," they said (v. 14). The king on his return said, "But as for these enemies of mine, who did not want me to reign over them, bring them here and slaughter them before me" (v. 27). The people of Israel were not wrong to see the rejection of God's chosen king as a very wicked thing. It is no less wicked today for people to reject Jesus, the King whom God has appointed (cf. Acts 2:36).

Notice that the people addressed their words to Samuel. Samuel's continuing authority, even over Saul, had been clear in 1 Samuel 10:25. The people had come out after Saul *and* Samuel in 1 Samuel 11:7. It was fully appropriate that the people who were now expressing their acceptance of Saul as king also recognized the standing of Samuel among them.

THEY DISCOVERED THE GRACE OF THE DAY OF GOD'S KING (v. 13)

It was Saul who responded to them, and in his response the people discovered the grace of the day of God's king: "But Saul said, 'Not a man shall be put to death this day, for today the LORD has worked salvation in Israel'" (v. 13).

This was an important moment ("this day," "today"). On a previous day a couple of other "worthless fellows" (1 Samuel 2:12 uses exactly the same expression for Eli's sons as we found in 1 Samuel 10:27) who had shown contempt for the things of God (compare 1 Samuel 2:17 and 10:27) were put to death (1 Samuel 4:11). This was the Lord's doing (see 1 Samuel 2:25, 34). "This day," however, was completely different from that earlier day. On this day the Lord had worked "salvation" in Israel. How very different from what the Lord worked in 1 Samuel 4! If the Lord had chosen to save and not to put to death, then far be it from Saul to countenance any contrary action.

The "worthless fellows" had asked, "How can this man save us?" (1 Samuel 10:27). Saul understood very clearly that the deliverance Israel had now experienced was the Lord's doing and answered their question.

God had proved himself again to be "your God, who saves you from all your calamities and your distresses" (1 Samuel 10:19). "This man" *could* save Israel, but not by virtue of his own abilities. *The Lord* had anointed him and empowered him to save his people (1 Samuel 9:16; 10:1).

The grace of Saul toward those who had opposed him was impressive. It was not unlike Jesus when he said, "If anyone hears my words and does not keep them, I do not judge him; for I did not come to judge the world but to save the world" (John 12:47). This did not mean that judgment would not come eventually to such people. It did mean that judgment was not the purpose of Jesus' first coming. He came to save, and those who have rejected him must hear that.

THEY HEARD THE CALL TO RENEW THE KINGDOM (v. 14)

It was Samuel's turn to speak: "Then Samuel said to the people, 'Come, let us go to Gilgal and there renew the kingdom'" (v. 14).

Gilgal was certainly an appropriate place to go after what had happened. It was one of the centers visited annually by Samuel as he "judged" Israel (1 Samuel 7:16). Gilgal's name was meant to be a perpetual reminder that through the exodus and the safe entry of the people of Israel into the land of Canaan God had "rolled away the reproach [or disgrace] of Egypt" (Joshua 5:9). Now the Lord had once again delivered Israel from threatened "disgrace" (1 Samuel 11:2). How fitting then to "go to Gilgal" once again!

More puzzling is what they were to do at Gilgal: "Let us . . . there renew the kingdom." It is worth spending some time reflecting on what Samuel meant by this call. It is fair to say that what was about to happen at Gilgal is the key for understanding the story of Saul. It is in fact critical for our understanding of the whole book of 1 Samuel. It is certainly important for seeing the consequences for the people of Saul's victory.

The defining questions are: (1) What "kingdom" did Samuel exhort the people to "renew"? and (2) What did it mean for the people to "renew" this kingdom?

"Kingdom" is a weighty word. It generally means "kingship, kingly office, royalty."[2] Therefore when we ask what kingdom Samuel meant, we are asking, *whose kingship* was he referring to? The word has occurred only twice previously in 1 Samuel, both times in the narrative of Saul, and on both occasions it contained an important ambiguity.

In 1 Samuel 10:16 the phrase "the word of the kingdom" (ESV, "the matter of the kingdom") was the narrator's way of describing Samuel's speech in 1 Samuel 10:1-8, although there Samuel had said nothing explicitly about a king. And so we may ask, whose "kingdom" did the narrator see as the subject of Samuel's speech? At one level we now know that Samuel's words would lead to Saul's acclamation as king (1 Samuel 10:24).

In this sense, Samuel's speech might be described as "the word of [Saul's] kingdom." However, at a deeper level the Lord was Israel's true King (see 1 Samuel 12:12). In his appointment of Saul, God was still acting as Israel's King. Although the people *intended* to reject God from being their king (see 1 Samuel 8:7; 10:19), the Lord had no intention of surrendering his claim on "my people Israel" (1 Samuel 9:16), "his heritage" (1 Samuel 10:1). Therefore the speech of Samuel in 1 Samuel 10:1-8 is appropriately described as "the word of *God's* kingdom."

In 1 Samuel 10:25 Samuel told the people about "the justice of the kingdom" (ESV, "the rights and duties of the kingship") and wrote this in a book that was laid up before the Lord. Again there was a subtle ambiguity. Whose "kingdom" did Samuel write about? Certainly what he wrote had implications for *Saul's* kingdom, acclaimed in the preceding verse. However, it is likely that Samuel wrote something like Deuteronomy 17:14-20, establishing the principle that a king in Israel must not be like the kings of the nations, for God was Israel's true King. The kingdom of which Samuel spoke and wrote in 1 Samuel 10:25 was therefore, again, *God's* kingdom — the heavenly King to whom a human king must submit.

I am not suggesting that we need to choose between these two senses of kingdom in these contexts, but rather that we should appreciate the subtle ambiguity. "The kingdom" was both Saul's kingdom *and* God's kingdom. This is the important issue behind the whole story of Saul. How could there be a human king *without* rejecting the heavenly King?[3]

If we have been correct to see at least an allusion to the kingdom *of God* in each of the previous references to "the kingdom," then when Samuel called the people to Gilgal to "renew the kingdom" in 1 Samuel 11:14, we should again recognize the important ambiguity. At one level Samuel's call could be understood in terms of reaffirming allegiance to Saul as king. After all, since "all the people" acclaimed him as king in 1 Samuel 10:24, there had been little evidence of confidence in his kingdom. The "men of valor" (1 Samuel 10:26) who went with Saul back to Gibeah, their hearts touched by God, appear to have been few.[4] The question of the "worthless fellows" ("How can this man save us?") seems to have better represented the wider attitude in the early part of 1 Samuel 11.[5] Now that Saul's ability to save had been so powerfully demonstrated, it was no doubt fitting to call the people to "renew the kingdom [of Saul]," that is, to reaffirm the acclamation of Saul as king that they had made in 1 Samuel 10:24.[6]

However, the location of this assembly in Gilgal (with its unavoidable associations; see Joshua 4:19-24) and the underlying problem that had been behind the whole push from the people for a king — namely, the fact that this was an expression of their desire to be rid of God as their King — suggests that Samuel's call to "renew the kingdom" at Gilgal had a deeper meaning as well. By all means they should reaffirm their recognition of Saul as the one chosen by God to be their leader, but more importantly they must reaffirm their recognition and acceptance of the Lord as their King. The kingdom that was most in need of "renewal" was the kingdom of God.

If this is correct,[7] then, the "renewal" Samuel called for was, fundamentally, the reestablishment of the people's acceptance of God as their king, after the foolish attempt to reject him in their demand for a king "like all the nations."[8] In 1 Samuel 12 we will see that this is exactly what happened at Gilgal.

Samuel's call brings to a climax the issue that had been in the air since the elders first approached Samuel with their request for a king. Could Israel have a human king without nullifying the kingly rule of God over his people?[9] Samuel's message would be that that is the *only* way in which Israel may have a king.

Samuel's call to "renew the kingdom" therefore anticipates Jesus' instruction to his disciples to pray "Your kingdom come" (Matthew 6:10) and his call to "seek first the kingdom of God and his righteousness" (Matthew 6:33).

THEY LEARNED THE GOODNESS OF GOD'S WAYS (v. 15)

First Samuel 11 concludes with a brief account of what happened at Gilgal, which will be elaborated in the following chapter:[10] "So all the people went to Gilgal . . ." (v. 15a).

The people (notice: "*all* the people," as in 1 Samuel 10:24) acted in obedience to Samuel's word. They went to Gilgal. This is very encouraging! It may seem a small thing, but it expresses a very different attitude to God's prophet from the one we saw in chapter 8, when "the people refused to obey the voice of Samuel" (v. 19).

The text emphasizes, by repetition, the name of the place to which they went. In verses 14, 15 "Gilgal" occurs three times and "there" (that is, Gilgal) four times. The location is important. In obedience to the word of Samuel all the people went to the place where the exodus from Egypt had reached its goal (see Joshua 4:19-24; 5:9-12).

At Gilgal something was done and something was said. What was done is briefly described here. The words, which as usual make sense of the actions, are reported in chapter 12. Here we note the simple but very important description of what was done: ". . . and there they made Saul king before the Lord in Gilgal" (1 Samuel 11:15b).

Far too much has been made of a tension that is perceived by some between the three accounts of how Saul became king. Firstly, there was the secret anointing by Samuel in 1 Samuel 10:1, which we must assume was for Saul's benefit, because he was the only one (apart from Samuel) who knew of it. Secondly, in 1 Samuel 10:20-24 Samuel publicly identified Saul as "him whom the Lord has chosen," and all the people shouted, "Long live the king!" (v. 24). After the terms of the kingdom ("the justice of the kingdom") were explained and written down by Samuel (1 Samuel 10:25), there seems to have been a cooling of the initial enthusiasm, even expressed in the doubting question, "How can this man save us?" (1 Samuel 10:27). It was clear at the beginning of chapter 11 that Saul was not acting as king, nor were the people expecting him to do so.[11] Thirdly, only now, in Gilgal, was Saul actually "made king."[12] This sequence of events is understandable in its own terms and is not at all contradictory.

It is very important, however, to notice that in Gilgal they made Saul king "before the Lord" (1 Samuel 11:15). He was not made a king like all the nations have, but he was made king before (that is, in the presence of, literally "to the face of") *the* King. Saul's kingdom was set in its proper relation to the Lord's kingdom.[13] This, as we will see, is precisely what will be proclaimed by Samuel in chapter 12. It is, if we have understood correctly, what was required for this kingdom according to Samuel's explanation of "the justice of the kingdom" in 1 Samuel 10:25.

This arrangement was good! At last the people had returned to the Lord after the apostasy of rejecting God as their King and Savior (1 Samuel 8:7; 10:19), and they knew well that this was something to celebrate: "There they sacrificed peace offerings before the Lord, and there Saul and all the men of Israel rejoiced greatly" (v. 15c).

The peace offerings signified "the fellowship and communion of God with his people."[14] The rejoicing was fitting for people whose relationship to their God had been restored. Notice again that "*all* the men of Israel" rejoiced.

In chapter 12 we will hear the powerful speech that Samuel gave there at Gilgal. In it Samuel will spell out the important fact that lies behind all that had happened since that day at Ramah when the elders had come to Samuel with their preposterous demand (1 Samuel 8:5):

> For the Lord will not forsake his people, for his great name's sake, because it has pleased the Lord to make you a people for himself.
> *(1 Samuel 12:22)*

The experience of the people of Israel in 1 Samuel 11 had the fingerprints of God all over it. It is an experience with which I hope you are familiar, though in deeper terms. Following the great victory that has been won for you by Jesus Christ, do you now recognize the wickedness of rejecting him as King? Have you seen that in him God has worked a great salvation, in the light of which you must now live and treat others? Come, then, let us go to the cross and there renew the kingdom! How good that is and a cause for great joy (see Luke 2:10; Jude 24)!

18

Kingdom Renewal
II

1 SAMUEL 12

The account of how Saul became Israel's first king has been a story of conflict. Power conflicts are familiar to all of us. It is difficult to imagine human life without conflicts of power. Such conflicts emerge from time to time, in various ways, in all human relationships and communities — from families to nations. Some power conflicts, of course, are much more serious than others. Conflict is often unavoidable and must be engaged in, not evaded.

The conflict we see in these pages of the Old Testament, however, is of particular importance. It was the conflict between the power of God and human power. The proposal, put up by the elders of Israel, had been to have a king *"like all the nations"* (1 Samuel 8:5) — a human king, with the power of a human king and the stability and security such power could provide. In that request, God himself said, "they have rejected me from being king over them" (1 Samuel 8:7). They were rejecting the kingdom (that is, kingship) of God for the power of a human king.

The conflict between the kingdom of God and human power is not unfamiliar to us. Christian people (by definition) are those who know that Jesus Christ is King over all things. His kingdom is the kingdom of God. He came into Galilee, a thousand years after Saul, "proclaiming the gospel of God, and saying, 'The time is fulfilled, and the kingdom of God is at hand'" (Mark 1:14, 15). He has called us to enter the kingdom of God by accepting him as Lord. We belong to the kingdom of God by belonging to Jesus. We look forward to the promise of the kingdom of God finally coming in all its fullness when Jesus returns. In the meantime we experience various forms of human power challenging the kingdom of God. Human wealth offers pleasures and security without any need for God. Human reason offers understanding of life and the world without reference to God. Human institutions offer purpose and value to people without necessarily resorting to God.

The conflict is not simple. Human power is not *always* godless, and the kingdom of God does not obliterate human activity. The Bible teaches us that human power, wealth, reason, and institutions have a legitimate place in God's good creation. There is not *necessarily* a conflict between the rule of God and the various forms of human power known to us. Those who belong to God's kingdom continue to live active, energetic, and effective human lives.

How, then, should the conflict we experience be resolved? If human power does in fact challenge the kingdom of God, how are the members of God's kingdom to regard human power? How are we to use whatever power God has given us as his human creatures?

Let me invite you to join the people of Israel at the climactic moment in the establishing of Saul as Israel's first king. Samuel had said to the people, "Come, let us go to Gilgal and there *renew the kingdom*" (1 Samuel 11:14).

What happened at Gilgal is told briefly at the end of chapter 11: "all the people went to Gilgal, and there they made Saul king *before the LORD*" (1 Samuel 11:15a): the human power (King Saul) *before* the heavenly King ("before the LORD"). This seems to be what Samuel meant by "renew the kingdom." Chapter 11 closes by informing us that "there Saul and all the men of Israel rejoiced greatly" (1 Samuel 11:15b).

What did it mean for Saul to be made king "before the LORD"?

In chapter 12 we are given a fuller account, in the form of Samuel's address there in Gilgal,[1] which had as its goal *the renewal of the kingdom*. We will hear the people's responses to what Samuel said. We will learn, therefore, how they "made Saul king *before the LORD*" and what it meant to "renew the kingdom." We will see how the conflict between human power and the kingdom of God was, for the time being, resolved.

THE SITUATION (vv. 1, 2a)

Samuel began by summing up the situation: "And Samuel said to all Israel, 'Behold, I have obeyed your voice in all that you have said to me and have made a king over you'" (v. 1).

The importance of this speech is indicated from the beginning. Samuel addressed "all Israel." This was a moment of national significance. Previously in 1 Samuel "all Israel" had been threatened by Nahash (1 Samuel 11:2), gathered by Samuel at Mizpah to return to the Lord (1 Samuel 7:5), gave a mighty shout when the ark of the covenant came into the camp (1 Samuel

4:5), heard the word of Samuel the prophet (1 Samuel 3:20; 4:1), and suffered under the wicked behavior of Eli's sons (1 Samuel 2:22). Now at Gilgal Samuel addressed "all Israel."

The speech began with a clear reference to the occasion at Ramah where the elders of Israel had first proposed the appointment of a king (1 Samuel 8:5). On the surface Samuel was presenting his act of making them a king as a response to their demand. "I have obeyed [or heeded] your voice." However, in saying this Samuel reproduced the very words God spoke to him on that earlier occasion: "Obey the voice of the people in all that they say to you" (1 Samuel 8:7). Therefore, at a deeper level we can see (although the people listening to Samuel at Gilgal may not have seen[2]) that Samuel was presenting his act of giving the people a king as an act of obedience to God. This paradox is an expression of the fact that at one level Saul was "your king, whom you have chosen for yourselves" (1 Samuel 8:18; cf. 12:13a); but at another level he was "him whom the LORD has chosen" (1 Samuel 10:24; cf. 12:13b). How could Saul be *both* of those things? Samuel's whole speech will answer that question.

Samuel's words, "I . . . have made a king over you," may refer to the event described in 1 Samuel 11:15, where the people "made Saul king before the LORD." There is no necessary contradiction between Samuel making Saul king and the people making Saul king. As in 1 Samuel 10:24, both Samuel and the people had a role in Saul's kingship being established and accepted. So it may have been in 1 Samuel 11:15. However, it is also possible (in my opinion more likely) that 1 Samuel 11:15 is a summary of what happened at Gilgal, which is then expanded in 1 Samuel 12. In that case Samuel may have been referring to the whole sequence of events leading up to the assembly at Gilgal, including the private anointing of Saul in 1 Samuel 10:1, the choosing of Saul by lot in 1 Samuel 10:21, his acclamation as king in 1 Samuel 10:24, and the writing of the terms of the kingdom in 1 Samuel 10:25. "I . . . have made a king over you" is a reasonable summary of these events.

Samuel continued: "And now, behold, the king walks before you, and I am old and gray; and behold, my sons are with you" (v. 2a).

In essence he was saying, "There is your king. Look at him — tall, good-looking, and (relatively) young (see 1 Samuel 9:2; 10:23, 24)! And here am I — old and gray" (see 1 Samuel 8:1).

It was as though Israel's future and past were represented by these two figures.[3] There is no difficulty in realizing which was the more attractive. Indeed it was Samuel's old age that the elders had advanced as one reason for their proposal that a king be appointed (1 Samuel 8:5).

The other reason they had advanced was the character of Samuel's sons (1 Samuel 8:5). Samuel mentioned them here too, though he did not say anything about their wickedness.[4] No doubt he had no need to. The character

of Samuel's sons was presumably as well known as that of Eli's boys (see
1 Samuel 2:23b). He simply reminded the people that the purported reasons
for asking for a king were still there, before their eyes.

With the new king and the old prophet/judge (and his sons) both on
display, it may have seemed obvious what was happening. The old order
was being *replaced* by the new. That, however, is precisely what was *not*
happening. Samuel's whole speech was intended to ensure that. Therefore
Samuel was setting this situation before the people in order to make them
think again, and think more deeply.

THE RIGHTEOUSNESS OF THE OLD ORDER (vv. 2b-11)

Samuel's powerful argument began with the vindication of the old order,
first of his own leadership of Israel, apparently about to be replaced by the
new impressive king, and then of the Lord's past dealings with Israel when
they had no king, which will cast a devastating light on their demand for a
king.

Of Samuel (vv. 2b-5)

First, Samuel spoke of himself: "I have walked before you from my youth
until this day" (v. 2b).

He was saying, "I[5] have walked before you [that is, lived and worked
openly before you[6]] for a long time." With the words "from my youth,"
Samuel points us to the story we have followed since the day he was given
to the Lord's service as a small boy (see 1 Samuel 1:26, 27; 2:11, 18, 21b,
26; 3:1, 8).[7] In the light of that long life of service he wanted the people now
to answer some serious questions. "Here I am; testify against me before the
LORD and before his anointed" (v. 3a).

The language suggests a court setting. Samuel put himself in the dock,
so to speak, and invited the people to bring accusations against him before
the Judge (the Lord) and a key witness (the new king).

For these proceedings to take place "before the LORD" would demand
honesty. "The LORD is a God of knowledge, and by him actions are weighed"
(1 Samuel 2:3b). To testify "before . . . his anointed" would mean that the
new king would be a witness to the righteousness of the old order.[8]

"His anointed" is a striking way to refer to Saul at this point. We (the
readers) have been prepared for this. It was the Lord who commanded Samuel
to anoint Saul (1 Samuel 9:16). When he did so, Samuel made it clear to
Saul that the anointing was the Lord's doing (1 Samuel 10:1). However, the
people had not heard either of these things. This is the first public reference
to Saul as the Lord's anointed, although they had heard Samuel call Saul
"him whom the LORD has chosen" (1 Samuel 10:24). This makes it clear at

the outset that the king had been put in place on the Lord's terms: he was *the Lord's* anointed. It also reminds us of the two earlier striking references to the Lord's anointed, one in Hannah's prayer (1 Samuel 2:10), the other in the prophecy of the man of God who came to Eli (1 Samuel 2:35).

Here are the questions the "accused" Samuel put to all Israel:

> *"Whose ox have I taken? Or whose donkey have I taken? Or whom have I defrauded? Whom have I oppressed? Or from whose hand have I taken a bribe to blind my eyes with it? Testify against me and I will restore it to you." (v. 3b)*

The questions amounted to this: had Samuel's power been exercised in an exploitative or oppressive manner? Had he abused his position to "take" from those he was supposed to be serving?[9]

That, of course, is how we commonly experience human power. This partly accounts for our resentment of another human having power over us. Samuel had earlier said to the people that this is precisely what they could expect from the king they were asking for: he would take, take, take (see 1 Samuel 8:11-18). On this day at Gilgal the new king and the old prophet were standing before all Israel. The question, with an obvious allusion to that earlier speech, was: Had Samuel in his many years walking before them ever acted like that?[10] "They said, 'You have not defrauded us or oppressed us or taken anything from any man's hand'" (v. 4).

Another would one day say, "I am among you as the one who serves" (Luke 22:27). Samuel had been like that. Human power among the people of God must always be like that (see Luke 22:26; 2 Timothy 2:24, 25; 1 Peter 4:11; 5:3). "And he said to them, 'The LORD is witness against you, and his anointed is witness this day, that you have not found anything in my hand'" (v. 5a).

The character of Samuel's leadership was vindicated in the sight of all (including, notably, the Lord's anointed, Saul). However, the vindication of Samuel meant the indictment of the people: "The LORD is witness *against you.*" Samuel had invited the people to testify against him (v. 3). Their failure to do so exposed their own guilt, which will be more fully detailed later in this speech. They would shortly find themselves in the dock.

Everyone acknowledged that the Lord himself was witness to the outcome of this stage of the proceedings: "And they said,[11] 'He is witness'" (v. 5b).

Literally what they said was, simply, "Witness." The one-word reply emphasizes that the people had nothing to say against Samuel. They could only agree by echoing his words.

Samuel had made his first point: the old style of leadership had served Israel well. No one could deny it.

Of the Lord (vv. 6-11)

Samuel turned to his second major point: "And Samuel said to the people, 'The LORD is witness, who appointed Moses and Aaron and brought your fathers up out of the land of Egypt'" (v. 6).

Literally Samuel said, "The LORD,[12] who made Moses and Aaron . . ." The Lord who was witness to Samuel's innocence (v. 5) was the one who had "made" leaders for Israel from the beginning (v. 6). Moses and Aaron had been leaders who, under the Lord, had led Israel out of their terrible oppression in Egypt (see, for example, Exodus 4:29, 30; 5:1; 6:13, 26, 27; 7:1, 10, 20; 10:3; 11:10; 12:28, 50). It is true that the leadership of Moses and Aaron was not utterly without fault (see Exodus 32:1-21; Numbers 20:12; 27:14; Deuteronomy 1:37; 3:26; 4:21; Psalm 106:32, 33). The point, however, is that in the matter of the deliverance from Egypt it would be difficult to find fault with their leadership. Just so the people had acknowledged that they could not criticize Samuel's leadership. What these leaders did for Israel was, of course, because of the Lord's goodness to his people. That was Samuel's second topic.

> *"Now therefore stand still that I may plead with you before the LORD concerning all the righteous deeds of the LORD that he performed for you and for your fathers." (v. 7)*

"Now therefore" represents exactly the same Hebrew expression as "And now" in verse 2. As there, it points to a conclusion to be drawn from what has been stated in the previous verse.[13] Having mentioned the Lord's provision of Moses and Aaron and the redemption from Egypt, it was time for all Israel to consider all the wonderful things that the Lord had done for them and their ancestors.

Here Samuel initiated a second stage in the rhetorical court proceedings, in which the roles were changed. The Lord was still the judge, but now Samuel would be the accuser and the people the accused.[14] The Hebrew for "plead" is a form of the important verb elsewhere translated "judge" (see, for example, 1 Samuel 4:18; 7:6, 15-17; 8:5, 6, 20).[15] The sense here is pleading a case, as one might do before a judge, who in this case was the Lord.[16]

Samuel called the things the Lord had done "righteous deeds" (literally, "righteousnesses"[17]). These deeds were expressions of the Lord's faithfulness to his people, the truthfulness of his promises, in other words, his "righteousness" in his dealings with Israel. God's *righteousness* is a major Bible theme (climactically see Romans 1:17; 3:21, 22). In the context of his relationship to Israel, the Lord's righteousness includes (but is not exhausted by) his fulfillment of the terms of the relationship. These terms had been laid down by the Lord himself in his promises and his law. The Lord's righteous deeds could include punishments for Israel's wickedness (see 1 Samuel 12:9), but typically involved his mercy and kindness toward them. This is why people in Israel appealed to the Lord for deliverance on the basis of his righteousness (see, for example, Psalm 5:8; 31:1; 36:10; 71:2; 88:12; 143:1).[18]

Samuel's purpose now was to bring the people to acknowledge all the Lord's acts of righteousness that Israel had been privileged to experience. In due course this would expose their own guilt.

He began with the exodus and the gift of the land:

"When Jacob went into Egypt, and the Egyptians oppressed them, then your fathers cried out to the LORD and the LORD sent Moses and Aaron, who brought your fathers out of Egypt and made them dwell in this place." (v. 8)

Samuel summarized the period covered from the end of the book of Genesis (when "Jacob went into Egypt," Genesis 46) through to the book of Joshua (when they came to dwell in the land, beginning here "in this place," namely Gilgal,[19] Joshua 4:19).[20]

The emphasis is on what the Lord did by means of the leaders he sent. In the Hebrew text it is clear that Moses and Aaron are the subject of "brought your fathers out" and "made them dwell." Although, of course, it was Joshua who actually led the people into the land of Canaan (see Deuteronomy 1:38; 3:28; 31:3, 7; Joshua 1:2), it is obvious that it was Moses and Aaron who made this possible.[21]

These events were the Lord's "righteousnesses" toward the fathers of Samuel's contemporaries. In other words, "Not one word of all the good promises that the LORD had made to the house of Israel failed; all came to pass" (Joshua 21:45). "Can you see," Samuel seems to have been asking, "how utterly righteous the Lord has been in his dealings with you?"

Mind you, the righteous deeds of the Lord toward Israel had not always been pleasant, for good reason:

But they forgot the LORD their God. And he sold them into the hand of Sisera, commander of the army of Hazor, and into the hand of the Philistines, and into the hand of the king of Moab. And they fought against them. (v. 9)

Trouble came, but who was to blame for that?

Israel had failed to heed the warning of Moses: "And you shall remember the whole way that the LORD your God has led you . . ." "Take care lest you forget the LORD your God . . . " (Deuteronomy 8:2, 11). The terms of the relationship between the Lord and Israel were clear: "If you forget the LORD your God and go after other gods and serve them and worship them, I solemnly warn you today that you shall surely perish" (Deuteronomy 8:19).

Therefore Israel's experience of being given over to their enemies was also the Lord's righteousness toward them. The episode with Sisera is recounted in Judges 4, 5 and with the king of Moab (Eglon) in Judges 3:12-30. Israel had experienced the hostility of the Philistines repeatedly (see Judges 3:31; 10:7; 13:1; 1 Samuel 4:1-11; 7:7). These are representative examples of the experience of Israel over a long period of time. Samuel's point was that in these times of oppression the Lord was still acting righteously toward Israel.

In the recent past there had been a period of some twenty years in which the people of Israel had apparently "forgotten" the Lord (1 Samuel 12:9) and suffered at the hands of the Philistines (see 1 Samuel 7:2, 3). This experience was of a piece with those mentioned here by Samuel.

However, there was even more to Israel's historic experience of the "righteousnesses" of the Lord. What happened when the people remembered the Lord again?

> *"And they cried out to the LORD and said, 'We have sinned, because we have forsaken the LORD and have served the Baals and the Ashtaroth. But now deliver us out of the hand of our enemies, that we may serve you.' And the LORD sent Jerubbaal and Barak and Jephthah and Samuel and delivered you out of the hand of your enemies on every side, and you lived in safety." (vv. 10, 11)*

Samuel was the last of the long line of leaders ("judges"), sent by God when Israel repented, to deliver his people from their enemies. Under these leaders they had enjoyed real security. Samuel again cited four representative examples. Jerubbaal (or Gideon, Judges 6:32) is the judge whose story is told in Judges 6–8. Barak's[22] adventure is in Judges 4, 5 (overcoming Sisera), Jephthah's in Judges 11:1–12:7. Of course, the account of Samuel began in 1 Samuel 1 and has included the defeat of the Philistines in 1 Samuel 7.

That was the most recent occasion of such repentance. At Mizpah "the people of Israel put away the Baals and Ashtaroth, and they served the LORD only" (1 Samuel 7:4). By Samuel the Lord then delivered Israel from the Philistines (1 Samuel 7:7-11). "You lived in safety" is an excellent description of the situation we saw in 1 Samuel 7:15-17, just before we heard of the people's demand for a king in chapter 8!

This, however, had been the pattern of the Lord's "righteous" dealings with Israel since the beginning.

Most recently, however, there had been a development.

THE FOOLISH WICKEDNESS OF THE
NEW ORDER (vv. 12, 13)

*"And when you saw that Nahash the king of the Ammonites came against
you, you said to me, 'No, but a king shall reign over us,' when the LORD
your God was your king." (v. 12)*

Here is a new piece of information. Nahash's threat was introduced to
us only in 1 Samuel 11:1. It seems we have one of those situations in the
Biblical narrative where the chronology is a little unclear. I am inclined to
think that the aggression of Nahash first mentioned in 1 Samuel 11:1 began
about the same time as the events of chapter 8. The siege of Jabesh-gilead
could have been protracted. As the long story of chapters 9, 10 was unfolding (but covering, perhaps, about a week[23]), the crisis of chapter 11:1b-11
(which apparently took a week, see 1 Samuel 11:3, 10) was developing —
the two story lines coming together when the news of the threat reached Saul
in Gibeah (1 Samuel 11:5).

We now learn that, according to Samuel, it was the Nahash threat that
had motivated the demand for a king back in chapter 8.[24] The Philistine menace from the west had, for the time being, been subdued (1 Samuel 7:13),
but apparently a new Ammonite danger had arisen from the east. Indeed,
we now see that when the elders asked for a king like the nations, they may
well have meant a king like Nahash! After all, we have already noticed that
the people of Jabesh-gilead actually tried to make Nahash himself their king
(1 Samuel 11:1)! This makes sense of the people's words back in chapter 8,
"that our king may . . . go out before us and fight our battles" (v. 20).

See what had happened. This time they did not "cry out to the LORD,
and say, 'We have sinned, because we have forsaken the LORD and have
served the Baals and the Ashtaroth. But now deliver us out of the hand of our
enemies, that we may serve you'" as they had before (1 Samuel 12:10). This
time, they said, "No, but a king shall reign over us." In this, they showed that
they no longer trusted the Lord their God as their King.

Samuel said to the people, in effect, "As you remember all the righteous
deeds the Lord your God has done for you, take a good look at your preferred alternative": "And now behold the king whom you have chosen, for
whom you have asked; behold, the LORD has set a king over you" (v. 13).

"And now," as in verses 2 and 7, introduces a conclusion to be drawn
from what precedes. "Now that you have asked for a king to replace the
Lord, can you see what you have done? Look at him ("behold")! Tall, good-
looking, young — he's all that — but he is not the Lord your God! What
kind of stupidity would exchange *the Lord your God* for *this*? What kind of
blind insanity would trust this young man *rather than* the Lord your God?

I don't care how tall and impressive he looks — this is madness! No, it is wickedness!" Such is the force of Samuel's argument.

The paradox (which has not yet been resolved) is forcefully expressed in Samuel's words. The king who was standing before them was, on the one hand, the one *they* had chosen, the one for whom *they* had "asked" (cf. 1 Samuel 8:10, 18). Even his name meant "Asked For"! This request of the people had been deeply wicked, a rejection of the God who had done so much for them (see 1 Samuel 8:7, 8; 10:19; 12:17, 19). On the other hand, "Asked For" (Saul) was the one whom *the Lord* had set over them (cf. 1 Samuel 9:16; 10:1, 24). Samuel had now twice referred to him as "[the LORD's] anointed" (1 Samuel 12:3, 5). What was Israel supposed now to do with this king, of whom both these things were true?

THE ULTIMATUM (vv. 14-18)

Samuel had summoned the people here to Gilgal to "renew the kingdom" (1 Samuel 11:14).

So the ultimatum was now issued:

> *"If you will fear the LORD and serve him and obey his voice and not rebel against the commandment of the LORD, and if both you and the king who reigns over you will follow the LORD your God, it will be well." (v. 14)*

That is to say, the only future for this new arrangement — "you and the king" — was if both they and their king feared and served and obeyed *the Lord*. They and their king had *another* King. It was time to renew *that* kingdom.

The phrase "it will be well" has been added by the translators in an attempt to make sense of the sentence here. However, the Hebrew could be translated:[25]

> *"If you will fear the LORD and serve him and obey his voice and not rebel against the commandment of the LORD, then both you and the king who reigns over you will follow the LORD your God."*

This is the language of following "a particular king in a situation where there was another possible alternative" (cf. 2 Samuel 2:10; 15:13; 1 Kings 12:20; 16:21).[26] With Israel and Israel's king following the Lord once again, *the* kingdom would be renewed or restored. *The* King would once again be properly recognized in Israel. The earlier rejection of the Lord as King (1 Samuel 10:19) would have been reversed.

In other words, what was required was repentance from the wicked rejection of the Lord that lay behind the request for a king and submission of the whole new arrangement to the rule of the Lord.

The alternative was disaster:

"But if you will not obey the voice of the LORD, but rebel against the commandment of the LORD, then the hand of the LORD will be against you and your king." (v. 15)

It was a simple choice. Will you and your king — you and your powerful king — you and the human power in which you have placed your hopes — will you submit to another kingdom, or will you not? The crucial test of truly having the Lord as your King was (as it is still, see John 15:14) obedience to his commands. The importance of heeding God's words is vividly expressed in the Hebrew of both verses 14 and 15, where the expression translated "rebel against the commandment of the LORD" is literally, "rebel against the mouth of the LORD."[27]

This was a critical moment in the history of Israel. If they now refused to return to the Lord but persisted with their rejection of him and went their own way with their king, then Israel would indeed become "like all the nations" (1 Samuel 8:20). The Lord would no longer be their God and Savior. Rather, they would find themselves like the Philistines in 1 Samuel 5, 6. Indeed Samuel's words echo the repeated references to the hand of the Lord being against the Philistines (see 1 Samuel 5:6, 7, 9, 11; 6:3, 5, 9).

This warning, as it appears in the Hebrew text, is even more devastating than in the ESV. The last word of verse 15 in the Hebrew is "fathers." The ESV has followed the Septuagint and replaced the word "fathers" with "king," presumably because this better fits the context.[28] However, striking (even puzzling) as it may be, the threat that "the hand of the LORD" would be "against you [the contemporary Israelites] *and your fathers* [their ancestors]" suggests a comprehensive rejection of Israel as a whole. The entire history of Israel would have come to nothing. The hopes of the fathers who had believed the promises of God to Israel would have been dashed. Rarely did the people of Israel ever face such a comprehensive threat as this. They were poised on a precipice. If they did not turn back, it would be the *end* for Israel (cf. Amos 8:2).[29]

While they considered the choice that had been set before them, Samuel offered a remarkable encouragement to decide well: "Now therefore stand still and see this great thing that the LORD will do before your eyes" (v. 16).

"Now therefore" represents a slight variation of the expression "And now" that introduced verses 2, 7, and 13. It may suggest the desperate urgency of this moment. Even now, as the people teetered on the very edge of the abyss, they were called to take notice of a great display of the Lord's power.

Samuel sounded rather like Moses when he announced the salvation the
Lord was about to work when he parted the sea so the Israelites could cross
(Exodus 14:13).[30]

> *"Is it not wheat harvest today? I will call upon the LORD, that he may
> send thunder and rain. And you shall know and see that your wickedness
> is great, which you have done in the sight of the LORD, in asking for your-
> selves a king." (v. 17)*

The promised miracle may not seem as grand as the crossing of the sea
in Exodus 14. Nonetheless it was impressive. The wheat harvest was early
summer, when no rain falls.[31] A thunderstorm in this season would have
been an unknown occurrence.[32]

The goal of God's great acts is typically knowledge of who he is and
his glory (see, for example, Exodus 6:7; 7:5; 8:10, 22; 9:14, 16, 29; 11:7;
16:6; 18:11; Deuteronomy 4:35, 39; Joshua 4:24). Here, however, the demonstration of the Lord's true power and greatness was to teach the people
("you shall know and see") the depth of their own wickedness in trying to
be rid of him.

"This great thing" (v. 16) would be a demonstration of the power of
the Lord God as King of all creation. It would therefore be a demonstration
of the foolish wickedness of Israel's seeking to replace the Lord their God
with a human king. The problem was not with the king as such, but with the
asking,[33] which had included the terrible purpose "that we also may be like
all the nations" (1 Samuel 8:20). "So Samuel called upon the LORD, and the
LORD sent thunder and rain that day, and all the people greatly feared the
LORD and Samuel" (v. 18).

They feared the Lord and Samuel, just as, after the crossing of the sea,
"the people feared the LORD, and they believed in the LORD and his servant
Moses" (Exodus 14:31).[34]

It is interesting and important to notice that Saul must be included here
with "all the people." The future of Israel depended on the people *and their
king* giving proper recognition to the Lord as their true King, and to Samuel
as his prophet. In this king and people were together.

However, imagine young Saul watching all this! To this point the young
man had found himself caught up in events very largely outside his control.
He didn't ask to be king. As old Samuel called to the Lord, and the thunder
crashed, and the rain teemed down, can you see Saul's wide-eyed wonder
— and fear?

REPENTANCE (v. 19)

The situation was deeply serious, and at last everyone could see it:

And all the people said to Samuel, "Pray for your servants to the LORD your God, that we may not die, for we have added to all our sins this evil, to ask for ourselves a king." (v. 19)

This was the response of "all the people" to Samuel's whole speech. They acknowledged Samuel's role: they were his "servants." They saw their need for him to pray for them. They recognized that they had forfeited the right to call the Lord "our God" and referred to him as "your [Samuel's] God." In 1 Samuel 7:8 (before they had asked for a king) the people had asked Samuel to "cry out to the LORD *our* God for us." The tragedy of the king business is captured in their preference now for "*your* God."

As I imagine the scene, it is difficult not to catch a glimpse of the tall, young man shuffling his feet at the awkwardness of his position. He had become Israel's king as a consequence of the nation's climactic evil act. No doubt he was included in the "servants" of Samuel who needed Samuel's prayers!

Despite such imaginings, it is important to appreciate that the interest of the narrative at this point is not on Saul. Indeed neither Samuel nor the people were focusing on Saul. The moment had come for *the kingdom to be renewed.*

THE RENEWAL OF THE KINGDOM (vv. 20-25)

And Samuel said to the people, "Do not be afraid; you have done all this evil. Yet do not turn aside from following the LORD, but serve the LORD with all your heart." (v. 20)

The logic of these words will only become clear in the astonishing verse 22. Until we hear it, what Samuel said must sound unreasonable. He told them (a) not to be afraid, (b) what they had done was indeed evil, (c) they should not do it again (that is, they should not again turn aside from following the Lord, as they had done in their demand for a king), and (d) they should now serve the Lord wholeheartedly.

What grounds could there possibly be for not being afraid? What they had done in asking for a king was not only evil, it was stupid: "And do not turn aside after empty things that cannot profit or deliver, for they are empty" (v. 21).

Again I wonder how Saul was feeling! The point, however, is that all forms of human power (including kingship) to which people turn when they turn away from the Lord must be seen for what they are — empty, pathetic substitutes for the Lord God. The language is powerfully vivid. "Empty" is the word used to describe the emptiness that preceded God's work of creation in Genesis 1:2 (ESV, "without form").

We still need to ask, why did Israel not need to be afraid, and how it is that there was still a future for this rebellious nation? Here is the reason:

"For the Lord will not forsake his people, for his great name's sake, because it has pleased the Lord to make you a people for himself."
(v. 22)

In the history of Israel there was something bigger at stake than the nation's well-being. The Lord had committed himself to this people, and "for his great name's sake" he would not forsake them. This is an astonishing statement. It expresses the absolute sovereignty of God's grace. This is not something that fits neatly into the human mind. While Israel's future had been brought to the very brink of disaster by her recent conduct, in the final analysis Israel's future rested on something utterly reliable — the gracious will of God to make a people for himself. The perplexing problem (to our minds) of the relationship between human responsibility and divine sovereignty arises here. The solution, however, must not be to deny the reality of either in order to make it all comprehensible to us. For his name's sake, that is, for the sake of his own reputation,[35] the Lord would not allow his good purposes for Israel to be destroyed, even by Israel's wickedness. He would bring them back to himself in repentance, and as they came they need not fear. (See similar expressions of this truth in Exodus 32:12-14; Numbers 14:15-19; Joshua 7:9; and especially Ezekiel 36:22-32.)

Ultimately this is why the kingdom had to be renewed or restored. The role of Samuel in the renewed kingdom would be crucial: "Moreover, as for me, far be it from me that I should sin against the Lord by ceasing to pray for you . . ." (v. 23a).

In God's kingdom Israel needed someone to pray for them. Samuel would do that. Indeed, he now tells them that he had never stopped doing so — and would never stop. " . . . and I will instruct you in the good and the right way" (v. 23b).

In God's kingdom Israel needed someone who would teach them the right way to live. Samuel would do that. Indeed he began to do it immediately: "Only fear the Lord and serve him faithfully with all your heart. For consider what great things he has done for you" (v. 24).

That is the way of life in the kingdom of God. Motivated by considering (not forgetting, 1 Samuel 12:9) the great things the Lord had done for them (1 Samuel 12:8),[36] they were to trust him and serve him. It is not sufficient to see the connection between this consideration and the behavior that will be motivated by it simply in terms of gratitude.[37] The "great things" demonstrate the power and righteousness of the Lord, and therefore the foolishness of turning from him: "But if you still do wickedly, you shall be swept away, both you and your king" (v. 25).

The way forward was now as clear as it could be. Israel would have a king. He had been given to them by God himself. However, he was never to *replace* the Lord and his prophet. On the contrary, both people and king were to submit to the Lord's great and good rule. Human power has its place, but only when it is exercised in humble obedience to the Lord.

This was the renewal of the kingdom (1 Samuel 11:14). It was how Saul was made king "before the LORD" in Gilgal (1 Samuel 11:15).

The kingdom of God has now come into this world more powerfully than it had in the days of Samuel. Jesus Christ is the Lord's anointed (or Christ) (see Acts 3:18; Revelation 11:15; 12:10). The kingdom has now been revealed with a fullness and a clarity unknown to Samuel's hearers. The roles of king and prophet are now faithfully exercised for us by Jesus. He prays for us (Romans 8:34; Hebrews 7:25; 1 John 2:1). He teaches us (see, for example, Matthew 7:24; Luke 6:47; John 6:68). We now wait for the day when that kingdom will certainly come with power and glory (see 1 Corinthians 15:24; 2 Timothy 4:1, 18). Nevertheless we find ourselves drawn and attracted and enticed by human power of various kinds. Whenever any form of human power replaces the Lord as the object of our trust and obedience, we need to hear what happened to Israel at Gilgal. Come, let us go to the feet of our Lord Jesus and there renew the kingdom.

19

The Fool

1 Samuel 13

The fool says in his heart, 'There is no God,'" (Psalm 14:1a; 53:1a). The trouble is, that is not what it looks like. It's not what it feels like. Those who deny God in their thinking, speaking, and living do not always (or even usually) seem to be fools.

The words of the psalm are not, of course, a statement about the intellectual capacity of atheists, nor about the rational validity of the proposition, "There is no God." There are many very clever atheists. The proposition "There is no God" can be defended with impressive, intelligent arguments. Some of the brightest people in the world today are atheists. The best arguments against the existence of God are not simply stupid.

Or are they?

My point, however, is that Psalm 14:1 does not say, "The fool says in his *mind*, 'There is no God.'" It is the one who says this *in his heart* who is scorned as a fool.

This is more serious, and more searching. Many may never say in their *mind*, "There is no God," but nevertheless say just that *in their heart*. The issue is the acknowledgment of God not just in my *understanding*, but in my consciousness, in my desires, in my anxieties, in my ups and in my downs, in my inmost thoughts — and therefore in my character and in the things I say and do. The psalm says that the person who *in his heart* says, "There is no God" is a fool.

The trouble is, that is still not what it looks like, is it? Some of the least foolish-looking people take no account of God. In fact, if we are honest, we would probably admit that it sometimes looks very foolish indeed to take God *too seriously*!

That is why most readers of the story of the young King Saul in

1 Samuel 13 feel considerable sympathy for him, and many readers (certainly many commentators) feel uncomfortable with old Samuel when he calls the new king a fool (1 Samuel 13:13). We will only appreciate the importance of this incident when we realize how outrageous and unreasonable Samuel's charge must have seemed. We will soon see that the narrator has used considerable skill in helping us to apprehend just that.

The account of how Saul became Israel's first king began rather unpromisingly in 1 Samuel 8. Through various twists and turns we have seen how Saul was eventually made king at Gilgal under the very clear terms that he and the people must still obey and serve the Lord (see 1 Samuel 11:15; 12:14, 15).

It is at this point in the account that the historian formally begins his account of Saul's rule. This is indicated, in a manner typical of later accounts of the reigns of kings, with a formal summary of Saul's reign. Such details as the age of the king when he took office and the length of his reign are typically recorded at the beginning of the account of a king's rule (see, for example, 2 Samuel 5:4; 1 Kings 14:21).

The problem is that the Hebrew text of 1 Samuel 13:1 tells us that Saul was, literally, "a son of a year" (which would usually mean one year old!) when he became king and that he reigned over Israel for two years. A literal translation of the Hebrew would be: "Saul was a son of a year when he reigned, and two years he reigned over Israel" (v. 1).

Most translations and commentators see a textual problem here and either propose emendations or indicate the problem in the translation, as does the ESV:[1] "Saul was . . . * years old when he began to reign, and he reigned . . . and two* years over Israel."

The ESV footnotes (*) then state, respectively, "The number is lacking in Hebrew and Septuagint" and "*Two* may not be the entire number; something may have dropped out."

An alternative and, in my opinion, far more satisfactory solution is possible.[2] Taking the Hebrew text as it stands, "a son of a year" may point not to Saul's actual age, but to the unusual circumstance whereby Saul became the one designated to become king. For Saul this was not at his birth (as would usually be the case for a crown prince), but only when Samuel anointed him (in 1 Samuel 10:1). It is possible, then, that the "year" of which he was a "son" was the time between that day (when, we might say, he became the crown prince) and the day that he began his reign at Gilgal in 1 Samuel 11:15 on the terms so clearly spelled out by Samuel in 1 Samuel 12.[3] It is then likely that the "two years" that 1 Samuel 13:1 tells us Saul reigned over Israel (which seems too short for all that happened while Saul was king, through to his death in 1 Samuel 31[4]) refers strictly to the period between his *becoming* king (1 Samuel 11:15) and his being finally *rejected* as king, which happens as soon as 1 Samuel 15:28.[5] The account of Saul's reign, strictly speaking, is then just the three chapters of 1 Samuel 13, 14, and 15.[6]

If this is right, the tragedy of Saul's kingdom is already indicated in this opening summary. After all the preparation, after all that had happened to circumvent the disastrous proposal of chapter 8 and to ensure that Israel's king would *not* be "like all the nations," after the promising start in chapter 11, after the real possibility held out in chapter 12, it really lasted only two short years. On this understanding, 1 Samuel 13, 14, and 15 cover these two years.

FEARFUL CIRCUMSTANCES (vv. 2-7)

The account of Saul's reign begins with a snapshot of the military situation. The people had asked for a king to "go out before us and fight our battles" (1 Samuel 8:20). The Ammonite threat from the east had been subdued (1 Samuel 11). However Saul had been chosen by God specifically to deliver Israel from *the Philistines* (see 1 Samuel 9:16). At his anointing Samuel had specifically mentioned the Philistine garrison at Gibeah (1 Samuel 10:5) and told Saul, in effect, to deal with them (1 Samuel 10:7). However, so far Saul had done nothing whatsoever about that garrison, stationed at or near his hometown, let alone address the general Philistine threat. It would be reasonable for us to expect that the first thing Saul would do, now that he was clearly and unambiguously Israel's king, would be to address the Philistine problem.

In order to understand the events as they unfold in this chapter, we need to recall the two instructions that Saul received at the culmination of the word of God spoken to him by Samuel in 1 Samuel 10. First, he was to attack the Philistine presence at Gibeah (the implicit meaning of 1 Samuel 10:7, as we have seen). Second, Saul was then to go down to Gilgal and wait for further instructions from Samuel (1 Samuel 10:8). Since Saul had not yet done anything about the Philistines, these two instructions were, as yet, unfulfilled.[7] If our understanding of 1 Samuel 13:1 is correct, these instructions were given about a year before the drama of the present chapter took place.[8]

Israel's Strength (v. 2)

Given the unresolved Philistine problem, it is no surprise that the account of Saul's reign begins with his formation of an army:

Saul chose three thousand men of Israel. Two thousand were with Saul in Michmash and the hill country of Bethel, and a thousand were with

Jonathan in Gibeah of Benjamin. The rest of the people he sent home,
every man to his tent. (v. 2)

It is possible that the choosing of the 3,000 men took place at Gilgal, at the conclusion of the proceedings described in 1 Samuel 11:15–12:25. The end of the verse then refers to the dismissal of the rest of the people at that time.

This is the first time we hear of Jonathan. Very soon he will be introduced to us properly, and we will learn that he was Saul's son (1 Samuel 13:16). We will hear much more of him.

Saul took his contingent to Michmash, situated directly west of Gilgal, up in the hills and on the north side of a deep valley that ran down to the southeast toward the Jordan River.[9] Michmash features in Biblical history most prominently in 1 Samuel 13, 14 (see also Nehemiah 7:31; 11:31; Isaiah 10:28). About four and a half miles to the northwest was Bethel, and about the same distance southwest, in the hills on the other side of the valley, was Gibeah, Saul's hometown (1 Samuel 10:26). It was here that Jonathan had his troops.

Saul had formed Israel's first standing army. The strategic reasons for the deployment described are not stated. However, it does look like preparation for some kind of action.[10]

Conflict with the Philistines (vv. 3, 4)

Surprisingly, however, it was Jonathan who initiated the long anticipated hostilities against the Philistines, who (as we have seen, 1 Samuel 10:5) had penetrated Israel's territory in these hills. "Jonathan defeated the garrison of the Philistines that was at Geba . . ." (v. 3a).

It seems most probable that this "garrison" was the one mentioned in 1 Samuel 10:5. Either it had moved from Gibeah to Geba (which some locate between Michmash and Gibeah) or (as some argue) Geba is an alternative name for Gibeah.[11]

"Garrison" could also be translated "governor." This may therefore have been an assassination. Otherwise it was a small-scale skirmish against a Philistine outpost. Was this an independent action by Jonathan or one ordered by Saul? We know that Saul had done nothing about the Philistines yet, and Jonathan was perfectly capable of independent action, as we will see in 1 Samuel 14:1.

Whatever Saul's involvement may have been, the first instruction of Saul's commission (1 Samuel 10:7) had now been accomplished, but not (at least directly) by Saul.

We are told, rather ominously, of the immediate consequence of Jonathan's action: ". . . and the Philistines heard of it" (v. 3b).

Down on the other side of the hills, to the west, on the coastal plain, "the

Philistines heard of it." It does not take a genius to guess that they were less than pleased! We can confidently expect that the Philistines would respond with an action such as we have seen before (see 1 Samuel 4:2, 10; 7:7).

Our attention is now taken back to Saul: "And Saul blew the trumpet throughout all the land, saying, 'Let the Hebrews hear'" (v. 3c).

The trumpet, or horn, was mostly used in war (see, for example, Joshua 6:4; Judges 7:8, 16).[12] This was presumably a call to arms. With the trumpet blast there was a message to be heard. To refer to his people as "the Hebrews" was a strange way for Saul to speak. It was often Israel's enemies and oppressors who called the Israelites "the Hebrews" (for example, Exodus 1:22; 2:6; 1 Samuel 4:6, 9; 13:7). It is as though Saul was addressing them as the Philistines saw them and as they may have been seeing themselves (as they certainly could soon become) — people under enemy oppression.

The message "the Hebrews" heard put a slight spin on what had happened but did not underestimate the seriousness of it: "And all Israel heard it said that Saul had defeated the garrison of the Philistines, and also that Israel had become a stench to the Philistines" (v. 4a).

Jonathan's action was heard as Saul's action. It seems that this is how Saul wanted the story told. After all, as we have seen, it was what he was supposed to do some time earlier. Be that as it may, the seriousness of the resulting situation would have been no surprise to anyone. As far as the Philistines were concerned, Israel now *stank*!

A major crisis was looming. What did Saul do next? "And the people were called out to join Saul at Gilgal" (v. 4b).

Why Gilgal? Gilgal was to the east, down in the Jordan Valley, the opposite direction from the Philistines to the west. Gilgal was where Samuel had called the people to "renew the kingdom" (1 Samuel 11:14) and delivered the speech in 1 Samuel 12. More importantly now, however, it was the place where Samuel had told Saul, a year or so earlier, to wait for him once the initial action against the Philistines had taken place:

> "Then *[after acting against the Philistines in Gibeah]* go down before me to Gilgal. *And behold, I am coming to you to offer burnt offerings and to sacrifice peace offerings. Seven days you shall wait, until I come to you and show you what you shall do." (1 Samuel 10:8)*

It seems that this second instruction to Saul had been remembered.

Curiously, at least in the way the account is told, Saul still remained remarkably inactive. We are not told who called the people to Gilgal, but it does not sound as though it was Saul. The text seems to indicate that Saul was now in Gilgal or on his way there[13] (presumably because of the earlier instruction), and somehow the people were summoned to join him there.[14]

Philistine Strength (v. 5)

Saul, remember, had an army of 3,000 chosen men (v. 2). Move back up from Gilgal into the hills, look west, and watch the Philistines:

> And the Philistines mustered to fight with Israel, thirty thousand chariots
> and six thousand horsemen and troops like the sand on the seashore in
> multitude. They came up and encamped in Michmash, to the east of Beth-
> aven. (v. 5)

This massive Philistine force had now occupied Michmash,[15] the very spot that Saul had just vacated. They had ten times as many chariots as Saul had men and twice as many horsemen![16] That was just the beginning of the Philistine force. There were more Philistines than could be counted.

Saul's reign began, therefore, in fearful circumstances. It was a terrifying situation.

Israel's Fear (vv. 6, 7)

That is exactly how the Israelites saw it:

> When the men of Israel saw that they were in trouble (for the people were
> hard pressed), the people hid themselves in caves and in holes and in rocks
> and in tombs and in cisterns, and some Hebrews crossed the fords of the
> Jordan to the land of Gad and Gilead. Saul was still at Gilgal, and all the
> people followed him trembling. (vv. 6, 7)

It is a pitiful scene. The consequences of provoking the Philistines were now all too plain. Saul's people (called "Hebrews" by the narrator, echoing Saul's word in verse 3) started to slip away, to go into hiding, to sneak across the Jordan to the lands of Gad and Gilead to the east, away from the terrible thing that was poised to happen.

However, Saul did not go into hiding. He was the king. He remained in Gilgal, as Samuel had instructed him. He probably had no idea what to do next. In any case Samuel had told him to wait in Gilgal for further instructions. All the people (that is, all who had not yet slipped away and gone into hiding) were right behind their king — trembling with terror!

THE FEARFUL FOOL (vv. 8-15)

Saul's situation was desperate. But he remembered well Samuel's direction of 1 Samuel 10:8.

Saul's Wisdom (vv. 8, 9)

Saul clearly took that direction seriously: "He waited seven days, the time appointed by Samuel" (v. 8a).

Time was precious, but Saul waited. Each day the Philistine advantage grew, but Saul waited. Seven days! Each day he must have anxiously inquired, "Has anyone seen Samuel?" Seven days because that is what Samuel had said. Seven days can pass quickly, but I am sure those seven didn't. Each day the anticipated appearance of Samuel did not happen: "But Samuel did not come to Gilgal . . ." (v. 8b).

The end of the seventh day approached, and there was still no sign of Samuel. All this time the situation was getting more precarious: ". . . and the people were scattering from him" (v. 8c).

How many were left now of the relatively tiny Israelite force he had started with? Yet Samuel was nowhere to be seen. It was a desperate moment. If he waited any longer Saul might have no army left at all. You can almost hear Saul's urgent inquiries of those around him on Day 7: "Where is Samuel?" "Has anyone seen Samuel? "Has anyone heard anything of Samuel?" "Does anyone have any idea where he is?"

There was no answer, no sign of Samuel.

At this desperate moment Saul decided he must act: "So Saul said, 'Bring the burnt offering here to me, and the peace offerings.' And he offered the burnt offering" (v. 9).

The king took action. A little later Saul would explain these sacrifices in terms of seeking "the favor of the LORD" in preparation for the confrontation with the Philistines (1 Samuel 13:12). However, the idea of offering a "burnt offering" and "peace offerings" was not Saul's. Samuel had told him that this is what he (Samuel) would do when he came to Gilgal (1 Samuel 10:8). Saul took the initiative, possibly now unsure about the purpose of these offerings.

What alternative did he have? He could have let his army disperse altogether and allowed the Philistines to walk in and take over the land and slaughter everyone. That, I take it, was the only alternative he could see. What kind of king would he then be?

Instead Saul took decisive action to prepare for the inevitable conflict. It is easy to see why we feel sympathetic toward Saul. It seems that he did what he had to do.

Saul's Judgment (vv. 10-13)

At the very moment Saul completed making the offering, what do you think happened? "As soon as he had finished offering the burnt offering, behold, Samuel came" (v. 10a).

Saul, I suspect, was quite relieved. He had thought Samuel was not going to show up. With that relieved look on his face, "Saul went out to meet him and greet him" (v. 10b).

I can imagine the smile on Saul's face. Samuel would know what to do. Samuel had dealt with the Philistines before. The smile quickly faded: "Samuel said, 'What have you done?'" (v. 11a).

Like the voice of God to Adam and Eve in the Garden of Eden after the couple had eaten from the forbidden tree (Genesis 3:9, 13) and to Cain after he had murdered his brother (Genesis 4:10), like the question to Achan when he had brought God's wrath on Israel by his greedy act (Joshua 7:19), Samuel asked Saul the accusing question, "What have you done?"

I can almost see Saul's bewildered face:

> And Saul said, "When I saw that the people were scattering from me, and that you did not come within the days appointed, and that the Philistines had mustered at Michmash, I said, 'Now the Philistines will come down against me at Gilgal, and I have not sought the favor of the LORD.' So I forced myself, and offered the burnt offering." (vv. 11b, 12)

"It is not as though I had any choice in any of these things," Saul seemed to say. "I could not stop the people from scattering. I had no idea where you were, Samuel. I could do nothing about the Philistines. And I was not going to go to war without seeking the Lord's favor. What do you mean, Samuel, 'What have I done?' I have done the only thing I could do in the circumstances![17] How was I to know you were about to appear out of thin air? (And by the way, where *were* you five minutes ago?)"

If Saul expected sympathetic understanding from Samuel, it was not to be: "And Samuel said to Saul, 'You have done foolishly'" (v. 13a).

What an astonishing thing to say! What was "foolish" about Saul's actions in these desperate circumstances? Would it not have been more foolish to do nothing? Samuel continued: "You have not kept the command of the LORD your God, with which he commanded you" (v. 13b).

And *that*, according to Samuel, is what only a fool does. The command that Saul had not kept was the command of 1 Samuel 10:8 (not to mention the fact that he himself had failed to keep the other instruction of 1 Samuel 10:7). The text is not clear whether Samuel had appeared in Gilgal late on the seventh day or on the eighth day. The former seems more likely, but in any case the instruction in 1 Samuel 10:8 was to wait "until I come to you and show you what you shall do."[18] Saul had *not* waited.

Feel the weight of this as this episode presents it to us. To obey God, for Saul, was an *extraordinary* thing to ask, considering the circumstances. We might reasonably say that it was close to impossible. Why? Because to obey

God in those circumstances would have required him to *trust God* against every instinct, against every evidence, and against every aspect of his experience at that moment. The Philistines were coming in massive numbers, the Israelites were slipping away, and everyone was terrified!

What a huge mistake it is to think that to obey God is an easy thing to do. Trusting God is neither straightforward nor simple.

The foolishness of disobeying God (the same foolishness that is spoken of in Psalm 14:1) cannot be seen by weighing the circumstances. In most circumstances it looks foolish to trust and obey God. The foolishness of disobedience and the wisdom of obedience can only be seen when we take into account something other than circumstances. Samuel therefore continued: "For then the LORD would have established your kingdom over Israel forever" (v. 13c).

It is in the light of God's promise that the utter foolishness of Saul's disobedience must be seen. In the light of his circumstances, Saul's action might seem wise and prudent. In the light of God's promise, it was the most foolish thing he could have done. Whether the act of disobedience helped the situation with the Philistines was irrelevant. What matters is that it forfeited the promise of God.

The Consequences (vv. 14, 15)

Samuel spelled out the consequences: "But now your kingdom shall not continue" (v. 14a).

The only king who can rule God's people Israel is a king who is obedient to God. Therefore:

> "The LORD has sought out a man after his own heart, and the LORD has commanded him to be prince over his people, because you have not kept what the LORD commanded you." (v. 14b)

The expression "a man after [God's] own heart" has entered Christian jargon, usually as a statement about the qualities of the person. In 1 Samuel 13:13, however, the expression is literally, "The LORD has sought for himself a man according to his own heart. . . ." This is about the place this man had in God's heart rather than about the place God had in the man's heart. It was a way of saying that God had chosen this man according to his own will and purpose.[19] We will consider this matter more fully when we meet this man in 1 Samuel 16 (especially 1 Samuel 16:7).

Here the point to be emphasized is that repeatedly the people had been presented with Saul as the king the people had asked for and had chosen *for themselves* (see 1 Samuel 8:10, 18; 10:19; 12:13). Things were about to change. The Lord had chosen a king *for himself*, a king on whom he had set

his heart. While it is true that Saul had been described as "him whom the
LORD has chosen" (1 Samuel 10:24) and "his anointed" (1 Samuel 12:3, 5),
this was always in the context of the people's demands. The striking new
thing is that the Lord would choose a king "for himself," "according to his
own heart." These things were never said of Saul.

However, the new thing the Lord was about to do is another story for
which we must wait. In the meantime:

> *And Samuel arose and went up from Gilgal.* The rest of the people went
> up after Saul to meet the army; they went up from Gilgal *to Gibeah of
> Benjamin. (v. 15a)*

The Hebrew text has only the italicized words (the rest have been
deduced from the Septuagint) and so only tells us that Samuel headed up
into the hills, not far from where the Philistines were gathering! If we follow
the Hebrew, we are left wondering where Saul and the rest of the people
went. This we will be told in the next verse. "And Saul numbered the people
who were present with him, about six hundred men" (v. 15b).

Just one in five of the original 3,000 were still with Saul. Even if "thousand" is not a number in 1 Samuel 13:2, but a term for a military contingent,
it is certain that verse 15 indicates a radical reduction in the Israelite fighting
force.

ISRAEL'S TROUBLING SITUATION (vv. 16-23)

In 1 Samuel 13:16 we learn that after the terrible encounter with Samuel in
Gilgal, Saul and Jonathan (the first time we are explicitly told that Jonathan
was "his son") had moved up from Gilgal in the Jordan Valley to "Geba of
Benjamin." We have already noted that Geba may have been an alternative
name for Gibeah or perhaps another location closer to Michmash. Either
way, it was where Jonathan had earlier inflicted damage on the Philistine
garrison (1 Samuel 13:3), stirring up the present troubles (1 Samuel 13:4).
A few miles to the northeast from Geba, across "a deep ravine,"[20] was
Michmash,[21] where the Philistines had assembled a force many times greater
than Saul had at his disposal (1 Samuel 13:5, 11). Saul, in Geba/Gibeah, had
just 600 fighters left of his original 3,000 (1 Samuel 13:2, 15b).

The Strategic Situation (vv. 16-18)

Try to take in the strategic situation we find at the end of 1 Samuel 13.

Saul, with his son Jonathan and those with them, were in Geba, across
the valley from the Philistine base: "And Saul and Jonathan his son and the

people who were present with them stayed in Geba of Benjamin, but the Philistines encamped in Michmash" (v. 16).

If Geba was the location closer to Michmash than Gibeah, then from there they would have been able to see movements from the Philistine camp. The narrator gives us the details of what they would have seen:

> And raiders came out of the camp of the Philistines in three companies. One company turned toward Ophrah, to the land of Shual; another company turned toward Beth-horon; and another company turned toward the border that looks down on the valley of Zeboim toward the wilderness. (vv. 17, 18)

In other words, the Philistines were sending raiding parties into the country to the north, the west, and the east. We can only guess at the strategic reasons for these raids.[22] But it is clear that Saul and his small band at Geba were powerless to do anything about it.

Israel's Disarmament (vv. 19-21)

That was not all. The Philistines' effective control at this time over Israelite life had very serious consequences:

> Now there was no blacksmith to be found throughout all the land of Israel, for the Philistines said, "Lest the Hebrews make themselves swords or spears." But every one of the Israelites went down to the Philistines to sharpen his plowshare, his mattock, his axe, or his sickle, and the charge was two-thirds of a shekel for the plowshares and for the mattocks, and a third of a shekel for sharpening the axes and for setting the goads. (vv. 19-21)

The Israelites were not permitted to make iron weapons and were dependent on the Philistines for the maintenance of their farming implements (with the Philistines making a solid profit from their monopoly).

The Strategic Situation (vv. 22, 23)

How long this had been going on we do not know, but the strategic consequences for the Israelites are clear:

> So on the day of the battle there was neither sword nor spear found in the hand of any of the people with Saul and Jonathan, but Saul and Jonathan his son had them. (v. 22)

"The day of the battle" sounds menacing. A battle has seemed inevitable since Jonathan had provoked the Philistines with his raid on the garrison that had been at Geba (1 Samuel 13:3). We cannot help imagining what kind of battle this will turn out to be, with not only the huge disproportion of numbers in favor of the Philistines, but among the Israelites only the king and his son had decent weapons!

Ominously we now read: "And the garrison of the Philistines went out to the pass of Michmash" (v. 23).

"The pass of Michmash" was apparently somewhere in the gorge that separated Michmash from Geba.

So the scene was set for the events that will unfold in chapter 14.

However we must now grasp something that is difficult for us to see. The really fearful situation for Saul and the Israelites was not the Philistines. It was the Lord God who had made it clear through his prophet that what he required of his people and their king was *obedience*. We find this hard to see because we are so like Saul. We sympathize with him because we, too, find that to obey God fully, to trust God fully, really is beyond us, in the circumstances in which we find ourselves.

King Saul could not help his people in this. He was a fool — like the rest of us.

It is therefore vitally important for us to hear this:

> *In the days of his flesh, Jesus offered up prayers and supplications, with loud cries and tears, to him who was able to save him from death, and he was heard because of his reverence. Although he was a son,* he learned obedience through what he suffered. *And being made perfect, he became the source of eternal salvation to all who obey him. (Hebrews 5:7-9)*

The obedient King has now come. This King is no fool. He is not like Saul, nor like us.

> *Let us then with confidence draw near to the throne of grace, that we may receive mercy and find grace to help in time of need. (Hebrews 4:16)*

20

A Leader Who Trusted God

1 SAMUEL 14:1-23

In this troubled world we are confused about what we value in leaders. We want leaders who can make a difference to the difficulties and complexities of life. But what attributes equip a person to be a good leader? What qualities do you look for in a leader? Intelligence? Decisiveness? Strength of personality? Energy? Commitment? Honesty? Strength of conviction? Competence? We could construct a long list, I am sure, of qualities that we want to see in our leaders.

The Biblical record of the reign of King Saul over Israel has shown us that Saul could be seen to have many of the qualities that we value. He was an impressive man (1 Samuel 9:2; 10:23, 24), militarily able (1 Samuel 11:5-11), and yet with an attractive humility (1 Samuel 9:21). He could be decisive, as he was when he defended the people of Jabesh-gilead against the Ammonites in 1 Samuel 11. But he was not one to take personal vengeance (see 1 Samuel 10:27; 11:12, 13).

Yet we have seen that Saul found himself disqualified from being king over God's people Israel (1 Samuel 13:14). The problem was not lack of intelligence or indecisiveness or weakness or laziness. It was that he had not been completely obedient to God's command to him.

The account in 1 Samuel 13 was astonishing. Saul's failure might have seemed to us to be a small thing — even, in the circumstances, a wise thing. In a desperate situation he had taken control. Isn't that what you expect from a king? But if we react in that way to the account, we must realize how different is our view of things from that of the narrator of this report, and of Samuel the prophet of God, and ultimately of God himself.

Still we were left wondering, I suspect, what Saul could have done differently. What kind of person would have acted differently from Saul?

In chapter 14 we find the sequel to the confrontation that took place between Saul and Samuel at Gilgal. It is a dramatic story in which our attention is focused on another man who displayed the very quality that Saul lacked. We will be following this account in two parts. In the first of these we will meet a leader who trusted God.

JONATHAN'S DAY OF ACTION (vv. 1-15)

First Samuel 14 begins (if I may translate a little more literally than most English versions): "And the day came . . ." "The day of the battle" mentioned in 1 Samuel 13:22 dawned. What a day it would turn out to be!

The Scene Is Set (vv. 1-5)

The first surprise is that our attention is drawn not to Saul and his dilemma on that day, but to his son, Jonathan.

The first appearance of Jonathan in the 1 Samuel story was in 1 Samuel 13:2, 3 — his attack on the Philistine garrison then in Geba. Keep in mind that it was that little adventure that had aroused the Philistines to their present hostile intentions toward the Israelites (1 Samuel 13:4).

JONATHAN'S PLAN (v. 1)

Chapter 14 opens with Jonathan at it again:

> *[And the day came, and]¹ Jonathan the son of Saul said to the young man who carried his armor, "Come, let us go over to the Philistine garrison on the other side." (v. 1a)*

That is, on the other side of the valley separating Geba and Michmash. You cannot help forming an impression of the kind of young man Jonathan was. He had a taste for adventure. He had succeeded the first time (if "succeeded" is the right word, considering the consequences that have developed). But now, with the huge enemy force massed in Michmash (see 1 Samuel 13:5), he proposed to try to do it again.

We are perhaps not surprised to read at the end of verse 1: "But he did not tell his father" (v. 1b).

This is the first clear hint that all may not have been well between this son and his father. Jonathan reasonably thought that Saul would not approve his plan. Those of us with teenage sons can probably see his point!

SAUL AND HIS COMPANY (VV. 2, 3)

We leave Jonathan for a moment, discussing his bold plan with his armor-bearer, and turn our eyes to Saul. What was Saul doing as his son was hatching his daring plans? "Saul was staying in the outskirts of Gibeah in the pomegranate cave at Migron" (v. 2a).

While Jonathan was planning audacious action, Saul was now further back up in the hills, further south, further away from the enemy, at "the outskirts of Gibeah." "Staying" could be translated "sitting," probably under a pomegranate *tree* rather than in a *cave*.[2] The contrast to the active, initiative-taking Jonathan could hardly be more stark.

Take a close look at the crowd with Saul as he sat there under the pomegranate tree:

> *The people who were with him were about six hundred men, including Ahijah the son of Ahitub, Ichabod's brother, son of Phinehas, son of Eli, the priest of the LORD in Shiloh, wearing an ephod. (vv. 2b, 3a)*

Jonathan had his armor-bearer. Saul had an ephod-bearer.[3] An ephod was a priestly garment that contained Urim and Thummim, devices not fully understood now, but that were used in ancient Israel to obtain divine guidance (see Exodus 28:6-30).[4]

We might have thought it was good that Saul had the priest Ahijah there with him, with the possibility of seeking God's guidance, if it were not for the fact that the narrator so pointedly reminds us that this priest's uncle was Ichabod. Who could forget Ichabod (1 Samuel 4:21, 22)? "Where is the glory?" He also reminds us of Ichabod's father, Phinehas. Can we forget those wretched brothers Hophni and Phinehas (1 Samuel 2:12-17)? Add their father, Eli, whose whole family fell under the terrible judgment in 1 Samuel 4 that in many ways lay behind everything that was now happening (see 1 Samuel 2:27-36; 3:11-14; 4:12-22). The "glory" departed from Israel then (1 Samuel 4:22), and here with Saul, the king who was rapidly losing his kingdom, was the nephew of "Where is the glory?"[5]

It is a scene with too many memories!

The 600 men with Saul were the remnant (1 Samuel 13:15) of the considerably larger fighting force he had assembled before Jonathan's first adventure (1 Samuel 13:2).

The end of verse 3 tells us: "And the people did not know that Jonathan had gone" (v. 3b).

They knew no more about Jonathan's escapade than did the king.

TOPOGRAPHY (VV. 4, 5)

We now return to Jonathan and his trusty companion, on the south side of the valley lying between them and the Philistines. We look with them across the steep and rugged valley at the terrain they will have to cross to reach the Philistine garrison on the other side, outside Michmash:

> *Within the passes, by which Jonathan sought to go over to the Philistine garrison, there was a rocky crag on the one side and a rocky crag on the other side. The name of the one was Bozez, and the name of the other Seneh. The one crag rose on the north in front of Michmash, and the other on the south in front of Geba. (vv. 4, 5)*

There was adequate cover, it seems, provided by these rocky crags (literally, "teeth of rock"). The two adventurers would perhaps be able, with care, to approach the other side of the valley undetected, hidden by Bozez and Seneh.

The Battle of Michmash (vv. 6-15)

So the scene is set. We are ready for the action to begin.

Before it does, we must listen to Jonathan again. We are about to see plenty of action, but we will only understand the action if we listen to Jonathan's words.

THE CONFIDENCE (VV. 6, 7)

> *Jonathan said to the young man who carried his armor, "Come, let us go over to the garrison of these uncircumcised. It may be that the LORD will work for us, for nothing can hinder the LORD from saving by many or by few." (v. 6)*

Did you hear that? Jonathan appears to have had no fear at all of the Philistines. He referred to them simply as "these uncircumcised" (cf. 1 Samuel 17:26).

This was not just teenage bravado. His courage was *faith in God*: "Nothing can hinder the LORD from saving by many or by few." Here in Jonathan's words we see the quality that Saul so clearly lacked. How very different this was from his father, just a little earlier, who had been thrown into panic because the people were scattering from him (1 Samuel 13:11). Here was Jonathan, with just *one* companion, confident that *God* can save with a mighty army or with no army at all.

We know he was right, of course — if we have been following the book of

1 Samuel. God had defeated the Philistines before, with and without military involvement from Israel (see 1 Samuel 7:10, 11 and 5:11 respectively).

The confidence we hear from Jonathan we will hear again when another young lad will face a giant of a Philistine and say, "The LORD who delivered me from the paw of the lion and from the paw of the bear will deliver me from the hand of this Philistine" (1 Samuel 17:37).

More importantly still, Jonathan was expressing the conviction that is basic to all true faith in God. God is of infinite power.[6] Again and again through the pages of the Bible we hear this truth. "Is anything too hard for the LORD?" (Genesis 18:14). "I know that you can do all things" (Job 42:2). "Nothing is too hard for you" (Jeremiah 32:17). "Nothing will be impossible with God" (Luke 1:37). "With God all things are possible" (Matthew 19:26). "Abba, Father, all things are possible for you" (Mark 14:36).

Do you know that *all things* are possible with God — that *nothing* is too hard for him — that he can do *anything*? That is what Jesus taught. It is what the whole Bible teaches. It is what makes faith in God possible, important, and wise. If you do not yet know this, then you will not be able to put your trust fully in God. True faith in God is possible because there is nothing that can hinder him.

Faith in God knows that he is of infinite power, but it does not *presume* on that power. When Jonathan said in verse 6, "*It may be* that the LORD will work for us," we might be reminded of another who, many years later, would say *first*, "Abba, Father, all things are possible for you," and *then*, "Yet not what I will, but what you will" (Mark 14:36). True faith in God knows his power to do all things but submits to his will, knowing that he is both wise *and* good.

Jonathan shows the essentials of such faith. This is precisely what Saul lacked in chapter 13. If he had believed in God's power, wisdom, and goodness, then he would not have disobeyed him, even though his situation was desperate. This is why his act of disobedience disqualified him from being king over God's people, Israel. God's king must trust God.

Jonathan's young armor-bearer shared his faith: "And his armor-bearer said to him, 'Do all that is in your heart. Do as you wish. Behold, I am with you heart and soul'"[7] (v. 7).

THE SIGN (vv. 8-12)

Jonathan had more to say:

> Then Jonathan said, "Behold, we will cross over to the men, and we will show ourselves to them. If they say to us, 'Wait until we come to you,' then we will stand still in our place, and we will not go up to them. But if they

say, 'Come up to us,' then we will go up, for the LORD has given them into
our hand. And this shall be the sign to us." (vv. 8-10)

See the plan? At an appropriate distance, somewhere in the valley, the
two would come out from the cover of the rocky crags and see what reaction
they provoked from the Philistines and take that reaction as guidance for
what to do next. Remember, they knew only that "it may be" that the Lord
would work for them.

They did as planned:

So both of them showed themselves to the garrison of the Philistines. And
the Philistines said, "Look, Hebrews are coming out of the holes where
they have hidden themselves." And the men of the garrison hailed Jonathan
and his armor-bearer and said, "Come up to us, and we will show you a
thing." And Jonathan said to his armor-bearer, "Come up after me, for
the LORD has given them into the hand of Israel." (vv. 11, 12)

Jonathan took the Philistine dare as a sign of God's intentions.

THE VICTORY (vv. 13-15)

Jonathan and his companion then scrambled on all fours up to the garrison
post, taking them completely by surprise:

Then Jonathan climbed up on his hands and feet, and his armor-bearer
after him. And they fell before Jonathan, and his armor-bearer killed them
after him. And that first strike, which Jonathan and his armor-bearer made,
killed about twenty men within as it were half a furrow's length in an acre
of land. And there was a panic in the camp, in the field, and among all the
people. The garrison and even the raiders trembled, the earth quaked, and
it became a very great panic. (vv. 13-15)

The hidden hand of God was clearly working for them. Just two young
Israelites, with the benefit of surprise, brought down about twenty Philistines!
But that set off such a panic through the garrison and well beyond that
chaos broke out. Even the raiding parties that had gone north, west, and east
(1 Samuel 13:17, 18) heard and were thrown into terror.

Leave them there in their trembling terror for the moment.

WHAT SAUL DID (vv. 16-23)

It is time to move back up, away from all this action, to the higher ground, further south, to Gibeah, where Saul was still sitting under his pomegranate tree.

What He Saw (vv. 16-19)

Saul did not himself see what was happening across the valley in Michmash. Presumably he was not watching. He had people to do that kind of thing for him! "And the watchmen of Saul in Gibeah of Benjamin looked, and behold, the multitude was dispersing here and there" (v. 16).

"Melting" is what the original says. That is a great metaphor. The solid, terrifying Philistine force had "turned to water," and it was running every-where!

Saul sparked up at this news. Perhaps he suspected what might have been happening:

> *Then Saul said to the people who were with him, "Count and see who has gone from us." And when they had counted, behold, Jonathan and his armor-bearer were not there. (v. 17)*

It is becoming clear that Saul was losing his grip. He knew nothing. He had not even noticed his son's absence.

When he learned that Jonathan was missing (with an obvious impli-cation if he can just remember back to the lad's earlier little escapade, 1 Samuel 13:3), Saul seemed to panic a little: "So Saul said to Ahijah, 'Bring the ark of God here.' For the ark of God went at that time with the people of Israel" (v. 18).

Was he planning to march into battle against the Philistines with the ark, as the Israelites had done (disastrously) before (1 Samuel 4:3, 10, 11)? Probably not. More likely he was thinking of seeking God's guidance at this point (cf. Judges 20:27).[8]

Whatever his intentions, he quickly changed his mind: "Now while Saul was talking to the priest, the tumult in the camp of the Philistines increased more and more. So Saul said to the priest, 'Withdraw your hand'" (v. 19).

In other words, "Don't worry about bringing the ark." The noise from across the valley apparently assured him that the Philistines were in big trouble, and so he dropped his interest in the ark.

What He Did (vv. 20-23)

This was obviously just the moment for a great king like Saul to get involved! "Then Saul and all the people who were with him rallied and went into the battle" (v. 20a).

They were not disappointed, and it took no effort on their part: "And behold, every Philistine's sword was against his fellow, and there was very great confusion" (v. 20b).

Unnecessary as they were, reinforcements were now obtained from an unexpected quarter:

Now the Hebrews who had been with the Philistines before that time and who had gone up with them into the camp, even they also turned to be with the Israelites who were with Saul and Jonathan. Likewise, when all the men of Israel who had hidden themselves in the hill country of Ephraim heard that the Philistines were fleeing, they too followed hard after them in the battle. (vv. 21, 22)

Those who had scattered earlier, in fear of the Philistines (1 Samuel 13:6, 7), returned now to join the victorious battle. Saul, of course, had nothing to do with all this. The narrator tells us plainly what really happened: "So the LORD saved Israel that day" (v. 23a).

What Jonathan knew *could* happen (1 Samuel 14:6) *did* happen. The Lord saved "by few." He proved himself again to be the God who saves his people (1 Samuel 10:19). It was a day like the earlier one when Saul had said, "Today the LORD has worked salvation in Israel" (1 Samuel 11:13). This time, however, Saul had very little to do with it.

The fighting continued:

And the battle passed beyond Beth-aven. (v. 23b)

That is, further to the west (see 1 Samuel 13:5).

That sounds like a great place to end the story, with the Philistines fleeing into the hills and the Israelites in hot pursuit. But the events of that day had only begun, and our second installment in 1 Samuel 14 will bring some very surprising developments.

Jonathan's leadership, by way of contrast, highlighted the failure of Saul. Our sympathies may still be aroused by Saul's tragedy. We know only too well how difficult, even impossible we find it to fully trust God. We know we would have done no better than Saul. But in Jonathan we are given a glimpse of the kind of leader we need — one who knows God's power, wisdom, and goodness enough to trust him wholly.

The Bible's message is that such a leader, such a king, has now come. He is the first man ever to fully trust and obey God (Philippians 2:8). He has become the pioneer and perfecter of our faith (Hebrews 12:2). Jonathan could have been one of the "witnesses" (Hebrews 12:1) celebrated in Hebrews 11 who, by his faith in God, points us to Jesus. Consider Jonathan. And then consider Jesus!

21

Disobedience and Foolishness

1 SAMUEL 14:24-52

The prophet Samuel confronted Saul on that fateful day in Gilgal and said to him "You have done foolishly" (1 Samuel 13:13). His words probably sound harsh to our ears. Saul's "mistake" seems so understandable — a small thing, a matter of timing, a judgment made in desperate circumstances. It is difficult to imagine that any of us would have done better than Saul in a similar situation. We witnessed Saul's struggle there in Gilgal, with his troops deserting him as the hours passed, with the hostile Philistines gathering their massive forces up in the hills at Michmash, with no sign of Samuel. What would *you* have done? Nothing? At least Saul acted. He took some initiative to save the situation. It is not obvious that Saul's action was "foolish," is it?

Yet that is what he heard from God's prophet Samuel: "You have done foolishly." He had not kept the command of the Lord, and Samuel allowed for no argument from special circumstances to soften his judgment. Saul was now disqualified from the kingship over God's people Israel. His kingdom would not continue. It would pass to another, to "a man after [the LORD's] own heart" (1 Samuel 13:14).

Unless you are a very unusual hearer of this story, you feel considerable sympathy for Saul. He did what *seemed* wise, but it was judged to be foolish. He did what seemed to be necessary but found himself condemned.

Our difficulties with the story of Saul should be taken seriously. We sympathize with Saul because we know all too well how difficult obedience to God can be. We find Samuel's judgment harsh because we are not always persuaded that obedience to God is the wisest course of action. If we were so persuaded, we would always obey.

In the first part of 1 Samuel 14 we saw, in the contrasting conduct of Saul's son Jonathan, that Saul's disobedience was a failure of faith in God. Jonathan believed that "nothing can hinder the LORD from saving by many or by few" (1 Samuel 14:6). If only his father had really believed that, he would not have been panicked into disobedience. But, once again, we sympathize with Saul. We know very well indeed that we find it difficult to put our trust in God's power, wisdom, and goodness.

Our problem goes back to the couple in the Garden of Eden, who believed the lie that disobedience to God is "to be desired to make one *wise*" (Genesis 3:6). We are the children of Adam and Eve. Have you noticed how we construct in our imaginations a caricature that makes wholehearted trust in God look naive — the very godly person who knows little about "real life"? Taking God too seriously (we think, without, of course, saying so) can only lead to naivete, not wisdom. As the saying goes, "They're so heavenly-minded, they are of no earthly use!"

This view is expressed in some contemporary debates about politics and religion. Those who take religion seriously can hardly be expected to have anything wise to say about politics. Politicians who have religious convictions would be wise to keep them private and not allow them to influence the performance of their public duties. There are circumstances in which we feel it is wise to disregard God.

If that is how our minds work, it is hardly surprising to find that we sympathize with Saul at Gilgal, for he found himself in circumstances where, he felt, he simply *had* to put the command of the Lord to one side. The difficulties we have with the story of Saul are evidence that to some extent and in some form we share his view of life: there *are* times (don't you think?) when the commands of God are best put to one side.

The Bible's remarkable teaching is that those who think like that, and therefore behave like that, are "foolish": " The fool says in his heart, 'There is no God'" (Psalm 14:1).

The psalm is not speaking just of the theoretical atheist, who argues philosophically against the existence of God. No doubt such a person is included, but the psalm speaks of all who *live* as though there is no God, who say *in their heart,* "There is no God." To disobey God's commands is the outward expression of this inward thought. Such a person, says the Bible, is a fool! And we all know that we have been such fools.

The account of Saul's reign as Israel's first king is one of the great demonstrations the Bible sets before us of the foolishness of disobeying God.

We left the account last time after seeing Jonathan doing the very opposite of saying in his heart that there is no God. He really did trust God. With the Philistines fleeing into the hills, the Israelites in hot pursuit, we can now see the *wisdom* of his faith.

SAUL'S OATH (vv. 24-35)

Pronounced (v. 24)

We take up the account of that day at 1 Samuel 14:24, where the narrator does something that Bible writers often do. He breaks into the story with a flashback, telling us now something that happened earlier, because now is when we need this information. "And the men of Israel had been hard pressed that day . . ." (v. 24a).

Previously, after Jonathan had launched his first attack on the Philistines and the Philistines responded by gathering a massive force at Michmash, we were told that "the people were *hard pressed*" (1 Samuel 13:6). They were, understandably, terrified of the Philistine threat. This highly stressed situation had led to many Israelites deserting Saul (1 Samuel 13:6, 7). Now in 1 Samuel 14:24 we are told that Jonathan's second attack (again, understandably) had the same effect at first. The reference seems to be to the initial reaction among the Israelites to the disturbances in the Philistine camp, before Saul and his people joined the fray.[1] In other words, 1 Samuel 14:24 looks back to the situation just prior to 1 Samuel 14:20.

Then we are told what Saul did, presumably to avoid the mass desertion he had suffered earlier (1 Samuel 13:6, 7):

> . . . *so Saul had laid an oath on the people, saying, "Cursed be the man who eats food until it is evening and I am avenged on my enemies." So none of the people had tasted food.* (v. 24b)

Once again we see Saul in desperate circumstances, taking desperate measures.[2] We cannot help noticing the contrast between his words and what we heard from Jonathan: "It may be that the LORD will work for us, for nothing can hinder the LORD from saving by many or by few" (1 Samuel 14:6). How different: "Cursed be the man who eats food until it is evening and *I* am avenged on *my* enemies." The man who did not obey God in chapter 13 now made no reference to God, expressed no confidence in God, and was obsessed with avenging *himself* on *his* enemies and coercing *his* people into supporting *him*.

Denounced (vv. 25-31)

All that was a flashback to help us understand what we are about to witness next. We now know that all the people who went into the battle with Saul

(1 Samuel 14:20) did so on empty stomachs, under Saul's oath to eat nothing
until the fighting was over.

Follow these hungry troops:

> Now when all the people came to the forest, behold, there was honey on
> the ground. And when the people entered the forest, behold, the honey was
> dropping, but no one put his hand to his mouth, for the people feared the
> oath. (vv. 25, 26)

It is one thing to be famished, quite another to then find yourself surrounded by sweet, dripping honey that you are not allowed to touch!

When Saul had pronounced this oath, Jonathan and his companion were
already among the Philistines. So Jonathan had not heard Saul's wretched
curse. In case we had forgotten this, the narrator reminds us and tells what
therefore happened:

> But Jonathan had not heard his father charge the people with the oath,
> so he put out the tip of the staff that was in his hand and dipped it in the
> honeycomb and put his hand to his mouth, and his eyes became bright.
> (v. 27)

That perked him up! After the exertion of that day, we can well imagine
that a mouthful of wild honey would do great good! But the people were
horrified:

> Then one of the people said, "Your father strictly charged the people with
> an oath, saying, 'Cursed be the man who eats food this day.'" And the
> people were faint. (v. 28)

The people, of course, had hardly done anything. The fighting itself
had been made easy by the terrified panic of the Philistines (see 1 Samuel
14:20b). But they were fainting from hunger, while Jonathan was invigo-
rated by his sugar hit.

The utter stupidity of his father's oath was clear to Jonathan:

> Then Jonathan said, "My father has troubled the land. See how my eyes
> have become bright because I tasted a little of this honey. How much bet-
> ter if the people had eaten freely today of the spoil of their enemies that
> they found. For now the defeat among the Philistines has not been great."
> (vv. 29, 30)

The tension between father and son that we noticed earlier in verse
1 (when Jonathan did not tell Saul of his plan to attack the Philistine gar-

rison) was becoming sharper. Jonathan was sounding like Samuel: "You have done foolishly" (1 Samuel 13:13). The one who did not obey God in chapter 13 and expressed no confidence in God when faced with his enemies had devised an idiotic plan to save himself. It had backfired. According to Jonathan the defeat of the Philistines that day could have been much greater, had it not been for Saul's stupid oath.

The fighting continued, however, and the Philistines were beaten: "They struck down the Philistines that day from Michmash to Aijalon" (v. 31a).

But predictably, the starved troops were wilting: "And the people were very faint" (v. 31b).

Unintended Consequence (vv. 32-35)

It is fair to assume that with the Philistines fallen and fleeing, Saul's abstinence oath no longer applied. Saul was "avenged on [his] enemies" (1 Samuel 14:24). The fainting troops therefore grabbed desperately for food from the spoils left by the fleeing Philistines:

> *The people pounced on the spoil and took sheep and oxen and calves and slaughtered them on the ground. And the people ate them with the blood. (v. 32)*

In their frantic grab for food, presumably because of the desperation caused by Saul's oath, the people overlooked a long-standing, God-given prohibition. It went back to the days of Noah (Genesis 9:4). It was clearly written in God's Law for Israel (Leviticus 7:26, 27, etc.). They were not to eat meat with blood still in it. Blood represented life and was to be used in atoning sacrifices (Leviticus 17:11).[3] But the people gave no thought to God's Law on this matter as they rushed to satisfy their craving for food.

So obedience to Saul's silly oath had now led to mass disobedience to God's Law. What would happen now?

> *Then they told Saul, "Behold, the people are sinning against the Lord by eating with the blood." And he said, "You have dealt treacherously; roll a great stone to me here." And Saul said, "Disperse yourselves among the people and say to them, 'Let every man bring his ox or his sheep and slaughter them here and eat, and do not sin against the Lord by eating with the blood.'" So every one of the people brought his ox with him that night and they slaughtered them there. And Saul built an altar to the Lord; it was the first altar that he built to the Lord. (vv. 33-35)*

The man who did not obey God in chapter 13 and expressed no confidence in God when faced with his enemies, who devised the crazy plan to save himself by starving his troops, now sounded so concerned about the people's act of disobedience! He tried to put it right by playing the priest, building an altar where the animals could be slaughtered and eaten properly.[4] But there is not the slightest suggestion that he saw how he had caused the problem.

SAUL ALONE (vv. 36-39)

Saul's Proposal (v. 36a-b)

However, he seemed to think that he had solved the problem because he immediately proposed to mop up what was left of the Philistines: "Then Saul said, 'Let us go down after the Philistines by night and plunder them until the morning light; let us not leave a man of them'" (v. 36a).

He still sounded very different from Jonathan, don't you think? Jonathan had said, "It may be that the LORD will work for us, for nothing can hinder the LORD from saving by many or by few" (1 Samuel 14:6). But there was no reference to God by Saul, no expression of faith in God.

The people were less than enthusiastic: "And they said, 'Do whatever seems good to you'" (v. 36b).

"Whatever *seems good to you.*" That was the measure of Saul's conduct now. Again, this was very different from Jonathan's careful trust in God.

Saul's (Delayed) Inquiry (vv. 36c, 37a)

Someone else had to remind Saul of God: "But the priest said, 'Let us draw near to God here'" (v. 36c).

There's a good idea! But why didn't Saul think of it?

> And Saul inquired of God, "Shall I go down after the Philistines? Will you give them into the hand of Israel?" (v. 37a)

At last Saul's thoughts turned to the God he had disobeyed in chapter 13, to whom he had apparently given no serious thought in chapter 14. But now, at the eleventh hour, when the Philistines were all but cleaned up, he (when prompted) asked God whether his (Saul's) plan was a good idea.

Saul's inquiry in all probability was done by means of the priest's Urim and Thummim. It is not entirely clear how this worked, but these objects were kept in the priest's breastpiece (Exodus 28:30; Leviticus 8:8) and were used in seeking God's guidance on important matters (see Ezra 2:63; Nehemiah 7:65).

Two Silences (vv. 37b-39)

Perhaps we are less than surprised to read: "But he did not answer him that day" (v. 37b).

Remember Samuel's warnings in 1 Samuel 8:18 about the troubles that a king would bring to the people. Samuel said then, "But the LORD will not answer you in that day."[5]

Saul's capacity to blunder was growing. He assumed that God's silence was someone else's fault:

> *And Saul said, "Come here, all you leaders of the people, and know and see how this sin has arisen today. For as the LORD lives who saves Israel, though it be in Jonathan my son, he shall surely die." (vv. 38, 39a)*

The irony is palpable. We have seen what looks like a growing tension between Saul and his son. We wonder whether Saul may have had some terrible inkling of what he was about to learn. But Saul met a second silence: "But there was not a man among all the people who answered him" (v. 39b).

Saul was alone. Not only did he meet silence from God — his people refused to answer him. The very thing that his oath had been designed to avoid, namely, the desertion of his people, had happened — perhaps not literally, but he had certainly lost their hearts.

SAUL VERSUS JONATHAN (vv. 40-46)

Saul Identifies the "Problem" (vv. 40-42)

Saul decided to force an answer. (In verses 41, 42 I am going to cite the NIV because here it follows the Hebrew text more closely than does the ESV[6]):

> *Then he said to all Israel, "You shall be on one side, and I and Jonathan my son will be on the other side." And the people said to Saul, "Do what seems good to you." Then Saul prayed to the LORD, the God of Israel, "Give me the right answer." And Jonathan and Saul were taken by lot, and the men were cleared. Saul said, "Cast the lot between me and Jonathan my son." And Jonathan was taken. (vv. 40-42)*

The scene is a kind of tragic comedy. The same process by which Saul had been identified as Israel's chosen king in 1 Samuel 10:20-24 (indeed the same process that had identified the thief Achan in Joshua 7:16-18) was now used to identify Jonathan as Israel's "problem," when it is all too obvious to us that the problems were caused by someone else.

Saul Deals with the "Problem" (vv. 43-45)

SAUL'S QUESTION (V. 43a)

That "someone" immediately interrogated Jonathan: "Then Saul said to Jonathan, 'Tell me what you have done'" (v. 43a).

This is reminiscent of Samuel's interrogating Saul in 1 Samuel 13:11 (and Joshua's interrogating Achan, Joshua 7:19). "What have you done?" The one who was condemned in chapter 13 was now the interrogator.

JONATHAN'S ANSWER (V. 43b)

Jonathan's reply brought the stupidity of the whole episode into focus: "And Jonathan told him, 'I tasted a little honey with the tip of the staff that was in my hand. Here I am; I will die'" (v. 43b).

The sarcasm is sharp: "Here is the extent of my crime: I *tasted* a *little* honey on the *tip* of my staff! Guilty me! Clearly a hanging offense! Execute me for my dastardly deed!"

SAUL'S VERDICT (V. 44)

Jonathan may have made a joke of the matter, but Saul was in no joking mood: "And Saul said, 'God do so to me and more also; you shall surely die, Jonathan'" (v. 44).

We were not mistaken to see a growing rift between father and son! We are witnessing the deterioration of Saul. The man who did not obey God in chapter 13 and then expressed no confidence in God when faced with his enemies and then devised the crazy plan to save himself by starving his troops and then sounded so very concerned about the people's act of disobedience was now prepared to kill his courageous and godly son because of his (Saul's) silly oath! In one of his few references to God in this chapter, he swore another oath!

JONATHAN'S REDEMPTION (V. 45)

The people knew better than their king:

> Then the people said to Saul, "Shall Jonathan die, who has worked this great salvation in Israel? Far from it! As the LORD lives, there shall not one hair of his head fall to the ground, for he has worked with God this day." So the people ransomed Jonathan, so that he did not die. (v. 45)

Jonathan had said, "It may be that the LORD will work for us" (1 Samuel 14:6). The people could see that his faith in God was vindicated: "He has worked with God this day." The wisdom of Jonathan's faith and the foolishness of Saul's efforts, which must be seen as faith-*less*, were clear to all.

The Real Problem Persists (v. 46)

The account concludes by noting that Saul failed to deal with the real problem that had been threatening him and his people all along: "Then Saul went up from pursuing the Philistines, and the Philistines went to their own place" (v. 46).

As Jonathan had said, "the defeat among the Philistines has not been great" (1 Samuel 14:30b).

A SUMMARY OF SAUL'S REIGN (vv. 47-52)

Although we have much more to hear about Saul (in particular there is a very important episode in chapter 15), there is a sense in which the essential story has now been told. And as though to signal this, the narrative provides at this point a summary of Saul's reign. Effectively Saul's reign was now over.

Saul's Accomplishments (vv. 47, 48)

The objectivity of this summary is striking, given the negative impression we have been given of Saul. Consider the outline of his accomplishments:

> When Saul had taken the kingship over Israel, he fought against all his enemies on every side, against Moab, against the Ammonites, against Edom, against the kings of Zobah, and against the Philistines. Wherever he turned he routed them. And he did valiantly and struck the Amalekites and delivered Israel out of the hands of those who plundered them. (vv. 47, 48)

Much more happened in Saul's time as Israel's king than is recorded in this book. This summary makes that clear. However, it also makes clear that if Saul was a failure as Israel's king (and he certainly was) it was not because of lack of military skill.[7] His failure, as we heard in chapter 13 and as we have seen played out in chapter 14, lay in his not trusting and obeying God.

Saul's Family (vv. 49-51)

Then we hear of Saul's family:

> Now the sons of Saul were Jonathan, Ishvi, and Malchi-shua. And the names of his two daughters were these: the name of the firstborn was

Merab, and the name of the younger Michal. And the name of Saul's wife was Ahinoam the daughter of Ahimaaz. And the name of the commander of his army was Abner the son of Ner, Saul's uncle. Kish was the father of Saul, and Ner the father of Abner was the son of Abiel. (vv. 49-51)

Of a number of these we will hear more in due course.

Saul's Legacy (v. 52)

Finally Saul's legacy is summed up. On the one hand: "There was hard fighting against the Philistines all the days of Saul" (v. 52a).

He never did deal with that problem. Indeed it will be in fighting the Philistines that Saul will meet his own end (1 Samuel 31). To save Israel from the Philistines had been the thing he was anointed for (1 Samuel 9:16).

On the other hand: "And when Saul saw any strong man, or any valiant man, he attached him to himself" (v. 52b).

That, of course, is what Samuel had said a king would do: "He will take your sons" (1 Samuel 8:11). One of the valiant men Saul will attach to himself will occupy our attention for many pages to come (see 1 Samuel 18:2).

Saul is one of the great tragic figures of world history and of world literature. We sense his tragedy because we know his weaknesses very well indeed. Saul failed as I have failed, as you have failed. We know what it is to forget God, to not really trust God, and to disobey God.

What we have seen, however, is that such lack of faith in God is, as Samuel had said at Gilgal, "foolish." Our schemes to save ourselves are likely to be as stupid as Saul's silly oath. Only God can save us from our real enemies. He can, and he will.

It is appropriate for us to see in Saul's story this lesson for our own lives. Let us not be like Saul. Let us not forget God. Let us trust him. Let us obey him.

But the deeper lesson for us to learn from Saul is that his failure should point us to the King who was everything that Saul failed to be. If we have seen Saul's foolishness, then let that point us to the wisdom of the one who said:

"Everyone then who hears these words of mine and does them will be like a wise man who built his house on the rock. And the rain fell, and the floods came, and the winds blew and beat on that house, but it did not fall, because it had been founded on the rock." (Matthew 7:24, 25)

22

The Leader Who Let Them Down

1 SAMUEL 15:1-11

It is a common human experience to be disappointed by leaders. Leaders who fail are more familiar to us than leaders who succeed. Leaders so often prove to be inept or unwise. Leaders make bad judgments or fail to make needed decisions. At worst we find leaders who prove to be dishonest or corrupt. Those leaders who do succeed, we cynically expect to do so only for a time. But the cynicism is born of experience that warns us that even good leaders can let us down sooner or later — and they usually do.

Why is it so rare to find a competent, wise leader who is appropriately decisive as well as honest and good?

In general terms Christian people will rightly answer that question in terms of the sinfulness of human nature. The human rejection of God has left us all morally weakened. We would be very foolish indeed to expect any of our merely human leaders to *never* let us down. We therefore ought not to put unqualified trust in such leaders. Those of us who are leaders ought not to expect others to *fully* trust us. We ought not to fully trust ourselves! Human sinfulness is the reason that we should welcome checks and balances, forms of accountability, limitations to power.

There are too many sad stories of Christian churches and groups that have suffered from improper use of power by leaders. Authoritarian leadership, centered on an individual or a small inner circle, beyond criticism and unaccountable, is one of the hallmarks of cult-like groups that have developed within or from Christian churches. A healthy understanding of the Bible's teaching about the sinfulness of human nature — including leaders — is an important protection from such dangerous and damaging developments. Wise leaders will make sure that they are open to the scrutiny of others (and not just those who like them!), while wise members of churches will graciously but firmly resist authoritarian, unchallengeable leadership styles.[1]

Christian people should be aware that improper forms of leadership are commonly associated with erroneous doctrine. The New Testament reminds us that false teaching typically involves exploitation (2 Peter 2:3). False teachers "despise authority" (other than their own) (2 Peter 2:10). They are "bold and willful, they do not tremble" (2 Peter 2:10). It is reasonable to assume that an inadequate doctrine of sin will be an important part of why false teaching and bad leadership go together.

The story of Saul in the book of 1 Samuel is a study in leadership failure. It is not, however, leadership in general terms that is under examination, but the leadership of the people of God, the Old Testament nation of Israel, constituted by God himself as his own people through whom he would eventually bring blessing to the whole world.

In the account we have been following, Israel's search for a leader led to the appointment of Saul as their first king. The analysis of Saul's failure in the Biblical record is remarkable. There are indications, as we have seen, that Saul had a number of significant accomplishments, especially in the military sphere (see 1 Samuel 14:47, 48). He was clearly a capable leader in certain respects. These, however, are mentioned with extreme brevity. Much more detailed attention is given to two critical incidents that might have been passed over in another kind of account of Saul's life. From the perspective of the Biblical historian they were decisive. Saul's failure as Israel's king consisted in this: *his disobedience to God's words to him.*

A chapter is devoted to each of two particular occasions of this failure (chapters 13, 15). We come now to the second of these, which should shock us into a radical reevaluation of the seriousness of sin and the inadequacy of a sinful leader.

First Samuel 15 begins abruptly after the end of the previous chapter, which concluded with a summary of Saul's whole reign (14:47-52). We have noted a number of times that Biblical narrative is less committed to chronological sequence than we are used to. There is no clear indication when the events recounted in chapter 15 took place. It is certain that it was after the events of chapter 13, for the rejection of Saul that took place then ("Now your kingdom shall not continue," v. 14) is brought to finality in chapter 15 ("The LORD has rejected you from being king over Israel," v. 26). By the end of chapter 15 the relationship between Samuel and Saul was finished ("Samuel did not see Saul again until the day of his death," v. 35). However, since Samuel did not appear at all in the dramatic events of chapter 14, the chronological relationship of the events of chapters 14, 15 is an open question.

That simply means that the time sequence of things was not, at this point, important as far as the Biblical historian was concerned. The summary of

Saul's life at the end of chapter 14 is followed by the detailed account we find in chapter 15 because, I take it, this incident, above all others, defined Saul's kingship. If you want to understand Saul, then the one incident you must comprehend is recounted in chapter 15.

The chapter unfolds in three scenes. Here we will consider the first two scenes (vv. 1-9 and 10, 11). The dramatic third scene (vv. 12-35) will occupy our next chapter.

SAUL AND THE AMALEKITES (vv. 1-9)

In Scene 1 we see one of Saul's many military victories (cf. 1 Samuel 14:47, 48). This one, however, is different. To understand the difference, we must hear what Samuel said to Saul before the action began.

The King Who Must Listen (v. 1)

Samuel spoke first of the character of Saul's unique kingship: "And Samuel said to Saul, 'The LORD sent me to anoint you king over his people Israel; now therefore listen to the words of the LORD'" (v. 1).

Saul was no ordinary king. There were three elements that made his kingship unique.

The first element was that *the Lord was the one who had made him king*. Saul was not king by virtue of some right of birth or position. He did not become king by his cleverness or strength, or even popularity. "Never forget, Saul, that you are king because and only because God chose to make you king" (see 1 Samuel 9:16; 10:1, 24). (We have noticed that through much of chapter 14 Saul seemed to give little thought to this fact.)

The second element was that *King Saul had to submit to the prophet Samuel*. This is clearer in the original Hebrew where the word "me" is emphasized. "It is *me* that the LORD sent to anoint you king," said the prophet (again see 1 Samuel 9:16 and 10:1). "Never forget, Saul, that even as king, you are not the ultimate authority around here. You are subject to God's prophet." (That, of course, was clear in chapter 13, when the prophet rebuked the king and told him he had been a fool!)

The third element that defined the uniqueness of Saul's kingship was that *the people over whom he reigned were not* his *people, but* God's *people* (see 1 Samuel 9:16 and 10:1). "Never forget, Saul, that Israel is *the Lord's* people." (That is something that Saul seemed to forget in chapter 14, when his talk was all about when "*I* am avenged on *my* enemies," v. 24.)

We had reason to think that this particular arrangement, whereby Saul's kingship was "before the LORD (1 Samuel 11:15), had been set out in writing by Samuel when he told the people "the justice of the kingdom" (1 Samuel

10:25, literal translation). Certainly it had been clearly explained at Gilgal (see 1 Samuel 12:14, 15).

If this was the unique character of Saul's kingship (appointed by God, subject to the prophet, over God's people), then one essential thing was required of this king: "Now therefore listen to the words of the Lord." Again the original is a little more vivid: "Hear the sound [or the voice] of the words of the Lord." Above all this king must *listen to the sound of the words of God.*

We find ourselves surrounded by many sounds. Lots of sounds are just background noise. Some sounds catch our attention. Some sounds affect us deeply: a piece of music, a baby's cry, an explosion, some news. Among all the sounds in the world, the people of Israel were privileged to have heard the sound of the words of God at Mount Sinai in the days of Moses. At that time God had said to Moses, "Gather the people to me, that I may let them *hear my words*" (Deuteronomy 4:10). Much later Moses reminded the people of that day: "Then the Lord spoke to you out of the midst of the fire. You *heard the sound of words*" (Deuteronomy 4:12). To be the people who *heard the sound of the words of God* was Israel's unique calling. A king over this people must therefore, more importantly than anything else, be one who *listens to the sound of the words of the Lord.*

This essential requirement for this peculiar king is the theme of 1 Samuel 15.

The Sound of the Words of the Lord (vv. 2, 3)

No sooner was this requirement spelled out in verse 1 than the sound of the words of the Lord rang out for Saul to hear:

> "Thus says the Lord of hosts, 'I have noted what Amalek did to Israel in opposing them on the way when they came up out of Egypt. Now go and strike Amalek and devote to destruction all that they have. Do not spare them, but kill both man and woman, child and infant, ox and sheep, camel and donkey.'" (vv. 2, 3)

Here is the deeply disturbing "sound of the words of the Lord."

Amalek was a grandson of Esau (Genesis 36:12). His descendants (referred to as Amalek or the Amalekites) had a long history of violent hostility toward the Israelites. They were the first human threat to the people of Israel after the exodus (see Exodus 17:8-16). On that occasion God told Moses to write down this promise: "I will utterly blot out the memory of Amalek from under heaven" (Exodus 17:14).

About four decades later, before the Israelites entered the promised land, Moses reminded them:

"Remember what Amalek did to you on the way as you came out of Egypt,
how he attacked you on the way when you were faint and weary, and cut
off your tail, those who were lagging behind you, and he did not fear
God. Therefore when the LORD *your God has given you rest from all your*
enemies around you, in the land that the LORD *your God is giving you for*
an inheritance to possess, you shall blot out the memory of Amalek from
under heaven; you shall not forget." (Deuteronomy 25:17-19)

Amalek was a people deeply and consistently set against God and his people. [2] Hostilities from Amalek continued after Israel entered the land of Canaan (see Judges 3:12-14; 6:3-5, 33; 7:12).[3] However the time had now come for the terrible judgment of God to fall on the Amalekites.

The sound of the words of God to Saul that day made it clear that God's king was the one appointed to bring, at last, God's judgment to the Amalekites.

Notice the terrible but clear terms of Saul's mission in 1 Samuel 15:3. "Devote to destruction" is one word in Hebrew. It is almost a technical term, sometimes referred to as the "ban," whose precise meaning is much discussed.[4] In this context the term refers to the destruction involved in divine judgment. No one was to be "spared." There was to be no escape.

There is no way to lessen the horror of this moment. The sound of the words of God to Saul that day was terrible. It must be remembered, however, that this was the holy and righteous judgment of God, "the LORD of hosts."[5]

Moments like this in the pages of the Old Testament must not be avoided. They must not, of course, be lifted out of context and caricatured. Sometimes such terrible Biblical incidents are condemned as "genocide" or "ethnic cleansing." This is to measure the events by modern moral categories, while disregarding the Bible's own evaluation of them. These episodes should remind us that God always has been and still is "the Judge of all the earth" who does only what is just and right (Genesis 18:25). Israel or Israelites could find themselves falling under this judgment (see Deuteronomy 13:12-18; Joshua 7:10-15), just as those to whom this judgment came could seek and find mercy (see, for example, Joshua 6:25).

Nor should we imagine that such episodes are Old Testament phenomena that are best forgotten now that the New Testament has come. Some Bible commentators attempt to come to terms with these horrors by suggesting that the morality of the Old Testament was provisional.[6] This fails to acknowledge that, according to the Old Testament, these discomforting episodes occurred at *God's* command. Are we to think that in Old Testament times God's morality was provisional?

A difference comes with the New Testament, but it is not some new morality that does away with the very idea of divine judgment. We will come to that difference in a few moments.

But let us return to 1 Samuel 15, where God's appointed king was called to bring God's long announced judgment on the Amalekites. We have seen the king who must listen to the sound of the words of God. We have heard the terrible sound of the words of God. What, then, did King Saul do?

What the King Did (vv. 4-9)

First we see him preparing to carry out the words of the Lord:

> *So Saul summoned the people and numbered them in Telaim, two hundred thousand men on foot, and ten thousand men of Judah. And Saul came to the city of Amalek and lay in wait in the valley. (vv. 4, 5)*

The location of Telaim is not now known. Neither is this "city" of Amalek.[7] What matters is that Saul with considerable forces appears to be preparing to obey the sound of the words of the Lord.

Then in verse 6 we see him taking considerable care to not go beyond the words of the Lord:

> *Then Saul said to the Kenites, "Go, depart; go down from among the Amalekites, lest I destroy you with them. For you showed kindness to all the people of Israel when they came up out of Egypt." So the Kenites departed from among the Amalekites. (v. 6)*

We should be impressed. Saul was taking care. The Kenites were not included in the terrible curse that was on the Amalekites. Indeed the account in Exodus 17 of the Amalekite aggression is followed by the description of the positive encounter between Moses and his Kenite father-in law, Jethro (Exodus 18:1-12).[8] Saul was not prepared to risk "collateral damage," and carefully, perhaps at some risk to his operation, he warned them to get out of the way.

Thirdly, with the Kenites safely out of the way, we see Saul begin to carry out his terrible task: "And Saul defeated the Amalekites from Havilah as far as Shur, which is east of Egypt" (v. 7).

We might shudder as we think of what was involved behind those brief words. We sense that King Saul was indeed bringing the long anticipated judgment on the people of Amalek.

But if the sound of the words of the Lord is still ringing in our ears, what we read next strikes a discord:

> *And he took Agag the king of the Amalekites alive and devoted to destruction all the people with the edge of the sword. But Saul and the people spared Agag and the best of the sheep and of the oxen and of the fattened calves and*

the lambs, and all that was good, and would not utterly destroy them. All that was despised and worthless they devoted to destruction. (vv. 8, 9)

That special Hebrew verb appears three times in these two verses. Saul *devoted to destruction* all the people with the edge of the sword, but there was quite a lot that Saul and the people would not *utterly destroy* (same word), although all that was worthless they *devoted to destruction*. Another word is repeated from verse 3, where God said, "Do not *spare* them": "Saul and the people *spared* Agag and the best" of the animals.

For the moment we can only see these actions as outside observers. We are told nothing about *why* Saul took Agag alive or *why* he and the people spared the better animals. We can just remember the sound of the words of the Lord: "Do *not* spare them."

The writer seems to be very careful to point out Saul's responsibility for the sparing that was done. The original suggests that it was Saul who "spared," and the people joined him.[9] The significance of this will be seen when we reach verse 15.

There is something very odd about this action. What would motivate sparing "the best" animals when all the people (except the king) and the worse animals were destroyed? The first scene in this drama leaves us wondering.

THE WORD OF THE LORD TO SAMUEL (vv. 10, 11)

Scene 2 is much briefer. It takes us from Saul and his troops to some other unspecified location where Samuel was.

The Lord's Regret (vv. 10, 11a)

The word of the LORD came to Samuel: "I regret that I have made Saul king, for he has turned back from following me and has not performed my commandments." (vv. 10, 11a)

Literally, "he has not fulfilled my words." In other words, his actions had been determined by something other than the sound of the words of the Lord. He had not listened to the sound to which he was obligated to listen. Something else had captured his attention.

That simple fact accounts for these terrible words from God: "I regret that I have made Saul king." A little later (when we reach verse 29) we will consider the implications of this remarkable statement that God "regrets" something.[10] For the moment we note that the translations seem to have struggled with the appropriate word to describe what God is doing here. The older RSV had, "I repent that I have made Saul king." This sounded so strange that the NIV put it, "I am grieved that I have made Saul king." The astonishing thing is that God so enters into his involvement with his creation, in particular with humanity, and even more particularly with his people, that their failures affect him. The Lord was so grieved by Saul's failure to listen to the sound of his words that he regretted making him king.

The depth of the tragedy recorded here may be appreciated if we recall the only other occasion where this language is used in this way.[11] In the days of Noah:

> The LORD saw that the wickedness of man was great in the earth, and that every intention of the thoughts of his heart was only evil continually. And the LORD was sorry that he had made man on the earth, and it grieved him to his heart. (Genesis 6:5, 6)

"The LORD *was sorry*" has exactly the same verb as "I *regret*" in 1 Samuel 15:11. It may well be appropriate to hear an echo from the days of Noah as God uttered these terrible words to Samuel. This day when God's appointed king did not listen to the sound of the voice of the Lord was like those far-off days when human wickedness came close to destroying all that God had made.

Samuel's Anger (v. 11b)

The tragedy was not lost on Samuel: "And Samuel was angry, and he cried to the LORD all night" (v. 11b).

We are not told what he cried. We are not told whether he was angry at God or at Saul or at the whole miserable situation. I suspect he didn't know either.[12] He was simply distraught. He had only reluctantly become involved in this king experiment. But Samuel knew the consequences of a disobedient king in Israel. He had warned the people at Gilgal:

> " . . . if you will not obey the voice of the LORD, but rebel against the commandment of the LORD, then the hand of the LORD will be against you and your king [or fathers]." (1 Samuel 12:15)

All that night Samuel cried out to the Lord. He understood the enormity of what had happened. The king the Lord had sent him to anoint over his people Israel had failed to listen to the sound of the words of the Lord.

What happened next was one of the most spectacular confrontations in the pages of the Bible, when the prophet Samuel met the defiant King Saul after the events we have just witnessed. We will witness that confrontation in our next chapter.

As we conclude, it is right, as always, to move from the Old Testament text to see its New Testament fulfillment. As we have seen before, Saul, the king who failed, points us to the King who did not fail. The difference that comes with the New Testament is the news that the one who will without fail bring God's judgment to the whole world has now been identified:

> *"[Jesus] commanded us to preach to the people and to testify that he is the one appointed by God to be judge of the living and the dead." (Acts 10:42; cf. 2 Timothy 4:1)*

The day has been set (Acts 17:31) when Jesus, as God's appointed king over the whole world (Revelation 11:15), will bring "the righteous judgment of God," "inflicting vengeance on those who do not know God and on those who do not obey the gospel of our Lord Jesus" (2 Thessalonians 1:5, 8). The gospel also includes the wonderful news that this same Jesus "delivers us from the wrath to come" (1 Thessalonians 1:10). This gospel both warns of the coming judgment and calls us to the Savior.

Saul's mission to judge the Amalekites was a local, small-scale anticipation of the judgment that will finally come on the whole world at the hands of God's appointed king.

Much modern "Christianity" wants to keep Christ but deny the divine judgment he has been appointed to bring. Such make-believe is a terrible distortion of the truth.

In these days of much religiously motivated violence, it is very important for us to understand that we are not living in the time of the Old Testament, when God's judgment was often brought on individuals and nations by war and other acts of physical violence.[13] The death and resurrection of Jesus announces the coming judgment of the whole world by the "man whom [God] has appointed" (Acts 17:31). We find ourselves living in a time when it is not up to Christian people to repay anyone evil for evil. So far as it depends on us we are to live peaceably with all, leaving all vengeance to the coming wrath of God (see Romans 12:18). Our warfare now is a spiritual battle for the proclamation of the gospel, in which physical violence has no place (see 2 Corinthians 10:3-6; Ephesians 6:10-20).

23

The Rejected King

1 SAMUEL 15:12-35

Saul was the leader whom God rejected. First Samuel 15 recounts the decisive events that led to Saul's rejection. The chapter is a brilliant study in the deceptive, corrupting power of sin. It reveals, therefore, the inadequacy that will plague all forms of human leadership. In particular it shows why God's people need a leader greater than Saul.

We have followed the first two of the three scenes of the drama in 1 Samuel 15. In Scene 1 we saw that King Saul had been sent to bring God's long anticipated judgment on the Amalekites (1 Samuel 15:2, 3). He went, and he won a decisive victory over the Amalekites (v. 7), but, for reasons not explained, he took their king, Agag, alive (v. 8), and he and the people "would not [better, "were not willing to"] utterly destroy . . . the best" of the animals (v. 9).

Scene 2 took us to some other unspecified location where God spoke to the prophet Samuel and said: "I regret that I have made Saul king, for he has turned back from following me and has not performed my commandments" (v. 11).

Literally this reads, "he has not fulfilled my words." Samuel was very distressed and spent the night crying out to the Lord.

In Scene 3 we now come to early the next morning. After his sleepless night, Samuel must have known that this would be a terrible day. He was not wrong!

SAUL'S MONUMENT (v. 12)

A dreaded confrontation with the king could not be put off: "And Samuel rose early to meet Saul in the morning" (v. 12a).

Of course, he had to find Saul first. Inquiries yielded the following information:

> *And it was told Samuel, "Saul came to Carmel, and behold, he set up a monument for himself and turned and passed on and went down to Gilgal." (v. 12b)*

This was not the famous Mount Carmel, but another Carmel well to the south, in Judah (see Joshua 15:55).[1] How Samuel's heart must have sunk to hear that Saul had erected a monument "for himself"! Notice those words: "a monument *for* [or *to*] *himself*." Presumably it commemorated his great victory over the Amalekites! After Moses had defeated the Amalekites, he had built a monument. It was an altar. That monument celebrated the Lord ("the Lord Is My Banner," Exodus 17:15).[2] Saul's monument was "to himself."[3] Did this man have no idea what he had done?! The inappropriateness of this monument will be apparent, even to Saul, before the end of this day.

INITIAL CONFRONTATION (vv. 13-16)

Samuel headed off, presumably toward Gilgal, and found Saul, apparently before he reached Gilgal.[4] Listen to the conversation.

Saul's Warm Greeting (v. 13)

Saul was the first to speak: "And Samuel came to Saul, and Saul said to him, 'Blessed be you to the Lord. I have performed the commandment of the Lord'" (v. 13).

Literally he said, "I have fulfilled the word of the Lord" — the very thing God had told Samuel that Saul had *not* done (v. 11). Imagine how these words sounded to Samuel. The previous night the Lord had anticipated exactly what Saul would say and, using the very same words, said to Samuel, "He has *not* fulfilled my words."

Saul had all the appearance of being blissfully unaware that anything at all was amiss. He showed no sign of a troubled conscience as he confidently greeted Samuel: "Blessed be you to the Lord!"

If we take Saul at face value — if we give him the benefit of the doubt and assume that he is not deliberately and consciously trying to cover up his failure to fully obey God's word — we see here something of sin's deceitfulness (cf. Hebrews 3:13). The very sinfulness that leads to disobedience often blinds the sinner to the reality of his or her disobedience. But as in the experience of Saul, a clear conscience is no guarantee of innocence. It can take the probing, searching work of the word of God to bring us to recognize our guilt (cf. Hebrews 4:11-13).

Samuel's Incriminating Question (v. 14)

Samuel could hear the incriminating sounds: "And Samuel said, 'What then is this bleating of the sheep in my ears and the lowing of the oxen that I hear?'" (v. 14).

There is a slight over-translation here. Literally Samuel said, "What then is this *sound* of the sheep in my ears and the *sound* of the oxen that I hear?" We recall from verse 1 of this chapter that the one thing this king had to do was listen to the *sound* of the words of God. The air was now filled with the *sound* of his failure to do so!

Saul's Deceived Defense (v. 15)

Listen to his response, and witness the depth of sin's deceitfulness:

> Saul said, "They *have brought them from the Amalekites, for* the people *spared the best of the sheep and of the oxen to sacrifice to the* LORD *your God, and the rest we have devoted to destruction."* (v. 15)

We noticed how in 1 Samuel 15:9 the narrator carefully told us that Saul *and* the people "spared" Agag, the Amalekite king, and "the best" of the animals, even suggesting that it was Saul who took the lead in this. But Saul's defense shifts the blame: "*They . . . the people* spared. . . ."

Where have we heard something like that before? "The man said, '*The woman* whom *you* gave to be with me, *she* gave me fruit of the tree, and I ate'" (Genesis 3:12).

Saul stood in the great tradition of sinners since Adam who deny responsibility for their own sin and blame others. We have all played that game, sometimes with utter sincerity. We convince ourselves that the blame is not ours. It's our parents, our circumstances, the system, the government — but it's not *our* fault.

Then, just in case he couldn't fully dissociate himself from the action, Saul minimized the seriousness of the disobedience by claiming that the people had a noble motive. It was done in order "to sacrifice to the LORD"! Again this is a game that we all know too well. We might have done the wrong thing, but we meant well! ("I cheated on my taxes so I could give more to my church!") Sin blinds sinners to sinfulness! In Saul's case the narrator has already told us in verse 9 that Saul and the people were *unwilling*[5] to destroy all the good animals, as the Lord had explicitly commanded (1 Samuel 15:3). Saul's noble motive was an illusion, as are the noble motives many of us have claimed.

Not only did Saul try to shift the blame to the people ("they" did it!) and play down the wrongness (it was "to sacrifice"), he then took credit for the part of what had been done that was obedient ("we" did that bit!): "the rest *we* have devoted to destruction."

Did you notice that in the course of this self-deceived defense, Saul let slip an indication of his real problem? His words betrayed his separation from the God whose voice he was meant to be hearing. He called him not "our God," certainly not "my God," but "*your* [Samuel's] God." Saul stood in the great tradition of sinners since Adam who minimize and deny the guilt of their actions *because* they have turned away from God. That, of course, is what God had said to Samuel the previous night: "He has turned back from following me" (1 Samuel 15:11).

Saul's one-sentence defense provides a brilliant study in the deceitfulness of sin.[6]

Samuel's Conversation Stopper (v. 16)

Samuel saw Saul's "defense" for what it was and shut him up: "Then Samuel said to Saul, 'Stop! I will tell you what the LORD said to me this night.' And he said to him, 'Speak'" (v. 16).

I rather suspect that Saul soon regretted that invitation!

SAMUEL'S ACCUSATION (vv. 17-19)

Samuel presented the case for the prosecution in three simple but important points that demolished Saul's attempted defenses.

Saul's Position (v. 17)

First, Samuel reminded Saul of his position: "And Samuel said, 'Though you are little in your own eyes, are you not the head of the tribes of Israel? The LORD anointed you king over Israel'" (v. 17).

This may be a reference to Saul's humility at an earlier stage of his life. When Samuel had first spoken to him, Saul had said:

> *"Am I not a Benjaminite, from the least of the tribes of Israel? And is not my clan the humblest of all the clans of the tribe of Benjamin? Why then have you spoken to me in this way?" (1 Samuel 9:21)*

And, of course, when the time came for Saul to be acclaimed king by the people, far from putting himself forward, he hid himself among the baggage (1 Samuel 10:22)!

More probably, however, Samuel was referring here to what Saul had just said, blaming "the people" for the sheep and the oxen that Samuel could hear.[7] "You might have subordinated yourself to the people, Saul. You may have made yourself 'in your own eyes' less than responsible for the behavior of the people. *But that is not who you are!* God has anointed you — 'messiahed' you — as king, as head over the people of Israel." That is the crucial point with which this chapter began (see 1 Samuel 15:1).

Saul's Mission (v. 18)

The second point in the case for the prosecution is the mission on which Saul had been sent:

> *"And the Lord sent you on a mission and said, 'Go, devote to destruction the sinners, the Amalekites, and fight against them until they are consumed.'"* (v. 18)

That is the sound (or voice) of the words of the Lord that this king was bound to hear (see 1 Samuel 15:2, 3). Calling the Amalekites "the sinners" emphasizes that Saul's mission was no ordinary military conquest. As God's anointed ("messiahed") king, Saul was to bring God's judgment on these "sinners." The terms of the mission were unambiguous and weighty.

Saul's Terrible Deed (v. 19)

These two points (Saul's position and his mission) provide the perspective for appreciating the seriousness of the third point: "Why then did you not obey the voice of the Lord? Why did you pounce on the spoil and do what was evil in the sight of the Lord?" (v. 19).

This "Why?" echoes Samuel's "You have done foolishly" on the earlier occasion (1 Samuel 13:13). Disobedience to the words of God is always foolish. *Why* do we do it? God is completely good, infinitely wise, all-powerful. *Why* do we human beings fail to obey him? Our sin makes no sense! Every time we disobey God's word, we demonstrate that we believe that he is *not* good, wise, and powerful. How foolish is that! But if every act of disobedience to the word of God is irrational, Saul's was all the more so. He was the one anointed by God as king over his people Israel. He had a clear and unambiguous word from God. *Why* did he not obey?[8]

His disobedience was "evil in the sight of the Lord." An almost identical phrase will be heard much later in the story of Israel's monarchy. After telling of David's acts of adultery and murder, the narrator will tell us, "the thing David had done was evil in the sight of the Lord" (2 Samuel 11:27, my translation).[9] Saul's disobedience in 1 Samuel 15 is fully comparable to David's sin with Bathsheba and Uriah. Both were "evil in the sight of the Lord."

Saul wanted to blame "the people." Samuel put all of the responsibility on Saul. The "you" in verse 19 is singular. Saul was, after all, the anointed king over this people.

Saul wanted to claim that the animals were spared in order "to sacrifice to the LORD." Samuel disregarded that claim: "Why did you *pounce* on the spoil?" That is what the people did in the previous chapter (1 Samuel 14:32) when they were famished and recklessly slaughtered the Philistine animals to satisfy their hunger.[10]

"*Why*, Saul, did you do it?"

SAUL'S DEFENSE (vv. 20, 21)

Saul responded by reiterating the defense he had already presented:

> And Saul said to Samuel, "I have obeyed the voice of the LORD. I have gone on the mission on which the LORD sent me. I have brought Agag the king of Amalek, and I have devoted the Amalekites to destruction. But the people took of the spoil, sheep and oxen, the best of the things devoted to destruction, to sacrifice to the LORD your God in Gilgal." (vv. 20, 21)

In the Hebrew of this text there is one word that can be translated "hear," "listen," or "obey." There is also one word that can be translated "voice" or "sound." Remember how in 1 Samuel 15:1 Saul had been told that he must "listen to the sound of the words of the LORD." Now he claimed that was exactly what he had done: "I *have* obeyed [or listened to] the voice [or sound] of the LORD." "I did what I was sent to do. I destroyed the Amalekites."

But did you notice the little piece of new information Saul slipped in in verse 20? "I have brought Agag the king of Amalek"! Up to now the interrogation had been about the animals. Samuel had said nothing about Agag. But presumably Saul was well aware that Agag's presence could not be hidden for long. He therefore took the initiative and presented this information with the best possible spin. He slipped it in between his assertion of obedience ("I *have* obeyed") and his claim to have destroyed the Amalekites.[11]

As for "pouncing on the spoil" as Samuel had put it, "that was the people, not me. And I repeat, their intentions were good: 'to sacrifice to the LORD *your* God.' So why am I on trial here?"[12]

SAMUEL'S VERDICT (vv. 22, 23)

Samuel's role now shifts from presenting the case for the prosecution to pronouncing the verdict.

> And Samuel said,
> "Has the LORD as great delight in burnt offerings and sacrifices,

as in obeying [or hearing] the voice of the LORD?
Behold, to obey [or hear] is better than sacrifice,
    and to listen than the fat of rams.
For rebellion is as the sin of divination,
    and presumption is as iniquity and idolatry.
Because you have rejected the word of the LORD,
    he has also rejected you from being king." (vv. 22, 23)

Only in the last line of this remarkable pronouncement is the penalty specified. The Lord had rejected Saul from being king. He could no longer be king because he had rejected the word of the Lord.

The rest of the speech is designed to expose what Saul seemed incapable of seeing — the fact and devastating seriousness of disobedience to God's word. The speech moves beyond the specific situation of Saul, his special office and the extraordinary task he had been given, to the fundamental reality of what God requires of man.

Saul's defense had included the implicit argument that the action of the people (which, of course, had nothing to do with *him*) was justified because their intention was to sacrifice the animals to the Lord. What kind of crazy idea is that! What kind of God do you think the Lord is? Does he delight in sacrifices more than hearing and obeying his voice?

Samuel's speech goes to the heart of Biblical faith, which is a response to the God who has spoken. In his word God has made known his will, in the form of promises and commands. Biblical faith consists in believing God's promises and obeying his commands. These are two sides of the one coin — the proper response to the God who has spoken, which the New Testament would call "the obedience of faith" (Romans 1:5; 16:26). But to think that disobedience to the word of God can somehow be compensated for by any amount of religious activity (such as Saul's proposed sacrifice of the animals taken in defiance of God's word) is utterly foolish.

Mind you, it is not at all uncommon to find precisely this attitude among modern religious people. Has it ever crossed your mind that you might compensate for some disobedience to God's word with regular churchgoing or generous giving or even disciplined praying and Bible reading?

Samuel's words should expose our foolishness just as they exposed Saul's:

"Has the LORD as great delight in burnt offerings and sacrifices,
    as in obeying the voice of the LORD?
Behold, to obey is better than sacrifice,
    and to listen than the fat of rams." (v. 22)

That is because disobedience is "rebellion" and "presumption" (v. 23).

If God has spoken, then to be unwilling to obey him is to *rebel against God* (cf. 1 Samuel 12:15). If God has spoken, then to fail to obey him is *presumptuous arrogance of the highest order*. If God has spoken, disobedience is in the same category as "the sin of divination"[13] and "iniquity and idolatry" — the effective rejection of God and the adoption of another religion.

Saul's disobedience was a rejection of the word of God, which was a rejection of God himself. The consequence was God's rejection of Saul as king over his people.

SAUL'S CONFESSION AND PLEA (vv. 24-33)

The Confession and Plea (vv. 24, 25)

The words of the prophet accomplished what Saul's conscience had failed to do. His guilt was exposed so that even he could see it:

> *Saul said to Samuel, "I have sinned, for I have transgressed the commandment of the LORD and your words, because I feared the people and obeyed their voice. Now therefore, please pardon my sin and return with me that I may worship the LORD." (vv. 24, 25)*

He had listened to the wrong voice, and now he knew it. The seriousness of the situation can only be appreciated if we remember the terms on which this king experiment had been allowed to proceed:

> *If you will fear the LORD and serve him and obey his voice and not rebel against the commandment of the LORD, and if both you and the king who reigns over you will follow the LORD your God, it will be well. But if you will not obey the voice of the LORD, but rebel against the commandment of the LORD, then the hand of the LORD will be against you and your king [or fathers]. (1 Samuel 12:14, 15)*

"Fear the LORD." But Saul had "feared the people." "Obey *his* voice." But Saul had "obeyed *their* voice." At last Saul sought pardon for his sin and the prophet's support in turning back to the Lord. It is not possible just from his words to make judgments about his sincerity. Against those who see utter sincerity here, we should not forget how slow Saul was to reach this point.[14] Too much should not be read into his desire to "worship the LORD." The verb means "bow down before"[15] and does not necessarily reveal anything about inner attitudes.

More important than reading between the lines here is the echo we hear from chapter 8. This whole king business began with the people demanding a king (1 Samuel 8:19) and the Lord's direction to Samuel to "obey their voice" (1 Samuel 8:22). Now we see where "obeying the voice of the people" has led. The king who was appointed by "obeying their voice" has failed precisely because he "obeyed their voice" (1 Samuel 15:24).[16]

The Refusal (v. 26)

However, among God's people this arrangement is simply not possible. For all the wonderful benefits of democracy as a system for organizing human government, democracy is no way for God's kingdom to be ruled.[17] The king who obeyed the voice of the people rather than the voice of God cannot be the king over God's people:

> And Samuel said to Saul, "I will not return with you. For you have rejected the word of the LORD, and the LORD has rejected you from being king over Israel." (v. 26)

The Torn Robe (vv. 27-29)

The tension must have been palpable. Saul was desperate. Samuel was implacable. Saul made one final despairing attempt to hold on to the prophet's favor: "As Samuel turned to go away, Saul seized the skirt of his robe, and it tore" (v. 18).[18]

It is a pathetic scene. Saul's attempt to hold on to Samuel results in the torn robe,[19] which becomes a sign of his tremendous loss:

> And Samuel said to him, "The LORD has torn the kingdom of Israel from you this day and has given it to a neighbor of yours, who is better than you." (v. 28)

We will be hearing more of this "better" neighbor next time. In what sense will he be "better"? Morally a "better" person? Or a "better" person for the office of the Lord's anointed king for some other reason? We will begin to see answers to these questions in chapter 16. At this point we cannot avoid recalling the earlier words of Samuel:

> "The LORD has sought out a man after his own heart, and the LORD has commanded him to be prince over his people, because you have not kept what the LORD commanded you." (1 Samuel 13:14)

As I said, we will learn more of that man when we examine 1 Samuel 16.

Samuel sealed the finality of this situation with the astonishing words: "And also the Glory of Israel will not lie or have regret, for he is not a man, that he should have regret" (v. 29).

These are astonishing words because we have already heard God say in verse 11, "I *regret* that I have made Saul king," and this chapter will close with the words, "And the Lord *regretted* that he had made Saul king over Israel" (v. 35).[20] This is one of those places where some claim to see an obvious contradiction in the text of the Bible.[21] The truth is, however, that both statements need to be heard. God did "regret" that he had made Saul king (vv. 11, 35). Saul's disobedience grieved him. But that does not mean that God had lied or that he had changed his intentions (v. 29). In the bigger picture,[22] all that has happened is exactly what God said would happen in 1 Samuel 12:15, *if* the king and the people did not obey the voice of the Lord.

The Confession and (Revised) Plea (vv. 30, 31)

In his last words in this chapter, Saul acknowledged his failure again but did not again seek pardon (did he realize that it was too late?). He just sought dignity:

> Then he said, "I have sinned; yet honor me now before the elders of my people and before Israel, and return with me, that I may bow before the Lord your God." (v. 30)

Even in this final confession Saul's inadequacy is evident. Two little pronouns betray him: "*my* people," "*your* God." For the sake of his own glory[23] he wanted to bow with Samuel before *Samuel's* God, before the elders of *his* (Saul's) people.[24] Saul had utterly failed to be the king described at the beginning of the chapter (1 Samuel 15:1, 2).[25]

For reasons that are not explained, Samuel relented from his refusal to go back with Saul (v. 26):[26] "So Samuel turned back after Saul, and Saul bowed before the Lord."

Samuel and Agag (vv. 32, 33)

Nothing is said about Samuel honoring or glorifying Saul before the people. On the contrary, Samuel seems to have taken over the royal prerogative and did the terrible deed that the king should have done.

> Then Samuel said, "Bring here to me Agag the king of the Amalekites." And Agag came to him cheerfully. Agag said, "Surely the bitterness of death is past." (v. 32)

Agag seems to have taken some heart from the sidelining of Saul. To be brought before the prophet gave him hope that perhaps the expected (and deserved!) death penalty had been averted. He could not have been more mistaken. It was God who had pronounced judgment on Agag and his people (1 Samuel 15:2, 3). Now the prophet of God, in the place of the failed king, carried out the terrible sentence:

> And Samuel said, "As your sword has made women childless, so shall your mother be childless among women." And Samuel hacked Agag to pieces before the LORD in Gilgal. (v. 33)

As we have seen previously, the horror of such scenes cannot be diminished. The words "before the LORD" remind us, however, that here again we are seeing the holy and righteous judgment of God, fully deserved, as Samuel's words emphasized.

The End (vv. 34, 35)

> Then Samuel went to Ramah, and Saul went up to his house in Gibeah of Saul. And Samuel did not see Saul again until the day of his death, but Samuel grieved over Saul. And the LORD regretted that he had made Saul king over Israel. (vv. 34, 35)

In a very important sense Saul's reign was now ended. The prophet departed from the king for good,[27] just as the king had turned away from following the Lord (1 Samuel 15:11).

We are right to see Saul's reign as a tragedy. At the heart of this tragedy was human sinfulness. In Saul we have seen that the leader chosen by the people and for the people was undone by his sinfulness.

How different was the day, many years later, when a voice was heard from Heaven saying, "This is my beloved Son, with whom I am well pleased" (Matthew 3:17). In Jesus we have a king who "humbled himself by becoming obedient to the point of death, even death on a cross" (Philippians 2:8). In complete contrast to the rejection of King Saul, the New Testament proclaims of Jesus:

> Therefore God has highly exalted him and bestowed on him the name that is above every name, so that at the name of Jesus every knee should bow, in heaven and on earth and under the earth, and every tongue confess that Jesus Christ is Lord, to the glory of God the Father. (Philippians 2:9-11)

PART THREE

David: The Leader
"According to God's Own Heart"

1 SAMUEL 16–31

24

Seeing as God Sees

1 SAMUEL 16:1-13

In any group of people there are as many points of view as there are individuals, on a whole range of things.

There are some subjects on which almost everyone has a point of view — a current political controversy, a celebrity scandal, a sporting triumph or failure. There are subjects on which many of us may have *similar* points of view, but even then it is likely that enough discussion between any two people would reveal at least some areas of difference on almost any subject. Certainly there are many issues — some of them very important — on which there are sharp differences in our points of view. You see it *this* way. I see it *that* way.

When that happens, what do we do?

More and more today it is believed that the right thing to do is to *accept* that we all have our own points of view and to *accept* all points of view as equally valid. It is wrong (so it is thought) to suggest that my point of view is in any way superior to yours or that yours is better than mine. Different *perceptions* of things, different *understandings* of things, are just, quite literally, *points of view*. *You* are looking at things from where *you* stand, with your background, your past experiences, your genetic makeup, and so on. *I* am looking at things — perhaps the *same* things — from where *I* am. We see things differently because we have different *points of view*. And the mature, sophisticated, postmodern, tolerant approach to differences is to try to understand and appreciate other points of view and accept their validity.

Let me suggest an important subject on which people certainly have different points of view — the person of Jesus Christ.

One point of view is that Jesus Christ is, in the purposes of God himself, the rightful ruler of the whole universe. He is the Savior all human beings need. He is the Judge of all people.

There are many *other* points of view about Jesus Christ. The other points of view have this in common: he is none of the things that the first point of view thinks he is.

In our mature, sophisticated, postmodern, tolerant age, those two opinions about Jesus Christ are thought of as points of view — just two ways of looking at things.

Perhaps you have relatives or friends who look on your Christian faith just like that. You hold your point of view about Jesus Christ because it is your *point of view* — your background makes you see it that way, your family, your friends, various influences on you, the kind of person you are. But it is only a *point of view*.

But is it?

Come with me to 1 Samuel 16 — back to the days when the nation of Israel had asked for and had been given a king. We have been reminded more than once that King Saul was the king *they* had chosen *for themselves* (1 Samuel 8:18; 12:13) so they could be like the nations — an impressive, efficient, powerful leader just like the nations had (1 Samuel 8:5, 20).

But Israel was *God's* people, through whom he had promised to bring blessing to the whole world. King Saul might have been able to win battles (1 Samuel 14:47, 48). He might have been able to rally the nation (1 Samuel 11:1-11). He might have been able to provide a focus for political strength and stability (1 Samuel 11:15). But he *disobeyed God* (1 Samuel 13, 15). He was therefore an *unmitigated disaster*. How can you live as *God's* people with a king who is disobedient to God?

In 1 Samuel 16 there is a dramatic new development, in the course of which we will find the key to the problem of points of view.

SAMUEL AND THE LORD: TWO POINTS OF VIEW (vv. 1-3)

The Lord's Rebuke (v. 1a)

In 1 Samuel 16:1 Samuel had returned to his home in Ramah after the final showdown with the disobedient Saul at Gilgal, and Saul had returned to his home at Gibeah (1 Samuel 15:34). Some unspecified time had passed. The Lord once again (see 1 Samuel 15:10) addressed Samuel: "The LORD said to Samuel, 'How long will you grieve over Saul, since I have rejected him from being king over Israel?'" (v. 1a).

The tragedy of Saul's failure distressed the prophet Samuel. We might say that Samuel had a point of view regarding what had happened. We saw something of that in chapter 13 when, faced with Saul's failure at Gilgal, Samuel cried, "You have done foolishly" (v. 13). We saw it more clearly in chapter 15 when the Lord told Samuel of Saul's more dramatic failure with the Amalekites, and "Samuel was angry, and he cried to the LORD all night" (v. 11). Chapter 15 concluded by noting, "Samuel grieved over Saul" (v. 35).

The great prophet Samuel — and make no mistake, he was a great prophet[1] — was not unaffected by the calamity over which he presided. We may reasonably assume that he had developed an affection for Saul. Saul would suffer from his failure, and Samuel wept. More than that, Samuel cared deeply for God's people. Remember how he had said to them, "Far be it from me that I should sin against the LORD by ceasing to pray for you" (1 Samuel 12:23). Israel would suffer as a result of Saul's failure, and Samuel wept. More even than that, Samuel knew that Saul's failure was a failure of faithfulness to the Lord who had done such great things for his people (1 Samuel 12:24). So Samuel wept.

In this he was not unlike Jeremiah who, because of the word of the Lord, could not sit in the company of revelers or rejoice but felt unceasing pain (Jeremiah 15:17, 18). Something like Samuel's agony would be experienced both by Jesus ("O Jerusalem, Jerusalem . . . ," Matthew 23:37) and the Apostle Paul ("I have great sorrow and unceasing anguish in my heart," Romans 9:2; see also Acts 20:31). All of these men of God grieved because of the consequences of sin, particularly on the people of God.

Pastors, preachers, Christian leaders, take note. One who loves God and his word will care deeply about sin and its terrible consequences. Like Samuel, you will find that you will weep.

However, on this day in Ramah, Samuel was rebuked by the Lord for his grief: "How long will you grieve over Saul?" (1 Samuel 16:1).[2] The tragedy of Saul's failure was real, but it was not everything. Samuel was not to be so overwhelmed by the calamity that he failed to see God's hand in it and God's purpose beyond the disaster: "How long will you grieve over Saul, *since I have rejected him from being king over Israel?*" (1 Samuel 16:1).

The word *rejection* could be the motto for Saul's kingship. You might recall that in chapter 8, when the people first asked for a king, the Lord said to Samuel: " . . . they have not *rejected* you, but they have *rejected* me from being king over them" (1 Samuel 8:7).

Saul's kingship had its origin in *rejection* — the people's rejection of the Lord as their king.

This was underlined when Samuel gathered the people to Mizpah to receive their king. Samuel said to them:

> " . . . *today you have* rejected *your God, who saves you from all your calamities and your distresses, and you have said to him, 'Set a king over us.'*" (1 Samuel 10:19)

In chapter 15 the rejection theme was taken further. Samuel said to Saul:

" . . . you have *rejected* the word of the Lord, and the Lord has *rejected* you from being king over Israel" (1 Samuel 15:26; cf. v. 23).

Now the time had come for Samuel to recognize the rightness of God's judgment. It was time to turn from his grief to God's future.

The Lord's Command (v. 1b)

Samuel was pointed to that future by the Lord's command: "Fill your horn with oil, and go. I will send you to Jesse the Bethlehemite, for I have provided for myself a king among his sons" (v. 1b).

Literally, "I have *seen* among his sons for myself a king."

Bethlehem was a town about eleven miles south of Ramah.[3] There is no reason to suppose that Samuel knew Jesse and his family, although they would certainly have known who Samuel was. In Bethlehem, among the sons of Jesse, the next stage in Israel's history was about to begin.

The precise words of God to Samuel ("I have seen among [Jesse's] sons for myself a king") are important. *Seeing* is a key theme of this chapter.[4] We will learn that God sees in a particular way. He has his own point of view. More about that shortly.

What should catch our attention is that God spoke of providing "*for myself* a king." What did he mean by that? Certainly he was indicating that the king from among Jesse's sons was going to be rather different from Saul. The record of Saul's appointment repeatedly emphasizes that he was the king chosen by the people *for themselves*. "Appoint *for us* a king," the elders had said to Samuel (1 Samuel 8:5). Samuel had referred to the king they demanded as "*your* king, whom *you* have chosen *for yourselves*" (1 Samuel 8:18). The Lord told Samuel to "make a king *for them*" (1 Samuel 8:22[5]). Saul was then described as "the king whom *you* have chosen, for whom *you* have asked . . . *your* king" (1 Samuel 12:13, 25). The people, when they realized what they had done, had acknowledged that they had asked for a king "*for ourselves*" (1 Samuel 12:19). While it is true that God retained his sovereignty over this development, so that Saul was also "chosen" by the Lord (1 Samuel 10:24), this does not lessen the emphasis that fundamentally Saul was appointed because of the people's demands "for themselves."

The time had come, the Lord now said to Samuel, for a different kind of king, "a king . . . for myself." There had been two earlier indications of what was about to happen. In chapter 13 Samuel had announced: "The Lord has sought out *a man after his own heart* . . . to be prince over his people" (v. 14).

In chapter 15 Samuel had told Saul: "The Lord has torn the kingdom of Israel from you this day and has given it to *a neighbor of yours, who is better than you*" (v. 28).

The time had come: "I have seen a king *for myself* among Jesse's sons."

Samuel's Fear (vv. 2, 3)

Samuel was a little reluctant to get involved with this king business again. Reasonably he figured Saul would be none too happy if he went and appointed another king: "And Samuel said, 'How can I go? If Saul hears it, he will kill me'" (v. 2a).

To get from Ramah to Bethlehem, Samuel would have to pass through Gibeah, Saul's town.[6] Relations between Saul and Samuel had broken completely. Samuel may have had God's authority over Saul, as we saw in chapter 15, but Saul had the troops and might well use them if Samuel took active steps to betray him.[7]

Such fears, however, were not to deflect Samuel from obeying the Lord's word. The Lord met Samuel's fear with a reiteration of his command, adding some details:[8]

> And the LORD said, "Take a heifer with you and say, 'I have come to sacrifice to the LORD.' And invite Jesse to the sacrifice, and I will show you what you shall do. And you shall anoint for me him whom I declare to you." (vv. 2b, 3)

TWO WAYS OF SEEING (vv. 4-10)

Samuel did what Saul had failed to do: he obeyed God:

> Samuel did what the LORD commanded and came to Bethlehem. (v. 4a)

There was some nervousness at the prophet's appearance. The conflict between the prophet and the king was no doubt known. The town leaders would hardly welcome the idea of being drawn into this clash.

> The elders of the city came to meet him trembling and said, "Do you come peaceably?" And he said, "Peaceably; I have come to sacrifice to the LORD. Consecrate yourselves, and come with me to the sacrifice." And he consecrated Jesse and his sons and invited them to the sacrifice. (v. 4b, 5)

It would have been reasonable for the elders to ask the purpose of this sacrifice. Why would the prophet have come to Bethlehem for a sacrifice? But they did not ask. Perhaps they did not want to know. Samuel didn't tell them the occasion that called for this sacrifice. He simply assured them that he had no hostile intentions toward them and told the elders to prepare to participate in the ceremony. He took a particular interest in inviting Jesse and his boys.

The scene is set for a remarkable moment in history. It involved two ways of seeing.

Seeing as Man Sees (v. 6)

When Jesse and his sons arrived, Samuel's eyes lit on one of them, the eldest (see 1 Samuel 17:13). Eliab was a tall, good-looking young man if ever there was one: "When they came, he [Samuel] looked on [literally, saw] Eliab and thought, 'Surely the LORD's anointed is before him'" (v. 6).

Samuel *saw*. Here is the second occurrence of this key word in 1 Samuel 16. Samuel saw Eliab in a particular way. From Samuel's point of view, this tall, good-looking young man seemed to be the kind of man God would choose to be king. However, do you remember the last tall, good-looking man we heard about in this story? It was Saul! ("There was not a man among the people of Israel more handsome than he. From his shoulders upward he was taller than any of the people," 1 Samuel 9:2; cf. 10:23.)

But from Samuel's point of view, he saw Eliab as the man God was likely to choose.

Seeing as the Lord Sees (vv. 7-10)

Now look carefully at verse 7, where we learn something very important about seeing.

> But the LORD said to Samuel, "Do not look on his appearance or on the height of his stature, because I have rejected him. For the LORD sees not as man sees: man looks on the outward appearance, but the LORD looks on the heart." (v. 7)

God has a point of view, and his point of view is different from the human point of view. If we take the text as it is translated here, it tells us that God is not *limited*, as humans are, in his point of view. He is not deceived by outward appearances. He sees a person's heart.

That, of course, is true. At least one reason that your point of view is different from my point of view is that we both have *limited* points of view. We have limited experience, limited understanding, limited knowledge, and we make mistakes. So it is hardly surprising that we all see lots of things differently. But *God* is not limited as we are limited. Therefore, if God has a point of view, that point of view will not be simply one more point of view among many others. His unlimited point of view will have an *absolute validity*.

But verse 7 is almost certainly saying even more than this. Translated more literally the last sentence of verse 7 goes like this: "For the LORD sees[9] not as man sees, for man sees according to the *eyes*, but the LORD sees according to the *heart*."[10]

That is, when God sees, he does not just see things with the eyes, as we do, taking in only impressions. God sees according to *his heart*. That is, God's point of view is determined by his own will and purpose. He sees according to his own intentions, his heart.

The fact of the matter is that Eliab — for all his good looks — was not the one God intended to make king. So God did not see Eliab in the same way that Samuel (just with his eyes) saw him.

This understanding of verse 7 is very important. In fact, it is, in my opinion, the key to understanding the whole of 1 and 2 Samuel! More than that, it is really the key to understanding life, the universe, everything!

It helps us understand the end of 1 Samuel 16:1, which literally reads, "I have *seen* for myself a king among [Jesse's] sons." God had *seen* a king for himself because God sees with his *heart*. In verse 1 God was therefore saying precisely what Samuel had said in 13:14: "The LORD has sought out a man *after his own heart. . . .*"

"A man after God's own heart" has been taken in popular Christian jargon to mean a particularly godly man, a man with a heart like God's. But I do not believe that the words can mean that. "A man after God's own heart" means *a man of God's own choosing*, a man God has set *his heart* on.[11] "A man after God's own heart" is — if I can put it like this — talking about the place the man has in God's heart rather than the place God has in the man's heart.[12]

These vital statements in 1 Samuel 13:14 and 16:7 are about God's gracious and sovereign purposes rather than some quality in a man. There is an illuminating statement by King David himself (the man who will turn out to be the "man after God's own heart") in 2 Samuel 7:21. By the time we reach 2 Samuel 7, of course, a great deal has happened. Just notice what David said about what God had done for him: "Because of your promise, and *according to your own heart*, you have brought about all this greatness, to make your servant know it" (2 Samuel 7:21).

"According to your own heart" here is the same expression as "after his own heart" in 1 Samuel 13:14.[13] That verse therefore asserts that the new king would be one whom God had sought out "according to his own heart." In 1 Samuel 16:7 the Lord told Samuel that the Lord *sees* not with eyes (taking in only impressions), but with his *heart* (his own personal intentions and purposes). David had a particular place in God's heart (God's purposes), and *that* is what made him so very different from Saul.

Come back to 1 Samuel 16, now that we understand the particular way that the Lord sees.

After Eliab, seven of Jesse's sons paraded before Samuel, and Samuel now saw as the Lord sees:

> *Then Jesse called Abinadab and made him pass before Samuel. And he said, "Neither has the LORD chosen this one." Then Jesse made Shammah pass by. And he said, "Neither has the LORD chosen this one." And Jesse*

made seven of his sons pass before Samuel. And Samuel said to Jesse,
"The LORD has not chosen these." (vv. 8-10)

The words have changed, but the idea is the same. None of these was the one the Lord had "seen" (according to his heart) as a king *for himself.*

The idea that has been expressed in various ways here is sometimes called the doctrine of election. God's good purposes arise out of his perfect and sovereign will. The Bible teaches that he chose Israel to be his people, David to be his king, and Jerusalem to be his city.[14] His purposes in all this will be fulfilled in Jesus Christ, his "Chosen One" (Luke 9:35; cf. Matthew 12:18; Luke 23:35; 1 Peter 2:4, 6). Christian believers know themselves to have been "chosen" in him (see Colossians 3:12; 1 Thessalonians 1:4; 1 Peter 2:9; Revelation 17:14).

The Biblical doctrine of election provides the firm foundation for Christian assurance and humility. God's good and gracious purposes depend ultimately only on his will. They are therefore certain but leave no room for human pride.

This doctrine of election has deep roots in the Old Testament. Just as God did not choose Israel or Jerusalem because of their "righteousness or the uprightness of [their] heart" (Deuteronomy 9:5; cf. 7:7, 8), he did not choose the new king because of his personal qualities. On the contrary, whatever outstanding qualities we might see in this new king are the *consequence of,* not the *reason for* God's choice of him.[15] The security of David's throne will rest on the solid foundation of God's promises, not on David's performance. That is what will make his reign so very different from Saul's.

THE ONE THE LORD "SAW" (vv. 11-13)

Come back again to 1 Samuel 16. The parading of Jesse's seven sons only revealed that none of them was the one chosen by the Lord. This left Samuel perplexed: "Then Samuel said to Jesse, 'Are all your sons here?'" (v. 11a).

The Unlikely One (vv. 11b, 12a)

I can imagine Jesse about to say, "Yes, they are all here" when he remembered the littlest,[16] the boy, the one they didn't normally include in adult company: "And he said, 'There remains yet the youngest, but behold, he is keeping the sheep'" (v. 11b).

"I didn't think you would want to see *him,* Samuel. He is still a child!" "And Samuel said to Jesse, 'Send and get him, for we will not sit down till he comes here'" (v. 11c).

And so they waited. Presumably it took some time. When he arrived, we are given a colorful description of his appearance: "And he sent and brought him in. Now he was ruddy and had beautiful eyes and was handsome" (v. 12a).

In this chapter that says so much about seeing, the boy's red complexion (or hair?), his beautiful eyes, and overall good looks[17] are probably a little ironic. We are not told of his height or stature, as we were with Eliab (v. 7) and earlier Saul (1 Samuel 10:23). The description is of an attractive-looking boy, but hardly a potential king.

The Lord's Command (v. 12b)

As is so often the case, the unlikely one (from a human point of view) turned out to be the one God had chosen: "And the LORD said, 'Arise, anoint him, for this is he'" (v. 12b).

This lad was to be anointed for one reason only: the Lord so willed it.

Samuel's Obedience (v. 13)

So Samuel anointed him ("messiahed" him) with oil, symbolically appointing him as God's chosen king. "Then Samuel took the horn of oil and anointed him in the midst of his brothers" (v. 13a).

This was the one on whom God had set his heart (1 Samuel 13:14), to be a king *for him* (1 Samuel 16:1). This is the sense in which David would be "better" than Saul (1 Samuel 15:28). As Samuel anointed the boy, David was empowered by God for the task that lay ahead: "And the Spirit of the LORD rushed upon David from that day forward" (v. 13b).

Verse 13 is the first time we hear the name *David* in the Bible, but we will hear much more about him! We will consider the importance of the Spirit of the Lord rushing upon him in our next chapter. This episode concludes: "And Samuel rose up and went to Ramah" (v. 13c).

We are aware that something very important happened in the little town of Bethlehem that day. It was not yet publicly known. Even the brothers of David who witnessed the anointing would have had little idea of the significance of what they had seen — if they saw only with their eyes.

They certainly could not have realized that what happened on that day in Bethlehem would eventually lead to another day for which the little town of Bethlehem gained its lasting fame (see Matthew 2:1-6; Luke 2:1-7, 15; cf. John 7:42). It was anticipated more than 200 years after the events of 1 Samuel 16, when the prophet Micah said:

> But you, O Bethlehem Ephrathah,
> who are too little to be among the clans of Judah,
> from you shall come forth for me
> one who is to be ruler in Israel,

whose coming forth is from of old,
    from ancient days. (Micah 5:2; see Matthew 2:6)

The only way that anyone can see the true significance of what happened in Bethlehem in the days of Samuel, Saul, and David, or "in the days of Herod the king" (Matthew 2:1) and Caesar Augustus (Luke 2:1) is to see these things from God's unique point of view.

Here is the Bible's astonishing answer to the problem of points of view, with which we began this chapter. Here, if I may put it like this, is the Bible's answer to postmodernism. It is the simple but powerful fact that *God* has a point of view. This is the reason that Christians cannot accept postmodernism. We welcome postmodernism's recognition of the provisional nature of human knowledge. But human knowledge is not the only knowledge. It is not that we want to impose *our* point of view on others, but we cannot accept that every point of view is equally valid. What we claim is that God's point of view has absolute validity because he is God. We human beings can only see properly as we learn God's point of view. That is precisely what the Word of God teaches us. It teaches us to see David as God sees him. So much more importantly, the Word of God teaches us to see David's greatest descendant as God sees him.

The shepherds who were "keeping watch over their flock by night" (Luke 2:8) a thousand years after Samuel anointed David learned to see properly. They heard the heavenly message:

> *"Fear not, for behold, I bring you good news of great joy that will be for all the people. For unto you is born this day in the city of David a Savior, who is Christ the Lord. And this will be a sign for you: you will find a baby wrapped in swaddling cloths and lying in a manger." (Luke 2:10-12)*

Then the shepherds said:

> *"Let us go over to Bethlehem and see this thing that has happened, which the Lord has made known to us." And they went with haste and found Mary and Joseph, and the baby lying in a manger. And when they saw it, they made known the saying that had been told them concerning this child. And all who heard it wondered at what the shepherds told them. . . . And the shepherds returned, glorifying and praising God for all they had heard and seen, as it had been told them. (Luke 2:15-20)*

Can you see properly? Or do you have no more than your own point of view?

25

Two Kings:
A Confusing World

1 SAMUEL 16:14-23

It is a confusing and uncertain world. It is confusing because the appearance of things does not always reveal reality. In the normal course of life we find ourselves making decisions and forming judgments on the basis of how things seem, only to discover in due course that the way things *seem* is very different from the way things *are*. The solid-looking house may turn out to be riddled with termites. The apparently sincere friend may prove to be a liar. The utterly confident businessman may be completely incompetent. Of course, it works the other way too. The unimpressive can turn out to be far better than we ever expected.

These common experiences illustrate the fact that human perceptions are profoundly unreliable. "Man sees according to the eyes," we heard God say in our literal translation of 1 Samuel 16:7.

The limitations of human perceptions are particularly evident when we try to see the meaning and significance of events. Who can tell with confidence the significance of the terrible events of September 11, 2001? Politicians and commentators often speak with unwarranted confidence. The truth is that none of us, by our imperfect powers of observation, can know enough to be sure of the meaning and significance of anything we see. "Man sees according to the eyes."

The confusion and uncertainty, however, is even deeper than this. For if God is really there, and if he is the Creator of all things and the Lord of all history, then any understanding of this world, or any part of this world or any event that occurs anywhere, that does not take into account God's power and purpose is bound to be at least inadequate, and more probably mistaken.

Our problem is that we cannot "see" God's power and purpose with our "eyes." That is why God's view of things is so different from ours. He sees, as we learned from 1 Samuel 16:7, "according to his heart." He sees all things and all people in the true light of his own will and purposes. The whole world looks very different from that perspective.

Who could have guessed the significance of what happened in Bethlehem in the days of Herod? Only those (like the shepherds) who were given some indication of God's purposes for the child who was born.

Who could have guessed the significance of what happened in that same town of Bethlehem in the days of Samuel, recorded in 1 Samuel 16?

As we take up the story at 1 Samuel 16:14, take a good look at what we can "see." Saul was still king, in his hometown of Gibeah. The lad from Bethlehem, David, was soon to become a minstrel for the king, doing the king's bidding (1 Samuel 16:21-23). If you see as man sees, you will just see Saul the king and David the servant musician.

THE SPIRIT OF GOD

The Bible invites us to learn to see things from a better point of view. The scene in 1 Samuel 16 is described by the Bible writer in terms that reveal to us what we could never see just with our eyes.

Samuel anointed David in Bethlehem as the one chosen by God to be a different kind of king from Saul. And "the Spirit of the LORD rushed upon David from that day forward" (1 Samuel 16:13b).

This astonishing statement deserves our attention. We cannot here fully explore the Bible's teaching about the person and work of the Spirit of God. We must notice, however, that the Spirit (or Breath[1]) of God is God himself. By his Spirit God accomplishes his purposes in his creation and for his people. In particular God's Spirit effectively sustains the leadership of God's people.[2]

In the earlier history of Israel the Spirit of God equipped the leaders of God's people for their formidable task.[3] In the period immediately prior to the introduction of the monarchy, the judges raised up by God were empowered by the Spirit or Breath of the Lord.[4] In particular we are specifically told of Samson:

> *Then the Spirit of the LORD rushed upon him, and although he had nothing in his hand, he tore the lion in pieces as one tears a young goat. (Judges 14:6a)*

Again: "And the Spirit of the LORD rushed upon him, and he went down to Ashkelon and struck down thirty men of the town . . ." (Judges 14:19a).

A little later:

Then the Spirit of the Lord rushed upon him, and the ropes that were on his arms became as flax that has caught fire, and his bonds melted off his hands. (Judges 15:14)

Saul himself had been promised and received this same empowering. Samuel had said to him: "Then the Spirit of the Lord will rush upon you, and you will prophesy with them and be turned into another man" (1 Samuel 10:6).

And when he came to Gibeah that is what happened: ". . . the Spirit of God rushed upon him, and he prophesied among them" (1 Samuel 10:10b).

Then when he heard of the threat from Nahash the Ammonite: ". . . the Spirit of God rushed upon Saul when he heard these words, and his anger was greatly kindled" (1 Samuel 11:6).

In each of these cases there is an emphasis on the fact that what happened to Samson and Saul came from beyond them. The power that "rushed" upon them came from elsewhere. This was the very opposite of a man gathering his inner strength to meet a challenge. These men were equipped to meet the need of the hour by God himself.

The observable effects of the Breath of God on these men varied. Samson tore a lion in pieces, struck down thirty men, and burst the ropes that bound him. Saul prophesied, became angry, and raised an army. In each case the Spirit of God enabled his appointed leader to do what was needed at the time and in the circumstances.

It is highly significant that when Samuel anointed David in Bethlehem, precisely the same words are used,[5] with an important addition. This boy was being equipped, as Samson and Saul had been equipped, to lead God's people, but with him there was a difference: "And the Spirit of the Lord rushed upon David *from that day forward*" (1 Samuel 16:13a).

The same Spirit of the Lord came upon (or perhaps into[6]) David, but not now as an empowering for a particular moment or specific task, but permanently.[7] Once again we are made aware that this new king will be different. David had become the one whom God had now equipped to be the leader of his people, or as the Lord had put it, to be "a king for myself" (1 Samuel 16:1).

It does not seem that there was an immediately observable effect of the Spirit at this time. If we saw only as man sees, we would not know that the Spirit had come to David in this way. Yet this coming of the Spirit was the most important thing that happened that day in Bethlehem.

The account of that day closed with Samuel's departure back to his home in Ramah (v. 13c).

THE PROBLEM WITH SAUL (vv. 14-18)

The scene shifts in 1 Samuel 16:14 to Gibeah, where Saul was. There is no indication of the time period between the events we have witnessed in Bethlehem and what we are about to see in Gibeah. As we will see when we reach chapter 17, it is possible that what we hear about in 1 Samuel 16:14-23 took place some considerable time later. Indeed there are reasons to think that the episode of 1 Samuel 16:14-23 occurred *after* the events of 1 Samuel 17. It is placed here, however, to show the consequences of David becoming the one chosen by God to be his king and the Spirit of the Lord therefore coming to David.

What would now become of Saul? His disobedience had led to his rejection (1 Samuel 13:14; 15:23, 26, 28). The new king had now been identified (albeit in a rather secretive way at this stage) and empowered for leadership (although that may not yet have been visible).

The Problem: The Departure of the Spirit (vv. 14, 15)

What the writer tells us about Saul at this point is remarkable. The immediate sequel to the Spirit rushing into David in 1 Samuel 16:13 is this: "Now the Spirit of the LORD departed from Saul, and a harmful spirit from the LORD tormented him" (v. 14).

As soon as we learn that the Spirit had "rushed" on David in this new way, we learn that the Spirit departed[8] decisively from Saul. This underlines the fact that God had rejected him. The Lord himself abandoned Saul[9] because Saul had abandoned the Lord (see 1 Samuel 15:23). Saul was no longer the one equipped by God for the leadership of Israel.

Years later, when David fully deserved to suffer in the same way as Saul did here, he prayed: ". . . take not your Holy Spirit from me" (Psalm 51:11).

I suspect that David had in mind this day when God did take his Spirit from Saul.[10]

You will have noticed that something else happened to Saul. "An evil [ESV, harmful] spirit from the LORD tormented him" (NIV). This, apparently, did have observable effects, which Saul's servants saw and interpreted, probably more truly than they knew: "And Saul's servants said to him, 'Behold now, a harmful spirit from God is tormenting you'" (v. 15).

The servants' words probably expressed the Israelite belief that God's hand is behind all the experiences of life. However, the narrator used almost the same words to describe Saul's troubles, but from him they were more than a pious expression. The "evil spirit from the LORD" was the other side of the fact that "the Spirit of the LORD had departed from Saul."

The precise form of Saul's suffering can only be guessed,[11] but his later behavior suggests a severe mental or emotional disturbance. We will see that this was not a permanent condition, but something that overcame Saul repeatedly.[12] At this point what we need to understand is not a psychiatric diagnosis of Saul's condition, but a theological understanding of its cause — the departure of the Spirit of the Lord.[13]

The word "evil" in this context should not be understood in moral terms but rather as an indication of the misery, distress, and harm this spirit or mood will cause Saul.[14] The "evil" (in this sense) that this condition brought to Saul came from God. In a different context Job recognized the hand of God behind the harm that came his way: "Shall we receive good from God, and shall we not receive evil?" (Job 2:10). Unlike Job, however, Saul's suffering was a consequence of his being rejected by God.

A Solution Suggested . . . (vv. 16, 17)

The servants of Saul offered a suggestion that might alleviate his troubled moods:

> *"Let our lord now command your servants who are before you to seek out a man who is skillful in playing the lyre, and when the evil spirit from God is upon you, he will play it, and you will be well." (v. 16)*

This sounds like a commonsense proposal. Music has a way of soothing the human spirit. A good musician would cheer up the king! "So Saul said to his servants, 'Provide for me a man who can play well and bring him to me'" (v. 17).

For the second time a speaker in the story uses words more telling than he could have known. Saul's words "Provide for me a man" strangely echo God's words in verse 1: "I have provided for myself a king."[15] In a few moments we will see that the man Saul sought to provide for himself will be the very man God had provided for himself!

. . . and Found (v. 18)

Astonishingly, there was a young man there who knew of just the right person to meet Saul's need:

> *One of the young men answered, "Behold, I have seen a son of Jesse the Bethlehemite, who is skillful in playing, a man of valor, a man of war, prudent in speech, and a man of good presence, and the LORD is with him." (v. 18)*

This is not the first time that Saul had been at a loss as to what to do and depended on the advice of a young man (see 1 Samuel 9:5-10).[16] What strikes us about the words of this young man, however, is the extraordinary description of the son of Jesse. Can this be the lad who was too small to be invited to the feast in Bethlehem? The explanation for this surprising description may lie in the time that could have passed between verse 13 and verse 14 of this chapter. If this is the case we must suppose that the events here took place after the events of chapter 17, where David was still a youth (1 Samuel 17:33, 56). However, it is also possible that the young man spoke in exaggerated terms, perhaps in order to impress Saul and persuade him to take on the son of Jesse.[17] Whatever the explanation for the remarkable description, it was, once again, truer than the speaker could have known. This son of Jesse would display musical and verbal skill that would last millennia. He would be "the sweet psalmist of Israel" (2 Samuel 23:1). He would be Israel's greatest warrior. As for "the LORD is with him," the irony and significance of this statement, in the light of verses 13, 14, could hardly have been appreciated by the young speaker.

THE SOLUTION FOR SAUL: DAVID (vv. 19-23)

We are to understand that no one with Saul knew what we know about David and the earlier happenings in Bethlehem. Certainly Saul was ignorant of these things. We wonder how this bizarre situation will work out — the rejected king unwittingly seeking the one who has been chosen as his replacement to come and serenade him!

Saul Summons David (vv. 19, 20)

But Saul knew more than we could, at this stage, have guessed. Listen to him: "Therefore Saul sent messengers to Jesse and said, 'Send me David your son, who is with the sheep'" (v. 19).

Saul knew David's name! As the narrative is unfolding this is a surprise. Saul — of all people! — is the first character in the narrative to name David.[18] The explanation for Saul's surprising knowledge may again lie in the chronological sequence of events, which (as we have noted) could differ from the sequence of the narrative. If this episode occurred after the dramatic events of 1 Samuel 17, then we have an explanation for Saul's knowledge of David's name, and even of the fact that he was "with the sheep" (see 1 Samuel 17:34).[19]

Be that as it may, the irony of this scene is palpable. Saul invited David (by name!) into his court! David came in obedience to Saul! Unwittingly Saul had summoned the very one who possessed the Spirit who, because of his departure from Saul, had caused Saul's present distress. To help him, Saul had unsuspectingly summoned the neighbor who was "better" than him and to whom the kingdom of Israel had been given (1 Samuel 15:28).[20]

The irony persisted as Jesse showed due deference to the authority of the king and sent his son, along with gifts to Saul: "And Jesse took a donkey laden with bread and a skin of wine and a young goat and sent them by David his son to Saul" (v. 20).

David Serves Saul (vv. 21, 22)

The resulting situation is astonishing. First we hear of David's obedient service:

And David came to Saul and entered his service. (v. 21a)

The chosen king was serving the rejected king!
Then we read of Saul's affection for David:

And Saul loved him greatly. (v. 21b)

While this no doubt means that Saul felt a strong affection for David (that, of course, carries its own irony, in view of the way in which this relationship would soon develop), the word *love* appears to have been used in the ancient world to describe a *political* relationship.[21] A king could demand the "love" of his subjects; an emperor could require the "love" of his vassals. This is a theme we will explore more fully in our study of 1 Samuel 18:1-6. The irony in 1 Samuel 16:21 may therefore have this added subtlety: Saul greatly "loved" David, whereas, at least politically, we might have expected it to be the other way around![22]

The sense of irony continues to build with the third element in 1 Samuel 16:21: ". . . and he became his armor-bearer" (v. 21c).

Although for the moment this seems unremarkable enough, in due course we will see that the handing over of arms will be the symbolic way in which Saul's son Jonathan will abdicate his position as successor to the throne to David (see 1 Samuel 18:4). Here Saul, unintentionally, and perhaps unnoticed by any of the participants in the events, does the same.

Saul, of course, saw none of the significance we now see in all of this. David was the kind of servant he was looking for: "And Saul sent to Jesse, saying, 'Let David remain in my service, for he has found favor in my sight'" (v. 22).

David and the Spirit (v. 23)

Our passage closes with a description of David's service:

And whenever the evil spirit from God was upon Saul, David took the lyre and played it with his hand. So Saul was refreshed and was well, and the harmful [evil] spirit departed from him. (v. 23)

Just as "the Spirit of the LORD [had] departed from Saul" (v. 14), so now, by the ministry of David (the one who now had received that Spirit), the "evil spirit" departed from him. Subtly we are being shown that Saul now depended on David for the needs of his spirit.[23] David was the one who could deal with "the evil spirit" brought on by the departure of the Spirit of the Lord because, of course, the Spirit of the Lord was in David.

God's purposes for the man from Bethlehem were hidden from all who saw only "as man sees" (v. 7). But the truth was that this man would become Israel's king. The Spirit of the Lord had come upon him for this purpose. And only when we realize that do we see this remarkable little episode in true perspective.

Many years after these events the prophet Isaiah would look forward to a day when another "shoot" would come from Jesse:

There shall come forth a shoot from the stump of Jesse,
*   and a branch from his roots shall bear fruit.*
And the Spirit of the LORD shall rest upon him,
*   the Spirit of wisdom and understanding,*
*   the Spirit of counsel and might,*
*   the Spirit of knowledge and the fear of the LORD.*
And his delight shall be in the fear of the LORD.
He shall not judge by what his eyes see,
*   or decide disputes by what his ears hear,*
but with righteousness he shall judge the poor,
*   and decide with equity for the meek of the earth;*
and he shall strike the earth with the rod of his mouth,
*   and with the breath of his lips he shall kill the wicked. (Isaiah 11:1-4)*

The day that the Spirit of the Lord rushed upon David became the background to this promise. The promise was fulfilled when Jesus came to John the Baptist:

And John bore witness: "I saw the Spirit descend from heaven like a dove, and it remained on him. I myself did not know him, but he who sent me to baptize with water said to me, 'He on whom you see the Spirit descend and remain, this is he who baptizes with the Holy Spirit.' And I have seen and have borne witness that this is the Son of God." (John 1:32-34)

God's purposes for this man from Bethlehem remain hidden from all who see only "as man sees." The truth is that this man has become Lord and Christ (Acts 2:36). He will judge the whole world (Acts 17:31). He will save those who belong to him (Matthew 1:21). The Spirit of the Lord came upon *him* for this purpose. Only when we realize that do we see the world, its history, and our own lives in true perspective.

26

The Enemy

1 SAMUEL 17:1-11

Are you an optimist or a pessimist? For you does every cloud have a silver lining, or does every silver lining have a cloud? If you are an optimist, no doubt you find the negativity of the pessimists a little trying. You need to know that the pessimists find you frustratingly unrealistic! Do you think Christians tend to be optimists or pessimists? We will return to these questions.

One of the Bible's most famous stories is the marvelous, unforgettable tale of David and Goliath. Many of us probably first heard it from a children's storybook. In the Bible, however, the account of what happened with David and Goliath takes us to a difficult moment in Israel's history. The leadership of the nation was in serious trouble. Saul had been appointed as the nation's first king, at the people's demand (see 1 Samuel 12:1). They believed that a king would bring stability and security in these precarious times and make them "like all the nations" (1 Samuel 8:20). However, Saul had been disobedient to God's commands and so had been rejected by God (1 Samuel 15:26), although he was still functioning as the people's king. A new king had now been chosen by God (1 Samuel 13:14; 15:28; 16:1). Secretly he had been anointed at Bethlehem by the prophet Samuel (1 Samuel 16:13a), and "the Spirit of the LORD rushed upon David from that day forward" (1 Samuel 16:13b).

Then comes the account of David and Goliath in 1 Samuel 17. It is one of the all-time favorites of all the stories in the world. It has the ingredients of drama and excitement, anticipation and the satisfaction of the good guy defeating the bad guy against all odds. The story is so skilfully told that it holds our attention and captures our imagination, no matter how familiar it has become.

In this exposition of 1 Samuel 17 I hope to add two dimensions to the familiarity with the story shared by almost all of us.

First, we are going to notice the importance of many of the details of the narrative that are easily overlooked. In order to give careful attention to these details, we will follow the story in four installments. We must be careful not to miss the forest for the trees as we listen to this wonderful narrative carefully, but listening carefully will enrich our appreciation.

Second, we will reflect on the significance of this story in its context. The story does not come to us in a children's storybook, with nothing before and nothing after. This story comes to us in the context of this critical period in Israel's history. Much in the story of David and Goliath is richly illuminated by the context in which the story is set.

Our first installment of the David and Goliath story (1 Samuel 17:1-11) will bring before us the massive threat to the people of Israel posed by the terrifying Philistines, especially by one particular terrifying Philistine. We will find that this wonderful narrative casts a brilliant light on our own lives. In this case it will challenge the optimism of optimists and the pessimism of pessimists.

It is important to remember that one reason (perhaps it was *the* reason really) that the people asked for a king in the first place was that their king might "go out before us and fight our battles" (1 Samuel 8:20). The people felt the need for a king because of the threat from their enemies. In other words, national security was a primary motivation behind their demand.

What Israel seemed to have forgotten was that their God had always been there to deliver them from their enemies. Only when they abandoned *him* did their enemies gain the upper hand (as so often in the book of Judges, and more recently in the encounter with the Philistines at Aphek, 1 Samuel 4:1-11). Whenever they turned back to the Lord and cried out for help, he delivered them (see 1 Samuel 12:6-11).

The threats from their enemies were the most obvious manifestation of Israel's insecurity. It is clear, however, from Israel's history that the more sinister threats to Israel did not come in the form of armies. Even more dangerous was the multifaceted, constantly present temptation to forget or forsake the Lord and to follow other gods. Israel feared the enemies they could see with their eyes. But the greatest threat to their security could not be seen in that way. As we begin to follow the most famous story in the book of 1 Samuel, we do well to notice that it began with a fearful and visible threat to the people of Israel.

That is the first point of connection between this story and our lives. We, too, face threats. Insecurity is part of life in this world. We are generally most vividly aware of the threats that we can see. How are we to think about the threats that face us? Indeed, are the dangers we fear the greatest dangers that threaten us? What should we fear? Where and how are we to find security?

As we follow the narrative in 1 Samuel 17, we will find once again that the theme of seeing properly (which was so important in 1 Samuel 16:1-13) is a key. We need to learn to see the threats that face us properly.

THE PHILISTINES AND THE ISRAELITES (vv. 1-3)

The Philistines (v. 1a)

The chapter opens with the ominous words: "Now the Philistines gathered their armies for battle" (v. 1a).

This is not the first time we have seen this situation develop. The Philistine threat has been in the background of the entire narrative of 1 Samuel so far and will be there until the end of the book and the end of Saul's life. Saul will die in conflict with the Philistines (1 Samuel 31). The Philistines first appeared (in this book) in chapter 4, where we read that at Aphek "the Philistines drew up in line against Israel" (v. 2). Hostilities on that occasion led to a double defeat of Israel, the capture of the ark of the covenant, and the deaths of Hophni and Phinehas and consequently of Eli. The remarkable story of how God brought the Philistines into submission without any assistance from Israel was told in the following two chapters.

Then in 1 Samuel 7 we heard how "the lords of the Philistines went up against Israel" at Mizpah (v. 7). It was very different this time, for Israel had returned to the Lord (1 Samuel 7:4), and Samuel prayed for Israel (1 Samuel 7:8, 9). The Lord dramatically delivered them from the threat (1 Samuel 7:10, 11).

The Philistine threat persisted, however, and provided much of the motivation for the people's demand for a king in 1 Samuel 8. When they were given their king, in the person of Saul, God said of Saul, "He shall save my people from the hand of the Philistines" (1 Samuel 9:16). While Israel had other enemies, it was the Philistines who, more than any other, threatened Israel's life. First and foremost, it was to save Israel from the Philistines that Saul was made king.

The opportunity for Saul to do just that came when "the Philistines mustered to fight with Israel" in Michmash (1 Samuel 13:5). However, Saul's foolishness led to a defeat of the Philistines that was "not . . . great" (1 Samuel 14:30).

The summary of Saul's reign at the end of chapter 14 told us that "there was hard fighting against the Philistines all the days of Saul" (v. 52).

Therefore 1 Samuel 17 begins with a situation that by now is all too familiar: the Philistines had gathered their armies once again for battle. These opening words vividly remind us of the failure of Saul to accomplish his mission as king. Israel's enemy was alive and well and threatening once again.

Their Location (v. 1b)

The location of the Philistine armies is given with some precision: "And they were gathered at Socoh, which belongs to Judah, and encamped between Socoh and Azekah, in Ephes-dammim" (v. 1b).

The Philistines were now further west than they had been in chapter 14,[1] as we might expect since on that occasion they had been pursued from central Israel (1 Samuel 14:23, 31). However, they were still encroaching on Israel's territory as the words "which belongs to Judah" point out.[2]

If Saul had been made king first and foremost to deal with the Philistine threat, this renewal of hostilities and its location remind us of opportunities lost. The Philistines were where they were because Israel had managed to drive them back (through Jonathan's, not Saul's, initiatives, 1 Samuel 13–14), but they were still a threat because of Saul's foolishness (see 1 Samuel 14:29, 30). We are right to wonder what will happen this time.

The Israelites (v. 2)

It is interesting that although the Israelite forces gathered to meet the renewed aggression of the Philistines, we are not told of any active leadership given by Saul: "And Saul and the men of Israel were gathered, and encamped in the Valley of Elah, and drew up in line of battle against the Philistines" (v. 2).

The grammar of the sentences conveys something of the difference between the two sides. The Philistines "gathered" (v. 1, active voice); Saul and the men of Israel "were gathered" (v. 2, passive voice). There is no sign of active leadership among the Israelites. Saul is just among those who "were gathered."

The Setting (v. 3)

The scene is strikingly similar to that in chapters 13, 14 where the two forces, one at Geba, the other at Michmash, faced each other across a ravine. We will be reminded of that earlier episode more than once.[3] This time we are given the explicit description: "And the Philistines stood on the mountain on the one side, and Israel stood on the mountain on the other side, with a valley between them" (v. 3).

The Valley of Elah was more open than the steep ravine of the previous episode[4] and provides a big setting for the big story that is about to begin with the appearance of a big man!

GOLIATH (vv. 4-10)

"The Man of the Between" (v. 4a)

On this occasion the Philistine threat was embodied in a single individual of terrifying appearance and equally terrifying speech. He is introduced in this way: "And there came out from the camp of the Philistines a champion named Goliath of Gath . . ." (v. 4a).

The word translated "champion" literally means "the man of the between,"[5] a vivid way of describing "anyone who comes forward from the front line [and] becomes a 'man between the battle lines' and is thus a sort of 'challenger' or 'champion.'"[6] Out from the Philistine camp, then, came "the man of the between."

HIS NAME

Surprisingly, we only hear the famous name "Goliath" twice in the whole story (here and in verse 23). Usually (and always in the speeches of the characters) he is referred to as "the" or "this Philistine."[7] There is no reason to suppose that the Israelite observers on their side of the valley knew the name, but as the story is told and the Philistine appears for the first time, the name has a menacing, foreign-sounding ring to it. "The man of the between" who emerged that day from the Philistine camp was named "Goliath."[8]

HIS CITY

We are told that Goliath was from Gath (v. 4). Gath was one of the five Philistine cities we saw in 1 Samuel 5 where there was a very great panic when the ark of the covenant arrived (vv. 8, 9). It was the Philistine city closest to Israelite territory, and the one closest to the scene of this confrontation. Gath was also mentioned in connection with the subjugation of the Philistines in 1 Samuel 7, when Israel took back cities and territory from the Philistines "from Ekron to Gath" (v. 14). The mention of Gath as Goliath's city reminds us that the previous suppressions of the Philistines had only been partial and temporary.[9] In the man from Gath, the Philistines were back!

His Appearance (vv. 4b-7)

However, if the name and the city of "the man of the between" suggest trouble, just hold your breath as you *see* him.

HIS HEIGHT (v. 4b)

First there was his height: ". . . whose height was six cubits and a span" (v. 4b).

He was huge! On the usual reckoning of cubits and spans, that would be about nine feet, nine inches![10] We may be reminded of the Lord's words to Samuel in the previous chapter — "Do not look on his appearance or on the height of his stature" (1 Samuel 16:7) — but we might well wonder whether those words could possibly apply now. Here was height and stature that were not easy to ignore!

HIS ARMOR (vv. 5, 6a)

Then there was his armor:

> *He had a helmet of bronze on his head, and he was armed with a coat of mail, and the weight of the coat was five thousand shekels of bronze. And he had bronze armor on his legs. . . . (vv. 5, 6a)*

There was lots of metal, mainly bronze, although the spearhead was iron (v. 7). The Philistines had had the monopoly on metalworking (1 Samuel 13:19-21). Their superior technology was on display in the figure that stood before the Israelites that day.

The detail given in this description is very unusual in Biblical narratives. Its purpose is clearly to impress. That it does!

Goliath's bronze helmet protected his head (but not, we might note, his face). What little we know of Philistine military dress suggests that they usually wore a feathered headdress.[11] There was nothing usual about this Philistine.

His upper body was covered with "a coat of mail" weighing 126 pounds (or fifty-seven kilograms)![12] Clearly he would not be susceptible to any weapon aimed at his chest. His legs were also protected by bronze armor.[13] In other words the man's defenses gave all the appearance of being impenetrable. He stood there like a one-man, indestructible fortress.

HIS WEAPONS (vv. 6b, 7a)

Goliath was not just massively protected, he was equipped with fearful offensive weapons.

> *. . . and a javelin of bronze slung between his shoulders. The shaft of his spear was like a weaver's beam, and his spear's head weighed six hundred shekels of iron. (vv. 6b, 7a)*

A javelin, or more probably a large curved sword,[14] was carried across his shoulders. A spear "like a weaver's beam" suggests to most modern readers (who have no idea what a weaver's beam might be!) a huge spear.

The spear was certainly massive. Its iron head weighed more than fifteen pounds,[15] but it is likely that the comparison with "a weaver's beam" or "rod" refers not to the size of such a rod (which was not remarkable) but to its shape and appearance. The part of a weaver's loom most probably referred to had loops of cord attached to it. Goliath's spear, then, would have been fitted with a thong for powerful and accurate slinging.[16]

The narrator has provided more precise detail of Goliath's defensive and offensive equipment than would have been apparent to those Israelites who first saw him. He has, in other words, given us a close-up view of this menacing giant. If we wonder how the narrator gained such detailed knowledge of what the Philistine wore and carried, we must wait until the end of the story to see how it all became available for close inspection!

HIS PROTECTION (v. 7b)

The description is rounded off by reference to the fact that he also had a shield so big that he had a servant to carry it for him. It was probably a large, rectangular, standing shield providing complete protection to the huge Philistine.[17] "And his shield-bearer went before him" (v. 7b).

The narrator has taken an unusual amount of space to give us this close-up view of Goliath. Try to form an impression in your mind of this colossal, powerful, apparently indestructible, menacing figure.

His Threat (vv. 8-10)

Now add to what you can *see* by *hearing* him. Across the Valley of Elah the voice of the Philistine thundered toward the Israelite lines.

A THREATENING QUESTION (v. 8a)

> He stood and shouted to the ranks of Israel, "Why have you come out to draw up for battle?" (v. 8a)

The question itself may have struck a chord if, as we have noticed, Israel was lacking clear and decisive leadership. Why indeed had they assembled for battle? Samuel had not summoned them, as earlier at Mizpah (1 Samuel 7:5). This was not really an Israelite initiative as previously at Michmash (1 Samuel 13–14). Although the answer to the question might seem obvious (they had drawn up for battle because the Philistines had drawn up for battle, 1 Samuel 17:1), the asking of it would be unsettling for the leaderless, directionless Israelites.

A Threatening Person (v. 8b)

The Philistine, however, had an alternative proposal to bloody battle between the two armies. First, let us be clear on who is speaking here and who is listening: "Am I not a Philistine, and are you not servants of Saul?" (v. 8b).

Literally he said, "Am I not *the* Philistine?" The pronoun "I" is strongly emphasized. "Am *I* — the one you see before you — the nine-and-a-half-foot-tall, metal-clad hulk, this powerful and violent figure — am *I* not the embodiment of *the* Philistine?"

"And *you* [again the pronoun is emphasized] are Saul's slaves." Why would Saul's slaves come out to fight the mighty Philistines? "Take another look at me, folks! Do *Saul's slaves* really want to fight *Philistines?*"

A Threatening Proposal (vv. 8c-10)

"Here's an idea that will save us all a lot of trouble": "Choose a man for yourselves, and let him come down to me" (v. 8c).

"Choose a man for yourselves"! Where have we heard those words before?

At the very beginning of the story of kingship, Samuel spoke to the people of "your king, whom you have *chosen for yourselves*" (1 Samuel 8:18, cf. 1 Samuel 12:13).[18] The Israelites had already "chosen a man for themselves." His name was Saul!

We presume that Goliath, like so many characters in this narrative, was not fully aware of the significance of his words, but as *we* hear them we can hardly fail to remember that Saul was the closest thing that Israel had to a Goliath. Remember what he looked like when the people chose him: ". . . when he stood among the people, he was taller than any of the people from his shoulders upward" (1 Samuel 10:23; also 1 Samuel 9:2).

And Samuel had said of him, "There is none like him among all the people" (1 Samuel 10:24).

There was only one candidate in Israel who had anything like apparent credentials to face the Philistine. And he was the one the people had (some time earlier) "chosen for themselves."

"And let him come down to me" — down from the mountainside, into the valley where "the man of the between" was laying down his challenge. "Let the man you choose for yourselves come and face *the* Philistine. Let *the* Israelite and *the* Philistine fight for their people, and let the winner take all:

> *"If he is able to fight with me and kill me, then we will be your servants.*
> *But if I prevail against him and kill him, then you shall be our servants*
> *and serve us." (v. 9)*

The story will eventually prove Goliath a liar. The Philistines will not submit to the Israelites even when their champion is slain. But at this point the possibility of that happening was so remote that no one would have given it any consideration.

We might imagine a brief silence after the words of verse 9 were uttered — a pause to let them sink in — a space in which (inconceivably) an Israelite might have come down into the valley to face the Philistine. But there was no movement from the Israelite lines.

The silence was broken by the thunderous voice again: "And the Philistine said, 'I defy the ranks of Israel this day. Give me a man, that we may fight together'" (v. 10).

"Defy" is too weak. "I *scorn* the ranks of Israel!" "I *mock* the ranks of Israel!"[19]

The Philistine was as powerful and threatening in his words as he was in his presence. Here was a truly terrifying enemy.

We are almost at the end of our first installment. Before we leave it, I want to step back and consider the significance of this astonishing figure in the Valley of Elah. Why has the Biblical historian given us such a full and detailed picture of "the man of the between"? What effect should this opening scene in the Valley of Elah have on us?

Goliath and the Philistines he represented are a particular instance of a major Bible theme. In the Valley of Elah we have been looking at and listening to a particular case of an important reality of which the Bible often speaks — the enemies of God and his people.

It would not be difficult to trace that theme through the Bible. We would certainly see that by the time we reach the New Testament, it is perfectly clear that the enemies of God and his people are more terrifying and powerful than even the menacing "man of the between" who stood that day in the Valley of Elah.

All of us face an enemy, an army of enemies, as real, powerful, and terrifying as Goliath. *Death* wields its terrible sword and mocks us all. *Sin* threatens to bring us down. *Satan* himself seeks whom he may devour.

Pessimists rarely see how terrible things really are. Optimists are ignoring reality.

That day in the Valley of Elah the people of Israel were taken beyond optimism and pessimism. They *saw* and *heard* the enemy.

FEAR (v. 11)

Our first installment of the Goliath story closes with the reaction of "Saul and all Israel": "When Saul and all Israel heard these words of the Philistine, they were dismayed and greatly afraid" (v. 11).

In the Valley of Elah that day, only a fool would pretend that things were not desperately serious.

What was it that God had said of Saul when the Saul story began? "He shall save my people from the hand of the Philistines" (1 Samuel 9:16). We see no sign of any such thing. There is in fact no distinction between "Saul" and "all Israel." Both he and they heard the words of the Philistine with the same ears, were dismayed (or "shattered") with identical alarm, and were equally greatly afraid.

This is not what it was meant to be like. Cast your mind back to Hannah and her prayer at the beginning of this book. She said:

> *"The adversaries of the LORD shall be broken to pieces*
> *[or dismayed, or shattered];* [20]
> *against them he will thunder in heaven.*
> *The LORD will judge the ends of the earth;*
> *he will give strength to his king*
> *and exalt the power of his anointed." (1 Samuel 2:10)*

How the tables have turned. It is the Philistines who should have been shattered, not Israel and their king! It is the Lord's anointed one who should have been given strength and power, not this hulking Philistine!

At this point we cannot help anticipating the outcome of this remarkable story. Eventually we are going to see that the words of Hannah proved to be astonishingly true. At this point, however, appreciate how much the words that will prove to be true did not *seem* to be true. The power that stood against the people of Israel was truly terrifying. It would be *astounding* if anyone could deliver Israel from this monstrous threat.

We need to understand that there are real threats that intimidate us. There are terrifying forces arrayed against us. This is true of human life generally, but it is particularly so for God's own people. There is much to fear.

Yet we know that the words of Hannah have proven true, even more astonishingly than in the days of Saul. Because of Jesus we can look at whatever we fear and say:

> *If God is for us, who can be against us? He who did not spare his own*
> *Son but gave him up for us all, how will he not also with him graciously*
> *give us all things? Who shall bring any charge against God's elect? It*
> *is God who justifies. Who is to condemn? Christ Jesus is the one who*
> *died — more than that, who was raised — who is at the right hand of*
> *God, who indeed is interceding for us. Who shall separate us from the*
> *love of Christ? Shall tribulation, or distress, or persecution, or famine,*
> *or nakedness, or danger, or sword? . . . No, in all these things we are*

more than conquerors through him who loved us. For I am sure that neither death nor life, nor angels nor rulers, nor things present nor things to come, nor powers, nor height nor depth, nor anything else in all creation, will be able to separate us from the love of God in Christ Jesus our Lord. (Romans 8:31-39)

27

The God of the Unexpected

1 SAMUEL 17:12-30

We left Saul and the men of Israel shattered and trembling on their side of the Valley of Elah, while the Philistine menace named Goliath hollered up at them from the valley below, "I defy the ranks of Israel this day! Give me a man, that we may fight together!" (1 Samuel 17:10)

God is the God of the unexpected. While he is all-powerful, and there is no power in all creation that comes close to matching his power, his power "is made perfect in weakness," as he told the Apostle Paul (2 Corinthians 12:9). In other words, God does and will break the bows of the mighty, bring down the proud, and shatter his enemies (cf. 1 Samuel 2:1-10), but he accomplishes his powerful purposes by means of the shameful death of Jesus on the cross, by the weakness of the proclamation of Christ crucified. Even as we are intimidated by whatever threatens us, we are called to put our trust in the God of the unexpected. God can be trusted, but he will act in ways that take us all by surprise. Who would think that the massive problems of the world and the troubles of human life have their ultimate solution in the execution of an innocent man in A.D. 33 outside Jerusalem and the preaching of the news about him to the nations of the world? God is the God of the unexpected.

Do you believe that? Or do you still think that power and wealth and cleverness can save us from whatever we need to be saved from?

We have already seen this in the book of 1 Samuel. The book opened, you may remember, in circumstances of grave national crisis for Israel — days of anarchy and instability, corrupt and ineffective leadership, and despair. The opening scene, however, took us to an obscure part of the country, to an unknown family and the distress of a childless woman. This was not exactly the place from which you would *expect* to see the answer to Israel's troubles emerge.

In a similar way, our second installment in the story of David and Goliath takes an unexpected turn. From the Valley of Elah, with its terror and excitement, we are suddenly taken about twelve miles to the east, into the hills of Judah, to the little town of Bethlehem.

DAVID AND HIS BROTHERS (vv. 12-16)

From the first word of verse 12 it is clear that we have left the drama in the Valley of Elah in order to meet David.[1]

Of course, we have met David already. We have been to Bethlehem before. On that occasion we saw how David was identified among the sons of Jesse in Bethlehem as the one chosen by God to be "a king for myself [God]" (1 Samuel 16:1, 12). We know that the Spirit of the Lord had rushed upon him "from that day forward" (1 Samuel 16:13). We have seen him "in the power of the Spirit" (if we may draw on a New Testament expression here, cf. Luke 4:14) driving out the evil spirit that troubled the rejected King Saul (1 Samuel 16:23).

However, in the new crisis that erupted in the Valley of Elah we have heard nothing yet of David. We have seen Saul and his army ("the men of Israel," 1 Samuel 17:2) gathered on one side of the valley, facing the Philistine forces on the opposite side. We have seen and heard *the* Philistine, with his massive armor and weaponry and his eloquent, thunderous threats. But David has not appeared in the first eleven verses of 1 Samuel 17.

We did note in passing as we examined the last part of 1 Samuel 16 that particular episodes of the narrative before us are not necessarily presented in chronological sequence. Of course, a narrative, by its nature, must generally move forward through time. Biblical narratives conform to the expectation that the overall movement of a story must be presented in chronological sequence. However, when it comes to particular episodes, chronological sequence is not always the most important way to see, say, two particular events in order to understand their significance. For this reason the Bible writers quite often appear to present particular episodes in a way that makes it difficult to be sure of the sequence in which things happened. Specifically, we have noted that it is not certain that David's involvement with Saul described in 1 Samuel 16:14-23 happened *before* the events of 1 Samuel 17.[2]

This may account for the surprising way in which David is introduced into the story in 1 Samuel 17:12. It almost sounds as though he is being introduced for the first time[3] precisely because this *is* the first time (chronologically speaking) that David became involved in Israel's national life.[4] Here, if you like, David is being introduced *publicly* for the first time, although we who have been reading the story have already had a *private* introduction in Bethlehem in 1 Samuel 16:1-13 (and have been given a glimpse into the future in 1 Samuel 16:14-23).

David's Family (v. 12)

With these things in mind, let us leave the Valley of Elah in order to meet David and his brothers:

> *Now David was the son of an Ephrathite of Bethlehem in Judah, named Jesse, who had eight sons. In the days of Saul the man was already old and advanced in years. (v. 12)*

Here is David's family. His father, Jesse, is now identified as an Ephrathite.[5] It is unlikely to be coincidental that as the book of 1 Samuel opened, in a similar relatively unimportant location, with Israel facing a major crisis, we were introduced to another father of a son who would become more famous than he,[6] who was described as an "Ephrathite" (1 Samuel 1:1). His name was Elkanah, the father of Samuel.

It so happens that the term "Ephrathite" has two meanings: a member of the tribe of Ephraim[7] and a member of a clan of the tribe of Judah[8] whose territory was around Bethlehem. Jesse was an Ephrathite in the latter sense. We saw earlier that 1 Samuel 1:1 may well have meant that Elkanah, and hence Samuel, had family connections with Bethlehem.

In the face of the Philistine threat, David's being another "son of an Ephrathite" is tantalizing. The last leader to thoroughly defeat the Philistines was the son of an Ephrathite. His name was Samuel.

However, David, we are reminded, was one of eight sons (cf. 1 Samuel 16:10, 11), and we now learn that his father was an old man.[9] The sons of old men have not done well in this story so far. Remember old Eli's boys (1 Samuel 2:12) and old Samuel's (1 Samuel 8:3).

Let us hear a little more about old Jesse's sons.

The Older Brothers (v. 13)

> *The three oldest sons of Jesse had followed Saul to the battle. And the names of his three sons who went to the battle were Eliab the firstborn, and next to him Abinadab, and the third Shammah. (v. 13)*

These are the three who were named in our earlier visit to Bethlehem (1 Samuel 16:6, 8, 9). Now they had joined the king's army and were among "the men of Israel" who were camped in the Valley of Elah (1 Samuel 17:2).

They were among "all Israel" who had seen and heard Goliath and were "dismayed and greatly afraid" (1 Samuel 17:11). Eliab, we remember, was the one with impressive height and stature (1 Samuel 16:6, 7).

We also know that of each of these brothers and four others it had been said, "Neither has the LORD chosen this one" (see 1 Samuel 16:7-10).

David (vv. 14, 15)

What about David? We are told (as we already know, of course), "David was the youngest" or the smallest (v. 14a) — too young (or perhaps also too small) to have joined the army. The smallness of David among his brothers has been emphasized for good reason, as we will see.

Our interest is focused on these three oldest boys but especially on the small one: "The three eldest followed Saul, but David went back and forth from Saul to feed his father's sheep at Bethlehem" (vv. 14b, 15).

David did not go with his older brothers into the army. He continued to look after his father's sheep but went to and from the troops under Saul's command with (as we will see) messages and packages from home.[10]

These few lines, reintroducing David to us, particularly in relation to his older brothers, have the effect of reminding us of what took place in Bethlehem in 1 Samuel 16:1-13. What happened then, of course, gives us reason to be very interested in David. It will also turn out to be the key to understanding the rest of this story. We know that despite all appearances to the contrary, this lad is the one chosen by God to be his king. By not mentioning this fact but subtly reminding us of it, the narrator has successfully kept this crucial piece of information well in the background, reflecting the fact that it was either unknown or not understood by the other characters in the story.[11]

Goliath's Continuing Threat (v. 16)

While we have been calmly reacquainting ourselves with the boy from Bethlehem, we do need to remember that in the Valley of Elah the Philistine troublemaker was continuing his performance: "For forty days the Philistine came forward and took his stand, morning and evening" (v. 16).

Twice a day, for forty days, Goliath repeated the routine we saw in 1 Samuel 17:8-10![12] During that time a small lad from Bethlehem would be making his way to the Valley of Elah — a small lad to whom *we* know there was more than met the eye!

DAVID AND THE PHILISTINE THREAT (vv. 17-27)

In order to follow this little development we are taken quickly back to Bethlehem where, we may presume, news of Goliath's antics had not yet been heard. It was an ordinary day in the life of a father, anxious about his three sons at the battlefront.

A Trivial Errand for the Boy (vv. 17-20a)

THE TASK (vv. 17, 18)

Not for the first time, we are to understand from verse 15, Jesse sent David on an errand out of concern for his boys:

> *And Jesse said to David his son, "Take for your brothers an ephah of this parched grain, and these ten loaves, and carry them quickly to the camp to your brothers. Also take these ten cheeses to the commander of their thousand. See if your brothers are well, and bring some token from them."* (vv. 17, 18)

In the scheme of things it was a menial, trivial task. The details here underscore the ordinariness and the unremarkable character of both David's family and the errand on which he was about to embark.[13] Parched grain and loaves of bread were simple enough fare.[14] A gift to the commander was the kind of thing many fathers would do — to the embarrassment of their sons! The request for some tangible sign of their welfare was also altogether natural.

THE DESTINATION (v. 19)

Just so we are quite clear about where Jesse was sending his youngest, we are reminded: "Now Saul and they and all the men of Israel were in the valley of Elah, fighting with the Philistines" (v. 19).

These words probably concluded Jesse's instructions to David. Replace "were" with "are" (which the Hebrew certainly allows),[15] and here we have Jesse informing David, perhaps for the first time, where his brothers were and what was going on there. Of course, we know better than did Jesse that Saul and the men of Israel were *not* fighting the Philistines at all. They were trembling with terror before *the* Philistine with his abuse, scorn, and threats (see v. 11).

THE OBEDIENT SON (v. 20a)

Neither Jesse nor David knew that yet. So David set out on his unremarkable chore: "And David rose early in the morning and left the sheep with a keeper and took the provisions and went, as Jesse had commanded him" (v. 20a).

The unimportant details keep us in suspense and force us to experi-

ence things from David's point of view. That David "rose" before he went
scarcely needs to be said. That he left "early in the morning" is hardly
more gripping. It is nice to know that he "left the sheep with a keeper,"
but we would not mind if we hadn't been told. All of this is how David
experienced the first part of that day — as an obedient son, doing as his
father told him.

Perhaps we find ourselves wondering now what the earlier episode in
Bethlehem meant. If this errand-running boy is the Lord's chosen king, if the
Spirit of the Lord has come upon this lad, it is difficult to see! He appears to
be no more than an obedient servant, doing his father's bidding.

The last time we heard of a trivial-sounding errand, performed by a
son in obedience to his father, was when Saul set out in search of donkeys
(1 Samuel 9:3). That rather ordinary task resulted in the appointment of a
king! Perhaps we have learned by now that very ordinary situations can be
the beginning of extraordinary things.

The Philistine Threat — in David's Hearing (vv. 20b-24)

DAVID'S ARRIVAL (vv. 20b, 21)

> *And he came to the encampment as the host was going out to the battle*
> *line, shouting the war cry. And Israel and the Philistines drew up for*
> *battle, army against army. (vv. 20b, 21)*

He arrived, after his twelve-mile trek with his considerable load, just as
some action was taking place. The army was lining up along the side of the
valley. There was shouting and much noise. The battle lines were drawn up.
The armies faced each other.

DAVID'S INTEREST (v. 22)

Any moment now the fighting would begin. David was too much of a
boy to miss seeing the action: "And David left the things in charge of
the keeper of the baggage and ran to the ranks and went and greeted his
brothers" (v. 22).

It was just as well his dad couldn't see him!

Without realizing it David was leaving behind old responsibilities as
he was about to take on a whole new and astonishing role. He had left the
sheep with a "keeper." Now he left the provisions he had brought with
another "keeper."

We might notice a curious contrast here between this small lad abandoning his burdensome load to "the keeper of the baggage" so he could
run forward to the scene of the action and a rather bigger lad who had

earlier tried to hide himself "among the baggage" to *avoid* the action (see 1 Samuel 10:22)!

DAVID'S SURPRISE (V. 23)

If David had rushed to the battle lines hoping to see some fighting, he was in for a surprise:

> As he talked with them, behold, the champion, the Philistine of Gath, Goliath by name, came up out of the ranks of the Philistines and spoke the same words as before. (v. 23a)

Here was "the man of the between." The repetition of the details we heard earlier (1 Samuel 17:4) — the designation "the Philistine," his name, Goliath, and the town, Gath — all contribute to the sense of Goliath being seen now *for the first time* not by us, nor of course by anyone else in the Valley of Elah, but *by David*.[16]

The Philistine menace repeated his now twice daily tirade:

> "Why have you come out to draw up for battle? Am I not the Philistine, and are you not slaves for Saul? Choose a man for yourselves, and let him come down to me. If he is able to fight with me and kill me, then we will be your slaves. But if I prevail against him and kill him, then you shall be our slaves and serve us. . . . I mock the ranks of Israel this day. Give me a man, that we may fight together." (1 Samuel 17:8b-10, my translation)

The only difference this time (a difference of monumental importance, though none could have guessed it at the time) is noted at the end of verse 23: "And David heard him" (v. 23b).

Just two words in the original: "David heard." Did anyone notice? Did anyone care that young David from Bethlehem "heard"? Of course not. But this was the turning point in Israel's fortunes, in Israel's history, and therefore in world history!

ISRAEL'S FEAR (V. 24)

As far as everyone on this side of the Valley of Elah was concerned, nothing had changed since the first time they heard the monster of Philistia: "All the men of Israel, when they saw the man, fled from him and were much afraid" (v. 24).

This paralleled the way they were "shattered and greatly afraid" the first time (see 1 Samuel 17:11, literal translation). They fled, much as they had fled from the Philistines when they had gathered in strength at Michmash in 1 Samuel 13:6, 7.[17]

In 1 Samuel 17:11 it had been the *hearing* that had led to the terror. This time it was when they "saw" him. Of course, the actual experience involved seeing *and* hearing on both occasions, but perhaps the mention of *seeing* in verse 24 should remind us of 1 Samuel 16:7. If so, we may entertain a thought: if the Israelites were seeing Goliath "as man sees" and were therefore terrified, what would Goliath have looked like to someone who saw *not* "as man sees," but as the Lord sees? What did the Philistine hulk look like *to God*? In a moment we will find out!

David's Response (vv. 25-27)

SAUL'S (RUMORED) RESPONSE (V. 25)

Before we hear David's response to what he had seen and heard, we hear of what Saul had done to counter the threat from Goliath. Had he decided to go and face the foe himself? Well, not exactly. Had he drawn up a battle plan, and would he lead his troops out to deal with the aggressors? Not exactly that either. In fact we do not learn of Saul's initiative from Saul himself. We just hear a rumor.[18]

> *And the men of Israel said, "Have you seen this man who has come up? Surely he has come up to defy [better, to mock] Israel. And the king will enrich the man who kills him with great riches and will give him his daughter and make his father's house free in Israel." (v. 25)*

We cannot be sure that the king *had* promised to do all this. All we are told is that this is what was being said.

DAVID'S FIRST WORDS: TWO QUESTIONS (V. 26)

David seems to have been unsure about this as well. He questioned the rumor. In asking his question, however, he revealed for the first time a rather different perspective on the terrifying figure in the valley:

> *And David said to the men who stood by him, "What shall be done for the man who kills this Philistine and takes away the reproach [or mockery] from Israel? For who is this uncircumcised Philistine, that he should defy [better, mock] the armies of the living God?" (v. 26)*

These are the first recorded words spoken by David in the Bible. He asked two questions. The first was to clarify the rumor: What is the reward for the man who puts an end to this mockery? The second was a rhetorical defiance of the Philistine arrogance. In the second question David sounds a little like Jonathan in 1 Samuel 14:6 ("Come, let us go over to the garrison of these uncircumcised").[19] More to the point, he sounds like nothing at all that had been heard from Saul or any other Israelite in the Valley of Elah. David spoke of *taking away* the mockery from Israel rather than being shattered by it. He expressed contempt, not terror, before the Philistine "man of the between." He saw, as apparently no one else saw, that the Philistine — this *uncircumcised* Philistine, this pagan worshiper of dead gods — was mocking not only Israel but Israel's God, who alone was "the living God."

We might recall the Philistine god. We saw him earlier in this book. Dagon was a dead god if ever there was one (see 1 Samuel 5:1-5)![20]

We now begin to see something of the effects of the Spirit who had "rushed upon David" some time previously in Bethlehem (1 Samuel 16:13). The Spirit-filled man was seeing Goliath differently! Could we even say that he seems to have been seeing "as the Lord sees"?

THE PEOPLE'S ANSWER TO QUESTION 1 (v. 27)

The people answered the first of David's questions with words previously heard: "And the people answered him in the same way, 'So shall it be done to the man who kills him'" (v. 27).

To David's second question there was no response.

DAVID AND HIS BROTHERS (vv. 28-30)

Actually there *was* a response. It came from those closest to David, those who knew him best. Our second installment of the great David and Goliath story closes as it began, with David among his brothers.

Eliab (v. 28)

In particular it was the oldest — big tall Eliab — who did the talking.

> Now Eliab his eldest brother heard when he spoke to the men. And Eliab's anger was kindled against David, and he said, "Why have you come down? And with whom have you left those few sheep in the wilderness? I know your presumption and the evil of your heart, for you have come down to see the battle." (v. 28)

We recall that David's brothers had witnessed his earlier anointing by Samuel in Bethlehem.[21] They may not have understood what they saw, but the singling out of the younger boy may well lie behind a sibling jealousy reminiscent of Joseph and his brothers (see Genesis 37:4).[22]

If that is the case, Eliab's hostility (like that of Joseph's brothers) is more disturbing than it may seem. Eliab was among the very few in Israel who had seen the prophet's anointing of David. His hostility was more than sibling rivalry. It was nothing less than opposition to God's chosen one and therefore to the living God himself. Eliab had unwittingly taken Goliath's side!

Eliab even sounded just a little like Goliath, with his accusing "Why have you come?" question, his scornful, belittling derision ("those few sheep" or "that bit of flock"[23]), and his presumed self-importance ("*I* am the one who knows . . ."[24]).[25]

There is irony in Eliab's suggestion that he was the one who knew the evil that was in David's heart, since we know that David was the one who has been chosen according to God's heart (1 Samuel 13:14; 16:7). Eliab knew nothing! He still saw "as man sees" and could only see "a presumptuous young rascal whose only purpose in coming here is to see the battle."[26]

David (vv. 29, 30)

And David said, "What have I done now? Was it not but a word?" (v. 29)

The NIV paraphrases the last question rather well ("Can't I even speak?"), but perhaps too clearly.[27] In Hebrew David's words have an ambiguity that may suggest evasiveness. He was not going to divulge his intentions to this hostile brother.

David moved away from his brothers and continued to ask his astonishing questions: "And he turned away from him toward another, and spoke in the same way, and the people answered him again as before" (v. 30).

We might imagine the youth moving from one group of soldiers to another, uttering his preposterously defiant questions. Perhaps he seemed to many to be a presumptuous young rascal.

God is the God of the unexpected. No one in the Valley of Elah that day (with possibly one exception) had any idea that this young man was the one through whom God would deliver his people.

God is the God of the unexpected. What he was doing in the Valley of Elah was the beginning of a sequence of events that can be traced through the Biblical record over about ten centuries. It came to its climax when a descendant of David appeared speaking words more provocative and apparently presumptuous than anything David said on that day in the valley. Those who knew him best, or who thought they did, those from his hometown said:

"Is not this the carpenter's son? Is not his mother called Mary? And are not his brothers James and Joseph and Simon and Judas? And are not all his sisters with us? Where then did this man get all these things?" And they took offense at him. (Matthew 13:55-57a)

It may be an understandable mistake, but it is a great mistake nonetheless to take offense at the unexpected ways of God. Who would think that Jesus, the teacher of parables, the healer of the sick, who was executed for blasphemy, is the King who saves his people and will rule the world? It is as unlikely as the boy from Bethlehem doing anything for the people who faced Goliath.

To trust God you must be prepared for the unexpected.

28

The Gospel of David

1 SAMUEL 17:31-40

The gospel of our Lord Jesus Christ is God's word to the whole world.

Attempts to revise, update, or otherwise improve the gospel are as foolish as they are common. It is an astonishing fact that so many who claim to be Christian believers have sought to modify the gospel message that has been given to us in the pages of the Bible. Such attempts always have the appearance of being well-meaning. They appear to be motivated by a desire to make the gospel relevant and acceptable to a particular culture or age. Aspects of the gospel considered unimportant, unacceptable, or unbelievable in a particular time or society are de-emphasized, ignored, or even denied. And so we have versions of Christianity that have no talk of sin or atonement, of resurrection or judgment, of Heaven or Hell. Indeed we have versions of Christianity that do not speak of God!

At the same time attempts are made to make the gospel address the needs of the day as they are currently perceived. So instead of forgiveness of sins we have meaning and purpose in life. Instead of holiness we have environmental responsibility. Instead of divine judgment we have the demand for social justice. Instead of God we have spirituality.

When the things that matter to *us* and to our culture are made the criteria for determining the gospel we proclaim, then we are engaged in the greatest foolishness imaginable.

I am not criticizing attempts to make the gospel *intelligible* to our culture, to express it in words that can be understood, rather than in the jargon of the Christian subculture. Proclaiming the gospel to the nations of the world will always involve the hard work of translating, explaining, and persuading. In turn that will require listening, empathizing, and understanding the thinking and concerns of the people to whom we are bringing the gospel.

I am simply saying that when explaining and persuading cross the line to *amending* the gospel in order to make it more relevant and credible, then we are no longer proclaimers of the gospel of Jesus Christ. We have become purveyors of a different gospel.

What does this have to do with the story of David and Goliath?

A great deal indeed. When Jesus is introduced in the first sentence of the New Testament as "Jesus Christ, the son of *David*" (Matthew 1:1), it should be clear that the story of David is part of the indispensable background to the gospel of Jesus. Essential aspects of the gospel have their roots in these much earlier days, when God, for the first time, chose and anointed "a king for myself" (1 Samuel 16:1). The most important thing for us to understand about the story of David and Goliath is that its gripping excitement has become the gripping excitement of the gospel of Jesus, the son of David.

In our third installment of this superb story we will see why the idea of changing the gospel can be so appealing, and why it must not be done.

The point we had reached was where David, the shepherd boy, had come to the Valley of Elah on an errand from his father — to bring provisions for his older brothers and to see how they were. On his arrival he had seen and heard the challenge of the Philistine-on-steroids and witnessed the terror among the Israelite troops. He heard that the king, Saul, had offered a reward to anyone who killed Goliath — wealth, his daughter's hand, and freedom for his family. The boy had expressed interest in the challenge with words that indicated not fear but outrage: "Who is this uncircumcised Philistine, that he should mock [my translation] the armies of the living God?" (1 Samuel 17:26). True, his brothers were unimpressed by his apparently presumptuous bravado. But word spread about the words this boy was speaking. It was not long before a report reached Saul.

THE CONVERSATION (vv. 31-37)

David's Words (v. 31)

> When the words that David spoke were heard, they repeated them before Saul, and he sent for him.[1] (v. 31)

"The words that David spoke" were words we heard earlier:

> "What shall be done for the man who kills this Philistine and takes away the reproach from Israel? For who is this uncircumcised Philistine, that he should mock the armies of the living God?" (1 Samuel 17:26)

Notice that David's words:

(1) acknowledged that the God of Israel was "the living God," who must be taken seriously by all people (including this Philistine minion, whatever he thinks!);

(2) recognized that Israel belonged to this God, her armies being "the armies of the living God" (who by implication could and should trust their God);

(3) saw the words of the Philistine for the blasphemous insult that they were (not just to Israel but to the living God); and therefore

(4) regarded the speaker of these insults as beneath contempt and unworthy of acknowledgment, let alone fear ("Who is this uncircumcised Philistine, that he should mock the armies of the living God?").

We cannot be sure how much of David's words were reported to Saul, but it was enough to catch the king's attention, and David was brought before him.

David's "Gospel" for Saul (vv. 32-37a)

Although we have seen David before the king earlier in the narrative (1 Samuel 16:21), I have been suggesting that encounter may have occurred later in time. If that is so, 1 Samuel 17:31 would be the first time that Saul and David met.[2]

The narrative leaves a great deal unsaid. However, enough has been said to ensure that we have not forgotten that Saul was the failed, rejected king. His inactivity in this chapter so far reminds us of his ineffective leadership in chapters 13–15 (see, for example, 13:3; 14:1, 2, 29-30, 45, 46; 15:9, 15, 21, 33). His specific failure on this occasion to respond to Goliath's challenge reminds us that he was the obvious one to do so (1 Samuel 10:23, 24) and that this was the very purpose of his kingship (1 Samuel 9:16). Even more clearly, we have been reminded of the earlier, somewhat secret happenings in Bethlehem, and so we are vividly aware of David's special status. Saul, of course, had no idea of this.

As the failed king unknowingly met the king-elect, in the person of a youth well under military age, it is astonishing to see how the young man took charge of the meeting. It is not too much to say that David proclaimed the gospel to Saul. It was not yet, of course, the gospel of our Lord Jesus Christ that he proclaimed, but listen carefully, and see if you can hear the gospel dimensions of his words.

"FEAR NOT — I WILL FIGHT" (v. 32)

And David said to Saul, "Let no man's heart fail because of him. Your servant will go and fight with this Philistine." (v. 32)

David's words were outrageous in exactly the same way that the gospel of Jesus Christ is outrageous. To grasp the preposterous nature of these words of David is to see something of the offense of the gospel. David's gospel had two outrageous points.

First, there was an imperative: "Let no human heart (including yours, Saul) fail on account of Goliath. Faced with the Philistine, do not be afraid!"

What kind of nonsense is that? Goliath embodied terror. To even think of his appearance and his threats was shattering to any human confidence. Faced with Goliath, there are many sensible things that could be said, like "Run for your life" or "Find a hiding-place" or "Try and think of a plan." But "Let no man's heart fail"? That is the most preposterous thing anyone could have said to Saul in those circumstances.

It is just like the gospel we know. Look at your great enemy, if you dare. Think of death — your death. Think of sin — your sin. Think of the devil and his claim on you. Yet the gospel of Jesus says, "Do not be afraid." That is the most preposterous thing anyone could say to sinners like us, don't you think?

Except, perhaps, for the second thing David said. It was an indicative, the reason why no man's heart need tremble at Goliath's threats. "I will fight him for you."

Right! There ought to be a better word than *preposterous* to describe that proposition and how it must have sounded to Saul. Here is this small youth. Skinny, I like to think. Too young to leave home. It would have seemed absurd for Saul, Israel's biggest and best, to even consider taking on the Philistine monster. That's why he didn't, of course. But for this kid to tell the king that he need not be afraid anymore because he, David, would fight the Philistine is either just stupid or breathtakingly audacious or . . . what?

It is rather nice to have the luxury (which I am sure Saul did not have) to reflect on the subtle nuances in David's words.

In the first place the expression he used for fear indicated heart failure.[3] We are aware that God himself has indicated that a false evaluation of another situation (which also involved seeing a man's size and stature) arose from a failure to see according to the heart (1 Samuel 16:7). We might reflect on the fact that the fear engendered by Goliath arises entirely from seeing Goliath "as man sees," namely, with the eyes. But what would Goliath look like if we could see him according to God's heart, if we could see him as God sees him? Fear of Goliath is altogether understandable. But it is a failure of the heart![4]

A second subtlety worth noting is David's self-designation: "your servant." The Philistine had derided the Israelites for being nothing more than Saul's slaves (or servants). David used the same word but gladly (it seems) accepted the role of Saul's "servant."[5] What for the Philistine was a demeaning insult (to be a servant) was David's accepted role. David proposed to serve Saul (and Israel) by fighting their terrible enemy.

This is what I am calling "the gospel of David": (1) "Do not be afraid," (2) "for I will fight."

The astonishing nature of these words is amplified when we recognize that they are reminiscent of an earlier gospel message, which we might call "the gospel of Moses." It was uttered on another terrifying day in the history of Israel, some half a millennium before this day. The Egyptian army had been advancing toward the Israelites who were trapped between the enemy forces and the sea. This was Moses' gospel:

> "Do not be afraid. Stand firm and you will see the deliverance the LORD will bring you today. The Egyptians you see today you will never see again. The LORD will fight for you; you need only to be still." (Exodus 14:13, 14, NIV)

Faced with Goliath, young David was speaking like Moses faced with Pharaoh! In similarly terrifying circumstances this was Moses' gospel: (1) "Do not be afraid," (2) "for the Lord (the God they could not even see!) will fight for you."

Do you see how these messages (David's to Saul and Moses's to the Israelites) are like the gospel of Jesus? Among the first to hear the latter were the shepherds. Do you remember the words they heard:

> "Fear not, for behold, I bring you good news of great joy that will be for all the people. For unto you is born this day in the city of David a Savior, who is Christ the Lord." (Luke 2:10, 11)

(1) "Do not be afraid." (2) "You will be saved from all your enemies by one who is wrapped in swaddling clothes and lying in a manger!"

People find it hard to take this gospel seriously for just the same reasons that Saul found it hard to take David's gospel seriously.

SAUL'S DISBELIEF (v. 33)

It is not difficult to relate to Saul's incredulity:

> And Saul said to David, "You are not able to go against this Philistine to fight with him, for you are but a youth, and he has been a man of war from his youth." (v. 33)

Saul could see what anyone could see: David was no match for the Philistine. It was a "youth" against one who had been "a man of war from his youth" — the implication being that was some time ago![6] That David should propose to fight a seasoned warrior of Goliath's experience was, to Saul's mind, preposterous. It was simply not possible.

Saul did not believe David's gospel. His unbelief was entirely reasonable. It focused on the doubtful ability of the youth before him to do what he proposed. "You are not able," said Saul.

There is a striking contrast between Saul's estimate here of the youth standing before him and the estimate given by another, earlier in the narrative. In 1 Samuel 16:18 one of Saul's "young men" described David as " . . . a man of valor, a man of war, prudent in speech, and a man of good presence, and the LORD is with him."

While I have suggested a number of times that the incident at the end of 1 Samuel 16 may well have occurred after the events of 1 Samuel 17, this does not gainsay the fact that the *narrative* has been arranged in such a way as to signal David's (later) "man of war" reputation *before* we hear Saul deny his capacity to go out against the Philistine "man of war." Quite simply, the narrative is ordered so that we know in advance that Saul's reasonable unbelief was wrong.

"I SAVED" (vv. 34-36)

David responded to Saul's unbelief by displaying another of the qualities identified by the youth in 1 Samuel 16:18, namely, his ability with words:

> But David said to Saul, "Your servant used to keep sheep for his father.
> And when there came a lion, or a bear, and took a lamb from the flock,
> I went after him and struck him and delivered it out of his mouth. And if
> he arose against me, I caught him by his beard and struck him and killed
> him. Your servant has struck down both lions and bears, and this uncir-
> cumcised Philistine shall be like one of them, for he has defied [mocked]
> the armies of the living God." (vv. 34-36)

David's words tell the story of his past exploits as a deliverer. David had delivered many a lamb from the clutches of deadly danger. At one level David could be understood to be displaying his credentials as a courageous and skillful fighter. Saul might have seen him as a mere, inexperienced youth, but David's youth had not been as empty as Saul may have supposed. The uncircumcised Philistine, who had threatened the armies of the living God, would be as the wild beasts who threatened the sheep under David's care.

It was Saul's turn to speak. But he said nothing.[7] Perhaps he was still being reasonable: "Wild beasts may be one thing, lad, but that fully armed,

totally protected monster out there in the valley is another story altogether."
Saving sheep is one thing; war is another.

"THE LORD WILL SAVE" (v. 37a)

The silence was broken by David. As though he had read Saul's reasonable
mind, he spelled out the meaning of his gospel in direct terms: "And David
said, 'The LORD who delivered me from the paw of the lion and from the paw
of the bear will deliver me from the hand of this Philistine'" (v. 37a).

David's earlier words were more than a testimony to his experience
and abilities. Behind the delivering hand of David had been the delivering
hand of the Lord. The Lord delivered David from the paws of the lion and
the bear. That is how David delivered the sheep from the clutches of the
beasts. And the Lord who delivered from the beasts was able to deliver from
this Philistine. And if the Lord delivered David from Goliath, David would
deliver Israel from the Philistines.

This is the first time in this chapter that God's covenant name has been
used. "The LORD," or in Hebrew *Yahweh*, is the name by which God had
made himself known to his people Israel (see especially Exodus 3:13-15).
In the long story of David and Goliath, it was David who named the name
of *Yahweh* — with one exception that we will note shortly.[8] The fear that
had gripped Saul's heart and all of the Israelites' hearts reflected their failure
to know *Yahweh*. David saw everything differently because he knew that
Yahweh delivers.[9]

As one writer has put it: "Quite a speech! Quite a young boy! Quite a
faith, not found anywhere else in Israel!"[10]

Even Jonathan had not expressed the confidence in God that we hear
in David's gospel. Jonathan had boldly said, "*It may be* that the LORD will
work for us" (1 Samuel 14:6), but David knew that "the LORD . . . *will* deliver
me."[11] The difference is that David was the anointed one on whom the Spirit
of the Lord had permanently come (1 Samuel 16:13).

As we read the story, we know very well that David was right because
we know that the Spirit of the Lord had rushed upon him. In the light of
the story so far, we are right to suspect that the Spirit had "rushed" upon
David for this very purpose, as he had on Saul in 1 Samuel 10:10 (cf. 10:6
and 11:6).

Saul's Acceptance (v. 37b)

David's gospel was very powerful. It produced these words from Saul: "And
Saul said to David, 'Go, and the LORD be with you!'" (v. 37b).

We have noticed how characters in this story often say more than they
realize. This is an arresting example. Remember the young man in 1 Samuel

16:18 who said of David, "The LORD is with him." Like that young man, Saul's words may be no more than a conventional pious expression. But the words can mean, "The LORD *will* be with you." And, more than Saul could have known, that was true![12]

THE ACTION (vv. 38-40)

At last, with Saul's "Go," we expect the action we have been waiting for since this story commenced to now begin.

Saul's Way (vv. 38, 39a-b)

However, there was a slight delay. Saul's failure to understand David's gospel was immediately apparent as he tried to equip the lad with his own considerable armor and weapons: "Then Saul clothed David with his armor. He put a helmet of bronze on his head and clothed him with a coat of mail, and David strapped his sword over his armor" (vv. 38, 39a).

Saul tried to equip David like Goliath! Goliath had a helmet of bronze, a coat of mail, and a sword (1 Samuel 17:5, 45, 51). Remember, Saul was the king that Israel got when they wanted a king "like all the nations" (1 Samuel 8:5). Saul was a king whose battle regalia was like Goliath's, only not nearly as good![13] A king "like all the nations" is what they got!

With more subtlety, however, we should appreciate this poignant moment. Saul the king was placing his royal (albeit inappropriately royal) garments on David. Without suggesting that Saul understood the full import of his actions, we may recognize that there was a symbolism to this act that corresponded to the truth we already know. Saul was the king on the way out. David was his designated replacement.[14]

But David would not be a king like Saul. He was not to be a king "like all the nations." So Saul's battle garb could not be used by him: "And he tried in vain to go, for he had not tested them" (v. 39b).

Saul's way could not be David's way. He had never used such equipment, and now was not the time to start!

David's Way (vv. 39c-d, 40)

> Then David said to Saul, "I cannot go with these, for I have not tested them." (v. 39c)

With *this* equipment Saul's earlier view would be correct. In verse 33 Saul had said, "You are not able to go against this Philistine." Now David said, "I cannot go *with these*."

So David put them off. Then he took his staff in his hand and chose five smooth stones from the brook and put them in his shepherd's pouch. His sling was in his hand, and he approached the Philistine. (vv. 39d, 40)

That is the point at which we will leave the story for now.

Can you now see with fresh clarity the foolishness of changing the gospel?

In the case of David it would be like suggesting that Israel's need of the moment was something other than deliverance from the Philistine threat or that the danger could be dealt with by someone or something other than David himself. The absurdity of David talking to Saul about anything *other than* the deliverance from Goliath is comparable to Christian preachers or teachers who want to major on something other than salvation from sin, death, and Satan. The foolishness of thinking there was or could be some other way of deliverance from Goliath than David's fighting the enemy is comparable to suggestions that people still entertain that human beings can live without the victory of Jesus Christ on the cross over our great enemies.

The gospel of Jesus Christ, like the gospel of David, addresses the *real need* with the *only solution*. Unlike the gospel of David, the gospel of Jesus is God's *eternal* solution to our *eternal* need.

29

David and Goliath

1 SAMUEL 17:41-58

"Death is swallowed up in victory."
"O death, where is your victory?
O death, where is your sting?"

The sting of death is sin, and the power of sin is the law. But thanks be to God, who gives us the victory through our Lord Jesus Christ. (1 Corinthians 15:54b-57)

The news about Jesus Christ is the news of an extraordinary victory. An enemy has been defeated. A very great liberation has been won. Jesus Christ has magnificently overcome the enemy, and those of us who belong to him rejoice in the victory he has won for us. The enemy is death. What makes death such a terrible enemy is sin. Sin means that death is not just the end of life but brings divine judgment. "The sting of death is sin" (1 Corinthians 15:56a).[1] What makes sin so serious that it deserves death is the Law of God. The Law means that sin is not just undesirable conduct but defiance of God's requirement of righteousness. "The power of sin is the law. But thanks be to God, who gives us the victory through our Lord Jesus Christ" (1 Corinthians 15:56b, 57).

The victory of Christ is breathtaking news. The demands of God's Law have been met in the perfect obedience of Jesus. The penalty for sin has been paid in the sin-bearing death of Jesus. The power of death has been broken in the mighty resurrection of Jesus from the dead.

"Death is swallowed up in victory."
"O death, where is your victory?
O death, where is your sting?" (1 Corinthians 15:54b, 55)

I wonder whether you appreciate the *victorious* nature of the Christian life. I am not speaking (as some have done using the language of "the victorious Christian life") of your own victorious living, but of the victory that has been *given* to us who belong to Christ because of Jesus' obedient life, atoning death, and victorious resurrection. Every Christian person should know the thrill of joining in Paul's words of praise: "But thanks be to God, who *gives* us the victory through our Lord Jesus Christ."

As we come to our fourth and final installment of the great story of David and Goliath, we come at last to the moment of victory. The story has been told at great length, mainly so we will appreciate the wonder of the victory we are to witness now. As David defeated that terrible enemy of God's people, we need to understand that God was doing (admittedly on a smaller scale and with more limited ramifications) what he has now done in Jesus' victory. Appreciate the victory of David over Goliath, and you should be able to say with excitement: "But thanks be to God, who gives *us* the victory through our Lord Jesus Christ."

We left the story at a rather intense moment. David, the lad from Bethlehem, had announced to Saul that no one need fear because he, David, would fight the monstrous Philistine who was terrorizing Israel, and the Lord would deliver David from the enemy. No one on the Israelite side of the Valley of Elah that day could fail to see that this news (if it was true) was the most important news they had ever heard. David had refused to don Saul's bulky armor (which so resembled Goliath's gear), but with his stick in one hand, five river stones in his pouch, and his sling in the other hand, he walked down into the Valley of Elah toward the nine-and-a-half-foot Philistine.

GOLIATH'S DISDAIN (vv. 41-44)

Picture the scene in the Valley of Elah. The armies, you may recall, were lined up on opposite sides of the valley. Goliath, the huge Philistine "man of the between" (literal translation of "champion," v. 4) came out from the Philistine lines twice each day and shouted his terrible challenge. This had been going on for some forty days. At last there was a response from the Israelite side of the valley. A young lad was walking out toward the Philistine.

Goliath's Approach (v. 41)

> And the Philistine moved forward and came near to David, with his shield-bearer in front of him. (v. 41)

I imagine the Philistine was moving forward because whatever was coming toward him was too small to see clearly!

We should call to mind the detailed description we were given at the beginning of this story (see 1 Samuel 17:4-7). See his massive size. Look at his impenetrable protective metal armor, from head to foot — bronze helmet, massive bronze mail coat, bronze leg coverings, and a shield as big as him carried by another man whose sole job was to hold up the shield in front of Goliath. Observe his deadly weapons — what was probably a large curved sword held across his shoulders and a massive spear designed for slinging.

The colossal Philistine and the wiry boy moved toward each other. Any moment now they would be close enough for the Philistine to be able to see the lad.

What Goliath Saw (v. 42)

And when the Philistine looked and saw David, he disdained him, for he was but a youth, ruddy and handsome in appearance. (v. 42)

The Philistine was, of course, "seeing as man sees" (see 1 Samuel 16:7). What he saw filled him with contempt. It was an affront to the seasoned warrior to see the Israelites sending out to meet him nothing more than a red-faced "youth."[2]

It is interesting that what Goliath saw is exactly what we were shown earlier, when David first appeared in the narrative, in Bethlehem, on the day he was anointed by Samuel. Then he had been described like this: "Now he was ruddy and had beautiful eyes and was handsome" (1 Samuel 16:12b).

What Goliath saw is described in almost the same words: "a youth, ruddy and handsome in appearance."[3] However, through Goliath's eyes, David's good looks were signs of weakness, inexperience, vulnerability, even childlikeness.[4]

Goliath's Curse and Threat (vv. 43, 44)

Goliath now voiced the offensive insult that this was to him: "And the Philistine said to David, 'Am I a dog, that you come to me with sticks?'" (v. 43a).

He was angry. The Israelites were not taking him seriously! How dare they send out such an unworthy opponent! An angry Goliath was no doubt even more terrifying than anything that had been seen in the Valley of Elah for the last forty days. "And the Philistine cursed David by his gods" (v. 43b).

Wittingly or not, by invoking the Philistine gods, Goliath signaled the true dimensions of this confrontation. More than Philistines versus Israelites, this was the gods of the Philistines versus the living God. It was a warrior who called on Dagon versus a lad who was the Lord's chosen one![5]

In the absence of any response from David, Goliath made his final threat: "The Philistine said to David, 'Come to me, and I will give your flesh to the birds of the air and to the beasts of the field'" (v. 44).

Goliath wielded the power of death. The language the Philistine used echoes the Old Testament vocabulary of death as curse and judgment (see Deuteronomy 28:26; Psalm 79:2, 3; Isaiah 18:6; Jeremiah 7:33; 8:1, 2; 15:3). Goliath's words remind us of what Hannah had said: "Talk no more so very boldly, let not arrogance come from your mouth" (1 Samuel 2:3). You will rarely hear arrogance to match what came from Goliath's mouth on that day!

As we see and hear him threatening David, and by implication all Israel, with death and destruction by his gods, the situation is complicated by the fact that these circumstances are related to the disobedience of Israel's king and his people to the word of the Lord.[6] As Saul had begun his reign, the prophet Samuel had warned:

If you will fear the LORD and serve him and obey his voice and not rebel against the commandment of the LORD, and if both you and the king who reigns over you will follow the LORD your God, it will be well. But if you will not obey the voice of the LORD, but rebel against the commandment of the LORD, then the hand of the LORD will be against you and your king [or fathers]. (1 Samuel 12:14, 15)

As had happened so often in Israel's history, when Israel forgot the Lord their God, he gave them up to the power of enemies (see 1 Samuel 12:9). Israel and their king, Saul, *deserved* the death that Goliath threatened in the Valley of Elah that day. It was the kind of death that would one day come to Israel. Many years after this day the people of Israel would cry out to God:

O God, the nations have come into your inheritance;
*   they have defiled your holy temple;*
*   they have laid Jerusalem in ruins.*
They have given the bodies of your servants
*   to the birds of the heavens for food,*
*   the flesh of your faithful to the beasts of the earth.*
They have poured out their blood like water
*   all around Jerusalem,*
*   and there was no one to bury them.*
We have become a taunt to our neighbors,
*   mocked and derided by those around us. (Psalm 79:1-4)*

That is the situation that all Israel faced several hundred years before the reality lamented in Psalm 79, in the Valley of Elah as David faced the angry mockery of Goliath.

DAVID'S GOSPEL FOR GOLIATH (vv. 45-47)

However, the threatened disaster was not going to happen on that day. Not, mind you, because Goliath was less powerful than he seemed, nor because Israel had the wherewithal to resist him, still less because Israel did not deserve this fate. They did deserve it. It did not happen that day because the Lord God of Israel had chosen a king for himself (1 Samuel 16:1), on whom the Spirit of the Lord had powerfully come (1 Samuel 16:13), and *he* was about to fight the Philistine (1 Samuel 17:32).

But first he proclaimed what I like to call "the gospel" to him! Previously we called 1 Samuel 17:32-37 "David's 'gospel' for Saul." Now we hear the same "gospel" announced to Goliath.

Two Powers (v. 45a-b)

First, David set the two powers that faced each other that day into perspective: "Then David said to the Philistine, 'You come to me with a sword and with a spear and with a javelin . . .'" (v. 45a). That is the Philistine side of this confrontation — weapons of destruction with the undeniable power to kill and maim. " . . . but I come to you in the name of the LORD of hosts, the God of the armies of Israel . . ." (v. 45b).

That is David's side. The Lord is named in thoroughly military terms: "the LORD of troops, the God of the battle lines of Israel" (literal translation). The name reminds us (even if it did not remind Goliath) of the whole history of the Lord's battles for his people. Beginning with the overthrow of Pharaoh in the days of Moses, and most recently the destruction of the Amalekites (1 Samuel 15), the Lord had again and again delivered his wayward people by defeating their enemies. It was in the name of this God that David came.

David's language is a mixture of old and new. This is the God who had been with his people Israel since their beginning, but never before had there been an individual who claimed to "come . . . in the name of the LORD."[7] This was not just a man of great faith in the Lord God speaking. This was the Lord's king, who came to Goliath "in the name of the LORD," as the Lord's representative, as the Lord's own king. This was the first time there had been such a person.

Notice then that David's gospel was *about David*. True, it was about David in relation to the Lord, but it was not a general religious truth. David's own identity was essential to David's gospel.[8]

Indictment (v. 45c)

The second element in David's gospel was his indictment of the Philistine. It is expressed in the last phrase of verse 45: " . . . [God] whom you have defied [mocked]" (v. 45c).

Goliath's mocking of Israel has been a theme through the story.[9] His mocking of the living God would be his undoing.

What Will Happen (v. 46a)

The third element in David's "gospel" for Goliath was his announcement of what would happen:

> *"This day the* Lord *will deliver you into my hand, and I will strike you down and cut off your head. And I will give the dead bodies of the host of the Philistines this day to the birds of the air and to the wild beasts of the earth. . . ." (v. 46a)*

As the one who came in the name of the Lord, David would strike down Goliath, cut off his head, and give the bodies of the Philistines to the birds and beasts. We notice again that what *David* would do was at the heart of his gospel!

The Purpose (vv. 46b, 47)

The fourth element of David's gospel for Goliath caps it all. What was the purpose of this extraordinary — and at this stage utterly incredible — victory? Was this a demonstration of Israel's superiority in some sense over the Philistines?

No. It was rather:

> " . . . *that all the earth may know that there is a God in Israel, and that all this assembly may know that the* Lord *saves not with sword and spear. For the battle is the* Lord*'s, and he will give you into our hand." (vv. 46b, 47)*

What was about to happen to Goliath was a consequence of the living God's will to be known. Here a major theme of the Bible impacts the story of David and Goliath. Like the exodus from Egypt (see, for example, Exodus 9:14-16), the victory over Goliath and the deliverance from his threats happened so that the people of Israel, and ultimately the people of the whole world, would know that the Lord is God.

There was David's "gospel" for Goliath:

(1) I come in the name of the Lord;

(2) You have mocked the Lord;

(3) I will destroy you;

(4) The world will know who God is.

This "gospel" (when proclaimed to Saul) was a call to trust in the Lord and not fear the nations. It was a call to the nations (the Philistines) to stop their foolish defiance of the Lord.[10]

DAVID'S VICTORY (vv. 48-54)

The time for action had come. In the narrative it has taken forty-seven verses to get to this point! But like the New Testament Gospels, when the critical moment arrives, the action is recounted with surprising brevity.

How It Happened (vv. 48, 49)

This is how it happened:

> When the Philistine arose and came and drew near to meet David, David ran quickly toward the battle line to meet the Philistine. And David put his hand in his bag and took out a stone and slung it and struck the Philistine on his forehead. The stone sank into his forehead, and he fell on his face to the ground. (vv. 48, 49)

Goliath fell, just as Dagon had fallen in Ashdod (1 Samuel 5:3, 4)![11]

How It Didn't Happen (vv. 50, 51a)

Before completing the account of the action, the writer underlines how the remarkable victory of David did *not* happen:

> So David prevailed over the Philistine with a sling and with a stone, and struck the Philistine and killed him. There was no sword in the hand of David. (v. 50)

There was nothing ordinary about this victory. "No sword was in the hand of David" reminds us that Saul and Jonathan had such weapons (see 1 Samuel 13:22). David's victory was more extraordinary than any accomplished by Saul and his son. The words more immediately remind us of verse 47 of this chapter. It was by the might of God, not the might of weapons, that David defeated Goliath. "Then David ran and stood over the Philistine and took his sword and drew it out of its sheath and killed him and cut off his head with it" (v. 51a).

The description of the action makes no direct reference to God. If we had witnessed the encounter without hearing David's "gospel," we might well have concluded that here was a remarkably brave, agile, skillful, and very lucky boy! In this sense, there was no visible miracle. "Only those who share the faith of David and who have heard his confession would know that he has a massive resource beyond his own power that operates for him: namely, the powerful, faithful, living God of Israel."[12]

The Reaction of the Philistines (v. 51b)

How did the Philistines respond to the fall of "the man of the between"? "When the Philistines saw that their champion was dead, they fled" (v. 51b).

They reneged on the deal. Remember, Goliath had said that if an Israelite could fight and defeat him, then the Philistines would be Israel's slaves (1 Samuel 17:9). Instead they fled for their lives.

The Response of Israel (and Judah) (vv. 52, 53)

What about the Israelites, those who so recently had themselves "fled" in fear and dread (see 1 Samuel 17:11, 24)?

> *And the men of Israel and Judah rose with a shout and pursued the Philistines as far as Gath and the gates of Ekron, so that the wounded Philistines fell on the way from Shaaraim as far as Gath and Ekron. And the people of Israel came back from chasing the Philistines, and they plundered their camp. (vv. 52, 53)*

They could have said, "Thanks be to God, who gives us the victory through our anointed king David" — except they did not know that secret yet.

Jerusalem (v. 54)

In one of the most striking examples of disregard for chronological sequence anywhere in Biblical narrative, the writer concludes the David and Goliath story by telling us: "And David took the head of the Philistine and brought it to Jerusalem, but he put his armor in his tent" (v. 54).

We have noted a number of times that in Biblical narrative the chronological sequence of events is sometimes disregarded in the interests of providing the reader with information at a point in the account where, for one reason or another, the writer wants to give it. If we take this feature of Biblical narrative seriously, then 1 Samuel 17:54 presents no difficulty. The writer simply tells us that David (eventually) brought the head of Goliath to Jerusalem. David will not get to Jerusalem for a long time yet (2 Samuel 5:6)! Indeed Jerusalem will not be mentioned again in this story until that day, recorded in 2 Samuel 5, when David, as king, will take Jerusalem to be his royal city. But at this point the writer connects the defeat of Goliath and David's coming to Jerusalem. It is as though he were saying, *this* is where David's journey to Jerusalem, to Israel's throne, began.

The rather less extraordinary statement that David put Goliath's armor "in his tent" underlines the fact that this victory was David's (not Saul's).[13] David had not taken Saul's armor, but he did take Goliath's, and he would soon take Jonathan's (1 Samuel 18:4).[14]

DAVID AND SAUL AGAIN (vv. 55-58)

The story is concluded, but there is a brief epilogue. The issue that will dominate the rest of the book of 1 Samuel is the relationship between the rejected king Saul and the one who we now know was on his way to Jerusalem. The epilogue to the David and Goliath story brings these two characters together again in a curious way.

Saul Did Not Know David (vv. 55, 56)

Again chronology is overridden. We have a flashback here:

> As soon as Saul saw David go out against the Philistine, he said to Abner, the commander of the army, "Abner, whose son is this youth?" And Abner said, "As your soul lives, O king, I do not know." And the king said, "Inquire whose son the boy is." (vv. 55, 56)

There is little value in speculating on the psychological or other reason that Saul, who had so recently spoken with David about the very exploit on which he now saw him embark, did not appear now to know who he was.[15] Here we have another example of the characters in this story saying more than they realize. The scene indicates a remarkable blindness on Saul's part. As David went out against Goliath, Saul could only see "as man sees," and he had no idea who this youth was. His ignorance was far deeper than his question!

Saul's "Introduction" to David (vv. 57, 58)

And Saul's ignorance would not yet be overcome.

> And as soon as David returned from the striking down of the Philistine, Abner took him, and brought him before Saul with the head of the Philistine in his hand. And Saul said to him, "Whose son are you, young man?" And

David answered, "I am the son of your servant Jesse the Bethlehemite."
(vv. 57, 58)

That is all Saul will be told for the moment. But for us the mention of Jesse the Bethlehemite takes us back to the events of 1 Samuel 16:1-13, where the explanation for all that has happened in 1 Samuel 17 is to be found.

As we conclude our reflections on the great story of David and Goliath, I want to suggest that we try to put ourselves in the position of those Israelites in the Valley of Elah on the day that David defeated Goliath. Stand there, however, with the understanding that the account of these events in 1 Samuel 17 has given us. You are aware, are you not, that something momentous has happened. Could you fail to say, "Thanks be to God"?

The unusual expression David used, when he said, "I come in the name of the LORD," occurs once again in the Old Testament. It is in a psalm written at a time when the speaker was threatened by enemies and when he "cut them off" "in the name of the LORD." That psalm then has these famous words: "Blessed is he who *comes in the name of the LORD!*" (Psalm 118:26).

Blessed, in other words, is God's king who defeats our enemies!

Psalm 118 appears a number of times in the New Testament, but in particular as Jesus approached Jerusalem and the crowds took up the words:

And the crowds that went before him and that followed him were shouting, "Hosanna to the Son of David! Blessed is he who comes in the name of the Lord! Hosanna in the highest!" (Matthew 21:9)

As the time for Jesus' death drew near, he lamented over Jerusalem, and he said: "For I tell you, you will not see me again, until you say, 'Blessed is he who *comes in the name of the Lord*'" (Matthew 23:39).

Jesus is the one who has now "come in the name of the Lord." He has won a victory that outshines David's, just as his kingship does. We have more in common with those Israelites in the Valley of Elah than we may ever have realized.

Thanks be to God, who gives us the victory through our Lord Jesus Christ.
(1 Corinthians 15:57)

30

Do You Love Him?

1 SAMUEL 18:1-16

One of the most precious descriptions of a Christian is one who "loves" the Lord Jesus Christ. Peter wrote to suffering believers, "Though you have not seen him, you love him" (1 Peter 1:8a).

He was perhaps recalling the words of Jesus that penetrated his own heart early on that unforgettable post-resurrection morning by the lake:

> *"Simon, son of John, do you love me more than these?" He said to him, "Yes, Lord; you know that I love you." (John 21:15)*

There is no more important question for any person to face than this: Do you *love* him?

It is an awkward question because it is so direct and personal.

Do you love him?

But it is a question that takes us to the very heart of the matter. It highlights the fact that Christianity cannot be reduced to formalities and externals, to words and actions alone, but has at its center the person of Jesus Christ.

Do you love him?

It is also a question that can be misunderstood. Few words have been more devalued in our time than the word *love*. Hollywood and the romantic novel have taught us that love is an overpowering emotion that we "fall into" and maybe "fall out of." The whole image of falling is associated with love in such a way that the question, do you love him? can be misunderstood to be merely a question about what feelings have overcome us.

But love is more than feelings and falling. Love is more than romance. We love in a wide range of contexts, and love means different things in different contexts. My love for my wife is not the same as my love for books. My love for my friends is different again and is not the same as my love for Mozart. There are different loves, appropriate to different objects. Some languages (like Greek) have a number of words for different kinds of love. Other languages (like English and Biblical Hebrew) seem to get by with the generally subconscious recognition that the word shifts in meaning depending very largely on its object.[1] "I love Australia" and "I love my grandson" mean different things.

Then what do we mean when we ask, do you love the Lord Jesus Christ? Jesus said:

> *"Whoever loves father or mother more than me is not worthy of me,*
> *and whoever loves son or daughter more than me is not worthy of me."*
> *(Matthew 10:37)*

So it is an important question. But how do we love him? What is that love like?

By now it may come as no surprise that love for Christ, like so much about Jesus, should be understood in the light of the story of Jesus Christ's great ancestor, David. It is interesting, and I believe it will be illuminating, to discover that David, who was then the Lord's anointed one (or "Christ"), was the object of love — much love, as we will see.

In 1 Samuel 18 Jonathan (vv. 1, 3), all Israel and Judah (v. 16), Saul's daughter Michal (vv. 20, 28), and Saul's servants (v. 22) are all said to have "loved" David. Earlier we were told that Saul "loved" David greatly (1 Samuel 16:21).[2]

Why did people love David? What did it mean to love David? Does this in any way help us understand what it means to love the Lord Jesus Christ?

The context of 1 Samuel 18 is very important. The youth from Bethlehem had killed Goliath. He had done what Israel's king was supposed to do, namely, fight Israel's enemies (see 1 Samuel 8:20; 9:16). David had not only fought, when no one else (including Saul) was prepared to fight — he had won!

To appreciate what happened next, we must be aware of the enormous impact that the defeat of Goliath would have had. Remember that the Philistines were the single greatest threat to Israel's existence, and a very real threat at that. For some forty days the Israelite troops had been quaking in terror at the abuse bellowed by the Philistine "man of the between" (literal translation of "champion" in 1 Samuel 17:4). It was clear that the Israelites were about to either become Philistine slaves or be exterminated. David, the unknown boy from Bethlehem, had single-handedly eliminated the threat, and launched VVE Day (Victory in the Valley of Elah!). Prior to that day

David had been a nobody in Israel. He could no longer enjoy obscurity. What he had done in the sight of all was extraordinary. It fully deserved the long account it has received in 1 Samuel 17 to celebrate it. At the end of chapter 17 he inevitably came to the attention of the king.

Chapter 18 follows immediately on from that conversation between King Saul and young David.[3]

The first five verses of chapter 18 will take us forward in time and summarize the situation that would develop over the years following VVE Day as David's reputation continued to rise. From verse 6 onward we are then taken back again to the Day itself, and the book will then trace, in the following chapters, specific events that took place over the years following the defeat of Goliath.

DAVID'S RISE (vv. 1-5)

Let's look first at the summary sketch of developments after the Goliath affair:

> *As soon as he [David] had finished speaking to Saul, the soul of Jonathan was knit to the soul of David, and Jonathan loved him as his own soul. And Saul took him that day and would not let him return to his father's house. Then Jonathan made a covenant with David, because he loved him as his own soul. And Jonathan stripped himself of the robe that was on him and gave it to David, and his armor, and even his sword and his bow and his belt. And David went out and was successful wherever Saul sent him, so that Saul set him over the men of war. And this was good in the sight of all the people and also in the sight of Saul's servants. (vv. 1-5)*

Jonathan and David (vv. 1, 3, 4)

The first relationship to develop with David after the Goliath affair was with the crown prince, Saul's eldest son, Jonathan. This was a remarkable relationship that was to be very important in David's life. In our passage, Jonathan is the first of many to be said to have "loved" David.

The relationship between David and Jonathan has often, and not inappropriately, been seen as an example of a wonderful and powerful human friendship. It was that, but it was more than that. We must not forget who these two young men were. David was the Lord's chosen and anointed one to be king "for himself" (for God), and he had just done a king's work, defeating Israel's enemies. Jonathan, on the other hand, was the one who by ordinary reckoning would have been the inheritor of Saul's throne. There were special dimensions to this friendship!

Perhaps I should say a word in passing (which is more than it deserves!)

about the view sometimes expressed that the David-Jonathan relationship may have had a sexual aspect.[4] The absurdity of that suggestion should be clear in this chapter. As one writer put it: "in this chapter everyone — apart from Saul, that is — loves David (vv. 16, 20, 22)! This particular consideration tends to be overlooked when David and Jonathan's relationship is presented in a less worthy light."[5] To see sex between the lines of the David-Jonathan story depends on our modern perception.[6] The texts themselves give no hint of sexual behavior.[7]

More important than what was *not* going on between Jonathan and David, let us look carefully at what *did* happen. It was very important indeed.

KNIT

First we are told that while the strange conversation with Saul (at the end of 1 Samuel 17) did not lead to any clear or decisive development between those two, it was another matter altogether with the king's son: ". . . the soul of Jonathan was knit to the soul of David . . ." (1 Samuel 18:1b).

Everything that has happened leads us to expect David and Jonathan to be rivals. The last time we heard of Jonathan, he was the one doing his father's work of attacking (and defeating) the Philistines (see 1 Samuel 13:3; 14:1-46). Jonathan was the one who had gained recognition from the people as the nation's savior (see 1 Samuel 14:45). David had now usurped both of those privileges. Furthermore, David's defeat of the Philistines was far more impressive than Jonathan's (also not to be sneezed at) accomplishments. Shortly we will see that David had also eclipsed any popularity Jonathan had enjoyed.

However, instead of rivalry, which could have been personal and you might think could at least have been political, we hear that "the soul of Jonathan was knit to the soul of David."

There is no doubt at all that this was the beginning of a deep and lasting friendship. What is emphasized here, however, is the unexpected *unity* between the two young men — unity where there was every reason for rivalry.

The language is very strong. Almost the same expression was used in the description of Jacob's relationship with his son Benjamin: Jacob's soul was knit with his young son's soul (Genesis 44:30).[8] In other words, it is language suitable to a family relationship. We might say that David and Jonathan became not rivals but brothers!

Nonetheless, to be a brother of the crown prince had political implications. As far as Jonathan was concerned, David was not the enemy of the royal family. He was, for him, in some sense a part of the family! Was he, even now, thinking of David as his *older* brother (not in age, but in rank)?

In fact, the word translated "knit" in verse 1 often refers to the binding together of people for political purposes. In other contexts it can refer to a political conspiracy, and it will have that sense later in the Saul-David story (1 Samuel 22:8, 13).[9]

The soul of Jonathan knit to the soul of David will have ramifications, you can be sure of that!

LOVED

Then we are told, "and Jonathan loved [David] as his own soul" (1 Samuel 18:1c).

These words probably do not add a lot to our understanding of the relationship. Once again they doubtless indicate the deep affection these two friends had for one another. In the context we must be struck by the surprise. Jonathan, as we have seen, had every reason to *hate* David. We know, as Jonathan probably did not yet, that God had chosen David to be Israel's next king. David had appeared as Jonathan's opponent. At least that is how it must have seemed. But Jonathan did not hate David. He "*loved* him as his own soul." There was to be no conflict of interest between them. Jonathan joined his life *to* David's rather than setting himself *against* him.[10]

We must take in the political dimensions of the astonishing fact that Jonathan loved David as his own soul. Whereas we tend to see only the emotional dimensions of the word *love*, the Bible (and the ancient Near Eastern world more generally) used the term in political contexts.[11] The political dimensions of Jonathan's relationship to David may not yet be clear, but that this relationship will have implications for nothing less than the kingship in Israel is obvious. In that context of potential power plays and struggles for supremacy, Jonathan *loved* David!

COVENANT

The third element in the description of this extremely important relationship in Israel is seen in verse 3: "Then Jonathan made a covenant with David, because he loved him as his own soul."

More details about this covenant[12] will become clear in later chapters (see 1 Samuel 20:8, 16; 22:8). A covenant is a binding agreement. What we should notice here is that the initiative for the covenant came from Jonathan.[13] At this stage Jonathan was the person of position and power. He was the crown prince. What kind of "covenant" would the prince make with the young Bethlehemite hero? All we are told here is that it was a covenant that expressed his love for David.

Robe

Any uncertainties we might have about the political dimensions to all this are dispelled by what happened next. This may well have been part of the covenant that was made between the two since it was common to have some symbolic action associated with the making of a covenant. "And Jonathan stripped himself of the robe that was on him and gave it to David, and his armor, and even his sword and his bow and his belt" (v. 4).

This is truly astonishing. It is the climactic moment in this scene. Jonathan's robe was his royal robe.[14] The Bible writer does not take us inside Jonathan's head. We do not know what he was thinking. We do know the significance that the act obviously has to any thoughtful observer. Jonathan was symbolically transferring his own royal rights and prerogatives (chief of which was his legitimate claim to the throne in Israel) to David. His passing over of his royal weapons and armor would have a similar significance.

This was nothing less than an act of abdication. It may not have been official, and it may not have been publicly known, but the covenant (v. 3), we may now reasonably suppose, had something to do with David and Jonathan's respective prospects for power in Israel. David would take precedence, and Jonathan would rejoice!

There is Jonathan's love for David.

Saul and David (vv. 2, 5a)

The other relationship of immense interest, of course, is that between Saul and David. Interspersed between the references to Jonathan and David in 1 Samuel 18:1 and 3, 4, and making a striking contrast with them, we have references to Saul and David in verses 2, 5.

Here there is much more ambiguity. The conversation immediately after the Goliath-felling had revealed that, surprisingly, David was a stranger to Saul. "Whose son are you, young man?" Saul had asked (1 Samuel 17:58). Once he learned the answer to that question, we are told that he did two things.

Kept

First, alongside the report that "the soul of Jonathan was knit to the soul of David, and Jonathan loved him as his own soul" we hear: "And Saul took [David] that day and would not let him return to his father's house" (v. 2).

Saul's taking and keeping David are not explained. If, as I have argued earlier, it was about now that the episode in 1 Samuel 16:14-23 occurred, then the explanation may lie there.[15] Be that as it may, Saul was acting in his usual way: "When Saul saw any strong man, or any valiant man, he attached him to himself" (1 Samuel 14:52b).

David was certainly such a man, and so Saul's action was not at all out of the ordinary. We note that Saul was also acting as Samuel had said a king would act in 1 Samuel 8:11. At this point the boy from Bethlehem had changed nothing as far as Saul was concerned.

How unlike Jonathan!

PROMOTED

Then, in contrast to Jonathan's dramatic symbolic abdication in verses 3, 4, we hear: "And David went out and was successful wherever Saul sent him, so that Saul set him over the men of war" (v. 5a).

Saul had a useful soldier on his hands, and he did with him what any king would do with a good soldier. He promoted him and made him as useful as possible. Again, unlike Jonathan, nothing had changed for Saul with the arrival of the Bethlehem hero.

David was successful wherever Saul sent him, as reported here, for many years to come, and those many years are summed up in verse 5.[16]

David and the People (v. 5b)

The third important relationship that developed after Goliath was defeated is that between David and the people: "And this was good in the sight of all the people and also in the sight of Saul's servants" (v. 5b).

GOOD!

Again this is a description of a situation that would prevail for many years to come. We should no doubt remember the words of Samuel to Saul that lie behind the dramatic developments of these days: "The LORD has torn the kingdom of Israel from you this day and has given it to a neighbor of yours, who is *better than you*" (1 Samuel 15:28).

As the successes of David were seen as "good" by the people, and even by Saul's servants, were they seeing that he was "better" than their king?

SAUL'S JEALOUSY (vv. 6-16)

But, of course, the most important relationship as far as David's future was concerned (humanly speaking) was the one that has been least explored in the outline of verses 1-5. It is time to go back to the day Goliath was killed and to see what happened in more detail in order to understand how things developed between Saul and David.

Popularity — Jealousy — Anger (vv. 6-11)

The day David returned from the fight in the Valley of Elah, word spread quickly, and there was excitement throughout the land. But it was an excitement that would have terrible effects on one man.

POPULARITY (VV. 6, 7)

Take a look at the excitement of the day:

> *As they were coming home, when David returned from striking down the Philistine, the women came out of all the cities of Israel, singing and dancing, to meet King Saul, with tambourines, with songs of joy, and with musical instruments. And the women sang to one another as they celebrated,*
> *"Saul has struck down his thousands,*
> *and David his ten thousands." (vv. 6, 7)*

There was another day, some time earlier, when a young man was greeted "with harp, tambourine, flute, and lyre" (1 Samuel 10:5). That was Saul, at Gibeah, when this king business had begun. But that had just been a group of prophets. This was something else! In Gibeah they had come up with a proverb: "Is Saul also among the prophets?" (1 Samuel 10:12). Now they were singing this rather more excited song:

> *"Saul has struck down his thousands,*
> *and David his ten thousands."*

If you understand the conventions of Hebrew poetry, and if you are not paranoid, you can appreciate that there may have been nothing deliberately sinister in the women's song. They were linking Saul and David together in this victory. The convention of putting a number in the first line and beefing it up in the second line was normal Hebrew poetic style.[17] It was as if they were to say, more prosaically, "Saul and David have struck down their thousands and tens of thousands." And they did mention Saul first!

JEALOUSY (VV. 8, 9)

Subtlety of interpretation was not, however, Saul's experience that day.[18] After all, on an earlier occasion when Jonathan had won a victory over the Philistines, all Israel had heard that *Saul* had done it (1 Samuel 13:4)! Does a king have to share his glory with another?

And Saul was very angry, and this saying displeased him. He said, "They have ascribed to David ten thousands, and to me they have ascribed thousands, and what more can he have but the kingdom?" (v. 8)

We have often noticed characters in this story saying more than they knew, but this one takes the cake! We cannot tell how much Saul understood clearly at this stage, but we can assume that the announcements of Samuel at Gilgal would not have been forgotten (1 Samuel 13:13, 14; 15:22, 23, 26, 28). Were his words a rhetorical flourish of anger, or had he begun to see why this boy had come to prominence in Israel?[19]

The contrast to Jonathan could not be greater. The jealousy we reasonably expected from Jonathan but did not see emerged with a vengeance from his father. "And Saul eyed David from that day on" (v. 9) — with an eye terribly distorted by his jealousy, as we will see.

HOSTILITY (vv. 10, 11)

It began the very next day:

The next day a harmful spirit from God rushed upon Saul, and he raved within his house while David was playing the lyre, as he did day by day. Saul had his spear in his hand. And Saul hurled the spear, for he thought, "I will pin David to the wall." But David evaded him twice. (vv. 10, 11)

We learned about this "harmful" or "evil spirit" in 1 Samuel 16:14. A terrible irony is now introduced. Whereas it had been the Spirit of the Lord who had "rushed on" Saul previously (1 Samuel 10:10; 11:6) and who had "rushed on" David recently (1 Samuel 16:13), now that the Spirit had departed from Saul (1 Samuel 16:14), a parody of the proper experience was his. The spirit that now "rushed on" Saul was evil, or harmful. Furthermore the effect of this spirit was apparently similar in some ways to the effect of the earlier experience. The word translated "raved" in verse 10 is exactly the same word as was translated "prophesied" in 1 Samuel 10:10, but as the translators recognize, there was now nothing positive about Saul's behavior, and so here "prophesied" is not the right English word.

There is a stark contrast now between Saul and David. One, we know, had the Spirit of the Lord; the other had this evil spirit. One had "in his hand"[20] his lyre, with which he could "refresh" Saul (1 Samuel 16:23); the other had "in his hand" his spear, with which he intended to do to David what David had done to Goliath![21]

Whatever initial "love" Saul had for David (1 Samuel 16:21) was all gone now. In Saul we see the opposite of the love for David we have seen in Jonathan.

Success — Fear — Love (vv. 12-16)

Our passage concludes:

> Saul was afraid of David because the LORD was with him but had departed
> from Saul. So Saul removed him from his presence and made him a com-
> mander of a thousand. And he went out and came in before the people.
> And David had success in all his undertakings, for the LORD was with him.
> And when Saul saw that he had great success, he stood in fearful awe of
> him. But all Israel and Judah loved David, for he went out and came in
> before them. (vv. 12-16)

This paragraph weaves a subtle texture of contrasting relationships. In the original the word "face" appears four times. Saul feared David's "face" in verse 12 and stood in awe of his "face" in verse 15. David went out and came in before the "face" of the people in verses 13, 16. It is a paragraph about how various people "faced" each other or, we might say, "faced off."

The key relationship is mentioned twice: "the LORD was with [David]" (vv. 12, 14).

The Lord was with David but had departed from Saul (v. 12). That, of course, is what we learned in verses 13, 14 of chapter 16. This represents God's rejection of Saul and his choice of David as his king. That is why, we are told, Saul was afraid of David's "face" (v. 12, literal translation).

The Lord was with David, and so David had success in all his undertakings (v. 14). Saul saw his great success, and it only intensified his fearful awe (v. 15). Saul was aware that David's success signaled something far more disturbing for him than that he had a gifted soldier.

Saul now sought to have David depart from him, just as the Lord had departed from him (vv. 12, 13).[22] He made him a commander of a thousand, which may have been a demotion from being "over the men of war" in verse 5.[23]

But David went out and came in before the "face" of the people (vv. 13, 16). This may refer to leading his troops in battle[24] or to life in the general community.[25] Either way, all the people — not just his own tribe, Judah, but all Israel — "loved" him (v. 16). His great success (we presume of a military kind), which put fear in the heart of Saul, aroused love from the people.

While there is no doubt that David was the object of the people's affection, their love for him was more than that. It was their response to *him* — the one whom the Lord was with, who was doing for them what their king had failed to do. Their love was "the kind of attachment people had to a king who would fight their battles for them."[26]

It is important to see that this kind of love is required of God's people for God himself. In the book of Deuteronomy the people are commanded to love God (Deuteronomy 6:5). This love is intimately related to a proper "fear" of the Lord and obedience to his commandments (Deuteronomy 10:12).[27]

The love of Jonathan and the love of the people for David, the Lord's anointed one, help us see more clearly the depth of the question, do you love the Lord *Jesus* Christ?

Do you love him?

He said, "If you love me, you will keep my commandments" (John 14:15).

He is, you see, the King. To love him is the kind of attachment that people have to a king who fights their battles for them. Do you love him?

"Whoever has my commandments and keeps them, he it is who loves me. And he who loves me will be loved by my Father, and I will love him and manifest myself to him." (John 14:21)

"If anyone loves me, he will keep my word, and my Father will love him, and we will come to him and make our home with him. Whoever does not love me does not keep my words. And the word that you hear is not mine but the Father's who sent me." (John 14:23, 24)

Do you love him?

31

Love Him or Fear Him

1 SAMUEL 18:17-30

It is not possible to adopt a neutral stance toward the Lord Jesus Christ. This would be the preferred option for many. It looks like the easy option: "No, I am not a believer, but neither would I describe myself as an unbeliever. I am not against Christianity, but neither am I enthusiastically for it. I am not convinced it is true, but neither could I say that I know that it is untrue. I'm neutral."

This is simply not possible. Jesus put it simply: "Whoever is not with me is against me" (Matthew 12:30a).

He also said, "For the one who is not against us is for us" (Mark 9:40).

It is not that it is undesirable or irresponsible or just plain lazy to refuse to make up your mind about the Lord Jesus Christ. It is *impossible*.

This has to do with who he is.

Our studies of the book of 1 Samuel should help us see that when we call Jesus "Jesus *Christ*," we are not just giving his name — we are saying something very important about him. He is the Christ, the Messiah, the anointed King in God's scheme of things. The significance of the title "the Christ" goes back to the days when God chose a king to reign over his Old Testament people, Israel. Just as the Old Testament experience of Israel, under God's great purposes, provided the meaning for such concepts as redemption, inheritance, covenant, blessing, law, holiness, and word of God, so when the New Testament speaks of "the Christ," the meaning of the words must be seen in the light of the Old Testament experience that gives them their meaning.

Therefore as we learn more about God's anointed king, David, we have been learning what it means to call Jesus "the Christ." David was the Lord's christ or messiah (anointed one). In due course we will see that

David failed to fulfill the role given to him, so that Jesus would be what David failed to be. Nonetheless in the story told in 1 Samuel we are following the Old Testament foundations of "the Christ," the title that now belongs to Jesus.

This means that we can confidently expect the story of David, and of Saul, to help us understand such questions as, why is it not possible to adopt a neutral stance toward the Lord Jesus Christ?

In 1 Samuel 18:1-16 we saw that as David became a public figure, many "loved" him. While that meant the affection of Jonathan's friendship and the adoration of the people, it was more than an emotion. It was the recognition and glad acceptance of David's role as the leader who saved Israel from her enemies. Jonathan loved him and therefore stripped off his own royal robe and placed it on David. The people loved him and therefore Saul feared for his kingdom.

It is this fear of Saul and its terrible expressions that will occupy much of the story from this point on, until Saul's death at the end of 1 Samuel. In that fear we see the impossibility of neutrality toward the Lord's Christ.

Look back at the development of Saul's attitude toward David after David came to his attention so effectively on that famous day in the Valley of Elah. In 1 Samuel 18:2 we saw that Saul "took" David into his service and did not allow him to return to Bethlehem. So far so good. That is what Saul did with able young men. In 1 Samuel 18:5 he appointed him "over the men of war," which again sounds like a sensible deployment of this remarkable young man. But then we are taken a little deeper into Saul's mind. In 1 Samuel 18:8 he expressed his angry jealousy of this young man who was receiving at least as much glory as he was for the defeat of the Philistines: "They have ascribed to David ten thousands, and to me they have ascribed thousands, and what more can he have but the kingdom?"

Then rather ominously we read: "And Saul eyed David from that day on" (v. 9).

The very next day Saul's troubled spirit, described as an evil or harmful spirit from God, overcame him (v. 10). He took hold of his spear and twice tried to pin David to the wall with it (v. 11).

We might say the relationship was deteriorating.

Then we learned of Saul's fear of David (v. 12), which led him to put him out from his presence and probably demote him (v. 13). But Saul remained in fearful awe of David (v. 15).

At this point we take up the story.

THE PLOT THAT FAILED (vv. 17-19)

One thing of which Saul could not be accused at this time was consistency. Having removed David from his presence in verse 13 because of his fear of him, the next thing we find is Saul speaking to David with a rather surprising offer considering the circumstances. We might be excused for suspecting that a plot of some kind was afoot.

The Plot (v. 17)

> Then Saul said to David, "Here is my elder daughter Merab. I will give her to you for a wife." (v. 17a)

If we are to believe the rumor that had circulated earlier in the Valley of Elah, this was one of three rewards that the king had promised to anyone who killed Goliath (1 Samuel 17:25). However, that is mere coincidence.[1] Saul was not offering his daughter as reward or recognition for David's great victory. His daughter had a price: "Only be valiant for me and fight the LORD's battles" (v. 17b).

This was not an unreasonable requirement, if we overlook the earlier offer of a reward. To marry the king's daughter a man could be asked to prove himself a brave and loyal subject.

However, there was more going on here than immediately meets the eye. It is possible that, in the peculiar way in which Biblical narrative can unfold, this is an elaboration of the brief statement in verse 13 that Saul removed David from his presence, making him "a commander of a thousand." The hand of his elder daughter may have been offered as an incentive for David to take on dangerous military responsibilities as "commander of a thousand." What is made clear to us is that Saul's intentions were entirely malevolent: "For Saul thought, 'Let not my hand be against him, but let the hand of the Philistines be against him'" (v. 17c).

The popularity of David with the people would have made it dangerous for Saul to pit himself directly and publicly against David. Although such qualms did not last, for the moment Saul was content to allow the Philistines to do his dirty work.

Saul's plan had as its object the elimination of David. The means to that end was David's (temporary) inclusion in the royal family. Saul did not seem to contemplate the possibility that the Philistines might not achieve his purpose. Then he would have his feared rival much closer than he wanted.

Saul's fear of David had twisted him. He was now hoping for a Philistine victory.

The Plot's Failure (vv. 18, 19)

It did not work. For reasons that may become clear a little later in our story, David was reluctant to accept the offer: "And David said to Saul, 'Who am

I, and who are my relatives, my father's clan in Israel, that I should be son-in-law to the king?'" (v. 18).

We presume that the irony of David's words was not intentional on his part, but as we hear them they sound strange. We have heard words just like them before:

> *"Am I not a Benjaminite, from the least of the tribes of Israel? And is not my clan the humblest of all the clans of the tribe of Benjamin?"*
> *(1 Samuel 9:21)*

That was Saul, protesting at the strange things he was hearing about himself from Samuel before he became a king. There was no irony then. But as David spoke similarly self-effacing words (no doubt, genuinely humble words), this was the Lord's chosen king addressing the rejected king.

It is possible, but not stated, that David's objection in verse 18 was a rejection of Saul's offer.[2] Or it may be that Saul reneged on the offer.[3] Whatever the reason, the plot came to nothing, and the marriage did not happen: "But at the time when Merab, Saul's daughter, should have been given to David, she was given to Adriel the Meholathite for a wife" (v. 19).

For the time being David remained in circulation, and Saul's fears had no relief. Saul's plot had failed.

THE PLOT THAT SUCCEEDED (vv. 20-27)

An unspecified time passed. The opportunity to reintroduce the plot arose, and Saul grasped it keenly.

The Plot (vv. 20-25)

The occasion for the renewed scheme was introduced by another of Saul's daughters: "Now Saul's daughter Michal loved David" (v. 20a).

First Samuel 18 indicates that Michal was not alone! *Everyone* loved David (see particularly v. 16)! That was Saul's problem.

Of course, Michal's love was the love of a woman for a man. But here, as we saw with Jonathan's love and with the people's love, there were other dimensions as well. It was the love of a princess for a national hero. More than that, we cannot help seeing Michal's love as consistent with the positive responses throughout 1 Samuel 18 to the one we now know was the Lord's anointed one.

The matter was reported to Saul. We might have expected him to explode with anger, but not so: "And they told Saul, and the thing pleased him" (v. 20b).

Literally, "the thing was right in his eyes." It was okay with him. No objections. If you are wondering why, read on: "Saul thought, 'Let me give her to him, that she may be a snare for him and that the hand of the Philistines may be against him'" (v. 21a).

It sounds like a rerun of the last scheme. Saul looks like a man singularly lacking in imagination. Do not be fooled. He had a trick up his sleeve. It started just like last time: "Therefore Saul said to David a second time, 'You shall now be my son-in-law'" (v. 21b).

This sounds rather audacious if it was Saul who reneged on the last deal. However, on the one hand we might remember Jacob and Laban (Genesis 29), and on the other hand the earlier refusal may have been David's.

In either case, the offer was made a second time. This time Saul arranged for some gentle persuasion to accompany the offer:[4]

> And Saul commanded his servants, "Speak to David in private and say, 'Behold, the king has delight in you, and all his servants love you. Now then become the king's son-in-law.'" (v. 22)

The addition of this level of persuasion may suggest that it was David who refused the earlier proposal.[5]

When the servants brought their message to David, he responded in a similar vein to the last time, but with something made explicit that may have been implied before:

> And Saul's servants spoke those words in the ears of David. And David said, "Does it seem to you a little thing to become the king's son-in-law, since I am a poor man and have no reputation?" (v. 23)

Was this the real reason for David's earlier refusal, or reluctance, to become Saul's son-in-law? He was a poor shepherd boy. How could he ever put together the bride-price for a king's daughter?[6] Of course, if Saul did make the promise of 1 Samuel 17:25, then David's poverty was testimony to Saul's failure to keep his word![7]

All this was reported back to Saul: "And the servants of Saul told him, 'Thus and so did David speak'" (v. 24).

Just what Saul was hoping to hear! He had apparently learned from the earlier exchange that the boy from Bethlehem would refuse his offer, and he appears to have understood why. Now he could set his trap:

> Then Saul said, "Thus shall you say to David, 'The king desires no bride-price except a hundred foreskins of the Philistines, that he may be avenged of the king's enemies.'" (v. 25a)

Assuming that the lovely Michal was too good for David to resist, Saul set the bait. "No need to worry about a bride-price, lad. One hundred Philistine foreskins is all the king asks." David had expressed his derision for Goliath by calling him twice "this uncircumcised Philistine" (1 Samuel 17:26, 36).[8] There is a certain nasty humor in Saul's suggestion that David might do something about that problem!

His intention was clear. *One lucky pebble from a sling against one big Philistine was one thing. Let's see how the boy goes against a hundred Philistines.*[9] *And if he beats them, let's see that he is so hated that they will get him in the end.* Just in case we are slow on the uptake, the narrator spells it out for us:

> *Now Saul thought to make David fall by the hand of the Philistines.* (v. 25b)

So there's the plot. More elaborate this time. Less likely to come unstuck, one might think.

David's Success (vv. 26, 27)

> *And when his servants told David these words, it pleased David well to be the king's son-in-law. (v. 26a)*

There is a subtle, almost tongue-in-cheek echo here. When Saul heard that Michal loved David, we heard, literally, "the thing was right in his eyes." Now David hears what we know to be Saul's plot, and the narrator tells us, literally, "the thing was right in David's eyes." This was okay with him! No objections from David!

David was not stupid. If Saul could hatch a plot, so could David. If Saul thought a hundred Philistines was a trap for David, he had another think coming. "Before the time had expired, David arose and went, along with his men, and killed two hundred of the Philistines" (vv. 26b, 27a).

Not 100, but *200!* "And David brought their foreskins, which were given in full number to the king, that he might become the king's son-in-law" (v. 27b).

I am sure that at this point we are meant to imagine Saul's face! I am not sure how the grisly trophy was presented to His Majesty, but there was no way he could back down on his offer. Whatever his reluctance or grumbling, his plot had backfired: "And Saul gave him his daughter Michal for a wife" (v. 27c).

Not only was David still alive and kicking, his reputation had gone up several notches, and he was about to be joined to the royal family.

At the beginning of this chapter Jonathan had, in effect, made David his (older?) brother (1 Samuel 18:1-4). This now happened officially, publicly, and legally thanks to Saul's miscalculation.

Saul's second plot had resulted in a success, but it was not his. It was David's.

DAVID'S SUCCESS, SAUL'S FEAR (vv. 28-30)

This success of David's was to have dire consequences, not for David, as Saul intended, but for Saul:

> But when Saul saw and knew that the LORD was with David, and that Michal, Saul's daughter, loved him, Saul was even more afraid of David. (vv. 28, 29a)

Here is the phrase we have seen several times already, the phrase that tells us what made David so utterly different from Saul: "the LORD was with David." Now we are told explicitly for the first time that Saul *knew* it. Previously we were told that Saul feared David "*because* the LORD was with him" (1 Samuel 18:12), but did Saul *know* that was the reason for his fear? We were told that Saul "saw" David's great success (1 Samuel 18:15), which was because "the LORD was with him" (1 Samuel 18:14), but did Saul *know* that was the reason for David's success? He did now.

Furthermore the love of Michal for David, which had been okay when it provided a pretext for Saul's plot (in v. 20), had now become the means by which the threatening presence of David would come closer to the paranoid king. What was now dawning on Saul made him "even more afraid of David."

The portentous conclusion to our present narrative is: "So Saul was David's enemy continually" (v. 29b).

The Hebrew word translated "enemy" is the participle of a verb that means "to be hostile to," "to hate." Saul had adopted the very opposite stance toward David from those who "loved" him — Jonathan, Michal, and the people.

There is a footnote to the story that tells us what the future was to hold:

> Then the princes of the Philistines came out to battle, and as often as they came out David had more success than all the servants of Saul, so that his name was highly esteemed. (v. 30)

Like the man of Psalm 1, "In all that he does, he prospers" (Psalm 1:3).

It was not possible for Saul to adopt a neutral stance toward David. We can perhaps now see that it was not possible for anyone in Israel to be neutral toward this remarkable man. If you were not with him, you were against him. If you were not against him, you were for him.

It had to do with who he was. The Lord was with him. If you did not throw in your lot with him, as Jonathan so gladly did, sooner or later you would fear him and hate him, as Saul so tragically did.

When we understand that Jesus is the Christ, is it any more possible to be neutral? As David's name was greatly honored, as he went from triumph to triumph, so it is with Jesus:

> *Therefore God has highly exalted him and bestowed on him the name that is above every name, so that at the name of Jesus every knee should bow, in heaven and on earth and under the earth, and every tongue confess that Jesus Christ is Lord, to the glory of God the Father. (Philippians 2:9-11)*

But it will not be possible to be neutral!

32

"... Against the Lord and Against His Anointed"

1 SAMUEL 19:1-10

We have all experienced (many times over!) the conflict of opposing wills. It is part of human life and human relationships to find the will of one to be against the will of another. A two-year-old child discovers the satisfaction of asserting his own will, only to find himself up against the will of a parent. The opposing wills of the leaders of nations can lead to war. Between these small and great conflicts of will we observe and experience innumerable other instances of the same phenomenon.

The Bible speaks of a conflict of wills that is of another order. On the one hand there is the will of God, the creator of and sovereign ruler over all things. His will is entirely good. On the other hand there are the wills of human beings, which are consistently set *against* the will of God.

The Bible shows us that this conflict is the reason that human wills are so often and typically in conflict with one another. If our wills were all in harmony with God's good will, we would be in harmony with each other. It is because we all seek to assert our own wills that we inevitably clash with one another. That is what causes quarrels, fights, and wars among us (see James 4:1-10).

This is not just a matter of morality. It is not simply that God wants humans to behave in certain ways, but humans want to be free from moral constraints. That is true, but it is a small part of the truth.

The gospel of Jesus Christ is the announcement to the whole world that the will and purpose of God is that all things should come under the rule of his anointed (or his Christ), his Son, Jesus, to whom all authority has been given (see, for example, Matthew 28:18; John 5:27; 17:2; Acts 2:36; Romans 14:9; 1 Corinthians 15:27, 28; Ephesians 1:10, 22; Philippians 2:9, 10; Colossians 2:10; Hebrews 1:2).

Every human will that is not aligned with Jesus being Lord of all is in conflict with the will of God.

In the day-to-day business of life it may not be obvious to us that our wills are set against the will of God. We want so many "good" things. Perhaps we act with moral probity much of the time. However, the will of God is not just that we should want and do good things. It is that Jesus Christ should be our Lord and the Lord of all people everywhere.

Wherever the gospel of Christ is proclaimed in the world, the resistance and opposition of human wills to God's will are encountered. Psalm 2 describes the situation (also see Acts 4:23-31):

> *Why do the nations rage*
> *and the peoples plot in vain?*
> *The kings of the earth set themselves,*
> *and the rulers take counsel together,*
> *against the Lord and against his Anointed. . . . (Psalm 2:1, 2)*

The marvelous wonder is that as the gospel is proclaimed by the power of God's Spirit, human wills can be turned to comply with the will of God — that is, to submit to the lordship of Jesus Christ. The gospel is God's call for us to change sides in this conflict of wills. Again Psalm 2 expresses this call:

> *Now therefore, O kings, be wise;*
> *be warned, O rulers of the earth.*
> *Serve the Lord with fear,*
> *and rejoice with trembling.*
> *Kiss the Son,*
> *lest he be angry, and you perish in the way,*
> *for his wrath is quickly kindled.*
> *Blessed are all who take refuge in him. (vv. 10-12)*

The clash between the will of God and human wills has a long history. It is spoken of in Psalm 2, composed centuries before the coming of Jesus into this world. In the background behind Psalm 2 are the events we have been following in the book of 1 Samuel, when God chose David to be his anointed king over his people Israel.

The story of David's kingdom being established long ago has many important parallels to the establishment of the kingdom of Jesus over all things. There are very significant differences, of course, but God's will at that time for his anointed, David, to reign over Israel and God's will now for all things to be brought under his anointed, Jesus, are expressions of his one good purpose for the world he has made. There is a profound unity, located in the will of God, binding the story of David to the story of Jesus. These stories stand at the beginning and end of the story of "the LORD and . . . his anointed."

We have reached the point in the story where David had been anointed in Bethlehem to be God's king. The Spirit of the Lord had come upon him for this future task (1 Samuel 16:13). Though still a youth, he had come to public attention by the remarkable feat of killing the great Philistine Goliath (1 Samuel 17). As a consequence he had come into King Saul's service (1 Samuel 18:2, 5; cf. 16:21). At first Saul, like many others, was positively disposed toward David (1 Samuel 16:21), but David's remarkable success against Israel's enemies aroused a terrible jealous fear in Saul (1 Samuel 18:8, 9, 12, 15). This fear became hatred, and Saul made a number of unsuccessful attempts to rid himself of the lad from Bethlehem (1 Samuel 18:11, 17, 21, 25, 29).

The tension through the rest of the book of 1 Samuel arises from the fact that the king who had been rejected by God (Saul) was still in power, while the king who had been chosen by God (David) was yet to begin his reign. The story of Saul now becomes a study of a will set "against the LORD and against his Anointed."

In 1 Samuel 19 the conflict intensifies. It is not clear how much Saul consciously understood that by setting himself against David he was opposing God.[1] Certainly he knew of his own decisive rejection by God because of his disobedience (1 Samuel 13:13, 14; 15:23b, 26, 28, 29). However, that David was to be the new king had not been told him explicitly. He had not witnessed the secret anointing by Samuel in Bethlehem (1 Samuel 16:13). He may not have understood that his own rejection involved the rejection of his potential dynasty (1 Samuel 13:13, 14). He may, therefore, have held some hope that his son Jonathan would be the one to take his place (see 1 Samuel 20:31). However, he must have had his doubts. He had seen David's remarkable, presumably divinely enabled victory over Goliath. He witnessed the continued successes of his now finest warrior. He had heard from others and had concluded from his own observations that "the LORD was with him" (see 1 Samuel 16:18; 18:12, 14, 28, cf. 17:37). "What more can he have but the kingdom?" (1 Samuel 18:8b). But we have not yet been told that Saul *knew* that David was the one of whom Samuel had spoken — the "man after [God's] own heart" (1 Samuel 13:14), "a neighbor of yours, who is better than you" (1 Samuel 15:28).

Those who reject and oppose the lordship of Jesus over their own lives and the advance of his kingdom over the lives of others by the proclamation of the gospel do not necessarily consciously understand that they have set themselves "against the Lord and against his Anointed." But that is what they are doing, as surely as it was what Saul was doing.

First Samuel 19 explores the conflict between the will of Saul (to be rid of David) and the will of God, known to us because we have read the previous chapters (to make David king). We find here four episodes, which turn out to be four short but brilliant escape stories. What can we learn here about human wills that are set "against the Lord and against his Anointed"?

Let us follow the first two escape stories.

DAVID SAVED BY SAUL'S SON (vv. 1-7)

The first episode brings Saul's son Jonathan back into the story. Last time we saw Jonathan, we had reason to believe that he knew something. His response to David was astonishing. He privately committed himself to David in a rare bond of friendship and loyalty (1 Samuel 18:1-4).

Open Hostility (v. 1a)

That bond was about to be tested. Saul's hostility to David broke free from any attempt at secrecy: "And Saul spoke to Jonathan his son and to all his servants, that they should kill David" (v. 1a).

Saul spoke to Jonathan because he was "his son." As yet Saul knew nothing of Jonathan's bewildering commitment to David. Saul was seeing David as a threat to his throne. "What more can he have but the kingdom?" he had muttered (1 Samuel 18:8b).

Further, we have seen:

> Saul was afraid of David because the LORD was with him but had departed from Saul. . . . And when Saul saw that he had great success, he stood in fearful awe of him. (1 Samuel 18:12, 15)

The last words of chapter 18 pointed clearly to Saul's problem:

> Then the princes of the Philistines came out to battle, and as often as they came out David had more success than all the servants of Saul, so that his name was highly esteemed. (v. 30)

Saul's previous attempts to be rid of David had either been private (1 Samuel 18:10, 11) or surreptitious (1 Samuel 18:9, 17, 21, 25). Now, however, his desperation drove him to enlist the involvement of his son (whose position was as much threatened by the boy from Bethlehem as was Saul's) and his servants (whose position was also dependent on Saul). He enlisted them all in his desire to kill David.

Jonathan's Intervention (vv. 1b-5)

However, it was not his position as son of the king that would determine Jonathan's conduct. He had embraced a higher loyalty.

Delight (v. 1b)

But Jonathan, Saul's son, delighted much in David. (v. 1b)

There is a gentle irony here. King Saul had earlier sent his servants to David with the message, "Behold, the king has *delight* in you" (1 Samuel 18:22). That was a lie. But Jonathan, "Saul's son" (notice how that point has been made twice in verse 1), "*delighted* much in David." That was the truth. He loved him as his own soul, he had made a covenant with him, and he had handed over his royal garments, armor, and weapons to the youth from Bethlehem (1 Samuel 18:1-4). It was this relationship that took precedence over Jonathan's being "Saul's son."[2]

Warning (vv. 2, 3)

Jonathan therefore went from his father to David. He set himself against his father's plans by warning David:

And Jonathan told David, "Saul my father seeks to kill you. Therefore be on your guard in the morning. Stay in a secret place and hide yourself. And I will go out and stand beside my father in the field where you are, and I will speak to my father about you. And if I learn anything I will tell you." (vv. 2, 3)

Notice how Jonathan's relationship to Saul is in the foreground here. Just as we were told twice in verse 1 that Jonathan was Saul's "son," Jonathan himself now three times refers to Saul as "my father." That is the relationship that is obvious and known to all. Everyone would expect Jonathan to act in accord with his sonship to King Saul. However, that is the relationship that created Jonathan's problem. Jonathan's father intended to kill the one to whom Jonathan was committed.[3]

So Jonathan warned him. "In the morning" David must be on his guard and in hiding.

Jonathan then put himself forward as a go-between on David's behalf.[4] He would take his stand "beside my father."[5] This meeting was to take place in the vicinity of David's hiding-place. Perhaps this was to give David an opportunity to observe the meeting and draw his own conclusions. Jonathan would then provide his own report of whatever he had learned.[6]

ADVOCATE (VV. 4, 5)

True to his word, Jonathan met with his father and raised the difficult subject of David. It seems clear that Jonathan had thought about what he would say. His argument was rhetorically vigorous, logically persuasive, morally convincing, and theologically powerful.

> *And Jonathan spoke well of David to Saul his father and said to him, "Let not the king sin against his servant David, because he has not sinned against you, and because his deeds have brought good to you. For he took his life in his hand and he struck down the Philistine, and the LORD worked a great salvation for all Israel. You saw it, and rejoiced. Why then will you sin against innocent blood by killing David without cause?" (vv. 4, 5)*

For all the formal deference in Jonathan's speech (which reminds us that Saul was a powerful figure[7]), he spoke very boldly. He called what Saul was contemplating against David "sin." How that word must have stung! "Sin" is not a word to be used lightly, and, as so often in this narrative, the speaker spoke more appropriately than he knew. The harm that Saul intended for David would be like that terrible day at Gilgal when Saul had been forced to confess to Samuel, "I have *sinned*" (1 Samuel 15:24). The story told in 1 Samuel has drawn attention to particularly dark occasions of sin that had cast their shadow over Israel's recent history. There was the "sin" of Hophni and Phinehas (1 Samuel 2:17; cf. verse 25) that in some ways lay behind all of the present troubles. There was the related "sin" that the people of Israel confessed at Mizpah (1 Samuel 7:6). But the climactic sin in this period of Israel's history had been the "sin" of asking for a king (1 Samuel 12:10, 19). Saul was about to add to that terrible sequence of sin. Jonathan pleaded, "Let not the king *sin* . . ."

Jonathan described David as Saul's "servant" who had *not* "sinned" against Saul, but on the contrary had "brought good" to him. The goodness of David's deeds must have stung Saul too. On that dreadful day at Gilgal, had not Samuel said that the Lord had torn the kingdom from Saul and given it to a neighbor who was "*better* than you"? I am not sure Saul wanted to hear about the goodness of David's deeds![8]

David's outstanding "good" deed, of course, was his smiting Goliath. Jonathan spoke of that incident in theological terms: "the LORD worked a great salvation for all Israel." Saul had seen it with his own eyes and "rejoiced," according to Jonathan. Here he may have been engaging in a little hyperbole![9] There had certainly been songs of joy at David's victory, but whatever joy Saul had felt was short-lived (see 1 Samuel 18:6-8). There had been a time when it was Saul who could promise Israel "salvation"[10] and through whom the Lord had worked "salvation in Israel" (1 Samuel 11:13).[11]

More recently, however, it had been not Saul but Jonathan who had "worked this great salvation in Israel" (1 Samuel 14:45). What was Jonathan saying about David by describing him as the one through whom the Lord had now done this?

Finally, Jonathan pointedly described Saul's intended violence against David as "sin against innocent blood . . . killing David without cause." The language is loaded. Special provisions had been made in Israel to avoid the shedding of "innocent blood" (Deuteronomy 19:4-10; cf. 27:25; Jeremiah 22:3).[12] When "innocent blood" was shed, retributive action was required (Deuteronomy 19:11-13), or else atonement was needed (Deuteronomy 21:1-9).[13] That Saul had no justification whatsoever for the violence he intended is reiterated in the expression "without cause."[14]

It was quite a speech!

David Safe Again? (vv. 6, 7)

It met its mark. Saul listened and responded reasonably: "And Saul listened to the voice of Jonathan. Saul swore, 'As the LORD lives, he shall not be put to death'" (v. 6).

Saul was often responsive to good advice, though he was rather short on wisdom of his own.[15] The oath he swore would not last long. This is the second time that Saul had threatened the apparent king-to-be with death (see 1 Samuel 14:44). On the previous occasion the king-to-be was Jonathan, and the people had intervened to redeem him (1 Samuel 14:45). This time it was Jonathan who intervened to save David.[16]

The crisis seemed to have passed. "And Jonathan called David, and Jonathan reported to him all these things. And Jonathan brought David to Saul, and he was in his presence as before" (v. 7).

Jonathan was the hero of the moment. *Jonathan* "called," *Jonathan* "reported," *Jonathan* "brought."[17] The son of Saul had delivered David from the threat of Saul — for the moment.

The will of Saul that had been set "against the Lord and against his Anointed" had not prevailed. It had been turned around — for the moment — by the goodness, the reasonableness, the rightness, the wisdom of Jonathan's words commending David.

DAVID'S ESCAPE FROM SAUL'S SPEAR (vv. 8-10)

Jonathan does not appear in the remaining three escape stories of this chapter. We might notice the way in which Jonathan appeared at the beginning of chapter 18 to introduce the theme of love for David, which was developed without further reference to Jonathan in the rest of that chapter. He has appeared again at the beginning of chapter 19 to introduce the theme of David's escapes from the threats of Saul. This theme is then developed through the rest of this chapter without Jonathan. Jonathan's leading role in positive responses to David is striking.

David's Success (v. 8)

We do not know how many days, weeks, or months elapsed between verse 7 and verse 8. It is difficult to imagine that it was years. The circumstance that brought to an end the peace Jonathan had won between Saul and David was David's doing more "good" for Saul (see v. 4): "And there was war again. And David went out and fought with the Philistines and struck them with a great blow, so that they fled before him" (v. 8).

Of course there was war again. On and off there had been war since the Philistines first attacked in 1 Samuel 4. Of course it was the Philistines. They had been causing trouble since the Goliath tactic had failed. And of course David thrashed them. That is what he did! None of this is surprising (see 1 Samuel 18:30).

Saul's Rage (vv. 9, 10a)

Furthermore we are not really surprised that David's successes got under Saul's skin. That is how it had been for some time now, since the king had heard the women singing their Saul-and-David song (1 Samuel 18:6-9).

What happened next is no surprise either, because it had happened before:

> Then a harmful spirit from the LORD came upon Saul, as he sat in his house with his spear in his hand. And David was playing the lyre. And Saul sought to pin David to the wall with the spear. . . . (vv. 9, 10a)

This is the third time we have heard of a harmful (or evil) spirit from the Lord afflicting Saul (see 1 Samuel 16:14-23; 18:10, 11).[18]

In 1 Samuel 16:14 we learned that the evil spirit from the Lord tormented Saul as a consequence of the Spirit of the Lord departing from him. The evil spirit was an aspect of God's judgment and rejection of Saul for his disobedience.

Now we learn that the evil spirit that came on Saul led, for the second time, to a violent attempt on David's life. This is like the hardening of Pharaoh's heart in the book of Exodus (e.g. Exodus 4:21; 11:10).[19] It is perplexing there to read that the Lord hardened Pharaoh's heart, leading to his cruel violence against the people of Israel — until we realize that Pharaoh hardened his own heart. In other words, God's judgment came in the form of giving Pharaoh up to his own willful stubbornness. If Pharaoh would harden his heart, then God would harden Pharaoh's heart and achieve his purposes through that hard heart (Exodus 10:1, 2)!

The evil spirit that came on Saul was the consequence of his setting himself against the Lord and his anointed.[20] God gave him up to his choice, just as he has given up sinners to their ways, according to Romans 1:18-32.

The wickedness of Saul's action is clear. Recently, in 1 Samuel 19:6, we heard him swear an oath guaranteeing David's safety. The only thing that has happened since then is David's success against Saul's enemies![21]

Notice again the scene: Saul with his spear in his hand (a spear is what Saul usually had in his hand) and David with his lyre in his hand.[22] As the evil mood seized Saul, he attempted to thrust the spear through David.

David's Escape (v. 10b)

But again he failed: ". . . but he [David] eluded Saul, so that he [Saul] struck the spear into the wall. And David fled and escaped that night" (v. 10b).

David never returned to Saul's court. For the rest of Saul's life, David would be on the run from him.

It was a terrible turn of events, reflected in the vocabulary used to describe it. Saul "struck" his spear into the wall, and David "fled." In 1 Samuel 19:8 David "struck" the Philistines, and they "fled."[23] Saul was attempting to do to David what David had done to the Philistines (for Saul!).

However, he failed again, and in that failure we see the madness of his hostility to the Lord and his anointed.

As we reflect on these first two of the four escape stories in 1 Samuel 19:

First, consider the contrast between Saul and Jonathan. Saul wanted to kill David. Jonathan delighted in David. The contrast is sharpened by the fact that whatever danger David posed threatened Jonathan and Saul equally. Only Saul, however, chose to see David as a threat. Jonathan saw his goodness.

When Jesus came, he encountered the same two responses. There were those who wanted to kill him. They saw him, in one way or another, as a threat. There were those who loved him. They saw his goodness.

Do you see the Lord's Anointed, Jesus Christ, as a threat? Or do you see his goodness?

Second, consider the motivation that drove Saul's hostility. It was not rational. He could not deny the goodness of David (v. 4) when that was set before him. Nevertheless it was David's goodness (his victories over the Philistines) that stirred Saul's jealous fears.

Those who hated Jesus were motivated by similar jealous fear. He was better than them in every way, and he called them to a way that was better than their own.

Do you recognize in your own heart an unwillingness to welcome the goodness, the grace, of the Lord's Anointed?

Third, consider the motivation that sustained Jonathan's faithfulness. How do you think Jonathan reacted when David went out again and thrashed the Philistines, more decisively than Jonathan himself had done? Although the narrative leaves it unsaid, there is no doubt at all that Jonathan rejoiced.

Those who delight in the goodness and the grace of our Lord Jesus Christ are those who will serve him faithfully.

Fourth, consider the foolish wickedness of Saul. There is little more to say. Certainly there was no room for Saul to blame anyone but himself. We have seen that even the "harmful spirit from the Lord" confirmed Saul's own choices. See the goodness of David, see the providential protection he clearly enjoyed, and you see that to set oneself against the Lord and his Anointed is both evil and stupid. Do not do it.

33

". . . The Lord Holds Them in Derision"

1 SAMUEL 19:11-24

Whenever one will is in conflict with another, the decisive question is, which will will prevail? The will of the stronger does not always have its way. The tiny two-year-old gets his way more often than many parents may wish. Circumstances beyond the control of either party can determine the conclusion to many more substantial conflicts of will.

When it comes to the great conflict between the will of God and the wills of those who set themselves "against the LORD and against his Anointed" (Psalm 2:2), we encounter an absurd situation. People speak and act as though there is some chance that the one enthroned in Heaven might be forced to back down! Of course, it does not always look absurd from our limited perspective. When persecution breaks out violently against Christians, all of the power can seem to be in the hands of the persecutors.

We must, however, learn to see this situation from a heavenly perspective. What does violent opposition to the Lord and his Anointed look like from God's point of view?

In 1 Samuel 19 we have seen the developing hostility of Saul toward David. Since at this time David was the Lord's anointed king-to-be, Saul's aggression was an expression of the general phenomenon with which we are familiar. There is a continuity from Saul's attempt to drive a spear through David to the crowds who cried out concerning Jesus, "Crucify him, crucify him!" to the threats of those who oppose the gospel of Jesus today (cf. Acts 4:23-30).

As we take up the third and fourth of the stories in 1 Samuel 19 we will find that the question of whose will prevails is answered decisively.

After Saul had failed to pin David to the wall with his spear, we read that "David fled and escaped that night" (1 Samuel 19:10b).

DAVID SAVED BY SAUL'S DAUGHTER (vv. 11-17)

However, the circumstances of David's flight and escape were a little more complicated than we have so far been told. It happened that night to be sure, but not before Saul had attempted to make up for the failure of his spear.[1]

Threat (v. 11a)

We are to understand that after evading Saul's spear, David went home. He had no reason to think that Saul's madness would threaten him there. But he was wrong: "Saul sent messengers to David's house to watch him, that he might kill him in the morning" (v. 11a).

Just as in verse 1, Saul recruited his servants into the mission of killing David.

Escape (vv. 11b, 12)

In verse 1 Saul's plan was interrupted by "But Jonathan . . . " This time it is "But Michal . . ." "But Michal, David's wife, told him, 'If you do not escape with your life tonight, tomorrow you will be killed'" (v. 11b).

Michal, of course, was Saul's daughter (1 Samuel 14:49; 18:20). However, she, like her brother Jonathan, was committed to David and saw this as a higher loyalty than that due to her father. Just like Jonathan, she came to David warning him of her father's scheme.

We do not know how Michal knew of Saul's plan. Had he shared it with her, presuming on her relationship as his daughter, as he had apparently presumed on Jonathan's relationship as his son? If so, Saul misjudged his daughter as badly as he had misjudged his son.

"So Michal let David down through the window, and he fled away and escaped" (v. 12), just as we have been told in verse 10. Perhaps David's house was built into the town wall, like Rahab's in Jericho, so that escape from the house by window also meant escape from the town (cf. Joshua 2:15).[2]

Deception (vv. 13-17)

In order to give David a chance to make good his escape, Michal put into place some smart delaying tactics: "Michal took an image and laid it on the bed and put a pillow of goats' hair at its head and covered it with the clothes" (v. 13).

This is a little perplexing. It reminds us of a similar ploy by Laban's daughter, Rachel, who deceived her father over something called "household gods" in Genesis 31 (see vv. 19, 34, 35). The same word is used here, though translated "an image." We might well wonder what an image (or idol) was doing in Michal and David's house. The same word is translated "idolatry" in 1 Samuel 15:23![3] Presumably the image belonged to Michal, and perhaps the use she put it to now showed how little regard she had for such an object![4]

Michal's trick of using a dummy to deceive Saul's messengers into thinking David was in the bed is simple enough to understand,[5] and effective. She added a lie to seal the deception: "And when Saul sent messengers to take David, she said, 'He is sick'" (v. 14).

The messengers took her word for it, could not apparently work out what to do, so reported back to Saul. Saul may have had suspicions about the claim that David was ill: "Then Saul sent the messengers to see David, saying, 'Bring him up to me in the bed, that I may kill him'" (v. 15).

The messengers soon discovered the deception: "And when the messengers came in, behold, the image was in the bed, with the pillow of goats' hair at its head" (v. 16).

It was, of course, too late. The trick had given David ample time to get away. Not surprisingly, Saul was not happy with his daughter's conduct: "Saul said to Michal, 'Why have you deceived me thus and let my enemy go, so that he has escaped?'" (v. 17a).

Unlike Jonathan earlier,[6] she had not tried to win him by persuasive speech. She had deceived him. Perhaps persuasive speech would no longer be effective. Saul had settled on the fact that David was his "enemy" (see 1 Samuel 18:29).

Then Michal deceived him again:[7] "And Michal answered Saul, 'He said to me, "Let me go. Why should I kill you?"'" (v. 17b).

This is not the first (or last) time in the Bible that a person who is clearly the hero (or heroine) of the moment achieves his or her noble purpose by telling a lie. Typically (as here) the Biblical narrative makes no explicit moral judgment concerning the rights or wrongs of the lie. One of the best known examples, which has other similarities to the present episode, is Rahab, the Canaanite prostitute of Jericho, who lied to the king's men about the whereabouts of the Israelite spies, thus enabling them to escape (Joshua 2:4, 5). Another example will come later in the book of 1 Samuel, when David will by his actions deceive (1 Samuel 21:13) and by his words lie to the Philistines (1 Samuel 27:10; cf. 29:8). It is right for us to pause and reflect on this puzzling feature of the Bible's story. The following points should be kept in mind:

(1) The Bible certainly places a high value on truth and truthfulness. That is why these incidents *should* shock us. Lies and deception are generally understood to be evil. As Samuel said earlier in our narrative, "The Glory of Israel will not lie" (1 Samuel 15:29). We must take very seriously indeed the fact that God does not lie.

(2) To lie is an act of hostility. When Rahab lied, it meant that she was taking the side of the Israelites and treating her own people as the enemy. This is why Michal's lie is so shocking. She lied to her father and so was treating him as an enemy. This, of course, was because he had made himself the enemy of David (1 Samuel 18:29b).

(3) When Rahab, Michal, and David lied (in the incidents about which we are thinking), that radically unfriendly act demonstrated that they had abandoned (or, in the case of David, never had) any allegiance or positive relationship to the one to whom they lied. Rahab had chosen to side with the Israelites and therefore became an enemy of those who opposed the Israelites. Michal had committed herself to David and was therefore against Saul. David will later appear to have joined the Philistines, but his lies to them will demonstrate that he was still their enemy.

(4) If these lies were justified (and this may still be debated), it is relevant to note that the ones who lied were the weak, threatened by a more powerful enemy. It may be that in extreme circumstances the weaker and threatened party may be justified in the defensive (though hostile) act of telling a lie to an enemy.

However, we must be careful not to moralize these Biblical incidents. The lies of the characters are part of their story because that is what they did. Whether we would ever be justified in doing likewise is another question. Certainly we must be people who love the truth, love to tell the truth, and hate lies — just as we must hate all acts of violence, even if sometimes they are justified or even required.

This has been something of a digression from our story. For the third time we have seen David saved from the violent intentions of Saul, this time with the help of Saul's daughter.

DAVID RESCUED BY THE SPIRIT OF GOD (vv. 18-24)

The fourth and final escape story in 1 Samuel 19 is the most remarkable of all and is a fitting climax to the four stories. We are no doubt expected to see the hand of God protecting his anointed one in each of the escapes recorded in this chapter. In the last of them, however, God's power is no longer behind the scenes, so to speak, but center stage.

David and Samuel (v. 18)

David's escape from Saul, referred to already in verses 10 and 12, is mentioned again in verse 18. We are clearly meant to take note of this departure. It will turn out to be permanent. David will not return to Saul's service.

Having left Saul, David made his way to the one who had set the extraordinary train of events in progress when he had come to Bethlehem and anointed Jesse's youngest son (1 Samuel 16:1-13):

> *Now David fled and escaped, and he came to Samuel at Ramah and told him all that Saul had done to him. And he and Samuel went and lived at Naioth. (v. 18)*

David did not flee far. Ramah was only about two miles from Saul's town of Gibeah. If he was in a hurry he could have been there in less than half an hour!

We have heard nothing of Samuel since his remarkable visit to Bethlehem in the first part of chapter 16.[8] We cannot tell how much time had elapsed since the Bethlehem anointing. It may have been a number of years. Events seem to have taken their course through this time without Samuel's direct involvement.[9] Of course, we know that Samuel's break with Saul at the end of chapter 15 meant that Samuel was no longer directly involved with Israel's reigning king (v. 35), but neither had he yet been publicly associated with the one he had privately anointed in Bethlehem.

David's coming to Samuel was therefore important. We have seen all along that God rules his people by his word. This has meant that, in terms of human agents, the ultimate authority in Israel would always lie with the prophet, not the king (see 1 Samuel 2:27-36; 3:1b, 19-21; 4:1; 9:27b; 12:23, 24; 15:10). Saul's disobedience to the word of the prophet had led to God's rejection of Saul, which in turn had resulted in the breech between Saul the king and Samuel the prophet. Likewise God's choice of David will be expressed in Samuel's support for David.

David's account of "all that Saul had done to him" must have been painful for Samuel to hear. Remember how Samuel had grieved over Saul's failure (1 Samuel 15:11b, 35; 16:1). However, I doubt that anything David reported was a surprise to the old prophet.

David and Samuel lived (or stayed) together at Naioth. No one is sure whether that is a place name. If it is, it is otherwise unknown. It could be a word referring to "pastures" or "dwellings" in or near Ramah.[10] This ambiguity matters little. What is important is how David will be kept safe from the violence of Saul, living so close to Gibeah.

Saul's Attempts to Kill David: Thwarted by the Spirit of God (vv. 19-21)

It did not take long for Saul to hear of David's new address: "And it was told Saul, 'Behold, David is at Naioth in Ramah'" (v. 19).

What would you expect Saul to do? "Then Saul sent messengers to take David . . ." (v. 20a).

Just as he had sent messengers to David's house, so he sent messengers to David's new home with Samuel. He had been outwitted once, but he was not one to give up. The messengers came to Ramah to take David.

They were in for a surprise:

> . . . and when they saw the company of the prophets prophesying, and Samuel standing as head over them, the Spirit of God came upon the messengers of Saul, and they also prophesied. (v. 20b)

We do not know a great deal about this "company of the prophets."[11] It appears to be the same "group of prophets" encountered by Saul at Gibeath-elohim in 1 Samuel 10:5. That group had been "prophesying" to the accompaniment of musical instruments. When Saul had met them, the Spirit of the Lord had rushed upon him, and he too "prophesied" with them and was "turned into another man" (1 Samuel 10:6, 10). We now learn what we might have suspected, that Samuel exercised some kind of leadership over this group.[12]

It is also not exactly clear what they were doing. It is called "prophesying," but "prophesying" could apparently take various forms. When the harmful spirit from God overcame Saul so that he "raved" in his house, the word used is, literally, "prophesied" (1 Samuel 18:10). On the other hand, when Samuel was established as a "prophet," he became the one who brought the word of the Lord to Israel (1 Samuel 3:20, 21). In other words, "to prophesy" means different things in different contexts.[13] What seems to be common to the various contexts is speech under the influence of a power beyond the speaker.[14] The activity of the company of prophets seems to be neither mad raving nor calm delivery of the word of the Lord. It appears to have been some kind of speaking activity, perhaps songs of praise,[15] under the influence of the Spirit of God.

The surprise for everyone was that as the messengers from Saul approached Samuel's band of prophets, the Spirit of God overpowered them, and they began to "prophesy." Whatever this was precisely, it seems to have meant that they were no longer capable of carrying out the king's command to "take" David.

Saul heard what had happened. He knew what it was like to be overpowered by the Spirit of the Lord and find yourself "prophesying." It had happened to him (1 Samuel 10:9-13).

He tried to retrieve the situation: "When it was told Saul, he sent other messengers, and they also prophesied" (v. 21a).

He made one more attempt: "And Saul sent messengers again the third time, and they also prophesied" (v. 21b).

It was as though the Spirit of the Lord had set up a protective shield around the one Saul was determined to destroy (compare 2 Kings 1:9-14)!

Saul Himself Thwarted by the Spirit of God (vv. 22-24)

The narrative now slows down, and we follow step by step what happened when Saul decided that if you want something done properly, you have to do it yourself! "Then he himself went to Ramah and came to the great well that is in Secu" (v. 22a).

We no longer know exactly where that was, but the original hearers of this story would have known. They could picture the well near Ramah and the determined king demanding an answer to his question: "And he asked, 'Where are Samuel and David?'" (v. 22b).

The powerful king was set on his purpose. His question, however, suggests that he was not as well informed as even the earlier messengers, who seem to have found Samuel and David easily enough. We do not know what Saul intended to do with Samuel when he found him, but we know very well his plans for David.

He got his answer: "And one said, 'Behold, they are at Naioth in Ramah'" (v. 22c).

Saul set off to locate his enemy: "And he went there to Naioth in Ramah" (v. 23a).

The powerful king, probably with accompanying armed men, approached the place where David was. We can sense the violent resolve in Saul's step. As he got close to where David was, this is what happened:

> And the Spirit of God came upon him also, and as he went he prophesied until he came to Naioth in Ramah. And he too stripped off his clothes, and he too prophesied before Samuel and lay naked all that day and all that night. (vv. 23b, 24a)

The powerful king was utterly powerless before the power of the Spirit of God. In this respect he was no different from his messengers, except that the Spirit of God overpowered the king before he had even reached Naioth. Stripping off his royal clothes was evocative. Yes, it showed him humbled (that is, humiliated) before the prophet.[16] But more, Saul here did unwill-

ingly what Jonathan had done gladly when faced with David (1 Samuel
18:4).[17] The disrobed Saul, and earlier Jonathan, testify that the marks of
royal office no longer belonged to the house of Saul.[18]

When this incident became known, new meaning was given to the proverb that had circulated about Saul: "Thus it is said, 'Is Saul also among the
prophets?'" (v. 24b).

Earlier this proverb had expressed the surprise that an unknown farm
boy had become associated with Samuel and the prophets (1 Samuel 10:12).
The Spirit of the Lord had then marked him out and empowered him as the
chosen king. Now, however, the same proverb seems to suggest that the
powerful king had been brought into submission to Samuel.[19] The Spirit of
the Lord had broken him and thwarted his wicked scheme.[20]

Think back over the four stories that have come to us in 1 Samuel 19:
(1) David rescued from Saul's murderous plan by Jonathan's good words,
(2) David rescued from Saul's spear by what might appear to have been a
lucky evasive move, (3) David rescued from Saul's henchmen by Michal's
deception, and (4) David rescued from Saul by the Spirit of God.

In each case the power appeared to be in Saul's hands. He had servants
at his command, while David just had a committed friend in Jonathan and a
faithful wife in Michal. Saul had a spear, while David just had a lyre. Saul
had plenty of men to send to Ramah, while David just had the old prophet
Samuel.

And yet the words of Psalm 2 ring true again:

> *He who sits in the heavens laughs;*
> *the LORD holds them in derision.*
> *Then he will speak to them in his wrath,*
> *and terrify them in his fury, saying,*
> *"As for me, I have set my King*
> *on Zion, my holy hill." (vv. 4-6)*

God will not be mocked! Those who set themselves against the Lord
and his Anointed will not prevail. They will be overthrown, just as Saul and
his men were stripped naked before the prophet of God.

Psalm 59 had its origin in these events. In that psalm we hear David's
trust in God:

> *Deliver me from my enemies, O my God;*
> *protect me from those who rise up against me;*
> *deliver me from those who work evil,*
> *and save me from bloodthirsty men. . . .*
> *But I will sing of your strength;*
> *I will sing aloud of your steadfast love in the morning.*

For you have been to me a fortress
and a refuge in the day of my distress.
O my Strength, I will sing praises to you,
for you, O God, are my fortress,
the God who shows me steadfast love. (vv. 1, 2, 16, 17)

The ultimate realization of this truth will come on the day that every knee will bow at the name of Jesus and confess that he is Lord, to the glory of God the Father (Philippians 2:9-11).

34

What Do You Fear?

1 SAMUEL 20:1-23

What do you fear? We may not like to admit it, but fear motivates many things we do. Certainly fear is not the only motivation for many of our actions, but it is at least part of the motivation for much in our lives. We work, at least partly, because we fear poverty. We exercise because we fear poor health. We even make friends, in part, because we fear loneliness. What do you fear?

Put like this, it is clear that fear is not necessarily a bad thing. To refrain from smoking because of a fear of lung cancer is wise. To be faithful to a spouse out of fear of the pain that unfaithfulness brings is good. A person who feared nothing and no one (if such were to exist) would be both a fool and a danger to others. Fear is an important, even valuable human experience. What do you fear?

Of course, there are unhealthy fears. Psychiatrists and counselors are kept in business by our harmful fears. These fears may be unnecessary — the thing feared is imagined or exaggerated, as when a teenager is terrified that everyone secretly dislikes him. They may be fears that instead of motivating wise and good behavior paralyze us or arouse inappropriate actions, as when a student's fear of exams makes him unable to concentrate and study.

What we fear and what we do because of our fears has a lot to do with the health of our human lives. What do you fear?

David feared Saul. And who could blame him? Saul was the king. Three times he had tried to thrust his spear through David (1 Samuel 18:11 [twice!]; 19:10). Twice he had tried to send David on such a dangerous mission that the Philistines would kill him (1 Samuel 18:17, 25). Three times he had enlisted his servants in various plots to do away with David (1 Samuel 19:1, 11, 20). The fact that so far none of these schemes had succeeded and even the apparently divine intervention to protect David on the last occasion did not allay David's fear of Saul.

The first half of 1 Samuel 20 brings us to a remarkable conversation between David and Jonathan, the son of Saul. It would not be right to say that the subject of the conversation was fear. Neither David nor Jonathan directly mention fear. But fear is present, and as we shall see, the big surprise in the conversation is what is feared and what is done because of the fear. David's fear of Saul was only the starting point for this dramatic conversation.

DAVID'S FEAR OF SAUL (vv. 1-11)

The first part of the conversation was dominated by David's fear of Saul. The immediate context was Saul's continued attempts to take David, who had sought refuge with the prophet Samuel in Ramah. As each band of Saul's emissaries came, they were remarkably overpowered by the Spirit of God and had not completed their mission (1 Samuel 19:20, 21). Saul himself was brought to the ground by the power of the Spirit and was humbled before Samuel (1 Samuel 19:23).

David's Fear (vv. 1-3)

Chapter 20 begins, "Then David fled from Naioth in Ramah . . ." This is a continuation of the story of chapter 19. That chapter had been about David's fleeing and escaping from Saul (see vv. 10, 12, 18). While we might have expected that David would have been safe in Ramah with Samuel, David's flight continued. We may suppose that the divine overpowering of Saul and his men at the end of chapter 19 was not permanent. What would happen when Saul recovered? Apparently David was not going to stay around to find out![1]

DAVID: INNOCENCE (v. 1)

From Ramah he sought out Jonathan:

> Then David fled from Naioth in Ramah and came and said before Jonathan, "What have I done? What is my guilt? And what is my sin before your father, that he seeks my life?" (v. 1)

Jonathan, we are never allowed to forget, was the king's son. David came "before Jonathan" as the subordinate that he was. A little later in this conversation he described himself as Jonathan's "servant" (see vv. 7, 8).

David was popular and was a successful warrior, but he conducted himself as a loyal subject, a servant.

In verse 1 we hear the first recorded words spoken by David to Jonathan. They are a formal protest to the king's son about the king's threats to his life.

David's innocence in relation to Saul will become a major theme of the closing chapters of 1 Samuel. The rhetorical question "What has David done?" will be asked of Saul again (see 1 Samuel 20:32; 26:18; 29:8). We know, and Jonathan knows, that David had only done "good" for Saul (1 Samuel 19:4). David's protest speech to Jonathan echoed Jonathan's own speech to Saul at the beginning of the previous chapter: "He has not sinned against you" (1 Samuel 19:4, 5).

That speech had resulted in a solemn vow from Saul that David would not be killed (1 Samuel 19:6). David's complaint was that Jonathan's father had broken the vow "without cause" (cf. 1 Samuel 19:5).

JONATHAN: REASSURANCE (V. 2)

Listen to Jonathan's response:

> *And he said to him, "Far from it! You shall not die. Behold, my father does nothing either great or small without disclosing it to me. And why should my father hide this from me? It is not so." (v. 2)*

Jonathan has not appeared in the story since 1 Samuel 19:7. He was apparently unaware of Saul's three subsequent attempts on David's life. The last Jonathan had heard about the matter was Saul's oath, which he was taking in good faith. Saul had said, "He shall not be put to death" (1 Samuel 19:6). So Jonathan now assured David, "You shall not die."[2] Jonathan believed his father and therefore did not believe that David was in any danger from him.[3]

Not only was David innocent in this situation, so was Jonathan. He honored his father and king by trusting him and offering David reassurance that all was well.

DAVID: FEAR (V. 3)

However, Jonathan had been deceived by his father, and it was very important, for reasons that we will see, for David to persuade him of that fact:

> *But David vowed again, saying, "Your father knows well that I have found favor in your eyes, and he thinks, 'Do not let Jonathan know this, lest he*

*be grieved.' But truly, as the LORD lives and as your soul lives, there is but
a step between me and death." (v. 3)*

David had begun by swearing his innocence; now he swore that the
danger of which he spoke was real.[4] We will see that David has read the situation well. Saul had, of course, realized that Jonathan (like almost everyone
else!) held David in high regard.[5] That is why, according to David, Saul had
not continued the open frankness with his son that had been the case at the
very beginning of chapter 19.

Jonathan had not been there, but three times there had *literally* been but
a step between David and death as he evaded Saul's hurled spear.[6] That was
also a reasonable metaphor for other threats that had come David's way.

David's Scheme (vv. 4-8)

Why was it so important to David to persuade Jonathan of the danger he was
in? He had a scheme that depended on Jonathan's taking his circumstances
seriously. This scheme would be revealed once Jonathan's goodwill had
been secured.

JONATHAN: WILLING (V. 4)

David's oath appears to have done the job: "Then Jonathan said to David,
'Whatever you say, I will do for you'" (v. 4).

This was the king's son speaking.[7] It was consistent with Jonathan's
earlier acts of commitment to David, but no less remarkable for that. The
king's son offered to do whatever David asked, a reversal of the expected
relationship between royalty and subjects.

DAVID: THE PLAN (VV. 5-7)

David revealed his plan:

> *David said to Jonathan, "Behold, tomorrow is the new moon, and I should
> not fail to sit at table with the king. But let me go, that I may hide myself
> in the field till the third day at evening. If your father misses me at all,
> then say, 'David earnestly asked leave of me to run to Bethlehem his city,
> for there is a yearly sacrifice there for all the clan.' If he says, 'Good!' it
> will be well with your servant, but if he is angry, then know that harm is
> determined by him." (vv. 5-7)*

The new moon, the beginning of a new month, was an occasion for
various festivities (see Numbers 28:11-15; 29:6; Ezra 3:5; Psalm 81:3).[8]

Despite the troubles of recent times, David was still Saul's son-in-law and an esteemed warrior and would be expected to join the king at his table.

David's plan appears to have been to determine, for himself as well as for Jonathan, whether Saul's murderous intentions toward him persisted. David needed to know this, for he could not return to Saul's presence unless the danger had passed. Saul had relented once, under the influence of Jonathan's persuasive words (1 Samuel 19:6). Perhaps the power of the Spirit of God (1 Samuel 19:23) had brought him to a better mind again. If so, David could return. If not, he dare not.

Hence the plan. David would absent himself conspicuously from the new moon festivities. This would certainly be noticed by Saul. Jonathan was to give an excuse. It was a dangerous excuse. At least it seems so to us as we hear the plan. Superficially there may have been danger in the idea of David returning to Bethlehem because Saul had forbidden him from doing so (1 Samuel 18:2).[9] More significantly, however, David's returning to Bethlehem for a sacrifice reminds us of the important day in Bethlehem when there had also been a sacrifice and David had been anointed by Samuel (1 Samuel 16:5, 13). As far as we know, this fairly private event had not become widely known. We may suspect that Jonathan had learned something about it, probably from David himself. But we have no reason (yet) to think that Saul knew of the anointing. His hostility to David is accounted for in the narrative by David's military success and great popularity.[10] Nonetheless, to suggest to Saul that David had run back to Bethlehem for a sacrifice when *we* know what happened last time he was in Bethlehem for a sacrifice seems to be playing dangerously.

There were two possible reactions from Saul, and which one occurred would indicate to David (and to Jonathan) what should be done.[11] If Saul was pleased, or at least satisfied, with the excuse offered, then his malice toward David had obviously abated, and David could enjoy (literally) "peace" (1 Samuel 20:7). If Saul was angry, it would be a clear sign that he had determined "harm." The word is literally "evil" as in "harmful [evil] spirit" (1 Samuel 16:14; 18:10; 19:9).

David: Appeal to Covenant (v. 8)

This was a lot to ask of the king's son. It did involve a lie. Jonathan had not lied to his father before this. His sister had (1 Samuel 19:17), and he had kept things from his father (1 Samuel 14:1), including, we presume, the extent of his commitment to David. But to lie to Saul for David was another big step in putting his relationship to David above his relationship to the king. Although he had done that once before, when he had warned David of Saul's plotting, he had not then deceived his father. On the contrary, he spoke honestly to him, with good effect (1 Samuel 19:1-7).

David was well aware of what he was asking of the king's son. The only basis that could justify such a request was Jonathan's commitment to David. To this David appealed:

> *"Therefore deal kindly with your servant, for you have brought your servant into a covenant of the LORD with you. But if there is guilt in me, kill me yourself, for why should you bring me to your father?" (v. 8)*

For the second time David humbly identified himself as "your servant." However, there was more to their relationship than that. Jonathan had initiated a relationship described here as "a covenant of the LORD." We saw the account of this at the beginning of chapter 18. The king's son initiated this formal (though secret) commitment between himself and David because of his love for David. We deduced from his actions at the time that this commitment involved, in some way, Jonathan's renouncing his right to Saul's throne and handing over that right to David. It was a "covenant of the LORD" in the sense that the Lord was witness to it and would watch over the parties to it.[12]

It is clear from the story, as it will unfold, that this agreement between Jonathan and David involved no suggestion of David's taking the throne from Saul by force. It is possible that part of the agreement was a renunciation of any such attempt. In due course it will be clear that David refused repeated opportunities to seize the throne through violence against Saul. When David said, "But if there is guilt in me," he apparently meant, "if I have broken this agreement, if I have threatened Saul in any way, if I have done him any harm." In that case the agreement between Jonathan and David would have been broken, and Jonathan would have no obligation toward David. He might as well kill him himself. There would be no need to hand him over to Saul.

However, David was asserting his innocence. He had done nothing to deserve Saul's hostility. Therefore, on the basis of the commitment between them, David asked Jonathan to "deal kindly" with him.[13] Here a famous Hebrew word is used. "Deal kindly" captures the sense well. It speaks of mercy shown to one in need by one with the power to help.[14]

Jonathan's Kindness (vv. 9-11)

Notice carefully that it was Jonathan, the king's son, who was asked by David, the one in danger, to "deal kindly." David was in need of mercy. Jonathan was the one to whom he looked for mercy because of the covenant between them. Jonathan responded with a firm promise that he would keep nothing from David.

JONATHAN: PROMISE (V. 9)

And Jonathan said, "Far be it from you! If I knew that it was determined by my father that harm should come to you, would I not tell you?" (v. 9)

With the same strong language ("Far be it!"[15]) as he had used to assert his confidence that his father kept no secrets from him (and therefore meant no harm to David), Jonathan asserted his commitment to keep no secrets from David (and therefore acknowledged David's innocence in this matter). "If I was forced to choose," Jonathan said in effect, "my allegiance to you, David, would take precedence over my allegiance to my father."

DAVID: BACK TO THE PLAN (V. 10)

But David had not raised the matter as a general question, but as a specific scheme to determine Saul's intentions toward him. And so David pressed his question within the specific circumstances he was proposing: "Then David said to Jonathan, 'Who will tell me if your father answers you roughly?'" (v. 10).

David was pressing for a specific assurance that should Saul respond to his absence as David expected him to, Jonathan would not abandon David but would inform him.

JONATHAN: MORE TO SAY (V. 11)

Now came a surprise. Jonathan did not give the assurance immediately: "And Jonathan said to David, 'Come, let us go out into the field.' So they both went out into the field" (v. 11).

Probably it was fear of being overheard that prompted Jonathan to take David outside for the rest of this remarkable conversation.[16] The reason was not that the things they had said so far should be kept secret, but what Jonathan was about to say to David certainly required the utmost care.

JONATHAN'S "FEAR" OF DAVID (vv. 12-17)

The first part of the conversation, apparently conducted somewhere indoors, was dominated by David's very understandable fear of Saul. Saul's spear and Saul's assassins had come too close for comfort, too often. We have seen David in need of Jonathan's kindness in these circumstances, to help him to know what to do next.

What we are about to hear is that Jonathan saw the situation in a rather different light. The conversation, as it proceeded out in the field, beyond

the possibility of being overheard, was astonishing! It was dominated by
Jonathan's "fear" of David.

Jonathan's Promise Now (vv. 12, 13a)

Jonathan took over the conversation. He began with the assurance David
had asked for:

> And Jonathan said to David, "The LORD, the God of Israel, be witness!
> When I have sounded out my father, about this time tomorrow, or the third
> day, behold, if he is well disposed toward David, shall I not then send and
> disclose it to you? But should it please my father to do you harm, the LORD
> do so to Jonathan and more also if I do not disclose it to you and send you
> away, that you may go in safety. (vv. 12, 13a)

Jonathan understood that the matter between them was of national
importance. There was much more at stake than had so far been mentioned
in this conversation. "The LORD, the God of Israel be witness!"

As far as the present situation was concerned, Jonathan would do exactly
what David had asked. Whatever happened, Jonathan would disclose all to
David. He would deal with David as he had thought his father was dealing
with him.[17]

Jonathan's Petition for the Future (vv. 13b-15)

But Jonathan had more on his mind than the present situation. He was looking to the future. If David had something to ask in the present, Jonathan had
something to ask for the future.

OF GOD (v. 13b)

First, he had something to ask of God: "May the LORD be with you, as he has
been with my father" (v. 13b), or better, "as he *was* with my father."

This is astonishing! This is more than a pious wish — "God be with
you!" Jonathan appears to understand something that may not yet have been
clear even to David — namely, that the Spirit of the Lord, who had rushed
upon David on the day of his anointing in Bethlehem, had departed from
Saul (1 Samuel 16:13, 14; 18:12). The Lord had been with Saul for the
purpose of his being king. He had been the one the Lord had chosen. For
Jonathan to ask that the Lord be with David as he had been with Saul was
to ask that David should become king.

The Hebrew is more ambiguous than our English translation. It could
be taken to be not a petition but a prediction: "The LORD will be with you, as

he was with my father." Understood in this way, Jonathan's words express a confidence (implicit even in the petition) that David *will* be king — God's king.[18]

Of David (vv. 14, 15)

Jonathan seems to have seen that future more clearly than David at this stage. As David found his present circumstances dominated by Saul's threats, Jonathan found himself dominated by the future reign of David. Looking forward to that future, he had two things to ask of David.

For Jonathan (v. 14):

> "*If I am still alive, show me the steadfast love of the* Lord, *that I may not die . . .*" (v. 14)

Jonathan used the Hebrew word that David had used in verse 8.[19] In the future it would be Jonathan who needed kindness and mercy, and David would be the one with the power to help. Jonathan understood the reversal that would take place, and so he looked to David for mercy, should he still be alive when David became king.

For Jonathan's house (v. 15):

> "*. . . and do not cut off your steadfast love from my house forever, when the* Lord *cuts off every one of the enemies of David from the face of the earth.*" (v. 15)

It is utterly astonishing that Jonathan seems to have seen that David's kingdom would be "forever." In the future that Jonathan saw, David would no longer be threatened by enemies. Remember that Saul had declared himself to be David's "enemy," and we have been told that Saul was "David's enemy continually" (1 Samuel 19:17; 18:29). The Lord would "cut off" every one of David's enemies from the face of the earth. Jonathan pleaded for mercy (it's that same Hebrew word again) for his descendants when that happened.

What a very strange speech this was, considering the circumstances in which it was spoken. Fear of Saul meant that it had to be uttered out in the field. Saul was the powerful one and to be feared. But Jonathan feared the one who was afraid! He understood that the day was coming when the despised one would be king. It was a speech of extraordinary faith.

A Covenant (vv. 16, 17)

That day, of course, had not yet come. Jonathan was still the king's son, and David was the king's subject. The future, however, was more important than the present, and Jonathan acted accordingly:

> And Jonathan made a covenant with the house of David, saying, "May the LORD take vengeance on David's enemies." And Jonathan made David swear again by his love for him, for he loved him as he loved his own soul. (vv. 16, 17)

A covenant with "the house of David" sounds a little premature! But Jonathan was speaking and acting with a remarkably clear vision of the future.

Jonathan declared himself to be not only *for* David, but also *against* David's enemies.[20] Whether he knew it or not, this set him against his father. But this could not be avoided. The point comes when those who love the future king must set themselves against his enemies, whoever they may be.

It is not clear in verse 17 who loved whom, but it matters little, because the love was mutual.[21] David swore, presumably, that when he came into his kingdom he would honor Jonathan's petitions in verses 14, 15. If you care to glance a long way ahead in the story to 2 Samuel 9:1 and 21:7, you will see that David kept the oath he swore this day.

This future that for the time being could only be talked about in whispers out in the field explains Jonathan's otherwise bizarre behavior.

JONATHAN, DAVID, AND THE LORD (vv. 18-23)

The long conversation concluded, still with Jonathan speaking, but coming back to the present crisis and the plan that had been proposed by David.

Jonathan and David (vv. 18-22)

All this seems rather mundane now that we have glanced at the future. It was nonetheless real enough, events would take their course, and Jonathan would do as he had promised:

> Then Jonathan said to him, "Tomorrow is the new moon, and you will be missed, because your seat will be empty. On the third day go down quickly to the place where you hid yourself when the matter was in hand, and remain beside the stone heap. And I will shoot three arrows to the side of it, as though I shot at a mark. And behold, I will send the young man, saying, 'Go, find the arrows.' If I say to the young man, 'Look, the

arrows are on this side of you, take them,' then you are to come, for, as
the LORD lives, it is safe for you and there is no danger. But if I say to the
youth, 'Look, the arrows are beyond you,' then go, for the LORD has sent
you away." (vv. 18-22)

At last Jonathan returned to David's question of verse 10 and his initial
reply in verse 12. Who would tell David the results of his proposed test?
Jonathan would, in the clandestine way he described.[22] The involvement of
a "young man" in the plan may be "designed to provide a witness who can
assure Saul that he did not meet David while out shooting."[23]

David, Jonathan, and the Lord (v. 23)

Jonathan concluded the conversation with these words: "And as for the matter of which you and I have spoken, behold, the LORD is between you and
me forever" (v. 23).

"The matter of which you and I have spoken" was surely the future
reign of David. That was a matter between David, Jonathan, and the Lord.
It would come in the Lord's time, in the Lord's way. What was required of
David and Jonathan in the meantime was faithfulness to the commitments
they had made to each other in the light of that future.

What do you fear?

The situation of David and Jonathan is profoundly like our own circumstances. There is much to fear in our present world. There are real dangers
and real enemies. We could perhaps look at David's plan to determine the
true nature of the threat against him and draw some kind of lesson about the
wisdom of realism and knowing your enemy.

However, our own circumstances are only really like the situation of
David and Jonathan when we see the future kingdom that is coming, just
as surely as David would one day reign. Jonathan took the future kingdom
seriously, more seriously, we might say, than the superficial aspects of the
present, real and terrible though they were. Jonathan "feared" the coming
king and made his peace with him as he had opportunity in the present. It
was a good fear. He loved the coming king. He knew his goodness. But he
was determined not to be found to be his enemy.

What do you fear? Whatever you fear should be seen in the light of the
future, when at the name of Jesus every knee will bow (Philippians 2:10).
Listen to Jesus' words about fear:

"So have no fear of them [that is, those who hate you because you belong
to Jesus], for nothing is covered that will not be revealed, or hidden that
will not be known. What I tell you in the dark, say in the light, and what
you hear whispered, proclaim on the housetops. And do not fear those who

kill the body but cannot kill the soul. Rather fear him who can destroy both soul and body in hell. Are not two sparrows sold for a penny? And not one of them will fall to the ground apart from your Father. But even the hairs of your head are all numbered. Fear not, therefore; you are of more value than many sparrows. So everyone who acknowledges me before men, I also will acknowledge before my Father who is in heaven, but whoever denies me before men, I also will deny before my Father who is in heaven." (Matthew 10:26-33)

35

"If Anyone Does Not Hate His Own Father . . ."

1 SAMUEL 20:24-42

"If anyone comes to me and does not hate his own father and mother and wife and children and brothers and sisters, yes, and even his own life, he cannot be my disciple." (Luke 14:26)

There are few more difficult sayings of Jesus than this. There are many reasonable things that can be said about these words of Jesus. We might point out that Jesus often spoke in hyperbole, so that "hate" should be understood as a stark and vivid word for loving family members *less* than we love Jesus. There is no doubt some truth in that observation. The same speech of Jesus concludes with the assertion that anyone who "does not renounce all that he has cannot be my disciple" (v. 33), but there is little evidence that his disciples or the early Christians considered that they had to *literally* abandon *all* possessions.

Likewise we might want to say that this aphorism of Jesus must not be isolated from the rest of his teaching, nor from the rest of the Bible's instruction, where obligations toward family members are clearly affirmed. Again this is true.

These reasonable observations, however, must not be used as a means of avoiding the shocking force of Jesus' words. These words should shake us into realizing, if it is not crystal-clear to us already, that Jesus of Nazareth cannot be reduced to a mere teacher of morality. What kind of morality is this that speaks of *hatred* toward mother, father, brothers and sisters, and even self? If we treat Jesus' teaching as mere ethical instruction, these words will be utterly unintelligible to us.

The teaching of Jesus was principally about *who he is* and *what he came to do*. He was not teaching simply about family relationships, but about what it means to "be *my* disciple." This difficult saying of Jesus must make us see more clearly who Jesus is, what he came to do, and what it means to be *his* disciple.

Jesus is the Christ, and he came to establish the kingdom of God.

In the story of the early days of the kingdom of God, in its expression in the history of Old Testament Israel, we have been seeing the beginning of the concept of "the Christ" and of "the kingdom." In the experience of Jonathan, faced with the Lord's Christ and the coming of his kingdom, we are about to see something of the background to Jesus' shocking words, "If anyone . . . does not hate his own father . . . he cannot be my disciple."

In the last chapter we examined the conversation between Jonathan and David, in which Jonathan clearly saw the coming kingdom of David and had set about ordering his commitments now in the light of that future.

THE TEST: DAVID'S ABSENCE (vv. 24-29)

David had proposed, and Jonathan had accepted, a scheme to ascertain Jonathan's father's attitude toward David, after the king's solemn vow that David would not be put to death (1 Samuel 19:6) and his subsequent repeated attempts to have him killed (1 Samuel 19:8-24). We take up the story at the point where the plan was being put in place.

Day One (vv. 24-26)

It was the new moon, a time apparently when King Saul was to hold a three-day feast, and David, his son-in-law and finest warrior, would be expected to be present. The plan was that David would absent himself from the festivities, Jonathan would make an excuse for him, and they would watch Saul's reaction (1 Samuel 20:5-7).

David's Absence (vv. 24, 25)

Day One of the feast began as planned:

> So David hid himself in the field. And when the new moon came, the king sat down to eat food. The king sat on his seat, as at other times, on the seat by the wall. Jonathan sat opposite, and Abner sat by Saul's side, but David's place was empty. (vv. 24, 25)

We can picture the table setting. The king's seat was by the wall as usual — perhaps providing him with some protection. Opposite him was Jonathan.[1] On one side of Saul was Abner, the army commander, whom we met after David had slain Goliath (1 Samuel 17:55-57; cf. 14:50). But there was an empty seat, with David's name on it.

This, of course, was the first part of the plan. Jonathan knew where David was (and so do we). He was hiding, as agreed between them, out in the field.

SAUL'S ASSUMPTION (v. 26)

Saul did not know anything about why David was absent. The empty seat did not provoke any comment on that first day. Saul assumed some simple explanation (simple to him, if not to us): "Yet Saul did not say anything that day, for he thought, 'Something has happened to him. He is not clean; surely he is not clean'" (v. 26).

Saul assumed that David was absent not on purpose, but by chance. Something beyond his control had happened, he thought, and kept him from the feast. It was apparently, after all, a religious festival requiring participants to be ceremonially "clean." According to Israel's God-given Law, many ordinary experiences could make a person unclean for a brief time (see Leviticus 11–15).[2] Saul assumed that something of that kind had happened to David.

We cannot help wondering at the fact that it did not seem to occur to Saul that three recent attempts by the king to murder David might have played a role in David's absence from the king's table that day! We should recognize that Saul's assumption indicates something of the power he at least thought he had over his subjects. Even though David must have known his life was in danger in Saul's presence (and Saul must have known that David knew), Saul assumed that David would not deliberately absent himself without the king's permission. Saul had become that kind of king.

Day Two (vv. 27-29)

DAVID'S ABSENCE (v. 27a)

And so Day Two of the festival dawned. We are to understand that everything began in the same way as on Day One. There was the king, in his place, and Jonathan and Abner — and one empty seat: "But on the second day, the day after the new moon, David's place was empty" (v. 27a).

Chance uncleanness could last until the evening.[3] The fact that David was absent the second day decreased the likelihood of this explanation.

SAUL'S QUESTION (V. 27b)

Saul therefore raised the matter with his son: "And Saul said to Jonathan his son, 'Why has not the son of Jesse come to the meal, either yesterday or today?'" (v. 27b).

We detect something of Saul's difficulty toward David in his avoidance of his name. Throughout this conversation and beyond, we hear Saul refer to David as "the son of Jesse" (see 1 Samuel 22:7, 8, 13; cf. 25:10). Unlike his son, Jonathan, Saul did not recognize the importance of David. He spoke of him as someone who was not yet a "name" in his own right.[4] The king demanded an explanation for the absence of David.

JONATHAN'S REPLY (VV. 28, 29)

David had concocted a reply that Jonathan was to give at this point. It was: "David earnestly asked leave of me to run to Bethlehem his city, for there is a yearly sacrifice there for all the clan" (1 Samuel 20:6).

Jonathan now embellished the proposed words a little:

> Jonathan answered Saul, "David earnestly asked leave of me to go to Bethlehem. He said, 'Let me go, for our clan holds a sacrifice in the city, and my brother has commanded me to be there. So now, if I have found favor in your eyes, let me get away and see my brothers.' For this reason he has not come to the king's table." (vv. 28, 29)

Perhaps Jonathan tried to make the excuse look as good as possible, by adding in the brother. It was David's obligation to his family that had kept him away. He was only obeying his brother's command. He had only gone to see his brothers. That is the reason, the only reason, that David's seat at the king's table was empty, said Jonathan.[5]

We know, of course, that this was a lie. David was hiding in the field, waiting for news of Saul's reaction to the fictional excuse for his absence.

There was one other slip that Jonathan made when he chose to embellish the story as it had been given to him by David. When he used the words "let me get away," he may inadvertently have given the game away. The word he used literally means "let me escape." It is the word that was used by the narrator repeatedly in the previous chapter to describe David's eluding of Saul's attempts on his life (1 Samuel 19:10, 11, 12, 17, 18). Saul himself had used this word when he rebuked Jonathan's sister: "Why have you deceived me thus and let my enemy go, so that he has *escaped*?" (1 Samuel 19:17).

Jonathan did not mean to, no doubt, but when he said that David had said, "Let me *escape* . . ." he gave a clue as to the real reason for David's absence.

THE RESULT: SAUL'S DECISION (vv. 30-34)

We cannot be sure whether that word stirred something in Saul's awareness or whether it was the emphasis on David's choice of a family obligation over his duty to the king or whether Saul's reaction would have been the same if Jonathan had stuck strictly to his script. What we see clearly is that the proposed test had a result. It was the result David had feared and Jonathan had hoped against hope would not be the case.

Saul's Rage at Jonathan (vv. 30, 31)

As David had set up this test earlier, he had predicted two possible reactions from Saul (1 Samuel 20:7). One was that he might say "Good!" This would be a sign that the danger for David had passed. To put it briefly, "Good!" is not what Saul said.

The other possibility anticipated by David was that he would be "angry." I think we can safely say that "angry" was putting it mildly!

JONATHAN HAD CHOSEN DAVID (v. 30)

Jonathan received the full blast of Saul's fury:

> *Then Saul's anger was kindled against Jonathan, and he said to him, "You son of a perverse, rebellious woman, do I not know that you have chosen the son of Jesse to your own shame, and to the shame of your mother's nakedness?" (v. 30)*

The abuse was extreme, verging on the obscene. The literal truth was, of course, that Jonathan *was* the son of a perverse, rebellious *man!*[6] But Saul was unlikely to express his insult in those terms.

Jonathan had not kept his high regard for David a secret, although the agreement between them, their covenant, appears to have been kept to themselves (cf. 1 Samuel 20:23). Jonathan had extravagantly commended David to Saul earlier, to good effect (1 Samuel 19:4-6). Saul was, however, more accurate than he may have known when he said, "you have *chosen* the son of Jesse." Actually, God had "chosen" the son of Jesse (see 1 Samuel 16:8-12), and Jonathan seems to have understood this. And Saul *knew.*

Saul saw Jonathan's attachment to David as an abuse of his family of origin ("the shame of your mother's nakedness").

JONATHAN HAD REJECTED SAUL AND HIS KINGDOM (V. 31a)

The reason for this sense of family betrayal became clear in Saul's next words: "For as long as the son of Jesse lives on the earth, neither you nor your kingdom shall be established" (v. 31a).

He was, of course, absolutely right. Jonathan's kingdom, which was Saul's kingdom, would not be established. Saul seemed to be remembering the terrible words of Samuel at Gilgal, "Now your kingdom shall not continue" (1 Samuel 13:14). And the son of Jesse had a lot to do with that. This is the first clear indication that Saul had some realization that David was the "man after [God's] own heart" of whom Samuel had spoken on that occasion (1 Samuel 13:14). What he failed to mention, however, was that Samuel had told Saul that if he had "kept the command of the LORD your God . . . *then* the Lord would have established your kingdom over Israel for ever" (1 Samuel 13:13). The son of Jesse was not to blame for the end of Saul's and Jonathan's kingdom. Neither was Jonathan. Saul was.

"SON OF DEATH" (V. 31b)

Saul's ranting rage concluded with the words, "Therefore send and bring him to me, for he shall surely die" (v. 31b) — literally, "for he is a son of death." "You, Jonathan, are the son of a rebellious woman, but the son of Jesse is a son of death!"

This was a direct command from Saul to his son to conspire with him to kill David. How clearly Saul understood what he was doing is difficult to say. What is clear, however, is that he was raging, plotting ("in vain" as it will turn out), taking counsel with Jonathan (if we can put it like that) and setting himself and if possible his son "against the LORD and against his Anointed" (see Psalm 2:1, 2).

Jonathan was faced with a terrible choice.

Jonathan's Defense of David (v. 32)

He did not, however, hesitate: "Then Jonathan answered Saul his father, 'Why should he be put to death? What has he done?'" (v. 32).

The focus remains on the father-son relationship.[7] We hardly need to be told yet again that Saul was Jonathan's father. But that is the point here. Jonathan was being forced to choose between David and his father, the king.

He was using the words of David from the beginning of this chapter: "What have I done?" (v. 1). His words were, in effect, a brief restatement of his earlier defense of David to Saul (1 Samuel 19:4, 5). They were very powerful because they were in the form of two questions to which Saul had no answer whatsoever.

What David had *done*, we have been told again and again was to kill Goliath and continue to do much damage to Saul's real enemy, the Philistines (see 1 Samuel 18:5, 7, 14, 27, 30; 19:8).

Saul's Threat to Jonathan (vv. 33, 34)

Jonathan's questions could not be answered reasonably, so Saul chose to answer them in another way.

SAUL'S VIOLENCE AND ITS MEANING (v. 33)

But Saul hurled his spear at him to strike him. (v. 33a)

As we would say, Saul lost it. A moment ago he was in a rage because the son of Jesse would rob Jonathan of his kingdom. Now he tried to take away his son's life!

The significant thing for us to see is that Saul now identified Jonathan with David. Three times that same spear had been hurled by that same hand at David. Now Jonathan, by his allegiance to David, had become the target of the spear.

With astonishing understatement the writer then informs us: "So Jonathan knew that his father was determined to put David to death" (v. 33b).

Saul "knew" that Jonathan had chosen David. Now Jonathan "knew," by the spear that had just missed him, that Saul was, after all, determined to destroy David. Again it is important that Jonathan understood that the attack on him demonstrated his father's hatred of David.

JONATHAN'S ANGER AND ITS CAUSE (v. 34)

Jonathan was still in a position to choose. His father's intimidation and the clear danger for himself of identifying with David could have persuaded him to relinquish his commitment to the son of Jesse.

But that is not what happened:

And Jonathan rose from the table in fierce anger and ate no food the second day of the month, for he was grieved for David, because his father had disgraced him. (v. 34)

"Grieved," just as David had earlier said he would be.[8] Whom Saul "disgraced" (Jonathan or David) is not clear, but it hardly matters, for he humiliated them both. Jonathan's allegiance to his father had been brought to an end.

THE OUTCOME: DAVID'S DEPARTURE (vv. 35-42)

The rest of the chapter tells us how Jonathan conveyed to David the news of Saul's reaction to the test and how the outcome was David's departure.

The Secret Message (vv. 35-40)

> *In the morning Jonathan went out into the field to the appointment with David, and with him a little boy. And he said to his boy, "Run and find the arrows that I shoot." As the boy ran, he shot an arrow beyond him. And when the boy came to the place of the arrow that Jonathan had shot, Jonathan called after the boy and said, "Is not the arrow beyond you?" And Jonathan called after the boy, "Hurry! Be quick! Do not stay!" So Jonathan's boy gathered up the arrows and came to his master. But the boy knew nothing. Only Jonathan and David knew the matter. (vv. 35-39)*

The message had been secretly conveyed to David as planned. Using the prearranged code of "beyond you," Jonathan signaled to David that "the LORD has sent you away" (1 Samuel 20:22).[9]

In a psychologically understandable departure from the plan, Jonathan (impulsively it would seem) moved to go beyond the secret signaling: "And Jonathan gave his weapons to his boy and said to him, 'Go and carry them to the city'" (v. 40).

That got rid of the boy. It also left Jonathan defenseless. Remember that Jonathan had just been told in no uncertain terms by his father that David was the family's number-one enemy. Jonathan was about to approach him *without his weapons*. On the one hand this signaled to David that Jonathan had no hostile intentions, despite his father. On the other hand, Jonathan was expressing his own confidence in David by approaching him in this way.

David and Jonathan (vv. 41, 42)

The reason for sending the boy away was so Jonathan and David could meet rather than just send signals.

DAVID'S GRIEF (V. 41)

That meeting was one of history's moving farewell scenes. We have previously emphasized that Jonathan's commitment to David had a political dimension. He recognized and welcomed David's coming reign as king. This should not diminish our appreciation of the personal affection they felt for each other. Nowhere is that clearer than in this scene:

> *And as soon as the boy had gone, David rose from beside the stone heap and fell on his face to the ground and bowed three times. And they kissed one another and wept with one another, David weeping the most. (v. 41)*

We notice that David continued to act as Jonathan's subordinate. He bowed three times. David was not yet king and would not claim the kingship for himself ahead of time. The twice repeated words "one another" represent a Hebrew expression that means literally, "a man, his friend (or neighbor)." The last word was the one used when Samuel told Saul that the kingdom had been given "to a *neighbor* of yours, who is better than you" (1 Samuel 15:28). Jonathan in this scene kissed and wept for this "neighbor."

The kiss, of course, must be understood in the context. In the Old Testament the kiss was an expression of friendship, but also of veneration.[10] Samuel had kissed Saul when he anointed him as king (1 Samuel 10:1). Kisses will appear in the story of David with a variety of political motives, both good and bad (see 2 Samuel 14:33; 15:5; 19:39; 20:9). Perhaps the most astonishing reference to kissing in the Old Testament is Psalm 2, where the kings of the earth are called to "kiss the Son" (v. 12), that is, the Lord's anointed King. There the kiss is an expression of submission and acknowledgment, a reversal of the raging and plotting against the Lord and his Anointed at the beginning of the psalm.

None of this is to suggest that the kissing at the farewell between David and Jonathan did not express genuine affection. It just suggests that it also involved a mutual recognition of their present positions and the future that Jonathan in particular could see. David's kiss was the very opposite of any form of hostility toward the heir to Saul's throne. Jonathan's kiss expressed his glad acceptance of David as the future king he knew that he would be.

What are we to make of their weeping? It is true that these tears must have been the tears of farewell between two friends. The events of this chapter had led them both to the conclusion that the Lord had "sent [David] away" (vv. 13, 22). More than this, however, it seems likely that the two friends wept at the circumstances that had made this departure necessary — namely, the hostility of Saul toward David that meant Jonathan had to choose between David and his father. Neither David nor Jonathan wanted enmity with Saul, but Saul had made it unavoidable. There was tragedy in that.

You might think that it was Jonathan who had lost the most in this situation, but David wept the most.[11] David had no desire to harm Saul, nor to destroy Saul's relationship with his son. The damage was all Saul's doing. It was no less tragic for that.

Jonathan's "Peace" (v. 42)

Jonathan had the final word (he was, remember, still the one with the position of power):

> *Then Jonathan said to David, "Go in peace, because we have sworn both of us in the name of the Lord, saying, 'The Lord shall be between me and you, and between my offspring and your offspring, forever.'" And he rose and departed, and Jonathan went into the city. (v. 42)*

Between Jonathan and David there was to be "peace." The cost of this peace, however, had been the enmity of Saul. The only way that Jonathan could have had "peace" with his father would have been to repudiate his commitment to David.

Jonathan and David were not to know whether they would ever meet again. As it happened they did meet one more time, in very difficult circumstances (1 Samuel 23:16-18). At this point, however, Jonathan looked again to the future kingdom of David and reiterated the commitment the two of them had made to peace forever.

In many ways, in the story that 1 Samuel tells, Jonathan is a model of a disciple of the future king. Jesus said, "If the world hates you, know that it has hated me before it hated you" (John 15:18), and we can well imagine David saying to Jonathan, "If Saul hates you, know that he has hated me before he hated you." As the spear whistled past Jonathan's ear, it would have made sense for him to hear the words of the later Christ: "If they persecuted me, they will also persecute you" (John 15:20).

Jonathan seems to me to be the Bible's clearest example of what Jesus meant when he said:

> *"If anyone comes to me and does not hate his own father and mother and wife and children and brothers and sisters, yes, and even his own life, he cannot be my disciple." (Luke 14:26)*

It was not simply a matter of comparative degrees of love — that Jonathan must love David *more than* he loved his father. It was a matter of choosing between the future king and his own flesh and blood when his own flesh and blood had chosen enmity to the future king.

We cannot know whether Jesus had Jonathan in mind when he spoke of hating one's own father, but I would not be at all surprised if he did. Jesus certainly knew himself to be living the life of the Christ, which David had done before him. We should, then, see ourselves as living the life of his disciples, which Jonathan has done before us.

36

"Have You Not Read
What David Did?"

1 SAMUEL 21:1-9

On a Sabbath, while he [Jesus] was going through the grainfields, his disciples plucked and ate some heads of grain, rubbing them in their hands. But some of the Pharisees said, "Why are you doing what is not lawful to do on the Sabbath?" And Jesus answered them, "Have you not read what David did when he was hungry, he and those who were with him: how he entered the house of God and took and ate the bread of the Presence, which is not lawful for any but the priests to eat, and also gave it to those with him?" And he said to them, "The Son of Man is lord of the Sabbath." (Luke 6:1-5)

It was a Sabbath day, and Jesus and his disciples were walking through the fields. As his disciples plucked some grain, they were doing something explicitly allowed by the Law:

If you go into your neighbor's standing grain, you may pluck the ears with your hand, but you shall not put a sickle to your neighbor's standing grain. (Deuteronomy 23:25)

It seems that Jesus and his disciples were being watched closely, for some Pharisees immediately raised the question of their doing something that was "not lawful to do *on the Sabbath*." It was not lawful to work on the Sabbath, and harvesting grain is work (see Exodus 34:21)! Were not the disciples harvesting grain?

Jesus' reply refused to argue on the Pharisees' grounds. As was his custom, he took over the conversation and turned it to his own purpose. He asked them to think about the episode in David's life that we are going to examine now.

About a thousand years before that Sabbath day, David had finally departed from Gibeah and began his life as a fugitive from Saul. Saul's hostility had been shown to be definite and determined. Even Jonathan, Saul's son but also David's friend, had reluctantly seen the impossibility of David staying safely around Saul. David's life on the run from Saul had begun.

It is probable that Jesus saw the developing hostility of the Pharisees and other Jewish leaders toward him as comparable to the growing animosity of Saul toward David. That could be one reason that Jesus' mind went to the incident we are about to study.

THE HUNGRY FED (vv. 1-6)

When David left Jonathan, presumably on the outskirts of Gibeah, he headed just a few miles south to Nob and Ahimelech the priest: "Then David came to Nob to Ahimelech the priest" (v. 1a).

There are historical details that would be fascinating to know but can only be pieced together by us from fragments of information. It seems likely that much earlier, after the Philistines had captured the ark and Eli and his sons had died (1 Samuel 4), the Shiloh sanctuary that we saw at the very beginning of 1 Samuel was destroyed.[1] Nob then seems to have become "the city of the priests" (1 Samuel 22:19), and the tabernacle had apparently been relocated there.

A little earlier David had sought refuge with Samuel the prophet at Ramah, and there he had been remarkably protected by the Spirit of God (1 Samuel 19:18-24). Now he came to Ahimelech the priest at Nob. Ahimelech was a great-grandson of Eli.[2] He was "the priest," that is, the chief priest. Although this encounter would be very different, it is significant that David found help and support from both the prophet and the priest. Both, in different ways, were not exactly on good terms with Saul.[3]

However, Ahimelech was hardly overjoyed to see David: "And Ahimelech came to meet David trembling and said to him, 'Why are you alone, and no one with you?'" (v. 1b).

Ahimelech "trembled" at the approach of David as his great-grandfather had "trembled" on the day the ark of God was lost, as the people of Israel had "trembled" before the Philistines, as the Philistines had in their turn "trembled" before the Israelites, and as the elders of Bethlehem had "trembled" when Samuel came on his secret mission (1 Samuel 4:13; 13:7; 14:15; 16:4; cf. 28:5). In other words, the term indicates a profound fear. Terror would not be too strong a word for what Ahimelech felt as he saw David approach. Why?

As when Samuel had come to Bethlehem to anoint God's new king, the terror seems to have been aroused because the visitor had, or may have, fallen out with King Saul. Seeing David alone, without any of his men or servants, seems to have suggested to Ahimelech that David was a fugitive. The sequel to this episode in the next chapter will show that Ahimelech had good reason to tremble.

For the moment, however, David sought to put the priest's fears to rest:

> *And David said to Ahimelech the priest, "The king has charged me with a matter and said to me, 'Let no one know anything of the matter about which I send you, and with which I have charged you.' I have made an appointment with the young men for such and such a place." (v. 2)*

This is probably what it seems to be — a fabricated story. Some have suggested there may have been a double meaning in David's words. They were almost true if we understand "the king" to be God, who has indeed charged David with a secret "matter," namely, the future kingdom.[4] That seems to me to be too subtle. It still leaves the last bit about an appointment with the young men unexplained.

More likely, David was doing exactly what he appears to have been doing — deceiving Ahimelech in order to calm his fears and win his trust.[5] The deception would have disastrous consequences in due course, which David would deeply regret (see 1 Samuel 22:22). The Biblical narrative does not pause to pass a moral judgment on David's lie one way or the other. It does show us, however, that David was not prepared to trust Ahimelech. Whether or not David's doubts were justified, we cannot now know.

David continued: "Now then, what do you have on hand? Give me five loaves of bread, or whatever is here" (v. 3).

Literally, David asked, "What is there under your hand?" David was interested in something that the priest had charge over.[6] What was he after? Well, he was hungry, so food would come in handy, but that would not be all.

As it happened, and as David would have known, the priest did have food in his care and charge: "And the priest answered David, 'I have no common bread on hand, but there is holy bread — if the young men have kept themselves from women'" (v. 4).

He had no ordinary bread "under his hand," only the bread that had been consecrated, set aside for use in the tabernacle. These were the twelve loaves baked according to the regulations in Leviticus 24:5-9. These loaves were, according to the Law, to be arranged on the table in the tabernacle every Sabbath day (Leviticus 24:8). It could be implied, therefore, that the day David came to Nob may have been a Sabbath day (like the day Jesus' disciples plucked the ears of grain).[7]

More directly to the point, according to the Law this bread was to be eaten by priests ("Aaron and his sons") "in a holy place" (Leviticus 24:9).

It is therefore puzzling that Ahimelech offered this bread to David and his purported young men on the condition that they had not engaged in sexual relations recently. There are two puzzles here. Behind Ahimelech's words is the Law in Leviticus that says that sexual intercourse temporarily rendered a person "unclean" (Leviticus 15:18; cf. Exodus 19:15). Why is that? Sex within marriage and the birth of children are clearly good gifts from God (Genesis 1:28; 9:7; Psalm 127:3-5; 128:3-6; not to mention the Song of Solomon!). It had to do with the symbolic system that those laws of Leviticus set up. In that system the loss of life liquids (blood or semen) symbolized death. Such a loss, in various life circumstances, rendered persons "unclean" until they had recovered from the loss, in the Leviticus symbolic system.[8] (It is important to understand that the Bible consistently regards sexual relations in marriage as good.)

The second puzzle in Ahimelech's words is, why did he offer the holy bread to David and his young men, even if he added the condition that they not be ritually unclean? They were not priests, and the Law provided that the bread was to be eaten by priests. Why was he apparently scrupulous about one aspect of the Law (the young men must not be unclean) and yet flexible on the other point? Let's leave that puzzle for the moment and follow the conversation between the priest and David:

> *And David answered the priest, "Truly women have been kept from us as always when I go on an expedition. The vessels of the young men are holy even when it is an ordinary journey. How much more today will their vessels be holy?" (v. 5)*

David kept up his story about having young men nearby.[9] Of course they had been kept from sexual relations, he said, as always on David's missions and especially on a mission as important as this secret one! The men, their clothes and their equipment were holy, not unclean.[10]

> *So the priest gave him the holy bread, for there was no bread there but the bread of the Presence, which is removed from before the LORD, to be replaced by hot bread on the day it is taken away. (v. 6)*

Anyone who knows the law of Leviticus still cannot help wondering why "the priest gave [David] the holy bread." What prompted Ahimelech to bend the Law that provided that this food was to be eaten by priests?

We cannot explain his action as careless disregard for the Law, for he took particular care with reference to uncleanness.

It does not seem at all likely that Ahimelech could or would have bent the rules for *any* hungry man who happened to ask for food. It was not, in other words, simply a case of loving his neighbor or putting compassion ahead of ritual, as some have suggested.[11] That it was *David* making the request made the crucial difference.[12]

I doubt that we can answer with confidence the question about Ahimelech's conscious motives. They are simply not revealed to us. However, *what* he did (as distinct from *why* he did it) was of greater significance than he probably knew. Just as Saul had been presented with loaves of bread by three men "going up to God at Bethel" in the immediate aftermath of his anointing as king (1 Samuel 10:3, 4), so David had now been given loaves of holy bread by the priest at Nob. The precise significance is elusive, but the suggestion that in some sense God was providing sustenance for his anointed king in each case is attractive.

More than that, we may sense that God's Law is intended to serve, not hinder, the coming of God's kingdom. It is possible, as the Pharisees of Jesus' day would prove again, to oppose God's king in the name of obedience to God's Law! Ahimelech, to his credit, did not do that.

DOEG THE EDOMITE (v. 7)

At this point we are told something that will turn out to be very important indeed when we come to the terrible sequel to this incident in 1 Samuel 22. While the conversation had been taking place between David and Ahimelech, in the background, in the shadows, was an almost unnoticed figure. But our attention is drawn to him:

> *Now a certain man of the servants of Saul was there that day, detained before the LORD. His name was Doeg the Edomite, the chief of Saul's herdsmen. (v. 7)*

Remember that name. We will meet Doeg again, though we will not be pleased to see him (1 Samuel 22:9)!

As our attention is drawn to him here, we should be alarmed. He was one of "the servants of Saul"! *All* of the servants of Saul had earlier been informed of Saul's intention to kill David (1 Samuel 19:1). And David had come to Nob because he had ascertained the firmness of Saul's intent.

Doeg was "the chief of Saul's herdsmen" or "the strongman of Saul's shepherds." There is perhaps a suggestion that Saul would prefer Doeg to David. David had been a shepherd.[13] Now this Doeg was Saul's shepherd strongman![14]

Furthermore Doeg was "the Edomite." Saul fought the Edomites (1 Samuel 14:47). Perhaps he had taken Doeg into his service after defeating them.[15] The Edomites were historic enemies of Israel. Descended from Esau (Genesis 25:30; 36:9), they had refused the Israelites safe passage in the days of Moses (Numbers 20:14-21). This unkind act against their brother people was not forgotten and was the pattern for Edom's later dealings with Israel (see Numbers 24:18; Judges 11:17; 2 Samuel 8:13, 14; 1 Kings 11:14-22; 2 Chronicles 28:17; Psalm 137:7; Isaiah 34:5-9; Jeremiah 49:7-22; Lamentations 4:21, 22; Ezekiel 25:12-14; 35; Amos 1:11; Obadiah). They had acted as the Amalekites had done, and we can vividly remember what happened to them (see 1 Samuel 15:2, 3). It is disturbing to see an Edomite servant of Saul, a strongman, lurking in the shadows at Nob.

We are told that he was there because he was "detained before the LORD," which sounds like some kind of punishment.[16] Be that as it may, the clear point is that Doeg was under Saul's control, and in due course we will see him do Saul's terrible will. For the time being, however, Doeg is left there in the shadows, ominously observing all that was happening.

THE DEFENSELESS ARMED (vv. 8, 9)

The conversation between David and Ahimelech continued. Food was not all that David wanted from the priest:

> *Then David said to Ahimelech, "Then have you not here a spear or a sword at hand? For I have brought neither my sword nor my weapons with me, because the king's business required haste." (v. 8)*

David was not only hungry, he was defenseless. He had indeed left the king in too much haste to either gather provisions or even collect his weapons. The circumstances were, however, very different from what he was leading Ahimelech to think.

Just as there had been food under the care and control of the priest,[17] was there perhaps a weapon? David asked. Perhaps a sword? That is a strange thing to ask a priest, except, of course, that just as David had known very well there was bread under Ahimelech's control, we strongly suspect that he knew full well that a sword *had* been entrusted to him. He was right:

> *And the priest said, "The sword of Goliath the Philistine, whom you struck down in the Valley of Elah, behold, it is here wrapped in a cloth behind the ephod. If you will take that, take it, for there is none but that here." (v. 9a)*

Again there is a story here that we are not fully told. At the end of the account of the slaying of Goliath we were told that David put the Philistine's "armor" or "weapons" in his tent. How and when the sword was entrusted to Ahimelech is not told, but it is likely that David would have known about it.

It seems very probable that this was the purpose of David's visit to Ahimelech all along. More important for the fugitive from Saul than five loaves of bread was the great sword of Goliath. Certainly he was eager to get it into his hands: "And David said, 'There is none like that; give it to me'" (v. 9b).

There was a time, not long previously in this narrative, when David had to refuse Saul's armor and weapons, but he had on that occasion put Goliath's sword to good use (1 Samuel 17:51)! Now he was no longer a shepherd boy with no experience of war. He eagerly took possession of Goliath's sword and (as we read in the next verse) rose and continued his flight from Saul.

Let us return to that Sabbath day a thousand years after this day when David came to Nob. Jesus said to the Pharisees who were accusing him:

> *"Have you not read what David did when he was hungry, he and those who were with him: how he entered the house of God and took and ate the bread of the Presence, which is not lawful for any but the priests to eat, and also gave it to those with him?" (Luke 6:3, 4)*

The exchange with the Pharisees could easily have become a debate about what was and wasn't lawful on the Sabbath and whether plucking some heads of grain and rubbing them in your hands constitutes harvesting and threshing. That is the kind of discussion the Pharisees had invited.

Jesus did not give them the satisfaction. Instead he accused them of not reading, or at least not understanding, the Scriptures. Jesus was doing what *David* had done.[18] In other words, Jesus' response to the Pharisees was not an argument about the interpretation of the Law or about the interpretation of his disciples' actions, but a claim to be one *like David*!

The events at Nob must be understood in the light of the fact that David was God's chosen king. Whatever Ahimelech was *thinking*, his *actions* were right. He served God's king. He did not attempt to set God's Law over against God's king. In due course we will see that he laid down his life for God's king.

In Jesus something *greater* than David had come. Jesus concluded this altercation with the Pharisees by saying, "The Son of Man is lord of the Sabbath" (Luke 6:5).

This son of David (Luke 3:31; 18:38, 39), who called himself the Son of Man, claimed an authority at least as great as the Law of God! And he was despised, opposed, and eventually killed.

The fugitive David found a few who believed in him. There were Jonathan, Michal, Samuel, and (at least in his actions) Ahimelech.

The Pharisees, in their hostility to Jesus, were more like Saul. In fact, in their sinister surveillance of Jesus and his actions, they were more like Doeg the Edomite! The resemblance became closer, for a few lines later in Luke's record, after Jesus had demonstrated his authority and power as lord of the Sabbath, we read: "But they were filled with fury and discussed with one another what they might do to Jesus" (Luke 6:11).

God's King is still despised and opposed. He is still less than impressive to many. Will you join the ranks of Saul, Doeg, and the Pharisees or the body of those who serve the King, whatever the cost?

37

Out of the Frying Pan . . .

1 SAMUEL 21:10-15

Approximately the last third of the book of 1 Samuel is devoted to the period in which David was on the run from King Saul. It might seem a little like the long chase scene at the end of some movies. The hero lurches from one crisis to the next. He escapes one threat, only to fall into deeper danger. How he will ever make it to safety is beyond us!

Perhaps because of the length and apparent repetitiveness of this part of the book, it is easy for Bible readers to miss its very great importance. Modern Bible readers can too easily impose their own ideas of what is interesting and valuable and become impatient with the Bible's priorities. If we are prepared to allow the Bible to teach us what is important, however, we will accept that something dealt with at length in the pages of the Bible may be more important than we initially realize.

One clue to the significance of these chapters of 1 Samuel is the fact that the book of Psalms contains no fewer than seven psalms that are explicitly associated with the events recounted here.[1] Many other psalms also reflect a situation of great distress that is not clearly and obviously identified, but it is very likely that a considerable number of these also originated in the dark days for David recounted in the latter part of 1 Samuel. If that is the case, we have the situation that not only are David's fugitive days treated at length in 1 Samuel, but also another part of the Bible — namely, the Psalms — draws our attention repeatedly to these experiences of David.

When we then notice that the New Testament frequently cites the book of Psalms to explain or proclaim Jesus,[2] we may begin to appreciate that David's fugitive years were very important indeed. At least some of the psalms referred to in the New Testament for this purpose probably originated out of David's experience on the run from Saul. Best known, perhaps, are the momentous words of Jesus from the cross, "My God, my God, why have you forsaken me?" (Matthew 27:46; Mark 15:34). These words were first David's and possibly originated in the period to which we are referring. Is it possible there is some connection between David's experiences fleeing from Saul and what happened when Jesus died on the cross?

The book of Psalms points us to these experiences of David as the context for much of the pain and suffering expressed in the psalms. Jesus and the New Testament point us to the psalms to explain that Jesus is the Christ and that he had to suffer and rise from the dead. Therefore we are going to see that David's experiences on the run from Saul, while exciting enough in their own right, are of monumental importance! Here we can expect to learn more deeply the meaning of the gospel message that Jesus is the Christ and the meaning of his suffering and his rising from the dead.

It may not, then, be coincidental that approximately a third of each of the Gospel accounts of the New Testament is devoted to the last week of Jesus' earthly life,[3] just as about the last third of 1 Samuel is about these troubles of David. These sufferings of David (and his deliverances) correspond in important ways to the sufferings of Jesus (and his resurrection).

David's flight from Saul began in 1 Samuel 19, when Saul for the third time tried to pin David to the wall with his spear and then sent a team of assassins to kill him at his home (vv. 8-17). David fled first to Samuel at Ramah (1 Samuel 19:18) and then, through his friendship with Saul's son Jonathan, took steps to discover whether Saul was really set in his purpose to kill him (1 Samuel 20). Once that was clear, David realized that he had no future around Saul. He went to Nob and obtained sustenance and a very impressive weapon from Ahimelech the priest (1 Samuel 21:1-9). He then continued his flight from Saul.

What David did next was dangerous and, some might say, reckless. The story is told briefly but vividly in 1 Samuel 21:10-15. That he should do what he did eloquently demonstrates the desperate peril he was facing from Saul. It is astonishing that David survived this experience.

Interestingly at least two psalms originated from this incident. They are Psalms 34 and 56. Psalm 56 is a cry from David in the terrifying plight in which he found himself. Psalm 34 is his relieved and thrilled expression of praise when it was all over.

We are going to follow what happened, as recounted in 1 Samuel 21, and at key points we will listen to the two psalms as they illuminate David's experience. We will conclude by reflecting on the connection we may then see between the experience of David here and Jesus.

DAVID FLED TO GATH (v. 10)

Nob, where David had met with Ahimelech and obtained food and a weapon, was only a short distance from Saul's town of Gibeah. Nob must have been a busy place. It was "the city of the priests" (1 Samuel 22:19), and we can imagine many people coming and going. If David could not stay safely with Samuel at Ramah (see 1 Samuel 20:1), he certainly could not stay long at Nob, particularly as he had presented himself there under the false pretense of being on an urgent mission from Saul (1 Samuel 21:2).

There have been a number of indications in the story so far of the considerable power of Saul. Just because Saul has moved somewhat to the background of the narrative, we should not imagine that he had lost his dominant sway or that David was in no real danger as long as he was careful. What David did next demonstrates that he was in desperate danger anywhere in Saul's kingdom: "And David rose and fled that day from Saul and went to Achish the king of Gath" (v. 10).

The boldness, or recklessness, of this move is stunning! We would like to know more details than we are told. Verse 10 says that David fled (literally) "from the presence of Saul." The implication is that Saul's presence could be felt, so to speak, throughout his kingdom, and the only way to escape "the presence of Saul" was to get out of Saul's dominion.[4]

Gath was about twenty-five miles southwest of Nob, down out of the hills, toward the coastal plain. Gath was, therefore, outside Saul's territory. That is the only positive thing that can be said for David's decision to flee from Saul to Gath, of all places. On the negative side is the fact that it was one of the five *Philistine* cities! What had David been doing in recent times? At every opportunity he had been fighting and inflicting serious damage on the Philistines (see 1 Samuel 18:27, 30; 19:8)! We can only suppose that David was so terribly desperate that he sought to hide from Saul in the last place Saul would expect him to be. He feared Saul more than he feared the Philistines![5]

He certainly did choose the very last place on earth that Saul would look for him, because Gath was not only one of the five Philistine cities, it was the hometown of Goliath (1 Samuel 17:4)! If there was one place on earth where you could confidently predict that David would be hated by all, it would be Gath. Saul was such a threat that David chose to take his chances in Gath rather than risk staying any longer in Saul's domain.

Do you remember what David was now carrying with him? He had taken from Nob the sword of Goliath. He had said to Ahimelech that there was none like it (1 Samuel 21:9). And now he chose to come into Gath carrying what must have been a rather difficult to hide distinctive weapon, with which he had previously very publicly cut off its Philistine owner's head!

We should appreciate the desperation that must have driven David to do something as risky as this. We can only presume that he hoped to enter Gath undercover and go into hiding as an unrecognized Hebrew fugitive.[6] The statement in verse 10 that he "went to Achish the king of Gath" probably means simply that he came into Achish's city rather than that he went and knocked on the king's door!

When we consider some words from David shortly from Psalm 56, we will see something of the terrible plight the man was in.

DAVID WAS RECOGNIZED IN GATH (vv. 11, 12)

If we have correctly understood David's thinking, he had seriously underestimated the intelligence network in Gath. His attempt to remain incognito was very quickly foiled. He was recognized, almost immediately it would seem, by Achish's men and reported to the Philistine king.

What they said to Achish is astonishing:

> And the servants of Achish said to him, "Is not this David the king of the land? Did they not sing to one another of him in dances,
> 'Saul has struck down his thousands,
> and David his ten thousands'?" (v. 11)

We have noticed many people in this story saying things that were more significant than they could have known. The words of Achish's servants could take the prize for unwittingly profound utterance.[7] Where did they get the idea that David was "the king of the land"? This was not a title used in Israel. Certainly no one in Israel was publicly calling David a king. But perhaps David's achievements in battle had given the Philistines the impression that he was, or was soon to become, the ruler of the land.[8] Perhaps, for them, Saul had already faded in importance. The narrator has already told us:

> Then the princes of the Philistines came out to battle, and as often as they came out David had more success than all the servants of Saul, so that his name was highly esteemed. (1 Samuel 18:30)

Rumors had evidently reached the Philistines about the song the women had sung that had so infuriated Saul. They apparently drew the same implications from the song as Saul did (1 Samuel 18:6-9).

Whatever the servants of Achish consciously thought, their words were truer than they knew. David *was* the one destined to be "the king of the land." David had now been acknowledged as the future king by God (in his word to Samuel, 1 Samuel 16:12), by the prophet Samuel (by anointing him, 1 Samuel 16:13), by Jonathan (by symbolically passing his robe to David, 1 Samuel 18:4; see also 20:13b-17), and now by the Philistine servants of Achish. It was the danger of being regarded as the future king in Saul's territory that had driven David to flee to Gath. Now that he had been recognized in Gath, any hope of safety there was gone. "And David took these words to heart and was much afraid of Achish the king of Gath" (v. 12).

Earlier Saul had hoped that the Philistines would do his dirty work for him

(1 Samuel 18:17, 21, 25). Unexpectedly, because of David's desperate flight to Gath, Saul's wishes may have come true. So it seemed at least to David.

David was "much afraid." We will see in the following lines that the Philistines seized him and brought him to Achish their king.

Psalm 56 is called "A Miktam of David, when the Philistines seized him in Gath."[9] In this psalm David speaks of the enemies threatening him. He seems to be thinking not only of his Philistine captors in Gath but also of Saul and his servants from whom he had fled. These oppressors are joined in David's mind.

> *Be gracious to me, O God, for man tramples on me;*
> *all day long an attacker oppresses me;*
> *my enemies trample on me all day long,*
> *for many attack me proudly. . . .*
> *All day long they injure my cause;*
> *all their thoughts are against me for evil.*
> *They stir up strife, they lurk;*
> *they watch my steps,*
> *as they have waited for my life. (Psalm 56:1, 2, 5, 6)*

"All day long," he cried. There seemed to be no end to the threats to David's life. Behind these words are the experiences of 1 Samuel 19–21 — one attempt after another to kill him. Then on the very day that he had fled from the presence of Saul, he found himself very afraid in the presence of Achish.[10]

The psalm emphasizes the *reality* of the threats and their *wickedness*. The verbs underline the reality: "tramples," "oppresses," "attack," "injure," "stir up strife," "lurk," "watch," "waited." This was David's experience "all day long." The wickedness of these threats is indicated by "proudly" and "for evil." We appreciate the wickedness of this hostility only when we remember who David was. Those who threatened him had set themselves "against the LORD and against his Anointed" (Psalm 2:2).

We have been told that in the presence of Achish, David was "much afraid" (v. 12). In the books of Samuel this is the only place in which we are told that David was afraid of the threats against him.[11] In Psalm 56 David speaks of this fear and perhaps explains why it is so rarely mentioned in the books of Samuel.

> *When I am afraid,*
> *I put my trust in you.*
> *In God, whose word I praise,*
> *in God I trust; I shall not be afraid.*
> *What can flesh do to me? (vv. 3, 4)*

There are various human responses to fear. David's response was to trust God![12] Trusting in God, he knows that he need *not* be afraid. This was not some kind of vague piety. The God he trusted was the God who had spoken, the God "whose word I praise." No doubt David knew and praised the word that God had spoken at Mount Sinai, which any Israelite could claim. But with David there was a more particular word. God had said, "Arise, anoint him, for this is he" (1 Samuel 16:12). I take it that this is the word that was particularly in his mind here. God's word had identified David as the one to whom the kingdom would be given (1 Samuel 15:28).[13] Trusting in the God who had spoken that word he asks, "What can flesh do to me?"

What indeed? If God was "for" him, who could be against him (cf. Romans 8:31)?

> *You have kept count of my tossings;*
>   *put my tears in your bottle.*
>   *Are they not in your book?*
> *Then my enemies will turn back*
>   *in the day when I call.*
>   *This I know, that God is for me. (Psalm 56:8, 9)*

Again, David's confidence that God was "for" him was not a pious wish. He was the Lord's anointed one (1 Samuel 16:13), the one "after [God's] own heart" (1 Samuel 13:14), whom God had "seen" (literal translation) for himself (1 Samuel 16:1).

The specific basis of David's trust in God, God's word concerning him, is a repeated refrain of the psalm:

> *In God, whose word I praise,*
>   *in the LORD, whose word I praise,*
> *in God I trust; I shall not be afraid.*
>   *What can man do to me? (vv. 10, 11)*

Psalm 56, therefore, casts a brilliant light on 1 Samuel 21:12, which says that David "was much afraid in the presence of Achish the king of Gath." His response to fear was to put his trust in the God whose word he believed.

DAVID ESCAPED FROM GATH (vv. 13-15)

We do not know the techniques that David used in most of his battles against the Philistines. We know, of course, the bold and skillful cunning with which he brought down Goliath. A perfectly placed stone from a slingshot was all that it took, and the nerve to land the shot! His victories since then have simply been reported without detail (1 Samuel 18:14, 27, 30; 19:8). We do not doubt, however, that David had become a courageous and highly competent commander.

David's escape from Achish was a matter of daring wit and cunning. This is what he did:

> *So he changed his behavior before them and pretended to be insane in their hands and made marks on the doors of the gate and let his spittle run down his beard. (v. 13)*

"In their hands" indicates that Achish's servants had seized David and brought him to their king.[14]

But what an act David put on for them! Slobbering hysterically, scraping the door with his nails, David put on the performance of his life. He contrived to change the fear and hatred of him to something else. Amazingly he succeeded:

> *Then Achish said to his servants, "Behold, you see the man is mad. Why then have you brought him to me? Do I lack madmen, that you have brought this fellow to behave as a madman in my presence? Shall this fellow come into my house?" (vv. 14, 15)*

David succeeded in stirring Achish to a mixture of pity and revulsion. The Philistine king could not believe that this dribbling, scraping thing was any threat to him. The accusations that he was "the king of the land" seemed absurd. Achish wanted this disgusting creature out of his sight. And as we learn from the first words of the next chapter, that is how David "escaped" from Gath.

The joke was on Achish and the Philistines. Achish himself testified that he was surrounded by idiots. The fact that Philistine Enemy Number One managed to escape from their grasp by just a bit of dribbling and scratching showed how right he was.

We might have doubted David's good sense in fleeing to Gath in the first place, but now we can hardly fail to admire his capacity for dealing with a most dangerous and difficult situation. We are amazed at David's daring and cunning.

However, if that is all we see here, we have not learned what we should from this episode. The two psalms from this day bring into sharper focus what is already implicit in the narrative of 1 Samuel 21. David's cunning is spectacular, but that is not the ultimate explanation for what happened.

At the end of Psalm 56 David said:

For you have delivered my soul from death,
    yes, my feet from falling,
that I may walk before God
    in the light of life. (v. 13)

Even before it had happened, it would seem, David expressed his confidence that God had delivered his anointed from the threats in Gath, just as he had delivered him repeatedly from Saul.

This deliverance led to the praise of Psalm 34. The title to that psalm indicates that it belongs to the occasion "when [David] changed his behavior before Abimelech [that is, Achish],[15] so that he drove him out, and he went away." David said:

I will bless the LORD at all times;
    his praise shall continually be in my mouth.
My soul makes its boast in the LORD;
    let the humble hear and be glad.
Oh, magnify the LORD with me,
    and let us exalt his name together!
I sought the LORD, and he answered me
    and delivered me from all my fears.
Those who look to him are radiant,
    and their faces shall never be ashamed.
This poor man cried, and the LORD heard him
    and saved him out of all his troubles.
The angel of the LORD encamps
    around those who fear him, and delivers them. (Psalm 34:1-7)

The prayer of Psalm 56 was answered, its trust was vindicated. I like to imagine David uttering this psalm in the cave of Adullam to which he fled after he escaped from Gath (see 1 Samuel 22:1). There his brothers and his wider family joined him, along with about 400 troubled people (1 Samuel 22:2). To these who had chosen to join the fugitive king-to-be he told the story of how God delivered this poor man from all his fears. He invited them to join him and exalt God's name together. He promised those who had joined him in the cave:

The LORD redeems the life of his servants;
    none of those who take refuge in him will be condemned. (Psalm 34:22)

The two psalms associated with David's escape from Gath point to the profound significance of this event.

As we look back on that day, not only in the light of the psalms, but also in the light of the gospel of our Lord Jesus Christ, we may see how the reality of the threats to David as the Philistines seized him foreshadowed the reality of the hostility encountered by Jesus. In other words, as the opposition grew to Jesus, he was reliving the experience of David, albeit significantly intensified. The hostility was real.

Jesus made it clear that those who followed him would encounter the same opposition:

> *"Beware of men, for they will deliver you over to courts and flog you in their synagogues, and you will be dragged before governors and kings for my sake, to bear witness before them and the Gentiles." (Matthew 10:17, 18)*

The hostility is *real.*

We also see how the wickedness of the threats against David anticipated the wickedness of those who opposed Jesus and eventually crucified him. We better understand the wickedness when we know who Jesus is, the Christ of God — they "crucified the Lord of glory" (1 Corinthians 2:8)!

Jesus taught that the wickedness of those who opposed him would be reproduced in opposition to his disciples:

> *"A disciple is not above his teacher, nor a servant above his master. It is enough for the disciple to be like his teacher, and the servant like his master. If they have called the master of the house Beelzebul, how much more will they malign those of his household." (Matthew 10:24, 25)*

The hostility is *wicked.*

As David put his trust in God that day in Gath, so in the depths of his suffering Jesus put his trust in his heavenly Father: "Father, into your hands I commit my spirit!" (Luke 23:46).

Christian, as you encounter the suffering that comes from the real and wicked hostility of those who oppose God and his Christ, do not be surprised:

> *Beloved, do not be surprised at the fiery trial when it comes upon you to test you, as though something strange were happening to you. But rejoice insofar as you share Christ's sufferings, that you may also rejoice and be glad when his glory is revealed. If you are insulted for the name of Christ, you are blessed, because the Spirit of glory and of God rests upon you. But let none of you suffer as a murderer or a thief or an evildoer or as a meddler. Yet if anyone suffers as a Christian, let him not be ashamed, but let him glorify God in that name. . . . Therefore let those who suffer according to God's will entrust their souls to a faithful Creator while doing good. (1 Peter 4:12-19)*

38

"God Chose What Was Low and Despised in the World"

1 SAMUEL 22:1-5

Who would want to be a Christian in today's world? Faith in Jesus Christ is not a passport to fame and fortune, or even pleasure and comfort. In many parts of the world it invites hardship and even persecution. While there are distorted forms of Christianity that promise health and wealth for the followers of Jesus, the Bible speaks repeatedly of the suffering that will come to those "who desire to live a godly life in Christ Jesus" (2 Timothy 3:12). While God's grace is freely given, and Jesus has paid the necessary sacrifice for us, Jesus himself taught those who would follow him to "count the cost" and to expect to suffer (for example, Matthew 5:11; Luke 14:25-33; John 16:1-4).

So who would want to be a Christian in today's world? In the first-century world, the Apostle Paul answered that question: not many impressive people by the world's standards.

For consider your calling, brothers: not many of you were wise according to worldly standards, not many were powerful, not many were of noble birth. But God chose what is foolish in the world to shame the wise; God chose what is weak in the world to shame the strong; God chose what is low and despised in the world, even things that are not, to bring to nothing things that are, so that no human being might boast in the presence of God. (1 Corinthians 1:26-29)

Most Christians will be unimpressive people in this world's terms. In this context Paul calls this God's *wisdom*. If not many of the famous, not many of the powerful, not many of the wealthy will want to be Christians in today's world, it does sharpen our question: Who *would* want to be a Christian in today's world? And where is the *wisdom* in God's doing things this way?

We are going to get a glimpse into these strange ways of God as we continue to follow David on the run from the powerful King Saul. At the end of 1 Samuel 21 we saw how in his desperation he had fled alone to the Philistine city of Gath, apparently thinking he could hide in that unexpected place. He was wrong and only escaped from the clutches of the Philistines by the skin of his teeth. David was in danger not only in Saul's territory but also now in the neighboring Philistine territory. Where could he go next?

DAVID AT ADULLAM (vv. 1, 2)

Chapter 22 opens with the answer to that question: "David departed from there and escaped to the cave of Adullam" (v. 1a).

Still alone, David had little choice but to find a hiding-place, out of the Philistine territory he had briefly tried, just over the western border of Judah. Adullam was about ten miles southeast of Gath, back into the foothills, but further south of Gibeah, where Saul was, than Nob, where David had briefly visited the priest Ahimelech.

From David's point of view he was in dire straits. The narrative so far has told us six times of David's "escaping" from Saul (1 Samuel 19:10, 11, 12, 17, 18; 20:29). Now he had "escaped" from the Philistines. Saul and the Philistines should have had very little in common, but as far as David was concerned they were equally dangerous.

David composed two more psalms from his experience in "the cave" (and it seems likely that it was this cave of Adullam).[1] Both Psalms 57 and 142 express David's trust in God "in the cave," just as he had put his trust in God in Gath. We hear David's sense of aloneness and helplessness, apart from the Lord, who was his only secure refuge. Listen to David "in the cave":

> *Be merciful to me, O God, be merciful to me,*
> *for in you my soul takes refuge;*
> *in the shadow of your wings I will take refuge,*
> *till the storms of destruction pass by.*
> *I cry out to God Most High,*
> *to God who fulfills his purpose for me.*
> *He will send from heaven and save me;*
> *he will put to shame him who tramples on me. Selah*
> *God will send out his steadfast love and his faithfulness!*

> *My soul is in the midst of lions;*
>> *I lie down amid fiery beasts—*
> *the children of man, whose teeth are spears and arrows,*
>> *whose tongues are sharp swords.*
> *Be exalted, O God, above the heavens!*
>> *Let your glory be over all the earth!*
> *They set a net for my steps;*
>> *my soul was bowed down.*
> *They dug a pit in my way,*
>> *but they have fallen into it themselves. Selah*
> *My heart is steadfast, O God,*
>> *my heart is steadfast!*
> *I will sing and make melody!*
>> *Awake, my glory!*
> *Awake, O harp and lyre!*
>> *I will awake the dawn!*
> *I will give thanks to you, O Lord, among the peoples;*
>> *I will sing praises to you among the nations.*
> *For your steadfast love is great to the heavens,*
>> *your faithfulness to the clouds.*
> *Be exalted, O God, above the heavens!*
>> *Let your glory be over all the earth! (Psalm 57)*

That was David's song in the cave of Adullam! Psalm 142 sounds a similar note.

Did you notice the words, "God who fulfills his purpose for me" (Psalm 57:2)? Consider how difficult it would have been to believe in God's purpose for David as he hid in the darkness of the cave of Adullam. What future could there be for this cornered fugitive? At the first opportunity Saul would kill him. The Philistines across the border would do the same if given another chance. Huddled alone in a cave was the only safe place he could find — and how long would that be safe? Yet he could speak of the "God who fulfills his purpose for me." We know that purpose: it was to give this poor man the kingdom.[2] How that could happen was beyond imagining. Nonetheless this man praised God's word and put his trust in him (Psalm 56:4, 10, 11), and so he knew the "God who fulfills his purpose for me."

His Family (v. 1b)

As David hid in the cave, news of David's hiding-place reached his family. Somehow he must have sent word to them. "And when his brothers and all his father's house heard it, they went down there to him" (v. 1b).

Things had changed somewhat since the day little David had appeared in the Valley of Elah to watch Goliath. On that day his older brother Eliab had angrily tried to put the young upstart (as he saw him) in his place (1 Samuel 17:28). Much had happened since that day. We are told nothing here of David's brothers' thoughts now. David had become a great and famous commander before becoming an enemy of the king.

Perhaps we should give them the benefit of the doubt and assume that their joining David in the cave expressed their solidarity with him. It might be unfair to labor the point that they probably had little choice. Saul's hatred of David was certain to spill over to his family. They, too, were on the run from Saul.

His Company (v. 2)

Very soon, however, it became clear that David's family were not the only ones suffering in Saul's kingdom. Before long the cave of Adullam became rather crowded. "And everyone who was in distress, and everyone who was in debt, and everyone who was bitter in soul, gathered to him" (v. 2a).

Before Saul had become king, Samuel had warned the people of the ways of the kind of king they were demanding. He had said:

> "These will be the ways of the king who will reign over you: he will take your sons and appoint them to his chariots and to be his horsemen and to run before his chariots. And he will appoint for himself commanders of thousands and commanders of fifties, and some to plow his ground and to reap his harvest, and to make his implements of war and the equipment of his chariots. He will take your daughters to be perfumers and cooks and bakers. He will take the best of your fields and vineyards and olive orchards and give them to his servants. He will take the tenth of your grain and of your vineyards and give it to his officers and to his servants. He will take your male servants and female servants and the best of your young men and your donkeys, and put them to his work. He will take the tenth of your flocks, and you shall be his slaves. (1 Samuel 8:11-17)

We will see a little later in this chapter that some benefited from Saul's reign (see v. 7), but they were not the ones who came to the cave of Adullam. It was the losers, the debtors, the downtrodden, the bitter, those disillusioned with such a kingdom. They were so dissatisfied with Saul that they joined the poor man hiding in the cave of Adullam. How desperate can one be?

This was not perhaps the kind of crowd David would have chosen for company, had he a choice. We might say that "not many were wise according to human standards, not many were powerful, not many were of noble birth" (cf. 1 Corinthians 1:26). Rather they were the weak and the despised. "Tax collectors and sinners," we might say (cf. Luke 7:34).

"And he became captain over them. And there were with him about four hundred men" (v. 2b).

No longer was David alone, but you could be forgiven for wondering whether he was not better off *before* he gained this crowd of nobodies. To be captain over this lot was not particularly promising. It was a far worse situation than when Saul had earlier demoted David to "a commander of a thousand" to get him out of his sight (1 Samuel 18:13).[3] Here he had only 400, and they were not exactly crack troops!

You will have noticed that we have returned to the idea with which we began. We might ask, who would want to join David in Saul's world? And here we see the answer. It was those who had nothing to gain in Saul's world, those who had lost out in Saul's world, those who were disillusioned with Saul's world. This is a point to which we will return.

Before we do, however, we will follow three movements made by David, so briefly reported that they could easily be overlooked.

DAVID IN MOAB AND THE STRONGHOLD (vv. 3, 4)

First, we are told that David went from the cave of Adullam to the east: "And David went from there to Mizpeh of Moab" (v. 3a).

This can be translated "the lookout of Moab."[4] To get to Moab, David would have had to cross the hills and the Jordan River. Moab was an eastern neighbor to Israel's territory, as the land of the Philistines was to the west. Moab is listed as one of the enemies of Saul, against whom he had successfully fought (1 Samuel 14:47). Was David hoping to find asylum as a fellow enemy of Saul? While he will craftily employ a tactic a bit like that later (see 1 Samuel 27), his purpose in visiting Moab was different: "And he said to the king of Moab, 'Please let my father and my mother stay with you, till I know what God will do for me'" (v. 3b).

Moab might have been Saul's enemies, but David had family connections. His great-grandmother was Ruth, the Moabite (Ruth 4:13, 18-22). Ruth's faithfulness bore fruit this day, more than a century later. David's journey to Moab was family business. He was taking care of his aging parents, getting them out of harm's way until the shape of the future became clearer.

We have seen Saul's disintegrating family relationships as the hostility grew between father and son. It is interesting to notice the reverse happening with David. It seems that his older brothers had joined him, and, in contrast to Saul, David's parents enjoyed their son's care and protection.

David was uncertain about "what God will do for me." He had the confidence we heard in Psalm 57 that ultimately God would "fulfill his purpose for me," but he did not know how that would happen or when, and he did not know what hardships lay ahead.[5]

He therefore did what he could to provide for the safety of his father and mother: "And he left them with the king of Moab, and they stayed with him all the time that David was in the stronghold" (v. 4).

The narrator seems to be in a hurry to get to the very important event that he recounts from verse 6, for he skips over details that were apparently less important. We do not know whether or not David took his 400 men with him to Moab. Either way, after the negotiations with the king of Moab he seems to have taken his men to a "stronghold," possibly in the rough terrain between Moab and Israel.[6] He stayed there for some time (as the words "all the time that David was in the stronghold" suggest), but we know nothing of what happened.

INTO THE FOREST OF HERETH (v. 5)

His third movement was prompted by the appearance of a prophet with a word for David: "Then the prophet Gad said to David, 'Do not remain in the stronghold; depart, and go into the land of Judah'" (v. 5a).

This is the first, but not the last, time this prophet is mentioned (see 2 Samuel 24:10-19; 1 Chronicles 21:7-19; 29:29; 2 Chronicles 29:25). In the next verse we will read that Saul heard news about David and his men. That may be the reason for the prophet's message. If so, it is interesting to see the prophet acting to protect David from Saul, just as we saw the Spirit of the Lord doing the same thing in a different way at Ramah (1 Samuel 19:18-24).

However, it was more than that. God was fulfilling his purpose for David, and for whatever reason that involved David's returning now to the land of Judah, the land he would one day rule. It was not just a matter of his safety, for it would have been safer to go east, into the land of Moab. In Judah David would encounter Saul's power again. He would suffer.

David did as the prophet said: "So David departed and went into the forest of Hereth" (v. 5b).

Who would want to be a Christian in today's world? is a question very like, who would want to join David in the days of Saul?

The reality was that to throw in your lot with David meant abandoning any hope of benefiting from Saul's power. It is not really surprising that those most likely to join David were those who had learned that Saul's power was never going to benefit them. If you held any hope that Saul would do you good, you would not make your way to the cave of Adullam.

The call of the gospel of Jesus Christ is no less radical. It is not at all surprising that not many of those who have great prospects in this world find themselves called into the kingdom of Jesus Christ. Perhaps it is understandable that Christians get very excited when a famous person becomes a Christian. We ought, of course, to rejoice whenever *any* sinner repents! But excessive attention to the few famous people who come to faith in Christ is mistaken. In his wisdom God has chosen to call *few* such people. Have we forgotten that if you hold any hope that this world will provide you with security and hope, you will not make your way to Jesus? How good it is that he receives the kind of people who came to David in the cave!

39

The Antichrist

1 SAMUEL 22:6-23

*For many deceivers have gone out into the world, those who do not confess
the coming of Jesus Christ in the flesh. Such a one is the deceiver and the
antichrist. (2 John 7)*

The letters of John in the New Testament contain the Bible's five references to "antichrist" (1 John 2:18 twice, 22; 4:3; 2 John 7), although the idea
is found more widely. While there have been various views among Christians
about the identity of *the* Antichrist, we should not miss the emphasis of John
that "many antichrists have come" (1 John 2:18) and that "the spirit of the
antichrist . . . is in the world already" (1 John 4:3). *Antichrist* means one
who opposes the Christ.[1] The ultimate antichrist is Satan, but John was keen
to alert his readers that they would encounter many antichrists. He was at
pains to ensure that they would recognize the spirit of antichrist wherever it
appeared: "Who is the liar but he who denies that Jesus is the Christ? This is
the antichrist, he who denies the Father and the Son" (1 John 2:22).

Jesus is the Christ, but a thousand years before Jesus, David was the
christ or the anointed. Just as we have been learning about Jesus by hearing
about his "father" David, so we should learn about the antichrist as we hear
about those who denied that David was the christ. A growing number of
people, in one way or another, were confessing David. Most important and
clear was Jonathan (for example, 1 Samuel 20:16). Most surprising were the
Philistines of Gath who spoke more than they knew (1 Samuel 21:11). Most
recently in our story 400 distressed people from Saul's kingdom had joined
David in the cave of Adullam (1 Samuel 22:2).

In 1 Samuel 22:5 we left David, presumably with his entourage of 400 men, hiding in the forest of Hereth, somewhere in Judah.

SAUL AT GIBEAH WITH HIS BENJAMINITE SERVANTS (vv. 6-10)

The narrative now leaves David. We will return to him at the end of this chapter, but before we do, we move north to Gibeah to see what Saul was doing. We were last in Gibeah in 1 Samuel 20, and our last sighting of Saul was when he hurled his spear at Jonathan in rage at his son's defense of David's innocence (vv. 32, 33). Since then we have followed the movements of David as he fled from Saul, first to Nob (1 Samuel 21:1), then to Gath (1 Samuel 21:10), then to the cave of Adullam (1 Samuel 22:1). Then came a side trip to Moab (1 Samuel 22:3), a period in an unidentified stronghold (1 Samuel 22:4), and hiding in the forest of Hereth (1 Samuel 22:5).

We arrive at Gibeah at an important moment for Saul: "Now Saul heard that David was discovered, and the men who were with him" (v. 6a).

This is probably at least a slight flashback. Saul probably heard about David and the men with him while they were in the stronghold referred to at the end of 1 Samuel 22:4, where David stayed for some time. This news reaching Saul would then be at least one reason for the prophet Gad urging David to move on from there (1 Samuel 22:5).[2] In any case, this was the first time since David fled from Ramah at the end of 1 Samuel 19 that Saul had received any reliable news about his enemy. David's attempts to keep away from Saul's attention had been successful for some time, but now Saul heard news of David. How much had he heard? What would he now do?

Saul heard about David "and the men who were with him." He therefore had learned something (we do not know how much) about the 400 losers who had joined David in the cave of Adullam, last mentioned explicitly in verse 2. Keep them in mind as the scene in Gibeah unfolds.

Saul Secure (v. 6b)

Take a good look at Saul: "Saul was sitting at Gibeah under the tamarisk tree on the height with his spear in his hand, and all his servants were standing about him" (v. 6b).

The scene makes a stark contrast to what we saw earlier in the cave of Adullam. Saul was at ease ("sitting"), out in the open ("under the tamarisk tree"), on the hill at Gibeah. The physical surroundings could not be more different from the cave in which David's men had assembled.

Saul had "his spear in his hand." The weapon of Saul's mad jealous rage was, as usual, in his hand — the very spear that had been repeatedly hurled at David (1 Samuel 18:11; 19:10) and more recently at Jonathan

(1 Samuel 20:33). Saul's spear represented what had forced David into his life as a fugitive.

Around Saul were "all his servants." How different they must have looked compared to the motley bunch that had gathered around David in the cave of Adullam.

We saw Saul in a scene like this earlier, before the menace of David had come into his life. On the day when Jonathan had slipped away to attack the Philistine garrison for the second time, we saw Saul, sitting under the pomegranate tree, just outside Gibeah, with 600 men around him (1 Samuel 14:2). As then, this scene had all the appearance of security. Saul had no need to hide in a cave. He did not need to beg a priest for a weapon. He did not have to accept the downtrodden as his company. Who would you rather be with, looking at these two scenes, Saul or David?

Saul's Insecurity (vv. 7, 8)

Appearances of security are, however, an illusion. Saul was full of fears. Listen to him address his servants: "And Saul said to his servants who stood about him, 'Hear now, people of Benjamin . . .'" (v. 7a).

This is literally "sons of Benjamin."[3] The first thing we notice is that Saul's servants were all apparently from his own tribe (see 1 Samuel 9:1, 2). Nepotism probably flowed from Saul's paranoia, which made it difficult for him to trust anyone. His fears, however, flowed even to these servants:

> " . . . will the son of Jesse give every one of you fields and vineyards, will he make you all commanders of thousands and commanders of hundreds, that all of you have conspired against me? No one discloses to me when my son makes a covenant with the son of Jesse. None of you is sorry for me or discloses to me that my son has stirred up my servant against me, to lie in wait, as at this day." (vv. 7b, 8)

He does not sound as secure as he looked, does he? Saul did not compose any psalms! Someone has described this as "the ranting and raving of a desperate man."[4] There was no evidence whatsoever that his servants were contemplating any form of disloyalty. Saul, however, was in the grip of his fears that had nothing to do with facts.

We cannot miss a critical note of irony here. Unwittingly Saul's words echoed what Samuel had said at the very beginning of this king business, when he had warned the people about what the king they were demanding would be like. He had said:

> "These will be the ways of the king who will reign over you . . . he will appoint for himself commanders of thousands and commanders of fif-

*ties. . . . He will take the best of your fields and vineyards and olive
orchards and* give them to his servants.*" (1 Samuel 8:11, 12, 14)*

Saul testified to the fact that he had indeed been that kind of king! The
beneficiaries of his ways were his fellow Benjaminites, with whom he had
surrounded himself.

The greater irony is that Saul unconsciously also testified to the fact that
the son of Jesse would *not* be that kind of king![5] Those who had gathered to
David in the cave of Adullam were no doubt those who had suffered under
the kind of king Saul had (on his own admission here) been. Those who had
stayed with Saul were his cronies who profited from his ways.

He could not trust them, however. Haunted by conspiracy theories, he
ranted.

We can imagine an embarrassed silence following his tirade. *No one
here thinks he would be better off with David. None of us has conspired
against you. No information has been withheld from you. No one here has
any idea what you are talking about!*[6] Those would have been the thoughts.
But no one dared say a word.

Saul's Friend: Doeg the Edomite (vv. 9, 10)

The silence was at last broken, not by one of the Benjaminite servants, but by
a foreigner we spotted a chapter earlier in another place (1 Samuel 21:7).

> *Then answered Doeg the Edomite, who stood by the servants of Saul, "I
> saw the son of Jesse coming to Nob, to Ahimelech the son of Ahitub, and
> he inquired of the LORD for him and gave him provisions and gave him the
> sword of Goliath the Philistine." (vv. 9, 10)*

At last Saul had found a friend who would not join the imagined conspiracy but would tell all he knew to the king.[7] And he had something to
tell!

We do not know how Doeg came to be in Gibeah. When we saw him at
Nob we were told that he was "detained before the LORD." Since we are not
quite sure what that means, it is perhaps idle to speculate how he came to be
in Saul's company now. We do know, however, that most of what he said
was true. He did see David come to Nob, to Ahimelech. He saw the priest
give David food and the sword of Goliath. However, no mention was made in
chapter 21 of Ahimelech inquiring of the Lord for David. If he had, and if it
was going to be important in this sequel, it is fair to assume that it would have
been mentioned. We may suspect therefore that Doeg added that element to
make his report to Saul even more in line with what Saul wanted to hear.[8]

Furthermore, what he did *not* say was as important as what he did say.

He did not mention that David had persuaded the priest to provide him with food and arms by a story about being on a mission for Saul. In other words, Ahimelech had given these things to David in the mistaken belief that David was serving Saul. We do not suppose that this vital piece of information would have made any difference to Saul, but that Doeg omitted it helps us to see what he was doing.

David reflected on this moment in Psalm 52:

> Why do you boast of evil, O mighty man?
>> The steadfast love of God endures all the day.
> Your tongue plots destruction,
>> like a sharp razor, you worker of deceit.
> You love evil more than good,
>> and lying more than speaking what is right. Selah
> You love all words that devour,
>> O deceitful tongue. (vv. 1-4)

That about sums up Doeg!

SAUL AT GIBEAH WITH AHIMELECH AND THE PRIESTS (vv. 11-19)

What happened next was not pretty. Saul now had a culprit on whom to vent his obsessive fury. The king summoned not only Ahimelech but all the priests of Nob to appear before him at Gibeah:

> Then the king sent to summon Ahimelech the priest, the son of Ahitub, and all his father's house, the priests who were at Nob, and all of them came to the king. (v. 11)

In another intriguing echo of what happened with David in the cave of Adullam, Ahimelech was summoned to Saul with "all his father's house." David's brothers had come to him in the cave with "all his father's house" (1 Samuel 22:1). The experience of the two families at the hands of the king and the king-to-be respectively could not have been more different.

Saul's mood must have been widely known, and so Ahimelech and the other priests would have come to Gibeah with considerable trepidation.

Saul's Paranoid Accusation (vv. 12, 13)

In the cave David's family found a man who would take steps to ensure the safety of his father and mother (1 Samuel 27:3). At Gibeah, Ahimelech and his family faced a furious and unreasoning king: "And Saul said, 'Hear now, son of Ahitub'" (v. 12a).

In "a shocking piece of rudeness,"[9] the king did not give the priest the dignity of his own name. As David was just "the son of Jesse" to Saul, so Ahimelech was "son of Ahitub."

The priest, however, replied with dignity and respect: "And he answered, 'Here I am, my lord'" (v. 12b).

Dignity and respect is not what came his way in return:

> *And Saul said to him, "Why have you conspired against me, you and the son of Jesse, in that you have given him bread and a sword and have inquired of God for him, so that he has risen against me, to lie in wait, as at this day?" (v. 13)*

Everyone, you will notice, was a part of Saul's elaborate conspiracy theory. Everyone was against poor old Saul. Everyone was on David's side — Jonathan, his servants, and now the priest. And, of course, David was out to get him.

Ahimelech's Truthful Defense (vv. 14, 15)

Whereas the servants of Saul had known better than to try to reason with the mad king, Ahimelech perhaps did not know him as well.

> *Then Ahimelech answered the king, "And who among all your servants is so faithful as David, who is the king's son-in-law, and captain over your bodyguard, and honored in your house?" (v. 14)*

The trouble, of course, with Ahimelech's defense was that it was true. David had served Saul faithfully and effectively. He had the support of Saul's daughter Michal, his wife. Saul had entrusted him with considerable military responsibilities. The reference to all Saul's house honoring him was also true but unfortunately provocative. Saul had nearly killed his son for his friendship with David. He had rebuked his daughter for helping her husband. There is an innocent naiveté about Ahimelech's truthful testimony.

As far as supplying food and a sword to David, Ahimelech had nothing to say. It was true. He did say something, however, about the charge of inquiring of God for David: "Is today the first time that I have inquired of God for him? No!" (v. 15a).

The trouble is, we cannot be sure what Ahimelech meant. Was he saying, "This is not the first time I have inquired of God for David. It has never been a problem in the past. Why accuse me now?"[10] More likely he was saying, "I have never inquired of God for David. Why would I start now?"[11]

Ahimelech concluded his eloquent and truthful defense with a deferential appeal to his and his family's innocence:

> *"Let not the king impute anything to his servant or to all the house of my father, for your servant has known nothing of all this, much or little."* (v. 15b)

He had no knowledge whatsoever of any conspiracy by David or by himself or by any of his fellow priests. We know that was absolutely true.

Saul's Unreasonable Verdict (vv. 16-19)

Ahimelech's defense did not move Saul, however. As accuser and judge, Saul pronounced his verdict and sentence without reference to anything that had been said.

PRONOUNCED (v. 16)

> *And the king said, "You shall surely die, Ahimelech, you and all your father's house." (v. 16)*

This king had become deadly. He had threatened his son with death twice. He had, of course, likewise threatened David. Neither of these threats had yet been successfully carried out. Would this terrible threat to kill all of the priests be different?

RESISTED (v. 17)

At first it seemed that the priests would be spared in much the same way that Jonathan had been spared when Saul first threatened him (1 Samuel 14:45). There was resistance to the king's unjust and wicked will:

> *And the king said to the guard who stood about him, "Turn and kill the priests of the LORD, because their hand also is with David, and they knew that he fled and did not disclose it to me." But the servants of the king would not put out their hand to strike the priests of the LORD. (v. 17)*

This was not a betrayal of Saul, but the servants, like the people in chapter 14, could see the disastrous foolishness and wickedness of what the king had ordered. They would not do this.

Executed (vv. 18, 19)

Saul, however, had one obedient hatchet man. He now turned to him:

> *Then the king said to Doeg, "You turn and strike the priests." And Doeg*
> *the Edomite turned and struck down the priests, and he killed on that day*
> *eighty-five persons who wore the linen ephod. And Nob, the city of the*
> *priests, he put to the sword; both man and woman, child and infant, ox,*
> *donkey and sheep, he put to the sword. (vv. 18, 19)*

Doeg exceeded the king's order, but we hear of no attempt from Saul to hold him back, and no protest from Saul at his wholesale slaughter. That day Doeg proved himself to be a true Edomite.[12]

What Doeg did to Nob, with at least Saul's tacit approval, is described in terms that echo the judgment of God on corrupt pagan nations.[13] Specifically it was like the judgment that God had commanded Saul to inflict on the Amalekites (1 Samuel 15:3). Now (through his Edomite henchman) Saul dealt with his own people as he had been commanded, but failed, to deal with the Amalekites! The dreadful corruption of Saul was complete. "The well-meaning farmer's son who became king has turned into a bloody tyrant."[14]

Saul, the king of Israel whom the people had chosen for themselves, but not the man after God's own heart, had become like Pharaoh in the days of Moses, the slaughtering destroyer of Israel. He had become like Herod in the days of Jesus, killing the infants of Bethlehem out of his fear of the Christ. He had become the antichrist.

There is an important footnote to this tragedy. While it was the wicked work of an evil king, it was not outside God's sovereign purposes. Evil never is. We must be very careful not to claim to know the mind and purpose of God when we see suffering. What we do know is that he is sovereign, and all things do work together toward his good purpose. In this case, however, we have a clear word from God about the event. Much earlier in our story a prophet came to old Eli with a terrible message. It included these words:

> *"Behold, the days are coming when I will cut off your strength and the*
> *strength of your father's house, so that there will not be an old man in*
> *your house. Then in distress you will look with envious eye on all the*
> *prosperity that shall be bestowed on Israel, and there shall not be an old*
> *man in your house forever. The only one of you whom I shall not cut off*
> *from my altar shall be spared to weep his eyes out to grieve his heart,*
> *and all the descendants of your house shall die by the sword of men."*
> *(1 Samuel 2:31-33)*

What happened in Nob that dreadful day was connected with the wickedness of Ahimelech's great-grandfather Phinehas and his brother Hophni, Eli's depraved sons.

THE ONE WHO ESCAPED: ABIATHAR (vv. 20-23)

We have one final scene, in which we follow a single escapee from the slaughter at Nob. In the prophecy, God had spoken of "the only one of you whom I shall not cut off from my altar" (1 Samuel 2:33). Now we see him.

Fleeing to David (vv. 20, 21)

Where do you think a lone escapee from the massacre in Nob would go? "But one of the sons of Ahimelech the son of Ahitub, named Abiathar, escaped and fled after David" (v. 20).

Somehow he found David, probably (as we will see) in the vicinity of Keilah (see 1 Samuel 23:6). "And Abiathar told David that Saul had killed the priests of the LORD" (v. 21).

With bitter irony, Abiathar's name means "my father remains."[15] Although, no doubt, God was the "father" of the name, it is deeply moving to see the man with *that* name come to David with his terrible news.

Safe with David (vv. 22, 23)

Now observe the contrast between the christ and the antichrist, between David here and Saul in the previous scene:

And David said to Abiathar, "I knew on that day, when Doeg the Edomite was there, that he would surely tell Saul. I have occasioned the death of all the persons of your father's house. Stay with me; do not be afraid, for he who seeks my life seeks your life. With me you shall be in safekeeping." (vv. 22, 23)

Whatever reasonable criticisms we might have of David's conduct at Nob, we cannot miss the contrast between the way he here takes responsibility for what had happened (in the sense that he should have foreseen it and somehow dealt with Doeg) and the utter lack of responsibility we have seen in Saul. David now took responsibility for the safety of Abiathar.

You would understand, wouldn't you, if Abiathar had just a little difficulty in seeing the logic of David's comfort: "he who seeks my life seeks your life. With me you shall be in safekeeping." But it is the logic of the gospel! The christ (David) is opposed by the antichrist, but with the christ you will be safe.

Only if you believe the gospel of the christ would you choose to leave Saul and join David. But it is obvious to us, isn't it, who will be king in the end. Can you entertain any doubt at all about whether Saul or David will triumph from this conflict? If we had been there, true enough, it would have been hard to find comfort in the message given to Abiathar. The tangible power was in the hands of Saul.

Likewise it may be hard for us to choose to be Christ's. But to stay with the antichrist makes no sense at all. Not when you see him as he really is.

40

The Christ Must Suffer

1 SAMUEL 23:1-14

Why? That tiny word is always uttered with urgency, earnestness, and even desperation when it is about *suffering*. When we suffer or we witness others suffer, it is hardly possible to suppress the question, why?

Mind you, we do not necessarily expect an answer. Some of us have cried out too often. We have learned that for all the urgency of the question, answers elude us. But still we ask, why? because we cannot escape the sense that life should not be like this. There should not be *such* suffering as there is in life, and there should not be so much of it. No one wants suffering. No one likes suffering. We all fear suffering. Yet suffering of so many different kinds is simply inescapable in this life. So we continue to ask, why?

In today's world it is generally assumed that suffering is *morally* random. We do not see any connection whatsoever between wickedness and suffering (or between goodness and not suffering). That much of the book of Job makes sense to us today. We do not think much of the arguments of Job's friends when they link his suffering with his supposed guilt. We rarely (if ever) make that connection when we see someone suffer or when we suffer ourselves. However, that is not so much because we have learned from the book of Job but because we have learned from our secular environment no longer to think in *moral* categories. If we do not struggle with the *moral* problem of suffering, it is probably because we have ceased to believe seriously in a moral universe.

Our perplexity about suffering has another dimension: we struggle with the relationship between *power* and suffering. This is not a distinctively modern problem, but it has modern expressions because human power has peculiar contemporary forms. Human power has always taken a variety of forms, from material wealth to physical health, from social standing to personal charisma. Although we no longer believe that *goodness* is any shield against suffering, we have come to a deep belief that *power* can protect us. Isn't that why we pursue power of various kinds? We have come to understand that money can buy private health care, fitness can ward off disease, status can protect you, and a powerful personality can save you from many troubles. Power, of various kinds, is our answer to suffering.

But, of course, it isn't. One of the most perplexing puzzles of human life for us is the fact that suffering appears to be not only morally random but also no respecter of human power. The rich can afford to hide their suffering but cannot escape from it. The physically fit avoid some diseases, only to fall to others. And so on. Whatever form of human power you rely on, it *will* let you down. It will not save you from suffering. And yet the myth that power can beat suffering persists and drives much of modern life.

I wonder whether we have understood with sufficient clarity that the Bible is a book about suffering. At least it is a book that has a great deal to say about suffering. From the third chapter of the first book to the last chapter of the last book the theme of suffering is never far from any page, and often it fills the page. The Bible understands humankind to be a suffering race. Old Testament Israel was a suffering nation, from Egypt to Babylon. The climactic moment of the whole Bible was a moment of perplexing suffering: "My God, why . . . ?" (Matthew 27:46; Mark 15:34).

What God says about suffering in the Scriptures is even more bewildering to our minds than the confusion of our experiences. And at the very heart of the Bible's words about suffering is the statement, "The Christ must suffer."

Jesus said:

> *"O foolish ones, and slow of heart to believe all that the prophets have spoken! Was it not necessary that* the Christ should suffer . . ." *(Luke 24:25, 26)*

> *"Thus it is written, that* the Christ should suffer . . ." *(Luke 24:46)*

This proposition confounded the disciples (see, for example, Mark 8:31-33). It scandalized the Jews, and it was foolishness to the Greeks (see 1 Corinthians 1:23). Yet, according to Jesus, it is the sure teaching of Scripture. It became central to the apostolic preaching. Peter said:

> *But what God foretold by the mouth of all the prophets,* that his Christ would suffer, *he thus fulfilled. (Acts 3:18)*

Or consider Paul in Thessalonica:

*. . . on three Sabbath days he reasoned with them from the Scriptures,
explaining and proving that* it was necessary for the Christ to suffer. *. . .
(Acts 17:2, 3)*

Paul stated before Agrippa:

*"I stand here testifying both to small and great, saying nothing but what
the prophets and Moses said would come to pass: that* the Christ must
suffer. . . ." *(Acts 26:22, 23)*

This is simply incomprehensible to our normal ways of thinking because
it turns the two possible ways we have of making sense of suffering upside
down. If the Christ must suffer, then goodness and suffering are not opposed
but linked, for the Christ is the Righteous One! If the Christ must suffer,
then power does not ward off suffering but submits to it, for the Christ is
the Mighty One!

In the chapters of 1 Samuel we have been studying, and the ones we will
soon examine, the most obvious thing to notice is that they contain so much
suffering. Chapter 22 was the worst so far. We have seen that these chapters
provide the background to many of the psalms, which speak so vividly of
suffering. At the center of this suffering was David, God's anointed one, or
messiah, or christ. That is how we must understand him since that day in
Bethlehem when, at the Lord's command, Samuel anointed him (1 Samuel
16:12, 13).

Although it is far from clear at this point in the story how God's purpose
for David will be realized, it is obvious that David was the one after God's
own heart — that is, the one on whom God had set his heart to be his king
(1 Samuel 13:14). He was, in this sense, the christ. These chapters are about
his suffering. I am confident that the Scriptures Jesus had in mind when he
said that the Christ must suffer included the pages before us now.

Last time we saw the stark contrast between Saul, who said to the priest
of Nob, "You shall surely die, Ahimelech, you and all your father's house,"
and David who said to the only priest to escape Saul's massacre, "Stay
with me; do not be afraid, for he who seeks my life seeks your life. With
me you shall be in safekeeping" (1 Samuel 22:16, 23). The antichrist and
the christ.

DAVID AND THE PHILISTINES (vv. 1-5)

There are reasons, which we will touch on shortly, for thinking that the
beginning of chapter 23 takes us back a little in time. I think it likely that
what we are about to see is what was taking place with David at the very
time that Saul was arranging the slaughter in Gibeah and Nob.[1] First Samuel

22 ended with Abiathar reaching David. We will catch up to that point in time in 1 Samuel 23:6.

As Saul was doing his ghastly work in Gibeah and Nob, what was David doing?

David the Willing Savior (vv. 1, 2)

> Now they told David, "Behold, the Philistines are fighting against Keilah and are robbing the threshing floors." Therefore David inquired of the LORD, "Shall I go and attack these Philistines?" And the LORD said to David, "Go and attack the Philistines and save Keilah." (vv. 1, 2)

Keilah was a town near the western border of Judah, near the edge of Philistine territory. It was just a few miles south of Adullam. There is some debate as to whether Keilah was an Israelite town at this time or not.[2] In the absence of any clear indication to the contrary, we may assume that a town David was sent to "save" was Israelite.

At about the same time as news reached Saul that David had been discovered (1 Samuel 22:6), news reached David of a Philistine attack on a border town, probably not too far from his own hiding-place in the forest of Hereth (1 Samuel 22:5). Since he had met Goliath, David's main task had been striking down Philistines. In this respect he had taken on the job that Saul had been appointed to do ("He shall *save* my people from the hand of the Philistines," 1 Samuel 9:16). It is remarkable that at the same time as Saul was becoming more and more obsessed with imagined conspiracies (and giving no attention at all to his primary responsibility as king, namely, the protection of his people), David, the one running for his life from Saul, cared enough about an Israelite town to pause and ask whether he should save them.

We can carry the comparison further. Remember Saul's speech in response to the news that reached him, that ranting tirade about everyone being against him (1 Samuel 22:7, 8). How different was David's response to the news that reached him — he prayed. He asked the Lord what to do.

Saul's answer and guidance (if you can call it that) came from Doeg the Edomite (1 Samuel 22:9, 10). David's came from the Lord: "Go and attack the Philistines and save Keilah."

This is an important moment. This is the first time in the story that we have heard direct communication between David and the Lord. The last time we heard the words "the LORD said" was that day in Bethlehem when "the LORD said [to Samuel], 'Arise, anoint him, for this is he'" (1 Samuel 16:12). As very often in the Bible, we are given no particular information about the manner of God's speaking. There have been times when the voice of God has been audible. That was the case at Mount Sinai (see Deuteronomy 4:12), and it was apparently the case in the boy Samuel's experience (1 Samuel 3:4, 6, 8, 10). It could have been the case here. We do not know.[3]

The *means* by which God spoke, however, is less important than the *fact* that he spoke and *what* he said. Since the departure of Samuel, Saul had been unable to receive guidance from God, though he had tried. There was an occasion when he had asked almost the same question David asked: "Shall I go down after the Philistines? Will you give them into the hand of Israel?" But he received no answer (1 Samuel 14:37). Since then, apart from the words of condemnation by the prophet Samuel — and even that was some time ago now (1 Samuel 15:16-23) — Saul had received no word from God. For information, he was dependent on the likes of Doeg the Edomite!

How different was David! He brought his question to the Lord and received an immediate answer. "Go and attack the Philistines and *save* Keilah." Though David himself was under threat, he was to do the work of God's king and save his people.

David's Fearful Followers (v. 3)

The proposal, however, did not find an enthusiastic response from David's men: "But David's men said to him, 'Behold, we are afraid here in Judah; how much more then if we go to Keilah against the armies of the Philistines?'" (v. 3).

Quite reasonably they found their situation demanding enough as it was. They may not have known yet that Saul had heard of their whereabouts, but they must have known that could happen at any time. They certainly knew of Saul's mood, and they may have had some idea of the ferocious violence he could display. It was dangerous enough in the forest of Hereth, with Saul to worry about. Was it really a good idea to take on the Philistines as well at this time?

They sounded a little like the disciples of Jesus later as he set his face to go to Jerusalem. Wasn't there enough trouble for them in Galilee? Was it really a good idea to head for Jerusalem at that time? (See Matthew 16:21, 22; Mark 10:32; Luke 9:51, 53; 18:31-34.)

Assurance, Obedience, Success (vv. 4, 5)

David's response was not to argue with the men but again to consult the Lord. The unwillingness of his men changed the situation somewhat. Did the Lord still want him to go against the Philistines?[4]

Then David inquired of the LORD again. And the LORD answered him, "Arise, go down to Keilah, for I will give the Philistines into your hand." (v. 4)

Can't get clearer than that! The promise already implicit in the earlier command was now made explicit. The word "I" is emphatic. Fears and apprehensions were answered by the promise of God — literally, "*I* am giving the Philistines into your hand."

Notice the close connection between the command and the promise. The command is to "Go" and do something that would normally be terrifying. The promise changes that: "*for* I am giving the Philistines into your hand." The command alone seems unreasonable and reckless, but if the promise is true, then the command is completely realistic!

The commands of God are always like this. They should never be isolated from the promises of God. Then God's commands seem burdensome, difficult, and even terrifying. Consider, in isolation, the Lord's command, "Go and make disciples of all nations." How do you think that sounded to the small group of men who first heard it? What could ever make such an extraordinary command acceptable? The promise attached to it: "*I* [the "I" is emphatic here too] am with you always, to the end of the age" (Matthew 28:19, 20).

God's promise to David introduced a theme that will run through this chapter with the word "hand."[5] "Hand" represents power. The Lord was giving the Philistines into David's "hand" or power.

The command and the promise met obedience: "And David and his men went to Keilah and fought with the Philistines and brought away their livestock and struck them with a great blow" (v. 5a).

In the obedience to the command, the promise proved true. "So David saved the inhabitants of Keilah" (v. 5b).

As Saul was overseeing the slaughter of the priests of Nob, David was saving the people of Keilah! Saul the destroyer — David the savior.

DAVID AND GOD (vv. 6-14)

The fundamental difference between Saul and David that the narrative is drawing to our attention in this chapter is that God spoke to David but no longer spoke to Saul.[6] This, of course, can be traced back to Saul's disobedience and God's choice of David to be a different kind of king.

David and Abiathar (v. 6)

In the astonishing way in which God is able to bring good out of the most terrible evil, Saul's slaughter resulted in a further expression of God's kindness to David — the arrival of Abiathar. Since Abiathar's survival from the Nob massacre was important to note as the conclusion to that story, Abiathar's meeting with David was movingly described at the end of 1 Samuel 22. I have been suggesting that 1 Samuel 23 takes us back a little in time and tells us what was happening with David as Saul was murdering the priests. If that is right, then Abiathar found David, as verse 6 indicates, in Keilah *after* he had fought the Philistines and saved the town.

I think, therefore, that verse 6 should be translated as the RSV and NRSV have done it (rather than the ESV and NIV, who use past perfect tenses):[7] "When Abiathar the son of Ahimelech fled to David to Keilah, he came down with an ephod in his hand" (RSV).

David, it seems, had various ways in which to receive God's communication to him. Earlier the prophet Gad had instructed him to move from "the stronghold" (1 Samuel 22:5). David could, it seems, seek answers directly from God, as he did about Keilah. Now the surviving priest had arrived with an ephod.

This seems to have been the ephod that belonged to the high priest,[8] Abiathar's murdered father, Ahimelech. All priests wore an ephod, called a "linen ephod,"[9] but the high priest's ephod was a more elaborate affair (see Exodus 28:6-14; 39:2-7).[10] Attached to this ephod was the breast-piece, which contained the Urim and Thummim (Exodus 28:30; Leviticus 8:8), associated with receiving revelation from God (see Numbers 27:21; 1 Samuel 28:6; Ezra 2:63; Nehemiah 7:65). We do not know the details of how this happened, probably because, once again, to the Bible writers the *fact* and the *content* of divine revelation were far more important than the mechanism.[11]

The important point here is that Saul's dreadful atrocity toward the priests of Nob had the unintended consequence of putting another means of consulting the Lord into the hands of David!

First Samuel 23:6 also has the second occurrence of the key word "hand" in this chapter. The power associated with the ephod had passed from Ahimelech to his son, who now made it accessible to David.

Saul's Threat (vv. 7, 8)

We turn now from David in Keilah back to Saul, presumably still in Gibeah, perhaps sitting under his tamarisk tree on the hill (cf. 1 Samuel 22:6). Saul received some more news in the only way in which he learned anything these days. Someone, but certainly not the Lord, told him: "Now it was told Saul that David had come to Keilah" (v. 7a).

This was the only kind of news Saul was interested in, and it cheered him up. Saul's *only* interest these days was the eradication of David. "And Saul said, 'God has given him into my hand, for he has shut himself in by entering a town that has gates and bars'" (v. 7b).

We do not hear Saul rejoice at the deliverance of Keilah from the Philistines! He praises God for giving[12] David into his "hand." The irony of the bloody tyrant (that is what Saul had become) claiming that God was working for him is bitter.

This third occurrence of "hand" introduces *Saul's* power to the chapter. His power was real and effective — for death and destruction. The blood of eighty-five priests proved it. He believed that David was now within the reach of his power.

And so Saul, with his terrible obsession, put himself again in the position of acting like the Philistines. Like them, he planned to attack Keilah: "And Saul summoned all the people to war, to go down to Keilah, to besiege David and his men" (v. 8).

David's Questions (vv. 9-12)

We move back to Keilah to see what David was doing as Saul was plotting his attack on the town. What we are told is delightful: "David *knew* that Saul was plotting harm against him" (v. 9a).

For Saul, knowledge about David was hard to come by. But as soon as he had received some news and formed a plan, David *knew!*[13] The fugitive David, with his band of misfits, had better intelligence services than the king!

What did he do with his information? "And he said to Abiathar the priest, 'Bring the ephod here'" (v. 9b).

There is little point in pondering why David consulted God one way, then another way. We know too little about the "ways" to comment. The important thing, once again, is *that* he consulted God. Threatened again by Saul, he prayed. Listen to what he asked:

> Then said David, "O LORD, the God of Israel, your servant has surely heard that Saul seeks to come to Keilah, to destroy the city on my account. Will the men of Keilah surrender me into his hand? Will Saul come down, as your servant has heard? O LORD, the God of Israel, please tell your servant." (vv. 10, 11a)

He addressed God as "O LORD, *the God of Israel.*" The threat against David was a crisis for the nation. David had two concerns. One was the threat Saul posed to Keilah. Was it true? Would Saul come against the city David had so recently delivered from the Philistines? The other concern was the threat that Keilah could pose to David. Would they deliver him up into Saul's "hand" (there's that word again)?

The Lord answered the first question: "And the LORD said, 'He will come down'" (v. 11b).

David repeated the second question: "Then David said, 'Will the men of Keilah surrender me and my men into the hand of Saul?' And the LORD said, 'They will surrender you'" (v. 12).

The power of Saul must have been terrible. No blame is laid by David, the Lord, or the writer on the people of Keilah. We are merely left with the impression that the fear of Saul's fury against anyone who aided David was greater than whatever gratitude they felt to the one who delivered them from the Philistines.[14] They had heard about Nob!

David's Escape (vv. 13, 14)

If David cared for Keilah, there was only one course of action open to him: "Then David and his men, who were about six hundred, arose and departed from Keilah, and they went wherever they could go" (v. 13a).

The 400 who had joined him in the cave of Adullam (1 Samuel 22:2) had grown by 50 percent. They all left Keilah but found themselves with nowhere to lay their heads. "When Saul was told that David had escaped from Keilah, he gave up the expedition" (v. 13b).

Thwarted again. "And David remained in the strongholds in the wilderness, in the hill country of the wilderness of Ziph. And Saul sought him every day, but God did not give him into his hand" (v. 14).

In case we are a little slow, the writer points out that what Saul had claimed ("God has given him into my hand," v. 7) was not true!

First Samuel 23:1-14 has not focused on David's suffering, but we should not lose sight of the fact that he was a threatened fugitive. He had nowhere to lay his head. His followers were afraid. He could not trust himself even to those he saved from the Philistines.

He was committed to the safety of his people, the defeat of their enemies, and doing the will of God. But his kingdom was bitterly opposed by the one with worldly power. So the christ must suffer.

If Jesus knew the story of David — and of course he did — it is not surprising, is it, that he should say "Thus it is written, that the Christ should suffer . . ." (Luke 24:46). He had nowhere to lay his head. His followers were afraid. He could not trust himself even to those he came to save. He was committed to the salvation of his people, the defeat of their enemies, and doing the will of God. His kingdom was bitterly opposed by the great Antichrist, the ruler of this world (John 12:31; 14:30; 16:11).

What a Savior we have in Jesus, the great son of David!

41

"Therefore We Do Not Lose Heart"

1 SAMUEL 23:15-29

Therefore, having this ministry by the mercy of God, we do not lose heart. . . . But we have this treasure in jars of clay, to show that the surpassing power belongs to God and not to us. We are afflicted in every way, but not crushed; perplexed, but not driven to despair; persecuted, but not forsaken; struck down, but not destroyed; always carrying in the body the death of Jesus, so that the life of Jesus may also be manifested in our bodies. For we who live are always being given over to death for Jesus' sake, so that the life of Jesus also may be manifested in our mortal flesh. So death is at work in us, but life in you. . . . So we do not lose heart. Though our outer nature is wasting away, our inner nature is being renewed day by day. For this slight momentary affliction is preparing for us an eternal weight of glory beyond all comparison, as we look not to the things that are seen but to the things that are unseen. For the things that are seen are transient, but the things that are unseen are eternal. (2 Corinthians 4:1, 7-12, 16-18)

In these words of the Apostle Paul we hear the astonishing and unparalleled Christian perspective on suffering, with its conclusion, "Therefore we do not lose heart." This is not stoicism, nor a stiff upper lip. There is no hint here of any kind of masochism — finding pleasure in suffering. Nor is there any element of denial — pretending the sharp reality of pain is less dreadful than it is. The pain is there. Suffering is awful. It hurts. Yet, "we do not lose heart." What is it that produces the Christian words, "we do not lose heart"? Where do they come from?

The key idea in the long narrative that occupies the last third of the book of 1 Samuel is the sufferings of David on his painful path to the throne. On every page from chapter 18 to the end of the book, we see David suffering and others suffering on account of David. We have discovered that many of the psalms are linked to this narrative and speak in their own way of the sufferings of David. We have also realized that as we listen to the story of David's sufferings in the context of the whole Bible, the theme of these pages appears again with astonishing simplicity and power in the New Testament message: "The Christ *must* suffer."

As we hear the Old Testament it is always important to both listen carefully to the text itself and also to listen to what happens to the text's truth in the New Testament. That is another way of saying that the life, death, and resurrection of Jesus Christ are so important that everything in the history of the world, before and after his coming, should be understood in the light of who he is, what he has done, and what he will yet do.

As we follow the story of David's troubles and listen to the echoes of his experience in the New Testament, we will understand why the sufferings of David are important, why it matters that the Christ must suffer, why we cannot be unmoved by the gospel that *Jesus* is the Christ, and why "we do not lose heart."

At the point we have reached in the story, the pressure on David had become immense. Saul's determination to eliminate David had become a nationwide manhunt. Saul was focused on discovering David's whereabouts. He was prepared to brutally punish any who offered David help. This had meant that David could not even trust himself to the people of Keilah, whom he had recently rescued from the Philistines. He was on the run and had headed south, further from Saul's base at Gibeah in the north.

The second half of 1 Samuel 23 brings us two episodes, distinguished by the characters and their very different dealings with David. In the first of these Jonathan met with David for the last time (1 Samuel 23:15-18). In the second Saul came within an inch of catching David (1 Samuel 23:19-29).

DAVID AND JONATHAN (vv. 15-18)

Saul's threat (v. 15)

Saul's threat to David still dominates the story: "David saw that Saul had come out to seek his life. David was in the wilderness of Ziph at Horesh" (v. 15).

Ziph was in southern Judah, about twelve miles south of Keilah, in the hills. The location will be important for the second episode.

Notice how the text says that "David saw" the hostile intentions of Saul. The enmity, from Saul's side, had been building since the day David killed Goliath, and the women sang, "Saul has struck down his thousands, and David his ten thousands" (1 Samuel 18:7). Anyone looking at this situation would see the terrifying, prevailing fact of Saul's determination to find David and take his life.

The text seems to be suggesting that this was a particularly low point for David. His location was depressing — the Wilderness of Ziph was not exactly a palace! His circumstances were depressing — would there be no end to Saul's obsessive hatred? David had been nothing but a faithful servant to the king, but there was nothing more he could do to turn Saul's enmity away.

David's Future (vv. 16, 17)

For the time being, Saul was unable to find his enemy. But someone else found him: "And Jonathan, Saul's son, rose and went to David at Horesh. . . ." (v. 16a).

Saul's son, Jonathan, was the best friend David had in the world. We last saw him at the end of chapter 20, when he and David had learned the depth of Saul's determined hostility toward David. David had left the region of Gibeah that day and had been on the run since — to Nob, Gath, Adullam, Moab, the forest of Hereth, Keilah, and now the Wilderness of Ziph. Jonathan was the person who had most clearly and gladly understood that David would take his place as the next king of Israel. Jonathan had committed himself to David, and David had committed himself to Jonathan.

When Jonathan found David in the Wilderness of Ziph, what did Saul's son do? ". . . [he] strengthened [David's] hand in God" (v. 16b).

What a moment that was! As Saul was seeking David's life, Jonathan "strengthened his hand in God."

This is the seventh time we have seen the word "hand" in this chapter. We have read of David's "hand" that defeated the Philistines, Abiathar's "hand" that brought the ephod to David, Saul's "hand" that longed to grasp David but so far had failed. The "hands" of the various characters represent the power struggle. The question in the air was, whose "hand" will prevail?

As David "saw that Saul had come out to seek his life," Jonathan came to him and "strengthened his hand *in God.*"

How did Jonathan do that?

And he said to him, "Do not fear, for the hand of Saul my father shall not find you. You shall be king over Israel, and I shall be next to you. Saul my father also knows this." (v. 17)

Have you noticed how often in the Bible we hear the words "Do not fear"? They are always spoken in terrifying circumstances, when *fear* is the natural and reasonable thing to do. The words, as we hear them in the Bible, are never an empty attempt at comfort but an expression of a reality that is more powerful than the terrifying circumstances (cf. 1 Samuel 17:32).

How could it be possible for David, *seeing* that Saul had come out to seek his life, to not fear? The hand of Saul was the hand that held and hurled the spear. He had done that to both of these men (1 Samuel 18:11; 19:10; 20:33). How could the hands of both David and Jonathan do anything but tremble with fear, seeing Saul's hand and its intentions?

Jonathan knew the answer: by hearing and believing the promise of God. "You shall be king over Israel." Jonathan strengthened David's hand in God by the promise of God. What David *heard* from Jonathan overcame what David *saw*. "The hand of Saul my father shall not find you." That is not what it *looked* like, until David took account of the promise: "You shall be king over Israel."

The difference the promise of God makes to what we *see* is very important. As Jesus approached Jerusalem, he could see what was coming, and he helped the disciples to see it too. "The Son of Man is about to be delivered into the hands of men, and they will kill him." That much the disciples *could* see, and "they were greatly distressed." If only they could hear the promise. He continued, "and he will be raised on the third day" (Matthew 17:22, 23).

We could compare this moment in David's experience with Jesus' time in the Garden of Gethsemane, where his hand was strengthened in God. "Your will be done" (Matthew 26:42).

We could also recognize in what Jonathan did for David an echo of the Christian experience of 2 Corinthians 4: "Therefore . . . we do not lose heart."

Jonathan believed the promise that David would be king over Israel and saw his own future in the light of it. "I shall be next to you" — more literally, "I shall be second to you." This was not, I think, Jonathan claiming a privileged place in David's kingdom,[1] but the heir to the throne giving way (again) to David and taking second place to him. Jonathan would have been able to say, "Therefore we do not lose heart."

Jonathan claimed that Saul, too, knew very well that David would be king. How different was Saul's response to this knowledge! He hated it, he fought it, and he would, if he could, deny it. Saul had not yet given any indication that he *accepted* the fact that David would be king.[2] He was determined to do all in his power to keep this from happening. He could *not* say, "Therefore we do not lose heart."

Covenant and Departure (v. 18)

The contrast between Jonathan and his father could not be greater. It is underlined by the strictly unnecessary repetition in verses 16, 17 of "Jonathan,

Saul's son," "Saul, my father," "Saul, my father." The difference between the two lies in the bond linking Jonathan and David and the enmity dividing Saul from David. The bond was reaffirmed that day: "And the two of them made a covenant before the Lord" (v. 18a).

There was nothing new here.[3] It was a reaffirmation of the commitment made at their first meeting (1 Samuel 18:3).[4] Jonathan and David reaffirmed their relationship "before the Lord" — that is, in full awareness of and trust in the Lord's promise.

The threat from Saul, however, meant that they had to part: "David remained at Horesh, and Jonathan went home" (v. 18b).

This was the last time they saw each other.

SAUL, DAVID . . . AND THE PHILISTINES (vv. 19-29)

The second episode shows that what David could "see" in verse 15 (Saul's hostility), while all too real, was not as fearful as it seemed. This is what Jonathan had said to David. What mattered much more than what was seen was what was unseen (God's invisible hand). As though to emphasize the point, the unseen hand of God is unmentioned in the text recounting this episode.

The Ziphites and Saul (vv. 19-23)

We are taken back from Horesh in the Wilderness of Ziph about twenty-five miles north to Gibeah to see what was happening with the one who was seeking David's life.

He must have thought it was his lucky day:

> Then the Ziphites went up to Saul at Gibeah, saying, "Is not David hiding among us in the strongholds at Horesh, on the hill of Hachilah, which is south of Jeshimon?" (v. 19)

Some Ziphites[5] came with just the kind of precise, detailed information the king was longing for. They told him exactly where to find his enemy — the general location ("the strongholds at Horesh), the actual hill where David was hiding ("the hill of Hachilah"), and its location ("south of Jeshimon"). They continued:

> "Now come down, O king, according to all your heart's desire to come down, and our part shall be to surrender him into the king's hand." (v. 20)

Saul could not ask for better subjects than these Ziphites, could he? They knew that the heart's desire of their king was to find David. They knew, of course, what Saul intended to do once he had David in that "hand" of his. They almost certainly knew what the hand of Saul had done to the priests of Nob. That, no doubt, was the reason for their excessive helpfulness.

Saul was moderately pleased to have found such friends: "And Saul said, 'May you be blessed by the LORD, for you have had compassion on me'" (v. 21).

Poor, paranoid Saul! How kind of these Ziphites to show pity on the unfortunate king — just as he had shown pity on Agag the Amalekite![6] That the powerful Saul saw himself as the victim when it was David who was hiding in caves and hills shows how out of perspective everything had become for him.

David had, of course, slipped from his grasp the last time Saul had received such intelligence as this. The king was determined that should not happen again. The detailed and careful information the Ziphites had brought was not enough for him:

> "Go, make yet more sure. Know and see the place where his foot is, and who has seen him there, for it is told me that he is very cunning. See therefore and take note of all the lurking places where he hides, and come back to me with sure information. Then I will go with you. And if he is in the land, I will search him out among all the thousands of Judah." (vv. 22, 23)

Fearful, desperate, but deadly and dangerous Saul.

The Chase (vv. 24-26)

The chase was on. The Ziphites went to do their king's bidding: "And they arose and went to Ziph ahead of Saul" (v. 24a).

Quickly we are taken to the thrilling chase that ensued: "Now David and his men were in the wilderness of Maon, in the Arabah to the south of Jeshimon" (v. 24b).

That was precisely where the Ziphites had said he was. "And Saul and his men went to seek him" (v. 25a).

That was precisely what Saul said he would do. "And David was told, so he went down to the rock and lived in the wilderness of Maon" (v. 25b).

David, too, had accurate intelligence. We know from earlier in this chapter that his sources of information were vastly superior to Saul's!

"And when Saul heard that, he pursued after David in the wilderness of Maon" (v. 25c). On this occasion Saul's spies did not let him down.

With the tantalizing brevity typical of much Biblical narrative, we hear how the chase moved toward its end: "Saul went on one side of the mountain . . ." (v. 26a).

Possibly we are to see Saul's troops executing a pincer movement: from one side of the mountain they moved in both directions toward David on the other side. ". . . and David and his men [were] on the other [far] side of the mountain" (v. 26b).

David was evidently aware of Saul's maneuver and was scrambling to get away before the pincer snapped shut: "And David was hurrying to get away from Saul" (v. 26c).

But Saul's men were getting closer and closer. In a moment more they would have him: "As Saul and his men were closing in on David and his men to capture them . . ." (v. 26d).

The Escape (vv. 27-29)

As we hold our breath, waiting for the axe to fall, at that very moment, ". . . a messenger came to Saul, saying, 'Hurry and come, for the Philistines have made a raid against the land'" (v. 27).

Who would believe it! The one thing that threatened Saul's kingdom as powerfully as he thought David did (the Philistines) could not be ignored.[7] "So Saul returned from pursuing after David and went against the Philistines" (v. 28a).

There is more than one irony here. Who was the man who earlier in this very chapter (not to mention numerous times previously) proved he could defeat the Philistines and save Israel from their threat? David. For mad Saul, however, both David and the Philistines were enemies.

"Therefore that place was called the Rock of Escape" (v. 28b).

This is probably better translated, "the Rock of Divisions" or "the Rock of Parting," for there David and Saul parted.

"And David went up from there and lived in the strongholds of Engedi" (v. 29).

This was on the rocky heights on the western side of the Dead Sea.

So the struggle would continue.

As we pause again to reflect on the events we have witnessed, we must be impressed that Jonathan was right to strengthen David's hand in God. At the center of this chapter (and the chapter should be seen as a whole) there is a sentence that sums it all up: "And Saul sought [David] every day, but God did not give him into his hand" (v. 14b).

David's future would not be determined by what he could "see" in verse 15 — Saul's ruthless, determined "hand." *God* would "give" David's future. This is not a general idea of providence, nor even a strong doctrine of divine sovereignty. These things are assumed, but with David there was more. It was because of the specific promise of God, which had David at its heart, that the enemies of David would not succeed. God would not give *him* into *their* hand.

The deliverance of David is a wonderful anticipation of the resurrection of Jesus. God would not abandon his Christ (cf. Acts 2:27, 31). But that is not the end of it! When we who know Christ hear the Apostle Paul say, "Therefore . . . we do not lose heart" (2 Corinthians 4:1), we understand the "therefore"! As we hear the story of David and its reverberations through the Scriptures, do we not find ourselves saying, in the face of whatever dreadful things the enemy may hurl our way, "therefore we do not lose heart." Is your hand strengthened in God?

42

"He Did Not Revile in Return"

1 SAMUEL 24

David's journey to the throne of the nation of Israel was long and difficult. Why? After all, God had rejected Saul and had chosen David. It is very clear from much of the account of 1 Samuel that God was, as always, sovereign over all the events. We wonder why the God who could arrange for the Philistines to attack Israel at just the right moment to force Saul to abandon his hunt for David (1 Samuel 23:27, 28) could not simply arrange for David to painlessly take over the kingdom immediately.

This is an aspect of a wider question that thoughtful people often ponder. If God's ultimate purpose for his creation is the new heavens and new earth where there will be no more tears, why is the journey to that kingdom so long and difficult? Why are there so many tears on the way?

The same question could be asked of Jesus. Indeed, it *was* asked of Jesus. "If you are the Son of God," the tempter said to him, then proceeded to suggest ways of coming into his kingdom quickly and without pain (Matthew 4:1-11; Luke 4:1-12; cf. Mark 1:12, 13). Jesus rejected the temptation, and he set out on the long and difficult journey that would take him to Jerusalem and to the cross. But even now all enemies are not yet under his feet (1 Corinthians 15:25). Why?

An important insight into these questions came on the day described in 1 Samuel 24. It was a day on which David could very easily have made his path to the throne quick and easy. If we can understand why he did not, we will learn something very important about why God is bringing in his kingdom in the way he is.

For some time Saul's pursuit of David had been intensifying. The first sign of his hostility toward David had been the spear he hurled at him (1 Samuel 18:11). Now, however, Saul was hunting David with his troops whenever he heard news of him.

Although until now Saul had been frustrated in his attempts to find, capture, and eliminate David, he always *seemed* to have the advantage over his prey. Despite his crazed paranoia, Saul was surrounded by servants, he had troops at his command, and he could sit under his tree at Gibeah whenever he chose. David, on the other had, was on the run for his life. Saul could fail to find David many times over and live to hunt another day. David only had to fail to elude Saul once, and that would be the end.

DAVID SPARES HIS ENEMY (vv. 1-7)

All that changed in a remarkable way on the day described in 1 Samuel 24.

Saul Against David (vv. 1, 2)

The chapter opens by telling us two things that remind us of Saul's apparent commanding position: "When Saul returned from following the Philistines, he was told, 'Behold, David is in the wilderness of Engedi'" (v. 1).

Details about the engagement with the Philistines, which had forced Saul to abandon his agonizingly close maneuver against David in the wilderness of Maon (1 Samuel 23:28), are not important. The implication is, however, that Saul was successful. It sounds as though his troops had pursued the Philistines. Saul still had the military power to deal with trouble from the Philistines.

He also had agents who were willing and able to inform him of David's whereabouts. After his narrow escape from Saul, David had gone up into the craggy hills overlooking the Dead Sea. The rocky terrain with supplies of fresh water near Engedi made the area "an ideal refuge."[1] He did not, however, escape Saul's detection for long.

With the power at his disposal and knowledge of his foe, Saul wasted no time in resuming the chase: "Then Saul took three thousand chosen men out of all Israel and went to seek David and his men in front of the Wildgoats' Rocks" (v. 2).

David had about 600 men with him at this time (1 Samuel 23:13).[2] That gave Saul a 5 to 1 numerical advantage, not to mention that he had "chosen men out of all Israel" — the nation's best. David's men, by contrast, were the downtrodden and oppressed (1 Samuel 22:2). He had hardly "chosen" them. Who would?

There is irony here. Saul had "chosen" 3,000 out of all Israel to hunt down the one whom the Lord had "chosen" out of all Israel (see 1 Samuel 16:8, 9, 10, 12).

Saul's forces arrived in front of the aptly named Wildgoats' Rocks. David and his 600 men could not hope to hide forever in these hills and rocks. It really must have seemed that Saul's moment of triumph was near.

Saul at David's Mercy (v. 3)

The narrative suddenly becomes remarkably detailed: "And he came to the sheepfolds by the way, where there was a cave, and Saul went in to relieve himself" (v. 3a).

This, I must say, is the kind of detail normally omitted from a story like this! These things are necessary, even for kings, but rarely essential to report. Presumably the king had ducked into many caves or other places for a similar purpose on his numerous expeditions, but we are normally spared being told about it!

The reason that the royal bathroom break on this occasion was interesting was because of the cave Saul happened to choose: "Now David and his men were sitting in the innermost parts of the cave" (v. 3b).

Of all the caves in the Engedi region (and I understand there were many[3]), Saul chose to come into this one, alone and vulnerable.

Of course, the men hiding there were vulnerable too. If Saul had raised the alarm, there were 3,000 troops outside, against whom David's 600 would be a poor match.

It was a tense moment of uncertainty. Picture the scene: the army outside the cave, armed and dangerous; David and his gang huddled deep in the darkness of the cave, hidden and no doubt more than a little nervous; and between the two, a short distance into the cave, Saul with his pants down!

Saul Spared by David (vv. 4-7)

In the darkness, deep inside the cave, there were whispers:

> *And the men of David said to him, "Here is the day of which the LORD said to you, 'Behold, I will give your enemy into your hand, and you shall do to him as it shall seem good to you.'"* (v. 4a)

Although the Lord had said no such thing, the sentiments of the men were understandable. In the previous chapter the Lord *did* say to David, "I will give *the Philistines* into your hand" (1 Samuel 23:4), which is pretty close to "I will give *your enemy* into your hand."[4] From the point of view of David's men, there was not a lot of difference these days between Saul and the Philistines! It is also true that Saul had branded David his "enemy"

(1 Samuel 19:17; cf. 18:29). The men were only drawing the obvious conclusion that if David was Saul's enemy, then Saul was David's enemy. So they made the reasonable movement of applying the Lord's promise to this enemy of David too.[5]

It was undeniable, moreover, that the tables had (however momentarily) been turned. Blissfully unaware, Saul was at the mercy of David. This damaging conflict could have been brought to an end at a stroke. It must have been as clear to the men in the back of the cave as it is to us that this turn of fortunes was the Lord's doing.

There was a silent movement at the back of the cave. Unseen and unheard, David crept forward in the darkness, sword in hand. The words are chosen to help us imagine what might have happened: "Then David arose and stealthily cut off . . ." (v. 4b).

Do you remember how Jonathan had pleaded with David, "Do not *cut off* your steadfast love from my house forever, when the Lord *cuts off* every one of the enemies of David from the face of the earth" (1 Samuel 20:15)? Is that what happened there in the cave? What did David "cut off"? ". . . a corner of Saul's robe" (v. 4c).

Is that all? What an anticlimactic moment! Just a corner of his robe!

The incongruity between the risk David was taking and the act he performed is stunning. Imagine the skill and stealth involved in this! Picture how sharp must the sword have been — and what else it could have done!

We are not told what went through David's mind *before* he did this. Was he caught up in the excitement of the men and only at the last minute restrained himself from doing something more drastic?[6] Did he know all along that he would not lay a hand on the king's person but decided to humiliate him? We are told what he thought *after* the event: "And afterward David's heart struck him, because he had cut off a corner of Saul's robe" (v. 5).

This may seem to us just a little wimpy! Saul would have had no qualms, if the roles had been reversed, in using his sword far more drastically on David. He had ordered David's assassination several times already (1 Samuel 19:1, 11, 20), and his ability to carry such a thing through had been dreadfully demonstrated with the priests of Nob (1 Samuel 22:17-19). Is it not a little too much that David's conscience should be devastated because he touched Saul's *robe*?[7]

There was more to it than a damaged garment. Whatever was going through David's mind *before* he cut the robe, it is certain that he immediately saw great significance in what he had done. It was like that day in Gilgal when a robe was torn between Samuel and Saul (1 Samuel 15:27).[8] That action was given massive symbolic significance by Samuel: "The LORD has torn the kingdom of Israel from you this day and has given it to a neighbor of yours, who is better than you" (1 Samuel 15:28).

Now, years later, in the cave of Engedi, that neighbor took it upon himself to slice Saul's royal robe. Symbolically, you see, he was laying claim to the kingdom. At least, what he had done could be seen that way.[9] For some reason that is far from clear at this stage, David was devastated that he had done such a thing.

> *He said to his men, "The Lord forbid that I should do this thing to my lord, the Lord's anointed, to put out my hand against him, seeing he is the Lord's anointed." (v. 6)*

The reasonable, understandable thinking of his men had been wrong. David (and Jonathan on David's behalf) had earlier pleaded that on no occasion had David shown anything but faithful service to Saul (see 1 Samuel 19:4, 5; 20:1, 32). Up until now David had never accepted Saul's claim that he was his enemy and had never treated Saul as his enemy. The symbolic act he had performed — or at least the symbolic significance that could be seen in the act — David renounced.

There was something very unusual going on here. David understood that the kingdom, which would certainly be his one day, was not for him to *take* by his own power. The kingdom had been *given* to Saul by God (in this sense "he is the Lord's anointed"), and it was up to God to take it from him, in his own time and in his own way. This was not politics as we know it. It was a power struggle, but different from the power struggles with which we are familiar. From David's side there was a determined refusal in this matter to "wage war according to the flesh" (2 Corinthians 10:3). The kingdom could only properly come to him as God's gift.

This was clearly very important to David. The ESV of verse 7 is a little mild: "So David persuaded his men with these words and did not permit them to attack Saul" (v. 7a). Literally the text says that David tore his men apart with his words.[10] They were utterly and completely wrong to think this was an ordinary conflict between men. With remarkable insight, David saw that "no one takes *this* honor for himself" (cf. Hebrews 5:4, which is about the priesthood, but the principle can be applied to David's situation).

The opportunity to bring the conflict with Saul to an end by ordinary means passed: "And Saul rose up and left the cave and went on his way" (v. 7b).

DAVID'S INNOCENCE AND GRACE (vv. 8-15)

That is the end of the *action* in this chapter, if by action we mean physical, observable deeds. However, it is far from the end of the chapter. It is typical of Biblical narrative to take us through the action quite briefly and then give much more space to what was *said*. The dramatic actions in the cave were really just the setting for two amazing speeches, which were more important on this occasion than the action.

Saul had moved some distance from the cave, perhaps down the hillside toward his troops. David came out to the mouth of the cave in a remarkably daring and risky move. If this did not work, David and his men would soon meet their end. "Afterward David also arose and went out of the cave, and called after Saul, 'My lord the king!'" (v. 8a).

David addressed Saul in a manner consistent with how he intended to treat him.

As you might imagine Saul stopped, turned around, and looked toward the voice. David added to his words appropriate gestures: "And when Saul looked behind him, David bowed with his face to the earth and paid homage" (v. 8b).

Again we have a tense moment. Picture the scene: David's men, still out of sight in the back of the cave; David at the mouth of the cave, bowing low, face to the ground; Saul, some distance away, presumably having not quite yet reached his troops.

Only the power of speech could save David from the might that Saul had at his disposal.

> And David said to Saul, "Why do you listen to the words of men who say, 'Behold, David seeks your harm'? Behold, this day your eyes have seen how the LORD gave you today into my hand in the cave. And some told me to kill you, but I spared you. I said, 'I will not put out my hand against my lord, for he is the LORD's anointed.'" (vv. 9, 10)

Just as David had repudiated "the words of men" in the cave,[11] he called on Saul to do the same. From all that we know, David was being rather too generous to Saul. We have no evidence that anyone, other than Saul himself, was saying that David was seeking to harm Saul. Indeed Saul had repeatedly been told the very opposite.

Of course, the fact that David was standing at the mouth of the cave was proof enough that only moments earlier he could have taken Saul by surprise. But David had further dramatic proof of his refusal to harm Saul, even though he had the opportunity:

> "See, my father, see the corner of your robe in my hand. For by the fact that I cut off the corner of your robe and did not kill you, you may know and see that there is no wrong or treason in my hands. I have not sinned against you, though you hunt my life to take it." (v. 11)

The symbolic significance of the torn piece of Saul's royal robe held high by David may have struck Saul, but it was overpowered by the fresh symbolic significance David gave to it as proof of the mercy he had shown to Saul. If David was holding the symbol of the kingdom in his hands, he was also holding the symbol of his innocence, his faithfulness, and his kindness toward Saul.

David had demonstrated that he would leave it to the Lord to deal with the differences between himself and Saul. He now called on Saul to do the same: "May the LORD judge between me and you, may the LORD avenge me against you, but my hand shall not be against you" (v. 12).

The speech could have stopped there, but a great deal depended on this speech, and David had a couple of last flourishes. Like many great orators, some of the power of the speech came from his willingness to sail very close to the wind: "As the proverb of the ancients says, 'Out of the wicked comes wickedness.' But my hand shall not be against you" (v. 13).

The obvious implication of the proverb is that Saul had acted wickedly because he was wicked, but David quickly deflected that implication by applying the proverb positively to himself: if David was wicked (as Saul seemed to believe), he would have done the wicked thing — lifted his hand against the king.

But ever so dangerously, David did turn the thought of the proverb toward Saul: "After whom has the king of Israel come out? After whom do you pursue? After a dead dog! After a flea!" (v. 14).

The question echoed the proverb almost too closely. "From the wicked *comes out* wickedness." "After whom has *come out* the king of Israel?"[12]

The thought was not allowed to develop, however, because David quickly again deflected it to his own insignificance. He was not so much pretending that he was a completely unimportant person as emphasizing the inappropriateness of Saul's hunting of him. He was no more a threat to Saul than a dead dog or a single flea on a dead dog!

Boldly David concluded by calling on God to decide the matter, and he had no doubt about which side God would come down: "May the LORD therefore be judge and give sentence between me and you, and see to it and plead my cause and deliver me from your hand" (v. 15).

That must have been the speech of David's life — so far at least. The man who had introduced David to Saul as "a man . . . prudent in speech" (1 Samuel 16:18) was not exaggerating! David's life now literally depended on the effect of these prudent words on Saul.

SAUL'S CONFESSION AND PLEA (vv. 16-22)

It was one of those moments when the course of history seemed to hang in the balance. We could speculate about what consequences would have followed if Saul had commanded his troops to rush up the hillside and slaughter

David. On any human assessment of this situation, that must have been a distinct possibility.

Instead, this is what happened: "As soon as David had finished speaking these words to Saul, Saul said, 'Is this your voice, my son David?'" (v. 16a).

The words of David, and all that they conveyed, appear to have hit Saul very hard. It had been a long time since Saul thought of calling "the son of Jesse" (1 Samuel 20:27, 30, 31; 22:7, 8, 13) "my son David"! For a moment he was overcome: "And Saul lifted up his voice and wept" (v. 16b).

Was this because of the shock of how close he had been to death himself? Was it the stabbing pain of an accusing conscience? Saul had much innocent blood on his hands from his hatred of David. Was it the realization, at last, that he could not stop this man from becoming king no matter what he did? Or was it all these things?

When he had recovered sufficiently, he spoke:

> *"You are more righteous than I, for you have repaid me good, whereas I have repaid you evil. And you have declared this day how you have dealt well with me, in that you did not kill me when the Lord put me into your hands. For if a man finds his enemy, will he let him go away safe? So may the Lord reward you with good for what you have done to me this day."*
> *(vv. 17-19)*

It is as though the shock of David's speech was working its way through Saul's consciousness. Every part of David's speech was undeniably true. Saul's walking out of that cave alive was irrefutable proof that David was not his enemy. Then what was he? For the first time, Saul put into words what he must have known for a long time now: "And now, behold, I know that you shall surely be king, and that the kingdom of Israel shall be established in your hand" (v. 20).

At long last we have heard it from Saul! His troops would have heard it too. We notice that this acknowledgment was not dragged out of Saul with a sword blade at his throat. It was forced out of him by David's righteousness and mercy!

There remained only one more thing for Saul to say to David: "Swear to me therefore by the Lord that you will not cut off my offspring after me, and that you will not destroy my name out of my father's house" (v. 21).

In other words, "Have mercy on me." Do we hear an echo of the sentiment in Saul's cry when people cried out to Jesus, "Have mercy on us, Son of David" (see Matthew 9:27; 15:22; 20:30, 31; Mark 10:47, 48; Luke 18:38, 39)? Belatedly Saul asked what Jonathan had asked previously. "Do not 'cut off' any more than the robe you hold in your hand!"

Considering what David had sworn to Jonathan, we are now not surprised to hear: "And David swore this to Saul" (v. 22a).

The episode concludes: "Then Saul went home, but David and his men went up to the stronghold" (v. 22b).

It is far from clear what would happen next.

In this remarkable episode we have been given a glimpse into the answer to the question about why David's kingdom was not established quickly and painlessly.

Quick and painless is the way in which we humans like most things to be achieved. The men in the cave wanted David to *take* the opportunity that had so unexpectedly come to him. His refusal to do so displayed an astonishing insight — namely, that God's kingdom is *God's* kingdom. It cannot be *taken* by human power. While God's kingdom will certainly entail the overthrow of evil and the just punishment of wickedness, that is God's business, not ours. It will happen at God's time and in God's way, not ours. If they wanted David as their king, they would have to put their trust in God, as he did.

Does David's godly patience and restraint in the cave remind you of someone else?

> *He committed no sin, neither was deceit found in his mouth. When he was reviled, he did not revile in return; when he suffered, he did not threaten, but continued entrusting himself to him who judges justly. (1 Peter 2:22, 23)*

Jesus no more grasped the kingdom violently than did David.

To have Jesus as our king calls for godly patience and restraint, like his. It is a long and difficult journey to the kingdom of heaven. Peter tells us that Jesus left us "an example, so that [we] might follow in his steps" (1 Peter 2:21). Behind the example of Jesus is the example of David.

43

Vengeance Belongs to the Lord

1 SAMUEL 25

Have you ever participated in a leadership training course? Perhaps you have been involved in conducting such a program. Even if you have not, use your imagination to consider what you think a curriculum to prepare people for leadership should involve. Time management? Goal-setting? Strategic thinking? Decisive assertiveness? Delegation?

By now you will understand that the book of 1 Samuel has an unusual approach to the subject of leadership. It tells the story of God's providing leadership for his people in Old Testament times, a story that eventually led to Jesus Christ who is the leader (or, to use the Bible's word, Lord) whom God has provided for all people who will come under his leadership (lordship).

The most important thing we are learning through our reading and reflecting on the story told in 1 Samuel is the kind of leadership God provides for his people — the kind of leadership he has now provided for us in Jesus.

What do you think God might include in a training course for the man he chose to be king for him over his people? What happened to David in the time between his anointing in chapter 16 and his becoming king can be seen as God's education of his chosen king. In chapters 24, 25, and 26 David learned a lesson I have never seen included in a leadership training course.

A critical moment was reached in the story of the rejected king, Saul, and the king-to-be, David, when Saul at long last publicly acknowledged the situation he had known for some time: "I know that you shall surely be king, and that the kingdom of Israel shall be established in your hand"

(1 Samuel 24:20; cf. 23:17). Since the day David was anointed by Samuel in Bethlehem, there had been a gradual recognition of David's future. Saul's son, Jonathan, was the first to see it clearly (1 Samuel 18:1-4). Then all Israel and Judah came to "love" David (1 Samuel 18:16). They may not at that stage have entertained thoughts of David becoming their king, but their love for him indicated the kind of regard a people should have for their king. Most remarkably the Philistines had, probably inadvertently, referred to David as "the king of the land" (1 Samuel 21:11). Through all of this the one person who was desperately hostile to the idea of David becoming king was, not surprisingly, Saul. His hostility began as angry jealousy, when the women seemed to ascribe greater glory to David than to Saul. Even then Saul, knowing as he did that God had rejected him, saw the terrible possibility: "What more can he have but the kingdom?" (1 Samuel 18:8).

However, it was not until the experience of being spared by David in the Engedi cave that Saul openly acknowledged that the kingdom would be David's: "I know that you shall surely be king."

At this significant moment in the story we hear the brief notice of Samuel's death: "Now Samuel died. And all Israel assembled and mourned for him, and they buried him in his house at Ramah" (v. 1).

We have heard very little of Samuel since he abandoned Saul at the end of chapter 15 and anointed David in chapter 16.[1] We have been aware that the old prophet was there, at his home in Ramah, no doubt watching the developing drama between the king he had condemned and the future king he had designated. Are we perhaps to understand that when Saul came to acknowledge the future that Samuel had been charged by God to inaugurate, Samuel's work was at last done?[2]

It is surprising that the notice of Samuel's death is so brief,[3] but there is no surprise that "all Israel assembled and mourned for him." His role as Israel's judge, prophet, priest, and anointer of kings had been remarkable.[4] His most important work was done in his old age (see 1 Samuel 8:1), and it had been tragically difficult work. His death came at a time when the monarchical institution he had constituted looked desperately unstable, and the future was far from clear. The stability represented by Samuel, even if he had been in the background for some time, was a significant thing to lose.[5]

Did Saul join the mourners? The lack of any reference to him in this context leaves us wondering how the fallen king reacted to the death of the prophet who had brought him down. But wondering is all we can do.

Was David among the mourners? Probably not. The settlement between Saul and David at the Engedi cave had not resulted in an invitation to David to return to public life. Saul had gone home to Gibeah, and David and his men had returned to "the stronghold," presumably in the Engedi hills (1 Samuel 24:22; cf. 23:29).[6] David evidently did not yet consider Saul safe. After the notice about Samuel's death, David's next recorded movement was:[7] "Then David rose and went down to the wilderness of Paran" (v. 1b).

This makes the most sense as David's reaction to Samuel's death.[8] Samuel's death must have been hugely significant for David. Paran was to the south, well away from Saul's influence, indeed beyond the land of Israel. The wilderness of Paran belonged to the period of Israel's wanderings in the days of Moses (see Numbers 10:12; 12:16; 13:3, 26; Deuteronomy 1:1). David seems to have gone alone. What went on for David in the wilderness of Paran we are simply not told.

NABAL'S FOLLY (vv. 2-13)

Time passed. We will learn shortly a little about the period between verse 1 and verse 2, where the next major episode of the story, after Samuel's death, begins. It will be packed with high drama, and even an element of romance. The characters are unforgettable, and the action is dramatic.

Nabal and Abigail (vv. 2, 3)

Two new characters will play a big part in this story:

> And there was a man in Maon whose business was in Carmel. The man was very rich; he had three thousand sheep and a thousand goats. He was shearing his sheep in Carmel. Now the name of the man was Nabal, and the name of his wife Abigail. The woman was discerning and beautiful, but the man was harsh and badly behaved; he was a Calebite. (vv. 2, 3)

Maon was the region in which Saul had pursued David and almost captured him (1 Samuel 23:24-29). Carmel was only a few miles away and was the site where Saul had earlier "set up a monument for himself" (1 Samuel 15:12). Saul will not appear in person in the episode recounted in this chapter, but the two locations mentioned in verse 2 remind us of his recent and not-so-recent activities. Much more in this chapter will remind us of Saul.

The man we meet here was "very rich," literally "very great." The translation is right, however, because he was one of those men whose greatness consisted in the abundance of his possessions. The occasion of the incidents about to be told was the shearing season, when the man's great wealth was in the process of becoming greater.

Two things should worry us about this man. The first is his name. In Hebrew it means "fool." The sense of the word can be appreciated from Psalm 14:1:

The fool [Hebrew, nabal] says in his heart, "There is no God."
They are corrupt, they do abominable deeds,
there is none who does good. (Psalm 14:1)

Isaiah spoke eloquently of the fool, in terms that fit Nabal remarkably:

For the fool [Hebrew, nabal] speaks folly,
and his heart is busy with iniquity,
to practice ungodliness,
*   to utter error concerning the LORD,*
to leave the craving of the hungry unsatisfied,
*   and to deprive the thirsty of drink. (Isaiah 32:6)*

The second worry is the description of his conduct, which fits his name (as well as Psalm 14:1 and Isaiah 32:6) too well: "the man was harsh and badly behaved."[9] We will see his abominable behavior very soon.

The last point made in his introduction is, "he was a Calebite." I suspect there is a note of bitter irony here. Caleb was no fool. Caleb was a model faithful Israelite at the time of the wilderness wanderings and the conquest of Canaan (see Numbers 13:30-33; 14:1-12, 24, 30, 38; Deuteronomy 1:36; Joshua 14:6-15; 15:13-19; Judges 1:11-15, 20). This man may have been a Calebite in name, but his character and conduct betrayed that noble heritage. In reality Nabal was no Calebite![10]

In a number of understated ways, there are hints that Nabal should remind us of Saul. We have already noted that Maon and Carmel remind us of Saul. Nabal was a "very great" man, as of course was Saul, the king. Nabal's name ("Fool") may remind us of the day that Samuel said to Saul, "You have done foolishly" (1 Samuel 13:13).[11] We will certainly be reminded of that day in the next chapter when Saul will confess, "I have acted foolishly" (1 Samuel 26:21).[12]

The second character introduced is Nabal's wife, Abigail. In short, she was everything he was not. He was a fool, she was "discerning" (literally, "good of understanding"); he was harsh, she was "beautiful" (literally, "beautiful of form"). Her wisdom and her beauty will play a major role in the events about to be told.

David's Request (vv. 4-9)

The action began with David hearing news of Nabal: "David heard in the wilderness that Nabal was shearing his sheep" (v. 4).

Typical of Biblical storytelling, we have not yet been given enough information to know why Nabal's shearing his sheep would be of interest to David. We are about to learn:

So David sent ten young men. And David said to the young men, "Go up to Carmel, and go to Nabal and greet him in my name. And thus you shall greet him: 'Peace be to you, and peace be to your house, and peace be to all that you have. I hear that you have shearers. Now your shepherds have been with us, and we did them no harm, and they missed nothing all the time they were in Carmel. Ask your young men, and they will tell you. Therefore let my young men find favor in your eyes, for we come on a feast day. Please give whatever you have at hand to your servants and to your son David.'" (vv. 5-8)

In other words, a lot *had* happened between verse 1 and verse 2 of this chapter! David had returned from the wilderness of Paran, joined his men, and spent time in the region of Carmel, where Nabal's shepherds kept his flocks. Taking David at his word,[13] he and his men did no harm to Nabal's shepherds or his sheep. Indeed, they assisted them so that, remarkably, no sheep at all were lost during this time. A little later we will learn that David's men had provided security against dangers, of which the wilderness had many.[14]

In other words, over a period of time David and his men had acted with kindness and generosity toward Nabal's shepherds and sheep.

The time had now come when Nabal was enjoying the benefits of that period of security for his flocks, while David and his men were in need. David sent ten of his young men to Nabal with a message of goodwill,[15] in David's name, and a request for some kindness and generosity from Nabal.

Remarkably, David subordinated himself to Nabal, referring to himself as "your son David." We are reminded of his speech to Saul a little earlier, when he addressed the king as "my father," and Saul had called David "my son David" (1 Samuel 24:11, 16).

The young men did as David had said: "When David's young men came, they said all this to Nabal in the name of David, and then they waited" (v. 9).

We should not overlook the emphasis on "in the name of David." The young men represented David. Their greeting was David's greeting; their message was David's message; their request was David's request.

They waited, presumably for their reasonable request "in the name of David" to be granted.

Nabal's Response (vv. 10-13)

Nabal's response to what was said to him "in the name of David" validated *his* name ("Fool"):

And Nabal answered David's servants, "Who is David? Who is the son of Jesse? There are many servants these days who are breaking away from their masters. Shall I take my bread and my water and my meat that I have killed for my shearers and give it to men who come from I do not know where?" (vv. 10, 11)

Nabal's questions suggest that he knew very well who David was! He knew enough to refer to him contemptuously as "the son of Jesse."[16] Everyone had now recognized that David, the son of Jesse, was Israel's future king. Even Nabal's wife understood this, as we will shortly see. Nabal's scornful words remind us of the only other person in Israel who had expressed hostility to David. Like Saul, Nabal asked who David was (cf. 1 Samuel 17:55-58). Like Saul, he referred to him disparagingly as "the son of Jesse" (cf. 1 Samuel 20:27, 30, 31; 22:7, 8, 13). Like Saul, he regarded him as a rebellious servant (cf. 1 Samuel 20:26-34; 22:7, 8).

Nabal, like Saul, held David in the opposite regard and esteem to virtually everyone else in Israel, who "loved" him (see 1 Samuel 18:1, 3, 16, 20, 28; 20:17). Nabal despised David and refused him any kindness.

Like many wealthy people, Nabal had a keen sense of *his* possessions — "*my* bread," "*my* water," "*my* meat," "*my* shearers." There was no way that he would "give" his possessions to such strangers as David and his men. "So David's young men turned away and came back and told him all this" (v. 12). David's response was swift and dramatic:

And David said to his men, "Every man strap on his sword!" And every man of them strapped on his sword. David also strapped on his sword. And about four hundred men went up after David, while two hundred remained with the baggage. (v. 13)

David was outraged at the insult his courteous approach had received. No description is given of his inner thoughts, but the actions speak for themselves. We do not need to be told what David intended to do with his force of 400 men.

At this point in the story, we might anticipate that Nabal's folly lay in scorning and insulting a man like David, who had up to 600 men at his disposal. He had provoked a potential friend into becoming an armed and dangerous enemy. Only ruin could follow. What a fool!

ABIGAIL'S WISDOM (vv. 14-31)

However, the story unfolded rather differently from what we might have expected. Before David and his men reached Nabal, events took a surprising turn.

Abigail's Action (vv. 14-19)

One of Nabal's young men, who had heard the exchange between David's young men and Nabal, took matters into his own hands:

> But one of the young men told Abigail, Nabal's wife, "Behold, David sent messengers out of the wilderness to greet our master, and he railed at them. Yet the men were very good to us, and we suffered no harm, and we did not miss anything when we were in the fields, as long as we went with them. They were a wall to us both by night and by day, all the while we were with them keeping the sheep. Now therefore know this and consider what you should do, for harm is determined against our master and against all his house, and he is such a worthless man that one cannot speak to him." (vv. 14-17)

This young man knew who David was, and he knew that Abigail would know too. He could see David's good intentions toward Nabal, and he testified to the truthfulness of David's claim to have served Nabal's interests well. Indeed he expanded the claim with the image of David's men being a "wall" for Nabal's shepherds and sheep. According to this young man, David had been "good" to Nabal, just as, according to Jonathan, David had been "good" to Saul (cf. 1 Samuel 19:4).

But the young man also knew the stupidity of his master and appealed to Abigail to think of what to do!

When this young man characterized Nabal as "a worthless man," he used the expression that our narrator used much earlier to describe the sons of Eli and the "worthless fellows" who originally despised Saul's kingship (1 Samuel 2:12; 10:27; cf. 1:16). Nabal, therefore, joined the infamous company of "sons of *belial*,"[17] whose contribution to this story has been to despise and scorn God's ways.

We have already been told that Abigail was "discerning" (v. 3; literally, "good of understanding"). She quickly understood the seriousness of the situation and worked out what to do:

> Then Abigail made haste and took two hundred loaves and two skins of wine and five sheep already prepared and five seahs of parched grain and a hundred clusters of raisins and two hundred cakes of figs, and laid them on donkeys. And she said to her young men, "Go on before me; behold, I come after you." But she did not tell her husband Nabal. (vv. 18, 19)

In the same way Jonathan had not told his father Saul of his plans on an earlier occasion (cf. 1 Samuel 14:1; also 22:8). Once again we find Nabal reminding us of Saul. He too had a family member who knew better than he did, particularly how to relate to David.

The gift Abigail prepared is described in detail and sounds substantial, but for David's 600 men it would not go far. It was more a token of goodwill. She sent it on ahead to make a favorable impression (cf. Jacob's similar strategy in Genesis 32:13-21), to signal her intentions before she encountered David.

Dangerous David (vv. 20-22)

Abigail set out. David was already on his way. As they approached one another, the tension mounts: "And as she rode on the donkey and came down under cover of the mountain, behold, David and his men came down toward her, and she met them" (v. 20).

In the way they moved on the mountain, for a moment she could see David, but he could not see her. It is possible that the words we now hear from David were overheard by Abigail in the moments before the two met. If that is what happened, she must have wondered whether there was any chance of making peace with this furious man.

> *Now David had said, "Surely in vain have I guarded all that this fellow has in the wilderness, so that nothing was missed of all that belonged to him, and he has returned me evil for good. God do so to the enemies of David and more also, if by morning I leave so much as one male of all who belong to him." (vv. 21, 22)*

The ferocity of David's words is lost a little in translation here. In the original his language had a vulgar edge to it that fitted his fury.[18] It was moral outrage. Nabal had returned "evil" for the "good" David had done him. Once again Nabal reminds us of Saul. In just the previous chapter Saul himself had acknowledged that David had done him "good" and received "evil" in return (1 Samuel 24:17). In that situation David had refrained from repaying the "evil," but that was not his intention this time. David was in a dangerous mood as he met Abigail. He swore[19] that he would kill every male of Nabal's household by dawn.

How different was David at this moment from the David we saw in the Engedi cave! There he agonized in remorse over cutting a corner from Saul's robe. Here he swore terrible vengeance on the one who wronged him. The similarities we have seen between Nabal and Saul highlight the difference in David's conduct toward the two.

Abigail's Plea (vv. 23-31)

The centerpiece of this chapter is undoubtedly Abigail's brilliant speech when she met David. In eloquence and moral depth it matches David's speech to Saul in the previous chapter.

HONOR FOR DAVID (vv. 23, 24)

First, she approached David with the respect and deference that Nabal had so conspicuously lacked: "When Abigail saw David, she hurried and got down from the donkey and fell before David on her face and bowed to the ground" (v. 23).

She bowed down to David as, in the previous chapter, David had bowed down to Saul (1 Samuel 24:8). Her words matched her posture: "She fell at his feet and said, 'On me alone, my lord, be the guilt. Please let your servant speak in your ears, and hear the words of your servant'" (v. 24).

David had sworn (possibly in Abigail's hearing) to eliminate every male in Nabal's service. By taking the guilt to herself, this resourceful female was attempting a dramatic change to the situation.[20] Presenting herself as his "servant,"[21] Abigail begged to be heard.

FIRST REQUEST: NABAL THE FOOL (v. 25)

She did not pause, however, for permission to be granted but pressed on:

"Let not my lord regard this worthless fellow, Nabal, for as his name is, so is he. Nabal is his name, and folly is with him. But I your servant did not see the young men of my lord, whom you sent." (v. 25)

Her first plea was that David should give Nabal the attention he deserved — namely, none. Fool by name, fool by nature. David would not have been so badly treated if only Abigail had known of the visit by his young men.

If we have rightly sensed David's mood, we may well think that she will have to do better than that to turn him from his fury.

SECOND REQUEST: A PRAYER (v. 26)

She did have more to say:

"Now then, my lord, as the LORD lives, and as your soul lives, because the LORD has restrained you from bloodguilt and from saving with your own hand, now then let your enemies and those who seek to do evil to my lord be as Nabal." (v. 26)

Abigail's second appeal was a prayer based on a very bold interpretation of her interception of David. The Lord himself had kept David from a disaster by putting Abigail in his path that day! She described the potential disaster from which he had been saved as "bloodguilt" and "saving [yourself] with your own hand."[22] The uncanny thing is that she was also describing what had happened to David in the Engedi cave. There, too, David had come close to shedding blood (Saul's) and "saving with [his] own hand." Her words, presumably far more than she knew, linked the situation David now faced with the situation he had faced in the cave.

Since the Lord had kept David from this disaster, Abigail seemed to argue, let all David's enemies, including Nabal (and implicitly Saul), be dealt with by the Lord.

THIRD REQUEST: ACCEPT THIS GIFT (v. 27)

Abigail's third request was that she might be allowed to do the good toward David[23] that Nabal had failed to do: "And now let this present that your servant has brought to my lord be given to the young men who follow my lord" (v. 27).

FOURTH REQUEST: FORGIVENESS (vv. 28-31)

It was Abigail's fourth and final petition that brought her speech to a stunning climax:

> *"Please forgive the trespass of your servant. For the LORD will certainly make my lord a sure house, because my lord is fighting the battles of the LORD, and evil shall not be found in you so long as you live. If men rise up to pursue you and to seek your life, the life of my lord shall be bound in the bundle of the living in the care of the LORD your God. And the lives of your enemies he shall sling out as from the hollow of a sling. And when the LORD has done to my lord according to all the good that he has spoken concerning you and has appointed you prince over Israel, my lord shall have no cause of grief or pangs of conscience for having shed blood without cause or for my lord taking vengeance himself. And when the LORD has dealt well with my lord, then remember your servant." (vv. 28-31)*

Abigail really did take on herself responsibility for her husband's offense, and now she begged forgiveness.[24] She based her appeal for forgiveness on the most astonishing prediction of David's coming kingdom. Such prophetic insight is matched in 1 Samuel only by Hannah's prayer in chapter 2 (see v. 10). Abigail's language anticipated the great promise that God would make to David (but had not yet made) through Nathan in 2 Samuel 7.

If the Lord brought Abigail across David's path that day, he also inspired her words. Abigail spoke as though she already knew in some detail the promises that God would make in 2 Samuel 7! This is the first time a "sure house" for David is mentioned in the Bible (cf. 1 Samuel 2:35, where there is reference to another "sure house," but not David's). Indeed it is the first clear reference to the dynasty of David. David's "sure house" is the climactic theme of the 2 Samuel 7 promise: "And your house and your kingdom shall be made sure forever before me. Your throne shall be established forever" (v. 16).

Abigail spoke in extravagant terms of the care the Lord would show toward David. As the Lord's king, who fights the Lord's battles, no harm would come to him.[25] Any who seek his life (Saul again comes to mind), the Lord will hurl away like the stone that David slung so effectively at Goliath (cf. 1 Samuel 17:49, 50). Like Hannah in 1 Samuel 2, Abigail spoke prophetically.

The point of her speech, however, was astonishing. She put forward the certainty of David's future kingdom and his secure dynasty as the basis on which David should now extend forgiveness to her on behalf of her pathetic husband. The connection between those two ideas is not immediately obvious. It lies in the unique kind of king David was to be. Since he would reign as God's king, he must not be one who sheds blood needlessly or takes vengeance into his own hands. David must be a man who trusts God. Vengeance is for God to take (Deuteronomy 32:35; cf. Romans 12:19; cf. also Deuteronomy 20:4; Judges 7:2). David must be one who entrusts his life "to a faithful Creator while doing good" (1 Peter 4:19). And Abigail, with her prophetic word, had been placed in David's path that day for that very purpose.

That being the case, she dared to hope that David would remember her when he came into his kingdom.

DAVID'S RESPONSE (vv. 32-35)

Abigail's speech was as effective as David's had been in the previous chapter. David's response to her now had echoes of Saul's response to him then:

> And David said to Abigail, "Blessed be the LORD, the God of Israel, who sent you this day to meet me! Blessed be your discretion, and blessed be you, who have kept me this day from bloodguilt and from avenging myself with my own hand! For as surely as the LORD the God of Israel lives, who has restrained me from hurting you, unless you had hurried and come to meet me, truly by morning there had not been left to Nabal so much as one male." (vv. 33, 34)

David's backdown is breathtaking — from blood-letting rage to apparently calm thankfulness to God for Abigail's intervention! He gratefully acknowledged the wisdom and goodness of everything that Abigail had said. He recognized the courage of her action. If God had not restrained him, such was his fury that he might have harmed her before shedding the blood of Nabal's men.[26] "Then David received from her hand what she had brought him" (v. 35a).

Accepting her gift was a recognition of the goodwill that had been established between them. "And he said to her, 'Go up in peace to your house. See, I have obeyed your voice, and I have granted your petition'" (v. 35b).

Remarkably Abigail's action had changed the situation to one of "peace," the very thing David had intended with his messengers to Nabal in 1 Samuel 25:6!

NABAL'S LOSS, DAVID'S GAIN (vv. 36-44)

The story has a kind of epilogue. God did deal with Nabal, and he did care for David.

Nabal's Death (vv. 36-38)

This is what happened to Nabal: "And Abigail came to Nabal, and behold, he was holding a feast in his house, like the feast of a king" (v. 36a).

Just as Nabal has several times reminded us of Saul, so he was now treating himself as though he were the king! We might recall how Hannah spoke of "those who were full" and how their fortunes would be reversed (1 Samuel 2:5). Nabal fits Hannah's prophecy well.

> And Nabal's heart was merry within him, for he was very drunk. So she told him nothing at all until the morning light. In the morning, when the wine had gone out of Nabal, his wife told him these things, and his heart died within him, and he became as a stone. (vv. 36b, 37)

He was ready for the Lord to "sling out as from the hollow of a sling" (v. 29)! "And about ten days later the Lord struck Nabal, and he died" (v. 38).

Nabal received his just deserts, but not from David's hand. "Vengeance is mine, I will repay, says the Lord" (Romans 12:19; cf. Deuteronomy 32:35).

David's Vindication (v. 39a)

David heard the news:

> When David heard that Nabal was dead, he said, "Blessed be the Lord who has avenged the insult I received at the hand of Nabal, and has kept back his servant from wrongdoing. The Lord has returned the evil of Nabal on his own head." (v. 39a)

In the previous chapter, David had called on God to be the judge and plead his case before Saul (1 Samuel 24:15).[27] Now he found that the Lord had judged the matter between him and Nabal. David had been vindicated by the one he had to trust to be his vindicator. It is as Hannah had said long ago: actions are weighed by the Lord (1 Samuel 2:3). That is why "those who were hungry [like David's men] have ceased to hunger" (1 Samuel 2:5).

There is no suggestion here that David's attitude was wrong. True, he needed the correction of Abigail's words earlier, but now we hear the words of David after he had learned his lesson.

This is one of those moments where we must be reminded that Bible narratives are not simply moral tales. We must remember here that David was God's king. Nabal's foolish behavior was more than a personal insult to the man David. He was scorning God's king.

David's Wives (vv. 39b-44)

Finally, these dramatic events had another outcome:

> *Then David sent and spoke to Abigail, to take her as his wife. When the servants of David came to Abigail at Carmel, they said to her, "David has sent us to you to take you to him as his wife." And she rose and bowed with her face to the ground and said, "Behold, your handmaid is a servant to wash the feet of the servants of my lord." And Abigail hurried and rose and mounted a donkey, and her five young women attended her. She followed the messengers of David and became his wife. (vv. 39b-42)*

At this point we are given more details of David's matrimonial situation: "David also took Ahinoam of Jezreel, and both of them became his wives" (v. 43).

What about Michal, the wife who loved David and had courageously saved him from Saul, her father (1 Samuel 18:20; 19:11-17)? "Saul had given Michal his daughter, David's wife, to Palti the son of Laish, who was of Gallim" (v. 44).

Let us not forget that though Saul has not appeared in this chapter (until this last verse), he was still the powerful king. The problem between David and Saul was far from over, as the next episode will reveal. Much later David will take Michal back, but that is another story (2 Samuel 3:13-16).

In 1 Samuel 25 we have seen a remarkable aspect of David's behavior in the days before he became Israel's king. He forgave his enemy. The fact that this only happened under the influence of Abigail's prophetic word underlines the fact that this is not the natural way for a powerful man to behave.

This remarkable aspect of David's conduct is strikingly similar to Jesus who did not come, in his first coming, "to condemn the world, but in order that the world might be saved through him" (John 3:17; cf. 12:47). The time will come for judgment (John 5:22). In the meantime Jesus Christ is in the business of forgiveness (Luke 24:47). Those who belong to him must be in the same business (see Romans 12:14-21).

44

Righteousness and Faithfulness

1 SAMUEL 26

It is not unusual in the Bible to find two incidents that are remarkably similar recorded quite close together. The Gospels have several examples. In Mark 6 we read of Jesus feeding the 5,000. Turn the page to Mark 8, and we find the feeding of the 4,000. The accounts are very similar, at some points identical. Critical scholars have often treated such similar narratives as doublets: two accounts of one incident that have been separated by some historical confusion. This misses the point seriously. In the case of the feeding miracles, it is important to understand that something very similar happened not once, but twice. The second incident takes on added significance precisely because it was the second time something just like this had happened. Therefore when Jesus had to say to his disciples the *second* time, "How many loaves do you have?" (Mark 6:38; 8:5), their slowness to understand was graphically illustrated and became the subject of his subsequent instruction.[1]

In our reading of 1 Samuel we come to a very similar situation in 1 Samuel 26. Two chapters previously we heard about the incident in the cave of Engedi, where David had, but did not take, the opportunity to put an end to his troubles by putting an end to Saul. In chapter 25 Saul briefly moved into the background of the narrative as we followed David's dealings with Nabal and Abigail and the powerful lesson he learned there. As we come to chapter 26 we find an incident remarkably similar to the Engedi cave episode, so similar that the critical scholars often propose that we have two versions of one story.[2] That is not possible, as we will see, but even more importantly it misses the point of the fact that after all that happened in chapters 24, 25 something very similar to chapter 24 happened *again*. The second incident takes on added significance precisely because it was the second time something just like this happened.

Let's follow the narrative and observe the added significance.

DAVID SPARES HIS ENEMY (AGAIN!) (vv. 1-12)

The action takes place in the first half of the chapter although, as so often in 1 Samuel, the point of it all comes out in the speeches we will hear in the second half of the chapter.

Saul Against David (Still!) (vv. 1-4)

The action begins with the first of two moments of déjà vu. The people of Ziph brought Saul information about the whereabouts of David:

> Then the Ziphites came to Saul at Gibeah, saying, "Is not David hiding himself on the hill of Hachilah, which is on the east of [better, in front of³] Jeshimon?" (v. 1)

Something very like this had happened before. It was in chapter 23:

> Then the Ziphites went up to Saul at Gibeah, saying, "Is not David hiding among us in the strongholds at Horesh, on the hill of Hachilah, which is south of Jeshimon?" (1 Samuel 23:19)

This led to the chase around the mountainside, from which David was only saved by the astonishingly timed attack by the Philistines elsewhere in the land (1 Samuel 23:25-29).

"Jeshimon" means "wasteland, wilderness." That is where David was. He was still a fugitive, driven out of society, deprived of the comforts provided by normal human community, living where no one would choose to live, in hiding, on the hill of Hachilah, in front of the wasteland. Like Jesus later, he had "nowhere to lay his head" (cf. Matthew 8:20).

The always-eager-to-please Ziphites, the inhabitants of the area, were politically astute. They could see on whose side it was prudent to be. They sent word to Gibeah, some twenty-five miles to the north, once again. I imagine Saul sitting under the tamarisk tree in Gibeah, spear in hand, surrounded by attendants (as we saw him back in 1 Samuel 22:6). The news from the loyal people of Ziph reached King Saul.

So our chapter opens with a scene we have seen before. However, the second time is different. The difference is that much had taken place since we first saw this scene. In particular, outside the cave of Engedi there was a crucial conversation between David and Saul in which, for the first time, Saul had acknowledged how wrong he had been to pursue David. He admitted that David had never done and never intended to do him any harm. He even conceded, for the first time, that David would surely be king and that the kingdom of Israel would be established in his hand. David had sworn, at Saul's request, that he would not destroy Saul's family when he became king (1 Samuel 24:17-22).

Therefore when the Ziphites brought their information to the king this second time, we do not know what will happen. If we believe Saul's words outside the cave, the hostilities were over. This second appearance in Gibeah of the informers from Ziph is the test that will prove whether Saul's confession in the wilderness of Engedi was real.

We are not kept in suspense for very long: "So Saul arose and went down to the wilderness of Ziph with three thousand chosen men of Israel to seek David in the wilderness of Ziph" (v. 2).

We do not get the impression that he was seeking David for a friendly chat! Despite the experience at Engedi, Saul did what he had done previously. He went down to the wilderness of Ziph, just as he had gone to the wilderness of Engedi in 1 Samuel 24:2.[4]

As on that occasion Saul took with him a massive force, considering the task at hand: "three thousand chosen men of Israel." Do not miss the power Saul had at his disposal. Three thousand of Israel's biggest and best! We recall that David initially had attracted 400 of Israel's rejects in the cave of Adullam (1 Samuel 22:2). That crowd had grown to 600 (1 Samuel 23:13),[5] but one could be excused for wondering whether an additional 200 of that caliber was really an improvement in his capacity. Saul outnumbered David five to one and outclassed his underdogs with crack troops.

The important point, however, is that Saul had clearly learned nothing that had changed him in the period covered by the previous two chapters.

Saul and his soldiers arrived at the spot where he had been informed David was in hiding: "And Saul encamped on the hill of Hachilah, which is beside the road on the east of [in front of] Jeshimon [or the wasteland]" (v. 3a).

However, this time the Ziphites' information was not quite accurate, or perhaps it was now out of date: "But David remained in the wilderness" (v. 3b) — not on the hill of Hachilah after all.

This time the tables were dramatically turned. What at first sight looked like Saul's great advantage (his powerful force) turned out to be impossible to conceal. Saul had no hope of a surprise element, and without surprise, the initiative fell to the cunning David: "When he saw that Saul came after him into the wilderness, David sent out spies and learned that Saul had come" (vv. 3c, 4).

David saw the massive camp on the Hachilah hillside. He presumably suspected who it was but needed to know for certain.[6] Unknown to Saul, David sent out spies and learned that it was indeed Saul. David could have been in no doubt about the purpose of Saul's expedition now. He had seen it all before.

If David had held any hope that Saul's confession at the Engedi cave meant a real change in the king, that hope was dispelled as the spies brought back news: "Yes, it is Saul. Yes, he has the army with him. Yes, they seem to be looking for someone!" David knew now that nothing had changed. He was in the same situation he had been in *before* the events at the cave of Engedi.

Saul at David's Mercy (Again!) (vv. 5-8)

This time, however, the initiative was in David's hands. The hunted became the hunter, and he found his prey:

> Then David rose and came to the place where Saul had encamped. And David saw the place where Saul lay, with Abner the son of Ner, the commander of his army. Saul was lying within the encampment, while the army was encamped around him. (v. 5)

It sounds as though David found some vantage point from which he could view Saul's camp. From this spot he could see Saul's resting-place, surrounded by the whole army, with Abner, the commander, guarding him.

What was David to do, now that he had located Saul and now that he knew that Saul's heart was unchanged? What would he do now that he knew that his earlier restraint and his appeal to Saul at Engedi had achieved precisely nothing? Saul's words could not be trusted. Reconciliation had proved impossible. What would David now do?

> Then David said to Ahimelech the Hittite, and to Joab's brother Abishai the son of Zeruiah, "Who will go down with me into the camp to Saul?" And Abishai said, "I will go down with you." (v. 6)

This sounded ominous for Saul.

Ahimelech the Hittite (not to be confused, of course, with the priest of Nob with the same name, whom Saul had slaughtered) is mentioned nowhere else in the Bible. The glimpse we are given of him here suggests something of the diverse composition of David's company. In contrast to Saul's 3,000 of Israel's best, David found beside him this foreigner, who had no reason apart from his own desperate circumstances (and we can only guess what they might have been) for being with David.[7]

On the other hand, Abishai was one of the three sons of Zeruiah, one of David's sisters (1 Chronicles 2:16). We hear much more about these nephews, the sons of Zeruiah — Abishai, Asahel, and Joab — as David's story unfolds in the second book of Samuel.[8] Here we make our first acquaintance with the strong-minded trio, whose loyalty to David was intense, but whose desire for blood would drive David to despair (see 2 Samuel 19:22).

Abishai volunteered to join David in a daring exploit "into the camp of Saul." The one Saul was seeking, with his 3,000 armed and dangerous men, proposed to go down *into* Saul's camp with one soldier accompanying him!

Events were unfolding very differently this time from the previous episode at the hill of Hachilah!

So David and Abishai went to the army by night. And there lay Saul sleeping within the encampment, with his spear stuck in the ground at his head, and Abner and the army lay around him. (v. 7)

It is a very strange scene. We will hear an explanation of it in a moment. But you cannot help wondering what kind of operation Saul was conducting. No sentries were on watch. The whole army, and Saul in the middle, were all sound asleep!

They found Saul easily because that spear of his was stuck in the ground near his head. David knew that symbol of Saul's violent power well. It had whistled past his ear three times (1 Samuel 18:11; 19:10; cf. 20:33). But now it was not in Saul's hand (see 1 Samuel 18:10; 19:9; 22:6). It was stuck in the ground, beside his sleeping and therefore vulnerable head.

Abishai won the prize for stating the obvious: "Then said Abishai to David, 'God has given your enemy into your hand this day'" (v. 8a).

This is the second déjà vu moment of the chapter. This is just what David's men had whispered to him in the depths of the Engedi cave, when Saul came into the cave alone, with his 3,000 waiting outside (1 Samuel 24:4)!

Abishai wins another prize for the most unoriginal proposal: "Now please let me pin him to the earth with one stroke of the spear, and I will not strike him twice" (v. 8b).

In the cave the men had suggested that David should do the deed and eliminate Saul. Abishai was not going to make that mistake again. He offered to perform the deed himself.[9] The spear in Abishai's hand would not miss its target as it had from Saul's hand. (The sons of Zeruiah remind us of the sons of Zebedee, "the sons of thunder," in the Gospels.[10]) To pin Saul to the earth was just the kind of proposal that came naturally to Abishai and his brothers.

The situation was uncannily similar to that which David faced in the cave of Engedi. David had Saul's life in his reach. Saul was momentarily defenseless before David and unaware of his danger. David's men (or in this case, man) were urging him to take the opportunity that God had clearly given him to bring his troubles to a swift and simple end.

Once again, however, we must appreciate the difference. In the cave David had spared Saul's life, with the effect that Saul seemed to renounce his hostility toward David. David had now learned, however, that Saul was not going to change. Mercy had achieved nothing. The fact that David had learned that makes the situation at the hill of Hachilah in chapter 26 very different from the cave of Engedi in chapter 24. What would David do *this* time? Abishai's proposal was more reasonable than the urgings of the men earlier, just because of Saul's proven belligerence.

On the other hand, since the Engedi cave, David had also learned from his experience with Nabal and Abigail. His lesson then was profoundly important. It was not up to him to save himself with his own hand (1 Samuel 25:26, 31, 33). Vengeance was God's business, not his. This was in tension with the logic that supported Abishai's proposition.

The experience of David in chapter 26 (immediately *after* the episode with Nabal and Abigail in chapter 25, and so similar in all essential aspects to the experience immediately *before*, at the cave in chapter 24) raises sharply the question whether the lesson learned from Abigail applies to the intractable situation with Saul.

Saul Spared by David (Again!) (vv. 9-12)

David was in no doubt about the answer: "But David said to Abishai, 'Do not destroy him, for who can put out his hand against the LORD's anointed and be guiltless?'" (v. 9).

For David, his experience with Nabal and Abigail had confirmed the fundamental rightness of what he had done (or, rather, not done) in the cave. His reason for restraint from harming Saul was not a forlorn hope that Saul might change. Nor, by the way, was it a simple ethic of nonviolence. Whatever you make of David, you cannot make him into a pacifist. Ask Goliath! He refused this particular act of violence, against this particular person, for this particular purpose.

It is, of course, puzzling. We know that ever since that day Samuel had come to Bethlehem, *David* had been the Lord's "anointed" or "messiah" (1 Samuel 16:12, 13). And since chapter 13 Saul had been the Lord's rejected one (1 Samuel 13:14; 15:26). So why here, and in the Engedi cave, did David so emphatically refrain from lifting his hand against Saul — from doing to Saul what Saul most certainly would have done to David, given the same chance?

The answer will come in the speeches shortly, but it is worth remembering those days when Jesus was in the wilderness, and the kingdom was held out to him if he would yield to the enemy (Matthew 4:1-11; Luke 4:1-13). It was there for the taking. But he would not *take* it. Not that way. Likewise David would not *take* the kingdom. Not Abishai's way.

Abishai offered no response to David's refusal to let him destroy his enemy. We might imagine his dumbfounded, bewildered expression.[11] Was David out of his mind? How could he pass up this God-given opportunity? Again!

So David continued:

> And David said, "As the LORD lives, the LORD will strike him, or his day will come to die, or he will go down into battle and perish. The LORD forbid that I should put out my hand against the LORD's anointed." (vv. 10, 11a)

David's restraint was because he trusted in *God*. David did not know how the Lord would deal with Saul, but trust in God means believing that God's promises will come to pass *in God's time* and *in God's way*. It was not for David to *take*, in Abishai's way.

But he did take something. He said to Abishai: "But take now the spear that is at his head and the jar of water, and let us go" (v. 11b).

And in that action, David once again won his strange victory over Saul.

However, David did not trust Abishai that close to Saul's head: "So David took the spear and the jar of water from Saul's head, and they went away" (v. 12a).

The spear and the water jar — the instrument of aggression and the source of sustenance in the desert. Without violence, David *symbolically* disarmed Saul and took his life. But the symbolic actions underlined his refusal to do the real thing (just like cutting off the corner of the king's robe in the Engedi cave).

The account of the action closes with a single sentence that sheds light on everything: "No man saw it or knew it, nor did any awake, for they were all asleep, because a deep sleep from the LORD had fallen upon them" (v. 12b).

This deep sleep was like that of Adam when the Lord created Eve, like that of Abram when he was given the promise (Genesis 2:21; 15:12; cf. also Job 4:13; 33:15; Proverbs 19:15; Isaiah 29:10).[12] David was right, you see, to trust God. No one could see it, but God kept his chosen king safe.

DAVID'S INNOCENCE (vv. 13-20)

The action in this chapter (as in chapter 24) is the backdrop for the speeches. We have already heard one important speech from David. It was whispered, heard only by Abishai. He had more to say for a bigger audience.

He moved to a place from which he could safely speak to that audience: "Then David went over to the other side and stood far off on the top of the hill, with a great space between them" (v. 13).

Abner's Guilt (vv. 14-16)

He did not begin, as at the cave, by addressing Saul. Perhaps he knew that speaking to Saul had proved pointless. "And David called to the army, and to Abner the son of Ner, saying, 'Will you not answer, Abner?'" (v. 14a).

By calling out to Abner, David may well have been implying that the real power in Israel was in his hands rather than Saul's.[13] If that was his implication, Abner, loyal servant that he was, would have none of it: "Then Abner answered, 'Who are you who calls to the king?'" (v. 14b).

David did not dispute the point of whom he was addressing. He had Abner's attention, and no doubt the attention of everyone in earshot:

> And David said to Abner, "Are you not a man? Who is like you in Israel? Why then have you not kept watch over your lord the king? For one of the people came in to destroy the king your lord. This thing that you have done is not good. As the LORD lives, you deserve to die, because you have not kept watch over your lord, the LORD's anointed. And now see where the king's spear is and the jar of water that was at his head." (vv. 15, 16)

Abner was a courageous and loyal servant of Saul, renowned in Israel. He had been Saul's commander from the beginning (1 Samuel 14:50). He had been at Saul's side the day that David killed Goliath and shared Saul's puzzlement at the identity of the remarkable young man (1 Samuel 17:55-57). Abner habitually sat at table by Saul's side (1 Samuel 20:25). Although he does not appear again in the narrative of 1 Samuel after chapter 26, he will play a major role in the early chapters of 2 Samuel, where his eventual death at the hands of the sons of Zeruiah is recorded (2 Samuel 3:26-30).

"You deserve to die" in verse 16 is, literally, "you are sons of death." We remember that earlier Saul had said that the son of Jesse was "a son of death" (1 Samuel 20:31, literal translation). Did Saul remember that? David seemed to pointedly proclaim that it was not he who was a "son of death," but those whom Saul trusted, Abner and his men. "*You* are the ones who deserve to die — not me!"

Who had saved Saul's life that day? Someone had come into Saul's camp ready, willing, and able to pin the king to the earth. "Just take a look, Abner. Where is the spear that was in the ground beside the king's head and his water jar? Who saved the king, Abner — while you slept?"

Saul's Guilt (vv. 17-20)

Abner had nothing to say. Stunned by what he'd heard, he said not a word. Someone else spoke: "Saul recognized David's voice and said, 'Is this your voice, my son David?'" (v. 17a).

Here we go again! That is exactly what he said outside the Engedi cave (1 Samuel 24:16).

> And David said, "It is my voice, my lord, O king." And he said, "Why does my lord pursue after his servant? For what have I done? What evil is on my hands?" (vv. 17b, 18)

(Actually the only evil in his hands was Saul's spear!)

> "Now therefore let my lord the king hear the words of his servant. If it is the LORD who has stirred you up against me, may he accept an offering, but if it is men, may they be cursed before the LORD, for they have driven me out this day that I should have no share in the heritage of the LORD, saying, 'Go, serve other gods.' Now therefore, let not my blood fall to the earth away from the presence of the LORD, for the king of Israel has come out to seek a single flea like one who hunts a partridge in the mountains." (vv. 19, 20)

David reminded Saul of his (David's) earlier words: "After whom has the king of Israel come out? After whom do you pursue? After a dead dog! After a flea!" (1 Samuel 24:14). It is not so much that David was claiming to be an insignificant person, but to be an insignificant threat to Saul. Saul had no more reason to fear David than to fear a flea or a partridge in the mountains!

If this went on, then he, David, would be driven from the land of Israel. To be driven from the Lord's land and the Lord's people would amount to being driven from the Lord's own presence. It would amount to sending him away from the presence of the Lord and therefore into the service of "other gods." What possible justification could Saul have for this evil?

SAUL'S CONFESSION AND PLEA (V. 21)

The answer is, none whatsoever. And once again Saul was driven to acknowledge that fact:

> Then Saul said, "I have sinned. Return, my son David, for I will no more do you harm, because my life was precious in your eyes this day. Behold, I have acted foolishly, and have made a great mistake." (v. 21)

Nabal, the fool, had a great companion in Saul, the fool. He had been a fool to disobey God, as Samuel had said.[14] Now he had multiplied his folly by his hostility to God's chosen one. Saul took the prize for understatement: he had indeed made a great mistake!

Saul's confession went further than what he had said outside the Engedi cave (1 Samuel 24:17-21) in one respect. This time he urged David to "return," presumably to Saul's service.

DAVID'S "RIGHTEOUSNESS AND . . . FAITHFULNESS" (vv. 22-25)

The last thing that David ever said to Saul was:

> *"Here is the spear, O king! Let one of the young men come over and take it. The LORD rewards every man for his righteousness and his faithfulness, for the LORD gave you into my hand today, and I would not put out my hand against the LORD's anointed. Behold, as your life was precious this day in my sight, so may my life be precious in the sight of the LORD, and may he deliver me out of all tribulation." (vv. 22-24)*

David's response to Saul's invitation to come back was devastating: "Here is the spear, O king!" "David knew, and Saul knew, the significance of the spear in their relationship."[15]

But David had understood the lesson of Abigail. For God's king,[16] what matters is *righteousness* and *faithfulness*, not cunning and cleverness, not power and control, not success and victory. *Righteousness* and *faithfulness*. David no longer expected or asked anything from Saul. The Lord would be his deliverer out of all his troubles.

Here is the high point of this chapter. We will return to it shortly.

The last thing that Saul ever said to David was: "Blessed be you, my son David! You will do many things and will succeed in them" (v. 25a).

Once again, even from the mouth of Saul, the righteousness and the legitimacy of David's coming kingdom were acknowledged (cf. 1 Samuel 24:20).

This was the last time that the two would see one another. David did not accept Saul's invitation to return with him. Saul could not be trusted. "So David went his way, and Saul returned to his place" (v. 25b).

David was still on the move. Saul went back to his tamarisk tree.

The harrowing experiences of the Engedi cave and then with Nabal and Abigail and now at the hill of Hachilah are summed up in two words: *righteousness* and *faithfulness*. David had been righteous in his behavior toward Saul, who was, after all, still king of Israel. David's refusal to lift a hand against the king was "righteousness." David had been faithful in his response to God. David's firm trust in God ("may he deliver me out of all tribulation," v. 24) was "faithfulness."

Righteousness and faithfulness are fundamental to God's own character (see Nehemiah 9:33; Psalm 85:10-13; 119:75, 138; 143:1) and therefore to God's kingdom (see 1 Kings 3:6; Psalm 89:14; 96:13; Isaiah 1:26; 11:5; 16:5; Zechariah 8:8).

The time would come when David's righteousness and faithfulness would fail (see 2 Samuel 11–12). For the moment, however, he had learned that the kingdom of God is a matter of righteousness and faithfulness (cf. Romans 14:17). This means that God's king must be righteous and faithful, and those who serve him must pursue righteousness and faithfulness.

The Lord Jesus did not fail. Without qualification he can be described as "the Righteous One" (see Acts 3:14; 7:52; 22:14; 2 Timothy 4:8; 1 Peter 3:18; 2 Peter 1:1; 1 John 2:1, 29; 3:7; Revelation 19:11). Likewise he is faithful (see 1 Thessalonians 5:24; 2 Thessalonians 3:3; 2 Timothy 2:13; Hebrews 2:17; 3:2, 6; Revelation 19:11).

It is no surprise, therefore, that for members of God's kingdom righteousness and faithfulness are essential. This wonderful reality comes to climactic expression in the gospel of our Lord Jesus Christ, in which "the *righteousness* of God is revealed from *faith* for *faith* [or faithfulness]" (Romans 1:17). "It was to show his righteousness at the present time, so that he might be just [righteous] and the justifier [the one who declares righteous] of the one who has faith in Jesus" (Romans 3:26).

45

Clever and Cunning Success

1 SAMUEL 27

The Bible is deeply honest and utterly realistic. If you come to the Bible looking for sentimentality or romantic heroism, you will be disappointed. The Bible is about real people and a real God. Real people have weaknesses as well as strengths, failures as well as successes, defeats as well as triumphs. The real God, while perfect in every way, deals with real people who do not always find his ways comfortable.

David is one of the real people whose story the Bible tells. As we reach 1 Samuel 27, we can look back and see that there has been much about David that is very impressive indeed. From his first public appearance in Israel, when he killed Goliath (1 Samuel 17), David made a powerful impact on everyone (see 1 Samuel 18:6, 7). He was consistently a winner in battles against Israel's enemies (1 Samuel 18:14, 27, 30; 19:8; 23:5). He won the love and trust of many in Israel (see especially 1 Samuel 18). Although Saul's bitter jealousy put his life at risk, he showed remarkable restraint in repudiating vengeance or violence against the man who still was his king (see 1 Samuel 24:6; 26:9).

There have been moments when we have glimpsed a darker side to David. He bitterly regretted cutting off a corner of Saul's robe in the Engedi cave. We might have been struck by the nobility of such a tender conscience but should not miss the fact that by his own measure, he regretted what he had done (1 Samuel 24:5, 6). More starkly, his violent anger against Nabal and his determination to take vengeance against him (1 Samuel 25:21, 22), was wrong. He didn't do it, but only because of the intervention of the courageous, prophetic, wise (not to mention, beautiful) Abigail (see 1 Samuel 25:23-35).

Nevertheless, by the end of chapter 26 "righteousness" and "faithfulness" are words that describe well what we have seen of David (1 Samuel 26:23). The young man who had commended David to Saul at the beginning was right about him: "a man of valor, a man of war, prudent in speech, and a man of good presence, and the LORD is with him" (1 Samuel 16:18). In particular the last point ("the LORD is with him") has been borne out. It is clear that David enjoyed the Lord's care, protection, and enabling. David, at his best, knew that.[1]

In chapter 27 something extraordinary happened. It is the kind of thing that clinches the case for the Bible's honesty and realism. In this respect it is like the Gospel records that include the failings of the disciples despite the very high esteem in which they were held by the early Christians. Here is an episode in the life of the great David that has been recorded for the simple reason that it happened and therefore contributes to the Bible's candid portrayal of one of its greatest characters.[2]

The chapter records a period when David chose to live under the protection of none other than the Philistines and, to a certain extent at least, collaborated with them. The severity of the scandal of this fact must be appreciated. The Philistines were the deadly archenemies of Israel. It is astonishing, to say the least, to hear that one who expected to become Israel's king should have this skeleton in his closet.

The chapter candidly answers three questions about this period.

WHY WAS DAVID AMONG THE PHILISTINES? (vv. 1-4)

At the end of chapter 26 we saw one of the high points in these difficult days for David. He had, for the second time, spared Saul's life. The pathetic Saul had acknowledged his foolish wickedness in seeking David's life (1 Samuel 26:21). David understood with brilliant clarity that the Lord could be trusted to protect him and deliver him out of all his troubles (1 Samuel 26:24). This was a moment of great moral and spiritual triumph. Against the odds, righteousness and faithfulness had prevailed (1 Samuel 26:23)! The Lord had kept David from guilt in regard to both Saul and Nabal (see 1 Samuel 25:26).

David's Decision (v. 1)

From this high point, David's thoughts took a rather different turn:

> Then David said in his heart, "Now I shall perish one day by the hand of Saul. There is nothing better for me than that I should escape to the land

*of the Philistines. Then Saul will despair of seeking me any longer within
the borders of Israel, and I shall escape out of his hand." (v. 1)*

The narrator makes no comment on this musing of David.[3] We are left
wondering what to make of it. It is puzzling.

One thing is clear. David did not believe that Saul's conciliatory words
at their last encounter could be trusted. In that he was undoubtedly right. "I
will no more do you harm," Saul had said (1 Samuel 26:21). He may even
have meant it. However, David knew well, from painful experience, that
it would only be a matter of time before Saul's bitter hatred overtook him
again.

The puzzle with David's words is that he imagined "the hand of Saul" to
prevail. He said, "I shall perish one day by the hand of Saul." His experience
through these admittedly difficult days had been that "Saul sought him every
day, but God did *not* give him into his hand" (1 Samuel 23:14). What made
David now think that God's protection of him would "one day" fail? Did he
think that God's protection was like luck that must sooner or later run out?
Had he forgotten the words of Jonathan at their last meeting ("Do not fear,
for the hand of Saul my father shall not find you," 1 Samuel 23:17a)? So far
Jonathan's words had proven to be astonishingly true. Why did David now
think the hand of Saul *would* find him? What reason did he have to doubt
that his prayer outside the Engedi cave ("May the LORD . . . deliver me from
your hand," 1 Samuel 24:15) would be answered?

The word David used of his impending fate ("perish") perhaps hints at
the depth of his anguish. It was not a common Hebrew word[4] and is used
only three times in the books of Samuel. In 1 Samuel 12:25 it described
the fate of Israel and their king if they disobeyed God: "you shall be *swept
away*." In 1 Samuel 26:10 David used the same word to describe one of
the ways in which God might deal with Saul: "he will go down into battle
and *perish*." That he should now think that this could be his fate "one day"
signals a significant change of perspective.

What is also troubling about David's words is that they sound like a
capitulation to Saul's evil intentions. David had protested that Saul's pursuit
of him was driving him away from "the heritage of the LORD," "away from
the presence of the LORD" (1 Samuel 26:19, 20). The implication was that if
Saul kept up his persecution, David would have to leave the land of Israel
and live in a pagan land where "other gods" were served (1 Samuel 26:19).
This potential outcome of Saul's policy was presented by David as proof of
its wickedness. By now proposing to "escape to the land of the Philistines,"
was David abandoning his "share in the heritage of the LORD" (1 Samuel
26:19) and fleeing "from the presence of the LORD" (1 Samuel 26:20), at
least in some sense? Was it a Jonah-like plan (see Jonah 1:3)? Was he turn-

ing his back on the word of the prophet Gad who had told him to "go into the land of Judah" (1 Samuel 22:5)?

And why the land of the Philistines, of all places? He had done something like this once before, and it had been a near disaster. He had fled to Gath, and just as quickly had to flee *from* Gath, escaping only by his quick wits and dribbling (1 Samuel 21:10-15)! Why the land of the Philistines again?

After the profound faith in the Lord and his good purpose for David expressed at the end of chapter 26, these words of David, with no reference to God,[5] appear to abandon hope. Literally he said, "There is no *good* for me" in the land of Israel. Had he forgotten the words of Abigail about "all the *good* that [the LORD] has spoken concerning you" (1 Samuel 25:30)?

The answers to our many questions are not given by the narrative. The questions, however, are sharply raised.[6] We might suspect that here David experienced the kind of crushing doubt that overcame Elijah many years later in the aftermath of his great day of triumph (see 1 Kings 18–19).[7]

David's Action (vv. 2, 3)

David was, however, as good as his words (or as bad as his words, depending on how you are seeing this): "So David arose and went over, he and the six hundred men who were with him, to Achish the son of Maoch, king of Gath" (v. 2).

There is almost something sinister in the words "went over."[8] David crossed a boundary that day, and not just a geographical one. He "went over" to the other side. This was quite different from the last time when he had gone to Gath alone, probably hoping to remain unnoticed. This time David brought with him his 600 men and (as we will see in the next verse) their families. The implication of "went over . . . to Achish" seems to be that David offered the services of his men to the Philistine king. Here was a fighting force that could be very useful to the king of Gath.[9] Who would know better how good they were? After all, they had fought and defeated the Philistines at least once since they had formed as David's band (1 Samuel 23:5).

The situation may have changed since David's last visit to Gath in another respect. Since then the hostilities between Saul and David had resulted in at least two incidents that may well have reached the ears of the citizens of Gath. Saul had slaughtered the priests and people of Nob (1 Samuel 22:17-19), and there had been the great chase in the wilderness of Maon (1 Samuel 23:24-29). If the bitter hatred of Israel's king toward David was now well known to Achish, then on the assumption that the enemy of my enemy is my friend, Achish may well have been better disposed toward David than we would otherwise have expected.

Whatever the full explanation might be, David and his band found a safe haven in the last place on earth that you would expect, Goliath's hometown of Gath:

> And David lived with Achish at Gath, he and his men, every man with his household, and David with his two wives, Ahinoam of Jezreel, and Abigail of Carmel, Nabal's widow. (v. 3)

With wives and children this could have been a group of 2,000 or 3,000 people.[10] They and David must have put themselves under the authority of Achish. You do not live "with" a king except under his sway. From the events that we will see in the following chapters, it seems clear that Achish understood David's men to be at his disposal. From Achish's point of view he had won a valuable, if surprising, vassal.

How would it have looked to anyone who heard about it in Israel? Again the narrative makes no evaluative comment.

David's "Success" (v. 4)

The extraordinary development *was* reported in Israel, specifically to Saul: "And when it was told Saul that David had fled to Gath, he no longer sought him" (v. 4).

In other words, David's escape had been successful. He had done it so that Saul would "despair of seeking me any longer within the borders of Israel, and I shall escape out of his hand" (1 Samuel 27:1), and that strategy worked. David was, it would seem, safe. His "fleeing" from Saul had gone on for such a long time (see 1 Samuel 19:12, 18; 20:1; 21:10; 22:17). Now it was over.

But at what cost? There is no mention here, as previously, of God's protective hand. Much had been said a little earlier in this narrative about the inappropriateness of David saving himself "with his own hand" (see 1 Samuel 25:26, 33). Should we consider whether this scheme falls into that category?[11]

The narrator has candidly answered the first major question about David's Philistine period. David was among the Philistines in order to escape from Saul. The answer, however, begs other questions.

HOW WAS DAVID TREATED BY THE PHILISTINES? (vv. 5-7)

Anyone who heard that David lived for a time among the Philistines would be bound to wonder how he was treated by them. This could be an indication of whether he really had "gone over" to the Philistines.

The disturbing answer provided by the narrative is that David and his band were treated very generously indeed by their hosts.

David's Request (v. 5)

This is demonstrated by what happened when David approached Achish with a very bold request:

> Then David said to Achish, "If I have found favor in your eyes, let a place be given me in one of the country towns, that I may dwell there. For why should your servant dwell in the royal city with you?" (v. 5)

The assumption of these words, of course, was that he *had* "found favor" in the eyes of Achish. There is irony in the fact that once David had "found favor in the eyes of " Saul (1 Samuel 16:22)![12] There is at least an apparent scandal in the idea that David had found "favor in the eyes of " the Philistine king. On the assumption that the friend of my enemy is my enemy, this would make David Israel's enemy!

On the basis of the good relationship with Achish, however, David's request had a certain logic to it. On the one hand, his very considerable company must have been "a rather burdensome presence in a modest-sized Philistine city."[13] On the other hand, David's service of the Philistine king, with the force he brought with him, surely warranted some payment. A royal land grant would seem a reasonable request.

However, it is the assumptions contained in these words that shock us. Did you notice how David described himself to Achish? "Your servant"! How would David ever live down this story? How could this man ever legitimately claim the throne in Israel? By his own mouth he had been a favored servant of Israel's bitter enemy.

David's Success (vv. 6, 7)

The proof that the assumptions in David's request were true lies in the fact that the request was granted: "So that day Achish gave him Ziklag" (v. 6a).

Although the location of Ziklag is not certain, a site some twenty-five miles south of Gath has been proposed. It was probably near the border of Philistine- and Judean-controlled areas.[14] We are not told why Achish gave him Ziklag. We do not know whether David had any say in where his town was to be. Subsequent events will give us reason to suspect that he may have. The simple fact is that Achish gave his "servant" David a significant land grant.

What do you think that did to David's reputation in Israel when word got out?

Of course, eventually word did get out. By the time this story was being written down, the fact that Ziklag had been in David's family for many years was well known. The writer made no attempt to deny it: "Therefore Ziklag has belonged to the kings of Judah to this day" (v. 6b).

The kings of Judah were, of course, David's descendants.[15] The writer points his original readers to the contemporary consequence of the awkward fact about David that has just been told. At the same time he reintroduces to the narrative the truth that this David, the apparent Philistine collaborator, *was* (as we should know by now) destined to become Israel's king. Achish did not know what he was doing in giving Ziklag to David. He was giving it to the future kings of Judah!

Be that as it may, what is quite clear is that David and his band were treated very well indeed by the Philistine king. There is nothing in the evidence so far to satisfy anyone who may have considered that this period raised serious questions about David. "And the number of the days that David lived in the country of the Philistines was a year and four months" (v. 7).

This was not a very long time, but it was long enough for David to realize his mistake (if that is what it was) and attempt to redress the situation.[16] It was also long enough to raise questions about what he did during that time.

HOW DID DAVID BEHAVE WHILE AMONG THE PHILISTINES? (vv. 8-12)

The third question that the uncomfortable fact of David's Philistine phase raises is about what he did during those sixteen months. It is possible that the first readers of this account had heard rumors that David's collaboration with the Philistines had extended to attacking his own people. If that were the case, his reputation would be irreparably damaged.

The narrator therefore sets out a frank, though brief, account of David's conduct in his Philistine days.

David's Battles (vv. 8, 9)

From his new base in Ziklag, David did what David did best: "Now David and his men went up and made raids against the Geshurites, the Girzites, and the Amalekites . . ." (v. 8a).

David was a military man of exceptional ability. He set about attacking and plundering the people of his locality. The Geshurites were a people group in the vicinity.[17] The Girzites are only mentioned here in the Bible, but from the context they were another people group nearby.[18] The Amalekites, of course, were an important part of Saul's downfall in chapter 15.

The first thing to notice about this behavior of David is that he did *not* attack Philistines. He attacked people who would have been hostile to the Philistines. In doing so he could be seen as a true servant of Achish![19]

In other words, the conduct of David in itself offered no reassurances to those who may have had concerns about his collaboration with the Philistines.

The narrator, however, points us in another direction: ". . . for these were the inhabitants of the land from of old, as far as Shur, to the land of Egypt" (v. 8b).

The implication is that the peoples David attacked were, when all is said and done, "the inhabitants of the land"[20] whom the Israelites were told by God, through Moses, to "devote to complete destruction" (see Numbers 33:50-56; Deuteronomy 7:1-5; 20:16-18).

The astonishing thing is that here is a possible explanation, perhaps even exoneration, of David's behavior. Was he, after all, fighting the battles of the Lord (cf. 1 Samuel 18:17; 25:28)? Under the *guise* of serving Achish, was he in reality fighting Israel's battles (cf. 1 Samuel 8:20)? What is astonishing is that the writer drops the hint of this possible explanation but does not elaborate.[21] If this is the explanation, the writer does not say so explicitly.

He does tell us, however, that David was ruthlessly thorough in his raids:

> And David would strike the land and would leave neither man nor woman alive, but would take away the sheep, the oxen, the donkeys, the camels, and the garments, and come back to Achish. (v. 9)

David therefore dealt with the people of these groups as God had commanded Saul to deal with the Amalekites (1 Samuel 15:3). However, he "took away" the animals — the very thing that Saul was forbidden to do.[22] It does not seem that David received any explicit word from God concerning this action, as Saul had done with regard to the Amalekites. It is possible that David believed he was acting according to the command that had been given through Moses concerning the original inhabitants of the land,[23] but this is not made clear.

David's Lies (vv. 10, 11)

Whenever David reported back to Achish, the Philistine king naturally wanted to know what his new subordinate had been doing. The conversation would go like this:

> When Achish asked, "Where have you made a raid today?" David would say, "Against the Negeb of Judah," or, "Against the Negeb of the Jerahmeelites," or, "Against the Negeb of the Kenites." (v. 10)

In other words he lied.

The Negeb was a large area to the south. The parts of it that David claimed to have attacked were occupied either by Judah or allies of Judah.[24]

Here is the first clear indication that David was not the faithful servant of Achish that Achish had been led to believe, although David's actual plundering activities did no harm to Achish's interests. On the contrary, as we have already noted, David attacked peoples who would have been as hostile to the Philistines as they were to the Israelites. If David had told Achish the truth, it would have done him no harm.

David chose, however, in a most calculating way to deceive Achish into thinking that he had spent his time and efforts attacking Judah's interests. He went to extraordinary lengths to ensure that his lies were believed:

> And David would leave neither man nor woman alive to bring news to Gath, thinking, "lest they should tell about us and say, 'So David has done.'" (v. 11a)

This is the only motive we are explicitly given for David's extreme policy in these raids. While this is not inconsistent with other motives (such as fulfilling the injunctions given through Moses), this motive is highlighted here.

This calculated policy persisted through David's time of purportedly "serving" Achish: "Such was his custom all the while he lived in the country of the Philistines" (v. 11b).

"Custom" is the word that was used to describe the ways of various leaders of Israel. In some contexts it may be translated "justice." We saw the "justice" of the sons of Eli in 1 Samuel 2:13. In 1 Samuel 8:3 Samuel's sons likewise perverted "justice." Samuel told the people the "justice" they could expect from a king like the nations in 1 Samuel 8:9, 11. In 1 Samuel 10:25 Samuel told the people of the "justice" of the kingdom. Now in 1 Samuel 27:11 we learn that David's "justice" during his Philistine period consisted in this cunning policy.

David's "Success" (v. 12)

The purpose of this deceptive two-timing is clear from the description of its success: "And Achish trusted David, thinking, 'He has made himself an utter stench to his people Israel; therefore he shall always be my servant'" (v. 12).

Achish (literally) "believed in David." It is exactly the same expression as we find after the crossing of the Red Sea, when the people of Israel "believed in" Moses (Exodus 14:31)! What an irony that was! The Philistine king trusted David on the basis of David's lies, supported by David's ruthless policy of extermination. He believed that David had become to the Israelites as the Israelites had earlier become to the Philistines (1 Samuel 13:4).

At the end of the chapter we are stunned at the political cunning and cleverness of David! The killer of Goliath (not to mention the countless other Philistines whose deaths he orchestrated) not only found safe refuge among the Philistines, but he deceived the king of Gath into utterly trusting him! Perhaps that was his plan all along. There are not many men who could pull off a stunt like that!

The story is not finished,[25] and we have yet to see what will come of Achish's misplaced trust in David. However, this is a convenient point to pause and reflect on the significance of what we have seen.

A little earlier in the story Saul had said of David, "It is told me that he is very cunning" (1 Samuel 23:22). We have now seen that Saul had been told the truth!

Nevertheless, 1 Samuel 27 should, I believe, puzzle and perhaps shock us. The cleverness of David in this chapter is very different from the "righteousness and . . . faithfulness" we saw in 1 Samuel 26. His cleverness included reflections at the beginning of the chapter that seem like a loss of confidence in God. His "going over" to Achish, while cleverly handled and apparently not the treacherous act it may have at first appeared, was not obviously an act of courageous faithfulness. His ruthless treatment of the peoples he chose to strike, while very effective and possibly justifiable in terms of God's revealed purposes, was motivated by the more questionable intention of covering his lies to Achish. Those lies, while they were told to Israel's archenemy and brilliantly achieved their purpose, had the dubious aim of dispelling any lingering doubts Achish may have had about David.

In other words, in chapter 27 we have begun to see what will become very clear in due course. The brilliantly gifted David was also a man "with a nature like ours" (cf. James 5:17). In himself he was more than capable of doubting God, of giving way to fear, and of self-protective action with no reference to God. The alarming conclusion (if we have understood this chapter fairly) is that David possessed all the weaknesses that led to Saul's downfall!

The chapter sets before us the apparent strength and success of cunning and clever David, in contrast to the apparent weakness and vulnerability of the righteous and faithful David we saw in the previous chapters. The sad truth is that the brilliantly gifted David eventually failed because of unrighteousness and unfaithfulness. The record of that failure becomes clear from 2 Samuel 11 onward. The seeds of that failure, however, can be seen in 1 Samuel 27.

We can see that Achish was a fool to put his trust in David. He had been duped by David's lies and ruthlessness.

The gospel calls us to put our trust in Jesus, in whom is to be found truth and life (cf. John 14:6). There are no lies with him. No ruthless cunning. Just righteousness and faithfulness.

46

"Having No Hope and Without God"

1 SAMUEL 28

Utter hopelessness is the darkest of all human experiences. It is the realization that there is absolutely no prospect of a future with anything positive in it. Hopelessness, when it overcomes a person, strips away motivation or enthusiasm for living because there is nothing, absolutely nothing, good to look forward to.

Even fear is better than hopelessness. When we are afraid, we usually dread something that *could* happen or that *may* be as bad as we imagine. But there is usually also the possibility that things will turn out better than we expect. There is, in other words, hope. Hopelessness is the experience of believing there is no future worth having.

The problem is that the human experience of hopelessness generally does not correspond to reality. This happens in two ways.

On the one hand, psychologists and counselors are kept busy helping people who have lost hope in the future because, in their depressed state of mind, they have become unrealistically negative. They need, perhaps, to see that there are people who love them and will continue to do so, that there is valuable work for them to do and that they can do it, that there are joys ahead for them to embrace. The terrible experience of hopelessness can be untrue, a kind of blindness. Christian believers are not immune from experiencing such dark times. Some of us need to be helped to see the goodness of God's sovereign purposes, the truth that "for those who love God all things work together for good" so that "the sufferings of this present time are not worth comparing with the glory that is to be revealed to us" (Romans 8:28, 18).

On the other hand there is a very different experience that is equally untrue. It is another kind of blindness, even more serious than the first, perhaps better described as shortsightedness. In this case there is no sense of despair, and there may be an entirely hopeful attitude to the future, but it is based on an unrealistically positive state of mind. Psychologists and counselors may see few of these people, because by the measures of these professions they are healthy, well-balanced men and women. The problem is only seen when we take seriously the brevity of life in this world and what lies beyond.

The Apostle Paul graphically described the utter hopelessness of all who are "separated from Christ" as "having no hope and without God in the world" (Ephesians 2:12).[1] He was not describing a conscious *sense* of hopelessness, but a real situation of hopelessness. To be in this transient world, but to be "without God" is indeed to have "no hope." The "healthy, well-balanced men and women" who are in this situation need to listen to the Bible's realism.

In 1 Samuel 28 we see the utter hopelessness of King Saul exposed. Though it is painful to watch, we will benefit by looking carefully at this man when he found himself "having no hope and without God in the world."

A DESPERATE SITUATION (vv. 1, 2)

The particular situation that provided the occasion for Saul's darkest night was, once again, the threat from the ever-aggressive Philistines:[2] "In those days the Philistines gathered their forces for war, to fight against Israel" (v. 1a).

This had, of course, happened many times in the past. Indeed we know that "there was hard fighting against the Philistines all the days of Saul" (1 Samuel 14:52). Saul had recently had some success against the Philistines.[3] The fact that the Philistines had once again initiated hostilities against Israel would not be particularly interesting except for one thing.

In 1 Samuel 27 we learned that David, the man who had always had far greater success against the Philistines than Saul (see especially 1 Samuel 18:30), "went over" to Achish, the Philistine king of Gath (1 Samuel 27:2). Although David's actions while in league with the Philistines, narrated in 1 Samuel 27, raise a number of puzzling questions, these fade into insignificance beside the question that is raised at the beginning of chapter 28. What was to happen when the Philistines attacked Israel, and David was not with Israel but with the Philistines?

Saul must have viewed this renewed Philistine aggression with greatly increased anxiety. He knew that David had joined the Philistines (1 Samuel 27:4). This was a crisis such as he had never faced before. Saul had two hated and feared enemies — David[4] and the Philistines.[5] On an earlier occasion Saul had been forced to choose to abandon dealing with one of these threats (David) in order to defend the land against the other (the Philistines) (1 Samuel 23:28). Did Saul now face an attack from the combined forces he feared most — Achish *and* David?

The narrator, however, leaves us (for the moment) to imagine Saul's desperation at this development because the renewed Philistine hostilities against Israel also brought about a desperate situation for David. He had duped Achish into trusting him by telling him that from his base in Ziklag he had been attacking Israelite interests, when in fact he had been doing nothing of the sort. Achish believed he had an ally who would now serve him faithfully always and never again be a friend to his own people (1 Samuel 27:8-12).

It is unlikely that David had guessed where Achish's trust in him would lead: "And Achish said to David, 'Understand that you and your men are to go out with me in the army'" (v. 1b).

It seems that David may have overplayed his hand. He had been so successful in deceiving Achish that the Philistine king now enlisted his support for the coming war against David's own people.[6] We know (although Achish did not) that David had renounced any hostile act against Saul (1 Samuel 24:6, 10-12, 22; 26:9, 11, 23). He had spent his time in Ziklag, not attacking Judah's interests as Achish thought, but Israel's ancient enemies (1 Samuel 27:9, 10). However, now he found himself required by his Philistine master to join the assault on Israel.

Had David been too clever for his own good? Had his crafty deceit landed him in an impossible dilemma? If he were to refuse to fight with Achish, his lies would be uncovered, and Achish would not hesitate to eliminate this deceiver. If he were to obey Achish and fight with the Philistines against Israel, his anticipated kingship over Israel would be undermined before it had begun. "David said to Achish, 'Very well, you shall know what your servant can do'" (v. 2a).

To Achish's ears, that must have sounded like "Splendid. You will see what I can do."[7] David encouraged that understanding by continuing to present himself to Achish as "your servant" (cf. 1 Samuel 27:5). To our ears, however, it was "an artful dodge."[8] In the original language "Very well" is less committal than it sounds in English.[9] "You will see what your servant can do" makes us wonder what, indeed, David would do with the dilemma in which his cunning had embroiled him.

David's predicament then deepened: "And Achish said to David, 'Very well, I will make you my bodyguard for life'" (v. 2b).

For Achish there could be no fuller expression of his confidence in David's loyalty than this. The Philistine king was entrusting his own life to the care of this Israelite renegade![10] We marvel at Achish's gullibility. As on the first occasion when David had appeared before Achish (1 Samuel 21:10-15), Gath's king was completely hoodwinked by David.[11]

In doing so Achish was putting himself in mortal danger. There is a shocking unconscious irony to Achish's words that is lost in English translation. In the original the expression for "my bodyguard" is literally "the guard of my head"! If I were a Philistine, I am not sure David is the one I would choose to "guard my head." He had quite a reputation for what he once did to another Philistine head (1 Samuel 17:51, 54)!

However, for David the appointment was hardly a welcome honor! The possibilities by which he might escape from his predicament were suddenly reduced. The freedom of movement, action, and deception he had enjoyed at Ziklag would no longer be available under the close surveillance involved in guarding the Philistine king.

How could David possibly get out of this pickle?

The narrator chooses to leave us in suspense on that question while he takes us forward in time to the eve of the battle with the Philistines. He does not yet reveal what happened with David in the meantime but is about to disclose how Saul was faring by the time that night fell. Only in chapter 29 will we be taken back to learn the outcome of David's difficulty.[12]

A DESPERATE SAUL (vv. 3-6)

On the evening that would turn out to be Saul's last night alive, he found himself in a depth of desperation he had not previously known. To help us understand his despondency the writer notes three aspects of the situation.

Samuel Dead (v. 3)

The first is something that had happened some time previously: "Now Samuel had died, and all Israel had mourned for him and buried him in Ramah, his own city" (v. 3a).

Samuel's death and burial had occurred earlier and was recorded in 1 Samuel 25:1. Saul had not had any significant contact with Samuel since the day the prophet had announced that the Lord had rejected Saul from being Israel's king (1 Samuel 15:26).[13] However, the moment had arrived when Saul's alienation from Samuel, now irreparable because the prophet had died, became unbearable.

The writer adds a surprising piece of information that will be important for understanding what he is about to narrate: "And Saul had put the mediums and the necromancers out of the land" (v. 3b).

The relevance of this fact is not immediately obvious. Following the mention of Samuel's death, however, it does remind us of Saul's better days. There had been a time when there were grounds for high expectations of Saul's reign.[14] This verse seems to go back to that time and reports a particular policy that enacted the one condition for this kingship to go well — namely, "If you will fear the LORD and serve him and obey his voice and not rebel against the commandment of the LORD" (1 Samuel 12:14). The commandments of God's Law were very clear about mediums, necromancy, and the like.

For example:[15]

"Do not turn to mediums or necromancers; do not seek them out, and so make yourselves unclean by them: I am the LORD your God." (Leviticus 19:31)

"If a person turns to mediums and necromancers, whoring after them, I will set my face against that person and will cut him off from among his people." (Leviticus 20:6)

"A man or a woman who is a medium or a necromancer shall surely be put to death. They shall be stoned with stones; their blood shall be upon them." (Leviticus 20:27)

"There shall not be found among you . . . anyone who practices divination or tells fortunes or interprets omens, or a sorcerer or a charmer or a medium or a necromancer . . . for whoever does these things is an abomination to the LORD." (Deuteronomy 18:10-12)

That Saul had at one time enacted a policy in accordance with these commandments of God is entirely to his credit. It may cast light on Samuel's words to him at their last encounter: "For rebellion is as the sin of divination" (1 Samuel 15:23).[16] Saul, we now learn, had once understood and effectively repudiated "the sin of divination." How terrible it must have been for the man who had eradicated mediums and necromancers from the land to hear that his failure with the Amalekites was "as the sin of divination"!

The immediate relevance of the fact that Saul had once proscribed such things will become clear shortly.

Philistines Gathered (vv. 4, 5)

The second factor that made Saul's situation so desperate was, of course, the latest Philistine initiative: "The Philistines assembled and came and encamped at Shunem. And Saul gathered all Israel, and they encamped at Gilboa" (v. 4).

This takes us forward in time from the conversation between Achish and David in verses 1, 2. The Philistines had now taken up their position at Shunem, located well to the north,[17] on the northern side of the Jezreel Valley that cut through the north-south ridge of mountains that was Israel's heartland. Apparently in response Saul had assembled his forces at Gilboa, on the southern side of the same valley.

The Philistine strategy seems clear. They were attempting to divide and conquer. The location of their assault potentially cut Saul off from the Israelites further to the north.[18] This could be the most serious attempt so far by the Philistines to break Israel.

We are not yet told what had happened to David since the crucial conversation with Achish back in Gath. Had he come north with the Philistines to Shunem? The effect of withholding that information for the time being is that as we hear the story, we share Saul's ignorance of this matter and may therefore appreciate his anxiety. "When Saul saw the army of the Philistines, he was afraid, and his heart trembled greatly" (v. 5).

Formerly this king had led his trembling people (1 Samuel 13:7). Now he was the trembling one. His world was collapsing. The present crisis was too much for him. He had lost the capacity to be king.

The Lord Silent (v. 6)

The third factor contributing to the desperation of Saul's circumstances was decisive:

> And when Saul inquired of the LORD, the LORD did not answer him, either by dreams, or by Urim, or by prophets.

This is a variation on the situation anticipated by Samuel on the day the people had first asked for a king: "And in that day you will cry out because of your king, whom you have chosen for yourselves, but the LORD will not answer you in that day" (1 Samuel 8:18).

Now the king they had chosen for themselves was himself crying out, and the Lord was not answering. Samuel was dead, and the Lord had sent no other prophet to Saul. The Urim was a means the priests used to seek God's guidance. Saul had slaughtered the priests. Dreams were sometimes a means of divine instruction, but there too Saul met silence.

The silence of God was not a new experience for Saul (see 1 Samuel 14:37),[19] but the time had come for King Saul when that silence was too much to endure. It meant that Saul was on his own. The God who had appointed him and had rejected him was not with him as he faced the greatest crisis of his life. He was utterly alone. What was he to do?

It is interesting to notice that the narrative has set before us both David and Saul in terribly desperate circumstances. Both are life-threatening. The outcomes of these two predicaments will, however, be very different.

A DESPERATE MEASURE (vv. 7-14)

The desperate Saul resorted to a desperate measure.

The Alternative Sought (v. 7)

The Lord was silent, and it is astonishing to hear of the alternative means of guidance to which Saul resorted: "Then Saul said to his servants, 'Seek out for me a woman who is a medium, that I may go to her and inquire of her'" (v. 7a).

The very commandment of God that Saul had once so diligently enforced in his kingdom, he now intended to break! Years later the prophet Isaiah would say to his contemporaries:

> And when they say to you, "Inquire of the mediums and the necromancers who chirp and mutter," should not a people inquire of their God? Should they inquire of the dead on behalf of the living? (Isaiah 8:19)

Saul's "decision to seek help from a medium is a measure of his moral exhaustion, his despairing faith, his failed life."[20] Here indeed was a man who had found himself "having no hope and without God in the world" (Ephesians 2:12).

Surprisingly his servants seemed both too willing and too able to help him: "And his servants said to him, 'Behold, there is a medium at En-dor'" (v. 7b).

How was it that there was still such a woman in Saul's kingdom? And how was it that Saul's servants had immediate knowledge of the fact? Was this evidence of the corruption that had come into the circle around the failing king?

There was a problem with the servants' advice. En-dor was north of Shunem.[21] From Saul's location in Gilboa it was across the Jezreel Valley and up into the hills beyond the Philistine forces in Shunem. It would be a risky business for the king to attempt to visit En-dor.

The Secret Request (vv. 8-11)

Once again Saul's desperation was displayed in his immediate decision to take the risk: "So Saul disguised himself and put on other garments and went, he and two men with him" (v. 8a).

His disguise was presumably needed to both escape detection by the Philistines whose position he had to pass and also to conceal his involvement in what was, after all, a crime. The indignity of discarding his royal attire, however, fits the circumstances as this failed king made his last effort to escape his doom.[22]

No details of the journey are given, just the fact of the destination reached: "And they came to the woman by night" (v. 8b).

It would have to have been "by night," of course, to avoid detection. However, the narrator seems to appreciate that darkness was appropriate for the incident he is about to tell.[23] "And he said, 'Divine for me by a spirit and bring up for me whomever I shall name to you'" (v. 8c).

The reference to the death of Samuel in 1 Samuel 28:3 is hint enough for us to guess who Saul wanted to reach through the medium. She, of course, did not know Saul's identity and did not yet know for whom he would ask.

Sensibly the woman was cautious with her unidentified night visitor:

> The woman said to him, "Surely you know what Saul has done, how he has cut off the mediums and the necromancers from the land. Why then are you laying a trap for my life to bring about my death?" (v. 9)

We should take the woman's words at face value. The last person in the world that she would have expected to approach her with this request would have been Saul. Her objection was genuine. She may well have feared that the stranger before her was an agent of Saul, but the idea that it was Saul himself would be far from her mind.

Her words should have struck a cord of conscience with Saul. His own policy was testimony to the Law of God, which he was now flagrantly breaking. However, Saul was in no mood for self-examination: "But Saul swore to her by the LORD, 'As the LORD lives, no punishment shall come upon you for this thing'" (v. 10).

The incongruity of swearing an oath by the Lord about this act of deep rebellion and disobedience to the Lord seems to have escaped Saul.[24] The woman, too, seems strangely, even naively, obliging. We might expect her to ask who this stranger was to offer such a guarantee against the king's decree. Instead we read: "Then the woman said, 'Whom shall I bring up for you?'" (v. 11a).

If we had any doubt about Saul's purpose, it is now revealed: "He said, 'Bring up Samuel for me'" (v. 11b).

Remember that the woman did not yet know Saul's identity. She probably had not yet guessed the identity of the "Samuel" requested.[25] Again it seems likely that the last person a woman such as this would expect anyone to ask her to conjure up would be the great prophet of the Lord who had forbade inquiring of the dead.

The Fearful Reply (vv. 12-14)

It is important to notice that the narrative gives us no precise details about what the woman then did. But between the end of 1 Samuel 28:11 and the beginning of 1 Samuel 28:12 Samuel appeared and scared the woman out of her wits: "When the woman saw Samuel, she cried out with a loud voice" (v. 12a).

This chapter of the Bible tells us nothing whatsoever about the practice of mediums and necromancy (except to remind us of the fact that the Law and the prophets forbade these practices). It is a mistake to try to draw conclusions on that subject from this chapter. Did the woman have the power to bring Samuel back from the dead? The text does not say so. It simply tells us that Samuel appeared. It seems far more likely to me that the Lord sent Samuel to Saul on this evening, just as on a very different occasion he sent Moses and Elijah to Jesus (Matthew 17:3). The dark powers of this woman (if she possessed such) were irrelevant.[26]

On recognizing the Samuel who appeared, the woman seems to have suddenly seen through Saul's whole scheme. Who in all of Israel would want to speak to the dead Samuel? The answer was now all too clear to her: "And the woman said to Saul, 'Why have you deceived me? You are Saul'" (v. 12b).

The woman now found herself in the presence of the king who had enforced the Law of God against her practices *and* the prophet who was God's mouthpiece. Her terror was completely understandable.

However, Saul meant her no harm. He had other things on his mind. He spoke now as the king: "The king said to her, 'Do not be afraid. What do you see?'" (v. 13a).

There is no point in speculating about why or how she could see Samuel, but Saul could not and had to ask. In response the woman gave a description, if we can call it that, of what she saw: "And the woman said to Saul, 'I see a god coming up out of the earth'" (v. 13b).

That was not particularly helpful.[27] So Saul tried again: "He said to her, 'What is his appearance?' And she said, 'An old man is coming up, and he is wrapped in a robe'" (v. 14a).

The old man and the robe were enough to identify the apparition to Saul:[28] "And Saul knew that it was Samuel, and he bowed with his face to the ground and paid homage" (v. 14b).

At their last encounter, that robe had become the symbol of Saul's lost kingdom. As Saul now bowed down, it is more than likely that he could remember seizing the robe and tearing it and hearing Samuel's last words to him (1 Samuel 15:27, 28).

This is the first (and only) time we have seen Saul bowing down before another human.[29] He had bowed before the Lord (1 Samuel 15:31), and others in the story had bowed,[30] but not Saul. The king had at last been brought to his knees.

SAUL BEFORE SAMUEL (AGAIN) (vv. 15-25)

Although the details are scant, it seems that the woman left Saul at this point.[31] The following moments seem to have been between Saul and Samuel alone.

Desperate Saul (v. 15)

Samuel was the first to speak. They were not words of comfort. "Then Samuel said to Saul, 'Why have you disturbed me by bringing me up?'" (v. 15a).

Samuel began this ominous conversation with the impropriety of Saul's initiative in seeking to "disturb" the dead. Saul's excuse was his desperation:

> Saul answered, "I am in great distress, for the Philistines are warring against me, and God has turned away from me and answers me no more, either by prophets or by dreams. Therefore I have summoned you to tell me what I shall do." (v. 15b)

The pathos of the scene is intense. It was too late. Out of the desperation of the Philistine threat and the Lord's silence Saul had taken this extraordinary step of trying to get the dead Samuel to tell him what to do.[32] It is striking that he failed to mention either his own disobedience, which lay behind his present predicament, or his nemesis, David, whose presence in Saul's world had been his undoing. These two omissions would soon be rectified by Samuel.

The contradiction involved in calling up from the dead Samuel, the great prophet of God, when God had turned away from Saul did not seem to bother the king.

Determined Samuel (vv. 16-19)

Samuel, however, was determined and firm.

THE LORD, YOUR ENEMY (v. 16)

He exposed the contradiction: "And Samuel said, 'Why then do you ask me, since the LORD has turned from you and become your enemy?'" (v. 16).

It was far too late. At this eleventh hour of his life, to seek guidance from God's prophet, by utterly illegitimate means, was Saul's final great folly.

DAVID THE KING (vv. 17, 18)

The two topics that Saul had avoided were now taken up by Samuel:

> *"The LORD has done to you as he spoke by me, for the LORD has torn the kingdom out of your hand and given it to your neighbor, David. Because you did not obey the voice of the LORD and did not carry out his fierce wrath against Amalek, therefore the LORD has done this thing to you this day." (vv. 17, 18)*

There was nothing new to be said. Samuel simply reiterated his message from that day at Gilgal in 1 Samuel 15. The only new item was David's name, but that was hardly news to Saul.

"YOU SHALL BE WITH ME" (v. 19)

The only news was that the consequences of that fateful day had now reached their end:

> *"Moreover, the LORD will give Israel also with you into the hand of the Philistines, and tomorrow you and your sons shall be with me. The LORD will give the army of Israel also into the hand of the Philistines." (v. 19)*

This was the announcement of the final failure of Saul's kingship. He had been appointed, in the Lord's words, to "save my people from the hand of the Philistines" (1 Samuel 9:16). Now both people and king were about to be given "into the hand of the Philistines." As Samuel had warned the people, the consequence of unfaithfulness and rebellion would be "the hand of the LORD will be against you and your king" (1 Samuel 12:15). The very next day it would happen.

Distraught Saul (vv. 20-25)

If it was utter hopelessness that had driven Saul to the actions of this night, it is difficult to find language to describe the depths to which he now sank.

> *Then Saul fell at once full length on the ground, filled with fear because of the words of Samuel. And there was no strength in him, for he had eaten nothing all day and all night. (v. 20)*

The once mighty Saul lay weak and helpless. The once tall and impressive king now lay full-length on the ground.

The only help available to him was a woman of pagan practices, who at this point returned:

> And the woman came to Saul, and when she saw that he was terrified, she said to him, "Behold, your servant has obeyed you. I have taken my life in my hand and have listened to what you have said to me. Now therefore, you also obey your servant. Let me set a morsel of bread before you; and eat, that you may have strength when you go on your way." (vv. 21, 22)

Israel's king had been reduced to being obeyed by a necromancer, who now urged him to obey her. "He refused and said, 'I will not eat'" (v. 23a).

See the helpless, hopeless man. "But his servants, together with the woman, urged him, and he listened to their words. So he arose from the earth and sat on the bed" (v. 23b).

The condemned man then enjoyed his final meal:

> Now the woman had a fattened calf in the house, and she quickly killed it, and she took flour and kneaded it and baked unleavened bread of it, and she put it before Saul and his servants, and they ate. (vv. 24, 25a)

It was a meal fit for a king. The trouble was, it was eaten by a man not fit to be king.

The chapter closes with the poignant words: "Then they rose and went away that night" (v. 25b).

"Separated from Christ" and "having no hope and without God in the world" (Ephesians 2:12) is a strikingly appropriate way to describe Saul that night. This was the ultimate consequence of his disobedience to God (1 Samuel 13, 15). If Paul's words in Ephesians 2:12 describe the situation of the Gentiles (that is, the nations), then Israel now indeed had a king "like all the nations" (1 Samuel 8:5)! In the hopelessness of Saul we should see the hopelessness of being separated from Christ and being without God.

Then we will appreciate the wonder of the gospel: "But now in Christ Jesus . . ." (Ephesians 2:13).

47

The "Trial" of David

1 SAMUEL 29

One of the great paradoxes in the history of the world occurred when Jesus Christ was put on trial before Pontius Pilate. The event is so significant for Christian faith that specific reference is made to it in the Apostles' Creed. In that most basic statement of belief, which appears to include only the bare essentials, we say "he suffered under Pontius Pilate."[1] Each of the New Testament Gospels provides details of the trial (Matthew 27:1, 2, 11-26; Mark 15:1-15; Luke 23:1-25; John 18:28–19:16). It is clear that an adequate account of the life of Jesus needs to include his trial "under Pontius Pilate."

With good reason Pilate was known, particularly among the Jewish people, as a cruel and evil oppressor.[2] Jesus was handed over to him by the Jewish authorities, accused of sedition for claiming to be a king.[3] Three times, in Luke's account, Pilate pronounced Jesus innocent: "I find no guilt in this man" (23:4); "I did not find this man guilty of any of your charges against him. . . . Look, nothing deserving of death has been done by him" (vv. 14, 15); "I have found in him no guilt deserving death" (v. 22).

Pilate, of course, was right. There was no guilt in Jesus, none whatsoever. He never did anything deserving of death; in fact, he never did any evil thing. The irony is that Pilate (hardly the model of a righteous judge) spoke more truly than he knew. Indeed, it seems that he announced Jesus' innocence largely because he did *not* understand.[4] Had he truly understood the claims of Jesus and taken them seriously, he may well have given a different verdict. Yet in the remarkable providence of God, Pontius Pilate's testimony to Jesus stands. It is one of the great paradoxes of history that in the hours before Jesus' death, the truth was proclaimed by the unrighteous and pagan governing authority: "nothing deserving of death has been done by him" (Luke 23:15).

It is quite remarkable to discover that once again the course of Jesus' life found a significant foreshadowing in the experience of his ancestor, David.[5] As the time for David to receive his kingdom approached, he was pronounced innocent (three times!) by the Philistine king Achish. Had Achish truly understood David, he would have given a very different verdict. Yet in the remarkable providence of God, Achish's testimony to David stands. The irony is that Achish (hardly the model of wisdom and insight) spoke the truth more profoundly than he could have known.

The circumstances in which this happened have been building since 1 Samuel 27. David had "gone over" to Achish, the king of Gath (1 Samuel 27:2). He had won the king's trust through the deceit and ruthlessness described in 1 Samuel 27. Despite the questions that may rightly be raised about David's conduct during this time, one thing is made clear by the account. David never acted against his own people or Saul their king. On the contrary, when Achish thought that he was doing so, David was in fact busy raiding Israel's ancient enemies (1 Samuel 27:8-10). David's "righteousness and . . . faithfulness" (1 Samuel 26:23, the theme of 1 Samuel 24–26) in refraining from violence against Saul or his own people (even in his own interests) was not undermined by David's conduct after he had "gone over" to the Philistines.

That had been the case until the Philistines themselves initiated hostilities once again against Israel (1 Samuel 28:1).[6] The trust Achish had (foolishly) put in David led to the inclusion of David and his men in the Philistine force. Not only that, but they were given the responsibility for guarding Achish himself (1 Samuel 28:2). At that point in the story it was far from clear whether David could any longer escape becoming involved in the Philistine hostilities against Israel.

The narrative left that uncertainty in the air and moved forward to the eve of the great battle, when the Philistines had assembled at Shunem and the Israelites at Gilboa, on opposite sides of the Jezreel Valley. That night a deeply troubled Saul secretly consulted the medium in Endor and learned from Samuel the prophet that in the next day's battle he and his sons would die, and Israel would be defeated (1 Samuel 28:3-25, particularly verse 19).

With that news, the seriousness of the question about David's involvement became acute. David had been required to join the Philistine forces as they prepared for the very battle in which Saul would die. Would David, after all, have a hand in the death of Saul? What would then be the worth of the "righteousness and . . . faithfulness" he had displayed at the cave of Engedi (1 Samuel 24) and the hill of Hachilah (1 Samuel 26)?

The answers to these questions are to be found in something that had happened earlier (perhaps a few days earlier) than the night of Saul's clandestine encounter in Endor. First Samuel 29 takes us back those few days to at last resolve the tensions that have been so effectively set up.

THE PHILISTINE OBJECTION TO DAVID (VV. 1-5)

We now return to an earlier stage in the battle preparations, when the Philistine forces had assembled but had not yet advanced to Shunem:[7] "Now the Philistines had gathered all their forces at Aphek. And the Israelites were encamped by the spring that is in Jezreel" (v. 1).

It now becomes clear that the Philistines were planning a massive assault on Israel. The assembling of "all their forces" suggests an all-out effort aimed at a decisive victory.[8]

The massing of the Philistine forces at Aphek, about thirty miles north of Gath, unavoidably reminds us of the much earlier conflict that began with the Philistines camped at this very site (1 Samuel 4:1).[9] That earlier confrontation had resulted in two terrible defeats for the Israelites (1 Samuel 4:2, 10). It was this disaster that, in many ways, had led to the appointment of Saul for the express purpose of saving Israel from the Philistines (1 Samuel 9:16). We know (from the preview of Saul's coming night at Endor in the previous chapter) that the approaching battle will be as dreadful for Israel as those earlier defeats and that for Saul it will be fatal. The failure of Saul's kingship could not be more vividly displayed than by this return to Aphek. What happened once at Aphek before Saul became king was about to happen again and bring his reign to an end. In the end the king "like all the nations," who would "go out before us and fight our battles" (1 Samuel 8:20),[10] had failed.

We are right to assume from the exchange between Achish and David at the beginning of chapter 28 that David and his men were among the great buildup of Philistine forces at Aphek.

The assembled Philistine army was about to advance another forty miles or so to the north, to Shunem, on the northern side of the Jezreel Valley (1 Samuel 28:4). The Israelites, we are told, were already camped "by the spring that is in Jezreel," at the foot of Mount Gilboa,[11] on the southern side of the Jezreel Valley. This suggests that Israel had some reason to expect the Philistine attack to come in that vicinity. Perhaps advance preparations by the Philistines at Shunem had been noticed or Saul had received some other intelligence.[12]

The Challenge (vv. 2, 3a)

As the Philistines moved on, the first question was raised about David and his men:

> *As the lords of the Philistines were passing on by hundreds and by thousands, and David and his men were passing on in the rear with Achish, the commanders of the Philistines said, "What are these Hebrews doing here?" (vv. 2, 3a)*

"The lords of the Philistines" were the rulers of the five Philistine cities, of whom Achish was one.[13] They were passing by with their military units.[14] It was not the lords, but the commanders,[15] the military men, who raised the question about the presence of a group of Hebrews[16] in the Philistine army that was preparing to overthrow Israel.

The Vindication (v. 3b)

Achish responded to the challenge from the military commanders with a strong defense of David:

> *And Achish said to the commanders of the Philistines, "Is this not David, the servant of Saul, king of Israel, who has been with me now for days and years, and since he deserted to me I have found no fault in him to this day." (v. 3b)*

On an earlier occasion it had been the servants of Achish who had said with alarm, "Is this not David the king of the land?" (1 Samuel 21:11a). Achish had been duped by David on that occasion, as he was duped now. As the servants had spoken more truly than they knew on the earlier occasion, so now Achish was more accurate than he realized when he said, "Is this not David, servant of Saul, king of Israel?" He did not mean, of course, that David was *still* Saul's servant. Achish believed that David had become *his* servant, having "made himself an utter stench to his people Israel" (1 Samuel 27:12). But that was not true. David had deceived Achish and had in fact done nothing to undermine his own claim to be Saul's faithful servant (1 Samuel 24:8, 10; 26:18, 19), a claim that had been powerfully supported by his conduct at Engedi and Hachilah.[17]

Achish seems to have taken some pride in the fact that this servant of Saul had been "with" the king of Gath for some considerable time. He exaggerated the time. David's total stay among the Philistines was one year and four months (1 Samuel 27:7), hardly "days and years." However, during that time, Achish claimed, "I have found no fault in him."

If Achish knew the truth, he would not have made this confident pronouncement. However, deceived as he was (we might even say, fool though he was), he uttered a truth more profound than he intended. David was without fault in a sense that Achish did not understand. He had *not* betrayed his king or his people. As their future king, his righteousness and faithfulness *were* intact!

The Verdict (vv. 4, 5)

The Philistine commanders were more astute than Achish. King though he was, the practical military men had little patience with his foolish gullibility: "But the commanders of the Philistines were angry with him" (v. 4a).

As well as being conned by David, Achish appears to not have had the respect of the commanders. The verb used for their anger almost always refers to the anger of a superior toward an inferior.[18] In their fury the commanders began to issue orders to the king:

> And the commanders of the Philistines said to him, "Send the man back, that he may return to the place to which you have assigned him. He shall not go down with us to battle, lest in the battle he become an adversary to us. For how could this fellow reconcile himself to his lord? Would it not be with the heads of the men here? Is not this David, of whom they sing to one another in dances,
> > 'Saul has struck down his thousands,
> > and David his ten thousands'?" (vv. 4b, 5)

The commanders displayed very good sense. Firstly, they had learned from experience. On a previous occasion Hebrews who had taken refuge among the Philistines had turned against their hosts when the opportunity arose (see 1 Samuel 14:12).

Secondly, they took David's reputation seriously. For the second time the David and Saul song was cited by Philistines (see 1 Samuel 21:11; cf. 18:7). They knew only too well that the song was talking about "thousands" and "ten thousands" of Philistine casualties! They were infuriated by the ease with which Achish had put his trust in this David.

Thirdly, they saw the very great advantage David could gain from becoming their "adversary."[19] The irony is that Achish had appointed David to (literally) "guard his head" (1 Samuel 28:2). The commanders could see that David had much to gain by doing something else with "the heads of the men here"!

It seems clear that the commanders understood David more truly than the foolish Achish and that their fears of betrayal were well-founded.

THE PHILISTINE DISMISSAL OF DAVID (vv. 6, 7)

Suddenly instead of David being in an awkward situation, it was the Philistine king who found himself embarrassed. He was apparently too weak to withstand the commanders but still held on to his belief in David.

The Vindication (v. 6a)

He therefore called David and attempted a diplomatic solution. First he
reiterated his own vindication of David:

> Then Achish called David and said to him, "As the LORD lives, you have
> been honest, and to me it seems right that you should march out and in
> with me in the campaign. For I have found nothing wrong in you from the
> day of your coming to me to this day." (v. 6a)

Remarkably Achish appears to have been very anxious to convince
David of his goodwill toward him. David's deceptions, and no doubt his
charm, had won Achish over utterly. He even swore an oath by David's
God![20] The content of the oath was David's honesty![21] Achish emphasized that as far as he was concerned, David's participation with him in the
Philistine campaign was (literally) "good." Again, this time before David
himself, Achish testified (literally), "I have found nothing evil in you from
the day of your coming to me to this day."

For the second time Achish had given a true verdict based on a deception. Achish had found no evil in David because he had been tricked. In
another sense altogether there *was* no evil in David (that is, no betrayal of
Saul and Israel). David *had* been "honest" to his obligations to Saul and
Israel, even while deceiving Achish. It is again an outrageous irony that the
testimony to David's goodness came from the lips of Achish.

The Challenge (v. 6b)

Having begun diplomatically, Achish had to broach the difficulty that had
arisen: "Nevertheless, the lords do not approve of you" (v. 6b).

Literally it was less diplomatic than that: "But in the eyes of the lords
you are not good."

Achish masked the fact that he had caved in to the demands of his sub-
ordinates, the commanders, by attributing the negative assessment of David
to his peers, "the lords."[22] They, he claimed, did not see David as "good."

Again the irony is acute. The lords (actually, of course, the commanders) were right, from their own perspective. As far as the interests of the
Philistines were concerned, David was *not* "good"! However, that is more of
a comment on the Philistine perspective than on the "goodness" of David!

The Dismissal (v. 7)

Then, under the guise of submitting to the majority view of his fellow lords,
Achish reluctantly urged David to return to Ziklag and behave well: "So

go back now; and go peaceably, that you may not displease the lords of the Philistines" (v. 7).

Again a more literal translation of the last words captures something important: ". . . and you will not do evil in the eyes of the lords of the Philistines." According to Achish, David's continued presence in the Philistine ranks (which, he had said, was "good in my eyes") would be "evil in the eyes of the lords."

Who was right?

DAVID'S "COMPLAINT" (vv. 8-11)

We might well imagine that David would welcome this providentially provided way of escape from an impossible dilemma. In a way he could not have orchestrated, he had been freed from the prospect of losing either the trust of Achish or his righteousness toward his people. David could remain "good" to Saul and Israel without becoming "evil" to Achish!

The "Complaint" (v. 8)

It is astonishing, then, to hear David complain:

> And David said to Achish, "But what have I done? What have you found in your servant from the day I entered your service until now, that I may not go and fight against the enemies of my lord the king?" (v. 8)

The cunning rascal! In fact, David is so cunning at this point that it is difficult for *us* to see what he was up to.

We have heard David protest like this before. "What have I done?" he had said to his older brother in the Valley of Elah (1 Samuel 17:29). "What have I done?" he had said to Jonathan (1 Samuel 20:1). "What have I done?" he had said to Saul (1 Samuel 26:18). Each time it had been a genuine protest of innocence. But what was he up to when he said, "What have I done?" to Achish?

Was he taking advantage of Achish's embarrassment and seeking to increase it by feigning offense at this slight on his "goodness"?[23] Or was he maintaining his earlier deceit because he had actually hoped to do what the Philistine commanders suspected he would do?

In either case, we are confident that calling himself Achish's "servant" was false. David was using Achish for his own purposes. Deceiving Achish into believing that David was his servant was part of his plan (see also 1 Samuel 27:5, and especially 1 Samuel 27:12).[24] Our difficulty is that we do not know the rest of David's plan, or even if he had a complete plan.

There may be a clue in his dangerously ambiguous words expressing his desire to "go and fight against the enemies of my lord the king."[25] Of course, Achish was to understand that "my lord the king" was himself and "the enemies" were the Israelites. He had been so thoroughly taken in by David, there was no risk of his taking the words any other way. However, we know that David had recently demonstrated his faithfulness to his lord, King Saul. "My lord the king" is the very expression David used to address Saul both outside the cave of Engedi and at the hill of Hachilah (1 Samuel 24:8; 26:17, 19)![26] When he rebuked Abner at the hill of Hachilah for failing in his duty, he called Saul "your lord the king" and "the king your lord" (1 Samuel 26:15). David had dramatically rejected the term "enemy" when it had been applied to Saul by his men (1 Samuel 24:4-6) and by Abishai (1 Samuel 26:8, 9) and insisted on calling him "my lord" and "the LORD's anointed" (1 Samuel 24:6, 10; 26:9, 11, 16, 18, 23). Saul had acknowledged that David did not see him as his "enemy" (1 Samuel 24:19). In view of the powerful proof in these earlier chapters that for David "my lord the king" was Saul, we may well suspect that David's words to Achish, expressing his desire to "fight against the enemies of my lord the king," had a different meaning for the speaker than the intended meaning for the hearer.[27]

If this is so, David's daring plan may have been to accompany the Philistines in their assault against Israel, but in some way to turn and do serious damage to these enemies of Saul and Israel. He may even have hoped to deliver Israel from their hand. He was genuinely trying to overturn the order to return to Ziklag.[28] This would fit with what we know of David's character and conduct prior to this. Previous experience should warn us against doubting the possibility of this remarkable man, the Lord being with him, succeeding in such an audacious exploit.[29]

What David did not know, however, was that the Lord had another plan for this battle. It was to be spelled out to Saul by Samuel on the eve of the conflict, although we have heard his message in advance:

> " . . . the LORD will give Israel also with you into the hand of the Philistines, and tomorrow you and your sons shall be with me. The LORD will give the army of Israel also into the hand of the Philistines." (1 Samuel 28:19)

Vindication (v. 9a)

If we have understood David's subtle intentions correctly, any lingering doubts about his faithfulness to his people, and even to Saul, should have been dispelled. Despite possible appearances, when David "went over" to the Philistines (1 Samuel 27:2), he did absolutely nothing to compromise his righteousness and faithfulness toward Saul and Israel that he had claimed and demonstrated earlier.

It is astonishing that Achish is the one who provided the assurance that this was so: "And Achish answered David and said, 'I know that you are as blameless in my sight as an angel of God'" (v. 9a).

Of course, Achish knew nothing of the sort. He had been deceived. Nonetheless, his words testifying, for the third time, to David's "goodness"[30] are true in a way he never intended. The hyperbole ("as good as an angel [messenger] of God") is astonishing. In his own mind, no doubt, Achish was still trying very hard to maintain David's approval, even adopting again the language of his faith. Inadvertently, however, he was describing "the man after God's own heart," the one whom God had appointed to be king "for him" (1 Samuel 13:14; 16:1). In a sense that Achish did not understand, David *was* a "messenger of God"!

Dismissal Confirmed (vv. 9b-11)

However, Achish was a weakling. He could not resist the pressure from his commanders. His own verdict on David had to be put to one side. The will of others would prevail. Achish therefore continued:

> *"Nevertheless, the commanders of the Philistines have said, 'He shall not go up with us to the battle.' Now then rise early in the morning with the servants of your lord who came with you, and start early in the morning, and depart as soon as you have light." (vv. 9b, 10)*

Perhaps the deluded Achish was confused, but a slip of the tongue once again unconsciously indicated David's true allegiance. He referred to David's men as "the servants of your lord," which sounds very much like an acknowledgment that David's lord was still Saul!

The chapter concludes by noting that the outcome of this remarkable verbal confrontation was that David headed south as the Philistines moved north to engage Saul for what would prove to be the last time: "So David set out with his men early in the morning to return to the land of the Philistines. But the Philistines went up to Jezreel" (v. 11).

So it was that in the remarkable providence of God, David was kept well away from the battle that would end Saul's life. In the same providential arrangement David's own desire (if we have correctly discerned his intentions) to save his people from the Philistines was, on this occasion, blocked.

The working of God, turning the hearts of kings wherever he will, like a stream of water in his hand (Proverbs 21:1), is clear in this chapter, though it is also hidden. That God's involvement in these events is not explicitly mentioned in the text reflects the nature of his providence. Often his sovereign will is achieved in ways that are unseen. Even David, in this episode, did not know God's purpose for the coming battle or his will that David should be free of blame for Saul's death. However, everything that happened worked together to bring about these things.

Within this remarkable course of events we have heard the threefold testimony of King Achish to the goodness of David: "I have found no fault in him" (1 Samuel 29:3); "You have been honest . . . I have found nothing wrong in you" (v. 6); "You are as blameless in my sight as an angel of God" (v. 9).

All this occurred as the time drew near for David to receive the kingdom.

Many years later, the time approached for Jesus to be exalted. The experience of David that we have followed in 1 Samuel 27–29 provides an interesting starting point to reflect on at least five aspects of Jesus' experience at this time.

First: David "went over" to the Philistines (1 Samuel 27:2). Jesus was "delivered up" to the Gentile nations (cf. Matthew 20:19; Mark 10:33; Luke 18:32). David's movement was the result of his rejection by Saul (1 Samuel 27:1). Jesus was delivered over to the Gentiles by the chief priests and scribes who had rejected him. The ambiguities in David's movement, however, were not part of what happened to Jesus. Jesus was being handed over to be killed.[31]

Second: David was accused before Achish of potential sedition. His accusers understood better than Achish the danger that David posed to them (1 Samuel 29:4, 5). Jesus was accused of subversion by those who understood only too well (e.g., Luke 23:2, 5). David's accusers knew only that he posed a serious threat to them. Jesus' accusers knew well that he had claimed to be the Christ.

Third: David was vindicated three times by Achish in extravagant terms that were more deeply true than he could know. Jesus was vindicated by Pontius Pilate (also three times, in two of the Gospel accounts). The truthfulness of David's vindication, however, was far surpassed by that of Jesus. David's "righteousness and . . . faithfulness" toward Saul and Israel had been maintained, but it had involved deceit and possibly doubt. Of Jesus, however, it could be truly said, without qualification, "He committed no sin, neither was deceit found in his mouth" (1 Peter 2:22; cf. Isaiah 53:9).

Fourth: Achish was weak and gave way to David's accusers. Pontius Pilate likewise gave in to Jesus' accusers. The consequences of these weak decisions were very different, at first sight. David was required to return to Ziklag. Jesus was crucified. The similarity lies in the fact that for both David and Jesus the outcome of their "trials" turned out to be an important step on their way to their respective kingdoms.

Fifth: The outcome, in each case, was the will of God for his anointed one. As we will see in 1 Samuel 30, David became, in a small but significant way, the savior of his people. Jesus, too, but in indescribably greater terms, became the Savior of the world.

48

A King Who Gives

1 SAMUEL 30

Power tends to corrupt, and absolute power corrupts absolutely." So said Lord Acton,[1] and his words rang so true to experience and observation that they have become proverbial.

Lord Acton was speaking specifically of political power — the power of rulers over their subjects. While it is clear that history and our own experience provide many examples of power being used for doing good and for overcoming evil, it is equally clear that greater power over others in the hands of an individual or group does tend to be dangerous. Absolute power becomes tyranny.

The Bible accounts for this distressing phenomenon that has been responsible for so much human misery. In short, the sinfulness of human beings means that power in human hands will tend to be used for evil purposes. It is not that power in itself is so terrible. In theory power could be used to do nothing but good. The reality is, however, that sinful people use power for sinful ends. Power in human hands provides the opportunity and the means to do greater evil.

It is easy to think of the corrupt dictators of world history. It is far more difficult to think of a person with similar power who used their power for good.

Early in the book of 1 Samuel the warning was given that a king, such as the elders of Israel demanded, would use his power to "take" from the people to benefit himself (1 Samuel 8:11-17). In other words, such a king would use his power for selfish purposes. Saul was made king on the condition that he (and the people) "fear the LORD and serve him and obey his voice and not rebel against the commandment of the LORD" (1 Samuel 12:14). In other words, power such as was being entrusted to Saul must be used in obedience to God rather than in self-centeredness.

We have followed the tragic account of Saul's failure to meet the condition of his kingship. From what might seem to be small acts of disobedience to the word of the Lord in 1 Samuel 13, 15, Saul eventually became the paranoid king who took from the people for the benefit of himself and his cronies. The senses in which Saul fulfilled the expectations of 1 Samuel 8:11-17 are alluded to in 1 Samuel 14:52, 15:19, and 22:7. He became the destroyer, not the deliverer, of his people (see especially 1 Samuel 22:6-19).

The failure of Saul raises the question whether absolute power (such as is implied by the idea of a king[2]) can be safely entrusted to a human being. After all, Saul started well. He showed great promise. His failure was, as we are inclined to say, "only human." However, what would the power of a king be like in the hands of one who *did* "fear the Lord and serve him and obey his voice and not rebel against the commandment of the Lord"?

As the story of Saul's decline has been told, we have been following the parallel story of David's rise. We have been given reason to expect that David would be a very different kind of king from Saul. He was the man the Lord had chosen to be king *for himself* (1 Samuel 16:1). David had a place in God's good purposes that Saul never enjoyed. He was the "man after his [God's] own heart" (1 Samuel 13:14). Already we have seen something of David's "righteousness and . . . faithfulness" (1 Samuel 26:23) in his dealings with Saul, which made a strong contrast to Saul's dealings with David.

The last five chapters of 1 Samuel present the final dark days of Saul in stark contrast to the experiences of David at this time. The stories of both are told in parallel. These days were dominated by the threat posed by the Philistines once again. Saul learned on the night before the approaching battle that he would die in that conflict (1 Samuel 28:19). This momentous event in Israel's history — the death of Israel's first king — will be recorded in chapter 31 and will conclude the book of 1 Samuel. In the meantime our attention has been focused on what was happening to David.

David and his men had been forced to "go over" to the Philistines, although they continued secretly, from their new Philistine home in Ziklag, to act in the interests of David's own people (1 Samuel 27). As the Philistines prepared for their assault on Israel, David and his men were required, at first, to accompany King Achish (at the beginning of 1 Samuel 28). However, when they reached Aphek, the Philistine commanders knew David's reputation well enough to insist that he and his men be dismissed and return to Ziklag before the actual hostilities against Israel began (1 Samuel 29). David protested at this development. We suspect that his intention had been to turn against his Philistine masters at some point, as the commanders in fact suspected.

However, in the purposes of God, which would be revealed to Saul the night before the battle (and have been revealed to us already in 1 Samuel 28), the Philistines were to prevail on this occasion. Therefore, the circumstances that forced David to be elsewhere when the fighting began must be seen as providential. God was not going to deliver Israel from the Philistines on this occasion. Therefore David (who *always* beat the Philistines!) was not to be present on this occasion.[3]

From Aphek there were two simultaneous movements. The Philistines advanced northward toward the Jezreel Valley for the final showdown with Saul. David headed south, toward Ziklag (1 Samuel 29:11). The distances involved were about the same. It is therefore possible that the two groups reached their destinations at about the same time. In 1 Samuel 30 we learn what happened when David reached Ziklag. Only in chapter 31 will we hear what happened further north when the Philistines reached the Jezreel Valley.

DAVID'S TROUBLE (vv. 1-6a)

David and his men covered the sixty miles or so from Aphek to Ziklag in not much more than two days. This suggests some haste. Perhaps they had heard a rumor of the trouble they were going to find when they reached their home.

From Amalekites (vv. 1-5)

This is what David discovered had happened while he and his men had been away: "Now when David and his men came to Ziklag on the third day, the Amalekites had made a raid against the Negeb and against Ziklag" (v. 1a).

The Amalekites have featured prominently in the story of Saul's reign. Most recently in the account we have heard Saul reminded that his failure had a lot to do with his treatment of the Amalekites. "Because you did not obey the voice of the LORD and did not carry out his fierce wrath against Amalek, therefore the LORD has done this thing to you this day" (1 Samuel 28:18, referring to the events of 1 Samuel 15). We are about to see how David dealt with these "enemies of the LORD" (1 Samuel 30:26).[4]

In time (since the word to Saul about the Amalekites was reported out of chronological sequence) the most recent involvement of the Amalekites in our story was David's early days in Ziklag, when he "made raids" against the Amalekites (among others) (1 Samuel 27:8, 9). During David's absence from Ziklag, the Amalekites had now retaliated. They "made a raid"[5] against the Negeb (which is what David had falsely claimed to have been doing when asked by Achish, 1 Samuel 27:10), and in particular against Ziklag.

Their raid, however, had been significantly different from David's earlier deadly raids:

*They had overcome Ziklag and burned it with fire and taken captive the
women and all who were in it, both small and great. They killed no one,
but carried them off and went their way. (vv. 1b, 2)*

Whereas David was at least partly motivated by the need to keep his
activities secret (1 Samuel 27:11), the Amalekites had no such necessity. The
fact that they did not kill should not, however, be understood as a humanitar-
ian virtue. For these raiders the captured women and children were booty,
possibly to be sold as slaves.[6]

The information given to us in 1 Samuel 30:1, 2 is more than David
could have known when he arrived at Ziklag. He and his men found the
city destroyed (although they would not yet have known by whom). They
deduced that their families had been taken alive, presumably because there
were no signs of killing: "And when David and his men came to the city,
they found it burned with fire, and their wives and sons and daughters taken
captive" (v. 3).

They could not have known at this stage who had done this, although
they surely had their suspicions. Given their earlier activities, the Amalekites
would certainly have been among their suspects, along with the Geshurites
and the Girzites (1 Samuel 27:8).

However, their immediate reaction, understandably, was grief: "Then
David and the people who were with him raised their voices and wept until
they had no more strength to weep" (v. 4).

As David had led his men in many things, he now led them in grief.[7]
He did so as one who shared their suffering: "David's two wives also had
been taken captive, Ahinoam of Jezreel and Abigail the widow of Nabal of
Carmel" (v. 5).

It looked as though the daring experiment on which David had led his
people, seeking a precarious safety among the Philistines, had ended in
disaster. David had brilliantly executed his deception of Achish and thereby
won the Philistine king's complete trust. The disaster, however, did not
come from the Philistines, but from the people David had used to deceive
the Philistines. David and his men had lost everything — wives, children,
and possessions.

This was the trouble David found when he returned from Aphek, at
about the same time as the Philistines must have been arriving in the valley
of Jezreel.

From His Men (v. 6a)

The disaster from the Amalekites was only the beginning of David's troubles when he arrived back in Ziklag. "And David was greatly distressed, for

the people spoke of stoning him, because all the people were bitter in soul, each for his sons and daughters" (v. 6a).

David's "distress" was not his emotional state but the dangerous predicament in which he found himself.[8] It is important to notice that David's circumstances are described with the words Saul used at about the same time in his dark meeting in Endor: "I am in *great distress*, for the Philistines are warring against me, and God has turned away from me and answers me no more . . ." (1 Samuel 28:15).[9]

Therefore at about the time Saul was experiencing his darkest hour of utter hopelessness, David was also in a very tight spot. The men he had so successfully led since the first 400 of them had joined him at the cave of Adullam (1 Samuel 22:2) now found themselves worse off than before they had attached themselves to him. All of his successes had been undone by this disaster. They were "bitter in soul" again.[10]

Their bitterness then turned to blame. David was, after all, responsible for the daring plan to find safety in Philistine territory, along with the scheme to "make raids" that had so terribly turned against them. It was not entirely unreasonable for the men to see David as responsible for their terrible loss.

They began to talk of venting their grief-stricken anger on their leader.[11]

David, who had escaped Saul and duped the Philistines, was in danger of being stoned by his own men! At first glance we might think that David's troubles there in Ziklag were as deep as those of Saul that night in Endor. But we would be wrong.

DAVID'S STRENGTH (vv. 6b-10)

David found strength that was simply no longer available for Saul. Saul turned, in his distress, to the medium and the forbidden world of necromancy, but David's response to his troubles could not have been more different: "But David strengthened himself in the LORD his God" (v. 6b).

This is what Jonathan had helped him do on an earlier occasion. Jonathan had "strengthened [David's] hand in God" by speaking God's promise to David (1 Samuel 23:16, 17). Here David found strength again in the one who had promised that he would be king over Israel. The strength David found was trust in God's promise. It was what we call faith.

This strength was not available to Saul because the only promise God now made to him concerned his destruction. God's promise to Saul filled him with fear: "there was no strength in him" (see 1 Samuel 28:20).[12]

Hearing God's Voice (vv. 7, 8)

Verses 7, 8 are probably best understood as an account of how David "strengthened himself in the LORD his God." Whereas Saul's despair at

God's silence toward him led him to seek the medium of Endor, David sought God's voice:

> *And David said to Abiathar the priest, the son of Ahimelech, "Bring me*
> *the ephod." So Abiathar brought the ephod to David. And David inquired*
> *of the LORD, "Shall I pursue after this band? Shall I overtake them?" He*
> *answered him, "Pursue, for you shall surely overtake and shall surely*
> *rescue." (vv. 7, 8)*

Abiathar, the son of the unfortunate Ahimelech, was the sole survivor of Saul's slaughter of the priests of Nob (1 Samuel 22:20; 23:6). One outcome of that terrible episode was that Saul had deprived himself of the priestly means of seeking God's guidance. Not, of course, that access to a priest guaranteed that God would speak, as Saul had learned on a previous occasion (1 Samuel 14:36, 37). Nor was the priest's ephod the only way in which God could be heard. It was only one God-given means of seeking God's guidance.

On the previous occasion when David had consulted God by means of Abiathar's ephod (see 1 Samuel 23:6-12) we noted that the precise process involved is no longer clear to us, probably because to the Bible writers the *fact* and the *content* of divine revelation were always far more important than the mechanics of how it occurred. Once again we do not know exactly how the ephod was used here in Ziklag, except that by means of it David asked the Lord about whether or not he should pursue the raiders and whether or not he would find them. He received God's answer in terms of an imperative ("Pursue"), supported by a doubly emphatic promise ("for you shall surely overtake and shall surely rescue").[13]

How very different from hopeless Saul! Perhaps it was at the very time that Saul made his clandestine visit to Endor under cover of darkness that David asked God for direction and received his emphatically encouraging answer.

OBEYING GOD'S VOICE (vv. 9, 10)

David strengthened himself in the Lord his God and was prompt to obey the voice of God once he heard it:

> *So David set out, and the six hundred men who were with him, and they*
> *came to the brook Besor, where those who were left behind stayed. (v. 9)*

The brook Besor was probably a few miles south of Ziklag.[14] David's 600 men had just completed the sixty-mile march from Aphek at a cracking pace. Some were simply too tired to press on with this presumably even faster chase into the southern desert. They stayed at the brook, with a useful task of which we will learn shortly.

> *But David pursued, he and four hundred men. Two hundred stayed behind, who were too exhausted to cross the brook Besor. (v. 10)*

The word from God had been "Pursue," and that is what David did. We will hear more about the 200 exhausted ones a little later.

Pause and notice the striking presentation of David — in deep trouble from enemies, and even from his own men, yet strengthened in his God, because he heard God's word and promptly obeyed.

DAVID'S DELIVERANCE (vv. 11-20)

It is interesting to notice that David's obedience to God's word did not mean there were no more decisions for him to make. He decided to leave the exhausted men at the brook. Presumably he also made the decision to head south, the direction from which he reasonably suspected the trouble had come. David's wit and wisdom would have been fully employed in the chase. However, the promise of God meant that the outcome did not depend ultimately on his abilities. Before long something happened he could not have engineered. It would turn out to be the key to the mission's success. The providential hand of God was surely behind this:

> *They found an Egyptian in the open country and brought him to David. (v. 11a)*

The Egyptian man was starving and parched (as we learn in verse 12). What help could this be? We know (even if David did not yet) that it was Amalekites who had raided Ziklag, not Egyptians. David's suspicions presumably focused on the peoples he had raided earlier. That did not include Egyptians. But, of course, there was the possibility that this fellow had seen something. There is also the possibility that no one yet realized he was an Egyptian. So they brought him to David.

> *And they gave him bread and he ate. They gave him water to drink, and they gave him a piece of a cake of figs and two clusters of raisins. (vv. 11b, 12a)*

He was, it seems, famished. We soon learn why: "And when he had eaten, his spirit revived, for he had not eaten bread or drunk water for three days and three nights" (v. 12b).

David had been in Aphek with the Philistines when this fellow had last eaten and drunk (see "the third day" in 1 Samuel 30:1). That at least suggests that he may have been in this vicinity at the critical time. The interrogation therefore began: "And David said to him, 'To whom do you belong? And where are you from?'" (v. 13a).

The man's Egyptian origin was apparently not obvious to David. He could, therefore, have supposed that he might have belonged to one of the suspected culprits. The man promptly explained and in a few words both dissociated himself from and involved himself in the troubles at Ziklag:

> He said, "I am a young man of Egypt, servant to an Amalekite, and my master left me behind because I fell sick three days ago. We had made a raid against the Negeb of the Cherethites and against that which belongs to Judah and against the Negeb of Caleb, and we burned Ziklag with fire."
> (vv. 13b, 14)

The last piece of information, of course, was the critical news. This man had been there. He said "we"! True, he was just an Egyptian servant, or slave, to an Amalekite. True, too, he had been abandoned to die by his Amalekite master. Therefore he was not exactly one of them.[15]

The Egyptian's report of the raiding activities of the Amalekites did not, of course, deliberately reflect the false reports that David had given Achish about his own exploits, as he created the impression that he was making himself "an utter stench to his people Israel" (1 Samuel 27:12). Neither did they correspond exactly to those reports. However, there is a striking correspondence between the actual activities of the Amalekites and David's pretended ones. The Amalekites had been operating in the Negeb, that large southern area in which David had claimed to do much damage (1 Samuel 27:10). While the Cherethites were not part of David's actual or pretended raids,[16] "that which belongs to Judah" is a fair summary of what David had deceived Achish into thinking he had done. In other words, these Amalekites had actually done what David pretended to have done. They *did* make themselves "an utter stench to [David's] people Israel"! The mention of "the Negeb of Caleb" is particularly telling. Nabal, the former husband of David's wife Abigail, was a Calebite (1 Samuel 25:3). David had very nearly attacked the Calebite Nabal and his men but had been restrained. The Amalekites did what David had not done. Among the very people where David had avoided bloodguilt (1 Samuel 25:26, 33), the Amalekites incurred it. These details add to what we already know about the Amalekites and support David's description of them in 1 Samuel 30:26 as "the enemies of the LORD."

Of most interest to David, however, was what the Egyptian said last: "and we burned Ziklag with fire." The usefulness of this man was now clear: "And David said to him, 'Will you take me down to this band?'" (v. 15a).

The Egyptian servant was not stupid. He probably knew something of David's reputation. His confessed involvement in the raids meant he was at David's mercy. But if he helped David, he could expect a traitor's penalty, should he fall again into his Amalekite master's hands. He therefore struck a bargain:

> And he said, "Swear to me by God that you will not kill me or deliver
> me into the hands of my master, and I will take you down to this band."
> (v. 15b)

David apparently accepted the terms of this agreement. So the man led them to the location of the Amalekite horde:

> And when he had taken him down, behold, they were spread abroad over all the
> land, eating and drinking and dancing, because of all the great spoil they had
> taken from the land of the Philistines and from the land of Judah. (v. 16)

What a sight confronted David and his men when they located the Amalekites![17] The impression is of a vast number, apparently well over a thousand,[18] perhaps several thousand. David had arrived with just 400 of his men. The enemy, however, was completely vulnerable. They were "spread abroad over all the land" — in other words, out of control and under no discipline,[19] gorging themselves with food, filling themselves with drink, and wildly celebrating[20] their booty. (Quite a contrast to the sick man they had left behind to starve to death!)

These Amalekites had taken their great spoil from the two peoples whose armies, probably at this very time, were engaged against each other far to the north in the valley of Jezreel. They had no idea that David and his small troop had returned. They were in for a surprise:

> And David struck them down from twilight until the evening of the next
> day, and not a man of them escaped, except four hundred young men, who
> mounted camels and fled. (v. 17)

The relatively small group who escaped was the same size as David's band that had won the victory in this surprise attack.[21] God's word to David had been, "you shall surely overtake and shall surely rescue" (1 Samuel 30:8). That is exactly what happened:

> David recovered [literally, rescued] all that the Amalekites had taken,
> and David rescued his two wives. Nothing was missing, whether small
> or great, sons or daughters, spoil or anything that had been taken. David
> brought back all. (vv. 18, 19)

David's rescue mission was a complete success. In addition to what was recovered, there was the spoil that the Amalekites had taken from other places. Specific mention is made in the next verse of the animals.[22] Verse 20 seems slightly awkward in the Hebrew (as the ESV note suggests), but it makes acceptable sense. Here is a quite literal translation: "And David took all the sheep, but the cattle they drove before those livestock, and they said, 'This is David's spoil.'"[23] (v. 20, literal translation).

This seems to indicate that the sheep[24] were separated from the larger cattle[25] in order to be allocated by the men to David. The larger cattle, presumably, were to be shared by all David's men. Not only had the trouble caused by the Amalekites been overcome, the trouble from the men's anger at David had been replaced by gratitude.[26]

At about the same time as the Philistines must have been engaging Saul and his army in the north, with the disastrous outcome we already know, David, by God's goodness, accomplished a great deliverance for his people. As Saul was being defeated, David was being victorious.

The contrast between King Saul and soon-to-be King David is underlined in two final scenes.

DAVID'S "JUSTICE" (vv. 21-25)

On the way back to Ziklag, with the rescued families as well as the considerable booty, the happy crowd came to the brook Besor and the 200 who must have been waiting anxiously for news of their wives and sons and daughters.

> *Then David came to the two hundred men who had been too exhausted to follow David, and who had been left at the brook Besor. And they went out to meet David and to meet the people who were with him. And when David came near to the people he greeted them. (v. 21)*

The scene has all the appearances of a joyful reunion. David himself was a powerful, uniting influence. "The people" in the last sentence of verse 21 seems to mean all the people, those who had just returned with David *and* those who were waiting at the brook. He greeted them all. Literally, he "asked them for peace."

The need for David's peacemaking initiative became clear immediately:

> *Then all the wicked and worthless fellows among the men who had gone with David said, "Because they did not go with us, we will not give them any of the spoil that we have recovered, except that each man may lead away his wife and children, and depart." (v. 22)*

There were troublemakers among the men who had gone with David. "Wicked and worthless" are the words used to describe them. We are reminded of Nabal who was "a worthless man" (1 Samuel 25:17, 25) and had treated David with contempt. Much earlier at the very beginning of Saul's reign he too had encountered "some worthless fellows" (1 Samuel 10:27). They had treated the new king with contempt. Earlier still there were the sons of Eli who were "worthless men" who treated the Lord "with contempt" (1 Samuel 2:12, 17)! The "worthless" men David now found among his people, like the others in this story, showed contempt for the ways of God, God's king or king-to-be. Their greed and self-interest was placed above the "peace" David called for.

David's response was remarkable:

> But David said, "You shall not do so, my brothers, with what the LORD has given us. He has preserved us and given into our hand the band that came against us. Who would listen to you in this matter? For as his share is who goes down into the battle, so shall his share be who stays by the baggage. They shall share alike." (vv. 23, 24)

Notice first that he called the troublemakers "my brothers"! Contrast Saul's treatment of his servants when he suspected them of causing mischief (see 1 Samuel 22:7, 8). David was a peacemaker among his people. The authority that David was beginning to assume was not that of a tyrant. His people, even these troublesome ones, were his "brothers."

This principle had been built into the rules for kingship in Israel from the beginning. In the Law it was written:

> One from among your brothers you shall set as king over you. You may not put a foreigner over you, who is not your brother . . . his heart may not be lifted up above his brothers. (Deuteronomy 17:15, 20)

This principle came to its most remarkable expression in Jesus, who "is not ashamed to call [us] brothers" (Hebrews 2:11; also v. 17; cf. Matthew 12:48, 49 [Mark 3:33, 34; Luke 8:21]; 23:8; 25:40; 28:10; Romans 8:29).

Second, David insisted that the spoils of war were "what the LORD has given us." Their survival, their victory, and the booty were all gifts from God. The dissenters saw it as "the spoil that we have recovered." Like the sons of Eli they did not "know" the Lord (1 Samuel 2:12). They excluded God from their thinking (cf. Romans 1:28).

This was an expression of the understanding of life given to Israel from the beginning. They had been solemnly warned by Moses of the great danger of forgetting the Lord their God by thinking that

"My power and the might of my hand have gotten me this wealth" (Deuteronomy 8:17; see verses 11-20). To forget the grace of God is to forget God.

To be a Christian is to have "understood the grace of God in truth" (Colossians 1:6). We know God as "the God of all grace" (1 Peter 5:10). The grace of God, experienced by Israel, recognized on that day by David, has come to its fullest expression in Jesus Christ. "By grace you have been saved . . . this is not your own doing; it is the gift of God" (Ephesians 2:8).

Third, David exposed greed and selfishness as an entirely unacceptable response to God's gifts. "Who would listen to you in this matter?" means "Who would agree with what you propose?"[27] The question is rhetorical, of course. The implication is that no one who understood the present situation, as David did, in terms of the Lord's goodness toward them all, could countenance greed and selfishness as a response.

This is the powerful logic of faith. Faith sees the grace of God and must draw the implications. The logic of David was essentially the same as that of Paul with the Corinthians: "What do you have that you did not receive? If then you received it, why do you boast as if you did not receive it?" (1 Corinthians 4:7).

Fourth, David established a radical principle of equity. We learn now that the exhausted members of the group had been given a job. They had watched over the baggage to enable the chase to proceed unhindered.[28] That task was obviously less strenuous than the chase of the Amalekites and the fighting. It was less dangerous too. The troublemakers had an apparently valid point.

They must have sounded rather like the laborers in a parable Jesus told. They had worked long and hard and then found themselves paid the same amount as others who had worked hardly at all. "These last worked only one hour, and you have made them equal to us who have borne the burden of the day and the scorching heat" (Matthew 20:12). It's not fair!

That's right. Grace is not about fairness. Since the booty had not been earned but was a gift from God, none had a greater claim to it than another. All shall "share alike." The grace of God, when known, demands a radical equity. "The last will be first, and the first last" (Matthew 20:16).[29]

Remarkably, this declaration by David can now be seen as the beginning of his kingly rule over Israel: "And he made it a statute and a rule for Israel from that day forward to this day" (v. 25).

This incident, and David's response to it, pointed to the kind of king he was to be and the kind of kingdom his power was to establish. The writer looks back and sees in this episode the beginning of a radical principle that operated in the kingdom until his own day.[30]

DAVID'S GIFTS (vv. 26-31)

In the last scene of this remarkable chapter we see David acting out the principles he had so clearly articulated:

> *When David came to Ziklag, he sent part of the spoil to his friends, the elders of Judah, saying, "Here is a present for you from the spoil of the enemies of the LORD." It was for those in Bethel, in Ramoth of the Negeb, in Jattir, in Aroer, in Siphmoth, in Eshtemoa, in Racal, in the cities of the Jerahmeelites, in the cities of the Kenites, in Hormah, in Bor-ashan, in Athach, in Hebron, for all the places where David and his men had roamed. (vv. 26-31)*

Commentators on this passage regularly delve into the political motives of David's generosity here. Was this reward for past favors? These "friends" of David were, after all, "the elders of Judah" in "all the places where David and his men had roamed."[31] Was it currying favor with those who would soon acknowledge David as king? The places mentioned, insofar as they can be identified,[32] lie in the general vicinity of Hebron, which was to be David's first royal city (2 Samuel 2:1-4). Was it compensation for those who had been plundered by the Amalekites?[33] Some of the places mentioned must have been included in "that which belongs to Judah" (v. 14), which had been the object of these Amalekite raids.[34]

The appeal of these proposals lies in their reasonableness. It is likely that David's actions here had some, at least, of the suggested effects. It is a mistake, however, to see this in terms of politically motivated maneuvering. We should note that David's distribution of spoil to the elders of Judah probably came from his own substantial portion, "David's spoil" of verse 20.[35] He was proving himself to be the very opposite of the king who "takes," described by Samuel so long ago (1 Samuel 8:10-18). Here was a king who *gives*!

The gift was given to "the elders of Judah," who were "his friends."[36] Cynicism may suggest that he gave the gifts to make them his friends, but cynicism is uncalled for here. "Friends" has an important meaning because of the contrast with the "enemies" of the Lord. David's relationships were being clarified. David's enemies were the enemies of the Lord; David's friends were the elders of Judah.

David described the gift as "a present [literally, a blessing, as in 1 Samuel 25:27] . . . from the spoil of the enemies of the LORD." The Lord's enemies were overthrown at David's hands. Out of that defeat David's friends were blessed.

By the time the events of this chapter had run their course, Saul had probably died on Mount Gilboa (see 1 Samuel 31). This chapter has revealed the kind of king who could replace him. He was a man who found his strength in God. He listened to God's voice and eagerly obeyed. God gave him decisive victory over his enemies, enabling him to save his people. He ruled in the knowledge of God's grace and therefore with equity and generosity. To be counted among the friends of this king was to be blessed. He was a king who gives.

The kind of king David might have been is a shadow of the kind of king Jesus is. On the night before his death Jesus told his disciples that he now called them his "friends" (John 15:15). To be counted among his friends is the greatest blessing a human being can know. "Greater love has no one than this, that someone lays down his life for his friends" (John 15:13).

49

The King Is Dead

1 SAMUEL 31

The Bible's account of the life, death, and resurrection of Jesus, who is called the Christ, is the greatest story ever told. It is a story that has become known as the gospel — the good news that all people everywhere need to hear. In the version provided by Matthew, the story concludes with the words spoken by the risen Jesus to his disciples on a mountain in Galilee. He said: "All authority in heaven and on earth has been given to me" (Matthew 28:18).

The one who died on the cross was raised from the dead and now reigns over all things. He is the King over all creation. He spelled out the necessary consequence of his all-encompassing authority:

> *"Go therefore and make disciples of all nations, baptizing them into [literal translation] the name of the Father and of the Son and of the Holy Spirit, teaching them to observe all that I have commanded you. And behold, I am with you always, to the end of the age." (Matthew 28:19, 20)*

This story, known as the gospel, is the means by which disciples are made from all nations. Hear this story, and you know the gospel that must be proclaimed to all people everywhere. Hear this story, and you know that Jesus has saved his people from their sins (cf. Matthew 1:21) and that death has been defeated. The resurrection of Jesus means that all peoples are now to be immersed into the knowledge of the triune God. That will happen as they are taught to live under the comprehensive authority that has been given to Jesus. The Lord Jesus Christ has promised to be with his disciples in the great task of proclaiming this gospel until the end of the age.

It *is* the greatest story ever told.

In the last chapter of 1 Samuel we read about events that occurred a thousand years before Jesus uttered those momentous words on a mountain in Galilee. In their own way the events of 1 Samuel 31 were momentous too. They took place on another mountain, Mount Gilboa, just south of Galilee.[1] The contrast between the events on these two mountains, a millennium apart, is stark. On Mount Gilboa we will not see the victory of the one who is called the Christ over death and his exaltation to reign over all things. First Samuel 31 tells of the tragic death of Saul, the one who had been called the christ, the anointed, and his humiliation. We will not hear the gospel of the Christ's resurrection to be proclaimed to the nations of the world by his disciples. In 1 Samuel 31 we will hear the gospel of Saul's death proclaimed by the Philistines in the house of their idols.

Yet, as we reach this dramatic moment in the long story of Israel's search for a leader, the death of Saul will point us not only to the coming kingdom of David, but also to the kingdom of the one descended from David according to the flesh who, a thousand years later, would be declared king in power by his resurrection from the dead (see Romans 1:1-4, where "Son of God" is a royal title, as in Psalm 2:7).

The brief closing chapter of 1 Samuel presents us with a great deal to ponder. It is a fitting conclusion to this extraordinary account of the reign of Israel's first king. There are numerous links back into the story that has been told as many threads are brought together.

A summary of Saul's life and achievements was given many pages earlier, in 1 Samuel 14:47-52. We observed at that point that it was the kind of review of this king's life that we might expect to appear after his death. In a paradoxical way it effectively signaled the end of Saul's reign. Through the long narrative that followed chapter 14, we have seen that this disobedient king was now incapable of properly ruling the people of Israel. Sixteen chapters have made clear that Israel needed a better future than this.

On the night before the events of 1 Samuel 31, at Endor, Saul heard from the dead and buried Samuel the devastating words that were to hang heavily over the following day:

> *"The LORD has done to you as he spoke by me, for the LORD has torn the kingdom out of your hand and given it to your neighbor, David. Because you did not obey the voice of the LORD and did not carry out his fierce wrath against Amalek, therefore the LORD has done this thing to you this day. Moreover, the LORD will give Israel also with you into the hand of the Philistines, and tomorrow you and your sons shall be with me. The LORD will give the army of Israel also into the hand of the Philistines."*
> *(1 Samuel 28:17-19)*

In one sense, therefore, the day of 1 Samuel 31 would bring no surprises. The death of Saul had been a long time coming, but it was not unexpected. And yet chapter 31 is riveting reading and is deeply moving. Part of its impact lies in its brevity. The events of the day unfold in four scenes. We are expected to pause and ponder the tragedy presented here.

PHILISTINE VICTORY — STAGE 1 (vv. 1-3)

The chapter begins with a slightly unusual construction in Hebrew. It indicates that what we are about to hear took place *at the same time* as the previously told events.[2] In other words, it was at the very time that David was striking down the Amalekites far to the south and rescuing his people from these "enemies of the LORD" (as we saw in 1 Samuel 30; note especially v. 26) that Saul was confronted by the Philistines in the northern valley of Jezreel, with a very different outcome (as we will see in 1 Samuel 31).[3]

The sequence of events that had led to this is easy enough to reconstruct, although in the preceding three chapters it has been presented out of chronological order, with particularly dramatic effect. In brief this is what had happened:

1. The Philistines made the decision to fight against Israel, and Achish insisted that David must come along (1 Samuel 28:1, 2).

2. In preparation for the assault, the whole Philistine fighting force assembled at Aphek, and there David was excluded (1 Samuel 29:1-10). At the same time the Israelites set up camp in the vicinity of the Jezreel Valley (1 Samuel 29:1).

3. From Aphek David then headed south to Ziklag (1 Samuel 29:11–30:1) as the Philistines moved north to the Jezreel Valley (1 Samuel 29:11).

4. The Philistines set up camp at Shunem on the northern side of the Jezreel Valley, and the Israelites assembled in the Gilboa hills on the south side of the valley (1 Samuel 28:4).

5. The terrified Saul secretly visited the medium at Endor by night (1 Samuel 28:5-25).

6. Meanwhile David reached Ziklag, discovered the catastrophe that had fallen at the hands of the Amalekites, and redeemed the situation (1 Samuel 30).

7. As David was dealing with the Amalekites more than a hundred miles to the south, the Philistines engaged the Israelites in battle in the valley of Jezreel (1 Samuel 31:1).

The Philistines and the Israelites (v. 1)

The military situation in the Jezreel Valley is summed up in the first verse of 1 Samuel 31: "Now the Philistines fought against Israel, and the men of Israel fled before the Philistines and fell slain on Mount Gilboa" (v. 1).

In those few words a catastrophe is presented. A hundred miles to the south it was Amalekites (the few who survived) who were "fleeing" from David (1 Samuel 30:17). In the Jezreel Valley the men of Israel were fleeing and dying before the Philistines.

If the fighting had begun on the level ground of the valley, this would have given a major advantage to the Philistines with their chariots (see 1 Samuel 13:5). Saul's troops were apparently forced to flee to the higher ground of Mount Gilboa, less accessible to the chariots.

Only twice before in the story told by 1 Samuel have the people of Israel "fled" before an enemy. The last time was in the Valley of Elah, when "all the men of Israel . . . fled" when they saw Goliath (1 Samuel 17:24). On that occasion, of course, the tables were turned by a young shepherd boy with a sling. It was then the Philistines who "fled" (1 Samuel 17:51).[4] That was the beginning of much fleeing by the Philistines before the shepherd boy who quickly became a great warrior (see 1 Samuel 19:8).[5]

The "fleeing" of the Israelites now, however, is more reminiscent of the much earlier occasion in 1 Samuel 4. Indeed the Philistine assembly point for the present assault was again Aphek, the very location of their camp on that previous momentous occasion,[6] although this time the battle would take place much farther north. On that earlier occasion Israel had "fled" before the Philistines (1 Samuel 4:10, 17; cf. v. 16) with disastrous consequences. Israel's failed leader and his sons were killed (1 Samuel 4:11, 18). The situation was summed up in the words, "The glory has departed from Israel" (1 Samuel 4:21, 22). That disaster had been the background to the Israelite demand for a king to "go out before us and fight our battles" (1 Samuel 8:20). Saul was that king. The tragic irony is that the last chapter of 1 Samuel has Israel in *the same situation* as 1 Samuel 4. This time they will not lose *the ark* — they will lose their *king*.[7] Once again Israel's failed leader will fall, with his sons, before the Philistines.

The Philistines pursued the fleeing Israelites onto Mount Gilboa, and many Israelites were slain.

The Philistines and Saul's Sons (v. 2)

The account now comes in closer to the action on Mount Gilboa and observes what was happening in more detail: "And the Philistines overtook Saul and his sons . . ." (v. 2a).

Among the Israelites scrambling up the slopes of Mount Gilboa, there was this small group in whom we have a particular interest. The Philistines also had a particular interest in them and "overtook" them.[8] What happened then? ". . . and the Philistines struck down Jonathan and Abinadab and Malchi-shua, the sons of Saul" (v. 2b).

Jonathan is the son of Saul with whom we have become most familiar through 1 Samuel. His death at this point is a terrible tragedy. Jonathan, Saul's eldest son, had responded in an exemplary manner to the purposes of God as they became clear to him. He seemed to have perceived Saul's failure to rule properly and took the necessary initiatives against the Philistines in Saul's place (see 1 Samuel 13:3; 14, especially v. 29). He was the first to recognize that David would be Israel's next king. He willingly, even gladly, committed himself to David (1 Samuel 18:1-4). He was faithful to that commitment and consistently, if reluctantly, took David's side in the conflict between Saul and David (1 Samuel 19:1-3; 20:1-42; 23:16-18). He risked his own life by testifying to Saul of David's innocence (1 Samuel 19:4-6; 20:26-34). Jonathan expected to play a role in David's coming kingdom (1 Samuel 23:17). His death, therefore, comes as a shock.

One of Saul's sons did not die on Mount Gilboa. His name was given as Ishvi in 1 Samuel 14:49.[9] We must assume either that for some reason he was not present on Mount Gilboa or that he somehow escaped. He will appear later in the story by the name Ish-bosheth (2 Samuel 2:8-10). For now our attention is focused on the three sons slain on Mount Gilboa.

The Philistines and Saul (v. 3)

We are now drawn closer still, and our attention is focused on the now lonely figure of Saul: "The battle pressed hard against Saul . . ." (v. 3a).

Literally this reads, "The battle was heavy toward Saul."[10] It was as though the whole weight of the conflict now pressed down on Saul. ". . . and the archers found him . . ." (v. 3b).

The Philistine chariots apparently had not been able to follow the Israelites up the slopes, but the archers sustained the pursuit. Against fleeing troops, the bow was particularly effective. We should remember Hannah's prayer: "the bows of the mighty are broken" (1 Samuel 2:4). There is irony in the fact that this faith is expressed at the beginning of 1 Samuel and the apparently contrary fact is found at the end.[11]

Saul was now in sight of the archers, and in their range. The text then says: ". . . and he was badly wounded by the archers" (v. 3c).

Some translations render this, "he was greatly distressed by reason of the archers."[12] With his sons dead at his feet, and the Philistine archers a short distance away and closing in, and perhaps with Samuel's words of the night before ringing in his ears, Saul trembled with terror.

SAUL'S DEATH (vv. 4-6)

For the second scene we come closer still and hear a terrible conversation between Saul and the only companion left to him.

Saul's Request (v. 4a-b)

Then Saul said to his armor-bearer, "Draw your sword, and thrust me through with it, lest these uncircumcised come and thrust me through, and mistreat me." (v. 4a)

A long time ago Saul's armor-bearer had been a young man named David (1 Samuel 16:21). Through Saul's mad, jealous, and wicked hatred, David was now many miles away, dealing with the Amalekites.

Saul appears now to have accepted the inevitability of his death this day but feared to be killed and abused by the despised Philistines.[13] Therefore Saul, whose life had twice been spared by his former armor-bearer (1 Samuel 24; 26), now asked his present armor-bearer to take his life. Of course, if David had been present we know very well that he would *not* have lifted his hand against Saul (see 1 Samuel 24:6, 10, 13; 26:9, 11, 23). Saul's present armor-bearer was no more willing: "But his armor-bearer would not, for he feared greatly" (v. 4b).

This armor-bearer proved himself to be remarkably like David, who had said, "The LORD forbid that I should do this thing to my lord, the LORD's anointed, to put out my hand against him, seeing he is the LORD's anointed" (1 Samuel 24:6).[14] Those words eloquently express what was probably behind the armor-bearer's great fear.

Therefore Saul found himself utterly alone. The tragedy of this moment is deeply moving. At the heart of the tragedy is what we do *not* hear from Saul. From him we do not hear, "My God, my God, why have you forsaken me?" That is what David cried on some occasion, perhaps on many occasions (Psalm 22:1). It was, of course, what Jesus cried from the cross (Matthew 27:46; Mark 15:34). Saul seems to have accepted his God-forsakenness and surrendered himself to it. The narrative itself corresponds to Saul's silence: it, too, makes no reference to God in the account of Saul's death.

Saul's End (v. 4c)

Utterly alone, Saul took the only course of action he could see: "Therefore Saul took his own sword and fell upon it" (v. 4c).

Just five words in the Hebrew text report the death of Israel's first king.[15] The momentous significance of the event does not require elaboration. The tragedy of this death does not need to be labored. The king who had failed was dead, by his own hand. His failure was now complete.

And Another (vv. 5, 6)

This second scene is concluded with yet another death and a solemn summary of what had happened on Mount Gilboa that day. "And when his armor-bearer saw that Saul was dead, he also fell upon his sword and died with him" (v. 5).

Was he overwhelmed with the hopelessness of the situation? Did he do this because he was responsible for the life of the king?[16] The reasons matter little. Another body fell on Mount Gilboa.

Listen carefully to the summing up of that day: "Thus Saul died, and his three sons, and his armor-bearer, and all his men, on the same day together" (v. 6).

It happened just as Samuel had said. King and people were swept away (see 1 Samuel 12:25).

At about the same time, many miles away to the south, David had succeeded as comprehensively as Saul had failed. "David brought back all" (1 Samuel 30:19)!

The death of any human being is tragic. The Bible describes death as "the last enemy" (1 Corinthians 15:26). Nothing speaks more powerfully of the corruption of God's good creation than death. As we witness Saul's death and that of Jonathan and his brothers, not to mention the many others who lay on the slopes of Mount Gilboa that day, it is appropriate to pause and recognize the tragedy of human death.

The Bible says nothing about the fact that Saul took his own life. We should be very clear, however, that such an act does not make things better. It never does. We should respect the Bible's silence here[17] and not condemn Saul for his final act, but neither should we think for a moment that the act had any sense in it. It magnified the tragedy; it did not lessen it.[18]

However, the death of Saul (like any human death, of course) had its own particular tragedy. In Saul's case this was extraordinary. He was the Lord's anointed — chosen by God to rule over God's people. Imagine what he might have been! In the very early days we had a glimpse of the possibilities. God's purpose for him was that he would save his people from the Philistines (1 Samuel 9:16). He was equipped for this task by the Spirit of the Lord who changed him into a new man (1 Samuel 10:6, 9, 10). He demonstrated his Spirit-empowered ability to deliver the people (1 Samuel 11), whom he then dealt with gently (1 Samuel 11:13).

The story of Saul has significant parallels to the story of Adam and therefore to the story of us all. Adam was created by God to rule over God's good creation (see Genesis 1:28). Imagine what might have been! In the Garden of Eden we are given a glimpse of the possibilities. God's purpose for Adam was freedom to enjoy God's good gifts (Genesis 2:16) and to exercise loving rule over God's creatures (Genesis 2:19, 20). Adam was equipped for this task by God's own breath and by being made in God's image (Genesis 2:7; 1:27). Briefly he was what he was made to be.

In the case of both Adam and Saul it was all undone by disobedience to the word of God (see Genesis 3:6, 13; 1 Samuel 15:26).

Therefore the tragedy of Saul's death reminds us of the tragedy of every human death at a deeper level. Human beings are made in the image of God to rule. Like the tragic Saul, what we might have been has been undone by our disobedience to the word of God.

We will think a little more about Saul's death when we have taken in the remaining two scenes of this chapter.

PHILISTINE VICTORY — STAGE 2 (vv. 7-10)

In the third scene we see how the horror we have witnessed on Mount Gilboa quickly had wider consequences as it became known. The Philistine victory was massive.

With the Israelites (v. 7)

Mount Gilboa was visible from the north, across the Jezreel Valley, and from the east, across the Jordan. The massacre was seen and reported:

> And when the men of Israel who were on the other side of the valley and those beyond the Jordan saw that the men of Israel had fled and that Saul and his sons were dead, they abandoned their cities and fled. (v. 7a)

The Israelites who knew that their king was dead abandoned hope and ran. We do not know how extensive this panic was or how many cities were deserted. It made the consolidation of the Philistine victory, however, a simple matter: "And the Philistines came and lived in them" (v. 7b).

The Philistines thus made deep inroads into Israelite territory. Their presence effectively cut off the northern tribes from Benjamin and Judah to the south.[19] Israel once again lived in territory occupied by the Philistines, the very situation that had led to Saul's appointment.[20]

With Saul and His Sons (v. 8)

Now we return to Mount Gilboa to see what the Philistines did the next day: "The next day, when the Philistines came to strip the slain, they found Saul and his three sons fallen on Mount Gilboa" (v. 8).

The practice of stripping the bodies of defeated soldiers was common.[21] It may have been only now that the Philistines realized that Saul and his sons were dead.

With Saul in Particular (vv. 9, 10)

Their attention, naturally, focused on the dead enemy king: "So they cut off his head . . ." (v. 9a), just as David had once done to a very large Philistine, ". . . and stripped off his armor . . ." (v. 9b).

This was the final divestment of Saul's royal garments. He had unwittingly offered his armor to David once. On another occasion he had stripped off his clothes and lay naked before Samuel. Most recently on the night before his death he had replaced his royal garb with "other garments" at Endor (1 Samuel 17:38; 19:24; 28:8).[22] Now his royal armor was gone forever, and the body of Israel's king lay naked on the hillside, completely vanquished. ". . . and [they] sent messengers throughout the land of the Philistines, to carry the good news to the house of their idols and to the people" (v. 9c).

The word "messengers" is not in the original. Literally it says, "and they sent throughout the land of the Philistines . . ." It is possible that they sent Saul's head or his body or perhaps his armor on this "missionary journey" with the "good news" that Saul was dead.

They proclaimed the "gospel" of Saul's death. That is the language used. It helps us to understand what proclaiming a gospel means. It is to announce momentous news to people. That day there was a gospel for the Philistines and a gospel for their idols! The king of the people of the God of Israel was dead! It was clear, was it not, that the gods of the Philistines had at last defeated the God of Israel? I doubt that many Philistines were ashamed of that gospel that day. What great news for the temple of Dagon! The humiliation of an earlier day had been overturned at last (see 1 Samuel 5:1-5).

What a gospel that must have been for the Philistine people! The many defeats they had suffered at Saul's hands were now a thing of the past (see 1 Samuel 14:47).

The news having been carried through the land, by whatever means, the signs of the victory were appropriately deposited: "They put his armor in the temple of Ashtaroth, and they fastened his body to the wall of Bethshan" (v. 10).

Just as they had once put the captured ark in the temple of Dagon (1 Samuel 5:2),[23] now the armor of the dead king was put in the temple of Ashtaroth, "the female deity worshipped alongside Dagon."[24]

The body of the king was another matter. Saul had feared being "mistreated" or abused by the "uncircumcised" Philistines (v. 4). His death did not spare him that indignity. His headless corpse was impaled on the wall in Beth-shan, a public object of horror and disgust. Beth-shan was in the Jordan Valley near where it meets the Jezreel Valley.

The humiliation could hardly be more complete. It was a great day to be a Philistine!

The Philistine gospel is still to be heard whenever human beings believe they have triumphed over God. Every mockery of God and his people, every expression of scorn toward the Lord Jesus and his followers, is a version of the Philistine gospel.

THE PEOPLE OF JABESH-GILEAD (vv. 11-13)

There is one final scene in 1 Samuel 31. It is rather surprising. The people who featured prominently in the very first of Saul's military exploits, which had had a far happier outcome for them than this one, appear again here at the end (see 1 Samuel 11:1-11). Their appearance reminds us of that earlier marvelous deliverance by the Spirit-empowered Saul. We cannot help seeing how different the circumstances were now.

What They Heard (v. 11)

> *But when the inhabitants of Jabesh-gilead heard what the Philistines had done to Saul . . . (v. 11).*

The Philistine gospel had reached their ears. But what was good news for the Philistines was a very different kind of news to the good people of Jabesh-gilead.

What They Did (vv. 12, 13)

> *. . . all the valiant men arose and went all night and took the body of Saul and the bodies of his sons from the wall of Beth-shan, and they came to Jabesh and burned them there. And they took their bones and buried them under the tamarisk tree in Jabesh and fasted seven days. (vv. 12, 13)*

Their all-night march through Philistine-occupied territory would have been dangerous. Taking the bodies (and now we learn that Jonathan and his brothers had suffered the same degradation as Saul) from the wall would have required stealth and courage.[25]

I wonder if they knew how fitting it was to bury Saul under a tamarisk tree. At Gibeah, remember, he used to sit under the tamarisk tree, spear in hand, powerful, surrounded by servants (1 Samuel 22:6). His story ends with his bones buried under a tamarisk tree, stripped at last of any shadow of power. The king was dead.

And so the book of 1 Samuel ends.

It is right that we do not move too quickly to 2 Samuel and the story of the new king. Indeed, if we did turn the page and begin to read the next book we would find that its first chapter points us back to this last chapter of 1 Samuel and forces us to reflect seriously on the tragedy we have witnessed before we move on to David's kingdom. David himself would take steps to see that these deaths were never forgotten. He composed a lament to be taught to the people of Judah (2 Samuel 1:17, 18).

Reflect again on the tragedy of death, as 1 Samuel 31 sets before us this tragedy. Death reigned that day.

Many years later another who was called the Christ was defeated by his enemies, or so it seemed. He, too, was handed over to the nations to be abused (Matthew 20:19; Mark 10:33; Luke 18:32). His body was also hung as a public object of horror and disgust (Matthew 27:31; Mark 15:20; Luke 23:33; John 19:18). In his case, too, there was someone who cared and came, at some risk to himself and took down his body and gave it an honored burial (Matthew 27:57-60; Mark 15:43-46; Luke 23:50-53; John 19:38-42).

The similarities between the death of Saul and the death of Jesus serve to highlight the stark difference. Saul died for his own failure to "fear the LORD and serve him faithfully" (1 Samuel 12:24). Jesus died as the righteous and faithful one, in complete obedience to his Father's will (for example, see Matthew 26:39; Romans 5:19; Philippians 2:8; Hebrews 5:7-10; 12:2).

Reflect then on the ultimate futility of human power. "There shall be a king over us, that we also may be like all the nations, and that our king may judge us and go out before us and fight our battles" (1 Samuel 8:19, 20). Now behold your king! Slain on Mount Gilboa. Slung on the wall of Beth-shan. Buried under the tamarisk tree in Jabesh. The foolishness of the demand, like the foolishness of all hopes placed in human power, can be starkly seen in Saul's end.

Reflect, thirdly, on hope. The story of Saul has been a story of the failure of human power and the failure of human schemes. It has been a story that ended in death. It has contained, however, another story. We could trace that other story back to Hannah's magnificent prayer at the very beginning of 1 Samuel:

> "The LORD kills and brings to life;
>> he brings down to Sheol and raises up. . . .
> The adversaries of the LORD shall be broken to pieces;
>> against them he will thunder in heaven.
> The LORD will judge the ends of the earth;
>> he will give strength to his king
>> and exalt the power of his anointed." (1 Samuel 2:6, 10)

We have been left in no doubt that it was ultimately the Lord who brought Saul down. He had become an "adversary of the LORD" and had been "broken to pieces." Where should we look for the other half of Hannah's insight? The Lord "brings to life," he "raises up," "he will give strength to his king and exalt the power of his anointed."

First Samuel has made clear that Israel's hope was David. Saul's failure was not the failure of God's purpose. The Lord had provided another whom he would "establish as king over Israel" and "exalt his kingdom for the sake of his people Israel" (2 Samuel 5:12).

All of this would turn out to be a shadow of the things to come. Israel's hope was David. In due course, however, David also failed, and David died. Israel's hope, and the hope of all mankind, in the face of the futility of human power and the inevitability of death is Jesus. Jesus' death was not the failure of God's purpose. In this case the Lord brought to life the one who had died, raised him up, and exalted him as both Lord and Christ. Here is the gospel that answers the false gospel of the Philistines:

> *"All authority in heaven and on earth has been given to me. Go therefore and make disciples of all nations, baptizing them in the name of the Father and of the Son and of the Holy Spirit, teaching them to observe all that I have commanded you. And behold, I am with you always, to the end of the age." (Matthew 28:18-20)*

Notes

CHAPTER ONE: THE LEADERSHIP CRISIS

1. As the book begins we will see that the leadership of the nation was in the hands of Eli. However, Eli is a relatively minor character in the book, quickly displaced by Samuel.

2. First Samuel is rightly seen as the immediate sequel to the book of Judges. In the Hebrew Bible 1 Samuel follows Judges. In English Bibles, following the Greek version known as the Septuagint, the book of Ruth has been placed between Judges and 1 Samuel because its story was set "[i]n the days when the judges ruled" (Ruth 1:1).

3. This refers directly to the books of Exodus and Numbers but applies in principle to the whole of the Old Testament Scriptures.

4. The NIV and NRSV follow an emendation of the Hebrew supported by the Septuagint: "There was a certain man from Ramathaim, a Zuphite. . . ." Likewise P. Kyle McCarter, Jr., *I Samuel: A New Translation with Introduction, Notes & Commentary*, The Anchor Bible, Vol. 8 (Garden City, NY: Doubleday, 1980), p. 51. Elkanah's being called a "Zuphite" tells us no more than that he belonged to a relatively unknown family line in the tribe of Ephraim. Zuph's only claim to fame in the text of the Old Testament is the territory named after him (see 1 Samuel 9:5).

5. The long name, Ramathaim-zophim, appears nowhere else in the Old Testament. It is identified by some with the New Testament's Arimathea (Matthew 27:57; John 19:38). Patrick Arnold identifies no less than five different towns called Ramah in the Old Testament. Patrick M. Arnold, "Ramah," in David Noel Freedman, ed., *The Anchor Bible Dictionary*, Vol. 5 (New York: Doubleday, 1992), pp. 613, 614. This one has been identified with at least four proposed sites, all about twenty miles north or northwest of Jerusalem. J. A. Thompson, "Ramah," in J. D. Douglas et al, eds., *The Illustrated Bible Dictionary*, Part 3 (Leicester, UK and Wheaton, IL: Inter-Varsity Press and Tyndale House, 1980), p. 1318. Prior to 1 Samuel, this Ramah has been mentioned in Joshua 18:25 (in a list of the cities of the children of Benjamin); Judges 4:5 (mentioned incidentally in the account of Deborah); Judges 19:13 (again incidental to the story of the Levite couple who chose not to stop there). This Ramah's greatest claim to fame, however, is its role in the story of Samuel, which begins and ends in Ramah (see 1 Samuel 1:19; 2:11; 7:17; 8:4; 15:34; 16:13; 19:18, 22, 23; 20:1; 25:1; 28:3). Joshua 19:8 mentions another Ramah to the south ("Ramah of the Negeb"), Joshua 19:29 another somewhere near Tyre, Joshua 19:36 yet another (a fortified city of Naphtali).

6. Lyle M. Eslinger, *Kingship of God in Crisis: A Close Reading of 1 Samuel 1–12*, Bible and Literature Series, 10 (Sheffield, UK: JSOT Press, 1985), p. 66. A number of commentaries seem to assume that the relatively long genealogy given for Elkanah is itself "impressive," indicating that "Elkanah has a proud past." Walter Brueggemann, *First and Second Samuel*, Interpretation: A Bible Commentary for Teaching and Preaching (Louisville: John Knox Press, 1990), p. 12; cf. Hans Wilhelm Hertzberg, *I & II Samuel: A Commentary*, Old Testament Library (London: SCM Press, 1964), pp. 22, 23; Peter R. Ackroyd, *The First Book of Samuel*, Cambridge Bible Commentary (Cambridge, UK: Cambridge University Press, 1971), p. 19; John Mauchline, *1 and 2 Samuel*, New Century Bible (London: Oliphants, 1971), p. 42; Robert P. Gordon, *1 & 2 Samuel: A Commentary* (Exeter, UK: The Paternoster Press, 1986), p. 72. This seems to seriously miss the point of verse 1. Granted that a person's genealogy is typically given to indicate his significant pedigree, the irony of 1 Samuel 1:1 is precisely that there is no one of

note in Elkanah's past. This genealogy perplexes us because it reveals an insignificant pedigree. That is its point!

7. A puzzle arises from 1 Chronicles 6:26-28, and especially verses 33-38 where Elkanah appears as belonging to the tribe of Levi. There is no hint of this in 1 Samuel 1:1, and if, as many argue, "Ephrathite" means "Ephraimite" (so NIV; RSV; NRSV; REB; Ralph W. Klein, *1 Samuel*, Word Biblical Commentary, 10 [Nashville: Word, 1983], p. 6; Mauchline, *1 and 2 Samuel*, p. 42), there is an apparent inconsistency. In this case only two explanations appear possible. Perhaps Elkanah was a Levite, and "Ephrathite" (= "Ephraimite") in 1 Samuel 1:1 refers to his place of residence. Some arguments in support of this are offered in M. J. Selman, *1 Chronicles*, Tyndale Old Testament Commentaries (Leicester, UK and Downers Grove, IL: InterVarsity Press, 1994), p. 111; see also C. F. Keil and F. Delitzsch, *Biblical Commentary on the Books of Samuel* (Grand Rapids, MI: Eerdmans, 1950), pp. 17, 18. Alternatively Elkanah was an Ephraimite who because of his famous son's priestly status was "adopted" into the Levitical line. So J. M. Myers, *1 Chronicles: A New Translation with Introduction, Notes & Commentary*, The Anchor Bible, Vol. 12 (Garden City, NY: Doubleday, 1965), p. 46; cf. H. G. M. Williamson, *1 and 2 Chronicles*, New Century Bible Commentary (Grand Rapids, MI and London: Eerdmans and Marshall, Morgan & Scott, 1982), p. 72. An alternative, considered in the next note, is that "Ephrathite" links Elkanah to Bethlehem rather than to the tribe of Ephraim. The inconsistency then dissolves (see Joyce Baldwin, *1 and 2 Samuel*, Tyndale Old Testament Commentaries [Leicester, UK: Inter-Varsity Press, 1988], pp. 50, 51). For our purposes in reading 1 Samuel, we simply need to note that here there is no hint of a connection with the tribe of Levi. Further reading on this subject is indicated in Gordon, *1 & 2 Samuel*, p. 331, note 2.

8. There is potential confusion here. Ephrathah is an alternative name for Bethlehem in Judah or for a region including Bethlehem (so Gordon J. Wenham, *Genesis 16–50*, Word Biblical Commentary 2 [Nashville: Word, 1994], p. 326; see Genesis 35:19; 48:7; Ruth 4:11; Micah 5:2; Psalm 132:6). "Ephrathite" can therefore mean a person from Bethlehem (1 Samuel 17:12; Ruth 1:2). In at least two other places, however, "Ephrathite" seems to mean "Ephraimite" (Judges 12:5; 1 Kings 11:26). It is often supposed that since Elkanah was from the hill country of Ephraim, "Ephrathite" in 1 Samuel 1:1 means "Ephraimite." Menahem Haran, however, mounts a good case that Elkanah may have been "of Bethlehem stock rather than an 'Ephraimite,' though he did dwell in the hill country of Ephraim." Menahem Haran, *Temples and Temple-Service in Ancient Israel: An Inquiry into the Character of Cult Phenomena and the Historical Setting of the Priestly School* (Oxford, UK: Clarendon Press, 1978), p. 308.

9. Cf. Eslinger, *Kingship*, p. 66.

10. The order in which they are mentioned suggests this, and the Hebrew word translated "the other" literally means "the second."

CHAPTER TWO: DOES GOD CARE?

1. Other locations could also be places of national assembly, such as Shechem (Joshua 24:1).

2. It is called "the house of God" in Judges 18:31, "the temple of the LORD" in 1 Samuel 1:9, "his dwelling at Shiloh, the tent where he dwelt" in Psalm 78:60, and "my place that was in Shiloh, where I made my name dwell at first" in Jeremiah 7:12.

3. This is the first occurrence in the Old Testament of the title for God variously translated "the LORD of hosts" (KJV, RSV, NRSV, REB, ESV) or "the LORD Almighty" (NIV). "Hosts" appears to refer to all the heavenly powers under God's almighty command. The title is often used to exhibit the Lord "as at all times the Saviour and Protector of his people (Ps. 46:7, 11)." G. T. Manley and F. F. Bruce, "God, names of," in J. D. Douglas et al, eds., *The Illustrated Bible Dictionary*, Part 1 (Leicester, UK and Wheaton, IL: Inter-Varsity Press and Tyndale House, 1980), p. 573. After Chapter 1 the expression occurs three more times in 1 Samuel: in connection with the ark ("the ark of the covenant of the LORD of hosts," 1 Samuel 4:4), in the solemn announcement of judgment on Amalek ("Thus

says the LORD of hosts," 1 Samuel 15:2), and in David's defiant challenge to Goliath ("I come to you in the name of the LORD of hosts," 1 Samuel 17:45).

4. As well as NKJV, NRSV, NIV. These translations follow an ancient Syriac version.

5. See RSV, NEB, REB. This aspect of the Hebrew text is supported by the Septuagint, which is followed by these translations.

6. It has to be admitted that difficulties remain with all available translations of this verse. See discussions in Robert P. Gordon, *1 & 2 Samuel: A Commentary* (Exeter, UK: The Paternoster Press, 1986), pp. 73, 74 and Lyle M. Eslinger, *Kingship of God in Crisis: A Close Reading of 1 Samuel 1–12*, Bible and Literature Series, 10 (Sheffield, UK: JSOT Press, 1985), pp. 71, 436, note 6.

7. Lyle Eslinger correctly insists that the repetition of the phrase "the LORD had closed her womb" (with a small variation in the Hebrew) in verses 5, 6 must be taken seriously, against a number of commentators who regard it as redundant (Eslinger, *Kingship*, p. 437, note 8). However, Eslinger treats the information in the phrase as reflecting simply the narrator's "omniscience" (p. 71) and stressing "that events on the human plane of the narrative are the product of an initiative from the divine plane" (p. 74). He fails, in my view, to appreciate that, while the observation is clearly made *by* the narrator, at this point he is signaling the point of view of the respective characters. Elkanah understands that the Lord has closed Hannah's womb and accepts this fact but treats his wife fairly (v. 5). Peninnah understands the same fact and torments Hannah because of it. For a discussion of this narrative technique see J. P. Fokkelman, *Reading Biblical Narrative: An Introductory Guide*, trans. Ineke Smit (Louisville and Leiderdorp, Netherlands: Westminster John Knox Press and Deo Publishing, 1999), pp. 147, 148.

8. The Hebrew syntax suggests that the shift from the account of what used to happen "year by year" to the particular episode that is about to be told begins with verse 8. Elkanah responded to Hannah's grief on one particular occasion with the words of verse 8, and the events of verses 9ff. ensued. KJV, RSV, NRSV, ESV ("said") reflect the Hebrew in verse 8 better here than the NIV ("would say"). If this is correct it would be better to make the paragraph break at the beginning of verse 8 rather than at verse 9.

9. Against, for example, John Goldingay, *Men Behaving Badly* (Carlisle, UK and Waynesboro, GA: Paternoster, 2000), p. 10 who sees Elkanah as "your average not-very-sensitive guy." There is a danger to be avoided in reading Biblical narrative of passing judgments on the actions of the characters from our (the readers') point of view. Unless this is also the point of view of the text (or the narrator), such judgments are unhelpful impositions that amount to misunderstandings.

10. The NIV begins verse 9, "Once when they had finished eating and drinking . . ." "Once" has no basis in the Hebrew text and is misleading if, as argued here, verse 8 is the beginning of Scene 2. The sense of the Hebrew would be better expressed if "Once" were moved to the beginning of verse 8.

11. Indeed the Hebrew could be translated, "After *she* had eaten and drunk . . ."

12. We know very little about what exactly is meant by "the temple" at Shiloh. It is generally considered that the tabernacle alone would not be referred to by this word, which presupposes a more substantial structure. For a helpful review of the evidence see Joyce Baldwin, *1 and 2 Samuel*, Tyndale Old Testament Commentaries (Leicester, UK: Inter-Varsity Press, 1988), pp. 65-68.

13. S. R. Driver, *Notes on the Hebrew Text and the Topography of the Book of Samuel with an Introduction on Hebrew Palaeography and Facsimiles of Inscriptions and Maps*, second edition (Oxford, UK: Clarendon, 1913), p. 12.

14. Contrary to Eslinger, *Kingship*, p. 77, who sees irony in the fact that Hannah prays to the Lord *without* knowing that it is the Lord who had sealed her womb. This is hardly possible with a woman of Hannah's evident piety. To confirm this point, if confirmation is needed, see 1 Samuel 2:5-8.

15. The language of God "looking" on the "affliction" of someone is also found in Genesis 29:32, when Leah gave birth to Reuben; Genesis 31:42, when God blessed Jacob despite Laban's ill treatment of him; 2 Kings 14:26, when the Lord had mercy on Israel in the

days of Jeroboam II; Job 10:15, in Job's cry to God out of his misery; Psalm 9:13, 25:18, 31:7, and 119:153 in the prayers of David in the face of his enemies; Lamentations 1:9, in Jerusalem's plea to God after her destruction.

16. This is the second occurrence in the Old Testament of the title "LORD of hosts." See verse 3.

17. More literally, "handmaid" (KJV) or "maidservant" (RSV).

18. On Nazirites see Numbers 6:1-21. A Nazirite could be a man or a woman (Numbers 6:2). Strictly speaking the expression translated "son" in 1 Samuel 1:11 (literally, "seed of men") is not gender specific (Gordon, *1 & 2 Samuel*, p. 75). It is not explicit that Hannah was praying for a *son*.

19. Literally "sons of worthlessness" (1 Samuel 2:12). The Hebrew idiom will appear again in 1 Samuel — in 10:27 (the "worthless fellows" who despised Saul), 25:17 (the "worthless man" Nabal), and 30:22 (certain "worthless fellows" among David's men). See also 2 Samuel 16:7; 20:1; 22:5 (where the word for "worthlessness" is translated "destruction"); 23:6.

20. Literally, "daughter of worthlessness."

21. So ESV. NIV, NRSV, RSV have "had no regard for the LORD."

22. It is not possible to reproduce the wordplay in English. The Hebrew asking words occur in verses 17 ("petition," "made"), 20 ("asked"), and 27 ("petition," "made"), and 28 ("lent" [twice]). The wordplay on the verb "to ask" extends, as we will see, to Saul, whose name means "Asked For." See 1 Samuel 9:2.

23. There is an ambiguity in the Hebrew. Eli's reply may have been a prayer (as the ESV has it) or a promise ("the God of Israel will grant your petition").

24. The vow of Elkanah in verse 21 is variously treated in the commentaries. Klein deletes it as a "gloss." Ralph W. Klein, *1 Samuel*, Word Biblical Commentary, 10 (Nashville: Word, 1983), p. 3. McCarter suggests the opposite course, expanding the text with some help from the Septuagint to read, "and to redeem his vow and all the tithes of his land." P. Kyle McCarter, Jr., *I Samuel: A New Translation with Introduction, Notes & Commentary*, The Anchor Bible, Vol. 8 (Garden City, NY: Doubleday, 1980), p. 55.

25. Indeed the Septuagint has "your word" rather than "his word" and is followed by NEB. See Gordon, *1 & 2 Samuel*, p. 77.

26. "Weaning was celebrated in ancient times as an important moment (see Gen. 21:8 for a feast at Isaac's weaning); it might well be postponed until a child's second or third year." Peter R. Ackroyd, *The First Book of Samuel*, Cambridge Bible Commentary (Cambridge, UK: Cambridge University Press, 1971), p. 28.

27. The thank offering may have been of even more generous proportions than the ESV indicates. The Hebrew has "three bulls," but since only one bull is mentioned in verse 25, the ESV and other translations have followed the Septuagint with the rendering, "a three-year-old bull" in verse 24. For details see Gordon, *1 & 2 Samuel*, p. 78.

28. "And the child was young" is puzzling in the Hebrew, which may be represented as, "And the child was a child." Alter has suggested the rendering, "and the lad was but a lad." Robert Alter, *The David Story: A Translation with Commentary of 1 and 2 Samuel* (New York and London: W.W. Norton, 1999), p. 7. The term translated "child" here and in verses 22, 25, and 27 (cf. 4:21) has a wider range of meanings than the English word *child*. In 1 Samuel it is most frequently used to refer to various servants (as in 1 Samuel 2:13, 15; 9:3, 5, 7, 8, 10, 22, 27; 10:14; 14:1, 6; 16:18; 20:21, 35-41; 21:2, 4; 25:5, 8, 9, 12, 14, 19, 25, 27; 26:22; 30:13). It appears to have this connotation when applied to Samuel in 1 Samuel 2:11, 18, 21, 26; 3:1, 8. It is also used of Jesse's sons (1 Samuel 16:11) and other youths (1 Samuel 2:17; 17:33, 42, 55, 58; 30:17).

CHAPTER THREE: THE GOD OF KNOWLEDGE

1. Note that according to 1 Samuel 2:21 Hannah bore five more children, in addition to Samuel. In her prayer she celebrates the fact that "The barren has borne seven" (v. 5), but that need not be a direct or literal reference to her own circumstances.

2. Exactly the same word is used in 1 Samuel 1:10 and 2:1 for Hannah's praying. The appropriate grammatical form of the same verb occurs in 1:26, 27, referring to the earlier prayer.

3. Robert Alter, *The David Story: A Translation with Commentary of 1 and 2 Samuel* (New York and London: W.W. Norton, 1999), p. 9.

4. The most serious loss here is the fact that the image is used again in verse 10, at the end of the prayer (this time translated "power" in the ESV). This echo of the beginning of the prayer at its end is lost, or at least dulled in our English translation. The NIV has retained "horn" in both places. We will note further significance in the "horn" metaphor when we reach verse 10.

5. Cf. Alter, *David*, p. 10; cf. Joyce Baldwin, *1 and 2 Samuel*, Tyndale Old Testament Commentaries (Leicester, UK: Inter-Varsity Press, 1988), p. 57; P. Kyle McCarter, Jr., *1 Samuel: A New Translation with Introduction, Notes & Commentary*, The Anchor Bible, Vol. 8 (Garden City, NY: Doubleday, 1980), p. 72. An alternative and less graphic interpretation is found in some commentaries and is reflected in most English translations. For example, "this connotes a rude, scornful opening of the mouth, sticking out of the tongue, and sneering 'Ha! Ha!' (Ps 35:21; Isa 57:4)." Ralph W. Klein, *1 Samuel*, Word Biblical Commentary, 10 (Nashville: Word, 1983), p. 15.

6. The second line begins with the Hebrew word often translated "for" ("because" in the last line of v. 1).

7. Compare the demand that Israel must be "holy" because the Lord their God is holy (e.g., Leviticus 19:2), which at least includes moral requirements. "Holiness is simply the moral reflection of the glory of the one absolute God." C. F. Keil and F. Delitzsch, *Biblical Commentary on the Books of Samuel* (Grand Rapids, MI: Eerdmans, 1950), p. 31.

8. Robert P. Gordon, *1 & 2 Samuel: A Commentary* (Exeter, UK: The Paternoster Press, 1986), p. 79.

9. God's knowledge is an important Biblical theme explored by Brian Rosner, "Known by God: C. S. Lewis and Dietrich Bonhoeffer," *Evangelical Quarterly* 77.4 (2005), pp. 343-352.

10. Since the "bows" of the Philistines are very far from "broken" by the end of 1 Samuel, it is clear that Hannah's prayer points beyond the pages of 1 Samuel.

11. We know that Hannah did eventually have (at least?) six children (see 1 Samuel 2:21). "The barren," however, should not be taken as a direct reference to herself, nor should "seven" be understood literally.

12. "Broken in pieces" represents the same Hebrew word as "broken" in verse 4. We recall again that by the end of 1 Samuel the Philistines (the quintessential "adversary of the LORD") will be very far from "broken in pieces." This is another clear indication that Hannah's prayer points us beyond the pages of 1 Samuel.

13. The word translated "judge" in verse 10 occurs only here in 1 Samuel (the noun form occurs in 1 Samuel 24:15) but is "to a great extent synonymous" with the much more common word for "judge" in 1 Samuel (1 Samuel 3:13 [ESV "punish"]; 4:18; 7:6, 15; 8:1, 5, 20; etc.). V. Hamp and G. J. Botterweck, *din*, in G. Johannes Botterweck and Helmer Ringgren, eds., *Theological Dictionary of the Old Testament*, Vol. 3 (Grand Rapids, MI: Eerdmans, 1978), p. 188.

14. The objections, found in many modern commentaries, that the prayer cannot be Hannah's precisely because it mentions a king (e.g., Klein, *1 Samuel*, p. 14; Alter, *David*, p. 9) claim to know too much of what Hannah could and could not have said. This is quite apart from their "utter denial of the supernatural saving revelations of God, and . . . consequent inability to discern the prophetic illumination of the pious Hannah. . . ." Keil and Delitzsch, *Biblical Commentary on the Books of Samuel*, pp. 29, 30. For a spirited criticism of the widely held view that Hannah's prayer has been added to the narrative secondarily (which is another issue) see Lyle M. Eslinger, *Kingship of God in Crisis: A Close Reading of 1 Samuel 1–12*, Bible and Literature Series, 10 (Sheffield: JSOT Press, 1985), pp. 99-102.

15. The first anointed king will be Saul (see 1 Samuel 9:16; 10:1; 15:1, 17), then David (16:3, 12, 13). It is noteworthy that the only other two occurrences of the word "horn" in 1 Samuel are in chapter 16 with reference to the anointing of David (vv. 1, 13).

CHAPTER FOUR: CORRUPTION AND INEPTITUDE

1. The omission of any mention of Hannah at this point is not as significant as Eslinger suggests, saying, "the text leaves the reader wondering about the place and action of . . . Hannah. Elkanah goes home and Samuel ministers to Yahweh, but where is Hannah and what is she doing?" Lyle M. Eslinger, *Kingship of God in Crisis: A Close Reading of 1 Samuel 1–12*, Bible and Literature Series, 10 (Sheffield: JSOT Press, 1985), p. 112. As 1 Samuel 1:3 clearly illustrates, the mention of Elkanah in such a context as this implies the rest of his family with him (with the one exception mentioned at the end of 2:11).

2. The Hebrew word behind "boy" here is the same as that translated "child" in 1 Samuel 1:22, 24, 25, and 27.

3. The verb (also in 1 Samuel 2:18; 3:1) is used particularly of priestly activities in service of God. See, for example, Exodus 28:35, 43; 30:20; 39:1; Numbers 4:12, 14; Deuteronomy 18:7; 1 Kings 8:11; 1 Chronicles 6:32; 16:4. Terence E. Fretheim, "*srt*," in Willem A. Van Gemeren, ed., *New International Dictionary of Old Testament Theology and Exegesis*, Vol. 4 (Carlisle, UK: Paternoster, 1996), pp. 256, 257. In the Hebrew the verb in verse 11 is a participle, which suggests the ongoing activity of Samuel at the same time as the corrupt behavior of the sons of Eli that will be described in the following verses.

4. The kind of duties that may have been involved are suggested by various passages, such as Numbers 3:5-10.

5. Possible examples of each of these meanings: death: 2 Samuel 16:7; 22:5 (=Psalm 18:4); Psalm 41:8; wickedness: Deuteronomy 15:9; Judges 19:22; 20:13; 1 Samuel 25:17, 25; 1 Kings 21:10, 13; Job 34:18; Psalm 101:3; Proverbs 6:12; 16:27; 19:28; Nahum 1:11; rebellion: Deuteronomy 13:13; 1 Samuel 10:27; 30:22; 2 Samuel 20:1; 23:6; 2 Chronicles 13:7; Nahum 1:15. See further Benedikt Otzen, "*beliyya'al*," in G. Johannes Botterweck and Helmer Ringgren, eds., *Theological Dictionary of the Old Testament*, Vol. 2 (Grand Rapids, MI: Eerdmans, 1975), pp. 131-136.

6. Other examples of "not knowing the LORD" include Judges 2:10; Jeremiah 9:3, 6; Hosea 5:4. Cf. John 1:10; 4:22; 7:28; 15:21; 17:25; 1 Corinthians 1:21; Galatians 4:8; 1 Thessalonians 4:5; 2 Thessalonians 1:8; 1 John 3:1; 4:8.

7. The word for "servant" is the same as "boy" in verse 11, sharpening the contrast between the lad Samuel, who ministered to the Lord at Shiloh, and the lads Hophni and Phinehas who carried out their contemptible customs.

8. Robert Alter, *The David Story: A Translation with Commentary of 1 and 2 Samuel* (New York and London: W.W. Norton, 1999), p. 12.

9. Some commentators argue that verses 13, 14 describe what the priests at Shiloh were *supposed* to have done, while verses 15, 16 describe the deviation from this "custom" by Hophni and Phinehas. So Eslinger, *Kingship*, p. 117. This understanding is reflected in the REB rendering of verse 14. Cf. comments by Robert P. Gordon, *1 & 2 Samuel: A Commentary* (Exeter, UK: The Paternoster Press, 1986), p. 82. Against this it may be argued: (1) The parallel with "the ways of the king" in 1 Samuel 8:11-17 supports the view that 1 Samuel 2:13, 14 describes exploitation. (2) The custom described is not supported in the Law, which has clear provisions for priests. (3) The detailed description of the three-pronged fork and the various utensils conveys the impression of "a frenzy of gluttony" (Alter, *David*, p. 12). (4) "All" that the fork brought up supports this impression, as does the fact that it was not given to the priests (as, for example, in Deuteronomy 18:3) but was "taken" by them.

10. The term certainly has a wide range of uses as the lexicons indicate, and in some contexts the connotation of "justice" may be remote or absent (e.g., Judges 13:12, ESV: "manner of life"). However, it is reasonable to see this connotation in a context where the word describes the conduct of community leaders.

11. See, for example Deuteronomy 1:17; Judges 4:5, where the term in question is rendered "judgment." For an example of the administration of such justice see 1 Samuel 7:15-17.

12. It is worth noting that the word translated "custom" will appear later in a very significant context, with certain similarities to this one. In 1 Samuel 8:11 Samuel will explain to the people "the ways of the king" for whom they had asked. "Ways" represents the same Hebrew word as "custom" in 1 Samuel 2:13. Furthermore "the ways of the king" according to Samuel would be characterized by "taking" from the people (the verb "take" occurs four times in 1 Samuel 8:11, 13, 14, 16), just as "the ways of the priests" according to 1 Samuel 2:14-16 involved "taking" from the people (the verb "take" occurs four times here!).

13. According to Leviticus 3:16, "All fat is the LORD's," and so not to be eaten (Leviticus 7:23-25).

14. "The gastronomical motivation for putting himself before Yahweh makes the priest out to be nothing more than a piggish lout." Eslinger, *Kingship*, p. 118.

15. The Hebrew is a little more tantalizing than the English translation, because "young men" is the plural of the word translated "servant" in verses 13, 15 (and "boy" in verse 11). The fact is that there were a number of "youths" at Shiloh. All but one were involved in the serious sinful behavior here described.

16. The linen ephod (1 Samuel 2:18; 22:18; 2 Samuel 6:14; 1 Chronicles 15:27) "was apparently a simple linen garment and thus distinct from the high-priestly ephod." Cornelius Van Dam, *The Urim and Thummim: A Means of Revelation in Ancient Israel* (Winona Lake, IN: Eisenbrauns, 1997), p. 145.

17. Cf. Eslinger, *Kingship*, p. 120. Note the use of the participle "ministering" again, as in verse 11, indicating that Samuel's faithful service was going on at the same time as the sons of Eli were abusing their privilege.

18. "Before" in verse 18 is exactly the same expression in Hebrew as "in the presence of" in verse 11.

19. In 1 Samuel 15:27 Saul tore Samuel's robe, and the incident occasioned a terrible message for him. In 1 Samuel 28:14 Samuel, brought back from the dead, was recognized by Saul because of his robe. Other significant events involving a robe are Jonathan's handing his robe to David (1 Samuel 18:4) and David's cutting off the corner of Saul's robe (1 Samuel 24:4, 11).

20. The strange pun on the name Saul that we saw in chapter 1 is repeated here. In Hebrew it sounds like "the *saul* that she *sauled* of the LORD."

21. In 1 Samuel 3:7 we will have to consider the surprising expression, "Now Samuel did not yet know the LORD."

22. It is appropriate to see in the lads' behavior a reenactment of the dreadful rebellion of the Israelites at Shittim; see Numbers 25:1. The terrible consequences of that event (read the rest of Numbers 25!), never forgotten in Israel (Deuteronomy 4:3; Joshua 22:17; Psalm 106:28-30; Hosea 9:10), may well cause us to shudder when we hear of the conduct of Hophni and Phinehas!

23. The translation indicates that the women were "serving." Alter takes another meaning of the verb and translates "the women who flocked to the entrance . . ." Alter, *David*, p. 13. However, Exodus 38:8 refers to "the ministering women who ministered in the entrance of the tent of meeting," where "ministering" and "ministered" represent the same verb as "serving" in 1 Samuel 2:22. The reference to the "tent of meeting" adds to our uncertainty about the nature of the structure at Shiloh, called "the temple of the LORD" in 1 Samuel 1:9.

24. The exact sense of the verb translated "mediate" is not clear. Suggestions include "mediate," "intercede," and "arbitrate." Gordon, *1 & 2 Samuel*, p. 84; Ralph W. Klein, *1 Samuel*, Word Biblical Commentary, 10 (Nashville: Word, 1983), p. 26.

25. Mauchline expresses this kind of misunderstanding: "To say that Eli's sons would not listen to rebuke and warning because it was God's will to destroy them is tantamount to saying that their sin was pre-determined and inescapable. In that case they could not be

held responsible for it; they could not be regarded as morally culpable." John Mauchline, *1 and 2 Samuel*, New Century Bible (London: Oliphants, 1971), p. 53. This statement makes two fatal errors: (1) It does not account for the fact that Hophni and Phinehas *are* held morally accountable by God. (2) It rests on the un-Biblical assumption that the sovereign rule of God over the affairs of men (as presented in such Biblical texts) excludes any freedom of choice on the part of man. Divine sovereignty and human responsibility are a problem for philosophical theology, but the solution is not so simple as denying the reality of one or the other. Eslinger's interpretation (Eslinger, *Kingship*, pp. 126-128) depends on a similar theological misunderstanding. He compares the sealing of Hannah's womb in chapter 1 with the prevention of Eli's sons from hearing their father's rebuke, without observing the moral difference between these situations. He sees the Lord presented "in an ugly mood" as a manipulator. However, Eli's sons are presented by the Biblical text as culpable (and they will be punished); Hannah has no culpability at all. God's sovereignty over all situations does not mean that all situations have the same moral character.

26. Robert Alter's quite literal translation brings out the point: "And the lad Samuel was growing in goodness with both the LORD and with men." Alter, *David*, p. 13.

27. It must be admitted that the echo is stronger in English than in the original languages. "In stature" is an implication of the Hebrew of 1 Samuel 2:26 but has no corresponding Hebrew expression. "In favor" in Luke 2:52 represents a Greek word often translated "grace"; in 1 Samuel 2:26 the Hebrew has the word for "good." Nonetheless the verses seem to be close enough in expression to see an allusion.

CHAPTER FIVE: GOD AND CORRUPTION

1. Robert P. Gordon, *1 & 2 Samuel: A Commentary* (Exeter, UK: The Paternoster Press, 1986), p. 84. Moses was called "the man of God" (Deuteronomy 33:1; Joshua 14:6; 1 Chronicles 23:14; 2 Chronicles 30:16; Ezra 3:2; Psalm 90 [title]). Subsequent prophets could be referred to as "the man of God" or "a man of God" (1 Kings 12:22; 13:1-31; 17:18, 24; 20:28; 2 Kings 1:9-13; 4:21-42; 5:8, 14, 15, 20; 6:6, 9, 15; 7:2, 17-19; 8:2, 4, 7, 8, 11; 13:19; 23:16, 17; 2 Chronicles 11:2; 25:7, 9; Jeremiah 35:4). Samuel would receive this appellation (1 Samuel 9:6, 7, 8, 10). An angel is called a "man of God" in Judges 13:6, 8. David is called "the man of God" in 2 Chronicles 8:14 and Nehemiah 12:24, 36. This background supports the view that "man of God" in its two occurrences in the New Testament (1 Timothy 6:11; 2 Timothy 3:17) does not simply mean "godly man" but suggests the prophetic role of the preacher/teacher of the gospel of Christ. Cf. J. N. D. Kelly, *A Commentary on the Pastoral Epistles: I Timothy, II Timothy, Titus*, Black's New Testament Commentaries (London: Adam & Charles Black, 1963), pp. 139, 140; Gordon D. Fee, *1 and 2 Timothy, Titus*, New International Biblical Commentary (Peabody, MA: Hendrickson Publishers, 1988), pp. 149, 154.

2. The ESV usually translates the expression, "Thus says the LORD." However, the rendering in 1 Samuel 2:27 is at least often preferable. The prophet typically delivers a message that the Lord has already spoken. Moses was the first to be instructed by God to introduce his message with this expression (Exodus 4:22). Subsequently it became a mark of prophetic speech (e.g., Samuel: 1 Samuel 10:18; Nathan: 2 Samuel 7:8; 12:7; Elijah: 1 Kings 17:14; Elisha: 2 Kings 3:16; see also Isaiah 8:11; Jeremiah 2:2; Ezekiel 11:5; Amos 1:3; Micah 2:3; Nahum 1:12; Haggai 1:2; Zechariah 1:3; Malachi 1:4).

3. C. F. Keil and F. Delitzsch, *Biblical Commentary on the Books of Samuel* (Grand Rapids, MI: Eerdmans, 1950), p. 40.

4. Contra P. Kyle McCarter, Jr., *1 Samuel: A New Translation with Introduction, Notes & Commentary*, The Anchor Bible, Vol. 8 (Garden City, NY: Doubleday, 1980), p. 89, who claims that Eli's father's house was the house of Moses. Ralph W. Klein, *1 Samuel*, Word Biblical Commentary, 10 (Nashville: Word, 1983), p. 26 follows Wellhausen, Cross, and others in the proposal of a connection with Moses or a line of Mushite priests (Numbers 3:33; 26:58). The arguments for the house of Eli being linked to Moses are not convincing, being based partly on the verse before us (see Frank Moore Cross, "Priestly

Houses of Early Israel," in *Canaanite Myth and Hebrew Epic: Essays in the History of the Religion of Israel* [Cambridge, MA: Harvard University Press, 1973], pp. 195-215). Hans Wilhelm Hertzberg, *I & II Samuel: A Commentary*, Old Testament Library (London: SCM Press, 1964), p. 37 says that "the house of your father" could mean either the tribe of Levi (so also Henry Preserved Smith, *A Critical and Exegetical Commentary on the Books of Samuel*, The International Critical Commentary [Edinburgh: T. & T. Clark, 1899], p. 22) or the sons of Aaron. However, the reference to revelation in Egypt and other Biblical data point to Aaron as the "father" of 1 Samuel 2:27.

5. The details of Eli's ancestry are not fully known. His great-grandson, Ahimelech (1 Samuel 21:1; see 22:9 and 14:3), is described as "of the sons of Ithamar" in 1 Chronicles 24:3. Since Ithamar was one of Aaron's four sons (Exodus 6:23), Eli was a descendant of Aaron in the line of Ithamar. Ithamar had a supervisory role over the Levites in the construction of the tabernacle (Exodus 38:21). On the subject of Eli's family tree (but irrelevant to our present text) there is an interesting argument that Jeremiah was probably a descendant of the house of Eli. This may account for the fact that he is the only Old Testament prophet to mention Shiloh, the site of his ancestor's priestly service (Menahem Haran, *Temples and Temple-Service in Ancient Israel: An Inquiry into the Character of Cult Phenomena and the Historical Setting of the Priestly School* [Oxford, UK: Clarendon, 1978], p. 87, note 2).

6. The promises of Exodus 29:9 (to Aaron and sons) and Numbers 25:13 (to Phinehas) promise priesthood, but not high-priesthood. Cf. Keil and Delitzsch, *Books of Samuel*, pp. 42, 43.

7. This proposal was advanced by Keil and Delitzsch, *Books of Samuel*, p. 39. Note that Baldwin adds to the confusion by mistakenly claiming that "Eli was called an Ephraimite in 1 Samuel 1:1" (Joyce Baldwin, *1 and 2 Samuel*, Tyndale Old Testament Commentaries [Leicester, UK: Inter-Varsity Press, 1988], p. 61). She has confused Eli with Elkanah.

8. In 1 Samuel 2:27 the Hebrew text does not have "subject" and emphasizes Pharaoh's ownership of the people. Lyle M. Eslinger, *Kingship of God in Crisis: A Close Reading of 1 Samuel 1–12*, Bible and Literature Series, 10 (Sheffield, UK: JSOT Press, 1985), p. 443, note 27.

9. See Haran, *Temples*, pp. 208, 241-245.

10. *Ibid.*, pp. 166-169.

11. Hertzberg, *I & II Samuel*, p. 37 suggests that the three duties comprise service in the forecourt, where that altar stood, in the inner sanctuary, where the altar of incense was, and the giving of oracles: "in other words, the cultus in its entirety."

12. The abusive and violent metaphor is used in a similar way of gluttonous contempt for God in Deuteronomy 32:15.

13. "You" at the beginning of this verse (like "yourselves") is plural, and so includes Eli and his sons. "Your" in "your sons," of course, is singular.

14. The Hebrew, a little awkwardly, has the word "dwelling" after "commanded." The NIV represents this with "for my dwelling." Various emendations have been proposed, including the deletion of the word (as ESV). See Gordon, *1 & 2 Samuel*, p. 86. Keil and Delitzsch, *Books of Samuel*, p. 41 render the word simply, "in the dwelling-place."

15. The perpetual priesthood of the house of Aaron was already implied in Exodus 27:21. On the gift of the priesthood to Aaron, see also Numbers 18:7.

16. Commentators often suppose that the promise had to do with the high priesthood and that here God was making a once unconditional promise conditional. Cf. Gordon, *1 & 2 Samuel*, p. 86. Walter Brueggemann, *First and Second Samuel*, Interpretation: A Bible Commentary for Teaching and Preaching (Louisville: John Knox Press, 1990), p. 23 accepts an alternative theory that the promise was to the Mushites. Even if Eli did serve as high priest, we have no evidence that the high priesthood was ever promised to Eli's house. It makes better sense of the evidence, and does not create artificial theological problems, to assume that verse 30 is speaking of Eli's inclusion in the broader general promise of priesthood (not high priesthood) to the descendants of Aaron.

17. Contra Brueggemann, *First and Second Samuel*, p. 23; Gordon, *1 & 2 Samuel*, p. 86.

18. The history of the priesthood in Israel is complicated and has suffered further from considerable scholarly speculation. Taking the Biblical evidence at face value, the subsequent history of the priesthood relevant to the judgment pronounced here can be summarized as follows:

(1) Eli, Hophni, and Phinehas died in connection with a great Philistine defeat of Israel, soon to be recounted (1 Samuel 4:11, 18).

(2) After the death of Phinehas, his wife gave birth to Ichabod (1 Samuel 4:20, 21).

(3) A son of Ichabod (therefore Eli's great-grandson) served as priest. This was Ahijah, and he acted as high priest with the ephod (1 Samuel 14:3, 18).

(4) Possibly because Shiloh was destroyed at the time of the Philistine defeat in 1 Samuel 4, the surviving priests relocated to Nob, under a great-grandson of Eli called Ahimelech, who may have been the same person as Ahijah (1 Samuel 21:1; 22:9).

(5) All but one of the eighty-five priests of Nob, with their families, were killed by order of Saul (1 Samuel 22:18, 19).

(6) The one who escaped was a son of Ahimelech, and therefore a great-great-grandson of Eli, named Abiathar, who served David as (high) priest (1 Samuel 22:20; 23:6, 9; 30:7).

(7) In David's service Abiathar was joined by Zadok (2 Samuel 15:24, 25, 29, 35; 19:11; 20:25). Zadok was a descendant of Aaron in the original high-priestly line of Aaron-Eleazar-Phinehas (a different Phinehas, of course, 1 Chronicles 6:3-8; 24:3).

(8) After David's death, in the struggle for the succession between his sons Adonijah and Solomon, Abiathar supported Adonijah, while Zadok supported Solomon (1 Kings 1:7, 8). Consequently, when Solomon became king he banished Abiathar, expelling him from the priesthood, "thus fulfilling the word of the LORD that he had spoken concerning the house of Eli in Shiloh" (1 Kings 2:26, 27).

(9) Solomon appointed Zadok "in the place of Abiathar" (1 Kings 2:35). Descendants of Zadok then dominated the priesthood in Jerusalem. We hear no more of any descendants of Eli.

19. This striking saying is just four words in Hebrew.

20. The Hebrew word for "honor" in verses 29, 30 can also be translated "make heavy" or "glorify." This vocabulary will play an important part later in the narrative. See 1 Samuel 4:18, 21, 22; 5:6, 11; 6:5, 6; 9:6; 15:30; 22:14; 31:3.

21. On God glorifying the one who glorifies him, see John 17:1.

22. This is a straightforward way of understanding the "you" in verse 32. The message is addressed not just to Eli personally, but to his "house." Similarly Gordon, *1 & 2 Samuel*, p. 87.

23. The words "with envious eye" in verse 32 depend on an emendation of the Hebrew. The NIV attempts to make sense of the unamended Hebrew: "you will see distress in my dwelling." Similarly Keil and Delitzsch, *Samuel*, pp. 43, 44.

24. Other suggested identities for the survivor include Samuel (so Eslinger, *Kingship*, p. 137). The historical fact is that Phinehas's son, Ichabod, survived his father, and his son Ahijah (=Ahimelech?) and grandson Abimelech served as (high) priests. The involvement of Eli's house in the priesthood only came to an end with the banishment of Abiathar by Solomon. The fulfillment of the prophecy in verse 33 seems to lie in the survival of this line, and particularly in the "distress" of Abiathar, as noted in 1 Kings 2:27.

25. The Hebrew lacks the word "sword" at the end of verse 33 and could be translated "die as men," which NIV interprets as "die in the prime of life."

26. Eslinger, *Kingship*, p. 138 points out that "faithful" in verse 35 is exactly the same word in Hebrew as "established" in 1 Samuel 3:20, applied there to Samuel as prophet.

27. Note that in the Hebrew "sure" and "faithful" in verse 35 are the same word.

28. "Forever" in verse 35 is, literally, "all the days."

29. Gordon, *1 & 2 Samuel*, p. 88.

Chapter Six: When God Speaks

1. "There was no frequent vision" is virtually synonymous with "the word of the Lord was rare," visions being a means by which the word of the Lord came to the prophets. Notice how the experience of Samuel is called "the vision" (different Hebrew word) in verse 15 of this chapter, although its essence was a verbal message. See Isaiah 1:1 ("the vision . . . which he *saw*") and 2:1 ("The word that Isaiah . . . *saw*"); cf. Amos 1:1; Obadiah 1; Nahum 1:1. See also Jeremiah 14:14; 23:16; Ezekiel 7:26; 12:22-24, 27; 13:16; Hosea 12:10; Habakkuk 2:2, 3; Psalm 89:19; Proverbs 29:18; Daniel 1:17; Lamentations 2:9; 1 Chronicles 17:15; 2 Chronicles 32:32. These verses all use the word translated "vision" in 1 Samuel 3:1, or related vocabulary.

2. The words in 1 Samuel 3:1, "in those days there was no frequent vision" (adopting a slight change in punctuation) may echo Judges 21:25, "In those days there was no king in Israel." In other words, the situation we now see is one of no established political leadership and no regular word from God. This was Israel's crisis.

3. Cf. Lyle M. Eslinger, *Kingship of God in Crisis: A Close Reading of 1 Samuel 1–12*, Bible and Literature Series, 10 (Sheffield, UK: JSOT Press, 1985), p. 146.

4. Cf. *ibid.*, p. 146, where Eslinger notes other subtle differences between 1 Samuel 2:11 and 3:1. The English translation suggests the development of the "boy" in 1 Samuel 2:11, 18 to the "young man" of 1 Samuel 2:21, 26, and 3:1. Unfortunately these represent the same word in Hebrew.

5. "At that time" in verse 2 is, literally, "on that day," which links the situation described with "in those days" of verse 1. Cf. Eslinger, *Kingship*, p. 147.

6. ". . . the reader recognizes the familiar image of a tired, old man who relies on the comfort and security of his own place." Eslinger, *Kingship*, p. 148.

7. After 1 Samuel 7:2 the ark is not mentioned again in the books of Samuel until 2 Samuel 6, with the one exception of 1 Samuel 14:18, about which there is some textual uncertainty.

8. R. E. Averbeck, "Tabernacle," in T. Desmond Alexander and David W. Baker, eds., *Dictionary of the Old Testament: Pentateuch* (Leicester, UK and Downers Grove, IL: InterVarsity Press, 2003), p. 814.

9. Eli's reference to Samuel as "my son" may raise our expectation that Samuel will be the one to survive the coming judgment on Eli's house and to become the "faithful priest" (1 Samuel 2:33, 35). The unfolding story, however, will show that the prophecy points beyond Samuel.

10. C. F. Keil and F. Delitzsch, *Biblical Commentary on the Books of Samuel* (Grand Rapids, MI: Eerdmans, 1950), p. 49. The words also speak of more than "a vivid sense of God's presence," contra Peter R. Ackroyd, *The First Book of Samuel*, Cambridge Bible Commentary (Cambridge, UK: Cambridge University Press, 1971), p. 43.

11. Cf. Robert Alter, *The David Story: A Translation with Commentary of 1 and 2 Samuel* (New York and London: W.W. Norton, 1999), p. 17.

12. In 2 Kings 21:12 we hear God announce the destruction of Jerusalem and Judah because of the wickedness of Manasseh: "Behold, I am bringing upon Jerusalem and Judah such disaster that the ears of everyone who hears it will tingle." Jeremiah spoke in similar terms of the disaster God was bringing on Judah and Jerusalem in Jeremiah 19:3.

13. The verb translated "tingle" is used of lips "quivering" in Habakkuk 3:16.

14. Eslinger, *Kingship*, p. 152.

15. See Barry G. Webb, *The Book of Judges: An Integrated Reading*, Journal for the Study of the Old Testament Supplement Series 46 (Sheffield, UK: Sheffield Academic Press, 1987), p. 111.

16. The verb translated "restrain" is based on the same Hebrew letters as "dim" in verse 2. Its use "is obviously meant to align Eli's failing in parental authority with the failing of his sight." Alter, *David*, p. 18. The precise meaning is disputed, and suggestions include "rebuke."

17. For example, verse 13 is the basis for Eslinger's argument that since the narrator told us
of Eli's rebuke in 1 Samuel 2:23-25, we (the readers) know that God was "not telling
the whole story to Samuel. As the reader watches the innocent young man being indoc-
trinated with an explanation of the ensuing disaster that is only partially true, he is once
again filled with foreboding about the future of the people whose fate lies in the hands
of this God." Eslinger, *Kingship*, p. 152.

A major thesis of Eslinger's interpretation of 1 Samuel rests partly on this point. He
insists on the normally unobjectionable principle that a narrator's perspective must be
distinguished from the perspectives of his characters. He applies this, however, with
rigor to drive a wedge between the narrator of 1 Samuel and God, as one of his characters. To the extent that this thesis rests on 1 Samuel 3:13, it must be seen as flimsy, since
Eslinger himself acknowledges that there are difficulties in ascertaining the meaning
of the critical verb in this verse. Eslinger, *Kingship*, pp. 445, 446, note 6. More fundamentally the proposition that the narrator of an Old Testament historical book would
present himself as having a perspective superior to that of God is fanciful. In some Old
Testament writings, to be sure, the writer questions, or even challenges, God's ways. Job
and Ecclesiastes might be cited as examples. In all such cases, however, the perspective
of the human questioner is seen to be inadequate, and God's ways are ultimately justified.
Eslinger's view of 1 Samuel 1-12 is quite different. He sees the narrator as profoundly
critical of God and his ways (and Eslinger agrees with the narrator!):

> Yahweh has engineered the unnecessary destruction of the Elides and
> now he is grooming his own pawn to take their place. If he had not desired to
> kill Eli's sons, perhaps they would have listened to their father, and if he told
> Samuel the truth about Eli's efforts to reform his sons perhaps Samuel would
> not be so dogmatically loyal to Yahweh. Eslinger, *Kingship*, p. 153.

Eslinger appears to have overlooked an important principle of interpretation,
expressed by Wayne Booth: "The author is present in every speech given by any character who has had conferred upon him, in whatever manner, the badge of reliability." Cited
by Francis Watson, *Text, Church and World: Biblical Interpretation in Theological
Perspective* (Grand Rapids, MI: Eerdmans, 1994), p. 318. note 7.

18. "May God do so to you and more also" was an idiom used in an earnest appeal or oath.
Cf. 1 Samuel 14:44; 20:13; 25:22.

19. This comparison is suggested by Robert P. Gordon, *1 & 2 Samuel: A Commentary*
(Exeter: The Paternoster Press, 1986), pp. 90, 91. Eslinger, based on his understanding of
the Lord's dubious dealings with Eli, rejects the understanding of Eli's words as humble
acceptance of just punishment and sees them as an expression of despair: "He is Yahweh,
he does as he pleases." Eslinger, *Kingship*, pp. 154, 155.

CHAPTER SEVEN: THE PROBLEM OF THE POWER OF GOD I

1. For a similar understanding of 1 Samuel 4:1a see Lyle M. Eslinger, *Kingship of God in
Crisis: A Close Reading of 1 Samuel 1–12*, Bible and Literature Series, 10 (Sheffield, UK:
JSOT Press, 1985), pp. 161, 162. Cf. C. F. Keil and F. Delitzsch, *Biblical Commentary
on the Books of Samuel* (Grand Rapids, MI: Eerdmans, 1950), p. 52, who, in my opinion, go too far in suggesting that "the word of Samuel" instigated Israel's movement
against the Philistines. Many commentators regard this sentence as a fragment belonging
with chapter 3 ("a final summary of Samuel's new authority at the end of his dedica-
tion story"), Robert Alter, *The David Story: A Translation with Commentary of 1 and
2 Samuel* (New York and London: W.W. Norton, 1999), p. 20; cf. Robert P. Gordon,
1 & 2 Samuel: A Commentary (Exeter, UK: The Paternoster Press, 1986), p. 92; P. Kyle
McCarter, Jr., *1 Samuel: A New Translation with Introduction, Notes & Commentary*,
The Anchor Bible, Vol. 8 (Garden City, NY: Doubleday, 1980), p. 95; Peter R. Ackroyd,
The First Book of Samuel, Cambridge Bible Commentary (Cambridge, UK: Cambridge
University Press, 1971), p. 45.

2. The Septuagint offers a longer text at this point that indicates it was the Philistines who started things. This may have been an attempt to supply information lacking in the Hebrew text rather than evidence of a longer Hebrew text.

3. Cf. Eslinger, *Kingship*, p. 163.

4. People called Philistines play a significant role in the stories of the Patriarchs (Genesis 21:32, 34; 26:1-18). There are reasons for thinking that these were not the same people group as the Philistines of later times. These probably came into the Palestine region from the west at about the same time as the Israelites entered from the east. They are often mentioned in the book of Judges. From the perspective of 1 Samuel 4, the most recent episode in the Bible records involving the Philistines is the story of Samson (Judges 15, 16). See further details in K. A. Kitchen, "The Philistines," in D. J. Wiseman, ed., *Peoples of Old Testament Times* (Oxford, UK: Clarendon Press, 1973), pp. 53-78; David M. Howard, "Philistines," in Alfred J. Hoerth et al, eds., *Peoples of the Old Testament World* (Grand Rapids, MI: Baker, 1994), pp. 231-250.

5. Here in chapter 4 the Philistines will take Israel's ark of the covenant; in chapter 31 they will take the body of Israel's king (1 Samuel 31:8-10).

6. In 1 Samuel these rulers are usually called "lords" (1 Samuel 5:8, 11; 6:4, 12, 16, 18; 7:7; 29:2, 6, 7), but Achish of Gath is called "king" in 1 Samuel 21:10, 12; 27:2; and possibly 1 Samuel 29:8.

7. Gordon, *1 & 2 Samuel*, p. 93.

8. It seems likely that the Ebenezer of 1 Samuel 4:1 is not the same place as the Ebenezer of 1 Samuel 7:12. The latter seems to have been named after the former.

9. Gordon, *1 & 2 Samuel*, p. 93. See John W. Wenham, "Large Numbers in the Old Testament," *Tyndale Bulletin* 18 (1967), pp. 19-53.

10. Cf. Eslinger, *Kingship*, p. 164.

11. Achan in Joshua 7 is a case in point. God's answer to Joshua's "Why?" (v. 7) was simply, "Israel has sinned" (v. 11). In the period of the Judges, the answer was essentially the same: "Because this people have transgressed my covenant . . . and have not obeyed my voice" (Judges 2:20).

12. Because of the three points listed I am unconvinced by Eslinger's argument that the people were "innocent" and that the elders were right (given what they knew) to question the Lord's covenant faithfulness "because they are aware of no sin on their part." Eslinger, *Kingship*, p. 165.

13. The ambiguity arises from the fact that in Hebrew "ark" is a masculine noun and could be the subject of the verbs "come" and "save." However, "the LORD" is a more suitable subject, certainly of the latter verb.

14. Contra Alter, *David*, p. 22.

15. Cf. Eslinger, *Kingship*, p. 166, from whom I have borrowed the last sentence in quotation marks.

16. Included in the rich symbolism of the ark was God's kingship. The ark was sometimes considered as the footstool to God's heavenly throne (1 Chronicles 28:2). There were two cherubim, made of hammered gold, at the ends of the cover of the ark (Exodus 25:18-22). While God reigns from Heaven, he promised to meet with Moses "from between the two cherubim that are on the ark of the testimony" (Exodus 25:22).

17. The Philistine version was a little muddled. The plagues were not in the wilderness. Nevertheless they seem to have heard about both the plagues *and* the wilderness, where other wonders were done for the Israelites.

18. An unusual word translated "plague" in verse 8 (for what God did to the Egyptians) is repeated in verse 10, translated "slaughter" (for what happened now to the Israelites).

CHAPTER EIGHT: WHERE IS THE GLORY?

1. Saul will be frequently identified with the tribe and land of Benjamin (1 Samuel 9:1, 16, 21; 10:20, 21; cf. 22:7). Indeed there is a Jewish tradition that the messenger in 1 Samuel 4:12 was Saul! Ralph W. Klein, *1 Samuel*, Word Biblical Commentary, 10 (Nashville:

Word, 1983), p. 43; P. Kyle McCarter, Jr., *I Samuel: A New Translation with Introduction, Notes & Commentary*, The Anchor Bible, Vol. 8 (Garden City, NY: Doubleday, 1980), p. 113. While there is no basis for this inference in the text, the mention of the messenger's tribal identity does at least two things: (1) It draws our attention to the tribe of Benjamin at this significant moment. A Benjaminite played an important role on this terrible day in the history of Israel. (2) When we meet another "man of Benjamin" later in the story, we may well be reminded of this Benjaminite and his awesome news. Attached to the Benjaminite Saul will be the hope that he will reverse the bad news brought by the earlier man of Benjamin: "He shall save my people from the hand of the Philistines" (1 Samuel 9:16). Cf. McCarter, *I Samuel*, pp. 113, 114, who raises the question of why the messenger is identified as a Benjaminite, noting that such details are not normally given "gratuitously." However, he says, "in this case the point escapes us."

2. On customary expressions of grief and mourning seen here, see Joshua 7:6; 2 Samuel 1:2, 11, 12; 13:31; 15:32.

3. On these proposals and the issues involved see Klein, *I Samuel*, pp. 38, 43; McCarter, *I Samuel*, pp. 111, 114. For all the difficulties, the usual English translation is close to the sense of the Hebrew text.

4. P. R. Davies argues that the verb translated "trembled" does not mean "be concerned" or "worry" but indicates fearful trembling. The preposition following the verb does not mean "for" but "on account of." "Eli is afraid *of* the ark and *for* his sons, because of their sins." P. R. Davies, "The History of the Ark in the Books of Samuel," *Journal of Northwest Semitic Languages* 5 (1977), pp. 12, 13. Cf. Lyle M. Eslinger, *Kingship of God in Crisis: A Close Reading of 1 Samuel 1–12*, Bible and Literature Series, 10 (Sheffield, UK: JSOT Press, 1985), pp. 177-181.

5. Robert Alter, *The David Story: A Translation with Commentary of 1 and 2 Samuel* (New York and London: W.W. Norton, 1999), p. 24.

6. The word is translated "plague" in 1 Samuel 6:4 (also in Exodus 9:14; Numbers 14:37; 16:48-50; 25:8, 9, 18; 26:1; 31:16; 2 Samuel 24:21, 25). Most of these texts refer to an affliction that killed.

7. Cf. Eslinger, *Kingship*, p. 180.

8. Cf. *ibid.*, p. 181.

9. "Judge" was still an important word to describe the leadership Israel needed. See 1 Samuel 7:6, 15-17; 8:1, 2, 5, 6, 20.

10. The precise meaning of the name is not unanimously agreed upon. Proposals include "No glory" (C. F. Keil and F. Delitzsch, *Biblical Commentary on the Books of Samuel* [Grand Rapids, MI: Eerdmans, 1950], p. 56; John Mauchline, *1 and 2 Samuel*, New Century Bible [London: Oliphants, 1971], p. 74; Peter R. Ackroyd, *The First Book of Samuel*, Cambridge Bible Commentary [Cambridge, UK: Cambridge University Press, 1971], p. 52); "Inglorious" (Henry Preserved Smith, *A Critical and Exegetical Commentary on the Books of Samuel*, The International Critical Commentary [Edinburgh: T. & T. Clark, 1899], p. 37); "Where is the glory?" or "Alas for the glory!" (McCarter, *I Samuel*, p. 116). The differences between these matter little here.

CHAPTER NINE: THE PROBLEM OF THE POWER OF GOD II

1. First Samuel 5:1 begins, literally, "And the Philistines . . ." The Hebrew syntax both signals a new episode and emphasizes the new subject.

2. Contra Eslinger who links the opening words of 1 Samuel 5:1 to the closing words of 1 Samuel 4:22 and says 1 Samuel 5:1 "introduces a new scene in a *chain* of events consequent to the Israelite defeat." Lyle M. Eslinger, *Kingship of God in Crisis: A Close Reading of 1 Samuel 1–12*, Bible and Literature Series, 10 (Sheffield, UK: JSOT Press, 1985), p. 189 (emphasis added). I am not arguing here for strict simultaneity of the two episodes (1 Samuel 4:12-22 and 5:1ff.). The events at Shiloh seem to have taken place on the same day as the defeat (1 Samuel 4:12, 16), while with the Philistines at least one day has passed by (1 Samuel 5:3). The point is that the sequences of events beginning

in 1 Samuel 4:12 and 1 Samuel 5:1 are in effect set side by side as the consequences, in different places, of the event in 1 Samuel 4:11.

3. "In the Ugaritic texts he is described as the father of Baal who, of course, appears as the arch-enemy of Yahweh at many points in the Old Testament." Robert P. Gordon, *1 & 2 Samuel: A Commentary* (Exeter, UK: The Paternoster Press, 1986), p. 98.

4. As it was called when first mentioned in this story, 1 Samuel 4:3.

5. It is worth noting that this particular description of the ark was used previously in this story only in 1 Samuel 4:6, at the point where the ark originally struck terror into the hearts of the Philistines. It will occur frequently from now on (1 Samuel 5:4; 6:1, 2, 8, 11, 15, 18, 19, 21; 7:1).

6. Robert Alter, *The David Story: A Translation with Commentary of 1 and 2 Samuel* (New York and London: W.W. Norton, 1999), p. 28.

7. Commentators often opt for an emendation of the Hebrew along the lines of the ESV. See Gordon, *1 & 2 Samuel*, p. 99.

8. Cf. Eslinger, *Kingship*, p. 193.

9. There is some uncertainty in the traditional Hebrew text as to whether the affliction was "tumors" or "hemorrhoids." For discussions of the issue (which makes little difference to the story), see Peter R. Ackroyd, *The First Book of Samuel*, Cambridge Bible Commentary (Cambridge, UK: Cambridge University Press, 1971), pp. 55, 56; P. Kyle McCarter, Jr., *I Samuel: A New Translation with Introduction, Notes & Commentary*, The Anchor Bible, Vol. 8 (Garden City, NY: Doubleday, 1980), p. 123; Ralph W. Klein, *1 Samuel*, Word Biblical Commentary, 10 (Nashville: Word, 1983), pp. 50, 51.

10. See Gordon, *1 & 2 Samuel*, p. 99.

11. Standard meanings for the Hebrew verb translated "terrified" are "devastated, ravaged, appalled."

12. Perhaps this was already Achish, King of Gath, whom we will meet much later in 1 Samuel (see 21:10-15; 27:1-12; 29:1-11). If so, there will be a later occasion on which he will be overruled by his fellow lords, or perhaps it was his commanders (see 1 Samuel 29:1-10).

13. This is the most natural reading of the Hebrew (as the English) sentence, but it is possible to construe the words as spoken by the lords themselves.

14. See the very similar description of the cry of the people of Israel in Exodus 2:23. Gordon, *1 & 2 Samuel*, p. 100.

15. For a development of this parallel see Eslinger, *Kingship*, pp. 197, 198.

CHAPTER TEN: KNOWING THE POWER OF GOD

1. The Hebrew for God's name is generally represented in English with the transliteration *Yahweh*. English translations of the Old Testament generally represent this name with "the LORD." See especially Exodus 3:13-17; 6:2-8. See G. T. Manley and F. F. Bruce, "God, names of," in J. D. Douglas et al, eds., *The Illustrated Bible Dictionary*, Part 1 (Leicester, UK and Wheaton, IL: Inter-Varsity Press and Tyndale House, 1980), pp. 571, 572.

2. Through the story in 1 Samuel 4–6 the ark is described in various ways, each with a different emphasis, appropriate to the context:

    (1) "The ark of *the covenant*," when the Israelites sent for the ark after their first defeat before the Philistines (1 Samuel 4:3; similarly "the ark of the covenant of God" at the end of verse 4), emphasizing that it was God's *covenant commitment* on which Israel was calling.

    (2) "The ark of the covenant of *Yahweh of hosts, who is enthroned on the cherubim*," when the narrator first mentioned the ark in his own words (1 Samuel 4:4), underlining *the exalted greatness and power* of the God of Israel.

    (3) "The ark of *the covenant of Yahweh*," as the ark was brought into the camp of Israel (1 Samuel 4:5), indicating how it was seen by the Israelites, and the cause of the great

shout from all Israel. The ark represented the *covenant* of *Yahweh*, the God who had made Israel his own people.

(4) "The ark of *Yahweh*," when the ark terrified the Philistines (1 Samuel 4:6), the narrator dropping the reference to the covenant. It was Israel's God, Yahweh, whom the Philistines feared. This title was used again when the Lord began to assert his power against the Philistines (1 Samuel 5:3, 4). It is noteworthy that this title, associated by its previous three uses with Philistine terror, is used in the summary statement in 1 Samuel 6:1 and then nine times through the rest of the story as the Philistines submit to Yahweh and the ark is returned to Israel (1 Samuel 6:1, 2, 8, 11, 15, 18, 19, 21; 7:1).

(5) When the ark was captured by the Philistines in 1 Samuel 4:11, the next nine references to the ark are just "the ark *of God*" (1 Samuel 4:11, 13, 17, 18, 19, 21, 22; 5:1, 2). It is as though the ark in Philistine hands could no longer signify the covenant, and it was no longer appropriate to link it to the name of Yahweh. This was also the narrator's term for the ark as the Philistines moved it around their country (1 Samuel 5:10, twice).

(6) Once the Philistines began to feel the heavy hand of Yahweh on them, they referred to the ark as "the ark of the God of Israel" (1 Samuel 5:7, 8 [3 times]; 5:10, 11; also 6:3).

(7) The ark is simply called "the ark" when it was sighted by the people of Beth-shemesh as it was returning to Israel (1 Samuel 6:13). The unqualified description suits the ambiguity of that moment from the observers' point of view. It occurs again at the end of the story to refer to the ark during its long (neglected?) sojourn at Kiriath-jearim (1 Samuel 7:2).

3. That this meeting took place in Ekron is confirmed in verse 16, when the lords *return* to Ekron. This means that 1 Samuel 6:2 picks up the story from the end of chapter 5. The seven months of 1 Samuel 6:1 is the whole period from the taking of the ark to Ashdod (1 Samuel 5:1) to its return to Israel in 1 Samuel 6:14-16.

4. The failed attempts by the Philistine people to call on the lords of the Philistines to solve the crisis were reported in 1 Samuel 5:8, 11. "The Philistines" seeking advice now from the priests and diviners are distinguished from their "lords" in 1 Samuel 6:4 by the words "you and your lords."

5. Hebrew words for divination appear at three important places in 1 Samuel — namely, 1 Samuel 6:2; 15:23; 28:8. The fact that divination was part of Philistine practice is worth remembering when we hear of such practices again (see 1 Samuel 15:23; 28:7). On divination, see Numbers 22:7; 23:23; Deuteronomy 18:10, 14; Joshua 13:22; 2 Kings 17:17.

6. English versions often render this verb in the exodus account as "let go." See also Exodus 3:20; 4:21, 23; 5:2; 6:1, 11; 7:2, 14, 16; 8:1, 8, 20, 21, 28, 29, 32; etc.

7. Robert P. Gordon, *1 & 2 Samuel: A Commentary* (Exeter, UK: The Paternoster Press, 1986), p. 101.

8. See Gordon Wenham, *The Book of Leviticus*, The New International Commentary of the Old Testament (Grand Rapids, MI: Eerdmans, 1979), pp. 103-112.

9. This same word is translated "an offering for sin [KJV; ESV, guilt]" in the highly significant text Isaiah 53:10.

10. Wenham, *Leviticus*, p. 111.

11. This picture is strengthened by the verb "return" in verses 3, 4, implying a debt that is to be repaid.

12. The Israelites will "know": Exodus 6:7; 10:2; 16:6, 12; Pharaoh and the Egyptians will "know": Exodus 7:5, 17; 8:10, 22; 9:14, 29; 11:7; 14:4, 18; all the earth will know: Exodus 9:16.

13. A measure of uncertainty is allowed in the Hebrew for "you will be healed" and is indicated by the context because in verse 5 the possibility of relief is only "perhaps," and in verse 9 the priests allow that the whole affair may have been a coincidence! A better translation would therefore be, "Then you may be healed . . ." Cf. C. F. Keil and F.

Delitzsch, *Biblical Commentary on the Books of Samuel* (Grand Rapids, MI: Eerdmans, 1950), p. 62.

14. Even more comical if they were (as we saw was possible in 1 Samuel 5:6) hemorrhoids!

15. Attempts to analyze the Philistine thinking further (sympathetic magic, Gordon, *1 & 2 Samuel*, p. 101; "like cures like," Peter R. Ackroyd, *The First Book of Samuel*, Cambridge Bible Commentary [Cambridge, UK: Cambridge University Press, 1971], p. 59; Hans Wilhelm Hertzberg, *I & II Samuel: A Commentary*, Old Testament Library [London: SCM Press, 1964], p. 58; "a supplication in symbolic form," John Mauchline, *1 and 2 Samuel*, New Century Bible [London: Oliphants, 1971], p. 78) are unnecessary.

16. The tumors and the mice may have been seen as attacks on the Philistine gods.

17. "In all cases [of the Hebrew word rendered 'perhaps'] an element of uncertainty prevails." Lyle M. Eslinger, *Kingship of God in Crisis: A Close Reading of 1 Samuel 1–12*, Bible and Literature Series, 10 (Sheffield, UK: JSOT Press, 1985), pp. 207, 208. Contra P. Kyle McCarter, Jr., *I Samuel: A New Translation with Introduction, Notes & Commentary*, The Anchor Bible, Vol. 8 (Garden City, NY: Doubleday, 1980), p. 134 who regards the "perhaps" as implying "an expectation of the desired (or feared) result."

18. The same verb (though in different conjugations) is used of Pharaoh hardening his heart and God hardening Pharaoh's heart in Exodus 8:15, 32; 9:7, 34; 10:1; 14:4, 17. The play on the ideas of "heavy" and "glory" appears in Exodus 14:4, 17, 18.

19. Ralph W. Klein, *1 Samuel*, Word Biblical Commentary, 10 (Nashville: Word, 1983), p. 58.

20. In Hebrew the calves are called "their sons," contributing to the story in which "sons" have played such an important role: the son of Hannah, the sons of Eli, and the son Ichabod. Alter elaborates on the resonance he sees with Hannah's story. Robert Alter, *The David Story: A Translation with Commentary of 1 and 2 Samuel* (New York and London: W.W. Norton, 1999), pp. 32, 33.

21. For further information about Beth-shemesh, see T .C. Mitchell, "Beth-shemesh," in J. D. Douglas et al, eds., *The Illustrated Bible Dictionary*, Part 1 (Leicester, UK and Wheaton, IL: Inter-Varsity Press and Tyndale House, 1980), p. 192.

22. There were forty-eight Levitical cities spread through the land allocated to the tribes of Israel in Joshua 13–21. Levites were to dwell in these cities and have use of adjoining pasturelands, although they remained the possession of the respective tribes (Joshua 21:2). See Marten H. Woudstra, *The Book of Joshua*, The New International Commentary on the Old Testament (Grand Rapids, MI: Eerdmans, 1981), pp. 303-313.

23. The same Hebrew word for "highway" occurs in 1 Samuel 6:12 and Isaiah 40:3. Cf. Walter Brueggemann, *First and Second Samuel*, Interpretation: A Bible Commentary for Teaching and Preaching (Louisville: John Knox Press, 1990), p. 43.

24. The repetition of "there" in the Hebrew emphasizes the location of the stone at the very place where the cart stopped. The role of the great stone in the ensuing events is not entirely clear. It is not explicitly stated that the burnt offering was made on the stone. The ark was set on it (v. 15), which may suggest that the subsequent burnt offering was not made on the stone. However, it is possible that the stone was *very* large and that the ark was on one part of it while the burnt offering was made on another part. Cf. Joyce Baldwin, *1 and 2 Samuel*, Tyndale Old Testament Commentaries (Leicester, UK: Inter-Varsity Press, 1988), pp. 76, 77.

25. Wenham, *Leviticus*, p. 63, who adds, "Its main function was to atone for man's sin by propitiating God's wrath." See Leviticus 1.

26. Cf. Eslinger, *Kingship*, pp. 214-216.

27. Gordon, *1 & 2 Samuel*, p. 102.

28. It is difficult to be precise about what the "sacrifices" added to the "burnt offerings." Keil and Delitzsch, *Books of Samuel*, p. 67 suggest, "In the burnt-offerings they consecrated themselves afresh, with all their members, to the service of the Lord; and in the slain

offerings, which culminated in the sacrificial meals, they sealed anew their living fellowship with the Lord."

29. So Keil and Delitzsch, *Books of Samuel*, p. 67.

30. Cf. Eslinger, *Kingship*, pp. 216, 217.

31. The ESV expresses the probable sense of a difficult Hebrew sentence but depends on two emendations. For details see Gordon, *1 & 2 Samuel*, p. 103.

32. ". . . here it no doubt signifies a foolish staring, which was incompatible with the holiness of the ark of God, and was punished with death, according to the warning expressed in Num. iv. 20." Keil and Delitzsch, *Books of Samuel*, p. 69.

33. There is a serious textual problem associated with the number. "Seventy" is followed in the Hebrew by "fifty thousand" in a way that does not make grammatical sense. Both numbers appear in the ancient versions, but most commentators recognize the larger figure to be some kind of textual error. Josephus supports this, giving the number as seventy. Keil and Delitzsch, *Books of Samuel*, p. 69; Gordon, *1 & 2 Samuel*, p. 103.

34. The number who died in 1 Samuel 4:10 was "thirty thousand."

35. It is possible that Shiloh was destroyed at about the time of the battle of Aphek in 1 Samuel 4 (see Psalm 78:60; Jeremiah 7:12, 14; 26:6, 9). If this was so, it would account for the ark not being sent back there. We must assume that the tabernacle had not yet been established at Nob (1 Samuel 21:1-6), but there is no evidence as to where it was at this time (cf. 1 Samuel 14:3). See J. B. Taylor, "Shiloh," in J. D. Douglas et al, eds., *The Illustrated Bible Dictionary*, Part 3 (Leicester, UK and Wheaton, IL: Inter-Varsity Press and Tyndale House, 1980), pp. 1437-1439.

36. Cf. Eslinger, *Kingship*, p. 227.

37. Brueggemann, *First and Second Samuel*, p. 47.

CHAPTER ELEVEN: EFFECTIVE LEADERSHIP

1. Remember that "thousand" may mean less than a thousand.

2. Lyle Eslinger's monograph, *Kingship of God in Crisis: A Close Reading of 1 Samuel 1–12*, Bible and Literature Series, 10 (Sheffield, UK: JSOT Press, 1985), is in many ways a stimulating and careful study of the text of 1 Samuel 1–12. The present exposition, as the endnotes reveal, has gained many insights from this incisive treatment. I must say, however, that I find his answer to the question before us (which he rightly sees as crucially important) is deeply disturbing. On what I judge to be very thin evidence he insists on the innocence of the people of Israel and the culpability of God! This, of course, is the very opposite of what any reader of Exodus, Numbers, and Judges would expect. It is not as though this is the first time Israel found itself on the wrong side of the Lord's wrath! On many previous occasions the reason is explicitly stated in terms of Israel's sinfulness. Eslinger bases some of his case on the absence of explicit criticism of the people up to this point in the story. That argument from silence is insufficient to overthrow the expectations created by the previous history of this people. Other quite subtle interpretations of particular texts that contribute to Eslinger's case are, in my opinion, far from compelling. In my opinion his entire interpretation of the narrative is deeply distorted by this judgment, which shapes much else, and illustrates a danger in close reading that can give more weight than is appropriate to a particular interpretation of a small detail of the text, which may then set a false agenda for the interpretation of much else. This, in my opinion, is the case with Eslinger's work.

3. The chapter divisions in the Old Testament familiar to us are not ancient. In many places (such as 1 Samuel 7:1) they divide the text contrary to the Massoretic divisions. They were apparently the work of Archbishop Stephen Langton, who divided the Vulgate into chapters early in the thirteenth century. His divisions were later transferred to the Hebrew Bible. The first printed Hebrew Bible to have these chapter divisions was published in 1517. The history is briefly sketched by Jordon S. Penkower, "The Chapter Divisions in the 1525 Rabbinic Bible," *Vetus Testamentum* 48 (1998), pp. 350, 351. A fuller examination of the matter is to be found in Christian D. Ginsberg, *Introduction to the Massoretico-Critical Edition of the Hebrew Bible* (London: Trinitarian Bible

Society, 1897), pp. 25-31. The work of Stephen Langton is examined in Beryl Smalley, *The Study of the Bible in the Middle Ages* (Oxford: Blackwell, 1952), pp. 196-263.

The chapter divisions usually stand at obvious literary breaks, but in a number of places, such as 1 Samuel 7, they seem incorrect. It does seem strange to put a break between 1 Samuel 6:21 and 7:1, 2. The three verses are tightly woven together, dealing with the request to Kiriath-jearim (6:21), their response (7:1), and the outcome (7:2). However, the chapter division, if it is allowed to influence the reader, will have the effect of highlighting (a) the request to Kiriath-jearim as the end of the story of the Beth-shemeshites, and (b) the bringing of the ark to Kiriath-jearim and its long sojourn there as the immediate background to events at Mizpah that chapter 7 is about to recount.

This raises the question of what weight should be given to the chapter divisions of the Bible. Most commentaries disregard them whenever they seem inappropriate to the literary divisions of the text. "Since the division into chapters was prepared a very long time after the writing of the text, it reflects late exegesis, and is not always precise" (Emanuel Tov, *Textual Criticism of the Hebrew Bible*, second revised edition [Minneapolis: Fortress, 2001], p. 52). On the other hand, it is precisely when the chapter divisions do not correspond to the "obvious" literary units that interesting questions arise about how the text was understood by those responsible for placing the divisions at unusual points. In this exposition we will not regard these divisions as authoritative but will consider whether and how the chapter divisions might draw attention to connections in the text. The chapter divisions are not, in other words, part of the inspired text of Scripture, but they may be evidence of an understanding of the text at various points that may be illuminating, though not authoritative.

4. The evidence advanced is (a) the ark would hardly be entrusted to the keeping of a non-priest, and (b) he gave his son, Eleazar, a good Aaronite name. Diana V. Edelman, "Abinadab," in David Noel Freedman, ed., *The Anchor Bible Dictionary*, Vol. 1 (New York: Doubleday, 1992), p. 22; John Mauchline, *1 and 2 Samuel*, New Century Bible (London: Oliphants, 1971), p. 82; P. Kyle McCarter, Jr., *1 Samuel: A New Translation with Introduction, Notes & Commentary*, The Anchor Bible, Vol. 8 (Garden City, NY: Doubleday, 1980), p. 137; C. F. Keil and F. Delitzsch, *Biblical Commentary on the Books of Samuel* (Grand Rapids, MI: Eerdmans, 1950), p. 70.

5. Eslinger, *Kingship*, p. 229; cf. Henry Preserved Smith, *A Critical and Exegetical Commentary on the Books of Samuel*, The International Critical Commentary (Edinburgh: T. & T. Clark, 1899), p. 50; Robert P. Gordon, *1 & 2 Samuel: A Commentary* (Exeter, UK: The Paternoster Press, 1986), p. 104.

6. An attempt to uncover the role of Kiriath-jearim (from a thoroughly historical-critical perspective) is made by Joseph Blenkinsopp, "Kiriath-jearim and the Ark," *Journal of Biblical Literature* 88 (1969), pp. 143-156. The suggestion that the ark was put at this relatively unknown site because of Philistine influence (e.g. Mauchline, *1 and 2 Samuel*, p. 82) is an argument from silence and contrary to the general sense of the narrative, which has shown the Philistines to have *no* power to control the ark or the God of the ark.

7. As we will note in due course, there are doubts about the text of this verse, since the Septuagint refers not to the "ark," but to the "ephod."

8. Apart from the seven months that the ark spent in Philistine territory (1 Samuel 6:1), there has been no explicit indication of the passage of time in the narrative of 1 Samuel so far. We might guess that two or three years passed from the birth of Samuel in 1 Samuel 1:20 to his weaning and presentation in Shiloh at the end of chapter 1. Chapter 2 seems to cover a period of about ten years or more, since by the time we reach chapter 3 Samuel is an articulate youth, possibly in his teens. The events of chapters 4–6 appear to have taken place within about a year. Now, however, a twenty-year period seems to pass by in one verse.

9. So Peter R. Ackroyd, *The First Book of Samuel*, Cambridge Bible Commentary (Cambridge, UK: Cambridge University Press, 1971), p. 65.

10. In particular I have in mind the indication in Acts 13:21 that Saul reigned for forty years and the fair comment by Joyce Baldwin, *1 and 2 Samuel*, Tyndale Old Testament Commentaries (Leicester, UK: Inter-Varsity Press, 1988), p. 77, "The period between the death of Eli and David's accession was almost certainly more than twenty years."

11. The Hebrew has a typical narrative sequence running through verses 2, 3 indicating a sequence of events, each one of which is consequent on the previous one: (a) the days became many; (b) they became twenty years; (c) all Israel lamented; (d) Samuel spoke. The syntax is helpfully analyzed by Keil and Delitzsch, *Books of Samuel*, pp. 70, 71. Cf. Robert Alter, *The David Story: A Translation with Commentary of 1 and 2 Samuel* (New York and London: W.W. Norton, 1999), p. 36; Ralph W. Klein, *1 Samuel*, Word Biblical Commentary, 10 (Nashville: Word, 1983), p. 65; Baldwin, *1 and 2 Samuel*, p. 77; Eslinger, *Kingship*, p. 230.

12. The Hebrew verb translated "lamented" occurs in only two other places in the Old Testament, and then in a different form (Ezekiel 32:18, ESV "wail"; Micah 2:4, ESV "moan"). A cognate noun has a similar meaning in Jeremiah 9:10, 18-20, "wailing," "lament"; Amos 5:16, "lamentation." It has been suggested that the verb in 1 Samuel 7:2 may mean "yearn after." See Mauchline, *1 and 2 Samuel*, p. 83.

13. Alter, *David*, p. 37. *Ashtoreth* (1 Kings 11:5, 33; 2 Kings 23:13) is itself a Hebrew wordplay with the vowels of a word meaning "shame" being added to the consonants of Astarte. See John Day, "Ashtoreth," in David Noel Freedman et al, eds., *The Anchor Bible Dictionary*, Vol. 1 (New York: Doubleday, 1992), pp. 491-494.

14. Eslinger rightly recognizes the importance of this question. His answer, with which I differ sharply, is that the Israelites only turned to these other gods *after* the ark had been put into "cold storage" in 1 Samuel 6:21–7:1: "with Yahweh dead and gone, Israel might well have turned to the reluctant worship of other deities . . . they turned to these other gods out of desperation." Eslinger, *Kingship*, p. 234. Eslinger, in my opinion, has failed to appreciate the power with which God's negative actions against Israel (in chapters 4, 6) raise the question for the Bible reader of what Israel had done. The reader's expectations are shaped by Israel's previous history, which gives us less optimism than Eslinger displays. However, we are kept in suspense and even perplexity until 1 Samuel 7:3. Now that the truth is out, however, we look back and reasonably suspect that it all began with the corruption of Eli's sons.

15. "The phrase, *to lament after God*, is taken from human affairs, when one person follows another with earnest solicitations and complaints, until he at last assents." Keil and Delitzsch, *Books of Samuel*, p. 71, citing Seb. Schmidt.

16. My suggestion that verses 3, 4 are a summary that is elaborated in what follows is not certain but seems to me to make best sense of the flow of the text. Cf. Walter Brueggemann, *First and Second Samuel*, Interpretation: A Bible Commentary for Teaching and Preaching (Louisville: John Knox Press, 1990), p. 50. Eslinger sees the matter very differently and in my opinion makes far too much of Israel's "immediate and unequivocal" response in verse 4. Eslinger, *Kingship*, p. 236. Once again he has not allowed the previous history of Israel to influence him as much as it ought. Any reader familiar with the book of Judges will have some doubts about the quick repentance of Israel reported in verse 4. The elaboration is therefore important.

17. Vocalized as Mizpeh.

18. Of course, we have already heard about the man of Benjamin who brought news of the Philistine victory to Shiloh (1 Samuel 4:12). Indeed some time after the assembly Samuel called in 1 Samuel 7, he will summon another gathering at Mizpah to appoint Saul of Benjamin as their king (1 Samuel 10:17).

19. "Mizpah" means "watchtower," and the term usually has the definite article, "the watchtower." It is hardly surprising, then, that several different places are referred to by this name. See Patrick M. Arnold, "Mizpah," in David Noel Freedman, ed., *The Anchor Bible Dictionary*, Vol. 4 (New York: Doubleday, 1992), pp. 879-881. A "Mizpah" had featured earlier in the story as the site of Israelite encampment or assembly (Judges 10:17; 11:11). The home of Jephthah was at "Mizpah" (Judges 11:34).

20. In Psalm 99:6 Samuel is associated with Moses and Aaron as among those who "called to the LORD, and he answered them." Similarly see Jeremiah 15:1. Ackroyd, *First Book of Samuel*, p. 66.

21. "There" subtly emphasizes that the words were spoken at the same place where the actions were done. Cf. Keil and Delitzsch, *Books of Samuel*, p. 73.

22. Gordon, *1 & 2 Samuel*, p. 107 suggests that the pouring out of the water before the Lord "may simply have formed part of the self-denial of the occasion as the participants solemnly proclaimed their abstention from even this necessity of life." This is not to deny that the actions would have symbolic connotations, especially when we recall such metaphors for a humble cry to God as "Pour out your heart like water before the presence of the Lord!" (Lamentations 2:19; the parallel is suggested by Keil and Delitzsch, *Books of Samuel*, p. 73; Hans Wilhelm Hertzberg, *I & II Samuel: A Commentary*, Old Testament Library [London: SCM Press, 1964], p. 67; Ackroyd, *1 and 2 Samuel*, p. 66). Cf. Psalm 22:14. Hertzberg, *I & II Samuel*, p. 67 also draws attention to the connection between water and repentance in the "baptism of repentance for the forgiveness of sins" (Mark 1:4).

23. Barry Webb draws attention to the failure of the Israelites in the earlier times to "listen to their judges" (Judges 2:17). This he takes to imply that the judges were not only military deliverers, but also proclaimers of the commandments of the Lord. Barry G. Webb, *The Book of Judges: An Integrated Reading*, Journal for the Study of the Old Testament Supplement Series 46 (Sheffield, UK: Sheffield Academic Press, 1987), p. 111. This was particularly true of Samuel who, alone among the judges of Israel, is also described as an intercessor for the people.

24. "Judging the people . . . [consisted] in the fact that Samuel summoned the nation to Mizpeh to humble itself before Jehovah, and there secured for it, through his intercession, the forgiveness of its sin, and a renewal of the favor of its God, and thus restored the proper relation between Israel and its God, so that the Lord could proceed to vindicate His people's rights against their foes." Keil and Delitzsch, *Books of Samuel*, p. 73. Marin Rozenberg has argued that the Hebrew verb translated "judge" in many places in the Old Testament has the general sense of "to exercise leadership." The precise nature of that leadership and the form that it takes varies with the context. Martin S. Rozenberg, "The *Sofetim* in the Bible," *Eretz-Israel: Archaeological, Historical and Geographical Studies* 12 (1975), pp. 77-86. Contra Mauchline, *1 and 2 Samuel*, p. 85 who understands the reference to judging in 1 Samuel 7:6 in judicial terms.

25. Contra Eslinger, *Kingship*, p. 237, who seems to overlook the twenty years and the indication in 1 Samuel 7:3 of recent Philistine hostilities.

26. I have slightly changed the ESV here to bring out the similarity between the two verses. The Hebrew has a different word for "hand" in the two verses.

27. Eslinger, *Kingship*, p. 239.

28. ". . . a basic function of the *burnt offering* was to make atonement (Lv. 1:4; *cf.* 2 Sa. 24:25; Jb. 1:5; 42:8)." Gordon, *1 & 2 Samuel*, p. 107.

29. Cf. Eslinger, *Kingship*, p. 240. Hannah's and Samuel's praying are described with the same verb in 1 Samuel 1:10 and 7:5 respectively.

30. See the full description in 1 Samuel 2:12-17.

31. The verb "thunder" in both verses represents exactly the same Hebrew word (in precisely the same form!).

32. The verbal correspondence of these expressions in 1 Samuel 4:2, 3 and 7:10 is unfortunately obscured in the ESV.

33. The precise location of Beth-car is unknown as this is the only mention we have. It seems clear, however, that it lay some distance to the west of Mizpah. Gordon, *1 & 2 Samuel*, p. 107.

34. We are not helped by the fact that the location of Shen ("the crag" or "the tooth") is unknown.

35. This way of putting it is suggested by Brueggemann, *First and Second Samuel*, p. 54.

36. We note that Saul will be appointed explicitly to "save my people from the hand of the Philistines" (1 Samuel 9:16). This does seem to imply some problem with the Philistines even before Samuel's exclusive leadership of Israel came to an end. Furthermore, according to Samuel, the true motivation for the request for a king in 1 Samuel 8:5, 19, 20 was the threat from Nahash, the king of the Ammonites (1 Samuel 12:12). Of course, once Saul became king, the Philistine threat was never far away (1 Samuel 14:52a) and would be responsible for his death in 1 Samuel 31.

37. "Ekron to Gath" represents the border between Israelite and Philistine territory.

38. Cf. Rozenberg, "*Sofetim*," p. 79.

CHAPTER TWELVE: THE LEADER ISRAEL WANTED

1. Barry Webb argues that Gideon's refusal must be seen in the light of "the specific terms in which the offer was made ([Judges] 8.22). Israel's future could not be secured by creating a new institution. Only wholehearted return to Yahweh could do that. . . ." Barry G. Webb, *The Book of Judges: An Integrated Reading*, Journal for the Study of the Old Testament Supplement Series 46 (Sheffield, UK: Sheffield Academic Press, 1987), p. 159. Even so, the situation in 1 Samuel 8 is sufficiently similar for Gideon's argument to apply here with equal force.

2. Cf. C. F. Keil and F. Delitzsch, *Biblical Commentary on the Books of Samuel* (Grand Rapids, MI: Eerdmans, 1950), pp. 81, 82; contra Robert P. Gordon, *1 & 2 Samuel: A Commentary* (Exeter, UK: The Paternoster Press, 1986), p. 109 ("his own little dynastic experiment").

3. Samuel's annual circuit from Ramah to Bethel, Gilgal, Mizpah, and back to Ramah (1 Samuel 7:16, 17) covered a relatively small central area of Israel's territory.

4. "Samuel's control over his sons and even his knowledge of their actions would always be at least two days after the fact." Lyle M. Eslinger, *Kingship of God in Crisis: A Close Reading of 1 Samuel 1–12*, Bible and Literature Series, 10 (Sheffield, UK: JSOT Press, 1985), p. 457, note 2.

5. Eslinger, *Kingship*, p. 253.

6. All twenty-three occurrences of this noun in the Old Testament refer to illegitimate or violent profit or gain, including bribes. Examples include Genesis 37:26 (ESV, "profit"); Judges 5:19 (ESV, "spoils"); Proverbs 1:19; Isaiah 33:15; 56:11; 57:17; Jeremiah 6:13; 22:17; Ezekiel 22:13, 27.

7. Diether Kellermann, *bs'*, in G. Johannes Botterweck and Helmer Ringgren, eds., *Theological Dictionary of the Old Testament*, Vol. 2 (Grand Rapids, MI: Eerdmans, 1998), p. 207.

8. The Hebrew verb translated "perverted" is a variant form of the verb rendered "turned aside" in this verse. We might say, colloquially, they were thoroughly "bent"!

9. Eslinger has, I believe, missed the simplicity of the structure of this passage as essentially two exchanges between the people and the Lord, with Samuel as mediator, by presenting it as "a remarkable network of correspondences and reversals in the roles of speaker and addressee," which he then sets out in a concentric diagram. Eslinger, *Kingship*, p. 258.

10. This is Eslinger's understanding of the thought of the elders. He argues that they knew that the earlier national catastrophe was Yahweh's doing because of Samuel's word to them (1 Samuel 4:1). In order to avoid this happening again, the elders proposed opting out of the covenantal arrangement with Yahweh altogether. "The request is a product of a defect in the theocratic system, a defect lying wholly on the side of Yahweh and his chosen mediators." Eslinger, *Kingship*, p. 255, also p. 457, note 3. Eslinger does not give sufficient weight, in my opinion, to the events of 1 Samuel 7, from which we learn that Israel's problems with the Lord were due to apostasy (this was understood and acknowledged by both Samuel and the people). Eslinger's view of the innocence of the people in all of this (which even the people did not believe, 1 Samuel 7:6) seems to have blinded him to the possibility that we are seeing history repeating itself not only in the old leader and his corrupt sons, but also in the apostasy of the people in this situation.

11. Cf. Hans Wilhelm Hertzberg, *I & II Samuel: A Commentary*, Old Testament Library (London: SCM Press, 1964), p. 72; Eslinger, *Kingship*, p. 255.

12. In attempting to grasp the meaning and connotations of the word "king," it is illuminating to consider the view of kingship presented in the book of Judges, which is assumed knowledge for the reader of 1 Samuel. In Judges the "king" vocabulary in chapter 1–8 refers only to kings of the non-Israelite nations. This is a sensible background to the phrase in 1 Samuel 8:5, "like all the nations." In Judges 9 a decidedly negative view is presented of the kingship that was introduced into Israel, although Barry Webb argues that here kingship "is not rejected in principle" (Webb, *Judges*, p. 159). In Judges 10–16 "king" vocabulary is used again only of the kings of the pagan nations. In Judges 17–25 the words are only found in the refrain "there was no king in Israel" (Judges 17:6; 18:1; 19:1; 21:25).

13. The conditions set out in Deuteronomy 17:14-20 included: (a) the king must be the Lord's choice; (b) he must be a brother, that is, a fellow Israelite under the same covenant with the Lord; (c) he must live in obedience to the law of the Lord. See Gerald Eddie Gerbrandt, *Kingship According to the Deuteronomistic History*, Society of Biblical Literature Dissertation Series, 87 (Atlanta: Scholars Press, 1986), pp. 109-112.

14. In this I agree with Eslinger. My disagreement is with his view that "the elders' drastic request seems entirely appropriate"! Eslinger, *Kingship*, p. 257.

15. For a fuller discussion of the meaning of "king," see H. Ringgren and K. Seybold, *melek*, in G. Johannes Botterweck and Helmer Ringgren, eds., *Theological Dictionary of the Old Testament*, Vol. 8 (Grand Rapids, MI: Eerdmans, 1997), pp. 346-374; Keith W. Whitelam, "King and Kingship," in David Noel Freedman, ed., *The Anchor Bible Dictionary*, Vol. 4 (New York: Doubleday, 1992), pp. 40-48.

16. Kingship is not necessarily hereditary but very commonly is so, and the principle of primogeniture often seems to be assumed. See Judges 8:22; 1 Samuel 20:31.

17. Alter understands the omission of the words "like all the nations" differently. ". . . the very phrase rejecting covenantal status that must especially gall him, 'like all the nations,' is suppressed." Robert Alter, *The David Story: A Translation with Commentary of 1 and 2 Samuel* (New York and London: W.W. Norton, 1999), p. 41.

18. Note that the Lord interprets the request of the elders as "the voice of the people."

19. Cf. Eslinger, *Kingship*, p. 262.

20. In context the words "they have not rejected you" (v. 7) must be understood to mean "they have not *merely* rejected you." Contra Eslinger who sees a contradiction here and, without textual evidence, emends the words in verse 8 to, "so they are also making a king." Eslinger, *Kingship*, pp. 264, 265.

21. In Hebrew there is a verb meaning "to be king" or "to reign" as well as a noun, "king." The verb is used in Exodus 15:18 and 1 Samuel 8:7. The noun is used in Numbers 23:21 and Deuteronomy 33:5 (also 1 Samuel 12:12).

22. Eslinger applies an otherwise sound principle (namely, that one must distinguish the views expressed by the characters in a narrative from the views of the narrator himself) unpersuasively to argue that while both Samuel and the Lord disapprove of the request for a king, the narrator sees it as fully justified. Eslinger, *Kingship*, pp. 259-262. He fails to reckon with the fact that in the Biblical historical narrative the reliability of God is well established!

23. The difficulty for translation is that the Hebrew word has a range of meanings that do not correspond to any one English word. This means that the wordplay in the Hebrew text cannot be readily reproduced in an English translation.

24. If the narrator wanted to indicate that Samuel was less than completely faithful in his mediatorial task here, as Eslinger argues (Eslinger, *Kingship*, p. 271), then he has hidden his intention remarkably well!

25. So Eslinger, *Kingship*, p. 461, note 24.

26. The delay created by Samuel's dismissal of the people may prepare us for the fact that the making of a king would not be a simple, single act. A somewhat involved process

will emerge in 1 Samuel 9–11. Cf. V. Philips Long, *The Reign and Rejection of King Saul*, SBL Dissertation Series, 118 (Atlanta: Scholars Press, 1989), p. 193.

27. Note that the section about the request for a king began with "the elders of Israel" (v. 4) and ends with reference to "the men of Israel" (v. 22). How could this people still be "Israel" if their request is granted?

28. Romans 3:21-26, my translation. I have deliberately used "justice" rather than "righteousness" and "King" instead of "Christ" in order to highlight the contrast with the proposed king of 1 Samuel 8.

CHAPTER THIRTEEN: LOST DONKEYS AND THE WORD OF GOD

1. The history of scholarly study of this section of 1 Samuel is well summarized by V. Philips Long, *The Reign and Rejection of King Saul*, SBL Dissertation Series, 118 (Atlanta: Scholars Press, 1989), pp. 173-194. Long persuasively challenges the widely held assumption that this narrative cannot be understood as a coherent account.

2. In Hebrew the first words of 1 Samuel 1:1 are identical to the words translated "There was a man" in 1 Samuel 9:1.

3. "A man of wealth" could perhaps be translated "a powerful man." P. Kyle McCarter, Jr., *I Samuel: A New Translation with Introduction, Notes & Commentary*, The Anchor Bible, Vol. 8 (Garden City, NY: Doubleday, 1980), p. 173. Some argue that the term translated "wealth" has military connotations. "Military ability and wealth go together"; H. Eising, *chayil*, in G. Johannes Botterweck and Helmer Ringgren, eds., *Theological Dictionary of the Old Testament*, Vol. 4 (Grand Rapids, MI: Eerdmans, 1980), p. 351.

4. "Like Samuel, Saul begins as a nobody who will become a somebody as a result of Yahweh's decision to make use of him." Lyle M. Eslinger, *Kingship of God in Crisis: A Close Reading of 1 Samuel 1–12*, Bible and Literature Series, 10 (Sheffield, UK: JSOT Press, 1985), p. 285. Contra Robert P. Gordon, *1 & 2 Samuel: A Commentary* (Exeter, UK: The Paternoster Press, 1986), p. 112, Joyce Baldwin, *1 and 2 Samuel*, Tyndale Old Testament Commentaries (Leicester, UK: Inter-Varsity Press, 1988), p. 87 and others who see the fact of the genealogy as an indication of importance.

5. The words "a man of Benjamin" refer to the land in which he lived; "Benjaminite" refers to his tribe. Eslinger, *Kingship*, p. 461, note 4.

6. The Hebrew expression for "man of Benjamin" is not precisely the same in 1 Samuel 4:12 and 9:1.

7. Translated "lent" in the ESV of 1 Samuel 1:28.

8. Robert Alter, *The David Story: A Translation with Commentary of 1 and 2 Samuel* (New York and London: W.W. Norton, 1999), p. 68. V. Philips Long goes further and suggests that the word should probably be translated "chosen (choice)" rather than "young man." Long, *Saul*, p. 204. Even if translated "young man," we should not interpret youthfulness in modern western terms. Saul may have been much older than "young man" suggests to us. By chapter 13 Saul will have a son old enough to engage in military leadership (v. 2), although it must be admitted that the length of time between chapters 9 and 13 is not clear.

9. McCarter argues that the Hebrew means that only some of Kish's donkeys, not all of them, had strayed. McCarter, *I Samuel*, pp. 173, 174.

10. Here we have the Hebrew word noted earlier that is variously translated "child" (e.g., 1 Samuel 1:22), "boy" (1 Samuel 2:11), "servant" (1 Samuel 2:13; 9:5, 7, 8, 10, 27) and, as here, "young man" (1 Samuel 2:21).

11. Cf. Eslinger, *Kingship*, p. 289.

12. The locations of Shalishah and Shaalim are not known. The hill country of Ephraim lay north of the land of Benjamin.

13. See Gerald J. Petter, "Zuph (place)," in David Noel Freedman, ed., *The Anchor Bible Dictionary*, Vol. 6 (New York: Doubleday, 1992), p. 1175.

14. The Hebrew word echoes the "glory" that departed from Israel (1 Samuel 4:21, 22).

15. Cf. Baldwin, *1 and 2 Samuel*, p. 88. "[I]t is possible that Saul's ignorance and Samuel's anonymity represent by a kind of metonymy the young man's complete unawareness of what lies ahead of him." Gordon, *1 & 2 Samuel*, p. 113.

16. "In short, it is the servant who initiates and facilitates movement toward Samuel. By contrast, Saul appears hesitant, passive, tending to impede rather than further the action . . . there is a certain misguidedness about Saul's action when compared to the servant. It is the latter's initiative and persistence that keeps the action moving in the providentially appointed direction." Long, *Saul*, p. 202.

17. Contra C. F. Keil and F. Delitzsch, *Biblical Commentary on the Books of Samuel* (Grand Rapids, MI: Eerdmans, 1950), p. 89; Alter, *David*, p. 50. The hints that the city is Ramah are: (a) the location in "the land of Zuph," and (b) the servant's knowledge that "there is a man of God in this city," suggesting that "this city" is the one known to be the place of this prophet (see 1 Samuel 7:17).

18. Robert Alter argues that these scenes belong to a particular "betrothal type-scene" that has a definite structure and content. See Robert Alter, *The Art of Biblical Narrative* (New York: Basic Books, 1981), pp. 51-62; also Eslinger, *Kingship*, pp. 297-299. In my opinion Alter's argument is somewhat circular. He establishes the elements of the type-scene from the Biblical examples and then draws conclusions from the fact that these elements are found in the very examples from which they were drawn! Furthermore he makes much of the fact that a scene like the one in 1 Samuel 9:11 turns out *not* to be a betrothal scene. I prefer to recognize the familiarity of the scene and the fact that such scenes have turned out to be important on a number of occasions in Biblical history, without suggesting that there is a necessary expectation of just what will happen here. Cf. Long, *Saul*, pp. 203, 204.

19. So Long, *Saul*, p. 198.

20. Eslinger, *Kingship*, p. 299.

21. Cf. *ibid.*, pp. 299, 300.

22. In an unusual construction the Hebrew of the last sentence of verse 13 emphasizes "him" by repeating the word.

23. This is the only reference to blessing a sacrifice in the Old Testament. Baldwin, *1 and 2 Samuel*, p. 89.

24. In verse 15 "revealed to Samuel" is literally, "uncovered the ear of Samuel."

25. Again we are reminded of the "man of Benjamin" in 1 Samuel 4:12.

26. "Prince" (ESV; KJV "captain"; NRSV "ruler"; NIV "leader") translates a Hebrew word (which occurs here for the first time in the Old Testament) that has no necessary royal connotations. The term has received a great deal of scholarly attention, and there is a variety of views. "It is a term that suggests the exercise of political power in a designated role of leadership rather than in the manner of the ad hoc charismatic leadership of the *shofet*, or judge." Alter, *David*, p. 49. "[T]he diversity of OT usage indicates that it became an honorific and specifically a title of nobility for people appointed to various positions." G. F. Hasel, *nagid*, in G. Johannes Botterweck, Helmer Ringgren, and Heinz-Josef Fabry, eds., *Theological Dictionary of the Old Testament*, Vol. 9 (Grand Rapids, MI: Eerdmans, 1998), p. 196. McCarter argues that the sense is "someone who though designated for an office has not yet begun to serve." McCarter, *I Samuel*, p. 178. For a survey of the main lines of the scholarly debate about the meaning of the term, see Baruch Halpern, *The Constitution of the Monarchy in Israel*, Harvard Semitic Monographs, 25 (Chico, CA: Scholars Press, 1981), pp. 1-11. Halpern understands the term to mean one designated by the Lord to be king: "the object of a divine promise of the throne" (p. 9). This, in my opinion, reads too much from the various contexts into the term.

27. So D. P. Wright and J. Milgrom, *'asar*, in G. Johannes Botterweck, Helmer Ringgren, and Heinz-Josef Fabry, eds., *Theological Dictionary of the Old Testament*, Vol. 11 (Grand Rapids, MI: Eerdmans, 1998), p. 311. Similarly KJV has "reign over"; NRSV has "rule over"; NIV has "govern."

28. This understanding has something in common with Eslinger's interpretation (Eslinger, *Kingship*, pp. 309, 310). However, I find Eslinger's understanding as a whole utterly

unbelievable, indeed blasphemous! He sees Yahweh as "sarcastic" and "vitriolic," even "manipulative," and expects the reader "to sympathize with the unsuspecting Israelites" (p. 313).

29. The sense I have followed here is suggested by the NIV ("And to whom is all the desire of Israel turned, if not to you and all your father's family?"). Cf. Long, *Saul*, 206. Alternatively, as the ESV suggests, "all that is desirable" may refer to all that is precious, suggesting that as king all the wealth of Israel will be his. So Keil and Delitzsch, *Books of Samuel*, p. 92; Alter, *David*, p. 50; McCarter, *I Samuel*, p. 179. Cf. "he will take" in 1 Samuel 8:11-17.

30. Contra Alter, *David*, p. 51, who sees this as the "etiquette of deference," whereas Saul's background was in fact far from so humble. Cf. Gordon, *1 & 2 Samuel*, p. 115. However see Baldwin, *1 and 2 Samuel*, pp. 89, 90.

31. First Samuel 9:24 presents some difficult textual problems. The sense, however, is clear enough and is adequately conveyed by the ESV. The NIV attempts a more literal translation of the unamended Hebrew. However, both the ESV and NIV attribute the spoken words to Samuel. The Hebrew suggests they may have been spoken by the cook!

32. The ESV follows the Septuagint, but for no compelling reason, since the Hebrew makes good sense. The Hebrew is supported by other ancient versions. See Keil and Delitzsch, *Books of Samuel*, p. 94, note 1 for a substantial argument of this point. Contra Gordon, *1 & 2 Samuel*, p. 116; Alter, *David*, p. 51.

CHAPTER FOURTEEN: THE SECRET OF THE KINGDOM

1. So Long expounds but does not argue for the longer reading. V. Philips Long, *The Reign and Rejection of King Saul*, SBL Dissertation Series, 118 (Atlanta: Scholars Press, 1989), pp. 206, 207. The Septuagint is also followed by Ralph W. Klein, *1 Samuel*, Word Biblical Commentary, 10 (Nashville: Word, 1983), p. 83; Walter Brueggemann, *First and Second Samuel*, Interpretation: A Bible Commentary for Teaching and Preaching (Louisville: John Knox Press, 1990), p. 74; John Mauchline, *1 and 2 Samuel*, New Century Bible (London: Oliphants, 1971), p. 97; P. Kyle McCarter, Jr., *I Samuel: A New Translation with Introduction, Notes & Commentary*, The Anchor Bible, Vol. 8 (Garden City, NY: Doubleday, 1980), p. 171; Henry Preserved Smith, *A Critical and Exegetical Commentary on the Books of Samuel*, The International Critical Commentary (Edinburgh: T. & T. Clark, 1899), p. 67. Robert P. Gordon, *1 & 2 Samuel: A Commentary* (Exeter, UK: The Paternoster Press, 1986), p. 116, is noncommittal.

2. Eslinger offers a substantial argument for retaining the Hebrew text. Lyle M. Eslinger, *Kingship of God in Crisis: A Close Reading of 1 Samuel 1–12*, Bible and Literature Series, 10 (Sheffield, UK: JSOT Press, 1985), pp. 467, 468, note 1. Cf. C. F. Keil and F. Delitzsch, *Biblical Commentary on the Books of Samuel* (Grand Rapids, MI: Eerdmans, 1950), p. 96, note 1. Alter follows the Hebrew without comment on the textual question. Robert Alter, *The David Story: A Translation with Commentary of 1 and 2 Samuel* (New York and London: W.W. Norton, 1999), p. 53.

3. As in the NIV.

4. The Septuagint's additional words may have been added under the influence of 1 Samuel 9:16.

5. The fact that the words *explain* the actions is even clearer in a more literal rendering of the Hebrew: "Is it not *because* the LORD anointed you to be prince over his heritage?"

6. E. Lipinski, *nahal*, in G. Johannes Botterweck, Helmer Ringgren, and Heinz-Josef Fabry, eds., *Theological Dictionary of the Old Testament*, Vol. 9 (Grand Rapids, MI: Eerdmans, 1998), p. 331.

7. The land is also called the Lord's "heritage" (possibly 1 Samuel 26:19), but the term is used more often of the people. Lipinski, *nahal*, p. 331; contra Joyce Baldwin, *1 and 2 Samuel*, Tyndale Old Testament Commentaries (Leicester, UK: Inter-Varsity Press, 1988), p. 90.

8. Eslinger, *Kingship*, p. 321.

9. The indication may be even more precise than appears in the ESV if we follow the NIV, which has Zelzah "on the border of Benjamin."

10. There are difficulties with identifying Zelzah (mentioned nowhere else in the Bible), and no less than eleven attempts to emend the Hebrew text at this point are outlined by Diana V. Edelman, "Zelzah," in David Noel Freedman, ed., *The Anchor Bible Dictionary*, Vol. 6 (New York: Doubleday, 1992), pp. 1073, 1074.

11. Gordon, *1 & 2 Samuel*, p. 117. Keil and Delitzsch dispute both points made here — namely, that Rachel's tomb was near Ramah (they locate it near Bethlehem) and that Saul met Samuel in Ramah (which they locate southwest of Bethlehem). Keil and Delitzsch, *Books of Samuel*, p. 97. Although the location of Rachel's tomb is disputed, Luker places it "in the territory of Benjamin S of Bethel and N of Ephrathah in the vicinity of Ramah (Gen 35:19-20; 48:7; 1 Sam 10:2; Jer 31:15)." Lamontte M. Luker, "Rachel's Tomb," in David Noel Freedman, ed., *The Anchor Bible Dictionary*, Vol. 5 (New York: Doubleday, 1992), p. 608.

12. Alter, *David*, p. 54.

13. It is tempting to think that the oak in Genesis 35:8 may have been the same as the oak mentioned by Samuel. However, this is far from certain and would be geographically awkward. See Keil and Delitzsch, *Books of Samuel*, p. 98, note 1.

14. Gordon, *1 & 2 Samuel*, p. 117; Baldwin, *1 and 2 Samuel*, p. 91; Mauchline, *1 and 2 Samuel*, p. 98; McCarter, *I Samuel*, pp. 181, 182. Contra Klein, *1 Samuel*, p. 91 who seems to identify Gibeath-elohim with Geba. Arnold prefers that Gibeath-elohim (a place name that is found only at 1 Samuel 10:5 in the Bible) "be regarded as the cultic name for the 'high place' in or near Gibeah/Geba." Patrick M. Arnold, "Gibeath-elohim," in David Noel Freedman, ed., *The Anchor Bible Dictionary*, Vol. 2 (New York: Doubleday, 1992), p. 1009.

15. For "garrison" the REB has "governor." See Long, *Saul*, p. 44, note 9.

16. The Hebrew has a plural noun, "garrisons."

17. The situation described in 1 Samuel 7:13 was therefore temporary.

18. Klein, *1 Samuel*, p. 91.

19. Long, *Saul*, p. 44, note 6.

20. The Hebrew word translated "spirit" also means "breath" and "wind."

21. Again it is not entirely clear what the activity of "prophesying" precisely was. Certainly a range of phenomena is referred to by this term. See, for example, Joseph Blenkinsopp, *A History of Prophecy in Israel: From the Settlement in the Land to the Hellenistic Period* (Philadelphia: Westminster Press, 1983), pp. 35-38. In the present context "prophesying" appears to be an ecstatic display under the influence of the Spirit of God. So Gordon, *1 & 2 Samuel*, p. 117. Cf. J. Lindblom, *Prophecy in Ancient Israel* (Philadelphia: Fortress, 1962), pp. 47-65.

22. "[S]urrender yourself to any impulse in the assurance that it is of divine origin." McCarter, *I Samuel*, p. 183.

23. Cf. Eslinger, *Kingship*, pp. 323, 324. However, I disagree with Eslinger's interpretation: "Samuel seems not to know precisely what is to happen; thus he leaves it open and tells Saul to improvise." Eslinger, *Kingship*, pp. 324, 325.

24. The parallel is suggested by Baruch Halpern, *The Constitution of the Monarchy in Israel*, Harvard Semitic Monographs, 25 (Chico, CA: Scholars Press, 1981), p. 155, who also points to similar expressions in Psalm 21:8; 1 Samuel 23:17; Isaiah 10:14.

25. My understanding of this important verse and the consequences that follow for understanding Saul's story are significantly influenced by V. Philips Long's excellent monograph. Long, *Saul*, see particularly pp. 51-55. An alternative understanding is that Saul's action in fulfillment of this instruction was his attack on the Ammonites in 1 Samuel 11. Gordon, *1 & 2 Samuel*, p. 118; Klein, *1 Samuel*, p. 92; Keil and Delitzsch, *Books of Samuel*, p. 101. Arguments against this interpretation are given by Long, *Saul*, pp. 51-54.

26. Long, *Saul*, pp. 64, 65.

27. In Hebrew the verb "go down" is repeated. A better translation of the second sentence of verse 8 would be, "And behold, I am coming down to you. . . ."

28. See R. L. Hubbard, Jr., "Gilgal," in Bill T. Arnold and H.G.M. Williamson, ed., *Dictionary of the Old Testament: Historical Books* (Downers Grove, IL and Leicester, UK: InterVarsity Press, 2005), pp. 334, 335.

29. Alter thinks that it is not implied that the transformation occurred immediately. Alter, *David*, p. 55.

30. The Spirit "rushing" on a man to prepare him to act as Israel's deliverer is familiar from the story of Samson in the book of Judges. In each of these cases the rushing of the Spirit is immediately followed by dramatic action (see Judges 14:6, 19; 15:14).

31. Cf. Eslinger, *Kingship*, pp. 331, 332.

32. Long argues that since the prophets are viewed positively in 1 Samuel, the people's surprise at Saul's association with them now amounts to a negative comment on Saul himself. Long, *Saul*, pp. 208, 209.

33. "Father" seems to be a reference to the leader of the group of prophets, who were also called "sons of prophets" (e.g., 1 Kings 20:35; 2 Kings 2:3). See also 2 Kings 2:12; 6:21; 13:14. Klein, *1 Samuel*, p. 93; McCarter, *I Samuel*, p. 184.

34. An alternative view, often espoused, is that the question is purely rhetorical and derogatory: these prophets are insignificant and lack a reputable leader. Gordon, *1 & 2 Samuel*, p. 119; cf. Alter, *David*, p. 57; Baldwin, *1 and 2 Samuel*, p. 92; Mauchline, *1 and 2 Samuel*, p. 100. Keil and Delitzsch propose that the question forms a very appropriate "answer" to the preceding question: "If those prophets had not obtained the gift of prophecy by inheritance, but as a free gift of the Lord, it was equally possible for the Lord to communicate the same gift to Saul." Keil and Delitzsch, *Books of Samuel*, pp. 104, 105.

35. The questions, in my opinion, express bewilderment rather than "amazement and wonder" (Klein, *1 Samuel*, p. 93).

36. Keil and Delitzsch, *Books of Samuel*, p. 105.

37. There is some debate about the meaning of the Hebrew term translated "uncle." Suggestions include "(paternal) uncle" (see 1 Samuel 14:50, where Ner, Kish's brother, is "Saul's uncle"), "kinsman," "loved one," "governor." Long, *Saul*, p. 209, note 61. The precise identity of the person concerned does not affect the point of the passage. One surprising suggestion is that the person was the commander of the garrison of the Philistines, or the Philistine governor, depending on the interpretation of the expression in verse 5 (see J. Sanmartin-Ascaso, *dodh*, in G. Johannes Botterweck and Helmer Ringgren, eds., *Theological Dictionary of the Old Testament*, Vol. 3 [Grand Rapids, MI: Eerdmans, 1978], p. 149). In my opinion decisive arguments against this speculative interpretation are provided by Eslinger. "Were this the intention of v. 14, one might wonder why the text would call this person 'Saul's governor' (v. 14) instead of 'the Philistine governor.' Moreover, why would the same words not be used as in 10.5 . . . to describe this governor?" Eslinger, *Kingship*, p. 334.

38. The suggestion that "the word of the kingdom" in 1 Samuel 10:16 means the word about *God's* kingdom will be strengthened when we consider the two further occurrences of the important term "the kingdom" in the following narrative: (literally) "the justice of the kingdom" (1 Samuel 10:25) and "renew the kingdom" (1 Samuel 11:14).

CHAPTER FIFTEEN: THE KING AND THE KINGDOM

1. Similarly C. F. Keil and F. Delitzsch, *Biblical Commentary on the Books of Samuel* (Grand Rapids, MI: Eerdmans, 1950), p. 106. Eslinger rightly takes seriously the choice of Mizpah for this assembly, in the light of the earlier assembly at this place. However, his interpretation of the significance of the choice is overly subtle and reads too much between the lines. For Eslinger, Mizpah was chosen on this second occasion as a ploy on Samuel's part to deceive the people into thinking that they were annulling the reconciliation previously made at Mizpah by rejecting the Lord in favor of a king when in fact they were being duped into accepting the Lord's appointee. Lyle M. Eslinger, *Kingship*

of God in Crisis: A Close Reading of 1 Samuel 1–12, Bible and Literature Series, 10 (Sheffield, UK: JSOT Press, 1985), p. 471, note 21. In my opinion Eslinger's interpretation, among other things, is inconsistent with the words "to the LORD" in 1 Samuel 10:17.

2. It is not clear where the quotation that begins "I brought up . . ." should end. The ESV closes the quote at the end of verse 18, presumably because the Lord speaks in the first person in verse 18, but is referred to in the third person in verse 19. It is possible, however, that the quote extends to the end of verse 19 (it is not unusual for a speaker to refer to himself in the third person). The point makes little difference, however. In this speech Samuel was speaking with the Lord's authority whether or not he was actually quoting the Lord.

3. "I" in "I brought you up . . ." is emphatic.

4. P. Kyle McCarter, Jr., *I Samuel: A New Translation with Introduction, Notes & Commentary*, The Anchor Bible, Vol. 8 (Garden City, NY: Doubleday, 1980), p. 192. Note that "today" does not mean that these words of Samuel were spoken on the same day as the events of chapter 8. They clearly were not. "Today" here is a general reference to "now." Contra Hans Wilhelm Hertzberg, *I & II Samuel: A Commentary*, Old Testament Library (London: SCM Press, 1964), p. 88, note a.

5. This is a critical part of the narrative for Lyle Eslinger's interpretation, which maintains that the people's demand for a king and rejection of the Lord was entirely justified because of the defeat of Israel at the hands of the Philistines at Aphek in 1 Samuel 4. He has to maintain that the narrator has a contrary understanding of events from both Samuel and the Lord. See Eslinger, *Kingship*, p. 342. This is far from persuasive. Eslinger's fundamental error, in my opinion, is to underestimate the significance of the Aphek incident as God's righteous judgment on Israel under corrupt leadership.

6. This typical logic in a prophet's speech announcing judgment has already been heard in 1 Samuel 2:27-36: (1) God's goodness to Eli was rehearsed (vv. 27, 28); (2) Eli's guilt was exposed (v. 29); (3) the consequent ("therefore") punishment was announced (vv. 30-36). Scholars describe prophetic speeches that follow this pattern "oracles of judgment." McCarter, *I Samuel*, p. 191.

7. Literally "And now," a different Hebrew expression from "Therefore" in 1 Samuel 2:30 (see previous note). The addition of "therefore" in the translation correctly underlines the fact that what follows is consequential on what precedes.

8. Cf. V. Philips Long, *The Reign and Rejection of King Saul*, SBL Dissertation Series, 118 (Atlanta: Scholars Press, 1989), pp. 215, 216.

9. We have noted on previous occasions that the Hebrew word translated "thousand(s)" probably refers to a less precise number of people. See 1 Samuel 4:2, 10. Here "thousands" seems to refer to a subunit of the tribes. Ralph W. Klein, *I Samuel*, Word Biblical Commentary, 10 (Nashville: Word, 1983), p. 98.

10. The parallel, but not its significance, is noted by Hertzberg, *I & II Samuel*, p. 88.

11. The ESV "was taken *by lot*" (vv. 20, 21) is interpretive. Precisely the same expression in Joshua 7:16, 17, 18 is translated simply "was taken." The same inconsistency is found in RSV and NRSV.

12. The Matrites, apparently the clan to which Kish's family belonged, are not mentioned elsewhere in the Bible.

13. "[T]he only other biblical instances of such drawing of lots among the tribes are in order to discover a culprit, and so Samuel has chosen a mechanism associated with incrimination and punishment." Robert Alter, *The David Story: A Translation with Commentary of 1 and 2 Samuel* (New York and London: W.W. Norton, 1999), p. 58. Alter fails to note, however, that there are only two other such instances (Joshua 7:16-18 and 1 Samuel 14:40-42).

14. Klein, *I Samuel*, p. 99; McCarter, *I Samuel*, p. 193.

15. A great deal has been made of this matter, and the precise wording of the question in verse 22. See the discussion in Long, *Saul*, pp. 211-215.

16. See McCarter, *I Samuel*, p. 193. Intriguingly "the baggage" features again in our narrative at 1 Samuel 17:22; 25:13; 30:24.

17. Others suggest something like "a fit of bashfulness." See Robert P. Gordon, *1 & 2 Samuel: A Commentary* (Exeter, UK: The Paternoster Press, 1986), p. 121; cf. Keil and Delitzsch, *Books of Samuel*, p. 108; Joyce Baldwin, *1 and 2 Samuel*, Tyndale Old Testament Commentaries (Leicester, UK: Inter-Varsity Press, 1988), p. 94. I agree with Eslinger that Saul's hiding presupposes that he knew (or suspected?) that the lot would fall on him. I disagree that he had necessarily made the connection between his anointing and the monarchy. Eslinger, *Kingship*, p. 347. Saul had already proven himself slow to grasp the significance of what was happening before his eyes (see 1 Samuel 9:18, 21, as well as the inaction of Saul when we expected it after 1 Samuel 10:10).

18. In his important study, V. Philips Long sees "several indications of ineptitude and timidity in Saul and of a reluctance to assume the office conferred on him by Yahweh. Saul's hiding seems to fit this picture exactly and to reflect badly on Saul." Long, *Saul*, p. 218.

19. Long plausibly argues that Saul was, nonetheless, guilty in his earlier failure to act against the Philistines. Long, *Saul*, pp. 216, 217.

20. "It would be overstating the case only slightly to say that this arrangement implies that the gift of a king is a kind of punishment . . . they shall have their king (v 19b), and (it is implied) this will be punishment enough!" McCarter, *I Samuel*, p. 195.

21. Samuel's words could well have been heard by the people as ironic. Cf. Long, *Saul*, p. 217.

22. KJV has "the manner of the kingdom"; NIV has "the regulations of the kingship"; REB has "the nature of a king."

23. So Keil and Delitzsch, *Books of Samuel*, p. 108; Gordon, *1 & 2 Samuel*, p. 340, note 57; Walter Brueggemann, *First and Second Samuel*, Interpretation: A Bible Commentary for Teaching and Preaching (Louisville: John Knox Press, 1990), p. 80. Cf. McCarter, *I Samuel*, p. 193. Contra Henry Preserved Smith, *A Critical and Exegetical Commentary on the Books of Samuel*, The International Critical Commentary (Edinburgh: T. & T. Clark, 1899), p. 74; Alter, *David*, p. 59.

24. Similarly Hertzberg, *I & II Samuel*, p. 90; Klein, *1 Samuel*, p. 100; Baldwin, *1 and 2 Samuel*, pp. 94, 95; Brueggemann, *First and Second Samuel*, pp. 80, 81.

25. The Hebrew of verse 26 could be translated: "And *even* Saul went to his home . . ." Eslinger, *Kingship*, p. 355.

26. See H. Eising, *chayil*, in G. Johannes Botterweck and Helmer Ringgren, eds., *Theological Dictionary of the Old Testament*, Vol. 4 (Grand Rapids, MI: Eerdmans, 1980), pp. 351, 352; Klein, *1 Samuel*, p. 100. Against this suggestion we might note that the same word is used of Saul's father, Kish, in 1 Samuel 9:1 (ESV, "wealth") without any obvious military connotations (although see Eising, *chayil*, p. 351).

27. Cf. Eslinger, *Kingship*, p. 356.

28. "[A] following who supported his style of kingship as it had been defined by Samuel." Baldwin, *1 and 2 Samuel*, p. 95.

29. So Eslinger, *Kingship*, pp. 356-358.

30. The ESV's "worthless fellows" represents exactly the same Hebrew expression as "worthless men" in 1 Samuel 2:12. Eslinger's interpretation, which thinks that the narrator is sympathetic to the dissenters, struggles at this point. Eslinger, *Kingship*, pp. 356-358.

31. More than this, it was not simply Saul's suitability *in himself* that they challenged, but Saul *as he had now been presented to them*. Contra Long, *Saul*, p. 212.

32. "Sons of *belial*" is a literal representation of the Hebrew. *Belial* is a Hebrew word we discussed when we considered 1 Samuel 2:12.

33. Note the echo of 1 Samuel 2:30 in the use of the verb "despise." Eslinger, *Kingship*, p. 358. The only other occurrence of this verb in 1 Samuel describes Goliath's disdain of David (1 Samuel 17:42).

34. The Hebrew is a little difficult (literally, "He was as one holding his peace"), and there is some textual uncertainty. See Gordon, *1 & 2 Samuel*, p. 122. Alter interprets the Hebrew,

"but he pretended to keep his peace." Alter, *David*, p. 59. Keil and Delitzsch, *Books of Samuel*, p. 109: "[H]e acted as if he had not heard."

35. Eslinger, *Kingship*, p. 358.

CHAPTER SIXTEEN: THE KINGDOM AT WAR

1. When we reach 1 Samuel 12:12 I will suggest that Nahash's aggression (1 Samuel 11:1) had begun about the same time as the events of chapter 8. This would mean a certain chronological overlap of the long story in chapters 9, 10 and the developing crisis in chapter 11. The two story lines then come together when the news of the threat reaches Saul (1 Samuel 11:5). The possibility that the events of chapter 11 are a flashback is mentioned by Lyle M. Eslinger, *Kingship of God in Crisis: A Close Reading of 1 Samuel 1–12*, Bible and Literature Series, 10 (Sheffield, UK: JSOT Press, 1985), p. 360, referring to the views of M. Buber. First Samuel 11:12 seems to refer back to the remarks of the "worthless fellows" in 1 Samuel 10:27, thus placing the events at the end of 1 Samuel 11 chronologically after the end of 1 Samuel 10. The Septuagint (supported by a manuscript from Qumran) has an alternative reading of 1 Samuel 10:27 that puts a gap of one month between the events of the two chapters. See REB. V. Philips Long, *The Reign and Rejection of King Saul*, SBL Dissertation Series, 118 (Atlanta: Scholars Press, 1989), p. 219, note 115 suggests that this longer reading is probably to be preferred. I am not persuaded of this.

2. The implication of 1 Samuel 12:12 is that Nahash had been involved for some time in hostilities against Israel. These appear to have predated the events of 1 Samuel 8.

3. This is the first reference to Nahash in the Bible. He subsequently appears in the record of David's life (see 2 Samuel 10:2; 17:25, 27; 1 Chronicles 19:1).

4. See J. A. Thompson, "Ammon, Ammonites," in J. D. Douglas et al, eds., *The Illustrated Bible Dictionary*, Part 1 (Leicester, UK and Wheaton, IL: Inter-Varsity Press and Tyndale House, 1980), pp. 40-43.

5. Jean-Michel de Tarragon, "Ammon (Person)," in David Noel Freedman, ed., *The Anchor Bible Dictionary*, Vol. 1 (New York: Doubleday, 1992), p. 195.

6. Cf. Hans Wilhelm Hertzberg, *I & II Samuel: A Commentary*, Old Testament Library (London: SCM Press, 1964), p. 92.

7. Cf. Eslinger, *Kingship*, p. 361.

8. We should note that the impression described in this paragraph is created by the sequence in which the narrative is told. It is probable that Nahash's aggression had begun earlier than the acclamation of Saul at Mizpah in 1 Samuel 10:24 (based on 1 Samuel 12:12). The bid for a treaty from the people of Jabesh may have occurred at about the same time as the Mizpah assembly. In any case by the time the messengers got to Gibeah, Saul was back there (1 Samuel 10:26; 11:4, 5).

9. Contra Long who argues that the silence of the Jabeshites about Saul was due to their intention to deceive Nahash. Long, *Saul*, p. 220.

10. Contra Robert P. Gordon, *1 & 2 Samuel: A Commentary* (Exeter, UK: The Paternoster Press, 1986), p. 123. C. F. Keil and F. Delitzsch, *Biblical Commentary on the Books of Samuel* (Grand Rapids, MI: Eerdmans, 1950), p. 111 suggest that the people of Jabesh had not heard of Saul's appointment as king. Cf. John Mauchline, *1 and 2 Samuel*, New Century Bible (London: Oliphants, 1971), p. 104. This is not what the text of 1 Samuel 10:18, 20, 24 implies with the repeated emphasis on the involvement of "all" the people in the process that led to Saul's acclamation as king.

11. Eslinger, *Kingship*, p. 363.

12. Nahash's granting of the seven days is not reported but is deduced by the reader from the simple fact that the messengers proposed in verse 3 do go in verse 4. Nahash's implied permission is variously interpreted as "Ammonite arrogance before Israelite impotence" (Gordon, *1 & 2 Samuel*, p. 123); "an additional opportunity to humiliate the Israelites" (Robert Alter, *The David Story: A Translation with Commentary of 1 and 2 Samuel* [New York and London: W.W. Norton, 1999], p. 61); "his feeling of absolute military

superiority" (Ralph W. Klein, *1 Samuel*, Word Biblical Commentary, 10 [Nashville: Word, 1983], p. 106); "his consciousness of the inferiority of Israel" (Hertzberg, *1 & II Samuel:* p. 92); "the easy insolence and contempt he showed" (Mauchline, *1 and 2 Samuel*, p. 104).

13. The alternative suggestion that the messengers may have deliberately gone straight to Gibeah because they had some hope in Saul (so Alter, *David*, p. 61; Hertzberg, *1 & II Samuel*, p. 92; Long, *Saul*, p. 221) does not seem likely in view of the way in which Saul is introduced to the narrative in verse 5 and the fact that he then had to ask for the news. Cf. Henry Preserved Smith, *A Critical and Exegetical Commentary on the Books of Samuel*, The International Critical Commentary (Edinburgh: T. & T. Clark, 1899), p. 78. It is, of course, possible that in the strange providence of God the messengers did go first to Gibeah, thus allowing a chronology such as that outlined by Long, *Saul*, pp. 221, 222, note 121.

14. Contra the Septuagint, which has "to Gibeah, to Saul" in place of "to Gibeah of Saul." Hertzberg, *1 & II Samuel*, p. 92.

15. Note that "of Saul" is the narrator's signal for the benefit of the reader but does not suggest that the messengers had any thought "of Saul" as they came to Gibeah.

16. Contra Long, *Saul*, pp. 223, 224 who argues that Saul may still have been the intended recipient of the message from Jabesh-gilead.

17. It is likely that Saul's work with the oxen was threshing rather than plowing. This fits well with several aspects of the context including the reference to "wheat harvest" in 1 Samuel 12:17. See J. Robert Vannoy, *Covenant Renewal at Gilgal: A Study of 1 Samuel 11:14–12:25: A Case for Literary and Theological Coherence* (Cherry Hill, NJ: Mack, 1978), p. 49.

18. Gordon, *1 & 2 Samuel*, p. 124.

19. Eslinger, *Kingship*, p. 366. Other interpretations of the double experience of the Spirit by Saul are outlined by Eslinger, *Kingship*, p. 476, note 5.

20. ESV's "messengers" in verse 7 follows the Septuagint; the Hebrew has "the messengers." Long, *Saul*, p. 222, note 125.

21. So Eslinger, *Kingship*, p. 366.

22. Baldwin goes so far as to say, "Saul's action was carefully calculated to be a reminder of the incident recorded in Judges 19." Joyce Baldwin, *1 and 2 Samuel*, Tyndale Old Testament Commentaries (Leicester, UK: Inter-Varsity Press, 1988), p. 97. It is more likely, in my opinion, that the narrator sees (and shows us) greater significance in Saul's actions than he himself knew.

23. "It is at least interesting to note that the gruesome action of the Levite in Judg 19 took place at a time when 'there was *no king* in Israel' [Judg 19:1; cf. 17:6; 18:1; 21:25]. Is there perhaps an insinuation in 1 Sam 11 that, due to Saul's inaction since his appointment to 'save Israel' [1 Sam 9:16; 10:1 (Septuagint). Cf. also the taunting question that immediately precedes chapter 11, "How can this one save us?" (10:27).], the situation has not yet much improved?" Long, *Saul*, p. 232.

24. Cf. Keil and Delitzsch, *Books of Samuel*, p. 112.

25. Eslinger, *Kingship*, pp. 368, 369; cf. Keil and Delitzsch, *Books of Samuel*, p. 112.

26. "Deliverance" in verse 9 should be rendered "salvation" (as it is in verse 13) to preserve the verbal echo in the Hebrew of "save" in verse 3.

27. Cited by Long, *Saul*, p. 220, note 116.

28. Keil and Delitzsch, *Books of Samuel*, pp. 112, 113; Smith, *Books of Samuel*, p. 79.

29. Long, *Saul*, p. 228.

Chapter Seventeen: Kingdom Renewal I

1. Contra Lyle M. Eslinger, *Kingship of God in Crisis: A Close Reading of 1 Samuel 1–12*, Bible and Literature Series, 10 (Sheffield, UK: JSOT Press, 1985), pp. 373, 374.

2. As distinct from a common meaning of the English word *kingdom*, the territory or realm ruled by a king. See Francis Brown, S. R. Driver, and Charles Briggs, *A Hebrew and English Lexicon of the Old Testament* (Oxford, UK: Clarendon Press, 1907), p. 574.

3. Cf. "The pivotal question which runs through the narratives in I Samuel 8–12 is that of how the monarchy was to be integrated with the already existing rule of Yahweh over Israel, without nullifying the latter." J. Robert Vannoy, *Covenant Renewal at Gilgal: A Study of 1 Samuel 11:14–12:25: A Case for Literary and Theological Coherence* (Cherry Hill, NY: Mack, 1978), p. 67.

4. So Eslinger, *Kingship*, p. 478, note 16.

5. Similarly *ibid.*, p. 378.

6. Several commentators see this and no more in the call to "renew the kingdom." So, in various ways, Robert Alter, *The David Story: A Translation with Commentary of 1 and 2 Samuel* (New York and London: W.W. Norton, 1999), pp. 63, 64; Joyce Baldwin, *1 and 2 Samuel*, Tyndale Old Testament Commentaries (Leicester, UK: Inter-Varsity Press, 1988), p. 98; C. F. Keil and F. Delitzsch, *Biblical Commentary on the Books of Samuel* (Grand Rapids, MI: Eerdmans, 1950), pp. 113, 114; Ralph W. Klein, *1 Samuel*, Word Biblical Commentary, 10 (Nashville: Word, 1983), p. 109; P. Kyle McCarter, Jr., *I Samuel: A New Translation with Introduction, Notes & Commentary*, The Anchor Bible, Vol. 8 (Garden City, NY: Doubleday, 1980), p. 205; Hans Wilhelm Hertzberg, *I & II Samuel: A Commentary*, Old Testament Library (London: SCM Press, 1964), p. 94; John Mauchline, *1 and 2 Samuel*, New Century Bible (London: Oliphants, 1971), pp. 105, 106.

7. Contra Eslinger who argues against Vannoy that all three occurrences of "the kingdom" refer to Saul's kingdom, although for him this also involves God's kingdom. Eslinger, *Kingship*, pp. 478, 479, note 17. Long argues more specifically against Vannoy that the kingdom on view in each case is the human kingdom of Saul. V. Philips Long, *The Reign and Rejection of King Saul*, SBL Dissertation Series, 118 (Atlanta: Scholars Press, 1989), pp. 226, 227. See also Gordon's brief dismissal of Vannoy's argument. Robert P. Gordon, *1 & 2 Samuel: A Commentary* (Exeter, UK: The Paternoster Press, 1986), p. 125.

8. I generally agree with the conclusions of J. Robert Vannoy regarding the meaning of 1 Samuel 11:14, 15. Vannoy, *Covenant Renewal*, pp. 61-91. Vannoy argues persuasively that the verb "renew" means that "something which was already established, but which subsequently had deteriorated, needed to be restored to the position of strength and validity which was proper to it." He maintains that, in the context, it was God's kingdom that needed to be "renewed" in this sense: "Strictly speaking it was not the kingdom which had deteriorated and needed renewal, but rather the recognition of the kingdom by the people." Vannoy, *Covenant Renewal*, pp. 65, 66. Long, *Saul*, pp. 227, 228 argues a contrary case that the "renewal" of the kingdom meant a public recognition that Saul's accession to the kingship was now back on track due to the victory over the Ammonites, which had overcome the problem created by Saul's failure to demonstrate his credentials earlier against the Philistines (as 1 Samuel 10:7 led us to expect). I do not think that the verb "renew" fits Long's interpretation as well as that of Vannoy.

9. Cf. Vannoy, *Covenant Renewal*, p. 67.

10. "I Samuel 11:15 is a condensed description of what took place at the Gilgal assembly. The verse functions as a sort of 'lead sentence' to the more detailed description of certain parts of the same ceremony which is contained in I Samuel 12:1-25." Vannoy, *Covenant Renewal*, p. 84.

11. "[N]owhere is it said in the report of the Mizpah assembly that Saul was 'made king,' nor is there any indication that he assumed the responsibilities and prerogatives of a newly installed king at that time." *Ibid.*, p. 87.

12. This expression "is consistently utilized to designate the official inauguration of someone's rule as king." *Ibid.*, p. 86.

13. Cf. Baldwin, *1 and 2 Samuel*, p. 98.

14. Vannoy, *Covenant Renewal*, p. 88. Vannoy also cites H. H. Rowley: "these sacrifices were for the maintenance or restoration of good relations with God." Vannoy, *Covenant*

Renewal, p. 90. Eslinger is more cautious about a specific understanding of these sacrifices but sees in this context that "the emphasis lies on the fact of reconciliation." Eslinger, *Kingship*, p. 479, note 19.

CHAPTER EIGHTEEN: KINGDOM RENEWAL II

1. The relationship between 1 Samuel 12 and its context is a matter of dispute among commentators. Some regard chapter 12 as an independent passage, with no connection to the assembly at Gilgal. See Ralph W. Klein, *1 Samuel*, Word Biblical Commentary, 10 (Nashville: Word, 1983), pp. 112, 113. Others recognize that the text as it stands seems to clearly imply that this speech was delivered at Gilgal. So C. F. Keil and F. Delitzsch, *Biblical Commentary on the Books of Samuel* (Grand Rapids, MI: Eerdmans, 1950), p. 115; P. Kyle McCarter, Jr., *I Samuel: A New Translation with Introduction, Notes & Commentary*, The Anchor Bible, Vol. 8 (Garden City, NY: Doubleday, 1980), p. 212; Hans Wilhelm Hertzberg, *I & II Samuel: A Commentary*, Old Testament Library (London: SCM Press, 1964), p. 97. Eslinger sees Samuel's speech in chapter 12 as his response to what the people did at Gilgal according to 1 Samuel 11:15. Lyle M. Eslinger, *Kingship of God in Crisis: A Close Reading of 1 Samuel 1–12*, Bible and Literature Series, 10 (Sheffield, UK: JSOT Press, 1985), p. 384. Vannoy understands Samuel in 1 Samuel 12:1 to be presenting the newly inaugurated king to the people. J. Robert Vannoy, *Covenant Renewal at Gilgal: A Study of 1 Samuel 11:14–12:25: A Case for Literary and Theological Coherence* (Cherry Hill, NJ: Mack, 1978), p. 10. It is more likely, in my opinion, that 1 Samuel 11:15 is a summary description of what happened at Gilgal, followed by a more detailed account in chapter 12. In other words, the people "made Saul king *before the LORD*" (1 Samuel 11:15) by their acceptance of Samuel's speech in 1 Samuel 12.

2. Perhaps the people *should* have seen this. Although they had not directly heard God's words to Samuel in 1 Samuel 8:7, Samuel had "told *all the words of the LORD* to the people who were asking for a king" (1 Samuel 8:10).

3. The comparison is stark in English, and even more so in the Hebrew. (a) "And now" points to a conclusion to be drawn from what has been stated in verse 1. See Francis Brown, S. R. Driver, and Charles Briggs, *A Hebrew and English Lexicon of the Old Testament* (Oxford, UK: Clarendon Press, 1907), p. 774. Compare verses 7, 10, 13, and 16 of this chapter. (b) "Behold" draws attention emphatically to what follows. (c) "The king" and "I" are both emphatic in the Hebrew. (d) Both "the king" (v. 2a) and "I" (v. 2b) are the subject of the same phrase, "walk before you," thus setting the "walk" of one beside the "walk" of the other.

4. Too much is often made of this silence by commentators (for example, John Mauchline, *1 and 2 Samuel*, New Century Bible [London: Oliphants, 1971], p. 107). A fact that is as well known as the corruption of Samuel's sons can be assumed without making the point explicit. Certainly it would not have been possible for Samuel to have *hidden* the failings of his sons by simply not mentioning their reputation. Contra Eslinger, *Kingship*, p. 386. Nor is it likely that Samuel could refer to his sons without reminding everyone of their infamy. Contra Keil and Delitzsch, *Books of Samuel*, p. 115; Hertzberg, *I & II Samuel*, p. 98; Henry Preserved Smith, *A Critical and Exegetical Commentary on the Books of Samuel*, The International Critical Commentary (Edinburgh: T. & T. Clark, 1899), p. 83.

5. "I" is emphatic in the Hebrew. Samuel was presenting himself and his "walk" in deliberate contrast to that of "the king."

6. Eslinger, *Kingship*, p. 480, note 3.

7. The Hebrew term translated in the ESV as "youth" in 1 Samuel 12:2 is cognate with the term translated "child" in 1 Samuel 1:27, "boy" in 1 Samuel 2:11, 18, and "young man" in 1 Samuel 2:21, 26; 3:1, 8.

8. Cf. Eslinger, *Kingship*, p. 388. Vannoy sees the king here as the one who "has now become the chief judicial officer in the land." Vannoy, *Covenant Renewal*, p. 14; likewise Keil and Delitzsch, *Books of Samuel*, p. 115; Robert P. Gordon, *1 & 2 Samuel: A Commentary* (Exeter, UK: The Paternoster Press, 1986), p. 126. This seems to overstate

the matter since Saul played no active role in the proceedings described in 1 Samuel 12. He is not even mentioned by name in this chapter.

9. Vannoy provides a more detailed analysis of the particular questions asked by Samuel, concluding that his purpose was "to establish publicly his adherence to the requirements of the covenantal law in the exercise of his leadership over the nation." Vannoy, *Covenant Renewal*, p. 17. The parallels he draws to particular Old Testament laws are not strong enough, in my opinion, to constitute definite allusions to these laws in Samuel's questions. Nonetheless we are hardly surprised to find that the crimes he cites are in one way or another prohibited by the Law.

10. Cf. Moses' similar self-vindication in Numbers 16:15. Vannoy, *Covenant Renewal*, pp. 15, 16.

11. The Hebrew verb is singular, probably because "all Israel," thought of as a united body, is the subject. Cf. Keil and Delitzsch, *Books of Samuel*, p. 116.

12. The Hebrew does not have "is witness." It is as though Samuel rather sharply completed the one-word reply by the people in verse 5b by identifying the one who was indeed "Witness": "The LORD, who . . . ." Cf. Eslinger, *Kingship*, p. 390. In this way he shifted the subject of his speech from his own conduct before the people to the Lord and his ways with them.

13. Eslinger proposes that "And now" introducing both verses 2 and 7 set the two sections (vv. 2-6 and 7-12 in his analysis) in relation to verse 1, "which gives the basic datum to which all of Samuel's reviews are related." *Ibid.*, p. 393. Attractive as this suggestion is, it does not, in my opinion, give sufficient weight to verses 1a and 6a as structural markers for the passage. This is not to deny that verse 1 is foundational to Samuel's whole speech.

14. Cf. Vannoy, *Covenant Renewal*, p. 25.

15. This is the last occurrence of this verb in 1 Samuel with a human subject. It occurs in 1 Samuel 24:12, 15 (Hebrew, verses 13, 16) with the Lord as subject.

16. Vannoy, *Covenant Renewal*, p. 24, note 42. Cf. Robert Alter, *The David Story: A Translation with Commentary of 1 and 2 Samuel* (New York and London: W.W. Norton, 1999), p. 66 who translates this, "that I may seek judgment with you . . ."

17. The expression (literally) "righteousnesses of the LORD" or an equivalent are only found in the Old Testament here and in Judges 5:11; Micah 6:5; Psalm 103:6; Daniel 9:16. Vannoy, *Covenant Renewal*, pp. 26-31.

18. Cf. E. R. Achtemeier, "Righteousness in the OT," in George Arthur Buttrick, ed., *The Interpreter's Dictionary of the Bible*, Vol. 4 (Nashville and New York: Abingdon Press, 1962), pp. 80-85. Also Vannoy, *Covenant Renewal*, pp. 27-31. Vannoy quotes John Calvin's illuminating comment on Daniel 9:16:

> Those who take this word "righteousness" to mean "judgment" are in error and inexperienced in interpreting the Scriptures; for they suppose God's justice to be opposed to his pity. But we are familiar with God's righteousness as made manifest, especially in the benefits he confers on us. It is just as if Daniel had said that the single hope of the people consisted in God's having regard to himself alone, and by no means to their conduct. Hence he takes the righteousness of God for his liberality, gratuitous favor, consistent fidelity, and protection, which he promised his servants. (John Calvin, *Commentaries on the Book of the Prophet Daniel, II* (Grand Rapids, MI: Eerdmans, 1948), p. 177.

19. This is not to deny that "this place" may also point to the land of Canaan as a whole. So Keil and Delitzsch, *Books of Samuel*, p. 117.

20. The Hebrew lacks the words "and the Egyptians oppressed them," which are found in the Septuagint. Since the oppression is implied in the people's cry for help, it seems more likely that the Septuagint has added the phrase than that the Hebrew text has omitted it. So Vannoy, *Covenant Renewal*, p. 31, note 62; Alter, *David*, p. 66. Contra McCarter, *I Samuel*, p. 210; Klein, *1 Samuel*, p. 111; Smith, *Books of Samuel*, p. 85.

21. In the very brief summary that we find in 1 Samuel 12:8, therefore, the proposition that "Moses and Aaron . . . made them dwell in this place" (compare Exodus 3:17) is not the

problem that many commentators make out. For example McCarter, *I Samuel*, p. 210; Smith, *Books of Samuel*, p. 85. In support of the Hebrew text see Vannoy, *Covenant Renewal*, p. 31, note 63; Klein, *1 Samuel*, p. 111.

22. The Hebrew text has the name "Bedan," where the Septuagint has "Barak." Since Bedan is otherwise unknown as a judge, many commentators conclude that "Bedan" in the Hebrew text is an error. So Keil and Delitzsch, *Books of Samuel*, p. 118; Smith, *Books of Samuel*, p. 86. Vannoy supports the suggestion that rather than an error, Bedan was another name for Barak, just as Gideon was also known as Jerubbaal. Vannoy, *Covenant Renewal*, pp. 32, 33, note 66. Alter prefers to accept that the list of judges in the book of Judges is not exhaustive. Alter, *David*, p. 67.

23. A possible chronology for the story in 1 Samuel 9, 10: Day 1: Saul set out in search for the donkeys (1 Samuel 9:3), and the Lord spoke to Samuel (1 Samuel 9:15, 16). Day 2: Saul met Samuel (1 Samuel 9:14, 17-21), and they ate together (1 Samuel 9:22-24). Day 3: Samuel anointed Saul and made known the word of God (1 Samuel 9:27–10:8), and Saul returned to Gibeah (1 Samuel 10:9-16). Day 4: the assembly at Mizpah occurred (1 Samuel 10:17-27). The news from Jabesh-gilead may have reached Saul (1 Samuel 11:5) on Day 5. However, there are also points where there may have been a longer time period (for example, between 1 Samuel 8:22 and 9:1ff., or between 1 Samuel 10:16 and 17).

24. In my opinion Eslinger is way off the mark in setting the narrator's account of the people's motivation *against* that of Samuel here. Eslinger, *Kingship*, pp. 401, 402. He fails to appreciate that (a) Samuel is established in this narrative as a true prophet of the Lord whose words can be trusted, (b) that in chapter 8 we only have the elders' word on the motive for their request (1 Samuel 8:5), and (c) the narrator, as we have seen, seems to reveal the absurdity of the elders' own argument for a monarchy (a dynastic system to solve the problem of corrupt sons). In my opinion it makes very good sense of the text to see Samuel now exposing the true motivation for the request. Cf. Vannoy, *Covenant Renewal*, pp. 38-40.

25. Following Vannoy, *Covenant Renewal*, p. 41; Eslinger, *Kingship*, p. 405.

26. Vannoy, *Covenant Renewal*, p. 42.

27. Eslinger makes the interesting suggestion that the Lord's "mouth" may be a reference to Samuel. Eslinger, *Kingship*, p. 413.

28. For a review of approaches to this difficult text critical problem see Eslinger, *Kingship*, pp. 485, 486, note 23. The emendation followed in the ESV is supported by Alter, *David*, p. 68, who regards the Hebrew as making "no sense." Similarly Gordon, *1 & 2 Samuel*, p. 129.

29. An alternative rendering of the Hebrew text is followed by the NIV, which retains "fathers" but interprets "and" in a comparative sense: "his hand will be against you, *as it was* against your fathers." Cf. Vannoy, *Covenant Renewal*, p. 46, note 104; Keil and Delitzsch, *Books of Samuel*, p. 119. This makes the threat less serious than I have suggested above, for then the apostasy involved in requesting a king would be just *like* the apostasy of the fathers referred to in verse 9. However, this interpretation of "and" is questionable (Eslinger, *Kingship*, p. 485, note 23; Gordon, *1 & 2 Samuel*, p. 129), and Samuel's speech seems to indicate that the evil of asking for a king surpassed all previous rebellions (see vv. 17, 19).

30. So Vannoy, *Covenant Renewal*, pp. 47, 48.

31. Alter, *David*, p. 68.

32. Eslinger, *Kingship*, p. 411.

33. So Eslinger, *Kingship*, p. 488, note 29.

34. Vannoy, *Covenant Renewal*, p. 50.

35. "The idea that Yahweh will do certain things for the sake of his own name is equivalent to saying that Yahweh will be faithful to his own self revelation. Yahweh cannot deny himself." *Ibid.*, p. 56.

36. Contra Eslinger, *Kingship*, pp. 423, 424 who limits this to the thunderstorm of 1 Samuel 12:18.

37. As Vannoy, *Covenant Renewal*, pp. 59, 60.

CHAPTER NINETEEN: THE FOOL

1. Likewise Robert P. Gordon, *1 & 2 Samuel: A Commentary* (Exeter, UK: The Paternoster Press, 1986), p. 132; Robert Alter, *The David Story: A Translation with Commentary of 1 and 2 Samuel* (New York and London: W.W. Norton, 1999), p. 70; P. Kyle McCarter, Jr., *I Samuel: A New Translation with Introduction, Notes & Commentary*, The Anchor Bible, Vol. 8 (Garden City, NY: Doubleday, 1980), pp. 222, 223; Ralph W. Klein, *1 Samuel*, Word Biblical Commentary, 10 (Nashville: Word, 1983), p. 122; Joyce Baldwin, *1 and 2 Samuel*, Tyndale Old Testament Commentaries (Leicester, UK: Inter-Varsity Press, 1988), pp. 102, 103; Hans Wilhelm Hertzberg, *I & II Samuel: A Commentary*, Old Testament Library (London: SCM Press, 1964), p. 103; C. F. Keil and F. Delitzsch, *Biblical Commentary on the Books of Samuel* (Grand Rapids, MI: Eerdmans, 1950), pp. 122-124.

2. Here I am indebted to a footnote in V. Philips Long's excellent monograph in which he points to the solution suggested by the medieval Jewish commentator Isaac Abrabanel. This is not Long's preferred solution (although he raises no objections to it). V. Philips Long, *The Reign and Rejection of King Saul*, SBL Dissertation Series, 118 (Atlanta: Scholars Press, 1989), p. 75, note 30.

3. The chronology of these chapters is far from clear (suggesting that it is not vital for understanding the narrative as it is intended to be understood). However, if we are looking for a time gap that would make the period from 1 Samuel 10:1 to 1 Samuel 11:15 a year, I would suggest between 1 Samuel 10:16 and 17.

4. It has been argued that the battles with the Philistines of 1 Samuel 13, 14 occurred in Saul's first year as king and that the battle in 1 Samuel 29–31, which was the Philistine response to these, took place in Saul's second year. See the summary in John Mauchline, *1 and 2 Samuel*, New Century Bible (London: Oliphants, 1971), p. 111.

5. One objection to this understanding is that the summary of Saul's reign found in 1 Samuel 14:47-52 seems to indicate a period much longer than two years. So Keil and Delitzsch, *Books of Samuel*, p. 124. However, 1 Samuel 13:1, coming immediately after the theologically loaded speech of Samuel in 1 Samuel 12, may view Saul's reign in strictly theological terms, whereas the summary at the end of 1 Samuel 14 comprehends "all the days of Saul" (v. 52).

6. John Mauchline supports this understanding of "two years" in 1 Samuel 13:1: "Saul remained king *de facto* even although he had ceased . . . to be king *de iure.*" Mauchline, *1 and 2 Samuel*, p. 111. Without following this understanding of 1 Samuel 13:1, Robert Gordon presents 1 Samuel 13:1–15:35 under the title "The Reign of Saul." "Saul's rule under Yahweh's aegis ends with ch. 15." Gordon, *1 & 2 Samuel*, p. 131.

7. In seeing the key significance of this twofold instruction for understanding the events of 1 Samuel 13, 14, I am following the thesis of V. Philips Long. See Long, *Saul*, p. 78.

8. Others suggest that many years separate the events of chapter 10 and those of chapter 13. So Gordon, *1 & 2 Samuel*, p. 133.

9. Patrick M. Arnold, "Michmash," in David Noel Freedman, ed., *The Anchor Bible Dictionary*, Vol. 4 (New York: Doubleday, 1992), pp. 814, 815.

10. For some suggestions see Long, *Saul*, pp. 82, 83.

11. So Alter, *David*, p. 70. See Long, *Saul*, p. 44, note 6.

12. Francis Brown, S. R. Driver, and Charles Briggs, *A Hebrew and English Lexicon of the Old Testament* (Oxford, UK: Clarendon Press, 1907), p. 1051.

13. More literally the Hebrew says, "the people were called after Saul to Gilgal."

14. Robert Alter captures the implied passivity of Saul in his translation: "And the people rallied round Saul at Gilgal." Alter, *David*, p. 71.

15. The mention of Beth-aven, the location of which is now disputed, is intended to clarify not so much the position of Michmash but of the Philistine camp. Long, *Saul*, p. 83, note 75.

16. Of course, we must remember that the Hebrew word translated "thousand" may not be a number but a reference to a military unit. See 1 Samuel 4:2.

17. V. Philips Long persuasively agues that "I *forced myself*, and offered the burnt offering" in 1 Samuel 13:12b should be rendered, "I *restrained myself* (i.e. *pulled myself together when the temptation was to flee*) and offered the burnt offering." "According to this reading, Saul would not be admitting to a breach of conscience, as commonly assumed, but, on the contrary, would be claiming to have acted in a self-controlled and even heroic manner." Long, *Saul*, p. 89.

18. Long, *Saul*, pp. 88, 89.

19. Similarly Gordon, *1 & 2 Samuel*, p. 134.

20. Baldwin, *1 and 2 Samuel*, p. 106.

21. This would be true of either location for Geba since Gibeah, the alternative site for Geba, and Michmash lay in approximately a straight line from the southwest to the northeast.

22. See Long, *Saul*, pp. 97, 98.

CHAPTER TWENTY: A LEADER WHO TRUSTED GOD

1. ESV and most English versions have here "One day."

2. Cf. NIV.

3. "Carried" in verse 1 and "wearing" in verse 3 represent the same Hebrew verb. See Robert Alter, *The David Story: A Translation with Commentary of 1 and 2 Samuel* (New York and London: W.W. Norton, 1999), p. 76.

4. See the helpful summary of the evidence concerning the ephod and the Urim and Thummim in C. Van Dam, "Priestly Clothing," in T. Desmond Alexander and David W. Baker, eds., *Dictionary of the Old Testament: Pentateuch* (Leicester, UK and Downers Grove, IL: Inter-Varsity Press, 2003), pp. 643, 644.

5. "His own glory gone, where else would we expect Saul to be than with a relative of 'Glory gone'?" D. Jobling, "Saul's Fall and Jonathan's Rise: Tradition and Redaction in 1 Sam 14:1-46," *Journal of Biblical Literature* 95 (1976), p. 368, cited by Long, *Saul*, p. 106.

6. See the perceptive study of this theme in D. Broughton Knox, *Selected Works, Volume I: The Doctrine of God*, ed. Tony Payne (Kingsford, Australia: Matthias Media, 2000), pp. 51-72.

7. Literally, "I am with you according to your heart," which means, "I am in agreement with your decision and purpose." This expression is worth comparing to the very similar one in 1 Samuel 13:14, where the new king will be, literally, "according to his [God's] heart."

8. There is no persuasive reason to prefer the Septuagint "ephod" over the Hebrew "ark" here, as many commentators do. For example Alter, *David*, p. 79.

CHAPTER TWENTY-ONE: DISOBEDIENCE AND FOOLISHNESS

1. V. Philips Long, *The Reign and Rejection of King Saul*, SBL Dissertation Series, 118 (Atlanta: Scholars Press, 1989), pp. 114, 115 provides a careful argument for the understanding represented here and reflected in the ESV.

2. NIV (following KJV, RSV) suggests that Saul's oath was the cause, rather than the consequence, of the people's distress. The Hebrew syntax, however, supports the ESV. "Syntactically, therefore, v. 24 suggests that the distress of the men of Israel may have *prompted* rather than resulted from Saul's oath." Long, *Saul*, p. 114.

3. See P. E. Hughes, "Blood," in T. Desmond Alexander and David W. Baker, eds., *Dictionary of the Old Testament: Pentateuch* (Leicester, UK and Downers Grove, IL: Intervarsity Press, 2003), pp. 87-90.

4. It is not at all clear, as most English versions imply, that Saul built other altars. Verse 35 could be translated literally: "So Saul built an altar to the LORD — that is, he began to build an altar to the LORD." For details see Long, *Saul*, pp. 121-123.

5. *Ibid.*, p. 124.

6. There are major textual issues in verses 41, 42. The ESV (like the RSV and NRSV) has largely followed the Septuagint, without indicating in its footnotes (as do the RSV and NRSV) the extent of its departure from the briefer Hebrew (the ESV footnote is misleading). The Hebrew is followed by the NIV. There are reasons to suspect that the priestly use of Urim and Thummim, as was probably done in verse 37, was different from casting lots, as was done in verses 41, 42 if the Hebrew text is followed. The distinction is unfortunately lost in the ESV. See Cornelis Van Dam, *The Urim and Thummim: A Means of Revelation in Ancient Israel* (Winona Lake, IN: Eisenbrauns, 1997), pp. 197-203.

7. Long, *Saul*, p. 130.

CHAPTER TWENTY-TWO: THE LEADER WHO LET THEM DOWN

1. Among many case studies of the damage that can come from leaders who assume too much power over their people is the recent account of a group in Melbourne, Australia by Morag Zwartz, *Fractured Families: The Story of a Melbourne Church Cult* (Boronia, Victoria, Australia: Parenesis Publishing, 2004).

2. "It is as a uniquely dangerous and perpetual challenger to the divine order of YHWH that the Amalekite nation appears in the Bible." Philips P. Stern, *The Biblical Herem: A Window on Israel's Religious Experience*, Brown Judaic Studies, 211 (Atlanta: Scholars Press, 1991), p. 174.

3. Gerald L. Mattingly, "Amalek," in David Noel Freedman, ed., *The Anchor Bible Dictionary*, Vol. 1 (New York: Doubleday, 1992), pp. 169-171.

4. Examples of the use of this term include Exodus 22:20; Leviticus 27:29; Numbers 21:2, 3; Deuteronomy 7:2; 20:17; Joshua 6:17, 18, 21; 7:1, 11-15. See A. C. Emery, "*Herem*," in T. Desmond Alexander and David W. Baker, eds., *Dictionary of the Old Testament: Pentateuch* (Leicester, UK and Downers Grove, IL: InterVarsity Press, 2003), pp. 383-387; Stern, *Herem*.

5. The title given to God here, "the LORD of hosts," appears four times in 1 Samuel (1:3; 4:4; 15:2; 17:45), and not before this book in the Old Testament. "Hosts" refers to the heavenly powers at God's command, as well as perhaps to the armies of Israel (see 1 Samuel 17:45) who are to do his work. While this title for God will be used many times by the prophets, there is something very solemn about this, its third occurrence in the Bible as his judgment on Amalek is announced.

6. E.g., "The institution of the 'ban', like the whole concept of the holy war, is far removed from the Christian code of the New Testament and must be seen in the context of the provisional morality of the Old Testament." Robert P. Gordon, *1 & 2 Samuel: A Commentary* (Exeter, UK: The Paternoster Press, 1986), p. 147. Gordon, however, goes on to helpfully qualify this statement.

7. For an argument that the Amalekites of 1 Samuel 15 were an enclave of the group occupying the hills of western Samaria, while the main Amalekite population was to the southeast of Judah, see Diana Edelman, "Saul's Battle Against Amaleq (1 Sam. 15)," *Journal for the Study of the Old Testament* 35 (1986), pp. 71-84.

8. Gordon, *1 & 2 Samuel*, p. 143.

9. The verb "spared" is singular, suggesting in Hebrew "that Saul is the principal actor and the troops only accessories." Robert Alter, *The David Story: A Translation with Commentary of 1 and 2 Samuel* (New York and London: W.W. Norton, 1999), p. 88.

10. "Repentance in God is not, as it is in us, a change of his mind, but a change of his method or dispensation. He does not alter his will, but wills an alteration." Leslie F. Church, ed., *Matthew Henry's Commentary on the Whole Bible in One Volume* (London and Edinburgh: Marshall Morgan & Scott, 1960), p. 302. "God is not slavishly bound by his own decisions, but is almighty to such an extent that he is Lord even of them. Just as he takes the action of men into consideration in his decisions, so that omnipotence never means that man is deprived of his responsibility, so, too, the election of the king is not irrevocable." Hans Wilhelm Hertzberg, *I & II Samuel: A Commentary*, Old Testament Library (London: SCM Press, 1964), p. 126. ". . . this does not express any changeableness in the divine nature, but simply the sorrow of the divine love at the rebellion of

sinners. . . ." C. F. Keil and F. Delitzsch, *Biblical Commentary on the Books of Samuel* (Grand Rapids, MI: Eerdmans, 1950), p. 153.

11. The particular Hebrew verb form used here appears a number of times in the Old Testament with God as subject. In several of these God "relents" (Amos 7:3, [= 6]) or does not "relent" (Jeremiah 4:28; 15:6; 20:16; Ezekiel 24:14; Zechariah 8:14) from some punishment he has announced. In just two contexts God "regrets" some other action: the creation of humanity (Genesis 6:6) and the appointment of Saul (1 Samuel 15:11, 35). See H. Simian-Yofre, *nhm*, in G. Johannes Botterweck, Helmer Ringgren, and Heinz-Joseph Fabry, *Theological Dictionary of the Old Testament*, Vol. 9 (Grand Rapids, MI: Eerdmans, 1998), pp. 340-355.

12. One commentator describes this as "a state of stress and anguish in which disappointment, anger and frustration were all intermingled." John Mauchline, *1 and 2 Samuel*, New Century Bible (London: Oliphants, 1971), p. 124.

13. A helpful study of the different approaches to physical violence in Islam and Christianity is Michael Raiter, *Contending for God in Islam and Christianity* (Lilydale, Australia: Bible College of Victoria, 2002).

CHAPTER TWENTY-THREE: THE REJECTED KING

1. This location is mentioned in 1 Samuel 25:2, 5, 7, 40; 27:3; 30:5. LaMoine F. DeVries, "Carmel," in David Noel Freedman, ed., *The Anchor Bible Dictionary*, Vol. 1 (New York: Doubleday, 1992), p. 873.

2. V. Philips Long, *The Reign and Rejection of King Saul*, SBL Dissertation Series, 118 (Atlanta: Scholars Press, 1989), p. 142.

3. Compare Absalom's arrogant monument "set up for himself" in 2 Samuel 18:18.

4. So Long argues in the light of verses 21, 25, and 30. Long, *Saul*, pp. 143, 144.

5. So, correctly, the NIV. See Long, *Saul*, p. 145.

6. Here I am disagreeing with both V. Philips Long ("In short: Saul is bluffing," Long, *Saul*, p. 146) and David Gunn ("there is essentially no failure on Saul's part to be accounted for, no failure, that is to say, for which he can be held seriously accountable." David M. Gunn, *The Fate of King Saul: An Interpretation of a Biblical Story*, Journal for the Study of the Old Testament Supplement Series 14 [Sheffield, UK: JSOT Press, 1980], p. 56). I propose that it is sin's deceitfulness that accounts for the fact that in the narrator's view Saul was certainly culpable (contra Gunn), but that it is quite possible that he was blind to his culpability (contra Long).

7. "The question seems to be a rebuke of Saul's self-confessed subservience to the people." Henry Preserved Smith, *A Critical and Exegetical Commentary on the Books of Samuel*, The International Critical Commentary (Edinburgh: T. & T. Clark, 1899), p. 136. "Samuel draws a contrast between Saul's apparent minimalist view of his royal responsibilities and what is actually required." Long, *Saul*, p. 147.

8. Cf. Achan (Joshua 7:25). See Diana Vikander Edelman, *King Saul in the Historiography of Judah*, Journal for the Study of the Old Testament Supplement Series 121 (Sheffield, UK: Sheffield Academic Press, 1991), p. 294; Meir Sternberg, *The Poetics of Biblical Narrative: Ideological Reading and the Drama of Reading*, Indiana Studies in Biblical Literature (Bloomington, IN: Indiana University Press, 1987), p. 498.

9. Unfortunately, most modern translations (ESV, NIV, NRSV) obscure this important verbal echo by translating 2 Samuel 11:27 with an expression like "the thing that David had done displeased the LORD" (ESV).

10. Saul's disobedient action is described in terms similar to the behavior of the people in 1 Samuel 14:32. According to an emendation of the Hebrew text at 1 Samuel 14:32 accepted by many (e.g., ESV, NIV, NRSV), the same verb (ESV, "pounced") is used in both places.

11. See Long, *Saul*, p. 149.

12. Cf. *ibid.*, p. 146.

13. Which Saul would later practice (1 Samuel 28). Robert Alter notes "Saul's repeated attempts to divine the future." Robert Alter, *The David Story: A Translation with*

Commentary of 1 and 2 Samuel (New York and London: W.W. Norton, 1999), p. 91. The pagan nature of divination was exemplified in the Philistine practice reported in 1 Samuel 6:2.

14. "Whatever favourable light now falls upon Saul for his candour is dimmed by the realization of how misguided, if not perjurious, his earlier asseverations had been." Long, *Saul*, p. 155.

15. Strangely the ESV (correctly) has "bow down before" in verses 30, 31. Verse 25 would be better translated "that I may bow down before the LORD." NIV and NRSV has "worship" in all three verses, which has the advantage of consistency but the disadvantage of over-interpreting Saul's action.

16. See Gunn, *Saul*, p. 74.

17. "Democracy is no more acceptable a replacement for prophetic theocracy than is monarchy!" P. Kyle McCarter, Jr., *I Samuel: A New Translation with Introduction, Notes & Commentary*, The Anchor Bible, Vol. 8 (Garden City, NY: Doubleday, 1980), p. 270.

18. The Hebrew here has a certain ambiguity, and there has been a debate as to who tore whose robe. However, the ESV makes best sense in context. See Long, *Saul*, pp. 157-163.

19. Note how Samuel's robe features at three critical points in his story: it was an expression of his mother's care in his days at Shiloh (1 Samuel 2:19); it became the symbol of Saul's lost kingdom here (1 Samuel 15:27, 28); it was the means by which Saul recognized the dead Samuel (1 Samuel 28:14). Saul will eventually have his own robe cut by another (1 Samuel 24:4, 11).

20. The Hebrew text has the same verb for "regret" in verses 11, 29, 35.

21. ". . . the contradiction of v 11 ('I [Yahweh!] repent . . .') that this statement ('Israel's Everlasting One . . . does not repent . . .') contains is so blatant that we must question its originality." McCarter, *I Samuel*, p. 268. Cf. Alter, *David*, p. 92.

22. We might say, "from an eternal perspective" because the expression "the Glory of Israel" may be better translated "the Eternal of Israel." Cf. Alter, *David*, p. 92.

23. The verb "honor" could be translated "glorify." It belongs to the same word group as "Ichabod" and "glory" in 1 Samuel 4:21, 22.

24. Long, *Saul*, p. 164.

25. Note the emphasis there that Israel was *the Lord's* people.

26. "Perhaps in recognition of the long-awaited candour of Saul's revised 'confession', or perhaps because he has unfinished business to attend to in Gilgal, Samuel reverses his earlier decision (v. 26) and consents to return with Saul (v. 31). After what has transpired, there is at any rate no longer any danger that Saul might misinterpret this action as a relaxation of his sentence." Long, *Saul*, p. 164. Strangely Robert Alter has argued (against all English versions) that verse 31 uses the same idiom as verse 11 and says "Samuel turned back *from* Saul": "Samuel is completing his rejection of Saul here by refusing to accompany him in the cult, shaming him by forcing him to offer the sacrifice without the officiating man of God." Alter, *David*, p. 93. Alter has missed the fact that verse 11 has the preposition "from," while verse 31 does not.

27. The fact that there was an encounter of sorts between Samuel and Saul in 1 Samuel 19:24 appears to account for the KJV rendering of 1 Samuel 15:35: "Samuel came no more to see Saul." The NIV has followed this attempt at harmonization ("he did not go to see Saul again"), but the effort is not necessary, nor is it justified by the Hebrew. The point is that "Samuel and Saul no longer have business in common, and a meeting like that recorded in 19:24 does not come into the reckoning." Robert P. Gordon, *1 & 2 Samuel: A Commentary* (Exeter, UK: The Paternoster Press, 1986), p. 147.

CHAPTER TWENTY-FOUR: SEEING AS GOD SEES

1. "A towering figure in Israel's history." Martin Kessler, "Narrative Technique in 1 Sm 16,1-13," *The Catholic Biblical Quarterly* 32 (1970), p. 547. See Jeremiah 15:1.

2. The implicit rebuke in the words "How long?" is seen in the use of precisely this expression in 1 Samuel 1:14; 2 Samuel 2:26. See *ibid.*, p. 547, note 21.

3. The word "city" in verse 4 should probably be translated more appropriately "town."

4. In Hebrew the verb "to see" occurs seven times in the chapter: once in verse 1 (ESV, "provided"), once in verse 6 (ESV, "looked on"), three times in verse 7 (ESV, "sees" and "looks"), once in verse 17 (ESV, "provide"), and once in verse 18 (ESV, "seen").

5. My translation.

6. Hans Wilhelm Hertzberg, *I & II Samuel: A Commentary*, Old Testament Library (London: SCM Press, 1964), p. 137.

7. Robert Alter, *The David Story: A Translation with Commentary of 1 and 2 Samuel* (New York and London: W.W. Norton, 1999), p. 95.

8. I doubt very much that the Lord was here giving Samuel "a cover story for his trip from Ramah to Bethlehem." *Ibid.*, p. 95. Gunn argues similarly: "The anointing of David is carried out by subterfuge involving, ironically, the pretence that the real purpose of Samuel's excursion is to offer sacrifice." David M. Gunn, *The Fate of King Saul: An Interpretation of a Biblical Story*, Journal for the Study of the Old Testament Supplement Series 14 (Sheffield, UK: JSOT Press, 1980), p. 77. On the contrary, however, the anointing of a king *would* involve offering sacrifices (see 1 Samuel 11:15), and here, therefore, Samuel's commission in verse 1 was simply reiterated with more details made explicit.

9. There is some textual uncertainty about the words "The LORD sees," but this does not affect the overall sense. See John Mauchline, *1 and 2 Samuel*, New Century Bible (London: Oliphants, 1971), p. 129.

10. This straightforward way of translating the Hebrew is rarely noted by commentators. However, see Alter, *David*, p. 96; Roger L. Omanson and John E. Ellington, *A Handbook on The First and Second Books of Samuel*, Vol. 1, UBS Handbook Series (New York: United Bible Societies, 2001), p. 339; and Diana Vikander Edelman, *King Saul in the Historiography of Judah*, Journal for the Study of the Old Testament Supplement Series 121 (Sheffield, UK: Sheffield Academic Press, 1991), p. 115 ("Yahweh's critical statement that he sees in accordance with the heart, whereas man sees in accordance with the eyes").

11. To be a little more technical, I am suggesting that in 1 Samuel 13:14 the phrase "after [or according to] his own heart" qualifies the verb "sought out," not the noun "man." This could be represented more clearly in English by "According to his own heart the LORD has sought out a man. . . ."

12. "This has nothing to do with any great fondness of Yahweh for David or any special quality of David . . . . Rather it emphasizes the free divine selection of the heir of the throne. . . ." P. Kyle McCarter, Jr., *I Samuel: A New Translation with Introduction, Notes & Commentary*, The Anchor Bible, Vol. 8 (Garden City, NY: Doubleday, 1980), p. 229. McCarter draws attention to Psalm 20:4 and Jeremiah 3:15 as examples of the same or a similar idiom. See also Robert P. Gordon, *1 & 2 Samuel: A Commentary* (Exeter, UK: The Paternoster Press, 1986), p. 134.

13. The only differences are the pronoun "his" and "your" (in each case referring to God), and a very slight difference in the Hebrew word for "heart." Importantly, "according to" in 2 Samuel 7:21 and "after" in 1 Samuel 13:14 represent the same Hebrew preposition.

14. The Lord also "chose" Aaron to be his priest (1 Samuel 2:28). We have already noted that the Lord "chose" Saul (1 Samuel 10:24), although Saul is first called the one "chosen" by the people (1 Samuel 8:18; cf. 12:13), and later the one *rejected* by God (1 Samuel 15:23). However, the Lord's "choice" of David becomes an important Biblical theme (2 Samuel 6:21; 1 Kings 8:16; 11:34; 1 Chronicles 28:4-6; Psalm 78:70; 89:19; cf. Deuteronomy 17:15), comparable to Israel as his "chosen" people (Deuteronomy 4:37; 7:6; 10:15; 14:2; 1 Kings 3:8; Psalm 33:12; Isaiah 14:1; 41:8, 9; 44:1, 2; Jeremiah 33:24; Ezekiel 20:5), and Jerusalem as his "chosen" city (Deuteronomy 12:5, 11, 14, 18, 21, 26; 14:23-25; 15:20; 16:2, 6, 7, 11, 15, 16; 26:2; 31:11; Joshua 9:27; 1 Kings 8:44, 48; 11:13, 32, 36; 14:21; 2 Kings 21:7; 23:27; Zechariah 1:17; 3:2; Psalm 78:68; 132:13; Nehemiah 1:9; 2 Chronicles 6:6, 34, 38; 7:12; 12:13; 33:7). The servant of the Lord, of whom Isaiah spoke, was the Lord's "chosen" (Isaiah 41:8, 9; 43:10; 49:7).

15. Here I am disagreeing in the strongest terms with an assessment such as that of David Hill: "The few references we have to the gift of the spirit to David and to Saul prove that the endowment of power for leadership came to them because they were of upright and obedient character, because they possessed the qualities necessary for kingship over the people of God." David Hill, *Greek Words and Hebrew Meanings: Studies in the Semantics of Soteriological Terms*, Society for New Testament Studies Monograph Series 5 (Cambridge, UK: Cambridge University Press, 1967), pp. 210, 211, note 2.

16. As the ESV notes in the margin, "youngest" in verse 11 could be translated "smallest."

17. "Handsome" is more literally "good appearance."

CHAPTER TWENTY-FIVE: TWO KINGS: A CONFUSING WORLD

1. In both Hebrew and Greek the word usually translated "spirit" also means "wind" or "breath." See John Woodhouse, "The 'Spirit' in the Book of Ezekiel," in B. G. Webb, ed., *The Spirit of the Living God: Part One*, Explorations, 5 (Homebush West, Australia: Lancer, 1991), pp. 1-22.

2. "Put shortly, the presence of the Spirit of God in the Old Testament is normally confined to the leadership of Israel and has in view the preservation of the concept of the theocracy; or otherwise stated, the theological function of the Spirit appears to be to implement and sustain the Old Testament notion of the Kingdom of God." W. J. Dumbrell, "Spirit and Kingdom of God in the Old Testament," *Reformed Theological Review* 33/1 (1974), p. 1.

3. With regard to Moses see Numbers 11:17, 25 (cf. Nehemiah 9:20); regarding Joshua see Numbers 27:18; Deuteronomy 34:9.

4. For example, Othniel (Judges 3:10), Gideon (Judges 6:34), Jephthah (Judges 11:29), Samson (Judges 13:25).

5. The only place in the Old Testament, other than those mentioned above, where we read of "spirit" "rushing" upon anyone is 1 Samuel 18:10, where "a harmful spirit from God rushed upon [or into] Saul."

6. There may be an additional hint of the difference in what happened to David in the fact that the preposition "upon" represents a different Hebrew word (which usually means "to" or "into") in 1 Samuel 16:13 than that found in the other texts about the Spirit rushing "upon" people.

7. "With David the spirit seems to be almost a direct result of the anointing, and it lasts permanently (cf. 30:25), and not spasmodically as it had with Saul." Ralph W. Klein, *1 Samuel*, Word Biblical Commentary, 10 (Nashville: Word, 1983), p. 162.

8. If, as I suspect, there was a considerable time period between verses 13 and 14, "departed" may be better translated "had departed" (as in NIV). So Robert Alter, *The David Story: A Translation with Commentary of 1 and 2 Samuel* (New York and London: W.W. Norton, 1999), p. 98; John Mauchline, *1 and 2 Samuel*, New Century Bible (London: Oliphants, 1971), p. 130.

9. Just as he had earlier abandoned Samson; see Judges 16:20 where "the LORD had left him" is, in Hebrew, a very similar expression to "the Spirit of the LORD departed from Saul" in 1 Samuel 16:14 (same verb, same tense, similar preposition).

10. Dumbrell has perceptively suggested that "take not your Holy Spirit from me" in Psalm 51:11 "may be an eloquent plea by David for the retention of the office of King, the Bathsheba incident being presupposed." Dumbrell, "Spirit," p. 5.

11. Guesses include: "bouts of Kierkegaardian melancholia" (Robert P. Gordon, *1 & 2 Samuel: A Commentary* [Exeter, UK: The Paternoster Press, 1986], p. 152); "some symptoms of paranoia, others of manic-depressive illness" (P. Kyle McCarter, Jr., *I Samuel: A New Translation with Introduction, Notes & Commentary*, The Anchor Bible, Vol. 8 [Garden City, NY: Doubleday, 1980], pp. 280, 281); "melancholia or a recurrent mania" (Mauchline, *1 and 2 Samuel*, p. 130).

12. Intriguingly a little later in the story we will read that "a harmful [that is, evil] spirit rushed upon" Saul (1 Samuel 18:10). See also 1 Samuel 19:9.

13. "Saul's suffering is described theologically, not psychopathetically or psychologically." Hans Wilhelm Hertzberg, *I & II Samuel: A Commentary*, Old Testament Library (London: SCM Press, 1964), p. 141.

14. We should be careful not to read too much into the reference here to "a . . . spirit." The word translated "spirit" can refer to a person's disposition or mood (examples include Genesis 26:35; 41:8; Exodus 6:9; Numbers 5:14; 1 Samuel 1:15; 1 Kings 21:5; Job 7:11; 21:4; Psalm 34:18; Proverbs 11:13; 14:29; 16:18, 19; Ecclesiastes 7:8; Isaiah 19:3, 14; 54:6; 66:2; Ezekiel 3:14; Hosea 4:12; 5:4). The "evil spirit from the Lord" that tormented Saul probably refers to Saul's distressed mood caused by the Lord. Cf. Deuteronomy 2:30. It is therefore not necessarily the case here that "evil spirits" are "beings sent by God to accomplish God's plan in the lives of individuals and the nation of Israel." Archie T. Wright, *The Origins of Evil Spirits: The Reception of Genesis 6.1-4 in Early Jewish Literature*, Wissenschaftliche Untwesuchungen zum Neuen Testament 2. Reihe 198 (Tübingen, Germany: Mohr Siebeck, 2005), p. 1. Wright cites, as examples of this meaning, Numbers 5:14, 15; 1 Kings 19:7; Isaiah 37:7; Hosea 5:4; Judges 9:23; Job 4:12-16; 1 Samuel 16:14-23; 18:10-12; 19:9, 10.

15. Noted by Klein, *1 Samuel*, p. 166 and Gordon, *1 & 2 Samuel*, p. 346, note 6. As we noticed previously 1 Samuel 16:1 literally says, "I have seen for me a king. . . ." With similar literalness Saul's words in 1 Samuel 16:17 are "See for me a man. . . ."

16. Alter, *David*, p. 98.

17. Alter's suggestion, however, seems a little far-fetched: "Is it possible that word of David's clandestine anointment has circulated among limited groups, and that the anonymous 'lad' may be a kind of pro-David mole in the court of Saul?" Alter, *David*, p. 98. More to the point is Hertzberg's comment: "The further mention of his valour and skills at arms is . . . quite pertinent, seeing that Saul was still on the look-out for good soldiers (14:52)." Hertzberg, *I & II Samuel*, p. 141.

18. As several commentators note. See Walter Brueggemann, *First and Second Samuel*, Interpretation: A Bible Commentary for Teaching and Preaching (Louisville: John Knox Press, 1990), p. 126; Klein, *1 Samuel*, p. 166, Gordon, *1 & 2 Samuel*, p. 152.

19. For a study of the difficulties, a review of proposals, and a rather more complex suggestion than mine, see John T. Willis, "The Function of Comprehensive Anticipatory Redactional Joints in I Samuel 16–18," *Zeitschrift fr die Alttestamentliche Wissenschaft* 85 (1973), pp. 294-314.

20. See Brueggemann, *First and Second Samuel*, p. 126, whose comments here are insightful (although he does not allow for the explanation of Saul's knowledge I have suggested here).

21. See, for example, 1 Kings 5:1. William L. Moran, "The Ancient Near Eastern Background of the Love of God in Deuteronomy," *Catholic Biblical Quarterly* 25 (1963), pp. 77-87.

22. "It is arguable that the verb ["love"] was carefully introduced at this point because of a certain ambiguity of meaning. It is the proper term to denote genuine affection between human beings, husband and wife, parent and child, friend and friend. But since the verb can also have political implications and since, as we shall argue, it is used in such a sense elsewhere in the narrative, we may suspect that already in 1 Samuel xvi 21 the narrator is preparing us for the later political use of the term." J. A. Thompson, "The Significance of the Verb *LOVE* in the David-Jonathan Narratives in 1 Samuel," *Vetus Testamentum* 24 (1974), p. 335. It must be admitted, however, that in verse 21 who loved whom is not as unambiguous in the original, which just has "he loved him greatly," as in most English translations.

23. In a way that English cannot express, the verb translated "refreshed" in verse 23 is cognate with the word usually translated "spirit."

Chapter Twenty-six: The Enemy

1. Socoh was about fourteen miles west of Bethlehem, while Azekah was a few miles northwest of Socoh according to McCarter. Ephes-dammim is of less certain location

but may have been about four miles northeast of Socoh. P. Kyle McCarter, Jr., *I Samuel: A New Translation with Introduction, Notes & Commentary*, The Anchor Bible, Vol. 8 (Garden City, NY: Doubleday, 1980), p. 290.

2. Joyce Baldwin, *1 and 2 Samuel*, Tyndale Old Testament Commentaries (Leicester, UK: Inter-Varsity Press, 1988), p. 124.

3. Edelman claims that the narrative "is deliberately framed to contrast with what was potentially Jonathan's previous unsuccessful testing during the battle at the Michmash pass in chs. 13-14." Diana Vikander Edelman, *King Saul in the Historiography of Judah*, Journal for the Study of the Old Testament Supplement Series 121 (Sheffield, UK: Sheffield Academic Press, 1991), p. 124.

4. *Ibid.*, p. 125. For a photograph of the valley see V. R. Gold, "Elah, Valley of," in George Arthur Buttrick, ed., *The Interpreter's Dictionary of the Bible*, Vol. 2 (Nashville and New York: Abingdon Press, 1962), p. 70.

5. In the Bible this expression occurs only in 1 Samuel 17. Robert P. Gordon, *1 & 2 Samuel: A Commentary* (Exeter, UK: The Paternoster Press, 1986), p. 154; Robert Alter, *The David Story: A Translation with Commentary of 1 and 2 Samuel* (New York and London: W.W. Norton, 1999), p. 101. McCarter, *I Samuel*, p. 291 argues that the word simply means "infantryman."

6. Hans Wilhelm Hertzberg, *I & II Samuel: A Commentary*, Old Testament Library (London: SCM Press, 1964), p. 148.

7. See verses 8 (literally "the Philistine"), 10, 11, 16, 26, 32, 33, 36, 37, 40, 41, 42, 43, 44, 45, 48, 49, 50, 51, 54, 55, 57.

8. Hertzberg, *I & II Samuel*, p. 148. Albright cites (with apparent approval) the long-held identification of Goliath's name as Lydian in origin. William Fox Albright, "Syria, the Philistines, and Phoenicia," in I. E. S. Edwards et al., eds., *The Cambridge Ancient History*, third edition, Vol. 2, Part 2 (Cambridge, UK: Cambridge University Press, 1975), p. 513.

9. Gath will feature significantly in the story of David (see 1 Samuel 21:10; 27:2).

10. Some doubt has been cast on the accuracy of the Hebrew text here by two Septuagint manuscripts and one of the Dead Sea Scrolls, which both give Goliath's height as "four cubits and a span" (about six feet, nine inches). Carl S. Ehrlich, "Goliath," in David Noel Freedman, ed., *The Anchor Bible Dictionary*, Vol. 2 (New York: Doubleday, 1992), p. 1073. This would nonetheless have been very tall in that culture. Walter Brueggemann, *First and Second Samuel*, Interpretation: A Bible Commentary for Teaching and Preaching (Louisville: John Knox Press, 1990), p. 127.

11. Ralph W. Klein, *1 Samuel*, Word Biblical Commentary, 10 (Nashville: Word, 1983), p. 175.

12. Baldwin, *1 and 2 Samuel*, p. 125.

13. Literally "bronze greaves." "On his legs he had form-fitting greaves, perhaps supplied with leather lining for comfort." Klein, *1 Samuel*, p. 175.

14. The word may be better translated "sword." Baldwin, *1 and 2 Samuel*, p. 126. It has been argued that the word here refers to a scimitar. Klein, *1 Samuel*, pp. 175, 176.

15. McCarter, *I Samuel*, p. 293.

16. This explanation, complete with pictures of looms and spears, was argued persuasively by Yigael Yadin, "Goliath's Javelin and the *mnwr 'orgym*," *Palestine Exploration Quarterly*, January-April 1955, pp. 58-69. A later work includes photographs of the relevant objects and the assertion, "the weapon could be hurled a greater distance with greater stability by virtue of the resultant spin." Yigael Yadin, *The Art of Warfare in Biblical Lands in the Light of Archaeological Discovery* (London: Weidenfeld and Nicolson, 1963), pp. 354, 355.

17. Baldwin, *1 and 2 Samuel*, p. 126; Klein, *1 Samuel*, p. 176.

18. Exact verbal correspondence depends on a slight emendation to the Hebrew word translated "Choose" in 1 Samuel 17:8. The emendation is advocated by S. R. Driver, *Notes on the Hebrew Text and the Topography of the Book of Samuel with an Introduction*

on Hebrew Palaeography and Facsimiles of Inscriptions and Maps, second edition (Oxford, UK: Clarendon, 1913), p. 140 and Henry Preserved Smith, *A Critical and Exegetical Commentary on the Books of Samuel*, The International Critical Commentary (Edinburgh: T. & T. Clark, 1899), p. 155 but rejected by McCarter, *I Samuel*, p. 287.

19. The translation needs to reflect the cognate word used by David in verse 26, "reproach" (ESV), "disgrace" (NIV), perhaps better "scorn" or "mockery."

20. In the books of Samuel this verb occurs only in 1 Samuel 2:10 and 17:11. Before this it occurs only in the encouraging exhortation *not* to be dismayed because of the Lord's promises (Deuteronomy 1:21; 31:8; Joshua 1:9; 8:1; 10:25). The only other occurrence of the word in the historical books is 2 Kings 19:26.

CHAPTER TWENTY-SEVEN: THE GOD OF THE UNEXPECTED

1. The first word of the Hebrew text in verse 12 is literally translated, "And David."

2. If this feature of Biblical narrative is taken seriously with respect to 1 Samuel 16–17, many of the problems raised by commentators (some of which we will note in our expositions) are simply solved. Other solutions have been proposed (e.g., see C. F. Keil and F. Delitzsch, *Biblical Commentary on the Books of Samuel* [Grand Rapids, MI: Eerdmans, 1950], pp. 176-178, note 1) but generally depend on the assumption that the events of 1 Samuel 16:14-23 must precede in time those of 1 Samuel 17.

3. I say "almost" because the words "Now David . . ." seem to assume that we know of David. Compare the very different way in which Saul was introduced to the readers for the first time in 1 Samuel 9:1, 2.

4. Gordon suggests that the manner of David's introduction here may be "a matter of narrative technique. Stories told in folkloristic mode sometimes reflect the view that a hero is more of a hero if he is an 'outsider.'" Robert P. Gordon, *1 & 2 Samuel: A Commentary* (Exeter, UK: The Paternoster Press, 1986), p. 155.

5. Literally "this Ephrathite," perhaps pointing readers to the man of Bethlehem we have already seen in the previous chapter.

6. Cf. the similar introduction of Kish, the father of Saul in 1 Samuel 9:1. P. Kyle McCarter, Jr., *I Samuel: A New Translation with Introduction, Notes & Commentary*, The Anchor Bible, Vol. 8 (Garden City, NY: Doubleday, 1980), p. 303.

7. Judges 12:5 and 1 Kings 11:26 (in both of which verses "Ephraimite" is literally "Ephrathite").

8. So Ruth 1:2; 1 Samuel 17:12. See Micah 5:2. Cf. 1 Chronicles 2:19, 24, 50; 4:4. The name of the clan (Ephrath or Ephrathah) was given to the clan's territory, which was around Bethlehem (see Genesis 35:16; Ruth 4:11; Psalm 132:6) and to Bethlehem itself (see Genesis 35:19; 48:7). See Lamontte M. Luker, "Ephrathah (Place)," in David Noel Freedman, ed., *The Anchor Bible Dictionary*, Vol. 2 (New York: Doubleday, 1992), pp. 557, 558, who describes the two meanings for "Ephrathite" as "an etymological coincidence." Also McCarter, *I Samuel*, p. 303.

9. The textual problem reflected in the ESV note does not significantly affect the meaning of the verse. All versions tell us that Jesse was an old man.

10. Many commentators regard verse 15 as "a verse designed to explain how David, who, according to 16:21, had been appointed armour bearer to Saul, was not in the Israelite camp when Goliath was issuing his challenge." Gordon, *1 & 2 Samuel*, p. 155. If, as I have suggested, David's appointment to Saul's staff happened *after* the events of chapter 17, then no explanation is needed. The verse then simply describes, from the point of view of the brothers at the front, the coming and going of their youngest sibling.

11. I would thus go further than Edelman: "The reminder seems to have been included to set the stage for the forthcoming exchanges between David and Eliab, and David and Saul." Diana Vikander Edelman, *King Saul in the Historiography of Judah*, Journal for the Study of the Old Testament Supplement Series 121 (Sheffield, UK: Sheffield Academic Press, 1991), p. 127.

12. "That Goliath appeared twice a day for forty days in full armour to hurl defiance at the Israelites was a remarkably sustained ritual which must surely have become, long before the expiry of that period, a farce or a pantomimic interlude." John Mauchline, *1 and 2 Samuel*, New Century Bible (London: Oliphants, 1971), p. 133.

13. "Every detail is meant to underscore the human insignificance of David and his family." Ralph W. Klein, *1 Samuel*, Word Biblical Commentary, 10 (Nashville: Word, 1983), p. 177.

14. So Klein, *1 Samuel*, p. 177, although Hans Wilhelm Hertzberg, *I & II Samuel: A Commentary*, Old Testament Library (London: SCM Press, 1964), p. 150 thinks parched grain was a delicacy. His reference to Ruth 2:14 does not prove the point either way.

15. So Robert Alter, *The David Story: A Translation with Commentary of 1 and 2 Samuel* (New York and London: W.W. Norton, 1999), p. 104; McCarter, *I Samuel*, p. 299; Henry Preserved Smith, *A Critical and Exegetical Commentary on the Books of Samuel*, The International Critical Commentary (Edinburgh: T. & T. Clark, 1899), p. 157; Keil and Delitzsch, *Books of Samuel*, p. 180.

16. Contrary to McCarter, *I Samuel*, p. 304, therefore, these words are not "superfluous here."

17. This comparison is made by Edelman, *Saul*, p. 125.

18. The Hebrew could be taken to indicate that the words of verse 25 were spoken by *one* Israelite man, presumably in the hearing, or partial hearing, of David. Alter, *David*, p. 104 translates verse 25 quite literally: "A man of Israel said . . ." This seems to me to make good sense in the narrative flow. Klein, *1 Samuel*, p. 169 states, "Someone had said, 'Men of Israel, do you see this man . . .'" Similarly McCarter, *I Samuel*, p. 299. However, the ambiguity does not substantially affect our understanding.

19. So Edelman, *Saul*, p. 126, who also draws out the contrast between Jonathan's provisional and David's absolute confidence in God.

20. Cf. Klein, *1 Samuel*, p. 178.

21. See 1 Samuel 16:13: "in the midst of his brothers."

22. Contrary, therefore, to those, like Klein, who claim "This account [1 Samuel 17] seems to be unaware of the anointing Eliab had witnessed." Klein, *1 Samuel*, p. 178. Eliab's words may well presuppose that earlier event.

23. Alter, *David*, p. 105. "A contemptuous reference to the little job which David did at home." Mauchline, *1 and 2 Samuel*, p. 134. This seems a more probable sense than "*Those few sheep* the loss of only one of which would be a very great loss to our family." Keil and Delitzsch, *Books of Samuel*, p. 181.

24. Alter, *David*, p. 106. Both Eliab and Goliath used the emphatic first-personal pronoun, albeit in slightly different forms.

25. Cf. Goliath's "Why have you come out?," his scornful reference to Saul's slaves, and his bold self-designation "Am *I* not the Philistine?" in 1 Samuel 17:8.

26. Mauchline, *1 and 2 Samuel*, p. 134. Cf. "Eliab saw the splinter in his brother's eye, and was not aware of the beam in his own. The very things with which he charged his brother — presumption and wickedness of heart — were most apparent in his scornful reproof." Keil and Delitzsch, *Books of Samuel*, p. 181.

27. The sentence is in fact very pithy and highly ambiguous, perhaps deliberately so. Suggestions include "Is it not a matter of importance?" (Smith, *Books of Samuel*, p. 159) and "Isn't this the matter/problem?" (Edelman, *Saul*, p. 129).

CHAPTER TWENTY-EIGHT: THE GOSPEL OF DAVID

1. The Hebrew is more abrupt: "and he took him," possibly reflecting Saul's desperation. Cf. 1 Samuel 8:11.

2. Contrary to the common assumption, reflected in most studies, that the events of 1 Samuel 16:14-23 preceded in time the events of 1 Samuel 17. E.g., Diana Vikander Edelman, *King Saul in the Historiography of Judah*, Journal for the Study of the Old Testament Supplement Series 121 (Sheffield, UK: Sheffield Academic Press, 1991), p. 129: "David is once again summoned before the king, as in 16.19. Without need of

a formal introduction because of his previous service in ch. 16, he reassures Saul that appearances are deceiving. . . ."

3. Literally, "Let not a human heart fall."

4. This is yet another case of a character in the narrative speaking more than he could know. We are not to suppose that David was deliberately alluding to God's words in 1 Samuel 16:7 (which he did not hear). However, the narrative frequently sets before us important points in speakers' words that they could not themselves have known. I therefore differ slightly from Edelman's comment that David was "hinting that the men would have no reason to fear if they would only follow their hearts instead of their eyes." Edelman, *Saul*, p. 129.

5. David uses the word "servant" again in verses 34, 36, and 58.

6. The range of meanings of the word translated "youth" here is examined thoroughly in John MacDonald, "The Status and Role of the *Na'ar* in Israelite Society," *Journal of Near Eastern Studies*, 35/3 (1976), pp. 147-170. MacDonald argues that the term very often refers to a status rather than an age. He appears to relate David's status as *na'ar* in 1 Samuel 17:33 to his appointment as Saul's armor-bearer in 1 Samuel 16:21 (p. 160). This assumes a chronological sequence of events that is questionable on other grounds. The Hebrew word was discussed when we considered 1 Samuel 1:24.

7. "Saul is nonplussed by these extravagant claims on the part of the young shepherd from Bethlehem, and he doesn't know what to say." Robert Alter, *The David Story: A Translation with Commentary of 1 and 2 Samuel* (New York and London: W.W. Norton, 1999), p. 107.

8. David will name Yahweh four more times in this chapter, all in the speech to Goliath in verses 45-47.

9. Cf. Walter Brueggemann, *First and Second Samuel*, Interpretation: A Bible Commentary for Teaching and Preaching (Louisville: John Knox Press, 1990), pp. 130, 131.

10. *Ibid.*, p. 131.

11. Cf. Edelman, *Saul*, p. 125. Contra Robert P. Gordon, *1 & 2 Samuel: A Commentary* (Exeter, UK: The Paternoster Press, 1986), p. 157: "The same faith in Yahweh that inspired Jonathan's deed of valour (14:6) is found in David."

12. I am unpersuaded by the argument of Edelman, *Saul*, pp. 130, 131 that these words (like the similar words in chapter 16:18) indicate that Saul (like the young man in 16:18) *knew* of David's anointing and his possession of the Spirit.

13. Brueggemann, *First and Second Samuel*, p. 131.

14. In the next chapter the heir apparent to the throne will make a more self-conscious but similar gesture (1 Samuel 18:4).

CHAPTER TWENTY-NINE: DAVID AND GOLIATH

1. Cf. C. K. Barrett's comment on 1 Corinthians 15:56: "Taking death as a given fact, sin is what embitters it, not only psychologically, in that it breeds remorse, but also theologically in that it makes clear that death is not merely a natural phenomenon, but a punishment, an evil that need not exist, and would not exist if man were not in rebellion against his Creator." C. K. Barrett, *A Commentary on the First Epistle to the Corinthians*, Black's New Testament Commentaries, second edition (London: A & C Black, 1971), p. 383.

2. We noted previously that the term translated "youth" might designate a person of a particular status or role in Israelite society rather than being simply a reference to age. If this is the case, "The Philistine apparently expected an Israelite lord to accept his challenge, according to the proper 'knightly' code, dressed in full armor, and he was disdainful when he saw that his opponent was only a *na'ar* and a very junior looking fellow at that." John MacDonald, "The Status and Role of the *Na'ar* in Israelite Society," *Journal of Near Eastern Studies*, 35/3 (1976), p. 161.

3. In Hebrew the vocabulary is even closer than appears in the English. An over-literal translation of 1 Samuel 16:12 would be: "And he was ruddy with beautiful eyes and good

of appearance"; according to 1 Samuel 17:42 Goliath saw that the youth was "ruddy with beautiful appearance" (literal translation).

4. ". . . only a boy, pink-cheeked and fair-complected at that!" Ralph W. Klein, *1 Samuel*, Word Biblical Commentary, 10 (Nashville: Word, 1983), p. 180.

5. Remember 1 Samuel 5–6! Diana Bikaner Edelman, *King Saul in the Historiography of Judah*, Journal for the Study of the Old Testament Supplement Series 121 (Sheffield, UK: Sheffield Academic Press, 1991), p. 132.

6. Although the accounts of Saul's disobedience in 1 Samuel 13, 15 concentrate on the king's failure, the involvement of the people is also clear, especially in chapter 15 (see especially v. 9).

7. The parallelism of the two parts of verse 45 suggests that the name of the Lord is the weapon with which David came. See 1 Samuel 12:22.

8. The very emphatic form of the Hebrew pronoun "I" is used by David in verse 45. The only other speaker to use this word in this story is Goliath (vv. 8, 43).

9. The Hebrew word for "mock" or "mockery" is in verses 10, 25, 26, 36, 45 (in all these verses, ESV, "defy"), 26 (ESV, "reproach").

10. "This is a 'missionary speech.'" Walter Brueggemann, *First and Second Samuel*, Interpretation: A Bible Commentary for Teaching and Preaching (Louisville: John Knox Press, 1990), p. 132.

11. Noted by Robert P. Gordon, *1 & 2 Samuel: A Commentary* (Exeter, UK: The Paternoster Press, 1986), p. 158 and Edelman, *Saul*, p. 133. We will not here pursue the interesting, but I think unconvincing, suggestion that the stone of David penetrated Goliath's shin or knee rather than his forehead. Ariella Deem, "'. . . and a stone sank into his forehead.' A Note on 1 Samuel XVII 49," *Vetus Testamentum* 28/3 (1978), pp. 349-351. Cf. Klein, *1 Samuel*, p. 181.

12. Brueggemann, *First and Second Samuel*, p. 133.

13. "Armor" here would include weapons. We are not told how and when Goliath's sword was entrusted to the priest at Nob (1 Samuel 21:9) but may presume that David knew of it. It is possible that the statement about Goliath's weapons in 1 Samuel 17:54, like the statement about his head, refers to some later time after David had retrieved the sword from Ahimelech.

14. "The passing of arms from the lesser to the greater so carefully described by the narrator, seems to have had political implications in the Ancient Near East." J. A. Thompson, "The Significance of the Verb *LOVE* in the David-Jonathan Narratives in 1 Samuel," *Vetus Testamentum* 24 (1974), p. 335, who cites 2 Kings 11:10; 2 Samuel 8:7, 11, 12. Also J. B. Pritchard, ed. *Ancient Near Eastern Texts Relating to the Old Testament: New Material* (Princeton, NJ: Princeton University Press, 1955), pp. 276, 281.

15. Explanations (apart from unsatisfying historical critical reconstructions [so John Mauchline, *1 and 2 Samuel*, New Century Bible (London: Oliphants, 1971), p. 135; Robert Alter, *The David Story: A Translation with Commentary of 1 and 2 Samuel* (New York and London: W.W. Norton, 1999), p. 110; Hans Wilhelm Hertzberg, *I & II Samuel: A Commentary*, Old Testament Library (London: SCM Press, 1964), p. 154; Gordon, *1 & 2 Samuel*, p. 159)] include: Saul knew David himself, he was just inquiring who his father was (because of the promised reward in verse 25?) (so Edelman, *Saul*, p. 134; Joyce Baldwin, *1 and 2 Samuel*, Tyndale Old Testament Commentaries [Leicester, UK: Inter-Varsity Press, 1988], p. 129; cf. C. F. Keil and F. Delitzsch, *Biblical Commentary on the Books of Samuel* [Grand Rapids, MI: Eerdmans, 1950], p. 186); Saul's failure to recognize David was an expression of his disturbed state of mind (1 Samuel 16:14) (so some older commentators according to Keil and Delitzsch, *Books of Samuel*, p. 186, note 1); Saul thought that David had backed out of the challenge by refusing the armor in verse 39 and so would not have presumed that he was the figure in the distance (so Robert Polzin, *Samuel and the Deuteronomist: A Literary Study of the Deuteronomic History. Part Two, 1 Samuel*, Indiana Studies in Biblical Literature [Bloomington, IN: Indiana University Press, 1993], p. 173, rejected by Edelman, *Saul*, p. 134).

CHAPTER THIRTY: DO YOU LOVE HIM?

1. C. S. Lewis's famous book, *The Four Loves* (London: Geoffrey Bles, 1960) is a classic study of a range of meanings of *love* with reference to corresponding Greek terms.

2. References to love for David are found elsewhere, but 1 Samuel 18 is the most concentrated set of such references. See also 1 Samuel 20:17; 2 Samuel 1:26; 1 Kings 5:1.

3. The chapter division is often criticized as interrupting the narrative unit of chapter 17, which, it is supposed, continues to 1 Samuel 18:5. So Robert Alter, *The David Story: A Translation with Commentary of 1 and 2 Samuel* (New York and London: W.W. Norton, 1999), p. 112. However, the chapter division makes very good sense thematically. So Walter Brueggemann, *First and Second Samuel*, Interpretation: A Bible Commentary for Teaching and Preaching (Louisville: John Knox Press, 1990), p. 135. The first five verses of chapter 18 introduce important ideas (especially love for David) to be explored in this chapter.

4. For example, Tom Horner, *Jonathan Loved David: Homosexuality in Biblical Times* (Philadelphia: Westminster Press, 1978), pp. 26-39; David F. Greenberg, *The Construction of Homosexuality* (Chicago: University of Chicago Press, 1988), p. 114. These references are cited by Robert A. J. Gagnon, *The Bible and Homosexual Practice: Texts and Hermeneutics* (Nashville: Abingdon Press, 2001), p. 146, note 232. Gagnon provides a thorough and judicious discussion of the relationship between David and Jonathan on pages 146-154. Proposals that find allusions to a sexual relationship between David and Jonathan have been "now generally recognized as being little more than romanticized misreadings of the far different cultural conventions of ancient societies — similar in fact, to the venerable (but scripturally unsupported) notion that Mary Magdalene was 'in love' with Jesus." L. R. Holben, *What Christians Think About Homosexuality: Six Representative Viewpoints* (North Richland Hills, TX: Bibal Press, 1999), p. 288, note 6. Even Phyllis Bird, hardly a conservative scholar on such matters, asserts, "Jonathan's love for David (1 Sam. 18:1) does not belong to the OT's understanding of homosexual relations." Phyllis A. Bird, "The Bible in Christian Ethical Deliberation Concerning Homosexuality: Old Testament Contributions," in David L. Balch, ed., *Homosexuality, Science, and the "Plain Sense" of Scripture* (Grand Rapids, MI: Eerdmans, 2000), p. 146, note 6.

5. Robert P. Gordon, *1 & 2 Samuel: A Commentary* (Exeter, UK: The Paternoster Press, 1986), p. 159.

6. "Only in our own day, removed as we are from ancient Near Eastern conventions, are these kinds of specious connections made by people desperate to find the slightest shred of support for homosexual practice in the Bible." Gagnon, *The Bible and Homosexual Practice*, p. 154. Also Peter Coleman, *Christian Attitudes to Homosexuality* (London: SPCK, 1980), pp. 44, 45. The text most often cited in this connection is 2 Samuel 1:26, where David described the love of Jonathan as "surpassing the love of women." Gagnon's comment is to the point: "Jonathan's repeated display of (non-sexual) kindness to David at a time when Jonathan was in a position of power, selflessly risking his own life and certainly his own kingdom, surpassed anything David had ever known from a committed erotic relationship with a woman. No more and no less than this is the point of David's eulogy of his dear friend." Gagnon, *The Bible and Homosexual Practice*, pp. 152, 153.

7. "The vast majority of occurrences of the noun 'love' and the verb 'to love' in the Old Testament have nothing to do with erotic love." Gagnon, *The Bible and Homosexual Practice*, p. 148, note 235. Gagnon provides a decisive response to the theory that the David and Jonathan narratives suppress the details of a homosexual relationship. Then why did they leave so much that is taken today as evidence for such a relationship? "The answer is obvious: nothing in the stories raised any suspicion that David and Jonathan were homosexually involved with one another." Gagnon, p. 154.

8. The verbal similarity cannot be seen in the ESV, which has, "his life is bound up in the boy's life." This parallel is suggested by Gagnon, *The Bible and Homosexual Practice*, p. 147.

9. See *ibid.*, p. 147; also Peter R. Ackroyd, "The Verb Love — 'Ahab in the David-Jonathan Narratives — A Footnote," *Vetus Testamentum* 25/2 (1975), pp. 213, 214, who argues that the verb in question (ESV, "knit") has (or suggests) the political sense of "conspire" found for the same root in 1 Samuel 22:8, 13 (where ESV has "conspire").

10. "Whatever happens to David happens also to Jonathan. If David hurts, Jonathan hurts. If David rejoices, Jonathan rejoices. Consequently, if David becomes king, Jonathan has every reason to rejoice." Gagnon, *The Bible and Homosexual Practice*, p. 147.

11. J. A. Thompson, "The Significance of the Verb *LOVE* in the David-Jonathan Narratives in 1 Samuel," *Vetus Testamentum* 24 (1974), pp. 334-338, drawing on the earlier key study by William L. Moran, "The Ancient Near Eastern Background of the Love of God in Deuteronomy," *Catholic Biblical Quarterly* 25 (1963), pp. 77-87.

12. This was "one of many covenants of one kind and another which were made over the years till David was finally securely established on the throne." Thompson, "*LOVE*," p. 334. See 1 Samuel 18:3 (with Jonathan); 2 Samuel 3:13 (with Abner), 21 (with all Israel); 5:3 (again, with all Israel).

13. This is more explicit in the grammar of the Hebrew sentence, but it is clear enough in the English where Jonathan is the active subject. Alter, *David*, p. 112.

14. Once again a "robe" features in this story. Hannah made a "robe" for her son Samuel (each year, 1 Samuel 2:19). The "robe" of Samuel became a symbol of the kingdom (1 Samuel 15:27, 28). Now Jonathan's "robe" symbolizes the kingdom and is transferred to David! In due course Saul's "robe" will represent his kingdom that David will refuse to take by force (1 Samuel 24:4, 11). The last appearance of a "robe" in 1 Samuel will be Samuel's robe again (1 Samuel 28:14).

15. It is notoriously tricky to try to reconstruct details of Biblical history that the text, for whatever reason, does not disclose. I have earlier asserted that the episode of 1 Samuel 16:14-23 may have occurred in time *after* the Goliath incident of chapter 17. This makes good and straightforward sense of a number of details of the account (namely, David was known in 1 Samuel 16:18 as a "man of valor, a man of war," but in chapter 17 he was too young to be a soldier; Saul knew David's name and his father in 1 Samuel 16:19 but appeared to know neither in 1 Samuel 17:55-58; David became Saul's armor-bearer in 1 Samuel 16:21 but appeared as an outsider in Eliab's view in 1 Samuel 17:28 and was unknown even to Abner in 1 Samuel 17:55). It remains difficult, however, to fit the episode into the events of 1 Samuel 18:1-5 — difficult, but not impossible. My tentatively held opinion is that the difficulties are typical of attempts to harmonize two incomplete accounts of contemporaneous happenings, but that the earlier recounted episode *did* occur in the time covered by 1 Samuel 18:1-4. The difficulties for harmonizers arise because the two accounts focus on different, though overlapping, interests. We might note that the "harmful [evil] spirit from the LORD" that was so significant in 16:14-23 is not mentioned in chapter 17 but reappears in 1 Samuel 18:10. Chronological unevenness in the narrative seems to me to be a far more satisfying account of the details of the text than the commonly adopted historical-critical hypotheses.

16. Verse 5 "is a summary meant to end the preceding tradition, but one which covers a long period of time. The succeeding chapters then go back in time and zero in on specific events that take place within that span of time." Diana Vikander Edelman, *King Saul in the Historiography of Judah*, Journal for the Study of the Old Testament Supplement Series 121 (Sheffield, UK: Sheffield Academic Press, 1991), p. 137, note 1.

17. The song "credits Saul and David with equal military honor." Edelman, *Saul*, p. 137. Also Brueggemann, *First and Second Samuel*, p. 137. Alter, however, believes that the convention was a vehicle to set David's triumphs above Saul's. Alter, *David*, p. 113.

18. "Saul hears the song through his jealousy." Brueggemann, *First and Second Samuel*, p. 137.

19. "Saul seems to have discerned in some inchoate way that the purpose of David's presence in his courts is eventually to seize the throne." *Ibid.*

20. The Hebrew has these words for both David and Saul.

21. The verb translated "pin" in verse 11 is the same as "struck down" in verses 6, 7.

22. The Hebrew makes this striking parallel. An over-literal rendering of verses 12b, 13a shows the point: "the LORD was with him [David], but from with Saul he had turned aside. And Saul turned him [David] aside from with him [Saul]."

23. John Mauchline, *1 and 2 Samuel*, New Century Bible (London: Oliphants, 1971), p. 139.

24. P. Kyle McCarter, Jr., *I Samuel: A New Translation with Introduction, Notes & Commentary*, The Anchor Bible, Vol. 8 (Garden City, NY: Doubleday, 1980), p. 313.

25. Mauchline, *1 and 2 Samuel*, p. 139.

26. Thompson, *"LOVE*," p. 337. ". . . the writer implies that the people at the point were already giving David a *de facto* recognition and allegiance, which his actual leadership and success in a sense justified." Moran, "Love," p. 81.

27. See this helpful description of love for God in the book of Deuteronomy, which is not unrelated to what we are seeing in 1 Samuel 18: "Love in Deuteronomy is a love that can be commanded. It is also a love intimately related to fear and reverence. Above all it is a love which must be expressed in loyalty, in service, and in unqualified obedience to the demands of the Law. For to love God is, in answer to a unique claim ([Deuteronomy] 6,4), to be loyal to him (11,1.22; 30,20), to walk in his ways (10,12; 11,22; 19,9; 30,16), to keep his commandments (10,12; 11,1.22; 19,9), to do them (11,22; 19,9), to heed them or his voice (11,13; 30,16), to serve him (10,12; 11,1.13). It is, in brief, a love defined by and pledged in covenant — a covenantal love." Moran, "Love," p. 78.

CHAPTER THIRTY-ONE: *LOVE HIM OR FEAR HIM*

1. Contra Robert P. Gordon, *1 & 2 Samuel: A Commentary* (Exeter, UK: The Paternoster Press, 1986), p. 161 who sees the offer as the redemption of the promise.

2. So Diana Vikander Edelman, *King Saul in the Historiography of Judah*, Journal for the Study of the Old Testament Supplement Series 121 (Sheffield, UK: Sheffield Academic Press, 1991), p. 140, based on her interpretation of the rest of the narrative.

3. So Hans Wilhelm Hertzberg, *I & II Samuel: A Commentary*, Old Testament Library (London: SCM Press, 1964), p. 161; Ralph W. Klein, *I Samuel*, Word Biblical Commentary, 10 (Nashville: Word, 1983), p. 186; Gordon, *1 & 2 Samuel*, p. 161.

4. The fact that Saul now communicated with David largely through intermediaries offers some secondary support for the idea that verses 13 and 17-19 may be parallel accounts of the same incident, by which Saul removed David from his presence.

5. So Edelman, *Saul*, p. 140.

6. So *ibid.*, pp. 140, 141.

7. *Ibid.*, p. 141.

8. "Uncircumcised" is a description applied to the Philistines also in 1 Samuel 14:6; 31:4; 2 Samuel 1:20.

9. The objection that David had 1,000 men at his disposal (1 Samuel 18:13) is probably not valid because the term "a thousand" may have referred to a contingent of soldiers of unspecified size, and on the basis of this story we may suggest that it could have been much less than 100 men! This goes a little further than John Wenham who suggested the meaning "the basic unit of the folk army, which went to war by its [thousands]." John W. Wenham, "Large Numbers in the Old Testament," *Tyndale Bulletin* 18 (1967), p. 24. He refers to the work of George E. Mendenhall, "The Census Lists of Numbers 1 and 26," *Journal of Biblical Literature* 77 (1958), pp. 52-66, who concludes that the Hebrew term "originally referred to a subsection of a tribe; the term was then carried over to designate the contingent of troops under its own leader which the subsection contributed to the army of the Federation," p. 66.

CHAPTER THIRTY-TWO: *". . . AGAINST THE LORD AND AGAINST HIS ANOINTED"*

1. ". . . none of the participants [in chapter 19] knows that Saul's protagonist is really Yahweh. Least of all does Saul recognize this. To an ordinary observer who does not, like us, have this privileged narrator to interpret and anticipate, the drama appears simply to be a deathly conflict over power between a king and his best warrior." Walter

Brueggemann, *First and Second Samuel*, Interpretation: A Bible Commentary for Teaching and Preaching (Louisville: John Knox Press, 1990), p. 141. On the other hand, Edelman concludes from 1 Samuel 16:19 that word of David's anointing had somehow reached Saul, and her exposition of the following narratives is significantly shaped by this view. Diana Vikander Edelman, *King Saul in the Historiography of Judah*, Journal for the Study of the Old Testament Supplement Series 121 (Sheffield, UK: Sheffield Academic Press, 1991), pp. 120, 121. In my opinion Edelman reads too much into 1 Samuel 16:19.

2. "The narrative . . . presents Jonathan acting against both his duty and his self-interest." Brueggemann, *First and Second Samuel*, p. 141.

3. We already noted that problems in the relationship between Saul and Jonathan were suggested in 1 Samuel 14:1, 29, 30.

4. In the Hebrew of verse 3 Jonathan twice uses the emphatic pronoun "I": "*I* will go out . . . *I* will speak . . ."

5. Literally "to the hand of my father," which "portrays Jonathan volunteering to 'stand up' to his father's power on behalf of David." Edelman, *Saul*, p. 141. Saul's "hand" is often associated with "his spear" (see 1 Samuel 19:9; cf. 1 Samuel 18:10; 22:6; 26:11).

6. The readiness of the historical critic to see difficulties where there need be none is illustrated by McCarter: "Jonathan's instructions contain a seemingly irreconcilable contradiction." P. Kyle McCarter, Jr., *I Samuel: A New Translation with Introduction, Notes & Commentary*, The Anchor Bible, Vol. 8 (Garden City, NY: Doubleday, 1980), p. 321. Similarly Hans Wilhelm Hertzberg, *I & II Samuel: A Commentary*, Old Testament Library (London: SCM Press, 1964), pp. 163, 164 who uses the expression "absolutely impossible to harmonize." The supposed problem is that David would not need a report from Jonathan if the meeting had taken place near him. The difficulty is grossly exaggerated as Robert P. Gordon, *1 & 2 Samuel: A Commentary* (Exeter, UK: The Paternoster Press, 1986), p. 163 shows.

7. "Saul's royal power is palpable in the dialogue, for his own son is careful to address him by title in the deferential third person." Robert Alter, *The David Story: A Translation with Commentary of 1 and 2 Samuel* (New York and London: W.W. Norton, 1999), p. 118.

8. McCarter argues that "good" in this context "may carry legal and political nuances." David "has acted consistently with the loyalty he owes his king." Cf. 1 Samuel 24:19. McCarter, *I Samuel*, p. 322.

9. The vocabulary of joy and rejoicing has been applied in 1 Samuel to people's response to God's work of salvation or deliverance, either before or after the event (1 Samuel 2:1; 6:13; 11:9, 15; 18:6; 19:5; cf. 2 Samuel 1:20).

10. First Samuel 11:9, where the ESV's "deliverance" translates the same Hebrew word as "salvation" in 1 Samuel 19:5.

11. Baldwin points out that Jonathan's words brought Saul back to the generous mind he had on that occasion when he had refused to punish his detractors (compare "Not a man shall be put to death this day" in 1 Samuel 11:13 and "he shall not be put to death" in 1 Samuel 19:6). Joyce Baldwin, *1 and 2 Samuel*, Tyndale Old Testament Commentaries (Leicester, UK: Inter-Varsity Press, 1988), p. 132.

12. However, these provisions did not achieve their purpose (Psalm 106:38; Isaiah 59:7; Jeremiah 7:6; 22:17).

13. The Lord hates "hands that shed innocent blood" (Proverbs 6:17). The supremely wicked king Manasseh "shed very much innocent blood" (2 Kings 21:16). It is interesting to notice that violence against God's servant is described in these terms in 1 Samuel 19:5 (David), Jeremiah 26:15 (Jeremiah), Jonah 1:14 (Jonah), and Matthew 27:4 (Jesus). Edelman draws attention to Saul's failure to shed *guilty* blood in 1 Samuel 15! Edelman, *Saul*, p. 145.

14. Compare 1 Samuel 25:31. David would often complain of those who hated him "without cause" (Psalm 35:7, 19; 69:4; 109:3; 119:161).

15. For Saul's dependence on the counsel of others at crucial moments when his own judgment would have led him astray, see 1 Samuel 9:5-10; 14:36, 37; 14:43-45; 16:15-19;

and especially 17:32-37. He was also capable of being led astray by others (1 Samuel 15:9, 15, 21). The exception, when Saul took good decisive action and even resisted the advice of the people, was when the Spirit of the Lord rushed upon him (see 1 Samuel 11:6, 7, 12, 13). Other examples of Saul's independent decisiveness are foolish (1 Samuel 13:12; 14:24).

16. "In each case, the apparent king-elect is under Saul's death sentence but is saved by external mediation to which Saul acquiesces . . . the echoes are intended to lead the narrative audience to contrast Jonathan's earlier situation with the one David is now experiencing. . . ." Edelman, *Saul*, p. 146.

17. "The repetition of Jonathan's name three times in the same verse is in fact surprising, and shows the desire of the author (or perhaps the desire of a scribe) to call especial attention to Jonathan's nobility of character." Henry Preserved Smith, *A Critical and Exegetical Commentary on the Books of Samuel*, The International Critical Commentary (Edinburgh: T. & T. Clark, 1899), p. 177.

18. There is a small variation in the Hebrew expressions used, but it is of no semantic significance.

19. Cf. Brueggemann, *First and Second Samuel*, p. 142.

20. "The thought expressed is, that the growth of Saul's melancholy was a sign of the hardness of heart to which Jehovah had given him up on account of his impenitence." C. F. Keil and F. Delitzsch, *Biblical Commentary on the Books of Samuel* (Grand Rapids, MI: Eerdmans, 1950), p. 195.

21. Ralph W. Klein, *1 Samuel*, Word Biblical Commentary, 10 (Nashville: Word, 1983), p. 196.

22. The Hebrew refers to the "hand" of Saul holding his spear and the "hand" of David playing music.

23. In 1 Samuel another verb is normally used for David's "fleeing" from Saul (so 1 Samuel 19:12, 18; 20:1; 21:10; 22:17; 27:4; cf. 22:20; 23:6). Only here (in 1 Samuel 19:10) do we find the verb that is otherwise used to describe the "fleeing" of defeated peoples in battle (the Israelites in 1 Samuel 4:10, 16, 17; 17:24; 31:1, 7; the Philistines in 1 Samuel 17:51; 19:8; cf. 30:17).

CHAPTER THIRTY-THREE: *". . . THE LORD HOLDS THEM IN DERISION"*

1. Verse 10b anticipates verses 12b and 18a. The details of what happened *before* the escape are given in verses 11, 12. This is noticed by C. F. Keil and F. Delitzsch, *Biblical Commentary on the Books of Samuel* (Grand Rapids, MI: Eerdmans, 1950), p. 195 and is an appropriate response to Smith, who asserts *"fled and escaped* is too strong language to use, if he simply went to his own house." Henry Preserved Smith, *A Critical and Exegetical Commentary on the Books of Samuel*, The International Critical Commentary (Edinburgh: T. & T. Clark, 1899), pp. 177, 178. This is another example of dramatic storytelling that results in chronological unevenness.

2. P. Kyle McCarter, Jr., *1 Samuel: A New Translation with Introduction, Notes & Commentary*, The Anchor Bible, Vol. 8 (Garden City, NY: Doubleday, 1980), pp. 325, 326.

3. The fifteen occurrences of this term in the Old Testament are briefly surveyed by Ralph W. Klein, *1 Samuel*, Word Biblical Commentary, 10 (Nashville: Word, 1983), p. 197.

4. "At least they [images] are useful for something in this Yahwistic account!" Walter Brueggemann, *First and Second Samuel*, Interpretation: A Bible Commentary for Teaching and Preaching (Louisville: John Knox Press, 1990), p. 143. It may well be appropriate to see in this incident a humorous mocking of idolatry (as in 1 Samuel 5, and earlier in Genesis 31). Cf. Peter R. Ackroyd, "The Teraphim," *The Expository Times* 62 (1950/51), pp. 378-380.

5. The gist of Michal's actions is clear enough, although there is debate over the details. Even the suggestion of Peter Ackroyd that what is referred to are "images designed to aid healing" does not significantly change the scene, in which Michal cleverly acted to deceive her father and protect her husband. Ackroyd, "Teraphim," p. 379. This interpre-

tation was developed in Peter R. Ackroyd, *The First Book of Samuel*, Cambridge Bible Commentary (Cambridge, UK: Cambridge University Press, 1971), p. 158 and filled out by Diana Vikander Edelman, *King Saul in the Historiography of Judah*, Journal for the Study of the Old Testament Supplement Series 121 (Sheffield, UK: Sheffield Academic Press, 1991), pp. 150, 151.

6. A little later in the narrative Jonathan, like Michal here, will seek to deceive Saul and, like Michal here, will become the object of his anger (1 Samuel 20:30-33).

7. Edelman argues that Michal was telling the truth in verse 17. Although she had warned David of the danger he was in, the escape plan was entirely his, and she did nothing but submit to David's instructions (and threats). Edelman, *Saul*, pp. 147, 148.

8. I do not think that Baldwin is correct in describing Samuel as "the prophet who had from the beginning been [David's] trusted guide." Joyce Baldwin, *1 and 2 Samuel*, Tyndale Old Testament Commentaries (Leicester, UK: Inter-Varsity Press, 1988), p. 133. There is no indication of any contact between Samuel and David since Samuel returned to Ramah from Bethlehem (1 Samuel 16:13).

9. Samuel's reappearance in the narrative now may "suggest that behind the events, as it were watching over them, is the figure of the prophet, the king-maker." Ackroyd, *First Book of Samuel*, p. 159.

10. *Ibid.*, p. 159. ". . . some special building in Ramah is the most probable conjecture — perhaps the cloister of the prophets," Smith, *Books of Samuel*, p. 181; "the *coenobium* of the pupils of the prophets, who had assembled around Samuel in the neighborhood of Ramah . . . this coenobium consisted of a considerable number of dwelling places or houses, connected together by a hedge or wall." Keil and Delitzsch, *Books of Samuel*, 196. McCarter, *I Samuel*, p. 328 translates this "the camps."

11. Even the word translated "company" is a problem. It occurs nowhere else in the Old Testament, and one suggestion is that it means "the aged" — "the aged prophets." John Mauchline, *1 and 2 Samuel*, New Century Bible (London: Oliphants, 1971), p. 143. For a thorough survey and analysis of the evidence concerning the constitution and operations of the variously described groups or bands of prophets, see Keil and Delitzsch, *Books of Samuel*, pp. 199-206.

12. This may have been the implied answer to the question in 1 Samuel 10:12, "And who is their father?" Ackroyd, *First Book of Samuel*, pp. 83-85.

13. Baldwin speaks of "the ambiguity of the gift of prophecy" and refers to 1 John 4:1. Baldwin, *1 and 2 Samuel*, p. 133.

14. "The actual phenomenon of prophecy is not clearly delineated here. Apparently 'prophecy' refers to some kind of ecstatic experience that causes the messengers to break out of normal, acceptable patterns of behavior and engage in frenzied or eccentric conduct not expected of the king's servants (cf. 10:9-10). This behavior is understood to be caused by the invasive, compelling power of God, who shatters all conventional categories of perception and conduct." Brueggemann, *First and Second Samuel*, p. 145. For an argument against the widely held view that prophesying was an ecstatic phenomenon, see Leon J. Wood, *The Prophets of Israel* (Grand Rapids, MI: Baker, 1979), pp. 37-65.

15. So *ibid.*, p. 92.

16. Leon Wood has argued that "Saul was overcome by a sense of despair" at his failure to deal with David and now seeing David under the protective favor of Samuel. *Ibid.*, p. 93.

17. The word "too" in verse 24 may indicate that the prophets and the messengers had also stripped off their clothes (a number of commentators are anxious to assure us that this probably means outer garments only!). This does not detract from the fact that for the *king* to strip off his clothes was particularly significant.

18. It is interesting to compare that day, when the Lord's anointed was threatened and the Spirit of the Lord came upon the hostile messengers, so that they prophesied and did no harm, with the Day of Pentecost, after God had made Jesus both Lord and Christ. The Spirit was poured out on those who had earlier demanded Jesus' death (Acts 2:1-41).

19. The statement in 1 Samuel 15:35 is not contradicted here, so long as we allow that the reference there is to normal human interactions. The incident in chapter 19 was not normal!

20. We must admit that there is some ambiguity surrounding these events. Mauchline argues that the proverb in 1 Samuel 10:12 was used disparagingly, "as if by people who were unable to believe that a man of good family like Saul had sunk so low." He then claims that when the proverb appears in chapter 19, "the intention rather is to show that Saul has become enthused as he once was (and may at other times have been) before the evil power took possession of him." Mauchline, *1 and 2 Samuel*, p. 144. I think this is mistaken. The king naked at the feet of the prophet is not a positive picture of the king!

CHAPTER THIRTY-FOUR: *WHAT DO YOU FEAR?*

1. Baldwin does not, in my opinion, take sufficient note of the word "fled" when she says, "The fact that Saul was out of action gave David the opportunity to seek out Jonathan." Joyce Baldwin, *1 and 2 Samuel*, Tyndale Old Testament Commentaries (Leicester, UK: Inter-Varsity Press, 1988), p. 134.

2. Edelman reads too much into the slight differences in wording between Saul's oath and Jonathan's reassurance here, seeing an "implication that Jonathan may not be able to guarantee David's safety or his father's honouring of his oath. . . ." Diana Vikander Edelman, *King Saul in the Historiography of Judah*, Journal for the Study of the Old Testament Supplement Series 121 (Sheffield, UK: Sheffield Academic Press, 1991), p. 153. In my opinion the differences actually point in the opposite direction!

3. Attempts to relocate this conversation, for example, after 1 Samuel 19:10 (Hans Wilhelm Hertzberg, *I & II Samuel: A Commentary*, Old Testament Library [London: SCM Press, 1964], p. 172) or after 1 Samuel 19:17 (P. Kyle McCarter, Jr., *I Samuel: A New Translation with Introduction, Notes & Commentary*, The Anchor Bible, Vol. 8 [Garden City, NY: Doubleday, 1980], p. 343) are plausible enough in that Biblical narrative can readily rearrange the chronology of events. However, this time it is a case of the critic destroying or at least lessening the dramatic effect of the narrative, which depends on Jonathan's surprising ignorance, obviously due to Saul's keeping a great deal from him since 1 Samuel 19:7. First Samuel 20:1 also indicates that in this case the incident belongs chronologically where it stands in the narrative.

4. Robert P. Gordon, *1 & 2 Samuel: A Commentary* (Exeter, UK: The Paternoster Press, 1986), p. 166 thinks "vowed again" cannot be correct because "there has been no mention of an oath before now." The text as it stands implies that David's questions in verse 1 were, in effect, a vow of innocence. This seems reasonable.

5. As had Saul himself at first. In 1 Samuel 16:22 exactly the same expression is used as here, when Saul said of David, ". . . he has found favor in my sight." Once again Edelman reads more into this than I think is there: "Jonathan's acceptance of David's status as king-elect has become public knowledge." Edelman, *Saul*, p. 154.

6. Twice in 1 Samuel 18:11 and once in 19:10.

7. Edelman draws an analogy to the words of Jonathan's weapons-bearer in 1 Samuel 14:7 and claims that Jonathan "now symbolically becomes David's weapons-bearer." Edelman, *Saul*, p. 155. This is far too much to read into a vague similarity between two statements. There is not much similarity in the wording at all.

8. The new moon was treated as an extra Sabbath (2 Kings 4:23; Isaiah 1:13; 66:23; Ezekiel 46:1; Amos 8:5; Colossians 2:16).

9. Edelman, *Saul*, p. 155.

10. Edelman's interpretation of the story is strongly affected by her view that 1 Samuel 16:19 indicates that Saul had heard a rumor of the anointing. So she says of the excuse Jonathan was to make that it "cannot but remind Saul of the rumoured circumstances of his anointing in Bethlehem at a sacrifice. . . ." Edelman, *Saul*, p. 155.

11. Compare the "sign" sought by Jonathan in 1 Samuel 14:8-10. Gordon, *1 & 2 Samuel*, p. 166.

12. *Ibid.*, p. 166.

13. "Therefore" in verse 8 (ESV), suggesting a logical link between David's appeal and what precedes, is unfortunate. The Hebrew simply has "And," and the basis for David's request is clearly what follows (the covenant) rather than what precedes (the harm that may or may not threaten David). NIV is better: "As for you, show kindness . . . for . . ."

14. There is a major debate surrounding the meaning of this word, one side arguing that it means "loyalty," suggesting that it is the outworking of the obligations involved in a preexisting relationship. So, for example, Katharine Doob Sakenfeld, *Faithfulness in Action: Loyalty in Biblical Perspective*, Overtures to Biblical Theology, 16 (Philadelphia: Fortress, 1985). The other side argues that the traditional sense of "mercy" or "kindness" is closer to the mark. See the important paper by Francis I. Andersen, "Yahweh, the Kind and Sensitive God," in Peter T. O'Brien and David G. Peterson, *God Who Is Rich in Mercy: Essays Presented to Dr. D.B. Knox* (Homebush West, Australia: Lancer Books, 1986), pp. 41-88.

15. The forcefulness of the expression can be sensed from other occurrences in 1 Samuel (2:30; 12:23; 14:45).

16. Hertzberg, *I & II Samuel*, p. 173 finds this suggestion "not convincing," but his argument is itself hardly persuasive.

17. The Hebrew idiom for "disclose" is "uncover the ear" (vv. 2, 12). It suggests a confidential, perhaps even whispered disclosure.

18. "Here Jonathan explicitly recognizes that the persecuted David is to displace Saul, his father." Robert Alter, *The David Story: A Translation with Commentary of 1 and 2 Samuel* (New York and London: W.W. Norton, 1999), p. 125.

19. It is unfortunate that English versions have quite different expressions in verses 8 (ESV, NRSV, "deal kindly") and 14, 15 (ESV, "show steadfast love"; NRSV, "show faithful love"), though the Hebrew is very similar. The NIV comes close with "show kindness" and "show unfailing kindness."

20. Alter, *David*, p. 126 includes all the words of verse 16 in Jonathan's speech, which is a little awkward because Jonathan then refers to himself by name. However, in favor of this rendering, it would mean that verse 16 refers to the one covenant with David rather than indicating that another was made. It is not clear why a further covenant would be needed when the covenant of chapter 18 was taken so seriously. The inclusion of all of verse 16 is also supported by the Septuagint, as reflected in the ESV margin.

21. "David swears by his *love* for Jonathan, for David *loved* Jonathan, as David *loved* his own life." Walter Brueggemann, *First and Second Samuel*, Interpretation: A Bible Commentary for Teaching and Preaching (Louisville: John Knox Press, 1990), p. 149. But David may have sworn by Jonathan's love, for Jonathan loved David as his own life (1 Samuel 18:3).

22. Some of the details in verses 18-22 are difficult in the original. The following expressions cover problems in the Hebrew that do not affect the overall meaning: "the third day," "quickly," "when the matter was in hand," "the stone heap." See Gordon, *1 & 2 Samuel*, p. 167.

23. Ackroyd, *First Book of Samuel*, pp. 164, 165.

CHAPTER THIRTY-FIVE: "IF ANYONE DOES NOT HATE HIS OWN FATHER . . ."

1. Actually the Hebrew here is a little obscure, and Alter insists that it cannot mean that Jonathan sat opposite the king. Robert Alter, *The David Story: A Translation with Commentary of 1 and 2 Samuel* (New York and London: W.W. Norton, 1999), p. 127. The Hebrew appears to mean that Jonathan "stood." The effect of the description of the table setting on the reader does not depend on precision, but on the fact that there is a detailed account of the various places at the table.

2. Robert P. Gordon, *1 & 2 Samuel: A Commentary* (Exeter, UK: The Paternoster Press, 1986), p. 168.

3. For the range of circumstances from which David might have become unclean "until the evening" see Leviticus 11:24, 25, 27, 28, 31, 32, 39, 40; 14:46; 15:5-11, 16-18, 19, 21-23, 27; 17:15; 22:6.

4. ". . . it is derogatory to call a man who is important in his own right merely by the name of his father." D. J. A. Clines, "X, X *ben* Y, *Ben* Y: Personal Names in Hebrew Narrative Style," *Vetus Testamentum* 22 (1972), pp. 266-287, 284.

5. Similarly Alter, *David*, p. 128.

6. Cf. the reference to Saul's "rebellion" in 1 Samuel 15:23.

7. Saul is referred to as Jonathan's "father" twelve times in this chapter, and twice we find reference to Jonathan as a "son."

8. David used the same word in 1 Samuel 20:3.

9. The shift from three arrows to one is not significant. "Hebrew narrative readily switches from multiple instances to a particular case." Alter, *David*, p. 129.

10. A helpful survey is K.-M. Beyse, *nasaq*, in G. Johannes Botterweck, Helmer Ringgren, and Heinz-Josef Fabry, *Theological Dictionary of the Old Testament*, 10 (Grand Rapids, MI: Eerdmans, 1999), pp. 72-76.

11. Although the Hebrew expression is difficult, this seems to be the sense.

CHAPTER THIRTY-SIX: "HAVE YOU NOT READ WHAT DAVID DID?"

1. The destruction of Shiloh is reflected in Jeremiah 7:12, 14; 26:6, 9 (cf. Psalm 78:60). None of these texts indicate when Shiloh was destroyed, just that its destruction was well-known.

2. Ahimelech was a son of Ahitub (1 Samuel 22:9), who was Ichabod's brother, a son of Eli's son, Phinehas (1 Samuel 14:3). Ahimelech could be the same person as Ahijah (1 Samuel 14:3). So Robert P. Gordon, *1 & 2 Samuel: A Commentary* (Exeter, UK: The Paternoster Press, 1986), p. 348, note 65; Hans Wilhelm Hertzberg, *I & II Samuel: A Commentary*, Old Testament Library (London: SCM Press, 1964), p. 179; John Mauchline, *1 and 2 Samuel*, New Century Bible (London: Oliphants, 1971), p. 150; C. F. Keil and F. Delitzsch, *Biblical Commentary on the Books of Samuel* (Grand Rapids, MI: Eerdmans, 1950), p. 217.

3. Cf. Hertzberg, *I & II Samuel*, p. 178.

4. Note how in 1 Samuel 20:39 "Only Jonathan and David knew *the matter*," namely, that the Lord had "sent [David] away" (1 Samuel 20:22). This understanding of David's words as "deceptively simple rather than simply deceptive" was advanced by Robert Polzin, *Samuel and the Deuteronomist: A Literary Study of the Deuteronomic History. Part Two, 1 Samuel*, Indiana Studies in Biblical Literature (Bloomington, IN: Indiana University Press, 1993), pp. 194, 195 and taken up by others — for example, Diana Vikander Edelman, *King Saul in the Historiography of Judah*, Journal for the Study of the Old Testament Supplement Series 121 (Sheffield, UK: Sheffield Academic Press, 1991), p. 163; Robert F. Youngblood, in *Expositor's Bible Commentary*, Vol. 3 (Grand Rapids, MI: Zondervan, 1992), p, 727.

5. Or was his motive "to protect the priest from any accusation of complicity in his flight from Saul"? Youngblood, *Expositor's Bible Commentary*, p. 728.

6. Edelman, *Saul*, p. 164.

7. This suggestion is strengthened by the reference to the removal and replacement of the bread in 1 Samuel 21:6 and the requirement of Leviticus 24:8 that the bread be arranged "before the LORD . . . every Sabbath day."

8. G. J. Wenham, "Why Does Sexual Intercourse Defile (Lev 15.18)?," *Zeitschrift fr die Alttestamentliche Wissenschaft* 95 (1983), pp. 432-434.

9. It has been argued that the incident in 1 Samuel 21:1-9 is out of chronological sequence and that the young men referred to are those whom David recruited in 1 Samuel 22:1, 2. Ralph W. Klein, *1 Samuel*, Word Biblical Commentary, 10 (Nashville: Word, 1983), p. 213. This could make sense if we had reason to assume that David was telling the

truth, but at this stage of the story David has proven to be a master of deception (see 1 Samuel 20:6; 21:13).

10. Argument about what "vessels" (admittedly a word with a range of possible meanings) refers to is probably settled by the quite common use of this term in 1 Samuel for a soldier's equipment, his weapons (1 Samuel 8:12; 14:1, 6, 7, 12, 17; 16:21; 17:54; 20:40; and especially, in this very story, 21:8). Mauchline is probably correct to insist that the word cannot mean "their bodies," despite the fact that this would fit the immediate context well. Mauchline, *1 and 2 Samuel*, p. 151.

11. ". . . for the sake of observing a higher commandment of love to a neighbor." Keil and Delitzsch, *Books of Samuel*, p. 218. "Human need takes priority over ceremonial law." Youngblood, *Expositor's Bible Commentary*, p. 728, citing F. F. Bruce.

12. "The point of the story must be that David is to receive the holy food as befits a king." Peter R. Ackroyd, *The First Book of Samuel*, Cambridge Bible Commentary (Cambridge, UK: Cambridge University Press, 1971), p. 170.

13. The same word used to refer to Doeg's occupation in 1 Samuel 21:7 (ESV, "herdsmen"; NIV, NRSV, "shepherd") is used to refer to David's former occupation in 1 Samuel 16:11; 17:15, 34, 40.

14. ". . . a foreigner has been put in charge of 'minding the flock' instead of Yahweh's chosen candidate, the trained shepherd David." Edelman, *Saul*, p. 165.

15. Joyce Baldwin, *1 and 2 Samuel*, Tyndale Old Testament Commentaries (Leicester, UK: Inter-Varsity Press, 1988), p. 138.

16. Baldwin, *1 and 2 Samuel*, p. 138. Intriguingly, a form of the same verb is used in 1 Samuel 21:5 ("women have been *kept from* us") and in 1 Samuel 9:17 ("He [Saul] . . . shall *restrain* my people"). Saul had "restrained" this Edomite, and very soon Saul's control over him would be all too evident (1 Samuel 22:18). Cf. Edelman, *Saul*, p. 165. Other suggestions for the meaning of Doeg's detention include: "detained at the sanctuary because of some ritual uncleanness" (Mauchline, *1 and 2 Samuel*, p. 151); "kept at the sanctuary by some religious (ceremonial) obligation" (Henry Preserved Smith, *A Critical and Exegetical Commentary on the Books of Samuel*, The International Critical Commentary [Edinburgh: T. & T. Clark, 1899], p. 198, 199); "in some way under constraint by the divine will" (Ackroyd, *First Book of Samuel*, p. 171); ". . . an act of penance, the performance of which was perhaps the cause of Doeg's later visible animosity against the priests" (Hertzberg, *I & II Samuel*, p. 181).

17. The unusual expression "under your hand" that we saw in verse 3 is repeated here.

18. Note that Jesus' reference to "those who were with him" simply means that Jesus was viewing the incident in terms of David's words to Ahimelech. This is how Ahimelech would have understood the incident. The fact that "those who were with him" were part of David's fictitious story rather than real characters in 1 Samuel 21 is not relevant to Jesus' purpose here.

CHAPTER THIRTY-SEVEN: OUT OF THE FRYING PAN . . .

1. Here I am referring to the indications in the so-called "titles" to Psalms 59 (referring to the incident in 1 Samuel 19:11); 34 and 56 (1 Samuel 21:10-15); 57 and 142 (1 Samuel 22:1 and/or 24:1-3); 52 (1 Samuel 22:9); and 54 (1 Samuel 23:19 and/or 26:1). Despite some controversy surrounding the subject, the "titles" are indisputably part of the Hebrew text of the Psalter and should be taken with full seriousness. A very helpful survey of the issues is given by Derek Kidner, *Psalms 1–72*, Tyndale Old Testament Commentaries (London and Downers Grove, IL: Inter-Varsity Press, 1973), pp. 32-35, 43-46.

2. For a very useful study of the New Testament's use of the Psalms, see Hans-Joachim Kraus, *Theology of the Psalms* (Minneapolis: Augsburg, 1986), Chapter 7: "The Psalms in the New Testament."

3. Counting the chapters from Jesus' entry into Jerusalem to the end of the Gospel, Matthew gives 29 percent of his account to this period, Mark 37 percent, Luke 25 percent, and John 48 percent. Average: close to one third!

4. Contra Smith who takes verse 10 as indicating that David's flight was directly from the presence of Saul and therefore makes more sense immediately after 1 Samuel 19:24. Henry Preserved Smith, *A Critical and Exegetical Commentary on the Books of Samuel*, The International Critical Commentary (Edinburgh: T. & T. Clark, 1899), p. 201. Cf. Hans Wilhelm Hertzberg, *I & II Samuel: A Commentary*, Old Testament Library (London: SCM Press, 1964), p. 182. "That day" makes it impossible to understand the text as it stands that way.

5. Again, 1 Samuel 21:10 literally says that David fled "from the presence of Saul."

6. Robert Alter, *The David Story: A Translation with Commentary of 1 and 2 Samuel* (New York and London: W.W. Norton, 1999), p. 133.

7. The older critical scholars can show a great lack of literary sensitivity. Smith described the words attributed to the Philistines here as "naively unhistorical." Smith, *Books of Samuel*, p. 201.

8. McCarter draws attention to the expression "kings of the land" in Joshua 12:1, 7 which, he says, means "local chieftains." P. Kyle McCarter, Jr., *I Samuel: A New Translation with Introduction, Notes & Commentary*, The Anchor Bible, Vol. 8 (Garden City, NY: Doubleday, 1980), p. 356.

9. Psalm 56, title. Suggestions concerning the meaning of the obscure term "Miktam" include "golden psalm," "atonement psalm," "secret prayer," "silent prayer," "indelible song," but there is no agreement. See Hans-Joachim Kraus, *Psalms 1–59: A Commentary* (Minneapolis: Augsburg, 1988), pp. 24, 25; Kidner, *Psalms 1–72*, p. 38.

10. First Samuel 21:10, 12 both have, more literally, "from the presence of" the respective kings.

11. In 1 Samuel fear of enemies is attributed to the Philistines (1 Samuel 4:7), the Israelites (1 Samuel 7:7; 17:11, 24), and Saul (1 Samuel 28:5). Saul was also said to fear the people (1 Samuel 15:24), David (1 Samuel 18:12, 29), and the words of Samuel (1 Samuel 28:20). The only other place in the books of Samuel where David is said to fear is 2 Samuel 6:9, where he was "afraid of the LORD." Fear of the Lord is a rather different theme (1 Samuel 12:14, 18, 24).

12. "Faith is seen here as a deliberate act, in defiance of one's emotional state. The first line might have too easily run, 'When I am at peace. . . .'" Kidner, *Psalms 1–72*, p. 203.

13. Cf. "all the good that he [the Lord] has spoken concerning you" (1 Samuel 25:30).

14. See also "you have brought this fellow" in verse 15. Hertzberg, *I & II Samuel*, p. 183; Peter R. Ackroyd, *The First Book of Samuel*, Cambridge Bible Commentary (Cambridge, UK: Cambridge University Press, 1971), p. 173. The title of Psalm 56 confirms this directly: "when the Philistines seized him in Gath."

15. The fact that Achish is referred to as Abimelech in the title to Psalm 34 is probably best explained by the suggestion that "Abimelech" may have been a cognomen of Philistine kings (like "Pharaoh" for Egyptian kings). Robert P. Gordon, "Abimelech," in J. D. Douglas et al, eds., *The Illustrated Bible Dictionary*, Part 1 (Leicester, UK and Wheaton, IL: Inter-Varsity Press and Tyndale House, 1980), p. 4.

CHAPTER THIRTY-EIGHT: *"GOD CHOSE WHAT WAS LOW AND DESPISED IN THE WORLD"*

1. It is possible that one or both of these psalm titles refer to the cave of Engedi (1 Samuel 24:1-4). The fact that Psalm 57 immediately follows Psalm 56, which is linked to the Gath episode, supports but does not prove the proposal that Psalm 57 belongs to David's time, immediately after he left Gath, in the cave of Adullam. One other piece of evidence in support of this is the fact that the word "fled" used in the title to Psalm 57 was used of David in the 1 Samuel narrative before and in the context of the cave of Adullam (1 Samuel 19:12, 18; 20:1; 21:10; 22:17), but rarely later in the story (only in 1 Samuel 27:4).

2. While it is true that the Hebrew lacks a word corresponding to "purpose" in Psalm 57:2, the sense of the line is captured by the English translation. It is not appropriate to generalize this as a statement about a God who "does things" (true as this undoubtedly is), for it is what God will do *for David* ("for me"), his chosen one, that is on view.

3. There is possibly a deliberate ironic allusion in 1 Samuel 22:2 to David's former role. The word translated "captain" here is the same as the word translated "commander" in 1 Samuel 18:13.

4. Diana Vikander Edelman, *King Saul in the Historiography of Judah*, Journal for the Study of the Old Testament Supplement Series 121 (Sheffield, UK: Sheffield Academic Press, 1991), p. 171.

5. Edelman is surely mistaken in describing David's claim to not know "what God will do for me" as a "ruse to secure his parents," not because David was incapable of such a thing, but because his confidence in the Lord's promises did not mean knowledge of the details. *Ibid.*, p. 172.

6. A similar suggestion is made by Robert Alter, *The David Story: A Translation with Commentary of 1 and 2 Samuel* (New York and London: W.W. Norton, 1999), p. 136. We simply do not know what happened to David's parents after this. Other attempts have been made to fill in the gaps in the account here. See, for example Ralph W. Klein, *1 Samuel*, Word Biblical Commentary, 10 (Nashville: Word, 1983), pp. 222, 223; Hans Wilhelm Hertzberg, *I & II Samuel: A Commentary*, Old Testament Library (London: SCM Press, 1964), pp. 184, 185.

CHAPTER THIRTY-NINE: THE ANTICHRIST

1. See Leon Morris, "Antichrist," in J. D. Douglas et al, eds., *The Illustrated Bible Dictionary*, Part 1 (Leicester, UK and Wheaton, IL: Inter-Varsity Press and Tyndale House, 1980), pp. 69, 70.

2. So Robert Alter, *The David Story: A Translation with Commentary of 1 and 2 Samuel* (New York and London: W.W. Norton, 1999), p. 136.

3. This is worth noting because Saul seems to address or refer to almost everyone as "son of . . .": David is "the son of Jesse" (vv. 7, 8, 13), Jonathan is "my son" (v. 8), Ahimelech is "son of Ahitub" (v. 12). Saul apparently found it difficult to give various people their own names!

4. Walter Brueggemann, *First and Second Samuel*, Interpretation: A Bible Commentary for Teaching and Preaching (Louisville: John Knox Press, 1990), p. 158.

5. Contra Ralph W. Klein, *1 Samuel*, Word Biblical Commentary, 10 (Nashville: Word, 1983), p. 224, who understands that David had promised these things, but Saul was questioning whether he would deliver. This, I think, is a misunderstanding.

6. This paragraph is based on Brueggemann, *First and Second Samuel*, p. 158.

7. McCarter's suggestion that Doeg presided *over* Saul's servants seems unlikely. P. Kyle McCarter, Jr., *I Samuel: A New Translation with Introduction, Notes & Commentary*, The Anchor Bible, Vol. 8 (Garden City, NY: Doubleday, 1980), p. 364.

8. ". . . looks like a fabrication — and one that would especially enrage Saul, who repeatedly had access to divine knowledge blocked." Alter, *David*, p. 137.

9. Alter, *David*, p. 137. Contra Peter R. Ackroyd, *The First Book of Samuel*, Cambridge Bible Commentary (Cambridge, UK: Cambridge University Press, 1971), p. 178 who insists that this "is not to be regarded as a scornful form of address."

10. So Brueggemann, *First and Second Samuel*, p. 159.

11. So Alter, *David*, p. 138.

12. It was behavior like this that would later produce responses like Psalm 137:7-9.

13. Compare, for example Joshua 6:21.

14. Alter, *David*, p. 139.

15. According to Alter, *David*, p. 139. Other meanings proposed include "father of excellence" and "the father is abundant."

CHAPTER FORTY: THE CHRIST MUST SUFFER

1. This is the view of J. Fokkelman and is cited with disapproval by Diana Vikander Edelman, *King Saul in the Historiography of Judah*, Journal for the Study of the Old

Testament Supplement Series 121 (Sheffield, UK: Sheffield Academic Press, 1991), p. 184.

2. For example, Edelman, *Saul*, pp. 186, 187 favors seeing Keilah as not Judean (that is, not Israelite). Walter Brueggemann, *First and Second Samuel*, Interpretation: A Bible Commentary for Teaching and Preaching (Louisville: John Knox Press, 1990), p. 162 assumes it to be Judean. In support of Brueggemann see Joshua 15:44.

3. The fact of quoted words that are themselves significant (in this case it is the Lord who introduced the important word "save") makes unlikely the common explanation that Urim and Thummim were used to give yes/no answers to questions. Contra Robert Alter, *The David Story: A Translation with Commentary of 1 and 2 Samuel* (New York and London: W.W. Norton, 1999), p. 141. See the helpful discussion of God's communication with David in this chapter in Robert Polzin, *Samuel and the Deuteronomist: A Literary Study of the Deuteronomic History. Part Two, 1 Samuel*, Indiana Studies in Biblical Literature (Bloomington, IN: Indiana University Press, 1993), pp. 200-203.

4. Some have suggested that the men did not realize that David had consulted the Lord the first time, and David may have made his second inquiry before them to reassure them. So Brueggemann, *First and Second Samuel*, p. 162.

5. The word "hand" appears nine times in 1 Samuel 23: David's hand (vv. 4, 16), Abiathar's hand (v. 6), and Saul's hand (vv. 7, 11, 12, 14, 17, 20).

6. "Chapter 23 illustrates the epistemological disadvantage under which Saul operates in his quest of David." Polzin, *Samuel and the Deuteronomist*, p. 200.

7. The ESV has, "When Abiathar the son of Ahimelech *had* fled to David to Keilah, he *had* come down with an ephod in his hand" (emphasis added). The past perfect tenses imply that Abiathar had come to David earlier. The NIV makes this more explicit by putting the whole verse in parentheses. The words "to Keilah" are difficult for this understanding (even though the Hebrew lacks "to"). C. F. Keil and F. Delitzsch, *Biblical Commentary on the Books of Samuel* (Grand Rapids, MI: Eerdmans, 1950), p. 229 offer a way of understanding the text as it stands along these lines, but it is awkward. Commentators who consider that Abiathar came to David before the salvation of Keilah often propose emending the text of verse 6 either to remove the reference to Keilah (Alter, *David*, p. 141) or, with support from the Septuagint, to indicate that Abiathar went down to Keilah *with* David (Hans Wilhelm Hertzberg, *I & II Samuel: A Commentary*, Old Testament Library [London: SCM Press, 1964], p. 189; P. Kyle McCarter, Jr., *I Samuel: A New Translation with Introduction, Notes & Commentary*, The Anchor Bible, Vol. 8 [Garden City, NY: Doubleday, 1980], p. 369 and Ralph W. Klein, *1 Samuel*, Word Biblical Commentary, 10 [Nashville: Word, 1983], p. 228). Edelman, *Saul*, p. 184 fails to adequately account for "Keilah" in verse 6.

8. This is argued at some length, along with a full discussion of the Biblical evidence concerning "ephod," by Cornelius Van Dam, *The Urim and Thummim: A Means of Revelation in Ancient Israel* (Winona Lake. IN: Eisenbrauns, 1997), pp. 140-153.

9. Samuel wore a "linen ephod" (1 Samuel 2:18), as did all eighty-five priests killed by Doeg (1 Samuel 22:18).

10. Arguments that the ephod in 1 Samuel is different from the ephod in Exodus are countered by Van Dam, *Urim*, pp. 143-145.

11. Van Dam offers a compelling argument against the commonly held view that using the Urim and Thummim was like casting lots. He considers that revelations by "Urim and Thummim" involved prophecy. See *ibid.*, pp. 215-232.

12. There are difficulties with the unusual Hebrew verb used here, but the context leaves us in little doubt of the general sense. Keil and Delitzsch, *Books of Samuel*, p. 229 argue for the sense "rejected," but most commentators emend the text.

13. As Polzin, *Samuel and the Deuteronomist*, p. 200 astutely notes, "The entire section comprising chapters 20-23 constitutes a meditation on the various effects of knowledge or the lack of it upon character and reader alike."

14. "The political paradox of the situation that has evolved is evident: David has achieved a victory against Israel's principal enemy; Saul now moves to destroy that victor, enlisting the aid of the people David saved." Alter, *David*, p. 142.

CHAPTER FORTY-ONE: *"THEREFORE WE DO NOT LOSE HEART"*

1. So Diana Vikander Edelman, *King Saul in the Historiography of Judah*, Journal for the Study of the Old Testament Supplement Series 121 (Sheffield, UK: Sheffield Academic Press, 1991), p. 189.
2. "Saul knows, but he does not yet know that he knows, and so his son Jonathan knows on his behalf." Walter Brueggemann, *First and Second Samuel*, Interpretation: A Bible Commentary for Teaching and Preaching (Louisville: John Knox Press, 1990), p. 164. See Saul's recognition of David as a *potential* king in 1 Samuel 20:31. I find unconvincing Edelman's argument (on which much of her interpretation of the narrative rests) that Saul had known the divine plan for David all along: "Saul's knowledge of the divine plan that calls for David rather than Jonathan to succeed him on the throne has already been revealed to the audience back in 17:37 and so is not news to David or the audience." Edelman, *Saul*, p. 188.
3. Contra Edelman, *Saul*, p. 189.
4. Strictly the Hebrew word for "covenant" in connection with Jonathan and David is used only in 1 Samuel 18:3 and 20:8 (clearly both referring to the same agreement). In 1 Samuel 20:16 and 1 Samuel 23:18 an abbreviated expression is used that lacks the word "covenant." This reinforces the impression that the latter two references are to reaffirmations of the agreement already settled in 1 Samuel 18:3 "because such mutual promises cannot be reiterated too often among real allies and trusting friends." Brueggemann, *First and Second Samuel*, p. 165.
5. Rather than "the" Ziphites. So Robert Alter, *The David Story: A Translation with Commentary of 1 and 2 Samuel* (New York and London: W.W. Norton, 1999), p. 144, although the reason for understanding the text this way is contextual rather than, as Alter says, the omission of the definite article. To illustrate the point, the definite article is frequently omitted from the Hebrew for "Philistines," but the context usually indicates that the sense is *"the* Philistines."
6. The same verb occurs in 1 Samuel 15:3, 9, 15 (ESV, "spared"), and nowhere else in 1 Samuel.
7. "[This] points up the madness of his obsessive pursuit of David: at a time when Israel's major national enemy is repeatedly sending troops against the territory Saul is supposed to be governing and protecting, he is devoting his attention, and his troops, to the pursuit of David." Alter, *David*, p. 145.

CHAPTER FORTY-TWO: *"HE DID NOT REVILE IN RETURN"*

1. G. G. Garner, "En-gedi," in J. D. Douglas et al, eds., *The Illustrated Bible Dictionary*, Part 1 (Leicester, UK and Wheaton, IL: Inter-Varsity Press and Tyndale House, 1980), p. 446.
2. David still had 600 men with him in 1 Samuel 27:2 and 30:9.
3. "There is no lack of caves in the wilderness of Judah; among them are some which run back, as it were, in sections: the immediate entrance gives way to further caves, often connected by half-blocked passages." Hans Wilhelm Hertzberg, *I & II Samuel: A Commentary*, Old Testament Library (London: SCM Press, 1964), p. 196.
4. It is even closer to the *Kethib* reading of the Hebrew, which has "enemies."
5. This understanding differs from commentators who think that the men were either "fabricating an oracle" (Robert P. Gordon, *1 & 2 Samuel: A Commentary* [Exeter, UK: The Paternoster Press, 1986], p. 179) or that "an earlier [unrecorded] divine promise to David is being quoted" (Peter R. Ackroyd, *The First Book of Samuel*, Cambridge Bible Commentary [Cambridge, UK: Cambridge University Press, 1971], p. 188; similarly Ralph W. Klein, *1 Samuel*, Word Biblical Commentary, 10 [Nashville: Word, 1983], p. 239).

6. Similarly Gordon, *1 & 2 Samuel*, p. 179.

7. The expression translated "David's heart struck him" is vivid and is used in only one other place, 2 Samuel 24:10, to describe David's remorse at ordering the census, another act that had a deeper significance than might at first appear. Robert P. Gordon, "David's Rise and Saul's Demise: Narrative Analogy in 1 Samuel 24–26," *Tyndale Bulletin* 31 (1980), pp. 37-64 (the significance of the cutting of Saul's robe is discussed on pages 55-57, and my exposition has benefited from this discussion).

8. In that text it is not unambiguously clear who tore whose robe. Although it seems most likely, from the context, that Saul tore Samuel's robe, perhaps the ambiguity supports the parallel noted here. In other words the important point in 1 Samuel 15 is that a robe was torn, not whose robe (it does not matter that it may have been Samuel's). In 1 Samuel 24 a robe was torn too (even if this time it was Saul's).

9. Gordon, "David's Rise," p. 56 supports "the complementarity of the two passages" by the fact that the Hebrew expression translated "a corner of [Saul's] robe" (1 Samuel 24:4 [Hebrew 5] and "the skirt of his robe" (1 Samuel 15:27) is not found anywhere else in the Old Testament. (Strictly he should have added 1 Samuel 24:11 [Hebrew 12] where the expression occurs twice, although this hardly weakens his point.)

10. The vividness of the metaphor can be seen from its literal use in Judges 14:6 where it is translated "tore" and "tears."

11. Gordon, *1 & 2 Samuel*, p. 180.

12. Following the word order in the Hebrew brings out an implicit parallel between "the king of Israel" and "wickedness."

CHAPTER FORTY-THREE: VENGEANCE BELONGS TO THE LORD

1. The only appearance of Samuel in the story since 1 Samuel 16:13 is the strange incident in 1 Samuel 19:18-24, where Samuel is in the background. No words or actions of Samuel are mentioned there.

2. "It is as though Samuel has lingered over the narrative, waiting until even Saul has finally acknowledged the turn of destiny. When Saul makes that drastic acknowledgment (24:20), Samuel's work is indeed completed and he may die. He has no more work to do." Walter Brueggemann, *First and Second Samuel*, Interpretation: A Bible Commentary for Teaching and Preaching (Louisville: John Knox Press, 1990), p. 175.

3. The brevity is perhaps compensated for by the fact that the notice is repeated in 1 Samuel 28:3.

4. "Since the days of Moses and Joshua, no man had arisen to whom the covenant nation owed so much as to Samuel, who has been justly called the reformer and restorer of the theocracy." C. F. Keil and F. Delitzsch, *Biblical Commentary on the Books of Samuel* (Grand Rapids, MI: Eerdmans, 1950), p. 238.

5. "But now [Samuel] is dead, and there is an imminent danger that there might be no more Israel." Hans Wilhelm Hertzberg, *I & II Samuel: A Commentary*, Old Testament Library (London: SCM Press, 1964), p. 199.

6. Contra Robert P. Gordon, "David's Rise and Saul's Demise: Narrative Analogy in 1 Samuel 24–26," *Tyndale Bulletin* 31 (1980), p. 181; John Mauchline, *1 and 2 Samuel*, New Century Bible (London: Oliphants, 1971), p. 166; and P. Kyle McCarter, Jr., *I Samuel: A New Translation with Introduction, Notes & Commentary*, The Anchor Bible, Vol. 8 (Garden City, NY: Doubleday, 1980), p. 385 who refer "the stronghold" at the end of chapter 24 to Adullam, presumably on the basis of the same word being used at 1 Samuel 22:4. But we have seen that "the stronghold" of 1 Samuel 22:4 was probably not Adullam because it was apparently not in Judah.

7. The traditional verse division suits the syntax of the Hebrew better than the splitting of verse 1 over two paragraphs as in ESV, NIV. The next episode begins with verse 2, not verse 1b. Cf. NRSV. Contra Mauchline, *1 and 2 Samuel*, p. 167.

8. The NIV follows the Septuagint and has "Maon" in place of "Paran." It is likely that the Septuagint, like a number of modern commentators (for example, Ralph W. Klein,

1 Samuel, Word Biblical Commentary, 10 [Nashville: Word, 1983], p. 245; Joyce Baldwin, *1 and 2 Samuel*, Tyndale Old Testament Commentaries [Leicester, UK: Inter-Varsity Press, 1988], 147; McCarter, *1 Samuel*, p. 388; Mauchline, *1 and 2 Samuel*, pp. 167, 168), linked verse 1b closely with what follows and thought Paran was then too far south. If the Hebrew text is followed here (as ESV), the syntax does not suggest a close sequential relationship between verse 1 and verse 2 and would be consistent with an implied but unspecified interval of time passing between David's journey to Paran and the next episode in Maon. The reference in verse 4 to "the wilderness" need not then be to "the wilderness of Paran" of verse 1b. After all, David had been in "the wilderness" in several places in these chapters ("the wilderness of Ziph," 23:14, 15; "the wilderness of Maon," 1 Samuel 23:24, 25; "the wilderness of Engedi," 24:1; as well as "the wilderness of Paran," 25:1).

9. "Badly behaved" is, more literally, "bad of deeds"; cf. "abominable deeds" in Psalm 14:1!

10. This differs from a number of commentators who suggest that the similarity between "Caleb" and the Hebrew word for "dog" (used in 1 Samuel 24:14) is the basis for a pun: "he was a Calebite/a dog." Diana Vikander Edelman, *King Saul in the Historiography of Judah*, Journal for the Study of the Old Testament Supplement Series 121 (Sheffield, UK: Sheffield Academic Press, 1991), p. 206; Robert P. Gordon, *1 & 2 Samuel: A Commentary* (Exeter, UK: The Paternoster Press, 1986), p. 182; Hertzberg, *I & II Samuel*, p. 199; Mauchline, *1 and 2 Samuel*, p. 168. Keil and Delitzsch, *Books of Samuel*, p. 239 propose understanding the term to be not a pun, but a word *meaning* "dog-like," citing support from the Septuagint, Josephus as well as the Arabic and Syriac. Alternatively the Hebrew text may be read as "he was like his heart," a possible allusion to Psalm 14:1. Robert F. Youngblood, "1 Samuel," in Frank E. Gaebelein, ed., *The Expositor's Bible Commentary*, Vol. 3 (Grand Rapids, MI: Zondervan, 1992), p. 754.

11. A different Hebrew word (not *nabal*) is used for foolishness in this verse.

12. More subtle is the fact that both Nabal and Saul are described with the word translated here "harsh" and in 1 Samuel 20:10 "roughly." Noted by Edelman, *Saul*, p. 206 and others.

13. Some commentators see David as involved in a "protection racket." E.g., Brueggemann, *First and Second Samuel*, p. 176; Henry Preserved Smith, *A Critical and Exegetical Commentary on the Books of Samuel*, The International Critical Commentary (Edinburgh: T. & T. Clark, 1899), p. 222. The comment of Bruce Birch is apt: "This view seems more influenced by old gangster movies than by the biblical narrative." Leander E. Keck, et al, eds., *The New Interpreter's Bible*, Vol. 2 (Nashville: Abingdon, 1998), p. 1166.

14. Compare David's own description of the dangers in 1 Samuel 17:34.

15. The Hebrew text at the beginning of verse 6 is difficult to translate and may simply be a form of greeting not otherwise preserved. See Gordon, *1 & 2 Samuel*, p. 182.

16. Here Nabal rejects David's respectful self-designation as Nabal's "son." Youngblood, *Expositor's Bible Commentary*, p. 755.

17. The precise sense of the expression is debated. One suggestion is "sons of destructiveness." J. A. Emerton, "Sheol and the Sons of Belial," *Vetus Testamentum* 37 (1987), pp. 214-217.

18. The vulgarity of the phrase in verse 22 translated in the ESV as "one male" is preserved in the King James Version literal rendering, "any that pisseth against the wall." The phrase occurs again in verse 34 and in 1 Kings 14:10; 16:11; 21:21; 2 Kings 9:8. Almost all more recent English translations avoid the offensiveness of David's language. This is a sensitive issue. McCarter suggests that the language of the KJV "has become vulgar in modern English." McCarter, *1 Samuel*, p. 398. But was it ever *not* vulgar? Birch is surely mistaken to call the Hebrew expression a "euphemism"! Birch, *New Interpreter's Bible*, p. 1168. Alter's comment is nearer the mark: "The phrase, of course, is a rough and vivid epithet for 'male,' and one that occurs only in curses. Its edge of vulgarity seems perfectly right for David's anger." Robert Alter, *The David Story: A Translation with Commentary of 1 and 2 Samuel* (New York and London: W.W. Norton, 1999), p. 156.

19. The form of David's oath has caused some discussion. The difficulty is that David was clearly expressing his strong intention to eliminate Nabal's men. Why would he

call down a curse on his enemies only if he *failed*? Some English versions follow the Septuagint ("May God deal with David, be it ever so severely . . . ," NIV; similarly NEB, RSV, NRSV). It makes more sense for David to call down a curse on *himself* if he failed. The Hebrew text has been variously explained as a scribal attempt to remove the idea that David, the great king, had cursed himself, given the fact that he did not in fact carry out his sworn intention here. Cf. Peter R. Ackroyd, *The First Book of Samuel*, Cambridge Bible Commentary (Cambridge, UK: Cambridge University Press, 1971), p. 197; McCarter, *I Samuel*, p. 394; Mauchline, *1 and 2 Samuel*, p. 169; Klein, *1 Samuel*, p. 245; Smith, *Books of Samuel*, pp. 225, 226. Gordon asserts, "*David's enemies* is almost certainly euphemistic for David himself." Gordon, *1 & 2 Samuel*, pp. 167, 184. How "David's enemies" can be a euphemism for "David" is not explained. The problem is exaggerated. The Hebrew text may lack precision, but it makes good sense. It may be understood to mean, "May God spare David's enemies if David spares any of Nabal's men," or "May God deal with David's enemies (including Nabal's men) if David fails to do so." Alternatively Keil and Delitzsch propose the sense, "as truly as God will punish the enemies of David, so certainly will I not leave till the morning. . . ." Keil and Delitzsch, *Books of Samuel*, p. 242.

20.   To the contrary, McCarter argues that Abigail's opening words have "nothing to do with Nabal's misbehavior" but are "simply part of the conventions of courteous and respectful behavior." McCarter, *I Samuel*, p. 398. Perhaps he is right about the language being conventional (although the parallels cited are not conclusive), but he is surely wrong to deny that a reference to "guilt" in this context (however conventional) would be linked by any hearer to the guilt that hung so heavily over the situation, namely, Nabal's guilt so emphatically denounced in verse 21.

21.   Literally "your maidservant" or "your handmaid," a term used by Abigail five times as she spoke to David (she called David "my lord" fifteen times!).

22.   ". . . the possibility that David may take matters into his own hand and thus make himself master of his fate, instead of letting it be guided by the Lord." Hertzberg, *I & II Samuel*, p. 204.

23.   "Present" in 1 Samuel 25:27 is literally "blessing."

24.   Baldwin suggests that the request for forgiveness is for any offense she may have implied by her gift. Baldwin, *1 and 2 Samuel*, p. 151; similarly Hertzberg, *I & II Samuel*, p. 204. McCarter interprets: "forgive me for speaking further." McCarter, *I Samuel*, p. 398, followed by Klein, *1 Samuel*, p. 250. Again, however, since the issue at hand is the terrible offense Nabal had given to David, it is probable that a reference to forgiveness of a trespass would be related to that matter.

25.   Regarding the probable sense of "evil shall not be found in you" (v. 28), "the thought that he might also be preserved from wrong-doing is not expressed till ver. 31." Keil and Delitzsch, *Books of Samuel*, p. 244.

26.   The same coarse expression is used at the end of 1 Samuel 25:34 as in verse 22.

27.   The echo of this verse in 1 Samuel 25:39 is masked in the translation. "Who has avenged" in 1 Samuel 25:39 represents the same Hebrew words as "plead my cause" in 1 Samuel 24:15. See Gordon, "David's Rise," p. 48.

CHAPTER FORTY-FOUR: RIGHTEOUSNESS AND FAITHFULNESS

1.   "Do you not *yet* understand?" (Mark 8:21).

2.   E.g., Peter R. Ackroyd, *The First Book of Samuel*, Cambridge Bible Commentary (Cambridge, UK: Cambridge University Press, 1971), p. 202; Henry Preserved Smith, *A Critical and Exegetical Commentary on the Books of Samuel*, The International Critical Commentary (Edinburgh: T. & T. Clark, 1899), p. 229; Ralph W. Klein, *1 Samuel*, Word Biblical Commentary, 10 (Nashville: Word, 1983), p. 236; P. Kyle McCarter, Jr., *I Samuel: A New Translation with Introduction, Notes & Commentary*, The Anchor Bible, Vol. 8 (Garden City, NY: Doubleday, 1980), pp. 385-387. Some of the weaknesses of the widely held critical position are discussed by John Mauchline, *1 and 2 Samuel*, New Century Bible (London: Oliphants, 1971), pp. 172, 173; also Robert P.

Gordon, *1 & 2 Samuel: A Commentary* (Exeter, UK: The Paternoster Press, 1986), p. 187; C. F. Keil and F. Delitzsch, *Biblical Commentary on the Books of Samuel* (Grand Rapids, MI: Eerdmans, 1950), pp. 247-249.

3. While the Hebrew expression can mean "east of," it also means "in front of" (as in 1 Samuel 24:2) or "before." First Samuel 23:19 has already indicated that the hill of Hachilah is "*south* of Jeshimon." An artificial contradiction is created by putting "east of" in 1 Samuel 26:1. Cf. Gordon, *1 & 2 Samuel*, p. 187; S. R. Driver, *Notes on the Hebrew Text and the Topography of the Book of Samuel with an Introduction on Hebrew Palaeography and Facsimiles of Inscriptions and Maps*, second edition (Oxford, UK: Clarendon, 1913), p. 205.

4. Note the almost identical wording in 1 Samuel 24:2: "three thousand chosen men out of all Israel . . . to seek David."

5. David's force remained at about that size (see 1 Samuel 25:13; 27:2; 30:9).

6. At the end of verse 4 the Hebrew has an expression (RSV renders it, "of a certainty") that the ESV has left untranslated. The turnaround of the Saul/David situation is subtly reflected in the fact that the same expression was used in 1 Samuel 23:23, when Saul insisted on getting "sure information." Cf. NIV, which has "definitely" in 1 Samuel 26:4 and "definite" in 1 Samuel 23:23. See Robert Alter, *The David Story: A Translation with Commentary of 1 and 2 Samuel* (New York and London: W.W. Norton, 1999), p. 163.

7. David's story will, of course, much later feature another Hittite in his service, by the name of Uriah. See 2 Samuel 11.

8. "David the warrior chieftain is surrounded by his three nephews, the three blood-minded sons of Zeruiah: two of them impetuous (Abishai and Asahel), the third, who is David's commander, ruthlessly calculating (Joab)." Alter, *David*, p. 163.

9. Diana Vikander Edelman, *King Saul in the Historiography of Judah*, Journal for the Study of the Old Testament Supplement Series 121 (Sheffield, UK: Sheffield Academic Press, 1991), p. 224.

10. James and John were the sons of Zebedee named "Boanerges, that is, Sons of Thunder" by Jesus (Mark 3:17). While it is true that the Gospel records give us little information about these brothers, perhaps their reactions in Mark 9:38 and Luke 9:54 indicate something of what lay behind their nickname. For details see R. T. France, *The Gospel of Mark: A Commentary on the Greek Text*, The New International Greek Testament Commentary (Grand Rapids, MI and Carlisle, UK: Eerdmans and Paternoster, 2002), pp. 161, 162.

11. Alter, *David*, p. 164.

12. There the same term for "deep sleep" occurs.

13. Walter Brueggemann, *First and Second Samuel*, Interpretation: A Bible Commentary for Teaching and Preaching (Louisville: John Knox Press, 1990), p. 185.

14. The same verb root is used for acting foolishly in 1 Samuel 13:13 and 26:21. Although it is not the same as the word for fool in the Nabal story, it may reasonably be regarded as a synonym (both are the antithesis of wisdom: compare Deuteronomy 32:6 and Ecclesiastes 2:19).

15. Robert P. Gordon, "David's Rise and Saul's Demise: Narrative Analogy in 1 Samuel 24–26," *Tyndale Bulletin* 31(1980), p. 60.

16. In verse 23 "every man" (see Driver, *Notes*, p. 209 in support of this rendering) is literally "the man" and is probably a slightly veiled reference to David himself. The following would be a fair rendering of the Hebrew syntax: "The LORD will return his righteousness and his faithfulness to the man into whose hand the LORD gave you today." Similarly Mauchline, *1 and 2 Samuel*, p. 176; contra Gordon, *1 & 2 Samuel*, p. 190. Cf. Keil and Delitzsch, *Books of Samuel*, p. 254: "Jehovah will recompense His righteousness and His faithfulness to the man into whose hand Jehovah hath given thee today. . . ."

CHAPTER FORTY-FIVE: CLEVER AND CUNNING SUCCESS

1. For David at his best, see 1 Samuel 26:9-11, 23-24.

2. "For those scholars who have argued that David is no more a historical figure than King Arthur, this whole episode constitutes a problem: why would such a later, legendary, and supposedly glorifying tradition attribute this act of national treachery to David? (It would be rather like the invention of a story that Winston Churchill spent 1917–1918 in Berlin, currying the favor of the kaiser.) The compelling inference is that the writer had authentic knowledge of a period when David collaborated with the Philistines; he was unwilling to omit this uncomfortable information, though he did try to mitigate it." Robert Alter, *The David Story: A Translation with Commentary of 1 and 2 Samuel* (New York and London: W.W. Norton, 1999), p. 168.

3. Literally the text says, "David said *to* his heart . . ." These are words David addressed *to* himself. Dale Ralph Davis suggests the importance of "talking truth to yourself, especially by speaking to yourself the truth about your God." This, he says, is what David failed to do here. Dale Ralph Davis, *Looking on the Heart: Expositions of the Book of 1 Samuel*, Vol. 2, Expositor's Guide to the Historical Books (Grand Rapids, MI: Baker, 1994), pp. 140, 141.

4. There are only nineteen occurrences in the Old Testament.

5. It is striking that there is no explicit mention of God anywhere in 1 Samuel 27.

6. In my opinion Edelman overstates her case but highlights the problem: "David has lost sight of his own special relationship with Yahweh as the king-elect and has lost faith in Yahweh's continued protection and support. . . . Why this sudden attack of nerves and development of an inferiority complex?" Diana Vikander Edelman, *King Saul in the Historiography of Judah*, Journal for the Study of the Old Testament Supplement Series 121 (Sheffield, UK: Sheffield Academic Press, 1991), pp. 232, 233.

7. After the great victory over the prophets of Baal at Mount Carmel, Elijah fled from the land because "they seek my life" (1 Kings 19:10). He, too, denied that there was now "good" for him (1 Kings 19:4, my translation).

8. Again Edelman may overstate the matter, while indicating the issue, when she describes the verb concerned as "a term that carries with it overtones of betrayal or transgression as well as the movement across physical space." Edelman, *Saul*, p. 233.

9. Alter, *David*, p. 168.

10. *Ibid.*, p. 169.

11. "Is he justified in using self-help to avoid a confrontation with Saul, or does the rule of avoiding self-help apply only to situations where one is aggressively confronting his enemy?" Edelman, *Saul*, p. 232.

12. The idiom in 1 Samuel 16:22 is identical to that in 1 Samuel 27:5, despite the variation in some English translations (ESV, "found favor in my sight" and "found favor in your eyes"; NIV, "I am pleased with him" and "I have found favor in your eyes").

13. Alter, *David*, p. 169.

14. Cf. Peter R. Ackroyd, *The First Book of Samuel*, Cambridge Bible Commentary (Cambridge, UK: Cambridge University Press, 1971), p. 206.

15. The statement at the end of verse 6 is *prima facie* evidence for dating the books of Samuel no earlier than the division of the kingdom after the death of Solomon (1 Kings 12) and no later than the Babylonian exile (2 Kings 25).

16. The year and four months mentioned here supports the view that 1 Samuel 13:1 cannot mean that Saul's entire reign was only two years long. Perhaps because of this apparent discrepancy the Septuagint omits "a year and" and implies that David's stay in Philistia was only four months.

17. Gordon cites Joshua 13:2 as evidence that they were neighbors of the Philistines. Robert P. Gordon, *1 & 2 Samuel: A Commentary* (Exeter, UK: The Paternoster Press, 1986), pp. 191, 192.

18. Hertzberg suggests that "Girzites" may be another form of the name "Girgashites." Hans Wilhelm Hertzberg, *I & II Samuel: A Commentary*, Old Testament Library (London: SCM Press, 1964), p. 214, note c.

19. "In doing so he is also serving Achish's purposes, for these peoples are also hostile to the Philistines (like the Israelites, latecomer interlopers in Canaan)." Alter, *David*, p. 169.

20. The Hebrew for "inhabitants" here is feminine. John Mauchline, *1 and 2 Samuel*, New Century Bible (London: Oliphants, 1971), p. 178 suggests that the literal meaning may therefore be, "for these were the inhabited areas of land."

21. The hint is really contained in the words "from of old" in verse 8 and is so brief that it is entirely eliminated by a small emendation of the Hebrew text that is followed, for example, by the NEB. See Gordon, *1 & 2 Samuel*, p. 192.

22. "Do not spare them," 1 Samuel 15:3.

23. The command to "devote to destruction" was sometimes applied to forbid the taking of booty (e.g., in Jericho, Joshua 6:21). On other occasions booty was allowed to be taken (e.g., in Ai, Joshua 8:2). It is not certain, therefore, that "David is not carrying out a 'ban' against these groups because he keeps all the livestock as booty." Alter, *David*, p. 170.

24. On Jerahmeelites and Kenites see 1 Samuel 15:6; 30:29. For details see F. F. Bruce, "Jerahmeel," and J. A. Motyer, "Kenites," in J. D. Douglas et al, eds., *The Illustrated Bible Dictionary*, Part 2 (Leicester, UK and Wheaton, IL: Inter-Varsity Press and Tyndale House, 1980), pp. 743, 849.

25. The story of David among the Philistines continues in 1 Samuel 28:1, 2, and then in chapters 29, 30. However, the new development of the Philistines' fresh hostilities against Israel in 1 Samuel 28:1 justifies the chapter division after 1 Samuel 27:12 and is important for the main story that chapter 28 has to tell.

CHAPTER FORTY-SIX: "HAVING NO HOPE AND WITHOUT GOD"

1. Note that in context Paul's words are applied specifically to the situation of *Gentiles* before they had come to Jesus Christ. See the nuanced discussion by Peter T. O'Brien, *The Letter to the Ephesians*, The Pillar New Testament Commentary (Grand Rapids, MI and Leicester, UK: Eerdmans and Apollos, 1999), pp. 187-190.

2. Many commentators treat 1 Samuel 28:1, 2 as the last part of the literary unit that began at 1 Samuel 27:1. So Robert Alter, *The David Story: A Translation with Commentary of 1 and 2 Samuel* (New York and London: W.W. Norton, 1999), p. 171; Walter Brueggemann, *First and Second Samuel*, Interpretation: A Bible Commentary for Teaching and Preaching (Louisville: John Knox Press, 1990), p. 191; Joyce Baldwin, *1 and 2 Samuel*, Tyndale Old Testament Commentaries (Leicester, UK: Inter-Varsity Press, 1988), pp. 157, 158; Hans Wilhelm Hertzberg, *I & II Samuel: A Commentary*, Old Testament Library (London: SCM Press, 1964), p. 215; Henry Preserved Smith, *A Critical and Exegetical Commentary on the Books of Samuel*, The International Critical Commentary (Edinburgh: T. & T. Clark, 1899), p. 237; P. Kyle McCarter, Jr., *I Samuel: A New Translation with Introduction, Notes & Commentary*, The Anchor Bible, Vol. 8 (Garden City, NY: Doubleday, 1980), p. 416; John Mauchline, *1 and 2 Samuel*, New Century Bible (London: Oliphants, 1971), p. 179; Ralph W. Klein, *1 Samuel*, Word Biblical Commentary, 10 (Nashville: Word, 1983), p. 265). However, while the continuity with 1 Samuel 27 is clear (and marked by the words "In those days . . ."), it makes good literary sense to see the renewed Philistine aggression in 1 Samuel 28:1, 2 as introducing the larger section, chapters 28–31, that is the denouement of the whole book. This Philistine assault is the occasion for Saul's dark night of fear in 1 Samuel 28:3-25 and his death in 1 Samuel 31:4-6. Cf. Diana Vikander Edelman, *King Saul in the Historiography of Judah*, Journal for the Study of the Old Testament Supplement Series 121 (Sheffield, UK: Sheffield Academic Press, 1991), p. 239, note 1.

3. This seems to be implied in 1 Samuel 24:1.

4. On Saul and David as "enemies" see 1 Samuel 18:29; 19:17; 24:4; 26:8; and possibly 20:15, 16; 24:19; 25:22, 26, 29.

5. On the Philistines as the "enemies" of Israel and Saul see 1 Samuel 4:3; 10:1; 14:24, 30, 47; 18:25.

6. Cf. Edelman, *Saul*, p. 239. Some argue that Achish was conducting a test to alleviate his lingering doubts about David. So Alter, *David*, p. 171. This, in my opinion, gives Achish more credit than is warranted by the narrative and gives 1 Samuel 27:12 less weight than it deserves.

7. Mauchline, *1 and 2 Samuel*, p. 179.

8. Alter, *David*, p. 171.

9. The Hebrew has the sense "that being so" and is intriguingly ambiguous, indicating either the fact of Achish's *requirement* for David's involvement ("You require that, but you will see what I can do") or David's *acceptance* of the requirement ("I will go out with you, and you will see what I can do").

10. I see no hint in the narrative that Achish harbored "a lingering doubt" about David and so was seeking "to maintain surveillance over David by an appointment that would keep him close to the court." Alter, *David*, p. 171.

11. Cf. Edelman, *Saul*, p. 240.

12. The literary structure of 1 Samuel 28–31 is important. Edelman describes it as "a non-sequential, nonlinear order to heighten audience suspense about David's possible role in Saul's death." Edelman, *Saul*, p. 238. The structure may be laid out as follows (cf. *ibid.*, p. 238):

    28:1, 2: The circumstances in which David became a potential killer of Saul.

    28:3-25: Forward in time to the eve of the battle: Saul's consultation with Samuel.

    29: Back in time to the battle preparations: David's dismissal from the Philistine ranks.

    30: At the time of the fateful battle: what David was doing.

    31: The fateful battle: the death of Saul.

13. See 1 Samuel 15:35: "Samuel did not see Saul again until the day of his death." The incident in 1 Samuel 19:24 apparently does not count, being so out of the ordinary. Certainly there was no communication between the two on that occasion.

14. See the divine promise of 1 Samuel 9:16, 17; 10:1; 12:14; the divine enabling of 1 Samuel 10:9; 11:6; the public support of 1 Samuel 10:24, 26; 11:12, 15; the success of 1 Samuel 11:11; 14:47, 48.

15. In the following citations from Leviticus I have replaced the ESV "wizard(s)" with "necromancer(s)" because the same Hebrew word is used as in 1 Samuel 28:3. See also Isaiah's condemnation of these practices in Isaiah 8:19-22.

16. "Divination" in this verse and "Divine" in 1 Samuel 28:8 represent cognate Hebrew terms.

17. Shunem was more than fifty miles north of Saul's town of Gibeah.

18. Robert P. Gordon, *1 & 2 Samuel: A Commentary* (Exeter, UK: The Paternoster Press, 1986), p. 194.

19. The last time Saul had heard the words of the Lord was from Samuel in chapter 15. The judgment on him then was that he had "rejected the word of the LORD" (1 Samuel 15:23, 26). Since the Spirit of the Lord then departed from him (1 Samuel 16:14), though Saul had continued to use the name of the Lord (1 Samuel 17:37; 19:6; 23:7, 21; 24:18-21), he had received no word from the Lord. In contrast David, on whom the Spirit had now come (1 Samuel 16:13), had access to divine instruction as needed (1 Samuel 22:5; 23:4, 11, 12).

20. Brueggemann, *First and Second Samuel*, p. 193.

21. More precisely, about four miles northeast of Shunem.

22. How very different from Jonathan's willing passing of his royal garb to David in 1 Samuel 18:4! Also compare the indignity of Saul's experience in 1 Samuel 19:24.

23. Note that the account ends with another reference to "that night" (1 Samuel 28:25).

24. "The irony of Saul's doing this in a negotiation with a conjurer of spirits is vividly caught by the Midrash: 'Whom did Saul resemble at that moment? A woman who is with her lover and swears by the life of her husband.'" Alter, *David*, p. 173.

25. So Edelman, *Saul*, p. 244; cf. Gordon, *1 & 2 Samuel*, p. 195; Baldwin, *1 and 2 Samuel*, p. 159.

26. Although the woman's fear seems to have arisen from the identity of the apparition rather than the mere fact of it, the estimate of the woman's powers by Keil and Delitzsch may still be valid: ". . . the woman saw an apparition which she did not anticipate, and therefore . . . she was not really able to conjure up departed spirits or persons who had died, but . . . she either merely pretended to do so, or if her witchcraft was not merely trickery and delusion, but had a certain demoniacal background . . . the appearance of Samuel differed essentially from everything she had experienced and effected before . . ." C. F. Keil and F. Delitzsch, *Biblical Commentary on the Books of Samuel* (Grand Rapids, MI: Eerdmans, 1950), p. 262.

27. The plural term translated "a god" (ESV) has been variously rendered: "a ghostly form" (REB); "a spirit" (NIV); "a ghost" (Mauchline, *1 and 2 Samuel*, p. 182); "a divine being" (NRSV).

28. Samuel's old age was first mentioned as long ago as 1 Samuel 8:1. He had therefore been an "old man" for the whole period of Saul's acquaintance with him. Samuel's robe, of course, Saul could never forget (see 1 Samuel 15:27, 28).

29. Edelman, *Saul*, p. 246.

30. David to Jonathan, 1 Samuel 20:41; David to Saul, 1 Samuel 24:8; Abigail to David, 1 Samuel 25:23, 41.

31. Notice how she "came to Saul" again in 1 Samuel 28:21.

32. Interestingly in his reference to the Lord's silence Saul failed to mention the Urim (see v. 6). Was this because of his "guilty recollection of his massacre of the priests of Nob"? Alter, *David*, p. 175.

CHAPTER FORTY-SEVEN: THE "TRIAL" OF DAVID

1. On the theological weight of these words, see Stephen Liberty, "The Importance of Pontius Pilate in Creed and Gospel," *Journal of Theological Studies* 45 (1944), pp. 38-56. For an argument that the words indicate the date and therefore essential historical character of the events concerned, see J.N.D. Kelly, *Early Christian Creeds* (London: Longmans, Green and Co., 1950), pp. 149, 150. See also the discussion of Jesus' trial before Pilate in Peter G. Bolt, *The Cross from a Distance: Atonement in Mark's Gospel*, New Studies in Biblical Theology, 18 (Leicester, UK and Downers Grove, IL: Inter-Varsity Press, 2004), pp. 116-121.

2. For a brief summary of Jewish testimony about Pilate (specifically Josephus and Philo), see D. H. Wheaton, "Pilate," in J. D. Douglas et al, eds., *The Illustrated Bible Dictionary*, Part 3 (Leicester, UK and Wheaton, IL: Inter-Varsity Press and Tyndale House, 1980), pp. 1229-1231. For a fuller account of the state of historical knowledge of Pilate, see Paul Barnett, *Jesus and the Rise of Early Christianity: A History of New Testament Times* (Downers Grove, IL: InterVarsity Press, 1999), pp. 143-148.

3. ". . . saying that he himself is Christ, a king" (Luke 23:2).

4. See particularly John's account of the exchange between Pilate and Jesus in John 18:33-38, where Pilate did not understand Jesus' words about his kingdom and asked the telling question, "What is truth?"

5. The suggestion of a relation between the accounts of Jesus' trial and 1 Samuel 29 is made by Walter Brueggemann, "Narrative Intentionality in 1 Samuel 29," *Journal for the Study of the Old Testament* 43 (1989), pp. 21-35. Brueggemann sees the respective narratives as "comparable 'type scenes' which make use of the same literary conventions" (p. 33). I am indebted to this article for a number of insights but will argue that the comparison has deeper roots than "comparable 'type scenes.'"

6. Although some have suggested that Saul may have initiated the hostilities on this occasion (Diana Vikander Edelman, *King Saul in the Historiography of Judah*, Journal for the Study of the Old Testament Supplement Series 121 [Sheffield, UK: Sheffield Academic Press, 1991], pp. 252, 253; Robert P. Gordon, *1 & 2 Samuel: A Commentary*

[Exeter, UK: The Paternoster Press, 1986], p. 197), the Philistine intentions are introduced without any suggestion of Israelite provocation.

7. As they had done by the night of Saul's visit to Endor (1 Samuel 28:4).

8. Cf. Robert Alter, *The David Story: A Translation with Commentary of 1 and 2 Samuel* (New York and London: W.W. Norton, 1999), p. 179.

9. Although there has been some debate about the location of this Aphek (e.g., Henry Preserved Smith, *A Critical and Exegetical Commentary on the Books of Samuel*, The International Critical Commentary [Edinburgh: T. & T. Clark, 1899], p. 243; C. F. Keil and F. Delitzsch, *Biblical Commentary on the Books of Samuel* [Grand Rapids, MI: Eerdmans, 1950], p. 270), Edelman is right: "If one accepts the author's deliberate non-chronological ordering of chs. 28–31 for purposes of heightening suspense . . . the alleged 'problem' of Aphek's location disappears." Edelman, *Saul*, pp. 252-254, note 1.

10. The positive assessment of 1 Samuel 14:47, 48 is therefore set in a context that makes it provisional and ultimately overthrown.

11. P. Kyle McCarter, Jr., *I Samuel: A New Translation with Introduction, Notes & Commentary*, The Anchor Bible, Vol. 8 (Garden City, NY: Doubleday, 1980), p. 427.

12. This seems more likely than the suggestion that the Israelite presence already in Jezreel indicates that Israel was the aggressor on this occasion (Edelman, *Saul*, pp. 252, 253). It is difficult to imagine Saul taking such an initiative at this stage, and his visit to Endor makes more sense as a response to an external threat than as anxiety about the outcome of his own initiative. If his own words can be taken seriously, they support this view ("the Philistines are warring against me," 1 Samuel 28:15).

13. Gordon, *1 & 2 Samuel*, p. 197. There were therefore five lords of the Philistines. Cf. 1 Samuel 5:8, 11; 6:4, 12, 16, 18; 7:7. Achish is the only one called a "king" (1 Samuel 27:2). Hans Wilhelm Hertzberg, *I & II Samuel: A Commentary*, Old Testament Library (London: SCM Press, 1964), p. 222.

14. "Hundreds" and "thousands" refer to military units, "roughly corresponding to the companies and battalions of modern use." John Mauchline, *1 and 2 Samuel*, New Century Bible (London: Oliphants, 1971), p. 184.

15. Contra Keil and Delitzsch, *Books of Samuel*, pp. 270, 271, who identify those here called "lords" as "commanders." The latter term is used of the military commanders that a king would appoint, according to Samuel (1 Samuel 8:12; cf. 1 Samuel 22:7), the army commanders — Sisera (1 Samuel 12:9), Abner (1 Samuel 14:50; 17:18, 55; 26:5), and David (1 Samuel 18:13; cf. 22:2), as well as the Philistine military commanders (1 Samuel 18:30).

16. "Hebrews" was the term typically used by foreigners to refer to Israelites, usually disparagingly. Ralph W. Klein, *1 Samuel*, Word Biblical Commentary, 10 (Nashville: Word, 1983), p. 277. The use of the term by the Philistines is another reminder of the disastrous events of 1 Samuel 4. See 1 Samuel 4:6, 9; cf. 1 Samuel 13:19; 14:11. For a suggestion about the connotations of the term, see Walter Brueggemann, *First and Second Samuel*, Interpretation: A Bible Commentary for Teaching and Preaching (Louisville: John Knox Press, 1990), p. 197.

17. Cf. 1 Samuel 25:10, 11. Edelman compares Achish with Nabal who also believed (foolishly) that David had abandoned loyalty to Saul. Edelman, *Saul*, p. 225.

18. In the narrative from Genesis to 2 Kings the term is invariably used of a superior's anger toward an inferior (with the one exception of 1 Samuel 29:4): Pharaoh toward his servants (Genesis 40:2; 41:10), Moses toward the people (Exodus 16:20; Leviticus 10:16; Numbers 31:14), Naaman, in his imagined superiority (2 Kings 5:11), Elisha toward Joash (2 Kings 13:19), and God's wrath (Leviticus 10:6; Numbers 1:53; 16:22, 46; 18:5; Deuteronomy 1:34; 9:7, 8, 19, 22; 29:28; Joshua 9:20; 22:18, 20; 2 Kings 3:27).

19. This context provides an illustration of the ordinary meaning of the term that became the title *Satan*.

20. Explanations in terms of courtesy or a "slip on the part of our Yahwistic narrator" (McCarter, *I Samuel*, p. 427; Klein, *I Samuel*, p. 277) are not convincing. We may note that the occurrence of this oath on the lips of a Philistine king helps us to see

that it may mean less than we might otherwise have thought on the lips of Saul. In 1 Samuel this precise oath is uttered by Saul (1 Samuel 14:39; 19:6; 28:10), the people (1 Samuel 14:45), Jonathan (1 Samuel 20:21), Abigail (1 Samuel 25:26), and David (1 Samuel 25:34; 26:10, 16).

21. The word translated "honest" indicates uprightness and integrity in a more general sense than mere truthfulness.

22. Cf. Alter, *David*, p. 181.

23. "Realizing the position of compromise that Achish has put himself in, David decides to make the Philistine grovel even further in order to assert his own superiority in a psychological game of 'King of the mountain.'" Edelman, *Saul*, p. 259.

24. While the whole episode of David's time among the Philistines has raised questions about his earlier claim to be Saul's "servant" (1 Samuel 26:18, 19), in the end the integrity of that claim survives.

25. The ambiguity is noted by several commentators, for example, Keil and Delitzsch, *Books of Samuel*, p. 272; Alter, *David*, p. 181; Klein, *1 Samuel*, pp. 277, 278; Peter R. Ackroyd, *The First Book of Samuel*, Cambridge Bible Commentary (Cambridge, UK: Cambridge University Press, 1971), p. 219. There is a discussion of possibilities in Mauchline, *1 and 2 Samuel*, pp. 185, 186.

26. The Hebrew expression for "my lord the king" and "my lord, O king" is identical in these verses.

27. So McCarter, *1 Samuel*, p. 427, followed by Klein who adds, "The word 'lord' is used three times in this chapter (vv 4, 8, 10) to designate David's relationship to a superior, and in each case the person indicated is probably Saul." Klein, *1 Samuel*, p. 277.

28. Contrary to the view of, for example, Alter: "in point of fact he must have been immensely relieved to escape from the intolerable position of battling against his own people." Alter, *David*, p. 181.

29. Cf. Joyce Baldwin, *1 and 2 Samuel*, Tyndale Old Testament Commentaries (Leicester, UK: Inter-Varsity Press, 1988), p. 165.

30. Literally, ". . . you are good in my eyes. . . ."

31. On the delivering of Jesus to the Gentiles/nations, see Bolt, *Cross*, pp. 56-58. Bolt persuasively argues that for Jesus to be handed over to the nations "is tantamount to being delivered over to the wrath of God" (p. 58).

CHAPTER FORTY-EIGHT: A KING WHO GIVES

1. Lord Acton (1834–1902), one of the great thinkers of the nineteenth century, was Regius Professor of Modern History at Cambridge University. He thought and wrote a great deal on the subject of liberty. The famous quotation belongs in that context: "Liberty is not a means to a higher political end. It is itself the highest political end . . . liberty is the only object which benefits all alike, and provokes no sincere opposition. . . . The danger is not that a particular class is unfit to govern. Every class is unfit to govern. . . . Power tends to corrupt, and absolute power corrupts absolutely." See http://questionitnow.com/educationb/2006/05/absolute-power-corrupts-absolutely.html.

2. Of course, we are speaking here historically. The modern constitutional monarchy, where the monarch is subject to law, is very different from what was implied by *king* in the ancient world and in the Bible. Indeed it is very different from what a king was understood to be in England only a few hundred years ago.

3. These chapters are often interpreted as a defense of David, demonstrating that he had never betrayed Israel and that he had played no part in the battle that killed Saul. The point that is often overlooked is that if David *had* gone with the Philistines, we can reasonably suppose that Saul would not have been killed. Everything we know of David's dealings with the Philistines supports this. See 1 Samuel 17; 18:27, 30; 19:8; 21:10-15; 23:1-5.

4. Robert P. Gordon, *1 & 2 Samuel: A Commentary* (Exeter, UK: The Paternoster Press, 1986), p. 198.

5. The use of the same verb for the Amalekites' action here as David's actions in 1 Samuel 27:8 "highlights the retaliatory nature of the strike." Diana Vikander Edelman, *King Saul in the Historiography of Judah*, Journal for the Study of the Old Testament Supplement Series 121 (Sheffield, UK: Sheffield Academic Press, 1991), p. 263.

6. Robert Alter, commenting on the verb translated here "carried off," suggests, "This rather brutal verb is typically used for driving animals, as in verse 20, and so highlights the rapaciousness of the Amalekites." He reiterates the point in his comment on the same verb in 1 Samuel 30:22. Robert Alter, *The David Story: A Translation with Commentary of 1 and 2 Samuel* (New York and London: W.W. Norton, 1999), pp. 184, 187. This overstates the case. While the verb can certainly be used for driving cattle (Genesis 31:18; Exodus 3:1; 1 Samuel 23:5; 30:20; 2 Samuel 6:3; 2 Kings 4:24; 9:20; 1 Chronicles 13:7; Job 24:3; but cf. Psalm 78:52; 80:1) and in other contexts that suggest harshness (Genesis 31:26; Exodus 10:13; 14:25; Deuteronomy 4:27; 28:37; 1 Chronicles 20:1; Psalm 78:26; Lamentations 3:2; Isaiah 20:4; 60:11), it can also be used in less brutal, even gentle contexts (1 Samuel 30:22; 2 Chronicles 25:11; Psalm 48:14; Ecclesiastes 2:3; Song of Solomon 8:2; Isaiah 49:10; 63:14; note Isaiah 11:6).

7. The Hebrew in verse 4 emphasizes David's leading role in this.

8. "Greatly distressed" might be better expressed, "in dire straits" (Alter, *David*, p. 184); "in a very tight place" (Walter Brueggemann, *First and Second Samuel*, Interpretation: A Bible Commentary for Teaching and Preaching [Louisville: John Knox Press, 1990], p. 201).

9. In Hebrew there is only a slight difference in the expressions "greatly distressed" (1 Samuel 30:6) and "am in great distress" (1 Samuel 28:15), one being adjectival, the other verbal. The words in 1 Samuel 28:15 were uttered by Saul on the eve of the battle in which he died, which must have been close to the time David reached Ziklag, assuming two or three days' journey for both David and the Philistines in their respective directions. Both men, at the same time, for different reasons, found themselves "greatly distressed."

10. The description of the people as "bitter in soul" in 1 Samuel 30:6 is a clear echo of the almost identical expression in 1 Samuel 22:2. David had led them back to the misery from which they had hoped he would deliver them.

11. Gordon draws attention to the similar plight of Moses in Exodus 17:4. Gordon, *1 & 2 Samuel*, p. 199. Also Brueggemann, *First and Second Samuel*, p. 201.

12. The Hebrew word for "strength" here is different from the verb "strengthened" in 1 Samuel 30:6 (but the same as "strength" in 1 Samuel 30:4).

13. The Hebrew construction behind the twice spoken "surely" is strikingly emphatic. This supports the view previously mentioned that God's guidance by means of the ephod (the Urim and Thummim) was not simply a form of casting lots.

14. Gordon, *1 & 2 Samuel*, p. 199.

15. "The act of abandoning a sick slave in the desert to perish of thirst and hunger dispels any illusions we may have harbored about the humanity of the Amalekites." Alter, *David*, p. 185.

16. It is uncertain who the Cherethites were. They may have been from Crete. See Peter R. Ackroyd, *The First Book of Samuel*, Cambridge Bible Commentary (Cambridge, UK: Cambridge University Press, 1971), p. 47; P. Kyle McCarter, Jr., *I Samuel: A New Translation with Introduction, Notes & Commentary*, The Anchor Bible, Vol. 8 (Garden City, NY: Doubleday, 1980), p. 435.

17. The term translated "behold" often marks a "transition from the narrator's overview to the character's point of view." Alter, *David*, p. 186. In other words, "behold" introduces a description of what David and his men saw and what it looked like to them.

18. Alter deduces this figure from the fact that 400 escaped the general slaughter according to 1 Samuel 30:17, and that was apparently a minority. Alter, *David*, p. 186.

19. "Spread abroad" is, more literally, "forsaken." It suggests a lack of control: they were "left to themselves over all the land." Francis Brown, S. R. Driver, and Charles Briggs,

A Hebrew and English Lexicon of the Old Testament (Oxford, UK: Clarendon Press, 1907), p. 643.

20. The word translated "dancing" is most commonly used of celebrating a feast. Gordon, *1 & 2 Samuel*, p. 200.

21. Edelman reflects at some length on the possible significance of the correspondence between the number of escapees and the size of David's force. Edelman, *Saul*, pp. 271, 272.

22. The reason that David was able to take booty from his attack on the Amalekites, whereas the taking of booty from these very people had been Saul's undoing (1 Samuel 15), is simply that Saul was under divine command to "devote to destruction all they have" (1 Samuel 15:3), but David was under no such commission.

23. This is my own translation, but it is close to the understanding of the Hebrew argued by Edelman, *Saul*, p. 273, note 1 (although there is a confusing error in her citations of the Hebrew).

24. The Hebrew word here designates smaller livestock, usually sheep and goats.

25. The Hebrew word here designates larger cattle, such as oxen. The word translated "livestock" refers to cattle in general and can include cows, sheep, horses, donkeys, and camels. Brown, Driver, and Briggs, *Hebrew and English Lexicon*, p. 889.

26. "This is David's spoil" could refer to all of the captured animals (so Gordon, *1 & 2 Samuel*, p. 200; Alter, *David*, 187), but the separation of the animals into two groups suggested by the Hebrew of verse 20 makes sense if its purpose was to allocate one group to David and the other to the people generally. This understanding is supported (though not proven) by the fact that in verse 22 a dispute breaks out over who is to receive the spoil. This makes less sense if it had already all been given to David.

27. So REB.

28. Compare the very similar situation in 1 Samuel 25:13. "The baggage" has appeared in the story of 1 Samuel a surprising number of times, at very significant points. See also 1 Samuel 10:22; 17:22.

29. Cf. Brueggemann, *First and Second Samuel*, p. 205.

30. "To this day" is an expression used quite often in the Biblical history to indicate present-day (from the writer's perspective) effects of the events recorded. The expression is used in this way four times in 1 Samuel (5:5; 6:18; 27:6; 30:25). Cf. 2 Samuel 4:3; 6:8; 18:18. It occurs more frequently in Joshua and Judges.

31. This is an allusion to 1 Samuel 23:13. Alter, *David*, p. 188.

32. See Gordon, *1 & 2 Samuel*, p. 201. It is significant that these places lie in the very region that David had falsely told Achish he had raided in 1 Samuel 27:10. Edelman, *Saul*, p. 277.

33. Hans Wilhelm Hertzberg, *I & II Samuel: A Commentary*, Old Testament Library (London: SCM Press, 1964), p. 229.

34. Edelman describes David's gifts as "a means of forging closer ties with his fellow countrymen, fellow citizens of Saul's state, who have shown him some respect at Saul's expense in the past . . . a bribe to convince them that he really is on their side, in spite of appearances." Edelman, *Saul*, pp. 276, 277. Cf. "The gifts which he sent to these people were at once an expression of gratitude for past favours, a renewal of the bonds of friendship, and a way of ensuring a continuance of the friendship in days to come." John Mauchline, *1 and 2 Samuel*, New Century Bible (London: Oliphants, 1971), p. 189.

35. So Edelman, *Saul*, p. 276.

36. Inexplicably the RSV, followed by the ESV, reverses the order of these phrases. The Hebrew word order, which provides the right emphasis, is "the elders of Judah, his friends."

CHAPTER FORTY-NINE: THE KING IS DEAD

1. Matthew does not identify the mountain of Jesus' Great Commission beyond the fact that it was "the mountain" in Galilee "to which Jesus had directed them" (Matthew 28:16). Traditionally it has been identified with Mount Tabor, about ten miles north of Mount

Gilboa, but this identification rests on no firm evidence. Donald A. Hagner, *Matthew 14–28*, Word Biblical Commentary, 33B (Dallas: Word, 1995), p. 884.

2. The Hebrew lacks the normal syntax for narrating a *sequence* of events. The word order and the use of a participle verb form are unusual at the beginning of a narrative unit. "The phrase has the force of a circumstantial clause and represents an action that occurred simultaneously with the previous action. . . ." Diana Vikander Edelman, *King Saul in the Historiography of Judah*, Journal for the Study of the Old Testament Supplement Series 121 (Sheffield, UK: Sheffield Academic Press, 1991), p. 279. The effect may be expressed in English: "And meanwhile the Philistines were fighting . . ." Cf. Robert Alter, *The David Story: A Translation with Commentary of 1 and 2 Samuel* (New York and London: W.W. Norton, 1999), p. 189; Hans Wilhelm Hertzberg, *I & II Samuel: A Commentary*, Old Testament Library (London: SCM Press, 1964), p. 230.

3. There is a certain irony to the fact that Saul's death is directly linked to his failure to properly deal with the Amalekites (1 Samuel 28:18) and took place at the very time that David was striking these same people!

4. The Philistines had "fled" before Saul and Jonathan in 1 Samuel 14:22.

5. There is irony in the fact that David was then forced to "flee" from Saul (1 Samuel 19:10).

6. Aphek is named in 1 Samuel only at 1 Samuel 4:1 and 29:1.

7. It is tempting to note that in 2 Samuel 1:19 David will lament the death of Saul and Jonathan with the words, "Your glory, O Israel, is slain on your high places!" However, the word translated "glory" is uncertain (Robert P. Gordon, *1 & 2 Samuel: A Commentary* [Exeter, UK: The Paternoster Press, 1986], p. 211) and in any case not the word used in 1 Samuel 4:21, 22. The "glory" of 1 Samuel 4 may, however, find an echo in 1 Samuel 31:3, which says, literally, "The battle was heavy toward Saul. . . ." "Heavy" and "glory" have the same Hebrew root. Cf. Edelman, *Saul*, p. 281.

8. Edelman, *Saul*, p. 281 draws attention to the use of the same verb in 1 Samuel 14:22 but fails to observe the preposition following the verb there, which gives it a different sense, according to Francis Brown, S. R. Driver, and Charles Briggs, *A Hebrew and English Lexicon of the Old Testament* (Oxford, UK: Clarendon Press, 1907), p. 180.

9. The situation is a little complicated. We seem to know of four sons of Saul: Jonathan, Ishvi (= Ish-bosheth), Abinadad, and Malchi-shua. This is supported by 1 Chronicles, which lists Saul's four sons in 8:33; 9:39 (where Ishvi/Ish-bosheth appears as Eshbaal). First Samuel 14:49 and 31:2 (= 1 Chronicles 10:2) each mention only three of these sons. For no clear reason Abinadab is omitted in 1 Samuel 14:49; Ish-bosheth is not mentioned in 1 Samuel 31:2 for the very good reason that he was not killed then. See Joyce Baldwin, *1 and 2 Samuel*, Tyndale Old Testament Commentaries (Leicester, UK: Inter-Varsity Press, 1988), p. 112; Hertzberg, *I & II Samuel*, pp. 120, 231; Peter R. Ackroyd, *The First Book of Samuel*, Cambridge Bible Commentary (Cambridge, UK: Cambridge University Press, 1971), pp. 120, 227; Ralph W. Klein, *1 Samuel*, Word Biblical Commentary, 10 (Nashville: Word, 1983), pp. 141, 142; Gordon, *1 & 2 Samuel*, pp. 142, 202. There are other ways of explaining these lists of names. For example C. F. Keil and F. Delitzsch, *Biblical Commentary on the Books of Samuel* (Grand Rapids, MI: Eerdmans, 1950), p. 149 consider the lists of three sons in 1 Samuel 14:49 and 31:2 to be the same, taking Ishvi as another name for Abinadab; Ish-bosheth is then not mentioned in 1 Samuel but appears for the first time in the narrative at 2 Samuel 2:8 and is the Eshbaal of 1 Chronicles.

10. As noted earlier, there may be an echo here of 1 Samuel 4:21, 22, "glory" and "heavy" having the same root in Hebrew. The "glory" departed from Israel in 1 Samuel 4; the only "glory" in 1 Samuel 31 was the "weight" of the battle against Saul.

11. The Hebrew text emphasizes the weapon: ". . . the archers, men with the bow, found him. . . ." See Alter, *David*, p. 189.

12. So RV, ASV. Alter follows this sense: "he quaked with fear of the archers." Alter, *David*, p. 189. The ESV and most English versions (including RSV, NRSV, NIV, REB) follow a small emendment to the Hebrew. For details see S. R. Driver, *Notes on the Hebrew Text and*

the Topography of the Book of Samuel with an Introduction on Hebrew Palaeography and Facsimiles of Inscriptions and Maps, second edition (Oxford, UK: Clarendon, 1913), p. 228.

13. In referring to the Philistines as "these uncircumcised" he echoed the view of Jonathan (1 Samuel 14:6) and David (1 Samuel 17:26, 36). The difference, of course, is that both Jonathan and David defeated the Philistines. Saul was referring to the Philistines as those who had defeated him. Cf. Edelman, *Saul*, p. 283.

14. Cf. Hertzberg, *I & II Samuel*, p. 232; Ackroyd, *First Book of Samuel*, p. 227; Baldwin, *1 and 2 Samuel*, p. 170. Other suggestions have been made as to why the armor-bearer feared to take Saul's life. For example, "he was supposed to be answerable for the king's life." Keil and Delitzsch, *Books of Samuel*, p. 279. It seems to me, however, that this armor-bearer's unwillingness should be seen in the light of the similar and recent refusal of David.

15. The brief Hebrew sentence does not specify "his own" sword; it has simply "the sword." Saul may have taken the armor-bearer's sword referred to in 1 Samuel 30:4a. This seems the most natural way to understand the Hebrew. The armor-bearer, then, took his sword back in 1 Samuel 30:5 in order to kill himself.

16. The armor-bearer's fear is all the more understandable if Saul had killed himself with his servant's weapon.

17. The Bible reports seven deaths by suicide, with no explicit comment on the act. More precisely one of these was Abimelech, who died at the hands of his armor-bearer (Judges 9:54). The others were Samson (Judges 16:30), Saul (1 Samuel 31:4; 1 Chronicles 10:4), Saul's armor-bearer (1 Samuel 31:5; 1 Chronicles 10:5), Ahithophel (2 Samuel 17:23), Zimri (1 Kings 16:18), and Judas (Matthew 27:5). For an informative survey of Jewish and Christian thinking about suicide, see A. J. Droge, "Suicide," in David Noel Freedman, ed., *The Anchor Bible Dictionary*, Vol. 6 (New York: Doubleday, 1992), pp. 225-231.

18. I profoundly disagree, therefore, with Edelman: "I tend to think that Saul's final act is to be viewed honorably, as a final surrender to Yahweh's will." Edelman, *Saul*, p. 286. Similarly Brueggemann: "Saul is a man with a last heroic gesture." Walter Brueggemann, *First and Second Samuel*, Interpretation: A Bible Commentary for Teaching and Preaching (Louisville: John Knox Press, 1990), p. 207.

19. Cf. Alter, *David*, p. 190.

20. Edelman, *Saul*, p. 288.

21. Gordon, *1 & 2 Samuel*, p. 203.

22. Cf. Alter, *David*, p. 190.

23. Notice how the sword of Goliath had been kept "wrapped in a cloth behind the ephod" in Nob (1 Samuel 21:9).

24. According to Ackroyd, *First Book of Samuel*, p. 228. See also 1 Samuel 7:3, 4; 12:10 for the place of the Ashtaroth in recent Israelite consciousness.

25. The burning of the bodies has occasioned some discussion. This is unusual in the Old Testament. One suggestion has been followed by the NEB, which has, "and anointed them there with spices" (REB has reverted to "and burned them"). For details see Gordon, *1 & 2 Samuel*, pp. 203, 204.

Scripture Index

General Index

Index of
Sermon Illustrations

Our schemes to save ourselves are stupid
— only God can save us from our real
enemies, 256

God
God is sovereign over all that happens in his
world and in our lives, 27
As a "Rock," God provides incomparable
protection and security, 43, 45
God is the of the unexpected — he can be
trusted, but acts in ways that take us all by
surprise, 313

God's Provision
God's answer to the crisis of the world comes
from the most unexpected quarter, 23
God's care for us all finds its fullest expression in Jesus Christ, 37
"My horn": an animal's horn is its glory and
power; Hannah uses this vivid animal
metaphor to acknowledge her being raised
up by God, 41

Gospel Message
If we amend the gospel to make it more relevant and credible, then we are no longer
proclaimers of the gospel of Jesus Christ,
325-326, 333
The words of the gospel message are the most
preposterous thing anyone could say to
sinners, 328-329
The call of the gospel of Jesus Christ is radical
— it goes out to those whom the world
views as despised, 430-431

Grace
"The last will be first, and the first last," 540

Hardness of Heart
Pharaoh hardened his own heart, and God
hardened Pharaoh's heart — it was a
matter of both his own choice and God's
judgment on him for that choice, 59, 116,
372-373

Hopelessness
Hopelessness is "having no hope and [being]
without God in the world," 507-508, 518

Hostility
Christians will encounter the suffering that
comes from the hostility of those who oppose God and his Christ, 422-423

Humility
We need to humbly recognize God's hand
behind all our circumstances, 27-28
We can only speak to God humbly, 31

Kingdom of God
The kingdom of God must prevail over all our
strategies, schemes, plans, training, abilities, and leadership models, 190

Listening to God
The people of God are called to hear the sound
of the words of God, 260

Losers
Losers are those who set themselves up
against God, 48

Love for the Lord Jesus Christ
To love the Lord Jesus Christ is the kind of attachment people have to a king who fights
their battles for them, 354-355

Missions/Service
"He has no other hands than our hands; he has
no other feet than our feet," 111, 122

Obedience
You cannot depend on God's promises while
paying no regard to his demands, 94
Sometimes, in the circumstances in which we
find ourselves, it is really beyond us to
obey God fully, 238
We are not always persuaded that obedience
to God is the wisest course of action,
247-248

Obscurity
God makes something out of nothing, life out
of death, rich out of poor, somebody out of
nobody, 21
God brings something important out of unimportance and "barrenness," 23

Point of View
We have limited points of view; but God's unlimited point of view has absolute validity,
286, 290, 291-292

Power
Whenever any form of human power replaces
the Lord, we need to remember what happened to Israel at Gilgal, 225
Lord Acton: "Power tends to corrupt, and
absolute power corrupts absolutely," 529

Prayer
We dare to speak to God because he has
    spoken to us, 30

Religion
Religion is the human attempt to harness
    God's power — which can't be done,
    85-86, 93

Revelation
Only when God reveals his purpose can any
    human know the purpose of God in human
    events, 162

Righteousness
David's refusal to lift his hand against Saul,
    who was still king, was righteousness,
    494-495

Sin
The very sinfulness that leads to disobedience
    often blinds the sinner to the reality of his
    or her disobedience, 268, 269
The sinner denies responsibility for his or her
    own sin and blames others, 269
One who loves God and his word will care
    deeply about sin and its terrible conse-
    quences, 283

Sinning against the Lord
There is little hope for those who show
    contempt for the very means God has pro-
    vided for their salvation, 58-59, 71, 78, 81

Status
No matter how high up the status tree you may
    think you have climbed (or think you will
    climb), there is always someone higher, 18

Suffering
The message of Scripture turns our ways of
    making sense of suffering — it is morally
    random and power can beat it — upside
    down, 443-445
In the midst of our suffering, "we do not lose
    heart," 453-454

Trust in God
Trust in God means believing that God's
    promises will come to pass in God's time
    and in God's way, 491

Vengeance
It is not up to Christians to repay anyone evil
    for evil — we must leave all vengeance to
    the coming wrath of God, 265

Victory
We can hold our heads high because of what
    God has done for us in the victory of Jesus
    on the cross, 134
We must never allow our longing for victory
    to tempt us into thinking that it may be
    won by worldly means, 191
The Christian life is a victorious life not be-
    cause of our victorious living, but because
    of the victory that has been given to us
    through Jesus' obedient life, atoning death,
    and victorious resurrection, 335-336, 344

Will of God
Wherever the gospel is proclaimed in the
    world, the resistance and opposition of
    human wills to God's will is encountered,
    365-366, 373-374, 375

Winners
Winners are the faithful ones, who belong to
    God, 47

Word of God
God's word to us is the word he has spoken by
    his son, Jesus Christ, 83
God speaks — his word expresses and enacts
    his purpose, 165-166
In the case of Adam and Eve, and of Saul,
    it was all undone by disobedience to the
    word of God, 549-550

About the Book Jacket

The design of the book jacket brings together the talents of several Christian artists. The design centers around the beautiful banner created by artist Marge Gieser. It is photographed on the jacket at about one-twentieth of its original size.

Concerning the Biblical message behind the banner for *1 Samuel*, Marge Gieser writes:

> The book of 1 Samuel opens with the nation of Israel facing a major leadership crisis. God cared about this crisis and took steps to address the problem. Samuel provided the first leadership that Israel needed. The result was peace and security. But the people were not satisfied and demanded a king "like all the nations." They asked for Saul, who failed as a leader because he failed to be obedient to God. Then God chose a leader for the people. He chose David out of his own grace and goodness — "a man after his [God's] own heart" (1 Samuel 13:14). David proved to be a man of righteousness and faithfulness.

The other artists contributing their talents to the creation of the jacket were: Bill Koechling, photography; Paul Higdon, design and typography; and Georgia Bateman, art direction.